The incarnation is the most accurate and articulate translation.

Any sincere student of classical music would sensitively seek to capture and interpret the piece, so as not to distract from the original sound of the composition.

To form a conclusion in the study of our origin would involve a peering over the Creator's shoulder as it were, in order to gaze through his eyes and marvel at his anticipation. His invisible image and likeness is about to be unveiled in human form!

The incarnation celebrates the fact that the destiny of the Word was not the page but tangible human life! The word of truth preserves God's original idea in the resonance of our hearts.

2 Corinthians 3:2 Instead of an impressive certificate framed on my wall I have you framed in my heart! You are our Epistle written within us, an open letter speaking a global language; one that everyone can ¹read and recognize as their mother tongue! (The word ¹anaginosko, from ana, upward and ginosko, to know upward; thus to draw knowledge from a higher reference; from above; to recognize; to read with recognition.)

3:3 The fact that you are a Christ-Epistle shines as bright as day! This is what our ministry is all about. The Spirit of God is the living ink. Every trace of the Spirit's influence on the heart is what gives permanence to this conversation. We are not talking law-language here; this is more dynamic and permanent than letters chiseled in stone. This conversation is embroidered in your inner consciousness. (It is the life of your design that grace echoes within you!)

Behold how beautiful
how valuable
how loved
you are!

In the Mirror,
Bible language becomes heart to heart
whispers of grace!

A work in progress

This is the sixth edition - March 2016

Mirror Word Logo by: Wilna Furstenburg

Cover Design by: Bryce Phelps and Sean Osmond
Published by Mirror Word Publishing

The Mirror Bible is also available as an iPhone or Android mobile app on the following website, www.mirrorbible.com

Should you wish to order printed copies in bulk, [10 or more] pls contact us at info@mirrorword.net

Contact us if you wish to help sponsor Mirror Bibles in Spanish, Shona or Xhosa.

Highly recommended books by the same author: Divine Embrace, God Believes in You, Done!, Children's book, The Eagle Story, by Lydia and Francois du Toit, beautifully illustrated by Carla Krige The Mirror Bible, Divine Embrace God Believes in You and The Logic of His Love are also abailable on Kindle

Francois' ministry page is www.mirrorword.net
Subscribe to Francois facebook updates http://www.facebook.com/francois.toit

The Mirror Translation fb group http://www.facebook.com/groups/179109018883718/

ISBN 978-0-9921769-0-7

THE MIRROR

The Mirror is a paraphrased translation from the Greek text. While strictly following the literal meaning of the original, sentences have been constructed so that the larger meaning is continually emphasized by means of an expanded text.

Some clarifying notes are included in italics. This is a paraphrased study rather than a literal translation. While the detailed shades of meaning of every Greek word have been closely studied, this is done taking into account the consistent context of the entire chapter within the wider epistle, and bearing in mind the full context of Jesus and his finished work, which is what the message of the Bible is all about

To assist the reader in their study, I have numerically superscripted the Greek word and corresponded it with the closest English word in the italicized commentary that follows. This is to create a direct comparison of words between the two languages.

I translated several Pauline epistles 25 years ago called the Ruach Translation. In 2006 I started with the Mirror Translation. This is an ongoing process and will eventually include the entire New Testament as well as select portions of the Old Testament.

Completed books as of February 2016 are:
John's Gospel, Romans, 1 Corinthians, 2 Corinthians,
Galatians, Ephesians, Philippians, Colossians,
1 Thessalonians, 2 Timothy, Titus, Hebrews, James, 1 John
In Progress: 1 Peter 1,2; 2 Peter 1.

© Copyright Francois du Toit 2012

To my darling Lydia and our amazing children,
Renaldo, Tehilla, Christo and Stefan

Jesus is God's language and message to mankind.

He is the context of Scripture.

To add anything to his completed work in revealing and redeeming the image of God in human form, or take anything away from what God spoke to us in him, is folly.

There is no perfect translation, there is only a perfect Word: the Logic of God.

The Bible is all about Jesus.

What makes the book irresistibly relevant, is the fact that

Jesus is all about you!

TABLE OF CONTENTS

Reflecting on any translation of Scripture gives one the opportunity to hear our Maker's voice and thoughts, filtered through the interpretation and language of the translator(s).

In this fresh Paraphrase, Francois du Toit has opened the curtain for readers of any age, culture or language to enjoy amazing insights into the heart-beat of Agape - where everyone feels equally loved, included and valued in the eyes of the Father - and fully redeemed in the union we come from! The Mirror underlines the fact that humanity did not merely begin in their mother's womb; we are the invention and idea of God!

To have this work now also available in Xhosa will mark a new era for young and old to rediscover the Bible afresh.

Archbishop **DESMOND TUTU** - *Legacy Foundation*

The Mirror Bible is a transforming paraphrased translation that is simplistic, accurate, detailed and comprehensive, captivating and at the same time exuding intriguing spiritual revelation; it is divinely insightful and contemporary.

It's a must read, a befitting guide and manual for all age groups for; Bible study, meditation, devotion, worship, teaching, instruction and scholarship.

Jesus Christ is the epicenter of the entire text.

Believers will not miss the centrality of the translation as there is a finite and delicate thread directing to the revealing and redeeming Christ.

Unbelievers will derive unrivaled comfort from the text as they get captivated by the reality and close proximity of Christ.

This is definitely a life giving and transforming translation. I am humbly convinced that Francois is chosen by God to serve this generation and the next with undiluted truth in the midst of incomprehensible compromises of worldly, heretical and traditional doctrinal interpretations and practices (religion) that have diverted humanity from the truth.

The Mirror Bible is a welcome revelatory and revolutionary development that is divinely sanctioned, inspired and directed. This translation is by no doubt a compelling grounding expository of our century.
To God be the Glory.

Rev. **ANOUYA ANDREW MUCHECHETERE**, *MBA, MA,*
Former Secretary General of the Evangelical Fellowship of Zimbabwe (EFZ).

The Mirror Translation is astonishingly beautiful. The union theme is outstanding. The gospel is not the news that we can receive Jesus into our lives; the gospel is the news that Jesus has received us into His. Once we discover this reality—and Francois du Toit has—beautiful, liberating, and life-giving questions emerge. Who is this Jesus who has received us into his life with his Father and the Holy Spirit? What is his life all about? How did he receive us? What does this mean for us, and for creation here and now, and hereafter?

The early followers of Jesus knew that he was the center of all creation, the plan from the beginning, the alpha and the omega, the author and finisher of faith. They wrestled deeply with these questions and the staggering implications of Jesus's very identity. They handed down clear and powerful and very relevant insights and answers. Francois has met the Jesus of the apostles, and through his wrestling with their light, is providing for us all a paraphrase of their work that is as thrilling as it is beautiful and true.

My imagination ignites reading your translation of 1 John and feeling mirrored! What a beautiful, breathtaking translation my brother. This is brilliant, and destined to relieve and liberate many. You sing John's heart, my brother. May the Holy Spirit continue to use the Mirror to reveal Jesus and his Father and us all around this world! I love it.

DR. C. BAXTER KRUGER
Author of "The Great Dance" and "The Shack Revisited"

I have been asked at times why God didn't make the Bible easier to understand. If He is able to inspire the writings of Scripture, couldn't He provide a key for unlocking its treasures for us? *The Mirror Translation* you hold in your hand opens the treasure-chest of understanding with that Key. The key to properly understanding the Bible is Jesus Christ. He is the source and subject of its pages. For years I have been asked why there isn't a Bible translation that presents the Scriptures from a pure grace orientation. It is a great encouragement to know that you now hold such a translation in your hands. Drawing not only from the literal meaning, but also the historical nuances of the Greek language, Francois Du Toit presents this translation in a way that will enrich your love for our Triune God and ground you in the grace expressed to us all through Jesus Christ. This is a translation you will read again and again. It is one you will share with your friends. I predict that *The Mirror Translation* will be widely accepted by those who are hungry to understand the Bible through the template of the lens of God's grace.

DR. STEVE McVEY - *Founder of Grace Walk Ministries, Tampa Bay, Florida*

The Bible is God's amazing conversation with mankind. Here we engage with God's words that crescendo in the revelation of his Son, Jesus Christ. The greatest joy is to discover and realize that you as an individual are included in this conversation. The Bible is all about Jesus, but everything about Jesus is about us. The message of the Bible reveals how God determined and succeeded to redeem his image and likeness in human form. By inclining our ear to this message we find the life that flows from it and discover the favorable opinion of God towards mankind.

Thank God for the many translations of the Bible that we have available today, as each one brings a dimension of God's communication in a specific way. However, some translations make it difficult for the reader to truly discover the heart of the Father. It was the mission of Jesus to reveal the Father; studying scripture outside of the context of the finished work of Christ on mankind's behalf causes one to miss out on understanding and appreciating the Father's loving intention with humanity.

The Mirror Translation brings a dimension in which this revelation is facilitated in a way that makes it not only easy to understand, but also life changing in its powerful impact as the revelation dawns in one's heart.

The Mirror Translation of these key books and chapters of the Bible is in all probability one of the greatest contributions in the last few years to the broader church. It is imperative that every Christ follower discovers their true identity declared in Christ Jesus. The most liberating revelation is the fact that we have not only died together with Christ, but that we were also raised with Him in resurrection life. Even going beyond this is to discover that we are seated with Him in a new position in heavenly places, where we function from a position of authority and influence within this world. The premise of the good news of the Gospel is that we are not required to strive to attain something through personal achievement, but rather to discover who we already are and what we already have in Christ, as revealed in the glorious Scriptures.

May The Mirror Translation impact your life as much as it has mine, and may it facilitate your spiritual journey to truly relocate your mind, living from the new vantage point of this glorious life in Christ.

ALAN PLATT - *Visionary leader of Doxa Deo International*

God has done the unthinkable ... the impossible, when He became human. Despite the limitations and constraints of a human body, the infinite One lived and moved and revealed himself, without constraint, in the person of Jesus Christ. The human body by itself is only flesh ... but united with God, it becomes the most holy place of sacred encounter.

In similar manner, God did the impossible in giving us the Scriptures: Despite the limitations and constraints of human language, God is able to reveal himself without constraint through these words. The words by themselves are simply human words appealing to nothing more than human intellect ... but united with God, they become spirit and create an environment for sacred encounter.

It is out of this place of sacred encounter that Francois brings us a fresh and exciting translation of the New Testament books. There is such a wealth of understanding contained within the variances and subtle meanings of the original Greek ... the sheer number of translations are testimony to that.

The Mirror Translation makes full use of the richness within the words themselves, but even more importantly, it is inspired by the revelation of Christ in us, the mirror encounter in which we see Jesus as the unveiling of our own identity.

Francois' translations of the Scriptures have inspired me for more than 20 years ... it is time that the world benefits from them!

ANDRE RABE - *Author and Bible Teacher*

When the 1611 King James team endeavored to compile their English version of the Bible, they quoted Augustine as proof "that variety of translations is profitable for the finding out of the sense of the Scriptures." As an avid collector of translations, I would highly recommend *The Mirror* as one of my favorites. Though every scholar attempts to present an objective portrayal of the text, each version is ultimately filtered through the translator's own theological lens. This is not wrong per se—it is impossible to convey the text apart from our own understanding of the work and nature of God.

Perhaps this is why Francois du Toit's work brings such a fresh perspective to the table. To rightly divide the Word of God, our interpretative lens must ultimately be the person of Christ Himself and His finished work. Christ is the ultimate Text. Each page of *The Mirror* drips with grace as we discover our own identity restored in the very Image of the invisible God, the Firstborn over all creation.

JOHN CROWDER - *Author of "Mystical Union" and "Cosmos Reborn"*

The *King James Version* of the Bible is widely considered to be the greatest piece of literature ever published in the English language. Known for its almost poetic expression of a literal translation from the original languages, the KJV is the most beloved rendering of the Bible in the English-speaking world. However, what lacks in a literal word-for-word translation is the ability of expression of the various nuances and meanings within each word. Many believe the *Amplified Bible* was the solution to what was missing from literal word-for-word translations.

However, while allowing for greater expression and therefore greater understanding of what is written in the text, the *Amplified* sacrifices the poetic majesty of Father's expression of Himself and us in Him. Father never intended for a written testimony of Himself to be rendered in cold, exact phrases; but rather, the scriptures are His love letter to all creation, the benevolent love of a Father to His children, and the passionate wooing call to His beloved bride—all in one.

It is a great pleasure to declare that *The Mirror Translation* is the perfect fusion of the poetic and powerful language of the *King James Version* with the expressiveness of the *Amplified*, clearly manifesting the scriptures as they were intended: to be a witness and testimony of Jesus and that by seeing and beholding Him as God, we consequently discover our own identity, having sprung forth from the logos (mind, thoughts) of God. *The Mirror Translation* is a poetically literal paraphrase packed with dunamis power spoken directly from the heart of the Father that reveals Jesus as what God has believed about mankind before the world began.

JEFF PATE - *Author of "I Am What I Am" and "Truth at First Light."*

A little boy who really wanted to show his family the roar of the Niagara Falls, caught some of its water in a bottle to take home. But when opening the bottle to show he said, "Oh no, it's dead!" Truth taken out of the stream of life - out of its original context -is a dead thing, but back in the stream of life it is an exciting thing ... never boring! For so long, Christians have read the Bible and completely missed the heart of the Father. If we read the scriptures in any other light than beholding Him, Jesus Christ, as in a mirror - we miss the point. *The Mirror* opens our understanding to know ourselves as we have always been known. My life has been enriched and many of my songs have been inspired by the fresh and beautiful revelation I have gained therein.

MARY-ANNE RABE

Once in a great while a person gets a chance to be associated with something of world changing significance. This is one of those rare moments for us! We are honored to endorse not only a great work, *The Mirror Translation*, but also two great people, Francois and Lydia du Toit. What they have accomplished in their beautiful translation of the New Testament has and will continue to shift the course of history. We are truly blessed to count the two of them as friends and family.

SCOTT & LORI SCHANG - *Author of "The Rhema Code"*

Mankind lost their greatest treausure when they lost the awareness of their true identity. It wasn't some sacred, ancient texts that went missing; it was more precious than that. When I met with Francois in Hungary in autumn of 2010, I found that great treasure. A veil fell from my eyes and all became clear. I realized that there was this latent 'treasure' inside me waiting to be awakened. When I discovered it, it became a vibrant, tangible reality! I was so happy. The Good News is that in Jesus God has taken away the veil from everyone, so they too can discover themselves mirrored in him. There is no veil in the Mirror Bible! This translation openly reveals YOU. See what God gave back to you: this greatest treasure that once was lost is now found again in YOU! As you read the Mirror Bible, you will enjoy how it reflects YOU in the original image and blameless innocence that God has always had in mind for you!

JOZSEF PALAVICS M.D.

See your identity clearly portrayed here in The MIRROR! Exhilarating, thrilling, breathtaking beauty overtakes you in this glorious translation. God's empowering, everlasting, all-compassing Gospel of Grace – Christ's Finished Work – is here revealed in depths and dimensions of joy that will rock your world. You are co-revealed in Christ! Co-crucified, co-included in His death and resurrection, co-buried, co-quickened, co- alive, co-seated "with Him in His executive authority in the Throne Room of the heavenly realm" (Eph. 2:6 The Mirror). Herewith, my highest recommendation for this new, powerful, mega-encouraging Bible translation, so rich with fresh, wide vistas of the mystery of our restored innocence in Christ. May The MIRROR Translation soon be treasured in every home, seminary and School of Ministry in the world!

REV. LANI LANGLAIS - *San Francisco, California*

I have been a follower of Christ for many years. With so many translations of the English Bible available, I have been privileged to discover many facets of God, but no translation has so powerfully revealed my true identity in Christ as *The Mirror Translation*. Being able to read the Scripture from a perspective that reveals and understands the finished work of the Cross has not only reshaped my thoughts of God, but it has transformed my view of God's opinion over me! *The Mirror* makes the Gospel easy to understand and it has become a regular reference in our Sunday celebrations and in our Church's conversations about God and themselves. Because of this translation's unique point of departure—Jesus came to reveal the Father to mankind—*The Mirror* has set itself out to affect change in people and not to perpetuate sameness of thought! My family and the life of our ministry is testimony to the power of this incredible gift that God has given us through *The Mirror Translation*!

IOANNIS DEKAS - *Pastor from Doxa Deo London*

The Mirror Reflects not who you can become, but who you already are. For ages, it has been God's desire for mankind to look deeply in the MIRROR of His word – to discover ourselves and stay under the influence of our true redeemed identity. Christ came to take away the veil from our faces so we can see ourselves in the same intent as God and to know ourselves just as we have always been known by Him. Every single page of this book oozes with irresistibly-attractive revelation; mankind is the heart-beat of Daddy God.

SHEPHERD MBATE - *Pastor, Mahalapye, Botswana*

All translators make choices... God cannot be contained exactly in our words. He is communicated Spirit to Spirit... Francois is sincere in revealing the original intent... He is translating this essentially "in public", open for comment, and gives his logic and notes for translation choices to let us see "under the hood"—whereas most other translations do not. The Mirror is an exhilarating, fresh look at familiar passages and a source of renewed passion to celebrate God!

ROD WILLIAMS - *Portland Oregon*

Thank you again for bringing this to all of us! We have found The Mirror Translation restores the power of the scriptures to life. The truth of our identity in His reflection brings back the joy of our salvation and we find ourselves "like children turned loose in the treasure room of the castle - we've got more than enough to keep us fascinated forever." Robert Capon.

THE SCHROEDERS - *Pastors, GoodNews Church, California*

My first experience with the Mirror Translation was hearing a preacher read Romans 6 from it. To say it was a poignant moment seems like a vast understatement! As soon as I got home, I started devouring this wonderful translation. Often, while reading the letters of Paul, I would find myself thinking, "This is how Paul himself would have written it in English." Verses I've read many times before seem to have come to life with the reality I was always meant to see. I used to think that the best translator would be an agnostic, Greek scholar who had no doctrinal biases; it is clear, however, when reading this amazing masterpiece, that the person best suited for the job is one whose heart is joyously pounding with excitement and passion in response to clearly seeing the revelation hidden for ages: Christ in you!

MARK PAULSON - *Fremont, California*

One day I had the pleasure of taking a famous photographer on a scenic boat trip in the bay of our hometown, Hermanus South Africa. I could tell by the size of his camera lenses and equipment that he was not your average tourist.

He explained to me that he needed to sell only two photographs a year to cover his budget! I was impressed to say the least and felt privileged and delighted to watch the artist at work. With fluent skill he would exchange lenses and film and go about his work.

After about two hours with the wonderful Southern Right whales we were on our way back to the harbor when we witnessed a flock of a few hundred Cape Cormorants.
The next moment they all took off in flight; the rhythm and unison of their wings were like a ballet reflecting on the water.

Our photographer friend was happily clicking away when suddenly he shouted, "I've got it! I've got it!"

It was amazing to witness the joy in the man's face. He knew that he had captured a moment that would be worth more than all the equipment in the boat. He immediately proceeded to pack away his expensive gear and carefully zipped up the waterproof bags. I then watched him relax and sit back, glowing with delight.

I couldn't help but reflect on what must have been the greatest moment when for the first time in the history of the universe the invisible Creator witnessed his image and likeness on display in fragile, tangible human form. And God saw everything that he had made and said, "Behold, it is very good." And God entered into his rest.

The Sabbath was a celebration of perfection rather than a break from a busy schedule to observe a religious ritual (Gen 1:31).

I became absorbed with the thought of photography; magic moments of light, shape, color and movement arrested and stored on film or in memory to be reproduced in a million glossy magazines or framed in art galleries. These exhibitions would be appreciated in any culture or language for countless years to come. I imagined how the artist would document these gems in a way that no virus would flaw the original detail, regardless of what would happen to the prints, whether they be framed, forgotten or destroyed—like words storing images of rare beauty to be repeated at any time in any language or thought.

In one of her classic novels, *Gentian Hill*, Elizabeth Goudge paints the picture of little Stella listening to her stepfather reading from the Bible:

"All through the Book, even in the dreadful parts, the language would now and then suddenly affect her like an enchantment. The peculiarities of Father Sprigg's delivery worried her not at all. It was as though his gruff voice tossed the words roughly in the air separate particles of no great value, and immediately they fell again transmuted, like the music of a peal of bells or raindrops shot through with sunshine and vista beyond vista of incomparable beauty opened before the mind. It was a mystery to Stella that mere words could make this happen. She supposed the makers of these phrases had fashioned them to hold their visions as one makes a box to hold one's treasure, and Father Sprigg's voice was the key grating in the lock, so that the box could open and set them free. That transmutation in the air still remained as unexplainable as the sudden change in herself, when at the moment of the magical fall her dull mind became suddenly sparkling with wonder and her spirit leaped up inside her like a bird ... ."

I am fascinated with words; language intrigues me. Mankind is in essence a communicator and an interpreter of thoughts and meaning. We live in the amazing age of a global communication explosion. Age-old traditions, interpretations and philosophies are "Googled" and questioned with deliberate scrutiny.

One wonders why Deity did not delay the spectacular event of the incarnation with two thousand years. Imagine our technology recording the Messiah on high definition mega pixel cameras and evidence his life, parables, miracles, love, his crucifixion and dramatic resurrection.

No technology yet to be invented in the far future could possibly match the enormity of human life. Consider the capacity and wonder of a single DNA strand with its three billion individual characters mirror repeated seventy five trillion times in the cells of one person. Just to count the individual characters in a single DNA strand at one character per second would take 96 years. This dwarfs any terabyte into insignificance.

Their inaudible voice resonates the light of life.

The hearing ear and the seeing eye, the Lord has made them both (Proverbs 20:12). Mankind is the god-kind, designed to live by the complete word that proceeds from the mouth of God.

The heavens are telling the glory of God; and the firmament proclaims his handiwork. Day to day pours forth speech, and night to night declares knowledge. There is no speech, nor are there words; their voice is not heard; yet their sound transmits through all the earth, and their words to the end of the world. In them he has set a tent for the sun, which comes forth like a bridegroom leaving his chamber, and like a strong man runs his course with joy. Its rising is from the end of the heavens, and its circuit to the end of them; and there is nothing hid from its heat (Ps 19:1-6 RSV).

All flesh shall see it together. Flesh was designed to exhibit the glory of God.

A voice cries: "In the wilderness prepare the way of the Lord, make straight in the desert a highway for our God (Isa 40:3 RSV).

Every valley shall be lifted up, and every mountain and hill be made low;

every crooked place shall be made straight, and the rough places smooth (Isa 40:4).

And the glory of the Lord shall be revealed, and all flesh shall see it together, for the mouth of the Lord has spoken (Isa 40:5 RSV).

In the incarnation God deleted every definition of distance; every possible excuse mankind could have to feel separated or even neglected by God was removed in one day, through one sacrifice, once and for all.

Life documented in the Rock of ages is now inscribed on hearts of flesh. Hear the echo, feel the resonance. Christ is all and in all.

You are living Epistles, known and read by all.

More than two thousand years ago the conversation that had begun before time was recorded—sustained in fragments of thought throughout the ages, whispered in prophetic language, chiseled in stone and inscribed in human conscience and memory—became a man. Beyond the tablet of stone, the papyrus scroll or parchment roll, human life has become the articulate voice of God. Jesus is the crescendo of God's conversation with humankind; he gives context and content to the authentic thought. Everything that God had in mind for mankind is voiced in him. Jesus is God's language. His name declares his mission. As Savior of the world he truly redeemed the image and likeness of the invisible God and made him apparent again in human form (Heb 1:1-3).

The destiny of the *logos* was not the printed page, but you! A mirror can only reflect the object; likewise, the purpose of the page was only to reflect the message which is "Christ in you." He completes the deepest longing of every human heart. The incarnation is the ultimate translation.

In the words of the song of Moses, "Give ear, O heavens, and I will speak; and let the earth hear the words of my mouth. May my teaching drop as the rain, my speech distill as the dew, as the gentle rain upon the tender grass, and as the showers upon the herb. For I will proclaim the name of the Lord, ascribe greatness to our God! The Rock, his work is perfect ... ." (Deut 32:1-4 RSV).

Mankind has forgotten their Maker and in the process, their identity. You were unmindful of the Rock that begot you, and you forgot the God who gave you birth (Deut 32:18 RSV).

The mission of Jesus was not to begin the Christian religion. His mandate was to reveal and redeem the image and likeness of God in human form.

While none of Jesus' brothers believed in him during the three years of his ministry, his brother, James, discovers his own true identity when Jesus appears to him after the resurrection (Jn 7:5, 1 Cor 15:4-7). James gives testimony to this life-changing discovery: We did not begin in our mother's womb! "It was God's delightful resolve to give birth to us; we were conceived by the word of truth." The incarnation reveals the logic of humanity's origin (Jas 1:18).

James continues in 1:23-25, "By being a mere spectator in the audience you underestimate yourself (you come to an inferior conclusion of who you really are). You are God's poem. The difference between a mere spectator and a participator is that both of them hear the same voice and perceive in its message the face of their own genesis reflected as in a mirror; they realize that they are looking at themselves, but for the one it seems just too good to be true, he departs (back to his old way of seeing himself) never giving another thought to the person he saw there in the mirror.

"The other one is mesmerized by what he sees; he is captivated by the effect of a law that frees mankind from the obligation to the old written code that restricted them to their own efforts and willpower. No distraction or contradiction can dim the impact of what he sees in that mirror concerning the law of perfect liberty (the law of faith) that now frees one to get on with the act of living the life (of their original design). This person finds a new spontaneous lifestyle, the poetry of practical living.

"The law of perfect liberty is the image and likeness of God revealed in Christ, now redeemed in mankind as in a mirror. Look deep enough into that law of faith that you may see there in its perfection a portrait that so resembles the original that he becomes distinctly visible in the spirit of your mind and in the face of everyone you behold."

Let us briefly consider these two words that James uses here, *parakupto* and *parameno.* I translated the word *parakupto* as "mesmerized" from *para*, a preposition which indicates close proximity, a thing proceeding from a sphere of influence, with a suggestion of union of place of residence, to have sprung from its author and giver, originating from, denoting the point from which an action originates, intimate connection; and *kupto*, to bend, stoop down to view at close scrutiny; *parameno*, to remain under the influence. The word often translated as freedom, *eleutheria,* means without obligation.

A word in any language can be most fascinating. A seed stores the life energy and the genetic detail of a plant species in much the same way as thoughts and concepts are concealed in words and language. Individual words can greatly influence the meaning and interpretation of any conversation.

For many years deliberate as well as oblivious errors in translations were repeated and have empowered the religious institutions of the day to influence, manipulate and even abuse masses of people.

Consider the word *metanoia,* consisting of two components, *meta,* together with, and *nous,* mind, suggesting a radical mind shift. This word has been translated regularly as "repentance," which is an old English word borrowed from the Latin, which means penance. Then they added the "re" to get even more mileage out of sin consciousness. Re-penance. This gross deception led to the perverted doctrines of indulgences, where naive, ignorant people were led to believe that they needed to purchase favor from an angry god. Most cathedrals as well as many ministries were funded with this guilt money.

English translations do little to help us understand what repentance truly is. Until Jerome's Latin Vulgate translation, the word *metanoia* was commonly used. For instance, Tertullian wrote in 198 A.D., "In Greek, *metanoia* is not a confession of sins but a change of mind." But despite this the Latin fathers begin to translate the word as "do penance" following the Roman Catholic teaching on doing penance in order to win God's favor.

In 1430, Lorenzo Valla, a Catholic theologian, began a critical study of Jerome's Latin Vulgate and Valla pointed out many mistakes that Jerome had made. Sadly, the "Vulgate-Only" crowd of Valla's day forced him to renounce many of the changes that he noted needed changing in the Vulgate including the poor translation of *metanoia.*

The business of religion desperately needs paying and returning customers. Jesus was crucified for this reason; the entire system of keeping people dependent on their hierarchy was challenged and condemned by him.

Isaiah 55:8-11 gives meaning to *metanoia:* "your thoughts were distanced from God's thoughts as the heavens are higher than the earth, but just like the rain and the snow would cancel that distance and saturate the soil to awaken its seed, so shall my word be that proceeds from my mouth."

The Greek preposition *meta,* together with, implies another influence. This is where the gospel becomes so powerful since it appeals to our conscience to reason together with our original design ... the authentic thought, the mind of God is realized again. The distance caused by Adam's fall, compared to the distance between heaven and earth, is cancelled in the incarnation. Metanoia suggests a co-knowing with God! It is an intertwining of thought; it is to agree with God about me.

Your belief in God does not define him; his faith in what he knows to be true about you defines you.

In Mark 11:22, Jesus says, "Have the faith of God." Unfortunately, most translations say, "Have faith in God." There is a massive difference between our beliefs and philosophies about God and God's persuasion about us! God's belief in you gives substance to your faith. Jesus is what God believes about you.

If our point of departure is not God's faith in the finished work of Christ we have no valid gospel to preach. If our faith is not sourced and sustained in him as the mirror image of God revealed and redeemed in us we are deceiving ourselves with yet another religious disguise called Christianity.

There are countless "errors" bound in expensive leather books, sold over many years under the notion of being "the authentic word of God." The book is not the word of God; but the message it contains certainly is. And in spite of the errors in text and translation millions of lives have been ignited, transformed and blessed by the Bible.

I salute the effort and contribution of the multitude of people who have painstakingly preserved, documented, gathered fragments of, scrutinized, compiled, copied and translated texts over the centuries; also those who translated and lost their lives in order to introduce the text in a language that ordinary people could understand.

The Mirror Bible does not replace any translation; it is simply a study tool that will assist both the casual reader as well as the student of scripture to gain highlighted insight into the promise and the Person documented and revealed in the Bible as the mirror image of the invisible God redeemed in human form.

Jesus blows our definitions and doctrines apart with one statement: "No-one knows the Father except the Son." Can you imagine how this shocked the Jews? They thought that they had copyright on God! Then he says, "If you have seen me, you have seen the Father." Whatever we thought that we knew about God that is unlike Jesus, is not God! (Mt 11:27, Jn 14:9, Lk 15.)

"If you have seen me you have seen the Father." This was his purpose, to resonate and redeem the *Abba* echo in every human heart.

"You have your heads in your Bibles constantly because you think you'll find eternal life there. But you miss the forest for the trees. These Scriptures are all about me!" (Jn 5:39, *The Message*. See also Lk 24:27, 44, 45.)

Jesus is what the Bible is all about, and you are what Jesus is all about. (John 5:39)

Every invention begins with an original thought. You are God's original thought. You are his initiative, the fruit of his creative inspiration, his intimate design and love-dream. The first Hebrew word in the Bible, *bereshet,* from *berosh,* literally means "in the head." God had you in mind from the beginning. You are his work of art; his poem, says Paul in the Greek text of Ephesians 2:10.

Every human life is equally valued and represented in Christ. He gives context and reference to our being as in a mirror; not as an example for us, but of us. The ugly duckling saw reflected in the water the truth that freed the swan.

Psalm 23 says, "He leads me beside still waters, and restores my soul" or "by the waters of reflection my soul remembers who I am." Psalm 22:27 says, "The ends of the earth shall remember and return to the Lord."

"He has come to introduce us to ourselves again, so that we may know, even as we have always been known." (Jer 1:5, 1 Cor 13:12)

Even when illiterate Peter learns to write, he declares, "we were born anew by the resurrection of Jesus from the dead." (1 Pet 1:3)

I love his motivation. In 2 Peter 1:13, he says, "I make it my business to thoroughly arouse you until these truths become permanently molded in your memory." He continues (vs 16-19): "We are not con-artists, fabricating fictions and fables to add weight to our account of his majestic appearance; with our own eyes we witnessed the powerful display of the illuminate presence of Jesus the Master of the Christ life." (His face shone like the sun, even his raiment were radiant white. [Mt 17:2])

"He was spectacularly endorsed by God the Father in the highest honor and glory. God's majestic voice announced, 'This is the son of my delight; he has my total approval.'"

"For John, James and me the prophetic word is fulfilled beyond doubt; we heard this voice loud and clear from the heavenly realm while we were with Jesus in that sacred moment on the mountain."

"For us the appearing of the Messiah is no longer a future promise, but a fulfilled reality. Now it is your turn to have more than a second hand, hearsay testimony; take my word as one would take a lamp at night; the day is about to dawn for you in your own understanding. When the morning star appears, you no longer need the lamp; this will happen shortly on the horizon of your own hearts." (2 Peter 1:16-19).

Now we all with new understanding see ourselves in him as in a mirror; thus we are changed from an inferior mindset to the revealed opinion of our true Origin.   (2 Corinthians 3:18)

By beholding the glory of the Lord as in a mirror you cannot but discover that you are his glory!

May this translation ignite many hearts with the light of life.

Francois du Toit ~ May 2012

The Incarnation Code

The Bible is a dangerous book! It has confused and divided more people than any other document. Yet its profound and simple message continues to appeal, overwhelm and transform the lives of multitudes of men and women of any age or culture. It is still the best seller on the planet.

Scriptures have been used to justify some of the greatest atrocities in human history. People were tortured, burned at the stake and multitudes murdered based on somebody's understanding of the scriptures! Jesus, Paul and believers throughout the ages faced their greatest opposition from those who knew the scriptures.

If it is such a dangerous document, how does one approach the book? What is the key that unlocks its mystery message?

The romance of the ages is revealed here. The heart of the Lover, our Maker is hidden in Scripture and uncovered in the pages of this book. He says in Isaiah 65:1, "I was ready to be found by those who did not seek me. I said, 'Here am I, here am I.'" (RSV) This sounds like mirror-language! Here I am echoes within us: "Here I am!"

What would it be that attracts God to engage with mankind?

Man began in God.

You are the greatest idea that God has ever had!

It is not our brief history on planet Earth that introduces us to God. He has always known us.

We are not the invention of our parents! Maybe your arrival was a big surprise to them, but according to Jeremiah 1:5, God knew you before he formed you in your mother's womb!

The Bible records how the invisible engineer of the universe found expression of his image and likeness in visible form in human life!

When God imagined you, he imagined a being whose intimate friendship would intrigue him for eternity. Mankind would be partner in God's triune oneness! His image and likeness would be unmasked in human life.

Jesus says in John 10:30, "I and the Father are one." None of the other disciples better captured the conclusion of the mission of Christ than John in John 14:20: "In that day you will know that I am in the Father and you in me and I in you." (RSV)

God has found us in Christ before he lost us in Adam. He associated us in Christ before the foundation of the world (Eph 1:4). He has always known us; now in Christ he invites us to know ourselves even as we have always been known (1 Cor 13:12)!

Jesus Christ is the context and meaning of Scripture; his work of redeeming the image and likeness of God in human form is what the Bible is all about (Col 1:13-15).

Christ reveals that there is no place in the universe where God would rather be; the fullness of Deity physically resides in him. Jesus proves that human life is tailor-made for God. He mirrors our completeness. (While the expanse cannot measure or define God, his exact likeness is displayed in human form. The human body frames the most complete space for Deity to dwell in.)

The whole Bible is about Jesus, and Jesus is all about you. This makes the Bible the most relevant book. Jesus is God's mind made up about "you-manity"! The meaning of his name declares our salvation. In him, God rescued his image and likeness in us.

Initially the prophetic shadow of the Old Testament introduces us to the Promise. The Promise points to the Person. He is the Messiah-Christ, the Incarnate Word.

He represents the entire human race. In the economy of God, Jesus mirrors humanity. The heart dream of God realized in the redemption of mankind; in one man, through one act of righteousness, in a single sacrifice, he rescued the human race!

The conclusion is clear. It took just one offense to condemn mankind; one act of righteousness declares the same mankind innocent. The disobedience of the one exhibits humanity as sinners; the obedience of another exhibits humanity as righteous (Rom 5:18, 19 *The Mirror*).

We see then, that as one act of sin exposed the whole race of mankind to judgment and condemnation, so one act of perfect righteousness presents all mankind freely acquitted in the sight of God (Rom 5:19 *J.B. Phillips*).

God has shown me that I should not call anyone common or unclean (Acts 10:28 RSV).

When Jesus joins the two confused disciples on their way back from Jerusalem, he introduces himself to them through the eyes of Scripture: "And beginning with Moses and all the prophets, he interpreted to them in all the Scriptures the things concerning himself" (Luke 24:27 RSV).

Then in Luke 24:44, he does the same when he appears to his disciples: "He said to them, 'These are my words which I spoke to you, while I was still with you, that everything written about me in the law of Moses and the prophets and the psalms must be fulfilled.'" (RSV) Luke 24:45 says, "Then he opened their minds to understand the Scriptures."(RSV)

Philip joins the chariot of the chief treasurer and asks him, "Sir, do you understand what you are reading?" (It is possible to read the right book and get the wrong message!) Then Philip opened his mouth, and beginning with this Scripture he told him the good news of Jesus (Acts 8:35 RSV).

The destiny of the Logos was not to be caged in a book or a doctrine but to be documented and unveiled in human life! Human life is the most articulate voice of Scripture. Jesus is God's language; mankind is his audience (Heb 1:1-3).

Diligent research and study is not the key to understanding the Scriptures; Jesus says, "You study and search the Scriptures thinking that in them you will find eternal life, but if you miss me, you miss the point."

The Message translation reads, "You have your heads in your Bibles constantly because you think you'll find eternal life there. But you miss the forest for the trees. These Scriptures are all about me"(John 5:39)!

> Jesus is the context of Scripture (Isa 53:4, 5).
> Long before the first line of Scripture
> was penned on papyrus scroll,
> the Word, unwritten,
> existed as the mind of God.
> Before the books were gathered
> collated as sacred text,
> the Word, intangible; invisible,
> was planning, was ordering
> the ages that were to come.
> This Word predates the Bible,
> this Word predates creation,
> this Word is alive and active
> and speaking still today.

— Andre Rabe

The mission of Jesus was not to begin the Christian religion or to win protest votes against Moses, Mohammed, or Buddha. His mandate was twofold; first to reveal and then to redeem the blueprint image and likeness of the invisible God in human form. Instead of an instruction manual, the Bible is a mirror revealing our redeemed identity.

We are not window-shopping the promises; we gaze into the mirror of our true likeness and discover the integrity of our redeemed innocence.

Any form of striving to become more like Jesus through personal devotion and diligence, no matter how sincere, bears the same fruit of failure and guilt.

Jesus did not come to condemn the world but to free the world. Religion has majored on guilt- and willpower-driven sentiment, which engaged mankind in futile efforts to save or improve themselves.

The Bible was never meant to be a manual; its message is all about Emmanuel! God with us! Every definition of distance is cancelled in Christ (Isa 40:4, 5). When Scripture is interpreted as a mere instruction manual for moral behavior its message is veiled.

2 Corinthians 3:15 says, "Whenever Moses is read the veil remains."

In John 1:17, "Moses represents the law; Jesus reveals grace and truth."

It is only in the mirror where the miracle transformation takes place and the blueprint image of our Maker is again realized in us (2 Cor 3:18)!

Jesus did not come as an example for us, but of us. Beholding Jesus in any other way, sentimentally or religiously, will bring no lasting change. Now in Christ we may know ourselves, even as we have always been known (1 Cor 13:12).

This is the truth that frees us to live the life of our design (John 8:32).

John writes that "this is not a new message; it is the word that was from the beginning. Yet it is new, for that which is true in him, is equally true in you" (1 Jn 2:7, 8).

We know that the son of God has come, and he has given us understanding to know him who is true; and this is the understanding, that we are in him who is true! (1 Jn 5:20).

Paul brands his gospel with the words grace and peace in order to distinguish the message of the revelation of the finished work of Christ from the law of Moses. It is a matter of grace vs. reward and peace vs. striving, guilt and condemnation. Grace and peace express the sum total of every beneficial purpose of God towards us realized in Christ.

To discover yourself in the mirror is the key that unlocks the door to divine encounter. Tangible beyond touch the genesis of our being is unveiled. Our most intimate and urgent quest is satisfied here.

The days of window-shopping the Bible are over. "And we all, with new understanding, see ourselves in him as in a mirror; thus we are changed from an inferior mind-set to the revealed opinion of our true Origin" (2 Cor 3:18).

As much as the world of science depends upon the senses to perceive, measure and calculate the facts to then form reliable conclusion, faith perceives the reality of God and extends the evidence to reason. Faith is to the spirit what your senses are to your body, while the senses engage in the fragile and fading, faith celebrates perfection. Faith is not wishful thinking; Jesus Christ is the substance of faith. He is both the author and conclusion of our faith. He is the accurate measure of the blueprint of our design.

The gift of Christ gives dimension to grace and defines our individual value. Grace was given to each one of us according to the measure of the gift of Christ (Eph 4:7).This is the mystery that was hidden for ages and generations; it is Christ in you (Col 1:27).

He is not hiding in history or in outer space, or in the future! He is *I am* in you!

Anticipate the revelation of Christ within you. There is no greater motivation for studying Scripture!

Jesus did not point to the sky when he gave the address of the kingdom of God; he said, "The kingdom of God is within you" (Lk 17:21).

In Matthew 13:44, he says, "The kingdom of heaven is like a treasure hidden in an agricultural field, which a man found and covered up. Then in his joy he goes and sells all that he has and buys that field." "He saw the joy of his image and likeness redeemed in mankind when he braved the cross and despised the shame of it." (Heb 12:2)

There is infinitely more to the field than what meets the eye. Jesus has come to unveil the real value of the field. Human life can never again be underestimated. The treasure exceeds any agricultural value that any harvest could possibly yield. The treasure defines the authentic value of the field.

Paul says, "We have this treasure in earthen vessels." (2 Cor 4:7 RSV). Yet our own unbelief veils our minds to keep us from recognizing the image of God, revealed in Christ, as the authentic reflection of our original identity (2 Cor 4:4).

We are not designed to live by bread alone. Bread represents the harvest of our own labor. Jesus invites us to look away from our own labor and to lift up our eyes and to see a harvest that is already ripe. A harvest is only ripe when the seed in the fruit matches the seed that was sown. The single grain of wheat did not abide alone. (Jn 12: 24, Jn 4:35, Jn 2:19-21, Hos 6:2, Eph 2:5).

The destiny of the word was not the book but the living epistle. Human life as revealed and redeemed in Christ is God's voice; humanity is his audience.

"You yourselves are all the endorsement we need. Your very lives are a letter that anyone can read by just looking at you. Christ himself wrote it—not with ink, but with God's living Spirit; not chiselled into stone, but carved into human lives—and we publish it." 2 Cor 3:2-3 —*The Message*

The Mirror Translation of 2 Corinthians 3:3 reads, "The fact that you are a Christ-Epistle shines as bright as day. This is what our ministry is all about. The Spirit of God is the living ink. Every trace of the Spirit's influence on the heart is what gives permanence to this conversation. We are not talking law-language here; this is more dynamic and permanent than letters chiselled in stone; this conversation is embroidered in your inner consciousness." *(It is the life of your design that grace echoes within you.)*

Any sincere student of classical music would sensitively seek to so capture and interpret the piece, so as not to distract from the original sound of the composition. To form an accurate conclusion in the study of our origin would involve a peering over the Creator's shoulder as it were, in order to gaze through his eyes and marvel at his anticipation. His invisible image and likeness is about to be unveiled in human form.

Personal opinion or traditional belief holds no ground against the fountain freshness of his thoughts. The word of truth accurately preserves his original idea in the resonance of our hearts.

My philosophy in doing the Mirror Bible is reflected in the following example: I do not read music, but have often witnessed our son, Stefan tackling a new piece. His eyes see so much more than mere marks scribbled on a page; he hears the music. His trained mind engages even the subtleties and the nuances of the original composition, and is able to repeat the authentic sound, knowing that the destiny of the music would never be reduced to the page; but is always in the next moment, where the same intended beauty is heard, and repeated again!

The best translation would always be the incarnation - the Word made flesh in you!

JOHN'S ENCOUNTER WITH JESUS

Sixty years after he last saw Jesus in the flesh, John, now in his nineties, reflects on the mystery that was revealed which transformed his life from an illiterate fisherman to a saint. He spent most of the latter part of his life (about 30 years) living in Asia Minor and more specifically at Ephesus; much of Paul's emphasis in teaching therefore reflects in John's writing. This he did both from Ephesus as well as from the Isle of Patmos where he spent some years in exile. *(Compare Col ossians 1:15-17, John 1:1-3,16-17, 1 John 5:20, "He has given us understanding to know him who is true and we are in him who is true!")*

None of the other disciples better captured the conclusion of the mission of Christ than John, *"In that day you will know that just as I am in my Father, you are in me and I am in you!" John 14:20*

He has no desire to outwit the others in giving an even more accurate historic account of Christ! The life that was manifest within his sacred gaze and now tangible embrace is a fellowship of the highest order! He must write; he must extend this reality to his immediate audience as well as the next generations! "I am writing this to complete your joy!" 1 John 1:4

Unlike Matthew and Luke who wrote 30 years prior to him, John did not bother to locate Jesus in the setting of his natural lineage. Instead he declares, "In the beginning was the Word!" Before history was ever recorded the Word was!

Mankind pre-existed in the Logic of God! He understands that the Word was both the eternal source and destiny of all things and that nothing could ever reduce or confine the Word to an isolated island experience, neither could the Word be trapped in human doctrine or tradition. No inferior translation or interpretation could compromise God's original intent. The authentic integrity of God's thought would forever be preserved and celebrated in the incarnation; human life would be the uninterrupted future of the Word.

Notice how often John uses the word, *egeneto*, from *ginomai*, meaning birth or origin in the first chapter: "In the beginning was the Word, and the Word was face to face towards God, and the Word was God. All things came into being *(ginomai, from genos, to give birth to)* through him; and nothing has any authentic existence outside of their origin *(ginomai)* in him.

In him was life and the life was the light of men. The light shone in the darkness, and the darkness could not comprehend it *(kata+lambano, to seize upon, to grasp)*. The true light that enlightens everyone has come into the world. The world was made *(ginomai)* through him, yet the world knew him not; he came to his own, and his own received him not *(para+lambano, to grasp, associate with)*.

But in everyone who by faith comprehends him to be their true origin (*lambano, comprehend, grasp, identify with*), in them he sanctions the integrity of their sonship (*didomi, in this case to give something to someone that already belongs to them, thus to return*), the fact that they already are his own, born from above, they have their beginning and their being in him (*eksousia, integrity, legality, authority, legal grounds*)! Jesus has come to reveal mankind's true sonship; he vindicated our origin and design.

"And the Word became (**ginomai**) flesh and now tabernacles in (**en**) us!" Not 'amongst us' as many translations would suggest! John 1:1-14.

"We are not preaching a new doctrine, but the word that was from the beginning; yet it is new: since everything that which is true in him is equally true in us!" 1 John 2:7, 8 As he is so are we in this world! 1 John 4:17.

In him we discover that we are not here by chance or accident, or by the desire of an earthly parent, neither are we the product of a mere physical conception; we exist by the expression of Elohim's desire to reveal their image and likeness in flesh. God said to Jeremiah, "I knew you before I formed you in your mother's womb." Jeremiah 1:5. The eternal, invisible Word, the Spirit-thought of God's face to face union, became flesh (**ginomai**, be born). James says: "Of his own will he brought us forth by the word of truth ... if anyone hears this word, he sees the face of his birth as in a mirror." James 1:17, 18, 23 RSV. Now we may know even as we have always been known. 1 Corinthians 13:12.

God never compromised his original thought. "The word became flesh and took up residence (tabernacled) in us, and we gazed with wonder and amazement upon the mystery of our inclusion in him (**theaomai**, to gaze upon, to perceive). We saw his glory (**doxa**, the display of his opinion); the glory as of the original, authentic begotten of the Father, full of grace and truth." (The original mind, or opinion of God, preserved and now revealed in Christ. He is both the "only begotten," **monogenes**, as in the authentic original mold, as well as the first born from the dead. Colossians 1:18, 1Peter 1:3.

He is the revelation of our completeness. "Of his fullness have we all received, grace against grace" (**garin anti garitos,** grace undeserved). "For the law was given through Moses, grace and truth came through Jesus Christ. He who is in the bosom of the Father, the only (original, authentic) begotten of the Father, he is our guide who accurately declares and interprets the invisible God within us." John 1:1-5, 9-14,16-18.

1 John 1:1 The Logos is the source; everything commences in him. The initial reports concerning him that have reached our ears, and which we indeed bore witness to with our own eyes - to the point that we became irresistibly attracted - now captivates our gaze. In him we witnessed tangible life in its most articulate form. (To touch, **psallo**, to touch the string of a musical instrument; thus to be deeply touched as in resonance.)

1 John 1:2 The same life that was face to face with the Father from the beginning, has now dawned on us! The infinite life of the Father became visible before our eyes in a human person! (In the beginning "was" the Word; **eimi**, timeless existence, "I am". The preposition **pros** says so much more than 'with,' it suggests towards; face to face. See John 1:1&2. Also John 1:14 "Suddenly the invisible eternal Word takes on visible form! The Incarnation! In him, and now confirmed in us! The most accurate tangible display of God's eternal thought finds expression in human life! The Word became a human being; we are his address; he resides in us! He captivates our gaze! The glory we see there is not a religious replica; he is the authentic begotten son. The glory (that Adam lost sight of) is now fully unveiled! Only grace can communicate truth in such complete context!" Also John 1:18 "Until this moment God remained invisible to mankind; now the authentic begotten Son, the blueprint of mankind's design who represents the innermost being of God, the Son who is in the bosom of the Father, brings him into full view! He is the official authority qualified to announce God! He is our guide who accurately declares and interprets the invisible God within us.")

1 John 1:3 We include you in this conversation; you are the immediate audience of the logic of God! This is the Word that always was; we saw him incarnate and witnessed his language as defining our lives. In the incarnation Jesus includes mankind in the eternal friendship of the Father and the Son! This life now finds expression in an unreserved union. (We do not invent fellowship; we are invited into the fellowship of the Father and the Son!)

1 John 1:4 What we enjoy equally belongs to you! I am writing this for your reference, so that joy may be yours in its most complete measure. (In all these years since the ascension of Jesus, John, now ninety years old, continues to enjoy unhindered friendship with God and desires to extend this same fellowship to everyone through this writing.)

1 John 1:5 My conversation with you flows from the same source which illuminates this fellowship of union with the Father and the Son. This, then, is the essence of the message: God is radiant light and in him there exists not even a trace of obscurity or darkness at all. (See James 1:17, "Without exception God's gifts are only good, their perfection cannot be improved upon. They come from above, [where we originate from] proceeding like light rays from the source, the Father of lights, with whom there is no distortion or even a shadow of shifting to obstruct or intercept the light; no hint of a hidden agenda. The word, anouthen, means, from above. John 3:3, 13. Mankind is not the product of their mother's womb; man began in God.")

John 3:7 Don't be so surprised when I say to you[manity] (plural!) You couldn't get here in the flesh unless you got here from above! (See John 1:13 These are the ones who discover their genesis in God beyond their natural conception! This is not about our blood lineage or whether we were a wanted or an unwanted child - this is about our God-begotteness; we are his dream come true! We are not the invention of our parents! [You are the greatest idea God has ever had!])

John 3:13 No one can fully engage in heaven's perspective, unless one's heavenly origin is realized! The son of man declares humanity's co-genesis from above!

Another pivotal reference John records is when Jesus defended his message when he declared, to the disgust of the religious leaders, "My Father and I are one!" (John 10:30) Jesus then quoted Psalm 82:6, "I say you are gods, sons of the Most High, all of you!"

In John 14:20 Jesus declares the conclusion of his mission where in his death and resurrection every possible definition of separation will be cancelled: "In that day you will know that I am in my Father, and you in me and I in you!" *(It is not our knowing that positions Jesus in the Father or us in them! Our knowing simply awakens us to the reality of our redeemed union!)*

1:1 To go back to the very ¹beginning is to find the ²Word already ³present there; ⁴face to face with God. The Word is ³I am; God's ²eloquence echoes and ⁴concludes in him. The Word equals God. *(In the beginning, ¹arche, to be first in order, time, place or rank. The Word, ²logos, was "with" God; here and again in verse 2 John uses the Greek preposition ⁴pros, towards; face-to-face.*

*Three times in this sentence John uses the active indicative imperfect form of the verb ³eimi, namely **aen [ἦv]** to be, [in the beginning 'was' the Word etc...] which conveys no idea of origin for God or for the Logos, but simply continuous existence, "I am." Quite a different verb **egeneto,** "became," appears in John 1:14 for the beginning of the Incarnation of the Logos. The Word 'became' flesh. The incarnation is not the genesis of Jesus. See the distinction sharply drawn in John 8:58, "before Abraham was [born, **genesthai** from **ginomai**] I am." The word **eimi,** I am; the essence of being, suggesting timeless existence.)*

1:2 The beginning mirrors the Word face to face with God. *(Nothing that is witnessed in the Word distracts from who God is. "If you have seen me, you have seen the Father." [John 14:9])*

1:3 The Logos is the source; everything commences in him. He remains the exclusive Parent reference to their existence. There is nothing original, except the Word! The Logic of God defines the only possible place where humankind can trace their genesis.

1:4 His life is the light that defines our lives. *(In his life mankind discovers the light of life.)*

1:5 The darkness was pierced and could not comprehend or diminish this light. *(Darkness represents mankind's ignorance of his redeemed identity and innocence [Isa 9:2-4, Isa 60:1-3, Eph 4:18, Col 1:13-15].)*

1:6 Then there was this man John *(Jesus' cousin)* **commissioned by God;**

1:7 his mission was to draw attention to the light of their lives so that what they witnessed in him would cause them to believe *(in their original life redeemed again).*

1:8 His ministry was not to distract from the light, as if he himself was the light but rather to point out the light Source.

1:9 A new day for humanity has come. The authentic light of life that illuminates everyone was about to dawn in the world! *(This day would begin our calendar and record the fact that human history would forever be divided into before and after Christ. The incarnation would make the image of God visible in human form. In him who is the blueprint of our lives there is more than enough light to displace the darkness in every human life. He is the true light that enlightens everyone! [Col 1:15; 2:9, 10; 2 Cor 4:6])*

1:10 Although no one took any notice of him, he was no stranger to the world; he always was there and is himself the author of all things.

1:11 It was not as though he arrived on a foreign planet; he came to his own, yet his own did not ¹recognize him. *(Ps 24:1, "The earth is the Lord's* *and the fullness thereof, the world and those who dwell in it [RSV]." The word,* [1]*paralambano, comes from* **para,** *a preposition indicating close proximity, a thing proceeding from a sphere of influence, with a suggestion of union of place of residence, to have sprung from its author and giver, originating from, denoting the point from which an action originates, intimate connection; and* **lambano,** *to comprehend, grasp, to identify with.)*

1:12 Everyone who [1]realizes their association in him, [6]convinced that he is their [2]original life and that [7]his name defines them, God [5]gives the assurance that they are indeed his [4]offspring, [2]begotten of him; he [3]sanctions the legitimacy of their sonship. *(The word often translated, to receive,* [1]*lambano, means to take in hand, to comprehend, to grasp, to identify with. This word suggests that even though he came to his own, there are those who do not* [1]*identify with their true* [2]*origin revealed in him, and like the many Pharisees they behave like children of a foreign father, the father of lies [John 8: 44]. Neither God's legitimate fatherhood of mankind nor his ownership is in question; mankind's indifference to their true* [2]*origin is the problem. This is what the Gospel address with utmost clarity in the person of Jesus Christ. Jesus has come to introduce mankind to themselves again; humanity has forgotten what manner of person they are by design! [James 1:24, Deuteronomy 32:18, Psalm 22:27].*

The word, [2]*genesthai, from* **ginomai,** *means to generate; to become; John employs this verb in the Aorist Infinitive tense, which indicates prior completion of an action in relationship to a point in time. Greek infinitives could have either a present or aorist form. The contrast between the two forms has more to do with aspect than with time. The present infinitive is used to express progressive or imperfective aspect. It pictures the action expressed by the verb as being in progress. The aorist infinitive however does not express progressive aspect. It presents the action expressed by the verb as a completed unit with a beginning and end. This is an important point since many translations of this verse suggests that God's ability to make us his sons can only be in response to something we must first do in order to trigger God into action! Our grasping [lambano] is simply the awakening to the fact that our genesis is already completed in the* **Logos.** *[See John 1:3] The* **Logos** *is the source; everything commences in him. He remains the exclusive Parent reference to their genesis. There is nothing original, except the Word. We are his offspring. [see also Acts 17:28]. "He has come to give us understanding to know him who is true and to realize that we are in him who is true." [1 John 5:20].)*

The word, [3]*exousia, often translated "power;" as in, he gave "power" to* [2]*become children of God, is a compound word; from* **ek,** *always denoting origin or source and* **eimi,** *I am; thus, out of I am! This gives* [3]*legitimacy and authority to our sonship;* [4]*teknon, translated as offspring, child.*

"He has given," [5]*didomi, in this case to give something to someone that already belongs to them; thus, to return. The fact that they already are his own, born from above and that they have their* [2]*beginning and their being in him is now confirmed in their realizing it! Convinced,* [6]*pisteo;* [7]*his name* **onoma,** *is mankind's family name. [see Eph 3:15].*

"He made to be their true selves, their child-of-God selves." — The Message)

1:13 These are the ones who discover their genesis in God, beyond their natural conception! This is not about our blood lineage or whether we were a wanted- or unwanted-child; this is about our God-begotteness. We are his dream come true and not the invention of our parents. You are indeed the greatest idea God ever had! *(See Jeremiah 1:5; 29:11 & John 3:2-7)*

1:14 Suddenly the invisible, eternal Word takes on ¹visible form - the Incarnation on display in a flesh and blood person as in a mirror! In him, and now confirmed in us! The most accurate tangible display of God's eternal thought finds expression in human life! The Word became a human being; we are his address; he resides in us! He ²captivates our gaze! The glory we see there is not a religious replica; he is the ³authentic begotten son. The ⁴glory *(that we lost in Adam)* returns in fullness! Only ⁵grace can communicate truth in such complete context! *(In him we discover that we are not here by chance or accident or by the desire of an earthly parent, neither are we the product of a mere physical conception; we exist by the expression of God's desire to reveal himself in the flesh. His eternal invisible Word, his Spirit-thought, ¹became flesh, ¹***ginomai***, as in be born and ²***theaomai***, meaning to gaze upon, to perceive. We saw his glory, ⁴***doxa***, the display of his opinion, the glory as of the original, authentic begotten of the Father, full of grace and truth. He is the "only begotten," ³***monogenes***; begotten only by the Father and not of the flesh; in him we recognize our true beginning, as in the authentic original mold. He is also the "first born from the dead", declaring our new birth. [Colossians 1:18, 1 Peter 1:3]. He is the revelation of our completeness.*

*And of his fullness have we all received, grace against grace, ⁵***garin anti garitos***, grace undeserved. For the law was given through Moses, grace and truth came through Jesus Christ. He who is in the bosom of the Father, the only original, authentic begotten of the Father; he is our guide who accurately declares and interprets the invisible God within us. Interesting that the revelation of the Incarnation in verse 14 doesn't follow verse 2 or 3, but verse 12 and 13! Genesis 1:26 is redeemed! See 2 Corinthians 3:17,18.)*

1:15 John the Baptist raised his voice to announce emphatically that Jesus was what his ministry and prophetic message were all about. He declared that Jesus, though younger than him, since he ¹witnessed his ²birth, ranks above him in prominence and in his Messianic mission - because in his I-am-ness, he always ³was preeminent. *(He was ²born ²in front of my eyes - I witnessed his birth, meaning he is younger than I; ¹***emprosthen mou*** ²***gegonen*** [from ***ginomai***] ***oti protos mou*** ³***ean*** [***eimi***] - but he ³was before I was ²born - Later Jesus reminds us that before Abraham was born, [***ginomai***] I am! [***eimi***]")*

1:16 He is the source of our completeness. Everyone may now realize his or her own completeness as evidenced in him. This is ¹grace where ²no grace was due! *(¹***garin*** ²***anti garitos***, grace undeserved. Grace prevailed against the tide of darkness due to Adam's fall. His fullness is the source of all that grace communicates as our portion, against all odds!)*

1:17 The law was given through Moses; grace and truth have their genesis in Jesus Christ. Against the stark backdrop of the law, with Moses representing the condemned state of mankind, Jesus Christ unveils grace and truth! *(Moses represents the system of performance as basis to one's standing before God; Jesus Christ is incarnate grace and truth! He is the life of our design on display in human form, as in a mirror.)*

1:18 Until this moment God remained invisible; now the [1]authentic, incarnate begotten Son, the blueprint of our design who represents the innermost being of God, the Son who is in the bosom of the Father, brings him into full view! He is the [2]official authority qualified to announce God! He is our guide who accurately declares and interprets the invisible God within us. *(Begotten only of God, [1]monogenes. Official guide, [2]eksegesato, from ek, preposition denoting source, and hegeomai, the strengthened form of ago, to lead as a shepherd leads his sheep; thus hegeomai means to be officially appointed in a position of authority.)*

1:19 The Jews sent a delegation of priests and Levites from Jerusalem to question John the Baptist; this is how he responded to them when asked, "So who are you really?"

1:20 Without hesitation he made it clear to them that he was not to be confused with the Christ.

1:21 "Could you possibly be the re-incarnate Elijah?" To which he answered, "No, I am certainly not!" Then you must be The Prophet Moses said would come? "No!" He said, "I am not." *[Deut 18:15; John 6:14; Acts 3:22]*

1:22 So who are you then? How shall we respond to those who sent us? What would you say about yourself.

1:23 I echo the prophetic voice of Isaiah, crying with urgency in the wilderness, "At once! Level the highway of the Lord! His appearance is apparent, without delay!"

1:24 These priests and Levites sent to question John were all of the Pharisee Party.

1:25 "So if you are not the Messiah, neither Elijah, nor that Prophet, what is the purpose and significance of your baptism then?"

1:26 John replied, "I baptize in water; but you do not even recognize him who is standing in your midst!

1:27 My baptism is preparing the way for this one coming after me; I am not here to distract from him in any way, or to make a name for myself! I do not even qualify to be the slave that unties his sandals!

1:28 This conversation was in Bethania, beyond the Jordan, where John was baptizing.

1:29 The next day John saw Jesus approaching him, and declared: "Behold the Lamb of God; this is the one who would [1]lift the sin of the cosmos like an anchor from the sea floor, for humanity to sail free!" *(This is unheard of! It is not about a revengeful god demanding a sacrifice; this is your Father and Creator providing himself as sacrifice. The ultimate sacrifice for sins would never be something we did, or brought to God to appeal to him; the shocking scandal of the cross, is the fact that mankind is confronted with the extravagant, embarrassing proportions of the love of their Maker; Father Son and Spirit would go to the most ridiculous extreme to finally convince us of their heart towards us! In order to persuade us of our worth, God speaks the most severe scapegoat language: "Behold the Lamb of God, who takes away the sins of the world!" This completely disarms religion! Suddenly there is nothing that we can do to persuade God about our sincere intentions; this is God persuading us of their eternal love dream! The word αἴρω - [1]airo, a primary verb; to lift; by implication to take up or away; specifically to raise the anchor to sail away.)*

1:30 Jesus is what my ministry and prophetic message are all about. Though younger than I, he ranks above me, since he always was! *(See John 1:15)*

1:31 I am not here to [1]introduce him merely as my cousin from a human point of view; my baptism in water is to publicly declare him to Israel as the Messiah whom their prophets have proclaimed! *([1]I do not know him; meaning my knowledge of him is not reduced to my opinion according to the flesh - I too only know him by revelation, according to the prophetic word. Even though John grew up within the dramatic context of his own supernatural birth, he didn't claim that his knowledge of himself or his cousin Jesus was anything he merely learnt by human opinion or instruction. See Luke 1:5-80.)*

1:32 Then John made this emphatic statement, "I [1]gazed with wonder and saw the Spirit descending [2]out of the heavenlies and resting upon him like a [3]dove, [4]endorsing her [5]abiding anointing on him, thereby uniting heaven and earth in the incarnate Christ!" *(John uses the word, [1]theaomai, to view attentively, to contemplate, to learn by looking; it suggests a gazing with wonder. See 1 John 4:13,14. The preposition [2]ek always denotes source or origin. The word for dove in the Greek, [3]peristeran is feminine. The preposition [4]epi suggests a continual influence upon; to superimpose, to have charge of; thus to endorse! The word [5]meno means to continue to be present in a seamless union; to abide. It is not as though the Spirit was absent in Jesus' life until now; this coming upon him was the prophetic moment of the Spirit's endorsing of his ministry; uniting heaven and earth in the incarnate Christ.)*

1:33 I did not merely take into account what I knew about Jesus as my cousin according to the flesh, but he who authorized me to immerse people in water clearly instructed me saying, the one upon whom you see the Spirit descends and abides, he is the one who [1]immerses in holy Spirit. *(John's baptism announces the incarnation; yet it communicates a mere prophetic picture of what Jesus' spirit baptism will fully interpret of mankind's co-inclusion and joint immersion into his death, resurrection and ascension. In the incarnation we have the prophetic word on exhibit, intercepting human history by assuming human form; thus we see divinity immersed into our humanity and declaring that* *there would be no stopping him from entering into our hell and deepest darkness. In dying our death, God would bring closure to every destructive mindset and futile fruit we inherited from Adam's fall. Just as he was raised out of the water in his baptism, we would be co-elevated together with him in his resurrection into newness of life! Hosea 6:2; Ephesians 2:5. The word [1]baptizo from bapto, to immerse, to overwhelm.)*

1:34 Having witnessed this exactly as I have told you, I confidently declare that Jesus is indeed the son of God!

1:35 The following day John was standing with two of his students,

1:36 while gazing intently at Jesus, he announced, "See for yourselves, the Lamb of God!"

1:37 These two students of John listened intently and were obviously intrigued by his words, thus they immediately[1]joined Jesus on his way. *(John uses the word akoloutheō from a, as particle of union plus keleuthos, a road, thus to join someone on the same road, to accompany.)*

1:38 Jesus turned around and looked them in the eyes and asked, "What is it that you are really looking for?" They answered him, Rabbi, which means, my Teacher, where do you [1]abide? *(John uses the word [1]meno more than anyone else in the New Testament. Meno means to continue to be present in a seamless union; to abide. This word points to so much more than a mere geographic location or physical address. It is a word key to John's understanding of the revelation of the incarnation; it locates us in that place where he has restored us to, so that we may be where he is, in the bosom of the Father; also that we may know, that just as he is in the Father, so we too are in him and he in us! John 1:18 and John 14:2,3,10 &20. See also 1 John 5:20 This is what has become distinctly clear to us: the coming of the son of God is God's mission accomplished! He is the incarnate Christ. The moment all of Scripture pointed to, has arrived! The son is present! In him God has given us the greatest gift, a mind whereby we may know him who is true; and in the same knowing, to find ourselves there in him who is true! Mankind is fully included and located in him, in his son Jesus Christ; this means that whatever Jesus is as son, we are. This is the true God; this is the life of the ages!)*

1:39 He replied, "Come along and [1]see for yourselves." They came, saw where he was [2]lodging, and ended up [2]remaining with him for the day. It was late afternoon when this happened. *(John uses the word ὄψεσθε - [1]op-sesthe from oraoo, you will see [perceive] for yourselves. Again the word [2]meno is used. Not long after this Jesus might have been homeless because of his public and controversial cleansing of the temple. See Mathew 8:20, "Foxes have dens and the birds have nests..." also Mathew 12:46, While Jesus was still speaking to the crowds, his mother and brothers stood outside requesting to talk with him.)*

1:40 Andrew, Simon Peter's brother, was one of the two.

1:41 He immediately fetched his own brother Simon, telling him, "We've found the Messiah" which in Greek means, "the Christ." *(Aramaic was the spoken language and Greek the academic language in which the New Testament was written.)*

1:42 When he introduced him to Jesus, he gazed intently at him and said, you are Simon the son of ¹Jonah; you will be ²known as Mr ³Rock. *(The Hebrew word **yona**, means dove. The word ²**kaleo** means to surname, to identify by name. **Kefas** is the Aramaic for ³**Petros**, a stone or chip of rock - a chip of the old block! See Mathew 16:13 - 18.*

This conversation beautifully reminds of the Song of Songs in chapter 2:14 "O my dove [yona], in the clefts of the rock, in the crevice of the cliff, let me see your face, let me hear your voice, for your voice is sweet, and your face is comely. The crevice of the cliff is the address and home of the rock pigeon! The birds have nests!)

1:43 The next day Jesus intentionally departed from there and went to Galilee. There he met Phillip along the way and asked him to accompany him.

1:44 Phillip was from Bethsaida, the hometown of Andrew and Peter. *(The word **koloutheo** is again used; from **a**, as particle of union and **keleuthos**, a road, thus to join someone on the same road, to accompany.)*

1:45 Phillip immediately went looking for Nathaniel and told him the news! We have found the one Moses wrote about in the Torah and he whom the prophets announced when they spoke about Jesus, *[the Savior]* **the son of Joseph from Nazareth.** *(See Deuteronomy 18:15, "The LORD your God will raise up for you a prophet like me from among you, from your brethren- him you shall heed. :18 I will raise up for them a prophet like you from among their brethren; and I will put my words in his mouth, and he shall speak to them all that I command him. Genesis 49:10, The scepter shall not depart from Judah, nor the ruler's staff from between his feet, until he comes to whom it belongs; and to him shall be the obedience of the peoples. Isaiah 7:14 Therefore the Lord himself will give you a sign. Behold, a virgin shall conceive and bear a son, and you shall call his name Immanuel. Also Isaiah 53:1-12; Isaiah 9:6,7 For unto us a child is born, unto us a son is given: and the government shall be upon his shoulder: and his name shall be called Wonderful, Counsellor, The mighty God, The everlasting Father, The Prince of Peace. Of the increase of his government and peace there shall be no end, upon the throne of David, and upon his kingdom, to order it, and to establish it with judgment and with justice from henceforth even for ever. The zeal of the LORD of hosts will perform this. Daniel 9:24-27; Jeremiah 23:5-6. See also Joh 5:39,40 You search the scriptures, because you think that in them you have eternal life; and it is they that bear witness to me; yet you refuse to come to me that you may have life. John 5:46, 47 If you believed Moses, you would believe me, for he wrote of me. But if you do not believe his writings, how will you believe my words?")*

1:46 To which Nathaniel answered, "How does Nazareth fit into into the picture of God's promised goodness? Phillip said to him, "Come and see for yourself!" *(The τι αγαθον, 'what good thing?' of Nathaniel refers to scriptures like Jeremiah 33:14 & 15 Behold, the days come, says the LORD, that I will perform that good thing which I have promised. In those days and at that time I will cause a righteous Branch to spring forth for David; and he shall execute justice and righteousness in the land. Also Micah 5:2 But you, O Bethlehem Ephrathah, who are the least among the clans of Judah, from you shall come forth for me one who* *is to be ruler in Israel, whose origin is from of old, from ancient days. Nathanael's question seems to imply, that not Nazareth, but Bethlehem, was to be the birthplace of the Messiah.)*

1:47 When Jesus saw Nathaniel approach him, he made the following observation, "Now here is a man of Israel, in whom there is no guile!" *(Note the wisdom of Jesus, instead of engaging Nathaniel in a doctrinal debate around the scriptures, he endorses him!)*

1:48 Nathaniel was surprised! How can you possibly know me if we have never met? Jesus answered him, "Long before Phillip spoke to you, I saw you under the fig tree!"

1:49 Nathaniel exclaimed, "Rabbi, you are the son of God! You are the king of Israel!"

1:50 Jesus said, "So you believe because I say I saw you sitting under the fig tree? You haven't seen anything yet!

1:51 Truly I say unto you *[singular],* **because of who I am, you** *[plural - You-manity - all the families in heaven and on earth]* **will surely see this communication between the heavenly sphere and earth thrown wide [1]open, and the angelic messengers of God ascending and descending upon the incarnate son of man. Heaven and earth meet in the incarnate one!** *(In him every definition of separation and distance is cancelled! Isaiah 55:10,11 "For as the rain and the snow come down from heaven, and return not there without saturating the earth [all flesh], so shall my word be that goes forth from my mouth; it shall not return to me empty, but it shall accomplish that which I purpose, and prosper in the thing for which I sent it. The prophetic word was destined to become flesh; every nook and cranny of human life is saturated in the incarnation! The word [1]aneogota, Perfect Active Participle Accusative Masculine Singular, 2nd Conjugation-form; the one who has led us upwards - from **anoigō, ana**, upwards and **agoo**, to lead! Jesus reminds Nathaniel of Genesis 28:12-14 And Jacob dreamed that there was a ladder set up on the earth, and the top of it reached to heaven; and behold, the angels of God were ascending and descending on it! And Jahweh said to him, I am Elohim of Abraham, your seed shall be like the dust of the earth, and you shall spread abroad to the west and to the east and to the north and to the south; and in you and your descendants have all the families of the earth been blessed! See Ephesians 3:15 also Ephesians 1:3 Let's celebrate God! He lavished every blessing heaven has upon us in Christ! See Ephesians 4:8-10, Scripture confirms that he led us as trophies in his triumphant procession on high; he repossessed his gift (likeness) in human form. (See Ephesians 2:6, We are also elevated in his ascension to be equally welcome in the throne room of the heavenly realm where we are now seated together with him in his authority. Quote from the Hebrew text, Ps 68:18, lakachta mattanoth baadam, thou hast taken gifts in human form, in Adam. [The gifts which Jesus Christ distributes to us he has received in us, in and by virtue of his incarnation. Commentary by Adam Clarke.]*

Ephesians 4:9 The fact that he ascended confirms his victorious descent into the deepest pits of human despair. (See John 3:13, "No one has ascended into heaven but he who descended from heaven, even the son of man." All mankind originate from above; we are anouthen, from above. [See James 1:17, 18])

Ephesians 4:10 He now occupies the ultimate rank of authority from the lowest regions where he stooped down to rescue us to the highest authority in the heavens, having executed his mission to the full. (Fallen mankind is fully restored to the authority of the authentic life of their design. [Ps 139:8])

"Jesus has united heaven and earth, the life of God and human life in himself. Just as it was planned before the time of the ages." Baxter Kruger.)

2:1 Three days later there was a wedding in Cana, a village in Galilee which Jesus' mother attended.

2:2 Jesus and his followers were also invited.

2:3 When Mary learned that they had run out of wine, she informed Jesus.

2:4 He responded with, "Well Ma'am, that's their problem - or do you want me to steal the show here at somebody else's wedding, when my hour of fulfilling my mission has not yet come? *(Religion has run out of wine – Jesus lived aware of his mission which was to redeem and restore the joyous celebration of the union and romance of the ages – marrying humanity and divinity! While he is the true joy and wine of the party, he fully understood what it would cost him to drink the cup of humanity's injustice and violence on the cross! See John 12:27 "Now is my soul troubled. And what shall I say? 'Father, save me from this hour'? No, for this purpose I have come to this hour.)*

2:5 Mary proceeded to line up the waiters to assist Jesus, "Do whatever he tells you to!"

2:6 Now there were six empty stone water pots used for the ceremonial cleansing of the Jews. They could hold approximately twenty gallons each.

2:7 Jesus asked the waiters to fill these stone jars with water, to the brim. *(Nothing would be left untouched by the effect of the incarnate Word impacting human life entirely - every nook and cranny - spirit soul and body! See Mirror note in John 1:51; also 1 John 5:18.)*

2:8 And then instructed them to immediately draw from the containers and present it to the governor of the feast; which they did without hesitation.

2:9 The host of the event tasted the water that has now become wine, but had no clue as to its vintage or origin. The servants didn't tell him a word, so he called the bridegroom.

2:10 "Why would you keep the best wine for last?" Everybody serves the better wine first, so that by the time the cheaper wine is served, no-one can tell the difference - and here you surprise us all by bringing this excellent wine from your storehouse. Even though we already had much to drink, it is impossible not to tell its superiority! *(Even minds intoxicated with inferior religious jargon can immediately tell the difference when the Holy Spirit transforms ordinary conversation into the wonderful, blissful wine of revelation and the merry celebration of life!)*

2:11 In this first of the signs which Jesus performed at a wedding in Cana of Galilee, he gave everyone a foretaste of the beauty and intention of his mission. And his disciples believed in him. *(The word [1]doxa often translated glory, from dokeo, to form an opinion, a view, an idea or intention - ideas become our eyes -the way we see things. [Baxter Kruger] If Jesus could do this to water - imagine how he can transform ordinary routine days into the invigorating adven-*

ture of living the life of our design! My friend Errol Meaney made this comment on my Facebook post, His 'FIRST' miraculous sign was a change within a vessel! A jar of stone. External washing has been upgraded to internal transformation of inner thought processes. Completely transformed to the "brim"! And, it wasn't even drinking water, but "the kind used for ceremonial washing!" There is nothing Jesus intended to leave out of this transformation. And, although it wasn't time for Jesus to give his wine that night at Cana. I believe it was no accident that it was the first miracle - Could there have been a more profound picture of his ministry and what his Wine would do in the lives of ordinary vessels? He thus revealed his Glory!

And here's a note from Mary Luti - "They have no wine." That's all Mary says to Jesus after noticing the newlyweds' embarrassment. Could she be more indirect? Yet he knows what she wants, and he's not feeling ready. He tells her it's not time to reveal his glory and suffer the consequences. The wine he could make would be free to the guests but cost him plenty. Mary marches right over to the serving table as if he'd said "no problem" instead of "no way." She once said a costly yes; she's not about to take no for an answer from him. Because they have no wine. It's human history she's talking about, life's disappointed guests milling around with empty glasses from time immemorial. She's waited long enough for the mighty to fall, for the poor to dance at the wedding, for the kingdom's elixir to flow. Three Persian potentates once bent their knees to him. Why is he still constructing cabinets in Nazareth? She wants him out of the house. He gives in and produces liquid heaven in preposterous quantities. He squanders it on us, the undeserving who can't distinguish rotgut from Rothschild. He becomes the wastrel we need him to be. - Thank you, Mary."

Prayer; When we are reluctant to act on our callings, O God, send Mary to remind us, "They have no wine." Get us out of the house.

Mary Luti is an Author, Blogger, Teacher, Theologian, and Interim Senior Pastor, Wellesley Village Church, Wellesley, Massachusetts.)

2:12 After this he joined his family and followers to go down to Capernaum and remained there for several days.

2:13 Jesus then went up to Jerusalem in time for the Jewish Passover.

2:14 When Jesus went into the temple he was shocked to find scores of traders selling their sacrificial items, cattle, sheep and doves. Even their money brokers were comfortably set up in the sanctuary. *(The business of sin-consciousness has taken over the mindset of religion - until Jesus arrives.)*

2:15 Then with a whip that he plaited of small ¹strands, he drove everyone with their sheep and oxen out of the temple and overturned the tables of the money brokers so that their money went flying all over the place. *(Jesus dramatically reveals that his Father has no delight in our religious sacrificial systems and its sin-conscious currencies. ¹σχοῖνος - schoinos perhaps from **skenos**, tabernacle or skin - leather thongs - a profound prophetic picture of his own broken skin that would become the whip to drive out sin-consciousness from our minds - the ultimate cleansing of the Temple - the sanctuary of God within us! 1 Peter 1:18,19.)*

2:16 He also drove the dove traders out with, "How dare you turn my Father's house into a shopping mall?"

2:17 This incident reminded his disciples of the scripture, "I am consumed with zeal for my Father's house!" *(Psalm 69:9. God is ablaze with zeal for you! You are the Temple of God - his address - his dwelling!)*

2:18 The Jews demanded to know from Jesus how, what he has just done in the temple, could possibly point to the significance of his Messianic mission. "Show us a sign!"

2:19 To which Jesus responded, "The temple will be completely demolished by you and in three days I will raise it up!" *(The word [1]lusate, to undo, demolish, is is in the aorist, passive, imperative case; the distinction between the aorist imperative and the present imperative is one of aspect, not necessarily tense. Thus, to get something over and done with!*

See Mathew 12:39,40 But he answered them, "An evil and adulterous generation seeks for a sign; but no sign shall be given to it except the sign of the prophet Jonah. For as Jonah was three days and three nights in the belly of the whale, so will the son of man be three days and three nights in the heart of the earth.

"Ask a sign of the LORD your God; let it be deep as Sheol or high as heaven. But you would not, therefore the Lord himself will give you a sign. Behold, a virgin shall conceive and bear a son, and shall call his name Immanuel." Isaiah 7:11-14. "For unto us a child is born, to us a son is given; and the government will be upon his shoulder, and his name will be called Wonderful Counselor, Mighty God, Everlasting Father, Prince of Peace. Of the increase of his government and of peace there will be no end." Isaiah 9:6,7.

In his resurrection on the third day, God would co-quicken humankind and co-raise us together with him! Hosea 6:2, Ephesians 2:5. Human life will again be the tabernacle of God! "On the third day Esther put on her royal robes and stood in the inner court of the king's palace, opposite the king's hall. The king was sitting on his royal throne inside the palace opposite the entrance to the palace; and when the king saw Queen Esther standing in the court, she found favor in his sight and he held out to Esther the golden scepter that was in his hand. Then Esther approached and touched the top of the scepter." Esther 5:1,2

"And beginning with Moses and all the prophets, he interpreted to them in all the scriptures the things concerning himself." Luke 24:27 "They said to each other, did not our hearts ignite within us while he talked to us on the road, while he opened to us the scriptures?" Luke 24:32 "Then he said to them, these are my words which I spoke to you, while I was still with you, that everything written about me in the law of Moses and the prophets and the psalms must be fulfilled. Then he opened their minds to understand the scriptures, and said to them, Thus it is written, that the Christ should suffer and on the third day rise from the dead" Luke 24:44-46; See also Psalm 22 and Isaiah 53.

Matthew 16:21 From that time Jesus began to show his disciples that he must go to Jerusalem and suffer many things from the elders and chief priests and scribes, and be killed, and on the third day be raised.)

2:20 The Jews responded with, "This temple was under construction for forty six years and you will rebuild it in just three days? Haha!"

2:21 They did not understand that the temple Jesus was pointing to, was his own human body. *(In him, the only true address of God was to be redeemed in human life in his resurrection! See Hosea 6:2 "After two days he will revive us, on the third day he will raise us up!" Also Ephesians 2:5 and 1 Peter 1:3; Acts 7:47-50 But it was Solomon who built a house for him. Yet the Most High does not dwell in houses made with hands; as the prophet says, 'Heaven is my throne, and earth my footstool. What house will you build for me, says the Lord, or what is the place of my rest? Did not my hand make all these things?'*

*The word **hieros** speaks of the greater temple building with all its outer courts etc. whereas the word Jesus uses here is **naos**, referring to the inner sanctuary - this is also the word Paul uses in 1 Corinthians 6:19 "Do you not realize that your body by design is the sacred shrine of the Spirit of God!" This is the most sacred place in the universe! There is nowhere in eternity that can match this! See John 1:14 "And the Word became flesh and now resides within us! And 14:20 In that day you will know that I am in my Father and you in me and I in you!"*

2:22 These words of Jesus as well as their significant prophetic connection with scripture gave such clear context to the disciples when they later, after his resurrection, recalled all these things.

2:23 Now during the Passover feast in Jerusalem, many believed in his Name - surely the signs he did confirmed his mission as the Messiah-Savior of the world?

2:24 Jesus however did not make much of their apparent support - he wouldn't entrust himself to them since he knew all things. *(He knew how their own faith would fail them in the end. He did not endorse their excitement about the signs they saw as a valid basis to their belief. Signs are not the source of faith - signs follow faith! Jesus' belief in the integrity of our inner being is what saves us from the lies that we believed about ourselves.)*

2:25 He knew that their brief belief was simply based on the surface hype of the moment and not upon that which he was about to redeem in their innermost [1]being. He knew them better than what they knew themselves! He had no need for anyone's theory about the [2]human species to confirm what he always knew to be true about them. *(Literal translation - "He had no need that any should testify concerning human life - he indeed knew what [1]was in the human being." [1]**eimi**, I am; our very beingness! Which was exactly why he came, not as an example for us but of us! So that we may know even as we have always been known! Mathew 13:44, 2 Corinthians 4:7. The word for the [2]human species, male or female is **anthropos**, from **ana**, upwards, and **tropos**, manner of life; character; in like manner. See John 1:51.)*

3:1 Now amongst them there was a man who was a prominent leader among the Jews, a Pharisee named Nicodemus.

3:2 He came to see Jesus under the cover of the night and said to him, "Rabbi, it is [1]**clear for all of us to see that you** [2]**come from God as a Teacher - the signs you perform are proof that God is** [6]**with you! **[3]**No one is** [4]**able to do these signs you do** [5]**if they are not in** [6]**union with God.** (*The thoughts from the following 6 words are repeated in the answer Jesus gives Nicodemus:* [1]*oidamen, from **eido**, to perceive, to see; to discern.* [2]***eleuthas**, from **erchomai**, to come from;* [3]***oudeis**, no one;* [4]***dunamis**, to be capable; able; to have the power to accomplish.* [5]***ean me**, unless; if not;* [6]***meta**, together with; to be included in; to be in union with.*)

3:3 Jesus answered him emphatically; no one would even be able to recognize anything as coming from God's domain unless they are born from above to begin with! The very fact that it is possible to perceive that I am in union with God, as a human being, reveals humanity's genesis from above! (*Notice from the previous verse how Jesus employs a play of words from the question of Nicodemus. Here Jesus uses the word anouthen meaning from above - see James 1:17, every good and perfect gift comes anouthen [from above]*)

3:4 Nicodemus did not understand this answer at all and said to him, "How can a person be born if they are already grown-up? Surely one cannot re-enter your mother's womb and be born a second time? (*Nicodemus looks at the subject merely from the physical side. His "second time" is not the same as Jesus' "from above." As Godet remarks, "he does not understand the difference between a second beginning and a different beginning."*)

3:5 Jesus answered, you have to get this, unless someone is born out of water (*the womb*) **and Spirit, there would be no possible connection with the realm of God!**

3:6 Whatever originates out of flesh is flesh; but what is sourced in Spirit is spirit! (*The Message says, when you look at a baby, it's just that: a body you can look at and touch. But the person who takes shape within is formed by something you can't see and touch--the Spirit*)

3:7 Don't be so surprised when I say to you[manity - plural!] **You couldn't get here in the flesh unless you got here from above!** (*See John 1:13 These are the ones who discover their genesis in God beyond their natural conception! This is not about our blood lineage or whether we were a wanted or an unwanted child - this is about our God-begotteness; we are his dream come true! We are not the invention of our parents! [You are the greatest idea God ever had!]*)

3:8 We can observe the effect the wind has and hear its sound whenever it touches objects - yet those objects do not define the wind; it comes and goes of its own accord - if life was not born out of spirit in the first place, it would not be possible to detect spirit influence at all! We are spirit-compatible by design! (*Spirit is our origin! Not our mother's womb! See 2 Corinthians 3:3 The fact that you are a Christ-Epistle shines as bright as day! This is what our ministry is all about. The Spirit of God is the living ink. Every trace of the Spirit's influence on the heart is what gives permanence to this conversation. We are not talking law-language here; this is more dynamic and permanent than letters* *chiseled in stone. This conversation is embroidered in your inner consciousness. (It is the life of your design that grace echoes within you!)*

3:9 To which Nicodemus responded, "How is this possible? What kind of birth can this be?

3:10 You are the teacher of Israel yet you do not know these things?

3:11 Nicodemus, hear me, [amen, amen,] our conversation stems from what we, humanity, have always borne witness to; we endorse what we have observed; how is it that your religious perspectives keep you so blinded to this? *(See Paul's reference in Romans 1:3 The son of God has his natural lineage from the seed of David; 1:4 however, his powerful resurrection from the dead by the Holy Spirit, locates and confirms his being and sonship in God. Then he says in verse 18 that we can suppress the truth through our own stubborn unbelief, yet 1:19 God is not a stranger to anyone; whatever can be known of God is evident in every human life. 1:20 God is on display in creation; the very fabric of visible cosmos appeals to reason. It clearly bears witness to the ever present sustaining power and intelligence of the invisible God, leaving mankind without any valid excuse to ignore him. See also Galatians 1:15 God's eternal love dream separated me from my mother's womb; his grace became my identity. 1:16 This is the heart of the gospel that I proclaim; it began with an unveiling of sonship in me; freeing me to announce the same sonship in the masses of non-Jewish people. I felt no immediate urgency to compare notes with those who were familiar with Christ from a mere historic point of view.)*

3:12 If I speak incarnate language to you *[Plural - you Jewish law-based-religious leaders)* **and you are not persuaded about our common origin, how will you be persuaded about heavenly things?** *(Here we are person to person - face to face - the prophetic word incarnate!)*

3:13 No one can fully engage in heaven's perspective, unless one's heavenly origin is realized! The son of man declares humanity's co-genesis from above!

3:14 *(This is my mission: See the prophetic relevance - this is how the veil will be removed!)* **Remember how Moses lifted up the serpent in the wilderness even so the son of man will be lifted up!** *(John 12:31 Now is the judgment of this world, now shall the ruler of this world be cast out; 12:32 and I, when I am lifted up from the earth, will draw all judgment unto me." 12:33 He said this to show by what death he was to die. John 3:13 and 14 are most significant since they point to the very essence of the Mission of Jesus - the co-begotteness of the human race now redeemed in our co-crucifixion and co-resurrection on the third day into newness of life! 1 Peter 1:3)*

3:15 In the same prophetic pattern, I will be lifted up for all to see and be equally persuaded in the echo of the life of the ages now redeemed within them!

3:16 The entire cosmos is the object of God's affection! And he is not about to ¹abandon his creation - the ²gift of his son is for humanity to re-

alize their origin in him who mirrors their [3]authentic birth - begotten not of flesh but of the Father! In this persuasion the life of the ages [4]echoes within the individual and announces that the days of regret and sense of [1]lost-ness are over! *(In Luke 15, in order to underline the value of the individual, Jesus tells the famous three parables of the lost sheep, coin and son; now all found, safe and sound! In everyone he repeats the word [1]lost,* **apollumi,** *to lose, to emphasize the fact that you cannot be lost unless you belong - to begin with! The word [1]apollumi, also suggests a sense of uselessness; that which comes to ruin and amounts to nothing! The word [2]didomi, to give, in this case to give something to someone that already belongs to them; thus, to return. The fact that they already are his own, born from above, they have their beginning and their being in him is now confirmed in their realizing it! He is the "only begotten," [3]monogenes; begotten only by the Father and not of the flesh; in him we recognize our true beginning - as in the authentic original mold. See my commentary note to John 1:12. The word [4]echo, to hold, or embrace, as in echo.)*

3:17 God has no intention to condemn anyone - he sent his son, not to be the Judge but the Savior of the world.

3:18 Faith and not flesh defines you! In the persuasion of your authentic sonship there is no [1]separation or rejection! For someone to prefer not to embrace this is to remain under their own judgment sustained by their futile efforts to define themselves through personal performance. In their stubborn unbelief they [1]reject what is revealed and redeemed in the Name of the son, begotten only of the Father and not the flesh. *(The word [1]krino, means to separate; to reject; to judge; to condemn. In naming his son Jesus, the Father openly announces his resolve, which has always been to rescue and redeem his image and likeness in incarnate sonship. As Paul says in Ephesians 3:15 Every family in heaven and on earth originates in him; his is mankind's family name and he remains the authentic identity of every nation. Also in Titus 2:11 The grace of God shines as bright as day making the salvation of humankind undeniably visible. Galatians 1:16 This is the heart of the gospel that I proclaim; it began with an unveiling of sonship in me, freeing me to announce the same sonship in the masses of non-Jewish people. I felt no immediate urgency to compare notes with those who were familiar with Christ from a mere historic and human point of view. See also Hebrews 1:1-3.)*

3:19 And this is the [1]crisis: the light is here right now, yet people are so addicted to their own darkness that they prefer a life of [2]labors, annoyances and hardships! *(The word [1]krisis, is often translated judgment. The word for evil, [2]poneros, translates, full of hardships annoyances and labors.)*

3:20 When someone is engaged in something [1]worthless, they often fear exposure and feel threatened by the light! *(The word, [1]phaulos means worthless; also used in James 3:16, all kinds of worthless pursuits)*

3:21 *(But I have good news for you Nicodemus! You won't ever need to hide in darkness again!)* **He who discovers the [1]poetry of truth, faces the light unashamedly - his lifestyle boldly displays the workmanship of union with God! His works speak for themselves -"Made in heaven - wrought in**

God!" *(Like Nicodemus there are many following at a "comfortable" distance, hidden in disguise - they too are invited to turn and face the redeeming light of the love of God!)*

3:22 From there Jesus and his followers went to the region of Judea and spend some [1]**bonding-time together -** [2]**immersed in conversation.** *(The word* [1]**diatribo** *carries the idea of a road well travelled; tarrying together - the text says and there he baptized - yet in chapter 4:2 John comments that Jesus himself did not baptize anyone. The word* [2]**baptitso** *means to immerse; for what it is worth, I thought to reflect on the bonding and cleansing that takes place in conversation, "You are already made clean by the word which I have spoken to you." Jn 15:3. I'm not disputing the fact that water baptism as a cleansing ritual is the context here; but Jesus' baptism shifts the emphasis from the prophetic water symbol to a baptism into words and spirit thoughts. He knows and communicates that his baptism into humanity's death, as the Lamb of God, is what John's prophetic baptism pointed to in the first place.)*

3:23 John and his disciples were not far from there at the Place of Springs, Aenon near Salim, which made it a popular location for baptism.

3:24 This was shortly before John landed up in jail.

3:25 Some of the disciples of John were disputing with a Jew, who was probably baptized by the disciples of Jesus. They debated about the meaning of these purifying rituals - comparing notes as to which baptism would be the most significant between Jesus and John's. *(See Hebrews 6:2 All the Jewish teachings about ceremonial washings (baptisms), the laying on of hands (in order to identify with the slain animal as sacrifice), and all teachings pertaining to a sin consciousness, including the final resurrection of the dead in order to face judgment, are no longer relevant. [All of these types and shadows were concluded and fulfilled in Christ, their living substance. His resurrection bears testimony to the judgment that he faced on humanity's behalf and the freedom from an obstructive consciousness of sin that he now proclaims. [Rom 4:25; Acts 17:31; Jn 12:31-33] Jesus said, "and when I am lifted up on the cross, I will draw all judgment unto me!" [Heb 9:28])*

3:26 They anxiously informed John that the one who was with him beyond the Jordan, whose life and mission he endorsed and bore witness to, is now attracting everyone to him - his baptism could put them out of business!

3:27 To which John responded, well, he obviously has heaven's backing, so let's not be jealous; everything we have is a gift!

3:28 You heard me when I said that I am not the Messiah - my mission was to introduce the Christ, not to compete with him!

3:29 The Bridegroom's best man does not compete for attention - he is appointed to support the groom and to greatly rejoice when he hears his voice! This is my joy - this is what I have come for!

3:30 The significance of my prophetic mission was simply to elevate him!

(See 1:15 John the Baptist raised his voice to announce emphatically that Jesus was what his ministry and prophetic message were all about. He declared that Jesus, though younger than him, ranks above him and was "born" before him, since he always was!)

3:31 We are dealing with two dimensions here, the one coming from above presides over all - while the reasoning from a mere earthly perspective is confined to communicate from an earthly point of view. The conversation realized as originating in heaven has the final say. *(See 3:13 No one can fully engage in heaven's perspective, unless one's heavenly origin is realized! The son of man declares humanity's co-genesis from above!)*

3:32 Even though I have seen and heard heavenly things, it seems to me that no one embraces what I have borne witness to! By trying to protect a fading prophetic perspective, you are missing the entire point! The shadow is eclipsed by the substance, not the other way around!

3:33 Whoever lays a hold of this testimony has the evidence of God's truth embossed like the impression of a signet ring resonating in their inner consciousness.

3:34 For the one sent from God communicates God's gift language from the limitless resource of the Spirit.

3:35 The theme of this conversation celebrates the extravagant love the Father has for the Son - and in him every gift of God is revealed - his hand extends God's touch; he is God's embrace of the human race!

3:36 To be persuaded about sonship as unveiled in the Son is to fully participate in the life of the ages! To be unpersuaded about sonship is to remain in blindfold mode to life itself in the here and now and to exchange fellowship with the Author of the life of our design for a fearful image of a vengeful, merciless god - quite the opposite of the loving Father the Son reveals!

4:1 Jesus heard the rumors that were spreading amongst the Pharisees, supposing that he was baptizing more people than John.

4:2 The fact was, he didn't baptize anyone himself, his disciples were.

4:3 He then decided to leave the area and go back to Galilee.

4:4 This meant that he had to travel through Samaria. *(At the time the land of Palestine was divided into three parts: Galilee on the north; Samaria in the middle; and Judea on the south.)*

4:5 En-route they approached Sychar, a Samaritan village bordering the field which Joseph inherited from his father Jacob.

4:6 The well which Jacob dug was still in operation. Since it was already midday and Jesus felt exhausted and thirsty from their day and a half walk, *[40 miles from Aenon]* he decided to wait at the well while his disciples would go into the village to buy food. *(Having left the Place of Springs, Aenon early the previous morning, one can just imagine how Jesus' mind drifted to the fountain theme!)*

4:7 When a local Samaritan woman finally arrived to draw water, Jesus immediately asked her for a drink.

4:8 There was still no sign of the disciples.

4:9 The woman obviously anticipated this request and was ready with her response, "You are a Jew, aren't you? So why would you expect to get anything for free from a Samaritan woman?" Within the politics of the day, Jews looked down upon the Samaritans and had no dealings with them. *(She knew very well how strategically en-route this precious well was and what political leverage it gave her over weary Jewish travellers!)*

4:10 *(Jesus was not at all intimidated or embarrassed by her political stance; he didn't allow his awareness of his weariness and desperate thirst, as well as an obvious opportunity to negotiate for a quick fix-drink, to distract from his Person and mission - instead of associating himself with the Jews as a mere Jew and endorsing the Samaritan's 'inferior' political identity, he immediately engaged her with a far superior conversation. He escaped the temptation to see himself or the lady reduced to a lesser identity. He knew who he was and what his mission was all about as the Messiah of mankind - by seeing himself he was able to see her in the same light. What he had to offer was not for sale!)* He looked her in the eye and said, "If you could see the generosity of God's grace gift, you would perceive who I am! *(I am so much more than a Jewish man and you are so much more than a Samaritan woman!)* So here I am asking you for a drink when you should be asking me and I would give you the water of life for free!

4:11 *(Just like Nicodemus in the previous chapter, she struggles to determine which source Jesus was pointing to!)* Sir, you have nothing to draw with and the well is deep! How would you reach this living water?

4:12 Whoever you are, ¹you are certainly not greater than our father Jacob who left us this well and its legacy as our inheritance? He bought this land and dug the well; he drank from it himself and it sustained his family and their livestock for centuries. How can you compete with that? (*[1]me su meitzon - The interrogative particle, me indicates that a negative answer is expected: Surely you are not superior... The σὐ, you, first in the sentence, is emphatic, and possibly with a shade of contempt.*)

4:13 Jesus answered her, "This well cannot quench the thirst that I am talking about. Anyone drinking from it will thirst again!" (*In her encounter with Jesus her familiar religious and historic identity is dramatically challenged. Everyone who drinks from the wells of religion and politics will thirst again! The business of religion desperately needs paying and returning customers! They crucified Jesus for this reason; their entire system of keeping people dependent on their hierarchy was challenged and condemned! So many sincere Christian ministries today fall into the same snare.*)

4:14 Whoever drinks from the source of this water that I shall give will never thirst again; because the water that I give becomes an artesian well bursting from within, [1]defining the life of the ages! (*The preposition [1]eis, into, indicating the point reached; conclusion; a defining moment. Unlike a man-made hole dug in the ground to access seepage water, Jesus speaks of a spring of water, an artesian well! In a later chapter this thought is reinforced when Jesus declares, "To drink from me is to be persuaded that I am what the Scriptures are all about [then you will discover that you are what I am all about] and rivers of living water will gush out of your innermost being!" John 7:37,38 Now this is economic and most effective ministry! In John 16:7 Jesus says, "It is to your advantage that I go!" This is what Paul knew when he wrote "Not only in my presence, but much more in my absence, discover the full extent of salvation in your own heart!" Philippians 2:12. There is something more beneficial to the individual than Paul's next epistle or even his next visit! It is discovering the fountain within your innermost being! The unveiling of Christ in you exceeds your every expectation! Col 1:27. Also Col 2:5 My physical absence does not distance me from you spiritually.*)

4:15 (*Again she did not understand!*) **Sir, then this is what I want! It will save me the trouble to return here again and again to bail out water for my thirst!**

4:16 Jesus said to her, (*you are missing the point! I am not talking about a thirst that water can quench!*) **Picture yourself back at home, you have discussed this with your husband, and before long you** (*you - singular*) **will be right back here, drawing water again from the same old well!**

4:17 The woman answered, "But I have no husband!" Jesus responded with, "This is an honest answer and confirms my point!"

4:18 Marriage does not define you. You could have failed five times and this time you're not sure about committing yourself to the guy you're living with!

4:19 She was shocked! "Sir! Now I know, you are a prophet!"

4:20 I'm also religious! Our forefathers worshipped here in this mountain; yet you Jews insist that everyone should worship in Jerusalem! *(Maybe feeling a bit vulnerable about her domestic life she tries to change the subject to again emphasize the religious tension between the Jews and Samaritans.)*

4:21 Jesus said unto her, "Believe me lady, the moment everyone was waiting for has come! From now on worship is no longer about a geographic holy mountain - or a sacred city in Israel experience! *(It is not whether you are a Jew in Jerusalem or a Gentile in Japan! The days of prophetic pictures are over!)*

4:22 You have been worshiping in ignorance all along while the Jews continue to anticipate the Messiah in their devotion, knowing that the promise pointing to the Savior of the world would be emerging from within. *(The Samaritans were a mixed race and only received the five books of Moses while they rejected the prophets. 2Kings 17:28-34)*

4:23 The end of an era has arrived - the future is here! Whatever prophetic values were expressed in external devotional forms and rituals are now eclipsed in true spirit worship from within, [1]face to face with the Father - acknowledging our genesis in him - this is his delight! The Father's desire is the [1]worshiper more than the worship! *(The word often translated worship, [1]proskuneo, from pros, face to face and, I would like to believe to be a derivation of koinonia, joint-participation; rather than the idea of kuneo, or kuon which means dog! I know, some tried to connect the idea of a dog licking its master's hand, which then became a possibility of kissing (!) - yet I would much prefer a face to face koinonia encounter to define true worship! This is the only reference to the noun [2]proskunētēs, worshipper, in the New Testament.)*

4:24 God is Spirit and not a holy mountain or a sacred city with man-made shrines! Return to your Source - the Father is our true fountain-head! *(You are not defined by your physical birth, your domestic life, your history, your culture or your religion!)*

4:25 The women then said, "I know the Messiah is coming, the one who is called the Christ and when he arrives he will declare everything to us from heaven's perspective!"

4:26 Jesus responded to her, "So here I am, speaking to you! I am the One you were longing for."

4:27 Just then his disciples arrived; they were quite surprised that he was in such deep conversation with a woman, but made no remarks.

4:28 Leaving her water pot behind she hurried back to the city to tell the people what happened at the well. *(No water pot can compete with a fountain bursting from within! Suddenly she understood that all people indeed share the same origin. The fountain of living water was not distant from her, beyond her reach, but waiting to awaken within her. Not any of her previous five marriages or even her religious tradition could quench her thirst. Not because she failed to meet 'Mr. Perfect' or the men in her life failed to meet her expectation, but simply be-*

cause of the fact that nothing external was ever meant to define or complete her life.

The life of our design is defined in Jesus Christ as in a mirror. Here, there remains no partner, politics or past experience to blame or compete with, only a new life within you to discover, explore, enjoy - and share. Your source will sustain you. "By the waters of reflection, my soul remembers who I am." Ps 23

Truth therapy does not attempt to untangle the complicated emotional hurts and traumas of the past; instead truth reveals the integrity of our original life redeemed in Christ. He is the fountainhead of our genesis. Paul did not say, "Behold the old! He said, "Behold all things are new!" 2 Cor 5:17

The end of an era has arrived! Return to your Source. "He is the Author and conclusion of faith." Heb 12:2.)

4:29 "Come quickly! I met a man who told me everything about my life! [1]Could this possibly be the Messiah?" *(With a woman's intuition she avoided* **ouk** *and uses [1]mēti, whether, at all, perchance. She does not take sides, but piques their curiosity. - Robertson's Word Pictures.)*

4:30 She arose their interest enough for them to leave the city at once to go meet this man for themselves.

4:31 In the mean while his disciples were urging him to take some food.

4:32 But he said, "I am feasting on food you cannot see!"

4:33 His disciples were baffled, "Who brought him anything to eat?"

4:34 Jesus told them, "My food is to fulfil the desire of him who commissioned me and to leave no detail undone!"

4:35 The bread you labor for takes four months from the day you sow the seed until it ripens in the ear, doesn't it? This is not the food that I am talking about. The fruit of your own toil and performance will never satisfy permanently; from now on, look at yourselves and everyone else differently; see them through your Father's eyes and you will know that they too are ripe and ready to discover how fully included they are in my finished work. They are perfectly mirrored in me! *(A harvest is ripe when the seed in the ear matches the seed that was sown! My mission is to reveal and redeem the image and likeness of God in human form!)*

4:36 This harvest reveals how both he who sows and he who reaps participate in the same joy of the life of the ages!

4:37 Just as the proverb says, "One sows and another reaps!"

4:38 I commissioned you to reap that which you did not labor for! Others labored and you tapped into the fruit of their toil!

4:39 Intrigued by the woman's testimony many of the Samaritans from that city believed! *(They were the first non-pure Jews who tasted the fruit of God's prophetic purpose revealed in Abraham and Israel's history wherein all the nations of the world would be equally included in the blessing of sonship!)*

4:40 They then approached Jesus and entreated him to remain with them longer, so he stayed over for two days.

4:41 When they heard him speak, many more believed.

4:42 They said to the woman, now we believe not just because of your word but we have heard for ourselves and can clearly see that this man is indeed the Christ, the Savior of the world!

4:43 After the two days with them Jesus left for Galilee.

4:44 Explaining why he was heading north to Galilee, John remembers how Jesus repeated the saying that a prophet is not honored in his own native land.

4:45 The Galileans welcomed him with open arms; they immediately recognized him for the spectacular things he did in Jerusalem where they too had been for the Passover feast.

4:46 So Jesus again visited Cana where he turned the water into wine and there met a man of the royal family whose son was sick in Capernaum.

4:47 This man heard the rumor that Jesus has returned from Judaea and was back in Galilee so he went looking for him. When he found him in Cana he entreated Jesus to urgently come with him to Capernaum to heal his son since he was at the point of death.

4:48 Jesus responded with "If your belief in me is merely based on the signs and miracles you can see, you miss the entire point of my mission!" *(See John 2:23-25 and my note on 2:24...Signs are not the source of faith - signs follow faith! Jesus' belief in the integrity of our inner being is what saves us from the lies that we believed about ourselves.)*

4:49 The nobleman urged him to come with him at once before it was too late!

4:50 Jesus then instructed him to return home on his own and said, "your son will live!" And the man believed the word that Jesus spoke and left. *(Here Jesus demonstrates that he didn't come to be restricted to his own human body and physical presence, but as the Word incarnate, his Word will continue to be as he is for all time and everyone! Jesus knows how a father would want to see his son return from the brink of death!)*

4:51 The man was still on his journey home when his servants met him to tell him the good news that his son lives!

4:52 He immediately asked them about the time that his son was healed and they told him it happened at the seventh hour the previous day! *(That is 1pm)*

4:53 The father knew that it was the very hour when Jesus declared his son alive! He and his entire household came to faith that day!

4:54 This Jesus did again as a second sign to mark the significance of his ministry beyond Judaea into Gallilee.

5:1 After these events there was another feast of the Jews in Jerusalem. Jesus determined to be there. *(Pentecost - 50 days after Easter)*

5:2 At the Sheep-gate in Jerusalem there was a pool called Bethesda; in Hebrew it means home of grace and kindness - it had five porches. *(Nehemiah 3:1 - the sheep gate would lead to the market where sheep would be sold for sacrifices - no wonder Jesus was attracted to go there - fifty days ago he was there whip in hand driving out the traders from the temple! [2:15] The pool of water reminds of the baptism theme so relevant in John's gospel. Multitudes are still waiting at the religious pools of mercy and kindness for some unpredictable, unmerited sign of favor to come their way! Sitting in the shade of their ideas of the 5 porches [or five-steps to receive blessings from God- ministries] waiting for another "flutter" or "move" of God! Jesus is not just another "move" of God! He is the Father made manifest in our human skin! He has come to awaken us out of our slumber!)*

5:3 Many ailing people were lying in the shade of these porches; blind, cripple and withered, waiting for the stirring of the water.

5:4 An angelic messenger would go down into the pool occasionally to stir the water; the first person to then enter the pool would be healed of whatever it was they were suffering from.

5:5 There was also a man who had an infirmity for thirty eight years.

5:6 Jesus saw this man and realized that he had been there for a very long time; he asked him, "Do you [1]really desire to be made well?" *([1]Theleis from thelo - to resolve, desire - not merely, do you wish, but are you in earnest?)*

5:7 The man answered him, "Sir, I have no one to help me get into the pool when the water is stirred; by the time I get there someone else has already gotten there before me!"

5:8 Jesus said to him, "[1]Awaken! Arise and pick up your bed and walk!" *([1]egeirō - to awaken from sleep.")*

5:9 And at once the man became whole ereand picked up his bed and began to walk! Now this was on the Sabbath day.

5:10 The Jews were immediately offended and rebuked the man for picking up his bed on a day where no work was allowed according to their law! *(Grace offends the legalistic mindset. See Romans 3:27)*

5:11 He answered them, "The man who healed me told me to pick up my bed and walk!"

5:12 They were very keen to know who this man was.

5:13 But the man didn't know who it was who healed him since Jesus already left unnoticed and there were throngs of people around.

5:14 Then a little later Jesus found him in the synagogue and said, "[1]See! You have become whole! Do not continue in your old [2]distorted mindset; then nothing worse can happen to you!" *(It is so important to [1]see your wholeness and not your distortedness! You reflect what you behold. To see yourself* *through God's eyes is the only way to escape the distortion of contradiction! The word* [1]*ide from* **horao** *means to see, to discern, to perceive. The word translated sin, is the word* [1]**hamartia**, *from* **ha**, *negative and* **meros**, *portion or form, thus to be without your allotted portion or without form, pointing to a disorientated, distorted identity; the word* **meros**, *is the stem of* **morphe**, *as in 2 Corinthians 3:18 the word* **metamorphe**, *with form, is the opposite of* **hamartia** *- without form. Sin is to live out of context with the blueprint of one's design; to behave out of tune with God's original harmony. See Deuteronomy 32:18, "You have forgotten the Rock that begot you and have gotten out of step with the God who danced with you!" Hebrew,* **khul** *or* **kheel**, *to dance. Many commentators have used this verse to conclude that God punishes people's sin with sickness! This is not the Father whom Jesus reveals! A few verses later [v 22) Jesus emphatically declares that The Father judges no-one! The religious mind has for so long connected God's judgment with disease and sickness! Jesus introduces us to the God who would rather become our distortions and diseases on the cross and go into our darkness and hell to deliver us from its claim, than to send sickness to us and send us to hell! In John 9:2 the followers of Jesus asks "Rabbi, who sinned: this man or his parents, causing him to be born blind?" And Jesus answered, "You're asking the wrong question. You're looking for someone to blame." [Message] Neither this man nor his parents were guilty! Then Knox translates the next sentence to read, "it was so that God's action might declare itself in him!" This has nothing to do with judgment! See also 9:34 for the typical opinion of the Pharisees! "You were born in utter sin - now you try to teach us!" Nothing makes a Pharisee more nervous and mad than when their sin- and judgment-paradigm gets taken out of the equation!)*

5:15 The man left and told the Jews that it was Jesus who healed him. *(Don't go testify in the wrong place at the wrong time to the wrong audience! That would be like casting pearls before swine!)*

5:16 Unwittingly, this man's testimony confirmed their suspicion and gave the Jews exactly what they wanted, a trigger to launch their persecution of Jesus! They were furious and immediately began to make plans to murder him! Their interpretation of a "Holy Day" was deeply offended! *(Reminds of many sincere Sabbath - keepers today!)*

5:17 Jesus replied, "My Father is working [1]**until** [2]**now, and so am I!"** *(This is not what the Jews wanted to hear! But Jesus is speaking about a different Sabbath! Just like John reminds us in chapter 2 that he had a different temple in mind; one that he would rebuild in 3 days! And in the next chapter with Nicodemus he points to a different birth; not his mother's womb, but our joint-genesis from above! Then the Samaritan woman in chapter 4 discovers a different well; one that bursts forth from within! So here in chapter 5 Jesus sees a different Sabbath to Jewish sentiment! The Sabbath of God points to his perfect work of both revealing and redeeming his image and likeness in human form. Every Sabbath continues to celebrate the perfection of our Father's work -* [1]*until* [2]*now! So when Jesus heals people on the Sabbath he is not contradicting it, but endorsing it! Jesus is what the Sabbath is all about! He is the substance of every prophetic shadow! In restoring someone's wholeness, the idea of the original Sabbath is reinforced and not compromised! When God introduced the Sabbath it was always meant to be a prophetic opportu-*

nity to celebrate his rest, which was him seeing his perfect work unveiled in us! He continues to invite us to enter into his Rest where we cease from our own works! The announcement, "You shall do NO WORK!" was to remind us again and again that his work is perfect, and we cannot improve on it! You cannot improve on you! You are his workmanship - his masterpiece! The deadly fruit of the "I am not Tree - system" had to be thoroughly uprooted! Hebrews 4:4 [Read the entire chapter 4 in the Mirror] Scripture records the seventh day to be the prophetic celebration of God's perfect work. What God saw satisfied his scrutiny. (Behold, it is very good, and God rested from all his work. [Gen 1:31, 2:2] God saw more than his perfect image in Adam, he also saw the Lamb and his perfect work of redemption! "The Lamb having been slain from the foundation of the world." [Rev 13:8] "That which has been is now; that which is to be, already has been" [Ecc 3:15] Also 2 Tim 1:9) Hebrews 4:10 God's rest celebrates his finished work; whoever enters into God's rest immediately abandons his own efforts to compliment what God has already perfected. (The language of the law is "do;" the language of grace is "done.")

Faith is God's language; God calls things which are not (visible yet) as though they were.

The word [1]heous is a conjunction linking God's work and intent in synchrony with the word [2]arti, which already suggests a continuation of a moment "until now!" [See note on arti in 1 Corinthians 13:12,13])

5:18 This was fuel for the fire of Jewish zeal in their determination to execute Jesus! Not only did he break their Sabbath, but now he has gone beyond all extremes! He calls God his own Father - who does he think he is - God's equal?

5:19 Jesus explained to them with utmost certainty that whatever they see the son does, mirrors the Father - he does not act independent of his Father - the son's gaze is fixed in order to accurately interpret and repeat what he sees his father does! The one reveals the other without compromise or distraction! *(The incarnation does not interrupt what the Word was from the beginning - face to face with God!)*

5:20 For the Father and the son are [1]best of friends! They have no secrets; the Father gladly lets his son in on everything he does and will continue to show him works of most significant proportions, which will astound you! *(The Father loves [[1]phileo] the son with fondness.)*

5:21 For just as the Father awakens people from their death-sleep and revitalizes them with zoe-life, even so it pleases the son to awaken people to life!

5:22 For the Father judges no-one but has given all judgment to the son!

5:23 The Father's desire is that all may value the son with the same honor with which they esteem him - there is no distinction - to dishonor the son is to dishonor the Father.

5:24 Most certainly do I say unto you that this is the vital transition from dead religion into the very life of the ages - embrace the Son's word with

the same persuasion as you would the Father's and you will not know any judgment - the Son gives voice to the Father! *(He is the Father's word made flesh.)*

5:25 Oh how I desire for you to get this! The prophetic hour has come! This is the moment for the dead to hear the voice of the Son of God - C'mon! Hear and live!

5:26 The [1]very self existence within the Father is what he has bestowed upon the Son in order for the Son to [2]radiate the same zoe-life. *(The word [1]hosper from hos, in that manner; and per , an enclitic particle significant of abundance [thoroughness], that is, emphasis; much, very or ever. The word [2]echo, to have possession of, reminds of the English word echo; thus to resonate, radiate.)*

5:27 The Father has also given the son of man [1]authentic authority to execute judgment on humanity's behalf! *(The word [1]exousia, often translated authority has two components, ek, out of, source and eimi, I am!)*

5:28 Do not be alarmed by this, but the hour is coming when those in the [1]graves will hear his voice! *(No-one who ever lived will escape the extent of his righteous judgment! Those who have [1]forgotten who they are will hear his incarnate voice! The word for grave, [1]mnēmeion, memory, suggests a remembrance! Like David prophesies in Psalm 22 when he sees the cross-crisis [krisis - judgment] a thousand years before it happens! His conlclusion in verse 27 sums up the triumph of God's resolve! "All the ends of the earth shall [1]remember and turn to the LORD; and all the families of the nations shall worship before him!" See 1 Corinthians 15:21,22 The same humanity who died in a man was raised again in a man. In Adam all died; in Christ all are made alive.)*

5:29 And they will come forth out of their graves - for those who have engaged themselves with that which is beneficial, it will be a resurrection to life - and for those who have done that which is worthless, it will be a resurrection unto [1]judgment. *(In the context of chapter 6:28 and 29 the work that is required is not a duty to be performed but a gift to be embraced - If our own good behavior could earn us salvation then there would be no point in Jesus dying our death! - This would be in conflict with the essence and crux of the gospel! It reminds of 2 Corinthians 5:10 "For we must all appear before the judgment seat of Christ, so that each one may receive good or evil, according to what he has done in the body!" Now read this verse in the Mirror - 2 Corinthians 5:10 For we have all been [1]thoroughly scrutinized in the [2]judgment of Jesus. We are [3]taken care of and restored to the life of our design, regardless of what happened to us in our individual lives, whatever amazing or meaningless things we encountered in the body. (See 5:14,16. We are mirrored in his life; his life reflects ours, not as an example for us but of us. See 2 Corinthians 3:18. The word, [1]phaneroo, means to render apparent, to openly declare, to manifest. Paul uses the aorist passive infinitive tense phanerothenai, not referring to a future event. The aorist infinitive presents the action expressed by the verb as a completed unit with a beginning and end. The word, bematos, comes from [2]bayma, means footprint, also referring to a raised place mounted by steps, or a tribunal, the official seat of a judge The word, [3]komitzo, comes from kolumbos, meaning to tend, to take care of, to provide for,*

*to carry off from harm. Paul's reference was not about how much abuse and afflic-
tion he suffered, neither was it the many good times he remembered that defined
him; "I am what I am by the grace of God!" If we are still to be judged for good
or bad deeds that we performed in the body, then the judgment that Jesus faced on
humanity's behalf was irrelevant. Galatians 2:21 I do not set aside the grace of God,
for if righteousness could be gained through the law, Christ died for nothing! NIV*

*See **Extended Commentary Notes** after the final chapter of the Mirror- Thoughts
on Judgment and Resurrection.)*

**5:30 The dynamic of my doing is in my union with my Father; my inti-
mate acquaintance with his voice is what inspires me - as I hear, I discern
and my judgment is just; there is no conflicting interest here - my Father's
commission is my mission in life!** *(Proverbs 20:12 The hearing ear and the
seeing eye, the LORD has made them both. See Hebrews 5:8 Acquainted with son-
ship he was in the habit of hearing from above; what he heard distanced him from
the effect of what he had suffered. (The word often translated as obedience is the
word, **upoakuo**, under the influence of hearing, or hearing from above. "By" the
things he suffered, **apo**, away from, distanced. "Then I said, I read in your book
what you wrote about me; so here I am, I have come to fulfill your will." [Heb 10:7]
Heb 5:9 By his perfect hearing he forever freed mankind to hear what he had heard.
[He now makes it possible for us to hear in such a way that we may participate
again in the full release of our original identity; the logos finding voice in the in-
carnation in us.])*

**5:31 If this was just about me trying to make a name for myself then you
can certainly reject my testimony as phony!**

**5:32 Yet there is someone else who endorses who I am and I recognize his
testimony of me as absolutely true.**

**5:33 You cross examined John and he too gave testimony to the truth of
who I am.**

**5:34 I do not draw my inspiration from your applause; I'm not here to win
a few votes for a noble cause - I am on a rescue mission!**

**5:35 John was a man on fire, a bright beaming light and for a brief mo-
ment you were jumping with joy in his radiance.**

**5:36 My testimony exceeds John's since the work which my Father has
ordained me to finish gives ultimate context to my mission.**

**5:37 The Father himself who has sent me continues to bear witness to me;
yet you are not familiar with his voice and did not discern his prophetic
utterance throughout ancient times and therefore you could not recog-
nize his image nor do you realize his appearance at this present time** *[in
the incarnate word.]*

**5:38 Your doubting him whom the Father has sent shows that you have
not taken his word to its full conclusion.**

5:39 You scrutinize the Scriptures tirelessly, assuming that in them you

[1]embrace the life of the ages - yet I am what the Scriptures are all about! (*[1]Echo, to hold, embrace, resonate*)

5:40 Still you refuse to resort to me as the very source of the life you seek. (*I echo the life of the ages within you!*)

5:41 I am not anchoring my belief in people's opinion.

5:42 But what I observe about you is that God's love does not resonate within you! (*You're so obsessed with the rule book that all you see in it is a god of judgment and wrath and miss out on God's love!*)

5:43 Here I am representing my Father and you have a problem with that; yet someone completely unknown to anyone would come in his own name and you will give him your full support. (*How strikingly has this been verified in the history of the Jews! From the time of Jesus Christ to our time, sixty-four false Christs have been reckoned by whom they have been deceived. [Bengel].*)

5:44 How is it possible for you to even venture into the dimensions of faith, if you already have your minds made up to go with popular opinion within your own ranks, while you show no desire to esteem him who proceeds directly from God?

5:45 No, I am not the one to accuse you before the Father - you stand condemned before your trusted friend Moses!

5:46 Had you discerned my Father's voice in Moses you would have been persuaded about me in his writings. (*The significance of the Scriptures is not in themselves but in who they point to! Genesis 3:15; Genesis 12:3 "in you shall all the families of the earth be blessed!" Compare John 8:56 & 58; Genesis 49:10; also Deuteronomy 18:15. "For he wrote of me" -* **peri gar emou ekeinos egrapsen.** *Deuteronomy 18:18. is quoted by Peter in Acts 3:22 as a prophecy of Christ and also by Stephen in Acts 7:37. See also John 3:14 about the brazen serpent and John 8:56 about Abraham foreseeing Christ's day. Moses most certainly wrote concerning him.*)

5:47 If you already doubt his words to begin with, my conversation will be irrelevant to you.

6:1 In the course of ¹time Jesus went from Jerusalem across the sea of Galilee which was also called Tiberias. *(With this... **meta tauta**, is John's favorite general note of the order of events; not necessarily in chronological order. ¹In the context and sequence of time, this would be the following year after the events described in the 1ˢᵗ 5 chapters.)*

6:2 By now a great multitude was following him because of the spectacular healings he performed.

6:3 Jesus went into the hills to be alone with his disciples.

6:4 This was again near the annual Passover. *(Here John reminds us of the economy of Jesus' ministry he knew very well the pivotal significance of his appointment with the ultimate Passover where he would lay down his life as the Lamb of God to be slaughtered by his own creation for their salvation.)*

6:5 There was no getting away from the crowds though; when Jesus saw the multitude arrive he said to Phillip, How do you think we are going to feed all these people?

6:6 This wasn't a trick question but simply to engage their faith; he already knew exactly what he was going to do! *(Jesus was not about to be distracted by the enormity of his mission where his body would be broken at the highest price in order to feed the multitudes of humanity with the true bread from heaven! Just like in Chapter 24 of Luke - the picture of a meal always translates into incarnation language - bread becomes flesh!)*

6:7 Phillip immediately concluded that this was impossible to do and far beyond a budget of any reasonable calculation; two hundred days wages could never buy enough for each person in the crowd to even get a little morsel of bread! *(Mankind cannot redeem themselves! Again Jesus leads the conversation into a different dimension - like with Nicodemus and the Samaritan woman - he points to a different source; not related to external reasoning or challenges to be met with personal contributions of our own toil or labor to define or defend ourselves but simply accessing the Father's limitless resources within. He has come to free our minds from the restrictions of a dimension that could never truly define us! He dramatically and very intentionally disengages us with every effort of our own to save ourselves! Our salvation is beyond our budget!*

BUT WAIT!! What about the little lad!? For unto us a child is born remember!)

6:8 Then one of his disciples, Andrew, the brother of Simon Peter

6:9 pointed to a little boy who had five small loaves of inexpensive barley bread and two small fishes and remarked how insignificant they appeared amongst such a multitude of hungry people!

6:10 Jesus asked his disciples to get everybody seated - the place was ideal for a picnic since it was spring and the grass was lush and green! Thousands of people gathered! *(In the Jewish custom where only the men were counted there happened to be 5000 of them let alone the multitudes of ladies and children!)*

6:11 Jesus took the bread and fish and thanked God for it, then distributed it amongst the people; everyone was free to take as much as they wanted!

6:12 When the crowd had eaten their fill Jesus said to his disciples to gather up all the broken pieces to make sure that nothing is lost. *(Every fragment and detail of God's masterful work of redeeming mankind in Christ is most significant!)*

6:13 So they did and filled twelve baskets with fragments after everybody had as much as they could eat!

6:14 The people who witnessed these signs [1]began to be more and more convinced that Jesus must truly be that Prophet, the one whom their scriptures pointed to. *(Deuteronomy 18:15 "The LORD your God will raise up for you a prophet like me from among you, from your brethren--him you shall heed-- The word [1]elegon is an inchoative imperfect form of the verb; thus, they began to say; the inchoative verb, sometimes called an inceptive verb, shows a process of beginning or becoming.)*

6:15 They were now ready to forcefully grab him and crown him as their King, but when Jesus saw their enthusiasm he slipped away and went higher into the mountain to be by himself.

6:16 In the evening his disciples went down to the sea;

6:17 they were hoping that Jesus would join them and waited until dark but then finally embarked the ship and proceeded to sail across to Capernaum.

6:18 En-route a massive storm hit them with huge swells and strong winds.

6:19 They were now about halfway across the six mile stretch of water, struggling with their oars against the wind and raging waters when they suddenly noticed Jesus coming towards them, walking on the stormy seas! They were horrified!

6:20 He spoke to them and said, Here I am - you have no reason to fear! *(ἐγώ εἰμι· μὴ φοβεῖσθε - His I amness is closer to you than any sense you could ever have of his absence!)*

6:21 They were very happy to take him on board and then miraculously reached their destination in no time!

6:22 The crowd that was left behind saw that there was only one boat and also noticed that Jesus did not leave with his disciples.

6:23 The next day other boats from Tiberias arrived near the area where they ate that bread which the Lord blessed.

6:24 When they realized that neither Jesus nor any of his disciples were around, they got into the boats to go to Capernaum hoping to find Jesus there.

6:25 They found him on the other side and wanted to know how he got there?

6:26 Jesus responded with, Surely the reason why you are so drawn to me is not because of the signs you've seen, but the contentment you felt within you when you ate the bread. *(The destiny of Jesus was not to merely engage people with the miraculous signs - as much as he desired to communicate the essence of his mission - which was to celebrate the incarnation! The bold exhibit of the image and likeness of our invisible Father in us in human form! Every meal is a celebration of the incarnation. In Luke's interview with the two followers on their way back to Emmaus, he finally records the climax of their encounter with the "stranger" when he broke the bread and their eyes were opened and they recognized him! The revelation of the incarnation is the point, not another ten miracles!)*

6:27 Living from meal to meal can keep you busy - there is so much more to life than survival - toiling merely for that which perishes is such a waste! The life of the ages requires a different kind of labor! This labor is not the kind which rewards you for something you have done but blesses you with the gift from humanity's son - this gift of sonship celebrates the authentic life which God the Father has endorsed from the beginning.

6:28 They immediately wanted the recipe! Tell us then what we must do in order to accomplish God's work?

6:29 This is the work of God; your belief in the One whom he has sent! *(Even your ability to believe is God's work! Realizing your authentic sonship on exhibit in Jesus is God's gift to you and cannot be earned! How can your labor compete with what God's rest celebrates as complete!)*

6:30 So Jesus, if it is your job to get us to believe, we need to see more signs!

6:31 How do you compete with Moses? Our fathers ate the manna in the wilderness - as it is written - He gave them bread from heaven to eat. *(The rabbis quoted Psalm 72:16 to prove that the Messiah, when he comes, will outdo Moses with manna from heaven. Robertson's Word Pictures.*

Ps 72:16 "There shall be a handful of corn in the earth upon the top of the mountains; the fruit thereof shall shake like the cedars of Lebanon: and they of the city shall flourish like grass of the earth. KJV [A handful of corn - five loaves here and in the following year's Passover Jesus' own body would be the bread broken on the mount of Golgotha!]

Deuteronomy 8:3 And he [1]treated you gently in the wilderness of your unbelief and fed your hunger there with manna, which you did not know, nor did your fathers know; that he might make you know that mankind does not live by the bread of their own labor, but that the life of our design hungers to be completely sustained by [2]that Word which proceeds out of the mouth of the LORD. [Some translations say, "[1]humbled you" but in 2 Samuel 22:36 the word [1]ANAH is translated, "Thou hast given me the shield of thy salvation, and thy [1]gentleness made me great." The Hebrew word KOL, often translated, "every" actually means the word in its most complete context = the INCARNATION!] He divorced them from that which does not satisfy!

You freed us from our slavery and led us gently like a Shepherd through the wilderness of our own unbelief and made known to us our authentic hunger not for the bread we labor for but for the word which mirrors our joint-genesis and eternal oneness!)

6:32 Jesus reminded them that it wasn't Moses who gave them the bread from heaven - My Father is the one who gives the real bread from heaven!

6:33 For the bread from God that comes down from heaven is that which gives life to the entire world!

6:34 They said, Oh Lord, this is the bread we crave! Give us this bread!

6:35 Jesus said, I am the bread of life! He that comes face to face with me shall never hunger and he who finds his faith resting in me shall never thirst!

6:36 But even though you have seen me, you are not persuaded. *(You might be happy with the healings and be entertained by the signs, but still you fail to understand who I am! I'm not here to impress you with me! I'm here to persuade you about you! Your sonship is what I am all about! And the only way that I can persuade you about you is to take you with me into your death and darkness and overcome your fear and hell and birth you again into newness of life in my resurrection!)*

6:37 Everyone whom the Father has given me will come [1]face to face with me! And here, mirrored in me they will see that I am not the Judge! I will not cast anyone out! *(The preposition **pros**, is used here again as in John 1:1.)*

6:38 For I have stepped down out of heaven, not to make a name for myself! I did not come to become a mere historic hero! I have come to communicate the resolve of him who sent me! *(I am here to demonstrate to you how persuaded my Father is about you!)*

6:39 My Sender's desire is for me to rescue every single individual - [1]this is his gift to me - that I will lose [2]no detail of mankind's original identity mirrored in me! My rescuing mission will conclude in humanity's co-resurrection! This is the [3]completeness of time! *(This is his gift to me, [1]ho dedoke moi. The phrase, [2]hina pan apoleso ex auto, meaning, that I should lose nothing out of it. In the conclusion/fulness of time - [3]te eschate hemera - This phrase occurs only in John - John 6:39, 6:40, 6:44, 6:54. See John 4:23 The end of an era has arrived - the future is here! Whatever prophetic values were expressed in external devotional forms and rituals are now eclipsed in true spirit worship from within - face to face with the Father - acknowledging our genesis in him - this is his delight! The Father's desire is the worshiper more than the worship!)*

6:40 And this is the desire of my Father, that every one who [1]sees the son, through his eyes, and finds the conclusion of (eis) their persuasion in him, will resonate (echo) the life of the ages! And I will [2]raise him up in

the final day! (*The word* [1]**theōreo** *means to gaze attentively. See Hosea 6:2 After two days he will revive us;* [2]*on the third day he will raise us up, that we may live before him.*)

6:41 The religious Jews were no longer paying any attention - they were shocked and offended at the idea that he said he was the bread from heaven!

6:42 They reasoned that since they knew his parents to be Joseph and Mary, he had no valid claim to any heavenly Source!

6:43 Then Jesus addressed them saying, Your murmuring and reasoning amongst yourselves will continue to veil me from you. (*Knowing me from a human point of view will not satisfy your quest.*)

6:44 No one is forcing you to believe - it is the Father who sent me who draws you to see me [1]**face to face - only once you've seen how in the mystery of God I mirror you, will you understand that I will co-raise you in the grand-finale of my mission!** (*The word* [1]**pros** *is used again, face to face.*)

6:45 It is written in the Prophets that every single individual will be taught of God. To hear the Father's instruction concerning me, is to come [1]**face to face with me.** (*The word* [1]**pros** *is used again. Isaiah 54:13; Jeremiah 31:34; Mica 4:1-4*)

6:46 No one has [2]**seen the Father except the one who** [1]**proceeds from him; he is most intimately** [2]**acquainted with the Father!** (*The word* [1]**para***, a preposition indicating close proximity, a thing proceeding from a sphere of influence, with a suggestion of union of place of residence; intimate connection; the word* [2]**horaō** *means to gaze; to see with the mind; to perceive; know; to become acquainted with by experience.*)

6:47 Of [1]**absolute certainty do I declare to you that anyone whose faith** [2]**ultimately rests in who I really am, in this one the life of the ages resonates.** (*In repeating the words,* [1]*amen amen - Jesus speaks mirror language in order to emphasize the radiance and resonance of certainty between himself and his audience - from faith to faith. The preposition* [2]**eis** *suggests a point reached in conclusion.*)

6:48 I am the bread of life!

6:49 Your fathers ate the manna in the wilderness and died there in the wilderness. (*The manna didn't kill them, their unbelief in themselves did. See Numbers 13:33 and Hebrews 4:2-6. The manna was a mere prophetic shadow of me.*)

6:50 This, what you have here in me standing face to face with you, is the very sustenance of your life; the bread descending out of the heavenly sphere for everyone to eat their fill and not die.

6:51 I am the living bread, I stepped out of the heavenly realm into this earth suit, in the incarnation, so that everyone may feast on the idea of their true incarnate identity mirrored in me and discover the life of the

ages incarnate in them! The bread that I will give is my own flesh; it will translate into life for the entire cosmos!

6:52 This brought about a war of words among the Jews! How can this man give us human flesh to eat? *(Just like Nicodemus and the Samaritan woman at the well they again got it all wrong! Jesus was pointing to a different womb, well and meal!)*

6:53 *(Instead of softening the blow by explaining to them what he really meant, Jesus made it a hundred times worse for their religious reasoning, by saying the following!)* **Amen amen, I say unto you that you have** *(echo)* **no real life in yourselves until you consume the flesh of the son of man and drink his blood.** *(The very core of our beingness is founded in our co-association with Jesus, the son of man; it is only in realizing and fully assimilating our oneness in flesh-incarnate context as the son of man, that we discover the truth of our oneness in our joint-genesis as sons of Deity. He is about to take humanity with him into their death, grave and hell and then victoriously co-quicken them and co-raise them into newness of life!)*

6:54 **To assimilate my flesh and absorb my blood - to digest me is to echo the life of the ages and to be co-risen with me in the final conclusion of my work of redemption.** *(The words* **ho trōgōn***, is in the present active participle form of the verb to emphasize a continual or habitual eating.)*

6:55 **My flesh is food in its truest form and my blood is drink in its truest form.**

6:56 **Eating my flesh and drinking my blood celebrates our seamless union - you in me and I in you - because you won't find you until you find me!**

6:57 **As the living Father has sent me and also sustains me so will I sustain the one eating me. I live through my Father - just like my daily food sustains me, so his life permanently resides in me - now you may also continually and habitually feast on me and live through me!**

6:58 **This is the bread that stepped down out of the heavenly sphere - there is no comparison with the manna your fathers received from heaven** *[which was merely a prophetic shadow pointing to me]* **they ate and they died** *[without completing their destiny]* **- now feast on me and celebrate the life of the ages.**

(Eating and drinking is most significant - every meal is both a reminder and celebration of the incarnation! Every time we face food we are reminded of our beingness in flesh and our seamless oneness with our Maker and one another. See 1 Corinthians 11:26 Your every meal makes the mandate of his coming [1]relevant and communicates the meaning of the new covenant. [Whether you eat or drink, you are declaring your joint inclusion in his death and resurrection, confirming your redeemed innocence. Some translations read, "until I come..." The word translated until is, [1]achri, from akmen, which means extremity, conclusion, the present time; Jesus is the conclusion of prophetic time! The word erchomai, to come is in the aorist tense, elthe - pointing to that which has already happened!]

The prophetic picture of the table was very strategic in the tent tabernacle in the wilderness - the priests had to daily place fresh bread on the table in the sanctuary. It was called Showbread, **lechem haPānīm**, *literally: Face-bread or Bread of the Presence. The Hebrew word for presence means face to face! While Jesus spoke to the two on their way to Emmaus in Luk 24, they did not recognize him, even though their hearts ignited while he was explaining the prophetic promise of mankind's redemption in all of scripture, from Moses through the Psalms and the prophets. In Luke's interview, he pressed them for the detail, he wanted to know exactly at what point in their meeting with Jesus did they recognize him in person! He writes in verse 28, "So they drew near to the village to which they were going. He appeared to be going further..." Wow! Should Jesus not at this point have given them an opportunity to make a commitment or at least say a "sinners prayer"? Not even the best Rabbi could take them any further, Luk 24:29 But they constrained him, saying, "Stay with us, for it is toward evening and the day is now far spent." So he went in to stay with them. Luk 24:30 When he was at table with them, he took the bread and blessed, and broke it, and gave it to them.*

Luk 24:31 And their eyes were opened and they recognized him; and he vanished out of their sight.

He vanished from their sight because Jesus can no longer be any more present in his person than what he is present in the Word incarnate in us!

The moment we discover Jesus in scripture as in a mirror, our hearts ignite and our very next meal becomes a celebration of our incarnate union! "Every time you eat or drink, remember me!" Every meal celebrates the temple! Your body is God's address on planet earth! He does not dwell in buildings made by human hands. You will never again need to employ your willpower to diet and get into shape! Willpower is the language of the law! Love and value-consciousness ignites belief. The revelation of the truth sets you free to be free indeed! The days of fast food and junk-food are over! The Table is sacred and celebrates your body as the sanctuary of your redeemed life, the life of your authentic design! Sitting around the table is a feast of friendship and delightful conversation. Eat food that blesses the temple! Most diseases are diet-related! Study nutrition! We have this treasure in earthen vessels! The vessel takes its value from the treasure it holds! Feast your mind on likeness realities - make Deity your diet - digest me! Face your Father!)

6:59 Jesus said these things in a synagogue while teaching in Capernaum.

6:60 Many of his followers said, this teaching is to tough to chew on!

6:61 Jesus perceived what they were murmuring about and said, So you take offence at this?

6:62 What if you see [1]humanity's son [representing the human race] **ascending to where he [2]was before?** (*The word for the [1]human species, male or female is* **anthropos,** *from* **ana,** *upwards, and* **tropos,** *manner of life; character; in like manner. See John 1:51. John 3:13: "No one has ascended into heaven but he who descended from heaven, even humanity's son." In the beginning [2]was the Word [[2]I* *am] and the word [2]was [[2]I am] face to face with God.)*

6:63 It is the Spirit that quickens the poetry of life - the flesh *(muscle and willpower)* **is useless without the spirit. The words that I speak unto you they are spirit and life! I communicate from a different dimension and perspective giving voice and substance to every prophetic shadow and purpose.**

6:64 I notice that there are those among you who are not persuaded about me. It was clear from the start that even amongst Jesus' close followers there were signs of unbelief and treason. *(And who it was that should betray him - **kai tis estin ho paradōsōn**. Same use of **estin** and note article and future active participle of **paradidōmi**, to hand over, to betray. John does not say here that Jesus knew that Judas would betray him when he chose him as one of the twelve, least of all that he chose him for that purpose. What he does say is that Jesus was not taken by surprise and soon saw signs of treason in Judas. The same verb is used of John's arrest in Matt 4:12. Judas was given his opportunity. He did not have to betray Jesus. Robertson's Word Pictures)*

6:65 I was addressing your hesitance to believe in me when I said to you that no one is forcing you to see yourself [1]mirrored in me - you do not need to go into make-believe-mode or fake your faith - it is the Father's gift to you! *(When you hear the words that I communicate with your heart you will encounter life-quickening faith. To try and decipher my words with your religious reasoning in your head is to miss the entire point of my mission and message. The preposition [1]**pros** - face to face, is translated here as mirrored in me.)*

6:66 Because of this conversation many of his followers went back to their old ways and would no longer be associated with Jesus.

6:67 So Jesus said to the twelve, "Don't feel obliged to stay - you are also free to go if you wish!"

6:68 Simon Peter said, Lord, who is there to go back to - which mirror should we gaze into? Your words resonate the life of the ages!

6:69 We believe and know without a doubt that you are the Messiah, the Christ, the son of the living God!

6:70 I have [1]pointed all twelve of you to your source and yet one of you remains trapped in the fallen mindset! *(The word **eklego** has traditionally been translated to mean election - I would prefer to emphasize the fact that **ek** is a preposition always pointing to origin or source and the verb **lego**, is associated with its noun **logos** as in the context of John 1:1 The original conversation! See Hebrews 1:1-3)*

6:71 He spoke of Judas Iscariot the son of Simon who was a man of Kerioth. *(He was not Galilean like the rest of the disciples and seemed to have struggled more than any of them to see the significance of the mirror likeness of Jesus as defining his true sonship.)*

7:1 Jesus concentrated most of his ministry activity in Galilee since the Jewish leaders in Judea wanted to kill him.

7:2 This was now about six months later when the Jewish Feast of Tabernacles was at hand.

7:3 His own brothers prompted him to go to Judea so that his followers there might again have the opportunity to witness his signs and teaching, they reasoned.

7:4 They figured that someone of his public importance and stature should not operate in secret! He should show himself off to the world and make a name for himself!

7:5 Yet none of his immediate family believed that he really was the Christ. *(It was only after his resurrection when Jesus also appeared to James that his brother's eyes were opened, 1 Corinthians 15:7 Galatians 1:19. This prompted James to write about seeing the face of your birth when you hear the authentic word of our co-begotteness by the Father of lights. James 1:17,23.)*

7:6 Jesus replied, "My [1]agenda is different from yours! You go ahead and feast with your Jewish friends! *([1]kairos, a fixed and definite time, the decisive epoch waited for.)*

7:7 It is me they hate not you! My testimony exposes their religious rituals and works of self-righteousness as [1]incompetent. *(The word often translated evil, [1]poneros suggests, to be full of labors annoyances and hardships! This word is associated with the system of works righteousness versus faith righteousness.)*

7:8 You go to this feast - I will go when its my time!"

7:9 So his family went to Jerusalem and left him behind in Galilee.

7:10 Then after they were gone he went there unnoticed and kept a low profile.

7:11 The Jews were looking out for him; constantly enquiring about his whereabouts.

7:12 Jesus was the topic of conversation among the people - everyone had an opinion about him. Some said that he was a good man - others thought him to be deceiving the crowds with trickery.

7:13 This was all hush-hush since no-one was prepared to openly oppose Jewish-sentiment.

7:14 Then Jesus surprised them all by showing up midway through the eight-day feast, teaching openly in their temple.

7:15 What amazed the Jews most was his knowledge of scripture while he never attended any of their schools.

7:16 To which Jesus replied, "My teaching is not the product of my own invention or human perception but by my Divine connection - my mission explains my Sender's purpose.

7:17 Anyone who has a desire to engage with God's heart dream will know without a doubt that what I teach is [1]sourced in God and not merely [2]my own ideas. *(The preposition [1]ek always points to the source or origin; whereas the preposition [2]apo points away from - both are translated "from" in English. See 2 Corinthians 3:18 and Romans 1:17 See also the use of para in verse 29; which is also translated "from.")*

7:18 He who communicates "[1]away from" his true self pursues his own [2]fame based upon popular opinion - but the one seeking the glory of his Sender *[Source]* finds truth unveiled in their individual I am-ness and their true righteousness. In this person there is no trace of [3]disharmony! *(Again the preposition [1]apo is used. The word [2]doxa means glory or opinion, here translated fame.The word [3]adikia refers to the system of unrighteousness; which is a system based upon self-righteousness according to personal pursuit and performance as opposed to the righteousness of our redeemed design. The two components of this word are, a, negative and dike meaning two parties finding likeness in each other; this is the stem word for righteousness, dikaiosune.)*

7:19 Did not Moses give you the law whereby you could measure your performance, yet not one of you get it right! I mean what about the "Thou shalt not kill" - part? And here you are devising ways on how you can murder me!"

7:20 The people responded with, "You talk like a madman! No one's trying to kill you! You sound like someone with a demon -connection rather than a divine one!"

7:21 Jesus answered them, I represent one single poetic expression of the sum total of God's work - compared to the multitudes of rules Moses left you with! And you are astounded at that! *(And still you want to confuse and compare me with Moses! See chapter 6:28-31)*

7:22 Lets take one of those rules: Moses represents circumcision as the tradition of the fathers and you are okay with performing the cut on the Sabbath;

7:23 now in order not to disappoint Moses you have made your circumcision rule superior to the Sabbath; when a boy is eight days old you have no problem with performing circumcision even when it coincides with the Sabbath and here I am making a man's entire body well on the Sabbath and you're ready to kill me and break another one of the ten commandments! *(See Genesis 17:12, "He that is eight days old among you shall be circumcised.")*

7:24 Do not cloud righteous judgment with your biased opinions and traditions."

7:25 The residents in Jerusalem were surprised that Jesus showed up publicly since it was common knowledge that the Jewish leaders sought opportunity to kill him.

7:26 Here he is as outspoken as ever and they are silent! Perhaps they too know deep inside that he is truly the Christ.

7:27 "But then again we know him and his family and are of the opinion that the origin of the Christ was supposed to be a mystery."

7:28 This provoked Jesus to raise his voice passionately while he was teaching in the temple, "You claim to know me and where I come from, yet you fail to recognize that I am not here on my own mission; you clearly show that you do not know him who sent me.

7:29 But I know him for I am his close companion and kinsman; he is the one who sent me." *(Again a different word to the English word "from" See verse 17 - para, is a preposition indicating close proximity, a thing proceeding from a sphere of influence, with a suggestion of union of place of residence, to have sprung from its author and giver, originating from, denoting the point from which an action originates, intimate connection - Jesus introduces the Holy Spirit in the same capacity: parakletos, meaning close companion, kinsman [John 14:16] - here it is used with kletos from kaleo, to surname - thus sharing the same family name.)*

7:30 This made them even more determined to seize him yet no one was able to touch him since his hour had not yet come.

7:31 Many in the crowds believed on him and reasoned that no Christ still to come could possibly begin to match the miracles which he already performed.

7:32 The Pharisees were extremely worried when they realized his popularity amongst the people, so with the support of their chief priests they ordered the temple police to arrest him.

7:33 Jesus then said to them, "I will only briefly remain with you where you can see me, then I will be on my way again, [1]sinking out of sight, to be [2]face to face with my Sender. *(The word [1]upago suggests a leading "under" as in under cover. Again John employs the preposition [2]pros.)*

7:34 You will search for me but not find me and where I am your religion cannot take you."

7:35 The Jews couldn't imagine where he would go where they wouldn't find him. Maybe he would join the dispersed Jews and go teach the Gentiles.

7:36 What would he mean by saying that we would seek him and not find him and "where I am you are powerless?"

7:37 On the final day, the crescendo of the eight-day Feast of Tabernacles, Jesus stood up and proclaimed with a loud voice, "If anyone is thirsty, let him come and stand [1]face-to-face with me and drink! *(John again employs the word [1]pros in order to emphasize the face-to-face fellowship we are invited into.)*

7:38 In your belief that I am what the scriptures are all about [1]you will discover uniquely for yourself, face to face with me, that I am what you are all about and rivers of living waters will gush out of your innermost being!" *(Jesus addresses the individual; [1]you singular. Here John records how Jesus witnessed the eighth day, the great and final day of the Feast of Tabernacles, when, according to custom, the High Priest would draw water from the Pool of Siloam with a golden jar, mix the water with wine, and then pour it over the altar while the people would sing with great joy from Psalm 118:25-26, See also the entire Psalm 118 which was obviously what Jesus reminded himself of and and also Isaiah 12:3; "Therefore with joy shall we draw water from the wells of salvation!" Then, Jesus, knowing that he is the completeness of every prophetic picture and promise, cried out with a loud voice: "If anyone is thirsty, let him come to me and drink! If you believe that I am what the scriptures are all about, you will discover that you are what I am all about, and rivers of living waters will gush from your innermost being!"*

7:39 Jesus spoke about the Spirit whom those who would believe that he is the conclusion of scripture were about to [1]grasp since who Jesus was in all of his majestic splendor was not yet fully acknowledged and thus the Spirit was not yet evident. *(The word often translated, to receive, [1]lambano, means to comprehend, grasp, to identify with.)*

7:40 Many lifted their voices from within the throngs of people and declared that this is indeed the Prophet.

7:41 Others openly announced that he is truly the Christ! Some said, "No this cannot be since he comes from Galilee!

7:42 Scripture clearly states that the Christ is of the seed of David and would be born in David's home town Bethlehem!" *(Micah 5:2; 1 Samuel 16:1)*

7:43 The difference of opinions in the crowd was loaded with tension and divided them.

7:44 Some were eager to arrest him yet no one could touch him.

7:45 At this point the temple police returned to the chief priests and Pharisees who were surprised that they came back empty handed, "Why did you not arrest him?"

7:46 The police officers answered, "We have never heard anyone speak like this before!"

7:47 The Pharisees were shocked, "Are you also deceived?

7:48 Surely we, your leaders should be your informed gauge to what you believe and none of our priests or any of the Pharisees believe in him!

7:49 But these ignorant crowds have no knowledge of the law and are accursed!" *(See Deuteronomy 27:26 "Cursed be every one who does not abide by all things written in the book of the law, and do them.")*

7:50 Then one of them, Nicodemus, who secretly came to see Jesus earlier, interposed,

7:51 "Does our law condemn someone without first giving them a proper hearing or acquainting ourselves thoroughly with his conduct?

7:52 They sneeered at him, "So are you also a Galilean? Search the scriptures and see for yourself that their is no mention of any future prophet arising out of Galilee!"

(Verses 53 and 8:1-11 are not in some of the oldest manuscripts - the reason could probably be that some copyists didn't feel comfortable with this dramatic account - we have no original MSS of the Bible - but thank God for the original authentic Logos and Spirit of Christ resonating in our hearts in the unveiling of Christ in us!)

7:53 Everyone went to their homes,

8:1 while Jesus proceeded to the mount of Olives.

8:2 Early dawn he was back at the Temple where many people sought to be near him to hear him teach - he sat down and taught.

8:3 Meanwhile the scribes and pharisees led a woman to him who was forcefully seized in the act of adultery and made her stand in the middle of the throng of people where everyone could stare at her.

8:4 They said unto him, "Teacher, this woman was caught committing adultery.

8:5 Now Moses commanded us in the law that adulterers should be stoned! What would you say?

8:6 They obviously had a clear agenda to snare him in their efforts to build a case of lawlessness against him. Jesus bent down and began to write with his finger on the ground, distracting attention from the girl.

8:7 They continued to interrogate him, then he stood up and looked them in the eyes, *(pros)* and said, "He who is without sin among you, let him cast the first stone at her!"

8:8 And he again bent down and continued writing on the ground.

8:9 They began to walk away one after the other beginning with the oldest. Until Jesus was left alone with the girl, still standing where here accusers dumped her. *("Being convicted by their own conscience" is probably an addition made by some copyist to explain the meaning, which is quite clear without it.)*

8:10 When Jesus stood up again, there was no-one there except the woman. So Jesus asked her, "Where are they? Has no-one condemned you?" *(Where are they, your accusers - your accusers was added by later copyists.)*

8:11 She answered, "No-one Lord!" And Jesus said to her, "Neither am I condemning you - go and sin no more - never again believe a lie about yourself!" *(The word translated sin, **hamartia** from **ha**, negative or without, and **meros**, portion or form; thus distorted pattern - the root of sin is to believe a lie about yourself. See Romans 6:14 Sin was your master while the law was your measure; now grace rules. [The law revealed your slavery to sin; grace reveals your freedom from it. Jesus didn't say to the lady, "Go and sin less," he said to her "Go and sin no more!" Jesus knew something about the life of our design that we had lost sight of! What he revealed, he also redeemed! Sin –consciousness is what empowers religion. It always amazes me how Simon could not receive the gift of the miraculous abundant catch that Jesus blessed him with; he felt more comfortable with the fact that he caught nothing the previous night because "I am a sinful man!" He accepted his fate as his due because his mind was educated under the law of blessings and curses! [Deuteronomy 28.] When he witnessed the word and the miracle of the catch, he slotted back into his familiar mode! "Depart from me Jesus! I am a sinful man! I am not worthy!" Luke 5:8.)*

8:12 And Jesus continued to say, "I am the light of the world - whoever journeys with me shall not walk in darknes but will ¹radiate the light of life!" *(The word ¹echo, to hold; resonate; in this case, radiate.)*

8:13 The Pharisees took offence at this and responded with, "You assume things about yourself; how can you expect us to believe your record to be true?"

8:14 Jesus answered, "Whatever I declare concerning myself is absolutely true because I know where I am from and where I am going. You have no clue where I come from and therefore cannot see where I am going.

8:15 You form your own judgment according to the flesh; I judge no-one.

8:16 And even if I do make a judgment, it is true since I am not making it up in my imagination or on my own accord, my record reflects the testimony of the Father who sent me.

8:17 That should settle it for you since it is written in your law that the testimony of two men is true! *(This combined witness of two is not true just because they agree, unless true in fact separately. But if they disagree, the testimony falls to the ground. Deuteronomy 17:6; and 19:15. - Robertson's Word Pictures)*

8:18 I am witness to who I am and my Father himself also bears witness to me.

8:19 Then they said to him, "So where is your Father?" And Jesus answered, "My Father is just as invisible to you as I am - if you perceived me you would have also seen my Father!"

8:20 Jesus spoke these words in the temple treasury; yet no-one arrested him since his time was still not due.

8:21 And again Jesus said unto them, "I will go on my way and ¹disappear from your view and you will still seek me, yet die in your ²sin; your belief-system keeps you trapped in blindfold-mode to make it impossible for you to reach me where I am - your religion is a cul-de-sac!" *(The word ¹upago, to lead under, as in a sinking out of sight, to disappear. The word for sin, ²hamartia is in the singular, suggesting not sinful acts but rather a condition of a distorted mindset - from ha, negative and **meros**, portion or form, thus to be without your allotted portion or without form, pointing to a disorientated, distorted identity; the word **meros**, is the stem of the word **morphe**, as in 2 Corinthians 3:18 where the word **metamorphe**, with form, [transform] is the opposite of **hamartia** - without form. Sin is to live out of context with the blueprint of one's design; to behave out of tune with God's original harmony.)*

8:22 The Jews reasoned that maybe he would kill himself in order to go to a different world because he said, "You cannot come with me."

8:23 Jesus said to them, "You draw your conclusions from the sense ruled world here below - my source points to a different dimension, a realm which is above the horizon of the senses. *(See Colossians 3:1-4)*

8:24 That is why I said that you will die in your sins because you are not convinced about who I am, you wouldn't know who you are! Your unbelief in my I am-ness will keep you trapped in this death-ruled dimension, the very dimension that I have come to deliver you from!"

8:25 They asked him again, "Then who are you really?" He answered, "I have told you from the beginning who I am!

8:26 I have many things to say to you and conclude about you in my personal capacity but since you do not believe in me it will mean nothing to you; but he who sent me is true, above your suspicious scrutiny. I speak to the world those things which I have heard from my close companionship with him.

8:27 They just could not make the connection - Jesus' claims about the Father made no sense to their reasoning at all.

8:28 "When you have lifted up the son of man, *[on the cross of your judgment]* then you will know and understand that I am and that my I am-ness is demonstrated in my doing; nothing that I do [1]distracts from that; my doing mirrors exactly what my Father has taught me even as my speech reflects his word. (*[1]apo, away from, and* **emautou** *myself. He constantly reminds them of the conclusion of his mission, see 3:14 And as Moses lifted up the serpent in the wilderness, so must the Son of man be lifted up.*)

8:29 And he who sent me on my mission also accompanies me; the Father has never [1]abandoned me for a moment! It is my delight to always do that wich [2]pleases him. (*[1]aphieimi - a word also used for a husband divorcing his wife. The word [2]arestos to please; it suggests to accommodate one's self to the opinions desires and interests of others.*)

8:30 Whilst listening to him, many were persuaded that he was indeed the Christ.

8:31 Jesus then said to those Jews who were believing in him, "To take my word to its complete conclusion and then to abide in seamless union with its logic is to truly be my disciples. (*Here he is not referring to some future "red-letter-edition Bible"; Jesus is speaking about the Logos defining his "I am-ness", face to face with God before time was, then documented in prophetic language in ancient scripture and now unveiled in incarnate human form, as in a mirror.*)

8:32 In this abiding you will fully know the truth about who you are and this knowing will be your freedom.

8:33 They answered him, "We are the seed of Abraham; we have have never been anybody's slaves! Why do you suggest that we are not free?"

8:34 Jesus answered and said, "I say unto you with absolute certainty that everyone engaging in the distorted mindset of sin is a slave to it!" (*Sin is not about things you do or don't do - sin is missing out on sonship! The sin-system is governed by the idea of justification by personal effort, performance and pretence; which is the typical fruit of the 'I am-not-mindset' which Peter refers to as the futile ways we inherited from our fathers. 1 Peter 1:18)*

8:35 The difference between the slave and the son is that the slave only works there; for the son the father's house is home!

8:36 With the freedom found in sonship there is ¹no pretence! *(Free indeed! The word, ¹ontoos, indeed is the opposite to what is pretended.)*

8:37 I know you are the seed of Abraham, yet you are seeking opportunity to kill me because my word finds no ¹resonance in you! *(The word χορός - choros relates to a ¹chorus, harmony in song or dance; the word could also derive from χώρα - choora, which refers to space between limits.)*

8:38 I observe my Father's voice with close attention; this inspires my every expression. You hear a different father's voice and behave accordingly!

8:39 They immediately responded with, "But Abraham is our father!" To which Jesus replied, "If you were conceived by Abraham's faith, you would mirror his behavior!

8:40 But here you are, desiring to destroy me because I declare to you the truth which I heard from a place of intimate acquaintance with God; this certainly does not reflect Abraham's faith!

8:41 Your actions clearly show who your father is!" They said unto him, "We are not conceived in fornication, God is our only Father!"

8:42 Jesus said, "If you were convinced that God was your Father, you would love me. Look, here I am! I did not arrive here by my own doing; I proceeded from him who sent me!

8:43 You do not understand my ¹language because you do not hear my logic! *(My dialect seems foreign to you because you are not familiar with the Logic of God. You might be acquainted with the scriptures but you are not acquainted with the Word! See 5:39,40 also 8:31. The word ¹lalia means dialect or language.)*

8:44 You are the offspring of a ¹fallen mindset and you desire to prove its diabolic parenthood in your willingness to execute its cravings. This "cast down" mindset is what kills the ²anthropos since the beginning - *[it violently opposes the idea of the image and likeness of God in human form.]* **The diabolos mindset cannot abide the truth. There is no connection with truth - lying is its ³language; in fact, the diabolos is the father of lies!** *(The word, ¹diabolos, devil, has two components, dia, because of or through, and ballo, to cast down; thus referring to the cast down condition mankind suffered in association with Adam's fall. The diabolos is a man-slayer, ²anthrōpoktonos from anthropos and kteinoo to kill. The word for the human species, male or female is anthropos, from ana, upwards, and tropos, manner of life; character; in like manner. See John 1:51, 2:25. The word ³lalia means dialect or language.)*

8:45 And here I am communicating that which is absolutely true but you are not at all convinced!

8:46 Is there anyone amongst you who can prove me guilty of sin? So if I am telling you the truth, why would you not believe me?

8:47 Whoever realizes their origin in God immediately recognizes the language of God; you do not make that connection since you don't realize your true origin in God!

8:48 The Jews snapped back at him, "We were right all along! You are a Samaritan dog and demon possessed!"

8:49 Jesus answered, "I do not have a demon and I honor my Father while you insult me!

8:50 I am not here to defend my own opinion; God is the judge of my glory.

8:51 Truly truly do I say unto you, that anyone who treasures my word will not consider death to be of any relevance beyond this age!

8:52 The Jews replied, "Now we are more convinced than ever, that you do have a demon! Abraham and the prophets died and you say that if someone treasures your word death will be of no relevance to them unto the age!

8:53 Are you greater than our father Abraham who is dead and the prophets who are dead? Who do you think you are?"

8:54 Jesus said, "If I honour myself, my honor means nothing; actually it is my Father who honors me, the one you claim to be your God!

8:55 You have never really known him; I know him personally and would lie if I'd say that I haven't seen him! I am not lying like you; I have seen him and treasure his logos! *(Deception is born in the "I am-not" idea)*

8:56 Your father Abraham was leaping with joy to see my day! What he saw made him exceedingly glad!

8:57 Then the Jews said, "Ha! You're not even fifty years old and you claim to have seen Abraham!"

8:58 "Most certainly do I say unto you that before Abraham was born, I am!" *(See note on John 1:1 Three times in this sentence John uses the imperfect of eimi, namely ane, to be, which conveys no idea of origin for God or for the Logos, but simply continuous existence, "I am." Quite a different verb egeneto, "became," appears in John 1:14 for the beginning of the Incarnation of the Logos. The incarnation is not the genesis of Jesus. See the distinction sharply drawn in John 8:58, "before Abraham was [born, genesthai from ginomai] I am." The word eimi, I am; the essence of being, suggesting timeless existence.)*

8:59 By now they were ready to stone him, but he slipped out of their sight and left the temple area.

9:1 On his way Jesus noticed a man who was born blind.

9:2 And his followers asked him, "Master, whose sin is responsible for this man's condition; is he punished for his own sins, or perhaps for his parent's sins? Why was he born blind?"

9:3 Jesus answered emphatically, "His condition has absolutely nothing to do with any sins committed either by himself or his parents! Neither him nor his parents were guilty of sin, this is an opportunity for God's action *(in Christ)* to be unveiled in him! *(Jesus again disarms the Karma-principle that religion hinges on!)*

9:4 [1]We together must occupy ourselves to accomplish the work of him who sent me - you must take sides with me! *(The best texts read* [1]ἡμᾶς, *us, instead of* ἐμὲ, *me. We cannot pull in two opposite directions in the same team! Grace and Karma do not go hand in hand!)*

9:5 The repeated presence of my "I am-ness" in the world is the light of the world! I am the light of the cosmos!" *(See my commentary on this word in Colossians 3:4, The word,* [1]otan, *often translated as "when" is better translated to read "every time." Thus, "Every time Christ is revealed we are being co-revealed in his glory." According to Walter Bauer Lexicon,* otan *is often used of an action that is repeated.)*

9:6 Having said that, he spat on the ground and made clay with the spittle; then he anointed the eyes of the blind man with the clay. *(The clay reminds of the Genesis 2 account of the creation of the earthen vessel of flesh - fafter the "fall", flesh represents the blindfold-mode, now to be washed off in the waters of spirit dimension.)*

9:7 And said unto him, "Go, and wash in the pool of Siloam. The Hebrew word means outflow. The man went there and washed and returned seeing! *(An outflow of waters [Vincent's Word Studies] which reminds of Jesus' urgent announcment at the pool of Siloam on the great day of the feast of tabernacles, "Rivers of living waters will flow out of your innermost being!")*

9:8 The people in the neighbourhood and those who knew him before said, "Is this not the blind beggar?"

9:9 Some agreed while others doubted but the he said, "Yes, I am!"

9:10 Then they asked him, "How did it happen that you received your sight?"

9:11 He answered, "A man named Jesus made clay and smeared it over my eyes and said to me to go to Siloam and wash, so I went there and washed and [1]looked up!" *(*[1]ἀνέβλεψα *- aneblepsa means to look up, as in Matthew 14:19 and Mark 16:4)*

9:12 They wanted to know where Jesus was, but the man did not know.

9:13 Then they took him to the Pharisees,

9:14 since it was Sabbath when Jesus made the clay and opened his eyes.

(They knew that the Pharisees would have something to say about their Sabbatical laws that were disregarded by this man Jesus!)

9:15 The Pharisees demanded to know exactly how it happened that he received his sight. He said, "He put clay on my eyes and I washed and now I see."

9:16 The Pharisees were divided in their opinion; some of them immediately said, "This man cannot be closely associated with God at all since he does not honor the Sabbath. Others were questioning this with, "How can someone who is an obvious sinner according to our law, do such miracles?"

9:17 They then asked the blind man, "So what do you say about this man who opened your eyes?" He said that he thinks Jesus is a prophet.

9:18 The Jews then began to doubt whether he was blind after all, so they addressed the parents.

9:19 "Is this your son who you say was born blind? How is it that he now sees?"

9:20 The parents said, "Of course we know that this is our son and that he was indeed born blind.

9:21 But how it is that he now sees and who it is who opened his eyes, we have no idea! He is a grown boy, why don't you ask him to speak for himself?"

9:22 They chose their words carefully for fear of offending the Jews since it was rumored that the Jewish leadership agreed to ban anyone from the synagogue should they confess Jesus to be the Christ.

9:23 For this reason the parents didn't want to commit themselves to an opinion put shifted the attention back to the boy himself, saying that he is of age and should be able to speak for himself.

9:24 Then they again called the man that was blind and said to him, "Give God the glory and agree with us that this man is a Sabbath breaker and sinner.

9:25 He said, "I cannot say whether he is a sinner or not, but one thing I do know is that once I was blind but now I see!"

9:26 They wanted to hear it again and asked him, "So what did he do to you, how did he open your eyes?"

9:27 He said, "But I have already told you and you are not hearing me; why would you want to hear it again, are you perhaps also desiring to become his followers?"

9:28 They scorned him and accused him to be a Jesus-disciple! "We are disciples of Moses!

9:29 We know that God communicated with Moses but who can tell where this fellow is from?"

9:30 The man answered them, "I am amazed that you just cannot see this; how can you not perceive where he is from? I mean, hello! He opened my eyes!

9:31 Are we not supposed to know that sinners don't dictate to God - but those who worship God and desires to perform his delight has a "hotline" to heaven.

9:32 Since the beginning of time no one has ever heard of anyone who opened the eyes of a man born blind!

9:33 If this is not proof of this man's close acquaintance with God, then what is - he would be powerless to perform anything on his own."

9:34 They replied, "You were born in utter sin and here you are trying to teach the saints!" And they cast him out.

9:35 Jesus heard that they cast him out and went looking for him; when he found him, he asked him, "Do you believe in the son of God?"

9:36 He answered, "Then who is he Sir, that I may believe in him?"

9:37 Jesus said, "You have seen him, and he is speaking to you!"

9:38 And he said, "Lord, I believe. And he worshipped him."

9:39 I have come to judge the world's blindness - so that they who are blind may see and those who think that they see may become blind.

9:40 Some of the Pharisees overheard him and said, "So, are we also blind?"

9:41 Jesus said, "If you were blind you would have no sin, but now you say you see and your sin continues!"

10:1 "I want to make this very clear to you, someone whose agenda is to steal and to plunder the sheep will not come through the gate of the sheepfold; they would climb over the wall or use some other obscure way.

10:2 The shepherd of the sheep enters by the door. *(In the context of Jesus' conversation he emphasises that the sheep wouldn't expect the Shepherd-Messiah to come from anywhere else but from the Father.)*

10:3 The gate warden lets him in and the sheep recognise his voice; he calls his sheep by name and leads them out. *(He leads them out of the prophetic enclosure - the fold of safety - into life - where my soul is restored in green pastures! By the waters of reflection my soul remembers who I am - and even if I go through the valley of the shadow of death I will fear no evil - Psalm 23!)*

10:4 And when he leads them out, he goes before them and the sheep follow him; for they are familiar with his voice.

10:5 They will never follow the stranger but flee from him since they do not know his voice."

10:6 Jesus told his disciples this illustration but they did not understand what he meant by it.

10:7 "Let me say it like this then,"Jesus continued, "I am the doorway of the sheep.

10:8 The so-called shepherds and saviors who preceded me are the thieves and plunderers but the sheep did not recognize their voices.

10:9 I am the door and the sheep who enter because of who I am is safe to roam freely and find pasture.

10:10 The thief "shepherd" has no other agenda but to steal, kill and he couldn't care less if he [1]lost some sheep. I have come with the sole purpose for you to have life in its most complete form. *The word [1]apolumi, to lose, is often translated to perish - see Luke 15.*

10:11 I am the shepherd, the good one who lays down his life for the sheep. *(Ez 34:23)*

10:12 In contrast, the hireling who is not the shepherd and owner of the sheep, sees the wolf approach and leaves the sheep unattended and flees for his life while the wolf kills and scatters the sheep at will!

10:13 The hireling is doing the job merely for the wage and not because of any affection for the sheep.

10:14 I am the Shepherd, the good one who knows what is mine and they know me!

10:15 My knowledge of the Father is anchored in his knowledge of me. Because I know my father's heart I lay down my life for the sheep.

10:16 I also have other sheep that are not from this fold; I must lead them too for them to hear my voice and so there will be one flock and one shepherd. *(Second aorist active infinitive of agō with dei expressing the urgency of his mission.)*

10:17 My Father's love is the compelling urgency of my mission which is to lay down my life and receive it again in my resurrection.

10:18 No one takes my life from me, I know who I am when lay it down and from that same place of my I am-ness, I take it up again. This is the ²conclusion of my Father's prophetic purpose which is what I am all about. *(The word often translated authority or power is the word **exousia**, from **ek + eimi**, out of I am. The word ²**entole**, which is often translated commandment or precept, has two components: **en**, in and **telos**, from **tello**, to set out for a definite point or goal; properly the point aimed at as a limit, that is, by implication, the conclusion of an act or state, the result; the ultimate or prophetic purpose. Strong's 5056 See 1 John 2:3 Mirror Bible)*

10:19 These words brought more division in their ranks.

10:20 Many of them said that he had a demon and was mad; so, "Why waste your time listening to him?"

10:21 Others said, "These words are definitely not the words of someone with a demon; also, demons do not open the eyes of the blind!"

10:22 Now in Jerusalem they were celebrating the feast of The ¹Renewal of the Temple - which was in winter. *(The feast of Renewal, or new beginnings - ἐγκαίνια - egkainia, ¹**en** + **kainos** - also known as the Feast of Dedication or the Feast of Lights - which was 3 months after the Feast of Tabernacles - today Hanukkah - meaning to understand, to teach - lasting eight days from the 25th day of Kislev (in December) and commemorating the rededication of the Temple in 165 BC by the Maccabees after its desecration by the Syrians. It is marked by the successive kindling of eight lights. It was instituted by Judas Maccabeus, his brothers, and the elders of the congregation of Israel in commemoration of the reconsecration of the Jewish Temple in Jerusalem, and especially of the altar of burnt offerings, after they had been desecrated during the persecution under Antiochus Epiphanes (168 BC). This happened on the day, 3 years after the destruction of the temple. The significant happenings of the festival were the illumination of houses and synagogues, and the singing of Psalm 30.*

Jesus lived and communicated from his awareness of the prophetic significance of his life's mission in laying down his life and in co-raising fallen humanity together with him in his resurrection - Hosea 6:2/ Ephesians 2:5. See John 2:19 To which Jesus responded, "The temple will be completely demolished by you and in three days I will raise it up!" See also my commentary note in Mirror Bible.

It is also interesting to note that the numerical value of the name Jesus is 888 - The name of Jesus in Greek is spelled I H S O U S (iota, eta, sigma, omicron, upsilon, sigma). Substituting in the Greek numeral system the equivalent numerical values to each letter in the name of Jesus and adding them up, the total is 888. The values of each letter are: iota, 10; eta, 8; sigma, 200; omicron, 70; upsilon, 400; sigma, 200. The sum of 10 + 8 + 200 + 70 + 400 + 200 is 888.)

10:23 Jesus was wandering around in the temple in Solomon's porch. *(A covered colonnade on the eastern side of the outer court of the temple - a relic of Solomon's days, which had remained intact in the destruction of the temple by Nebuchadnezzar. Very much in the forefront of Jesus' mind must have been the knowing that at the next Jewish festival - 4 months later - he would fulfil John 1:29 and 2:19 as the Lamb of God to be slaughtered by his own people - for his Father to raise him up on the 3rd day and for humanity to be rebooted into newness of life! En kainos!)*

10:24 Suddenly the Jews closed in on him and demanded to know, "How long will you keep our soul suspended in mid-air? If you are the Christ then tell us plainly!"

10:25 Jesus answered them, "I have told you and you would not believe; all I do is endorsed by my Father and in his name and these works confirm my words."

10:26 Your unbelief shows that you are from a different shepherd's flock, *[as I've told you, you have made deception your shepherd.]*

10:27 My sheep hear my voice and I know them and they follow me.

10:28 And I give them the life of the ages and they shall never be lost neither shall anyone wrestle them out of my hand.

10:29 As for my Father, what he has given me is most precious and no-one can snatch them out of his hand! *(See Westcott and Hort text. The greatness of the value of the flock, is the ground of their safety. See also Weymouth NT "What my Father has given me is more precious than all besides; and no one is able to wrest anything from my Father's hand.")*

10:30 My Father and I, are one!"

10:31 This filled the Jews with renewed rage and they picked up stones to stone him.

10:32 Then Jesus questioned them saying, "I have openly shown you many good works confirming my union with my Father; for which one of these works do you stone me?"

10:33 They said, "We are not stoning you for something that you have done but for what you have just said! You have blasphemed God! You are a mere man and you make yourself equal with God? *(The penalty for blasphemy was death by stoning - Leviticus 24:16)*

10:34 Jesus said, "Is it not written in your law, 'I said you are gods?' *(Psalm 82:6)*

10:35 And if he called them gods, unto whom the word of God came, and scripture cannot be dissolved;

10:36 dare you say of him whom the Father has consecrated and commissioned into the world, "You blaspheme!" because I said that I am the son of God?

10:37 If I was not doing my Father's works then you would have reason not to believe me;

10:38 But if I do, then even if you do not believe me believe the works; then you will understand and be convinced that the Father is in me and I am in him!"

10:39 And again they sought to seize him as they had tried repeatedly in the past, but he escaped out of their hands.

10:40 Meanwhile he went back across the Jordan into the region called Peroea to the place where John first baptized, and remained there.

10:41 Many people followed him saying, "John didn't do any miracles, but everything he said about him is true!"

10:42 And many in that region believed in him.

11:1 Now the brother of Martha and Mary from Bethany was sick.

11:2 This was the same Mary who anointed the Lord with perfumed oil and dried his feet with her hair. *(John looks back from the end of the century as he writes this commentary - even though the anointing is only recorded in chapter 12)*

11:3 So the sisters sent someone to tell Jesus, "Lord, your dear friend Lazarus is sick."

11:4 His sickness is not to face death but to face the glory of God triumph over and above death! And the son of God will be glorified because of that. *(pros, face to face; uper, over and above.)*

11:5 Jesus loved Martha, her sister and Lazarus.

11:6 After he heard of Lazarus' sickness he did not go immediately but remained where he was for another two days. *(In his deliberate delay here, again, his mind must have been occupied with his mission - knowing that soon he would enter humanity's death for two days and face the horror of their judgment)*

11:7 Then he said to his disciples, "Let's go into Judea again."

11:8 His disciples were surprised, "But Master we've just come from there and the Jews wanted to stone you! Now you want to go there again?"

11:9 Jesus replied, "Are there not twelve hours in the day? To walk in the light of day is to walk freely without obstruction.

11:10 But someone who walks in the night would stumble because there is no enlightenment in him.

11:11 Having said this he added, "Our friend Lazarus is not dead but sleeps and I am going to wake him up out of his sleep."

11:12 His disciples responded with, "But Lord if he is only sleeping he should be okay?"

11:13 Yet Jesus meant that his death was nothing more than being asleep but they thought that he meant that he was just taking a rest in a deep sleep.

11:14 So Jesus said it plainly, "Lazarus is dead.

11:15 And for your sakes I am glad that I wasn't there so that you may believe; nevertheless let's go to him."

11:16 Then Thomas said to his fellow disciples, "Let us also go so that we may die with him!" *[Aramaic te'oma meaning twin, or didumos in Greek]*

11:17 When Jesus arrived Lazarus was already in the tomb for four days.

11:18 Now Bethany was only about two miles from Jerusalem.

11:19 Many Jews came to comfort the two sisters.

11:20 Martha immediately went out to meet Jesus when she heard of his arrival, while Mary was waiting in the house.

11:21 Martha said to Jesus, "Lord, if you'd been here earlier my brother would not have died.

11:22 But I know that even now whatsoever you would ask of God he will give it to you."

11:23 Jesus said to her, "Your brother shall rise again."

11:24 Martha said, "Yes I know that he shall rise again in the conclusion of time."

11:25 Jesus said, "I am the resurrection and the life - he that believes in me shall live even though he died.

11:26 And whoever is alive in the life that I am, shall never die. Do you believe this?"

11:27 Yes Lord, I believe that you are the Christ, the son of God, who was destined to come into the world.

11:28 Martha then called Mary secretly away from the attention of the mourners, saying, "The Lord is here and he wants to tell you something."

11:29 Mary immediately jumped up and went out quickly to meet him.

11:30 Jesus was not yet in the town where they lived but waited in the place where Martha met with him.

11:31 The Jews who had come from Jerusalem to console her, saw her getting up quickly to leave the house; they thought that she was going to weep at the grave so they followed her.

11:32 When Mary came to the place where Jesus was waiting for her, she fell down at his feet saying to him, "Lord if only you were here, my brother wouldn't have died!"

11:33 When Jesus saw her weeping and also the Jews mourning with her, he groaned in his spirit and was deeply moved.

11:34 He asked, "Where is the tomb?" They said, "Lord come and we'll show you."

11:35 Jesus wept.

11:36 The Jews remarked, "He really loved him very much!"

11:37 Some of them reasoned, "Why could this man, who opened the blind eyes of a stranger, not prevent his friend's death?"

11:38 Jesus again groaned in himself as he arrived at the grave; it was a cave with a stone upon it's opening.

11:39 Then Jesus asked for the stone to be taken away. Martha warned that by this time there would be a stench since it was already four days since he passed away.

11:40 Jesus answered, "Did I not tell you that in your believing you see the glory of God - [not in your doubting!] (Believing opens the horizon of your spirit to see beyond the immediate!)

11:41 Then they removed the stone from the cave where the dead was laid. Jesus lifted up his eyes and said, "Father I thank you that you have heard me.

11:42 I am persuaded that you always hear me; but I am saying this for the sake of those who are standing by so that they too may come to believe that you sent me."

11:43 And after he spoke these words, he raised his voice and hollered, "Lazurus! Come out!"

11:44 And the dead man appeared with his hands and feet swathed in linen cloths also his face was covered in a cloth. Jesus said to them, "Unwrap him and so that he can move around freely."

11:45 Then many of the Jews who accompanied Mary to the grave believed in him when they witnessed what he just did.

11:46 But some of them went and reported what had happened to the Pharisees.

11:47 The chief priests and Pharisees immediately called a council meeting. "What do we do now? For this man is doing many miracles.

11:48 If we let him alone everyone will believe in him. Then the Romans will come and dispossess us from our land and our national heritage! (Feeling threatened rather than endorsed in their core identity - thus missing the entire point of the Messiah's mission!)

11:49 And one of them, Caiaphas who was the High Priest at the time, said, "You don't know what you're talking about.

11:50 If you merely reasoned about this you would have known that it is to our advantage that one should die instead of an entire nation."

11:51 This he said without realizing that in the office of the High Priest he was prophesying Jesus' sacrificial death as the scapegoat of the entire nation.

11:52 And this was not for Israel only but in Jesus laying down his life as the true Shepherd of mankind, he would lead together into one family all the children of God from wherever they have been scattered (into places and circumstances where they have lost their true identity. His death would bring closure to every lie that mankind believed about themselves.)

11:53 Then from that day they took counsel together to put him to death.

11:54 And so Jesus no longer moved about publicly in Jewish circles. He withdrew into the hill country bordering the desert where he remained with his disciples in the village of Ephraim. (Near Bethel)

11:55 The Jewish passover was coming up and many people were making their way to Jerusalem to participate in the ceremonial purification before the Easter celebrations.

11:56 Jesus was the topic of conversation among the people in the temple courts. Everyone was curious about his whereabouts and wondered whether he would show up during Passover.

11:57 **The Chief priests and Pharisees** [the Sanhedrin] **decreed that anyone with information must disclose it so that they can arrest Jesus.** (They were seeking Jesus six months before at the feast of tabernacles [John 7:11], but now they were ready to kill him.)

12:1 Six days before Passover Jesus arrived at Bethany where Lazarus whom he raised for the dead lived.

12:2 There they prepared supper for him. Lazarus joined him at the table while Martha was serving them.

12:3 In the meantime Mary took a pound of very expensive spikenard oil and massaged Jesus' feet and wiped it with her hair. The entire house was filled with the fragrance.

12:4 One of his disciples Judas Iscariot, who betrayed him, was shocked at this and said,

12:5 "Why this waste! The perfume could have been sold for a years wages and the money given to the poor!"

12:6 He couldn't care less about the poor! He was a thief and while he was entrusted with the money bag, he would help himself to it!

12:7 Then Jesus said, "Do not hinder her! She has preserved this for the preparation of my burial.

12:8 You will always have the poor to minister to with you but you will not always have me with you.

12:9 A large crowd of Jews heard that Jesus was in Bethany and went there not only to see Jesus but Lazarus who was raised from the dead.

12:10 So the chief priests determined to kill Lazarus as well.

12:11 They knew that because of him many were leaving their faith to join Jesus.

12:12 The following day many people were flocking to the feast because they learned that Jesus was coming to Jerusalem.

12:13 They gathered palm branches and went to meet him while continually shouting, Jahshana - salvation now! Well spoken of is the king of Israel who comes in the name of the Lord!" *(connected with the Feast of Tabernacles. eulogeō. Quotation from Psa 118:25., written, some think, for the dedication of the second temple, or, as others think, for the feast of tabernacles after the return (Ezr 3:1.). It was sung in the processional recitation then as a welcome to the worshippers. Here the words are addressed to the Messiah as is made plain by the addition of the words, "even the king of Israel")*

12:14 Having found a young colt, Jesus sat on it and fulfilled that which was written prophetically about him in scripture.

12:15 Fear not daughter of Sion; rejoice exceedingly! Pay attention! Your king is coming, humbly riding a donkey, a mere colt of a donkey. *(Zec 9:9)*

12:16 The disciples did not immediately realize the profound significance of this moment; it was only after he was glorified that the full impact of what was written of him and what they did to him dawned on them.

12:17 The people who witnessed the raising of Lazarus from the dead gave testimony to what they have encountered.

12:18 This was also part of the reason why so many people came out to meet him since they too have heard about the miracle.

12:19 The Pharisees were perplexed about this and said, "Look, we are gaining no ground against him! The entire world is running after him!"

12:20 There were also a number of Greeks who came to worship at the feast because of the rumors they have heard.

12:21 They approached Phillip who was from Bethsaida in Galilee and asked him, "Sir, we would be delighted to see Jesus. Is there perhaps any chance that you could introduce us to him?"

(He had a Greek name and the Greeks may have seen Philip in Galilee where there were many Greeks)

12:22 Phillip went and told Andrew and the two of them told Jesus.

12:23 Jesus, immediately understanding the prophetic significance of the moment, knew that he, the Messiah was who all the nations were longing for! and answered, "The hour is here for the son of man to be glorified! *[Jesus studied scripture as in a mirror - he knew that "in the book, it is written about me!"Haggai 2:7 and the desire of the nations shall come...]*

12:24 Most certainly shall the single grain of wheat fall into the earth and die - if it doesn't die it remains alone - but in its death it produces much fruit. *(It bears an innumerable harvest of its own kind! Seed always produces after its kind.)*

12:25 To hold on desperately to a mere life defined by the soul realm is to lose it; but to abandon the soul substitute for the real deal is to observe your spiritual life which is the life of the ages.

12:26 Whoever continues to minister to me, let him keep on following me; where I go you will share unhindered companionship with me. This shared union is what Father greatly values. *(Note, **ean** with present active subjunctive of **diakoneō**, keep on serving with dative **emoi**; let him keep on following" - present active imperative of **akoloutheō**. Literally, **eimi egoo ... ho emos estai**, to be where I am - see John 14:20, in that day you will know that I am in my Father and you are in me and I am in you!)*

12:27 My soul is exceedingly perplexed right now! What shall I say, "Father! Rescue me [1]out of the clutches of this hour!" No! This hour is the very culmination of my destiny! *(Greek preposition, [1]**ek**, out of; source; origin.)*

12:28 "Father! Glorify your name!" And immediately there came a voice out of the heavenly realm saying, "I have glorified it, and I will glorify it again!"

12:29 The crowd heard the voice and said that it had thundered; others thought it was the voice of an angel.

12:30 Jesus replied, "This voice was not for my sake but for yours! *(Signs are for unbelievers. 1 Corinthians 14:22)*

12:31 This is the judgment of this world; it is the moment where the authority of the world-system is cast out! *(The serpent's head is about to be crushed! Genesis 3:15; Colossians 2:14,15)*

12:32 When I am ¹lifted up from the earth, I will draw ²all judgment to me! *(¹He would be lifted up on a cross, descend into the depths of our hell, then, according to the prophetic word in Hosea 6:2, after two days be lifted up as representative of the human race, out of the lowest parts of the earth and elevated to the highest heavens! Ephesians 4:8,9; see also Ephesians 2:5,6 and Colossians 3:1-3. ²All things include all of mankind and their judgment. The subject of the sentence as from the previous verse is the judgment of the world - thus the primary thought here is that in his death, Jesus would draw all judgment upon himself! John 3:14; John 8:28; Act 2:33. 1 John 3:5 We have witnessed with our own eyes how, in the unveiling of the prophetic word, when he was lifted up upon the cross as the Lamb of God, he ¹lifted up our sins and broke its dominion and rule over us! [John 1:29 "Behold, the Lamb of God, who ¹takes away [airo] the sin of the world! The word ¹airo means to lift up.])*

12:33 This he said to point to the way in which he would die. *(See John 19:15 - Lift him up! Lift him up! Crucify him!")*

12:34 The people answered him, "We understood from the law *[the Scriptures]* **that the Christ remains forever. On what basis would you say then, that the son of man would be lifted up? Who is this son of man?"**

12:35 Then Jesus said, "Yet a little while the light is in your midst; walk in accordance with the light that you have, *(resonate with; echo)* **then you will not be overtaken by darkness. For the one who walks in darkness has no idea where to go.**

12:36 So long as you have *(echo; resonate)* **the light, live persuaded ¹in the conclusion of light; oh that you ²might realize your authentic origin as the sons of light!** *(The preposition ¹eis points to conclusion; a point reached. The word ²genesthe from ginomai, to be born, to become is in the Aorist Subjunctive Mood, which is similar to the Optative expressing a wish. The Mood of the Greek verb expresses the mode in which the idea of the verb is employed. This wish is consistent with the theme of John's conversation in this book, see John chapter 1. See also 2 Peter 1:19 For us the appearing of the Messiah is no longer a future promise but a fulfilled reality. Now it is your turn to have more than a second-hand, hearsay testimony. Take my word as one would take a lamp at night; the day is about to dawn for you in your own understanding. When the morning star appears, you no longer need the lamp; this will happen shortly on the horizon of your own hearts.*

To walk in the light as he is in the light means to see your life and everything that concerns you, exclusively from your Father's point of view. You are indeed the focus of your Father's attention and affection. To be convinced of your origin in God and Father's initiative in redeeming your mind from all the lies you believed about yourself, is the vital energy of the law of liberty. To reflect the opinion of God in your attitude and conversation makes your life irresistibly attractive.

12:37 Even though he had done so many miracles in front of their eyes they were still not persuaded about him.

12:38 Their persistent unbelief reminds of what Isaiah said, "Lord, who has believed our report? To whom has the arm of the Lord been revealed! Who understands how God has reached into our world?

12:39 They were incapable of faith since Isaiah also said,

12:40 "He has blinded their eyes and hardened their heart so they cannot see with the eyes nor perceive with the heart and be transformed where I shall heal them." *(See Romans 9:17-33; also 11:7 The very thing Israel sought to obtain through their diligent labor they failed to get; yet those who embraced grace as God's original intent hit the bull's eye every time, leaving the rest groping around in the dark like blindfolded archers. (eklego: the original reasoning, logic, word.)*

Romans 11:8 Isaiah said that God has given them a spirit of slumber, causing their eyes and ears not to function. This drowsiness seems to prevail even to this day. (Unbelief and religious ritual are blindfolds. "And the Lord said, this people draw near to me with their mouth and honor me with their lips but remove their hearts and minds far from me, and their fear and reverence for me are a commandment of men that is learned by repetition ... ." [Isa 29:10 - 14])

Isa 29:10 For the LORD has poured out upon you a spirit of deep sleep, and has closed your eyes, the prophets, and covered your heads, the seers.

Isa 29:11 And the vision of all this has become to you like the words of a book that is sealed. When men give it to one who can read, saying, "Read this," he says, "I cannot, for it is sealed."

Isa 29:12 And when they give the book to one who cannot read, saying, "Read this," he says, "I cannot read."

Isa 29:13 And the Lord said: "Because this people draw near with their mouth and honor me with their lips, while their hearts are far from me, and their fear of me is a commandment of men learned by rote;

Isa 29:14 therefore, behold, I will again do marvellous things with this people, wonderful and marvellous; and the wisdom of their wise men shall perish, and the discernment of their discerning men shall be hid."

Isa 29:15 Woe to those who hide deep from the LORD their counsel, whose deeds are in the dark, and who say, "Who sees us? Who knows us?"

Isa 29:16 You turn things upside down! Shall the potter be regarded as the clay; that the thing made should say of its maker, "He did not make me"; or the thing formed say of him who formed it, "He has no understanding"?

Isa 29:17 Is it not yet a very little while until Lebanon shall be turned into a fruitful field, and the fruitful field shall be regarded as a forest?

Isa 29:18 In that day the deaf shall hear the words of a book, and out of their gloom and darkness the eyes of the blind shall see.

Isa 29:19 The meek shall obtain fresh joy in the LORD, and the poor among men shall exult in the Holy One of Israel.

Isa 29:20 For the ruthless shall come to nought and the scoffer cease, and all who watch to do evil shall be cut off,

Isa 29:21 who by a word make someone out to be an offender, and lay a snare for the one who reproves in the gate, and with an empty plea turn aside the one who is in the right.

Isa 29:22 Therefore thus says the LORD, who redeemed Abraham, concerning the house of Jacob: "Jacob shall no more be ashamed, no more shall his face grow pale.

Isa 29:23 For when he sees his children, the work of my hands, in his midst, they will sanctify my name; they will sanctify the Holy One of Jacob, and will stand in awe of the God of Israel.

Isa 29:24 And those who err in spirit will come to understanding, and those who murmur will accept instruction.")

12:41 Isaiah said these things when he saw the beauty of God on exhibit in the Messiah. *(And he could not understand that the people of Israel wouldn't see this for themselves!)*

12:42 Many of the chief rulers believed that Jesus was the Messiah but because of the Pharisees they would not openly confess him since they knew that they would be thrown out of the assembly.

12:43 They loved the ¹opinion and recognition of people more than the opinion of God. *(The word often translated, glory, doxa from dokeo, to form an opinion.)*

12:44 Jesus cried out and said, "To believe in me is not proof that I won your vote; it proves your belief in the one who sent me!

12:45 To see me is to see him who sent me.

12:46 I have come to enlighten the world so that anyone who believes in me should no longer abide in darkness.

12:47 If any one hears my words and rejects them, I do not judge that person; for I did not come to judge the world but to save the world!

12:48 The one who rejects me and my words has one who judges him, the very Word that I have spoken to him is the final judge. No-one will escape the ultimate scrutiny of the Word!

12:49 I have not conjured up what I have spoken to you but the Father who sent me has given me specific instruction to say what I do in the way that I do it.

12:50 And I know that this instruction is the life of the Ages - the detail of what I say echoes exactly what I've heard my Father say.

13:1 Now Jesus having known, before the feast of the passover, that this was his hour; he knew very well that he would step out of this world into his Father's embrace. *[pros - face to face]* He drew much love-energy from his own who would remain still in the world after his departure; He loved them completely.

13:2 It was supper time and the [1]diabolos already had the heart of Judas Iscariot in sync with his own, which was to betray Jesus. *(During supper - deipnou ginomenou, which is the correct text, present middle participle of ginomai - [not genomenou, second aorist middle participle, "being ended"] The devil, dia because of and ballo, cast down; because of the fall; referring to the fallen mindset - the one that will be crushed by the Seed of the woman - 'put into the heart of Judas, 'ballo eis kardia'... thus Judas' heart was in sync with the fallen mindset.)*

13:3 Jesus was fully aware of the fact that his Father has given all things into his hands; he knew that he came from God and that his destiny was to return face to face with God. *(As the incarnate word he knew that he is the exhibit of the thoughts of God in human form; he knew that he fulfilled what Isaiah saw when he spoke about the thoughts of God that would come down from heaven like rain and snow to saturate the earth, making it bring forth and sprout, giving seed to the sower and bread for food, before it returns again to heaven. "So shall my word be, that proceeds from my mouth, it shall not return to me empty but prosper in my purpose!" He has come to mirror God's mind towards mankind.)*

13:4 So he got up from the table and took off his outer garments and wrapped a towel around him.

13:5 He then poured water into a basin and began to wash the feet of his disciples and dried them with the towel around his waste.

13:6 When he came to Simon Peter, Peter protested saying, "Lord do you want to wash my feet?"

13:7 Jesus answered, "You might not appreciate it now but afterward you will understand the significance of what I am doing!"

13:8 Peter refused and said, "I will never allow you to wash my feet!" And Jesus replied, "If I do not wash you then you have no participation with me."

13:9 Then Peter said, "Lord, not only my feet but also my hands and head!"

13:10 But Jesus answered, "He that has already taken a bath only needs to wash his feet for he is completely clean. And you are already clean, yet not everyone of you.

13:11 For Jesus knew who would betray him - that is why he said, "you are not all equally clean." *(Not all of you have given the word the same opportunity to wash your minds! According to custom the guest was supposed to bathe (louō) before coming to a feast and so only the feet had to be washed (niptō) on removing the sandals.)*

13:12 So when he was done he put his robe back on again and reclined at the table and asked them, "Do you understand what I just did?"

13:13 You call me your Instructor and Lord and its good, for so I am;

13:14 If I, your teacher and Lord have washed your feet; you too ought to wash one another's feet!

13:15 For I have demonstrated an example for you to mirror.

13:16 For I would want you to know most certainly that the servant is not greater than his Lord and the one sent is not greater than the one who sent him.

13:17 To know these things is to find your joy in expressing them in your lifestyle.

13:18 I am not talking about all of you; I have chosen you and know that one of you will kick me like a horse, just as it is written, "Even my trusted friend, who ate bread with me has turned his heel against me." *(Psalm 41:9)*

13:19 I'm telling you this in advance so when it happens you may be persuaded about me.

13:20 I also assure you that whoever can identify with your mission, identifies with me and therefore identifies with him who he sent me." 1lambano, means to comprehend, grasp, to identify with.

13:21 Having said this Jesus was again deeply disturbed in his spirit and said, "I am telling you now that one you is about to betray me!"

13:22 The disciples were confused, looking at one another and wondering who this person could possibly be.

13:23 One of the disciples was leaning against the bosom of Jesus, cuddled up in his love;

13:24 Simon Peter prompted him to ask Jesus who it was.

13:25 So he did, "Jesus, who is it?"

13:26 Jesus relied, "It is the one I'll give the morsel of bread to once I have dipped into the broth." He then dipped the morsel and handed it to Judas Iscariot, Simon's son.

13:27 Wrapped up in that morsel was the opportunity for Satan to now fully engage the mind of Judas. Then Jesus said to Judas, "Do what you've got to do and get it over and done with ." *(Literally, ¹meta, together with the morsel...)*

13:28 Even now the other disciples did not suspect Judas in the least. *(Amazing how Jesus never treated Judas any differently even though he knew that he was stealing money from them.)*

13:29 Some thought that since Judas was their treasurer Jesus asked him to go and buy necessities for the feast, or perhaps to go and give some money to the poor.

13:30 With that, Judas left immediately; and it was night.

13:31 Then, with Judas gone, Jesus said, "This seals the glorification of the son of man, as well as God's glorification in him.

13:32 In this joint glorification God is glorified in himself - In God glorifying mankind in himself, his personal glory is not diminished at all, but fully endorsed! This is happening immediately and seamlessly! *(Whatever God accomplished in Jesus the incarnate Christ is of immediate consequence to the human race.)*

13:33 Little children, I am with you for a very little while, then you will seek me, but as I said to the Jews, where I go you cannot join me; so now I say to you,

13:34 I give you a new commandment, keep on loving one another just as I have loved you - my love for you is the source of your love for one another. *(The word entole, which is often translated commandment or precept, has two components: en, in and telos, from tello, to set out for a definite point or goal; properly the point aimed at as a limit, that is, by implication, the conclusion of an act or state, the result; the ultimate or prophetic purpose. Strong's 5056)*

13:35 I this environment of your love for one another everyone will come to know your discipleship unto me.

13:36 Simon Peter then asked him, "Lord, where are you going?" Jesus answered, "Where I am about to go, you are not able to accompany me right now, but you will afterwards. *(See 14:1 I go to prepare a place for you that where I am you may be also!)*

13:37 Peter said, "But Lord, why cannot I follow you right now? I will give my life for you!"

13:38 Jesus said, "Will you give your life for me? I say to you now, most certainly will you have contradicted me three times before the cock crows."

14:1 Set your troubled hearts at ease by letting your belief ¹conclude in God as you rest your confidence in me. *(The preposition ¹eis, means a point reached in conclusion.)*

14:2 What makes my Father's house home, is your place in it! If this was not the ultimate conclusion of my mission why would I even bother to do what I am about to do if it was not to prepare a place for you? I have come to persuade you of a place of seamless union where you belong. *(See John 8:35 The difference between the slave and the son is that the slave only works there; for the son the father's house is home! 8:36 With the freedom found in sonship there is ¹no pretence! [Free indeed! The word, ¹ontoos, indeed is the opposite to what is pretended.] What Jesus is about to accomplish in his death and resurrection will forever shift the idea of religious works and pretence and performance from the typical slave-mentality to the freedom and reality of sonship!)*

14:3 The proportions of what I will accomplish are astonishing! I will ¹prepare a highway for you, just as in the Oriental custom, where people would go before a king to level the roads to make it possible for royalty to journey with ease and comfort. By ²fully identifying myself with you I would fully identify you with me so that you may be completely at home where I am! *(Jesus sees the full scope of his work: by submitting himself to our judgment and hellish fury, he would enter our death and gloom and thereby strip every principality and dominion of its judgment and power-play over the human race. Colossians 2:14,15. The word ¹hetoimazō suggests a levelling of the road to make it passable for kings! [Isaiah 40:3-5] The word ²paralambano, carries two components, para, a preposition indicating close proximity, a thing proceeding from a sphere of influence, with a suggestion of union of place of residence, to have sprung from its author and giver, originating from, denoting the point from which an action originates, intimate connection; and lambano, to comprehend, grasp, to identify with. He would lead us in his triumphant procession on high out of our darkness into his marvellous light, where we may now participate in the union of the ages - "and take you to myself so that you may be where I am, face to face with the Father! " Hosea 6:2; Ephesians 4:8; Colossians 1:13. John 1:1,2. See John 1:18 Until this moment God remained invisible to mankind; now the authentic, incarnate begotten son, the blueprint of our design who represents the innermost being of God, the son who is in the bosom of the father, brings him into full view! He is the official authority qualified to announce God! He is our guide who accurately declares and interprets the invisible God within us.)*

14:4 And where I go you know the way. *The best texts omit the second ye know, and theand before the way;*

14:5 Thomas said, "No, we don't get it; we have no idea where you are going with this - how could we possibly know the way?"

14:6 Jesus said, "My I am-ness *[mirrored in you]* **is your way; this is your truth and also your life! Every single person can now come face to face with the Father entirely because of my doing."**

14:7 If you had known me for who I really am, you would have immedi-

ately recognized my Father in me. Now, with me bringing you back face to face with the Father, you will certainly know him and [1]become fully acquainted with him. *(The word [1]horao implies encounter.)*

14:8 Phillip said to him, "Lord, [1]show us the Father, then we will be satisfied." *([1]Aorist imperative - denoting aspect, not tense; once and for all.)*

14:9 "Phillip, I have been with you for a long time, and yet you haven't really known me? To see me is to see the Father! How can you still say, "Show us the Father?" *(Phillip was the one who introduced Nathaniel to Jesus in the beginning of their walk with Jesus. "We have found him of whom Moses in the law and the prophets did write" John 1:46. The Father cannot appear in any more visible or tangible manner than what he did in Jesus, the incarnate Word. Any idea one could possibly have about God that is unlike Jesus, is not the Father! He is the radiant and flawless expression of the person of God. He exemplifies the character and every attribute of God in human form. Hebrews 1:3)*

14:10 Are you not convinced that I am in the Father and that the Father is in me? We are in seamless union. The words that I speak to you are not my independent opinion or ideas; the Father in me addresses you; this conversation then translates into the Father's action unveiled in my doing.

14:11 The fact that the Father seems distant or invisible to you does not mean that he is absent. In me he is very present with you! You cannot claim to know me while you ignore him - we are inseparable. Humanity, I dare you *[plural]* to believe that I am in the Father and the Father in me - if it seems far fetched, then believe me because of what I have done and what I am about to do. It is the Father in me who defines me. My works exhibit his resolve. *(Jesus did not come to persuade the Father about us, he came to persuade us about the Father. There is nothing in the incarnate Word that is in conflict with who God is! John 1:1-3 If you underestimate me, you underestimate my father - and you underestimate you!)*

14:12 I want you to be fully convinced about this, anyone whose belief concludes in who I am will also do the works I do. And because of my going to my Father the works that the believer will do will be of greater proportion and of global influence; the Father is as present in you as he is in me because of my going to do what I am about to do.

14:13 And whatever you desire in my name, that will I do that the Father may be glorified in the son. Your sonship is endorsed in my sonship. *(The first occurrence of the phrase, In my name, en tōi onomati mou. See also John 14:26; 15:16; 16:23, 16:24, 16:26. "If this name, Jesus Christ is in the believer's consciousness, the element in which the prayerful activity moves; so that thus that Name, embracing the whole revelation of redemption, is that which specifically measures and defines the disposition, feeling, object, and contents of prayer. The express use of the name of Jesus therein is no specific token; the question is of the spirit and mind of him who prays" Meyer)*

14:14 If you ask me anything, in knowing what my name entitles you to,

that will I perform. *(The use of 'me' here is supported by Aleph B 33 and the Vulgate Syriac Peshitta manuscripts. Aleph is the famous Sinaiticus, the great discovery of Constantine von Tischendorf, the only surviving complete copy of the New Testament written prior to the ninth century; [4th century] and the Vulgate Syriac Peshitta, of AD 150. Called the "Queen of Versions" because of it's beauty and simplicity. There are 177 of these MSS, most in the British Museum. This was the translation used by the church at Antioch.)*

14:15 In your loving me you will greatly value and treasure ¹the prophetic conclusion of my ministry. *(The word ¹entole, which is often translated commandment or precept, or assignment, has two components, en, in and telos, from tello, to set out for a definite point or goal; properly the point aimed at as a limit, that is, by implication, the conclusion of an act or state, the result; the ultimate or prophetic purpose. Strong's 5056. See 1 John 2:3)*

14:16 And I will agree with the Father to give you another ¹close companion to be with you - in such an intimate way that my immediate presence will be fully perceived by you within the timeless zone of the ages! *(Notes on **parakletos:** Romans 1:12 And so we will be mutually refreshed in the ¹participation and reflection of our common faith. (The word, ¹sumparakaleo, comes from sum, together; para, is a preposition indicating close proximity, a thing proceeding from a sphere of influence, with a suggestion of union of place of residence, to have sprung from its author and giver, originating from, denoting the point from which an action originates, intimate connection, and kaleo, meaning to identify by name, to surname; thus, alongside, closest possible proximity of nearness Jesus introduces the Holy Spirit in the same capacity, **parakletos,** meaning close companion, kinsman [Jn 14:16]. Romans 12:8 or to just be there ¹alongside someone to remind them of their true identity; always let faith set the pace. You are ³intertwined with your ²gift, wrapped up in the same parcel. Lead with passion; minister mercy cheerfully. [¹**parakaleo,** alongside, closest possible proximity of nearness; ²**metadidomi** [see note on Romans 1:11], and ³**haplous** from ha, a particle of union and pleko, to plait, braid or weave together. You cannot distance yourself from your giving! What God now has in us is gift wrapped to the world [Eph 4:11]. 2 Corinthians 1:4 There is no contradiction of any proportion that we can possibly face that has what it takes to exasperate us or distance us from God. Our consciousness of his inseparable nearness immediately reinforces us to extend the same tangible ¹closeness to you in your difficult times, and together we snuggle up in the ¹comfort of his intimate embrace! [Paul uses the word, ¹**parakaleo,** which comes from para, close proximity, and kaleo, to identify by name; often translated, to comfort.] Philippians 2:1 In Christ our ¹association is most intimate; we ²articulate his love story; entwined in spirit communion and tender affections. The word ²**paramuthion,** is from para + muthos, a myth or tale, a story of instruction, told in heart to heart language. Philippians 2:2 Your Christ mindedness completes my delight! You co-echo the same agape; we are soul mates, resonating the same thoughts.] 1 Thessalonians 4:10 I know your affection for your fellow family throughout Macedonia. From this place of our close union in our ¹common origin we anticipate the ever ²increasing impact of love's irresistible impression. [Our common origin, ¹**parakaleo.**] 1 Thessalonians 5:11 Continue, as you so eloquently* *do, to edify one another by cultivating the environment of your [1]close association in your joint-genesis. [The word [1]parakaleo is here translated as our joint-genesis])*

14:17 Your eternal companion is the Spirit of truth who cannot be grasped by the world since their visual horizon is veiled and they are not able to understand what they cannot see. But you know because you are already acquainted with the Spirit in me and this same Spirit will reside within you. *(Spirit dimension is not a foreign place neither is the Spirit a foreign person to you!)*

14:18 At no time will you be orphaned or abandoned by me; I come to abide [1]face to face with you. *(I come to be no less face to face with you than what I've always been face to face with the Father from the beginning for all eternity. The Holy Spirit does not replace but reinforces the presence of Jesus and the nearness of the Father. Again John uses the word [1]pros, face to face. See John 1:1)*

14:19 In yet a little while and the world will no longer see me but I will be tangibly visible to you in the very life we share together.

14:20 In that day you will know that just as I am in my Father, you are in me and I am in you! *(Now picture 4 circles with the one fitting into the other - The outer circle is the Father, then Jesus in the Father, then us in Jesus, and the Spirit in us! This spells inseparable, intimate oneness! Note that it is not our knowing that positions Jesus in the Father or us in them! Our knowing simply awakens us to the reality of our redeemed union! Gold does not become gold when it is discovered but it certainly becomes currency!)*

14:21 Whoever [1]resonates and [2]treasures the [3]completeness of my prophetic purpose cannot but fall in love with me and also find themselves to be fully participating in my Father's love and I will love this one and make myself distinctly known and real to each one individually. In this embrace of inseparable union love rules! *(Intimacy is not the result of suspicious scrutiny but the inevitable fruit of trust! [1]Echo, to have; to hold; to resonate. [2]Tereo, to treasure ; to safeguard. [3]Entole, see note in 14:15.)*

14:22 Judas, not Iscariot, said to him, "Lord, how is it that you will make yourself visible to us and not to the world?" *(This is the fourth interruption of the talk of Jesus (by Peter, 13:36; by Thomas, 14:5; by Philip, 14:8; and now by Judas.)*

14:23 Jesus answered, "This is so much more than a mere casual, suspicious or indifferent observation, whoever loves me will treasure my words and know my Father's love and we will come face to face with this one and make our abode with [para] each one individually." *(We will make our abode, [1]mone, the same Greek word that is rendered mansions in the KJV in the former part of this chapter. God doesn't dwell in buildings made by human hands - God has no other address but 'you'-man life!)*

14:24 To be indifferent to me and my words is to be equally indifferent to my Father's word; and I am commissioned by him.

14:25 This has been my constant conversation with you in our time together.

14:26 The Holy Spirit is about to become your close companion, sent by my Father in my name to represent me, to teach you all things and remind you of everything that I have spoken to you. Thus my word will continue to find a voice in you.

14:27 Peace be with you! I give you my own peace - this is not the kind the world gives - this is peace in the midst of troubled times; therefore you have nothing to fear! Let not your hearts be timid.

14:28 You have heard me say that I go away to come to be face to face with you; now if you're in love with me you would not be threatened by the idea of my departure, but you would rejoice since I'll be going to the Father and my Father is greater than me. From now on we will be present in a much closer capacity to you than what I could ever be while I am with you in the flesh!

14:29 What I now tell you is to prepare you for what is about to happen, so that when it happens, you will not be shaken in your belief but stand strong.

14:30 In my going *[into your judgment,]* my silence should not disturb you; *[like a lamb led to slaughter, he opened not his mouth]* the ruler of this world-order come but this "voice" has nothing in common with mine - there is no [1]resemblance or resonance! *(The word [1]echo, to have, to hold, to resonate.)*

14:31 Thus the world will understand my love for my Father and it will be clear to them that I have accomplished his [1]prophetic purpose. Arise, let's go! *(See note in 14:15 for [1]entelomai. They rose from the table, left the city, and went towards the garden of Olives, or garden of Gethsemane, on the road to which, a part of the following discourse was delivered. It was now about midnight, and the moon was almost full, it being the 14th day of her age, about the time in which the Jewish passover was to be slain. Adam Clark)*

15:1 I am the authentic ¹vine! My Father is the farmer. *(The word ¹ampelos, grapevine; from amphi, around and halōn, from the base of heilissō, to roll up or together; thus a vine coiling about a support. "On the Maccabean coinage Israel was represented by a vine". Jesus is the genuine Messianic vine. Robertson. Not the empty vine Hosea 10:1 mentions. See also Mathew 21:33)*

15:2 Every offshoot in me that does not bear fruit, he ¹lifts up from the ground and fastens it to the stake and every fruit bearing part he ²dresses in order to maximize its yield. *(The words ¹airei and ²kathairei are employed to suggest the lifting of the branches as well as the dressing process which includes pruning. Airei, from airoo, to elevate, to lift up, to air; katharei, from kata, in this case signifying intensity, and again airoo. Lifting up to manage a grape vine's canopy which will influence not only the potential yield of the crop but also the quality of the grapes due to the access of air and sunlight needed for the grapes to ripen fully and for preventing various grape diseases. When the Greeks began to colonize southern Italy in the 8th century BC, they called the land Oenotria which could be interpreted as "staked" or land of staked vines, growing upwardly. The grapevine is attached to stakes, or posts, thus making sure the branches grow up-wardly. They are also dressed and pruned to be positioned in such a way that their fruit would be easily accessible. **Hina karpon pleiona pherēi**, purpose clause with **hina** and present active subjunctive of **pherō,** "that it may keep on bearing more fruit" (more and more). The Father's vineyard tool is his Word, incarnated in son-ship; as in Hebrews 1:1-3 and 4:12. Hebrews 1:1 Throughout ancient times God spoke in many fragments and glimpses of prophetic thought to our fathers. 1:2 Now, the sum total of this conversation with us, has finally culminated in a son. In his sonship, God declares him heir of all things. He is, after all, the author of the ages. 1:3 Jesus is the crescendo of God's conversation with humankind; he gives context and content to the authentic thought. Everything that God had in mind for mankind is voiced in him. Jesus is God's language. Jesus is the radiant and flawless expression of the person of God. He makes the glorious intent of God visible and mirrors the character and every attribute of God in human form. 4:12 The message God spoke to us in Christ, is the most life giving and dynamic influence in us, cut-ting like a surgeon's scalpel, sharper than a soldier's sword, piercing to the deepest core of human conscience, to the dividing of soul and spirit; ending the dominance of the sense realm and its neutralizing effect upon the human spirit. In this way mankind's spirit is freed to become the ruling influence again in the thoughts and intentions of the heart. The scrutiny of this word detects every possible disease, discerning the body's deepest secrets where joint and bone-marrow meet. (The mo-ment we cease from our own efforts to justify ourselves, by yielding to the integrity of the message that announces the success of the Cross, God's word is triggered into action. What God spoke to us in sonship (the incarnation), radiates his image and likeness in our redeemed innocence. [Heb 1:1-3] This word powerfully penetrates and impacts our whole being; body, soul and spirit.)*

15:3 Your personal pruning and dressing already happened in our con-versation; The word made flesh in my person and language is how the Father prepares and sets you up for fruit bearing.

15:4 Our seamless union, you in me and I in you, is pictured in the vine:

the shoot cannot bear fruit outside of this union. In its abiding in the vine, fruit happens naturally - as with your abiding in me.

15:5 I am the vine and you are the branches; it is the one who understands this mutual union that naturally bears much fruit - which is impossible to happen apart from me.

15:6 [1]Every area of human life that does not continue to be entwined in this place of seamlessness in me, [2]was already cast forth where it has [3]withered away and is gathered to be burned as [4]firewood. *(The word [1]tis is an enclitic indefinite pronoun; some or any person or object. So, instead of 'every-one' I chose to see* **tis** *here as referring to everything, meaning every area of your life. As mentioned in verse 2, the 'dressing' or 'pruning' is not in judgment but in order to maximize the yield! God's faith sees humanity fully associated, included and represented in the incarnation. He called things which were not yet visible as though they were, because they are! Romans 4:17! "When God changed Abram's name to Abraham, he made a public statement that he would be the father of all nations. (Genesis 17:5) Here we see Abraham faced with God's faith; the kind of faith that resurrects the dead and calls things which are not (visible yet) as though they were." Human failure in every tense and sense of the word was dealt with in Jesus death, burial and resurrection. The Aorist Passive tense, [2]**eblethe**, denoting a momentary act in the past tense, indicates that it was cast forth. The next verb is also in the Aorist Passive, [3]**exeranthe**, it was withered away, from* **xerainoo**, *to wither. The incarnate Christ is about to enter into humanity's judgment and hell and bear the ultimate victorious fruit in co-raising us together with him. The single grain of wheat did not abide alone but bore much fruit! John 12:24. See also 12:31 and 32, This is the judgment of this world; it is the moment where the authority of the world-system is cast out! [The serpent's head is about to be crushed! Genesis 3:15; Colossians 2:14,15] See Colossians 3:1 Engage your thoughts with your co-crucifixion and co-resurrection and co-seatedness in Christ! And 12:32 When I am lifted up from the earth, I will draw all judgment unto me! [4]From living fruit-bearing branches to firewood, which becomes recycled energy again! See Extended Commentary Notes after the final chapter of the Mirror - Thoughts on Judgment and Resurrection.)*

15:7 My words find voice in you. With your abiding in me and my words abiding in you a conversation is inspired where you will request that which arises in your desire from our union and it shall come to pass for you!

15:8 These union-inspired desires bear the very fruit that endorses the Father's glory! This is where true discipleship is born. *(The aorist tense; was glorified. As in Joh 15:6, marking the point when the Father's glory was realized in the perfect union of the believer's will with Christ's.)*

15:9 The love of the Father for me is my love for you - abide in my love for you!

15:10 By [1]treasuring the [2]prophetic conclusion of my life you will remain constantly engulfed in my love even as I treasure the completeness of

my Father's prophetic purpose and abide in his love embrace. (*tereo, to treasure, to guard; entole, see note in 14:15.*)

15:11 I have spoken these things unto you so that my joy will continuously infuse you - you don't have to invent your own if you can tap into mine! This is the ultimate bliss!

15:12 I *advise you to discover your love for one another mirrored in my love for you; this is the *conclusion of my mission. (*The word often translated assignment or commandment, *entole, from en in and telo, complete. See note in 14:15*)

15:13 There is no greater expression of love than the love that leads someone to lay down his life for his friends. (*"Self-sacrifice is the high-water mark of love." Dods*)

15:14 Our friendship is endorsed in your continual engagement with *the conclusion of my mission. (*Again the word *entole, assignment or conclusion.*)

15:15 I do not communicate with you on a slave - boss basis; slaves have no clue what their Master is about to do. I talk to you as my friends telling you everything that I have heard in my conversation and *intimate association with my Father. This I explain to you in the *clearest possible terms. (*The preposition *para is used here, pointing to close companionship; the word *gnoritso means to have thorough knowledge of.*)

15:16 I did not begin in you; you began in me! I am not your idea; you are mine! I have strategically positioned you in order that you may abound in much fruit bearing, wherever life leads you - fruit that would ceaselessly continue this same incarnate life of union with me! From within this place, anything you desire has already been granted you by my Father. (*The word, *eklegomai, traditionally associated with the idea of election, has two components, ek, a preposition that indicates source or origin and lego, meaning to communicate ideas; thus, the original blueprint-word, the logos; see John 1:1-3 and 12. The word becomes flesh in the fruit you eat! The many are called, [kaleo] but few are "chosen" eklegomai thus, The masses are defined by my name but few realize their origin in me!*)

15:17 All these things are the conclusion of my assignment to you and find their context in your love for one another.

15:18 Know that the world-system hated me first whenever you encounter their resistance against you.

15:19 If your lives were the product of the world-system you would enjoy their *applause and friendship; but they can't stand you because their mold no longer has any hold on you, now that you have discovered your authentic identity in my *declaration of who you are by design. (*Phileo, friendship. Again the word *eklegomai is used. See 3:31 We are dealing with two dimensions here, the one coming from above presides over all - while the reasoning from a mere earthly perspective is confined to communicate from an earthly point of view. The conversation realized as originating in heaven has the final say. Also*

3:13 No one can fully engage in heaven's perspective, unless one's heavenly origin is realized! The son of man declares humanity's co-genesis from above!)

15:20 Remember that I told you that within the environment and association of servant and Master, what happens to the Master happens also to the servant - the servant is not treated any differently - if they hunted me down, they will hunt you down; if they treasured my word they would also treasure yours.

15:21 They will do all these things unto you because of your association with me, since they have no regard for him who sent me.

15:22 My arrival and my conversation, *[the logos becoming flesh]* **removed any possible excuse of ignorance they could have had to continue in a distorted pattern of life. In my absence they would have had no sin, but now they have no valid excuse.**

15:23 To dishonor me is to dishonor my Father.

15:24 If I had not accomplished in them the works which nobody else has ever performed they would have had reason to remain trapped in their distorted pattern of life; yet, inspite of what they have witnessed with their own eyes, they continue to despise my Father and I.

15:25 Their hatred for me fulfils the word of their own law. *(As recorded in Psalm 69:4, They that hate me without a cause and in Psalm 35:19 Let not those rejoice over me who are wrongfully my foes, and let not those wink the eye who hate me without cause.)*

15:26 But when the close Companion comes, who I shall send to you from the immediate presence of the Father, the Spirit of the truth who originates and proceeds out of the Father, this One will confirm everything about me.

15:27 You also will confirm everything about me since you are with me from the beginning. *(You now know your joint I am-ness together with me from the beginning.)*

16:1 I have communicated these things to you so you will not be embarrassed about your scandalous association with me.

16:2 You will be kicked out of their synagogues and there will be times where those who kill you will think that they have done God a favor!

16:3 They will do these things because they know neither the Father nor me.

16:4 I have told you all this in advance so that when it happens you will remember this conversation. While I was with you there was no need for me to tell you about these things.

16:5 But now I am going away to be face to face with him who sent me! And here you are not even asking me to explain to you what I am about to do,

16:6 since you are so worried about your own future!

16:7 Now listen up! Hear me, my departure is not to disadvantage you; everything that is about to happen, brings conclusion and bears together what the prophets pointed to! This will be to your absolute advantage! If I do not go away, your [1]Companion cannot come to you, but if I go I will send to you One to be [2]face to face with you defining your very being. (*[1]Parakletos, from para and kaleo; redefining our original being in the closests possible association and kindred companionship; closer to you than your breath! Again the word [2]pros is used!*)

16:8 In this capacity of close companionship with you, Holy Spirit comes to convince the world concerning sin, righteousness and judgment:

16:9 Holy Spirit in you will persuade them concerning their sin, which boils down to a bankrupt, distorted identity due to their indifference to me. (*The world's unbelief and indifference to Jesus is the very cause of their bankruptcy! The word for sin, [1]hamartia from ha, negative and meros, portion or form, thus to be without your allotted portion or without form, pointing to a disorientated, distorted or bankrupt identity; the word meros, is the stem of the word morphe, as in 2 Corinthians 3:18 where the word metamorphe, with form, [transform] is the opposite of hamartia - without form. Sin is to live out of context with the blueprint of one's design; to behave out of tune with God's original harmony.*)

16:10 In this union with you, the great Companion will also convince the world of righteousness because in my disappearing out of sight, to be face to face with the Father, the Spirit of truth will interpret the conclusion of my mission which is mankind's association in me and their redeemed innocence! The intimate union with my Father that I displayed while present with you in my physical body will now be made visible in you!

16:11 Then the world will be convinced that the judgment that was their due was accomplished when the ruler of this world system was judged. (*In Jesus dying humanity's death, closure was brought to the system of the law of works and performance as dictating and defining human life. In mankind's co-cru-*

cifixion and joint-descent in Jesus into their hell and in their co-resurrection and co-elevation to be seated together with him in heavenly places! See John 5:21,22; John 12:31-33; Hosea 6:2, Ephesians 2:5,6; Colossians 3:1-3; Romans 4:25; Acts 17:29-31; 1 Peter 1:10,11; Hebrews 1:1-3.)

16:12 I have so much more to tell you but you would not be able to handle it now.

16:13 But when she [5]is come, the Spirit of truth, she will [1]take you by the hand and guide you into the path of all truth. She will not draw attention to herself but will communicate and [1]unveil everything she hears and discerns from a heavenly perspective about the things that is [4]about to happen [3]within you. *(While spirit is in the neuter gender, truth is feminine. In Hebrew, the word for spirit is ruach which is feminine. The word [1]οδηγησει, from odos, the pathway and hegeomai, the strengthened for of agoo, to lead, thus officially appointed Guide. The word anangellei, from ana, upwards, above and angello, to announce; [3]umin, personal pronoun, you in the Dative case, also pointing to location "in." The things about to happen, [4]erchomena, the Present Participle describes an action thought of as simultaneous with the action of the main verb, [5]elthay, is come, When she, the Spirit of truth, is come [hotan elthēi ekeinos, to pneuma tēs alētheias]. Indefinite relative clause [hotan and the second aorist active subjunctive of erchomai, whenever she comes." The Mood of the Greek verb, in this case the subjunctive, expresses the mode in which the idea of the verb is employed. See commentary note to Hebrews 10:14 in the Mirror Bible.)*

16:14 Holy Spirit will endorse my [1]opinion of you by taking that which is mine and [2]interpreting it [3]in you. *(The word often translated glory, [1]doxa from dokeo, to form an opinion. The word [2]anangello, from ana, upwards and angello to announce or declare. The preposition ana always points upwards to the things that are above the earth's perspective. [3]Umin, personal pronoun, you in the Dative case, also pointing to location "in.")*

16:15 The Father and I enjoy all things in common - even to the finest detail - because this is so, I said that the Close Companion esteems my glory and [2]lays a hold of that which is within me and declares it within you from [1]heavens point of view. *([1]Ana, upwards; The best texts read [2]lambanei λαμβάνει, takes, instead of λήψεται, lempsetai, shall take. The relation between the Son and the Spirit is present and constant. Vincent's Word Studies.)*

16:16 For a brief while will I be absent from your [1]view; then in another brief while you [2]will see and know me. *([1]Ye shall not see - ou [negative] theorete - the present tense: "you behold me no more." - [theōreō - English, theorize] Then again you will [2]see me, opsesthe, Future, middle Deponent Indicative of the verb horao. A different verb for seeing is used here. [1]Theoreo, emphasizes the act of vision, [2]horao, the result. Theoreo a derivative of theaomai, denotes deliberate contemplation conjoined with mental or spiritual interest. "The vision of wondering contemplation, in which they observed little by little the outward manifestation of the Lord, was changed and transfigured into sight, horao, in which they seized at once, intuitively, all that Christ was. As long as his earthly presence was the object on which their eyes were fixed, their view was necessarily imperfect. His* *glorified presence showed him in his true nature." - Westcott.*

Paul beautifully prays that the eyes of our understanding be flooded with light so that we may know the full conclusion of his death and resurrection and how fully included we are in it.

The best texts omit, "Because I go unto the Father." Although it is present in the next verse.)

16:17 Some of his disciples said to each other, "What does he mean? He tells us that in a little while we won't see him. Then he tells us that in a little while we will see him again and then he would return to be face to face with the Father."

16:18 What does he mean by a little while? This just doesn't make sense to us at all.

16:19 Jesus perceived that they were confused about this and asked them, "Are you still trying to figure out what I mean by this brief time where you will no longer see me and then the next moment you will really see me?"

16:20 During this brief time of my apparent absence you will mourn and grieve but while the religious world rejoices, your pain will give birth to joy!

16:21 The anguish a woman suffers when her hour has come to give birth, is soon forgotten and replaced with delight when another [1]human life is born! *(The word for the human species, male or female is [1]anthropos, from ana, upwards, and tropos, manner of life; character; in like manner.*

16:22 Just like with childbirth where joy eclipses the labor pains, so your present sorrow will be vanquished and your hearts will erupt in joy when you realize how you captivate my [1]gaze! And no one will be able to take this joy away from you! *(Again the word [1]οψομαι is used, from horaoo, to look at something with wide open eyes as in gazing at something remarkable! In the mirror reflection of his gaze, we see ourselves and now we know even as we have always been known!)*

16:23 In that day of your awakening to our inseparable union, you shall ask me no more [1]questions; instead you should certainly [2]ask the Father directly in my name, knowing that my name represents the extent of all the Father has already accomplished on humanity's behalf and he will happily grant you your requests and take all questions of possible doubt or uncertainty out of the equation. *(To question is the primary meaning of the verb [1]erotao. Another verb for ask occurs in the following sentence, [2]aiteo, to make a request.)*

16:24 Until now you have not required anything in my name - when you realize what is yours in my name, then make your requests and lay a hold of that so that your joy may burst its banks!

16:25 I have used [1]examples to illustrate these things in figurative speech

but the hour comes when the illustrations will be replaced with [2]unreserved utterance and I will [3]declare to you openly, heavenly things about the father. (*[1]Paroimiais, from para and oiomai, to make like ("The kingdom of heaven is like a treaure hidden in an agricultural field..."), that is, imagine: - suppose, think; parable or illustration. The word [2]parrhēsia, openly, frankly, without concealment. The word [3]anangello, from ana, upwards and angello to announce or declare. The preposition ana always points upwards to the things that are above the earth's perspective.*)

16:26 In that day you will make your [1]requests in my name without a middleman - there will be no need for me to [2]question the Father on your behalf. (*Again, as in verse 23, the words [1]aiteo, to make a request and [2]erotao, to question are used.*)

16:27 The Father himself is so fond of you and is pleased with your affection for me and your belief that I proceeded from his [1]immediate presence. (*The preposition [1]para, indicates close proximity, a thing proceeding from a sphere of influence, with a suggestion of union of place of residence, to have sprung from its author and giver, originating from, denoting the point from which an action originates, intimate connection.*)

16:28 I have indeed proceeded from the [1]immediate and intimate presence of the Father to come to the world and return again to be [2]face to face with the Father. (*Again John beautifully uses the words [1]para and [2]pros to communicate the level of intimacy within the Trinity.*)

16:29 The disciples said to him, "You are coming through loud and clear without the aid of a parable.

16:30 Now we see what you have seen all along! To be persuaded that you indeed proceeded from the Father brings an end to all our speculations and uncertainties!"

16:31 To this Jesus responded with, "Just when you think you now finally believe that I am who I claim to be,

16:32 then suddenly you will all scramble and run for your lives and abandon me! But I am never forsaken because my Father is always with me!

16:33 I have spoken these things to you that in me you will know the sweet and assured resonance of my peace! In the world you encounter extreme and stressful times, but be of good courage, I have conquered the world-order!"

17:1 Having said these things Jesus lifted up his eyes into the [1]heavenly sphere and spoke, "Father, the hour has come; this is the culmination of time! Glorify your son; endorse your opinion of your son so that the son may mirror his opinion of you and cause your dignity and worth to be made renowned and rendered illustrious in order to become manifest and acknowledged throughout! (*The word [1]ouranos, heavenly sphere; from oros, mountain, from airō, to raise, elevate, to lift up. Here there exists no conflict of interest - only glory repeated in the other!*)

17:2 Within the [1]mirror reflection of glory you co-[2]echo [3]every nook and cranny of flesh on exhibit in the son's [4]authentic 'I am-ness'! In order that every detailed aspect of what it takes to live life in the flesh may be be [5]endued with the life of the ages. (*The word, [1]kathos, from kata, downward impression and hōs, as, like, even as, the same as; kathos follows on the previous thought of the co-exhibition of glory; the original image and likeness in the glory of the Father is again repeated and impressed in sonship. The word [2]echo, to have in hand, to echo, resonate; the word [3]pas, suggests each and every detail of all things; the whole, everyone, all things, everything. The word [4]exousia, often translated authority, from ek, out of, source, and eimi, I am. The word [5]didomi, to give, to endue, to return something to someone that already belongs to them. See John 1:14.*)

17:3 This life of the ages, invites them to engage in the [1]inexhaustible adventure of knowing you, the only true God and Jesus as the Christ whom you have commissioned! (*The word, [1]ginōskōsin, to learn to know, to perceive, to understand; in the Present Active Subjunctive form with hina [subject clause], "should keep on knowing."*)

17:4 I have caused your dignity and worth to be made renowned and rendered illustrious in order to become manifest and acknowledged throughout the earth by accomplishing the work which you have given me to do.

17:5 And now, o Father, bestow the most intimate nearness of your own person upon me with the glory that I shared in your immediate presence even before the world was.

17:6 I have displayed your name and exactly who you are with distinction to those whom you have given me; they were yours in the first place then you gave them to me; they are also those who have treasured your word [incarnated in me].

17:7 Now they too have come to know that everything you have given me originate in their own I am-ness in you! (*Man began in God!*)

17:8 I have given them the very [1]words which you have given me in our conversation, which words they have embraced and have come to know that surely I also proceeded from you and are commissioned by you! (*Here the word rhemata [plural] is used and not logos like in verse 14 and most other references in John - rhema refers to the spoken word in conversation as such.*)

17:9 I pray specifically for them - those who know that they are yours to begin with and that you gave them to me. I'm not here to debate with those who still see themselves defined by the world-system!

17:10 I am greatly esteemed in our shared friendship with every individual person - all those who are mine are also yours and what is yours is mine.

17:11 I am no longer in the world but they are - I am proceeding to be face to face with you holy Father; I ask for the protection of those whom you have given me in your name that they also may be one even as we are.

17:12 While I was with them in the world I guarded over the ones you have given me in your name and did not lose any, except the lost son who fulfilled what was written prophetically.

17:13 And now I come to be face to face with you Father; I speak these things while I am still in the world that they may have my joy fulfilled in themselves.

17:14 I have given them your Logos and now the world hates them because they have lost their manipulative, performance-based hold over them - these now know that they did not originate in the kosmos but in the logos, even as I did not begin in the kosmos!

17:15 I do not request that you take them out of the world but that you keep them from the [1]evil performance-based system of hardships, labors and annoyances! *(The [1]poneros-system is the system that is referenced in the Tree of the knowledge of good and evil (poneros) which is a system based on performance as the defining reference to human life - Jesus came to reveal and redeem our authentic value, identity and innocence as defining our lives.)*

17:16 They are not defined by the kosmos-system even as I am not defined thereby.

17:17 [1]Define them in your truth - your logos is the unveiled truth. *(The word [1]hagiazo speaks of a sanctification, a setting apart as in a defining moment.)*

17:18 Just as you have commissioned me into the world so I send them on their mission into the world!

17:19 For their sakes do I sanctify myself to be high above the kosmos-sytem so that their true set apart-ness *[from the performance based systems of the world]* will be mirrored in me.

17:20 I do not pray for them exclusively but also for those who would come to believe in me because of their word.

17:21 That they all may be one, exactly as you Father are mirrored in me and I in you, that they also will be exactly mirrored to be one in us - then the entire world will believe and be persuaded about your mission upon my life!

17:22 And I, *[the Incarnate word]* have endued them with the same glorious esteem that you have given me so that their oneness may mirror ours.

17:23 I am in them as you are in me, and on this basis their seamless oneness may be entirely concluded. Thus the world will acknowledge your commission upon my life and know that my love for them mirrors your love for me.

17:24 Father I desire that [1]what you have given me in them may cause them to be where I am so that they may see what I see and gaze attentively upon the splendor of my glory which you have given me *[in them]* because you loved me before the [2]fall of the world. Thus the world will be persuaded that your love for them was never compromised because of the fall - you continued to love them the same! *(The best texts read, [1]ho not hous - that which. The word, [2]katabalo, means "to fall away, to put in a lower place," instead of themelios, meaning "foundation" [see Ephesians 2:20]; thus, translated "the fall of the world," instead of "the foundation of the world.")*

17:25 Father of righteousness, while the world has not known you, I have known you and these here have come to know that you sent me.

17:26 And I have made the essence of your being known to them so that they may know you by name; and I will also give them understanding to know that the same love with which you have loved me is in them even as I am in them!

18:1 When Jesus concluded his prayer he and his disciples crossed over the brook Cedron into a garden.

18:2 Judas, who betrayed him was familiar with this place since Jesus often gathered there with his disciples.

18:3 Judas was given a Roman military cohort of about 600 soldiers to accompany him; they came together with temple officers from the chief priests and Pharisees with torches, lanterns and their weapons.

18:4 Jesus, fully aware of everything that was coming upon him, went forward to meet them and said, "Who are you seeking?"

18:5 They said to him, "Jesus the Nazarene." Jesus answered, "Here I am." And there Judas was, standing with them.

18:6 Just when Jesus said, "I am," they stumbled backwards and fell to the ground!

18:7 He asked them again, "Who is is that you are seeking?" They said, "Jesus of Nazareth,"

18:8 Jesus said, "I already told you who I am; if its me you are after then let the others go."

18:9 He said this to confirm to his disciples that he would protect them so that none of them would be implicated.

18:10 Simon Peter thought that it was a good idea to defend themselves and drew his sword and struck at the high priest's servant, Malchus' head, who ducked away and lucky for him only lost an ear.

18:11 Jesus told Peter to put away the sword and said, "Do you think that I am not going to drink this cup the Father gave me?"

18:12 Then the soldiers under their captain's command together with the Jewish police arrested Jesus and tied him up.

18:13 They first took him to Annas, the father-in-law of Caiaphas who was the High Priest that year.

18:14 It was Caiaphas who advised the Jews that in order to save the entire nation, it was inevitable that one person should die.

18:15 Peter and another disciple followed Jesus; the High Priest knew the one disciple and he was allowed to enter the courtyard.

18:16 Peter remained outside at the entrance. Then the other disciple who knew the High Priest went to speak to the lady at the door and asked permission for Peter to join him inside.

18:17 The lady who guarded the door said to Peter, "Are you not also one of this man's disciples?" He said, "No I am not." *(She obviously recognized John as a disciple.)*

18:18 The slaves and temple police were huddled around a coal fire to warm themselves; Peter also joined them to get out of the cold.

18:19 The High Priest then began to question Jesus about his disciples and his teaching.

18:20 Jesus replied, "I have spoken openly to the world and frequently taught in the synagogue and temple to a Jewish audience and have said nothing in secret.

18:21 Why would you question me? Talk to my audience if you wish to find out about my teaching; they are familiar with what I teach."

18:22 When he said this one of the temple police slapped him in the face and scolded, "How dare you speak to the High Priest in this manner?"

18:23 Jesus answered, "If I said anything evil then tell me; but if I have spoken only that which is beautiful, why do you strike me?"

18:24 Annas sent him bound to Caiaphas, the High Priest. *(The proper place of this verse is immediately after the 13th.)*

18:25 In the mean time Peter was still warming himself at the fire when he was asked again if he was not one of the disciples of Jesus. He emphatically objected and said that he was not.

18:26 Then a relative of Malchus whose ear Peter chopped off also recognised him and said, "Did I not see you with him in the garden?"

18:27 Again Peter disclaimed it and just then, the cock crowed!

18:28 Then they led Jesus from Caiaphas into the the praetorium, the Roman governor's judgment hall - it was still early in the day so the Jews didn't go into the court room for fear of contracting some impurity, which would have obliged them to separate themselves from eating the Passover.

18:29 Then Pilate went outside to face them and asked, "What accusation do you bring against this man?"

18:30 They answered, "If he wasn't an evildoer we wouldn't have wasted your time with this court case in the first place.

18:31 Then Pilate said, "Take him and judge him according to your law." They said, "Our law does not allow a death sentence."

18:32 This was also to confirm what Jesus said about his manner of death. *(I would be lifted up - crucifixion was not a Jewish punishment - 1 John 3:5 We have witnessed with our own eyes how, in the unveiling of the prophetic word, when he was lifted up upon the cross as the Lamb of God, he lifted up our sins and broke its dominion and rule over us! (John 1:29 "Behold, the Lamb of God, who takes away [airo] the sin of the world! The word airo means to lift up. John 3:13 No one can fully engage in heaven's perspective, unless one's heavenly origin is realized! The son of man declares humanity's co-genesis from above! John 3:14 (This is my mission: See the prophetic relevance - this is how the veil will be removed!)*

Remember how Moses lifted up the serpent in the wilderness even so the son of man will be lifted up! (John 12:31 Now is the judgment of this world, now shall the ruler of this world be cast out; John 12:32 and I, when I am lifted up from the earth, will draw all judgment unto me." John 12:33 He said this to show by what death he was to die. John 3:13 and 14 are most significant since they point to the very essence of the Mission of Jesus - the co-begotteness of the human race now redeemed in our co-crucifixion and co-resurrection on the third day into newness of life! 1 Peter 1:3) John 3:15 In the same prophetic pattern, I will be lifted up for all to see and be equally persuaded in the echo of the life of the ages now redeemed within them!)

18:33 Than Pilate went back into the court room and summoned Jesus to him and asked him, "Are you the king of the Jews?"

18:34 Jesus responded, "Are these your own thoughts or did others suggest this about me?"

18:35 Pilate replied, "Am I a Jew, why would I bother to speculate about you? Your own people and priests handed you over to me. What have you done to make them do this?

18:36 Jesus answered, "My kingdom has nothing in common with the political or religious systems of this world; it does not originate out of their structures. If it did my subordinates would fight for me and resist my handover to the Jews."

18:37 Pilate then said, "So you are a king?" Jesus replied, "You say that I am a king. My destiny was to be born in the flesh and for this purpose have I come into the world to bear testimony to the truth. Everyone who recognizes their true origin, hears my voice." *(The truth about mankind's authentic sonship and the image and likeness of the invisible Father of the human race is evidenced in me and confirmed in my work of redeeming the human race from the futile ways they inherited from their fathers.)*

18:38 Pilate then asked him, "What is truth?" Without giving him a chance to respond, he went outside again to face the Sanhedrin and said to them, "I find no cause for any accusation in this man."

18:39 But since it is custom that I should release one of your prisoners during your festive time, would you be happy for me to pardon the King of the Jews for this Passover?"

18:40 They shouted back, "No, not this one, but Barabbas!" Barabbas was a Jewish freedom fighter, probably the leader of the band which included the other two who were crucified with Jesus.

19:1 Then Pilate took Jesus and gave order for him to be scourged. *(Scourging was the legal preliminary to crucifixion, but, in this case, was inflicted illegally before the sentence of crucifixion was pronounced, with a view of averting the extreme punishment, and of satisfying the Jews. The punishment was extreme, the victim being bound to a low pillar or stake, and beaten, either with rods, or, in the case of slaves and provincials, with scourges, called scorpions, leather thongs tipped with leaden balls or sharp spikes. The severity of the infliction in Jesus' case is evident from His inability to bear His cross. Vincent)*

19:2 The soldiers plaited a crown of thorns and placed it on his head; they also threw a purple garment over him.

19:3 Then they positioned themselves in front of him and scorned him, saying, "Hail King of the Jews!" while continually slapping him in the face.

19:4 Then Pilate again went outside to the Sanhedrin saying, "Behold I am leading him out to you; I want you to know that I find no valid cause to condemn him."

19:5 Then Jesus came out of the Praetorium wearing a crown of thorns and the purple robe while Pilate announced, "Behold the man!" *(Idou ho anthrōpos; this exclamatory introduction of Jesus in mock coronation robes to the mob was clearly intended to excite pity and to show how absurd the charge of the Sanhedrin was that such a pitiable figure should be guilty of treason. Pilate failed utterly in this effort and did not dream that he was calling attention to the greatest figure of history, the Man of the ages. Robbertson's word pictures.)*

19:6 When they saw him, the chief priests and the temple police shouted with rage, "Crucify! Crucify!" Pilate told them, "You take him and execute the crucifixion yourselves, I find no fault in him."

19:7 The Jews answered him, "We have our own law and by this law he must die because he made himself out to be the son of God!" *(See John 5:18 This was fuel for the fire of Jewish zeal in their determination to execute Jesus! Not only did he break their Sabbath, but now he has gone beyond all extremes! He calls God his own Father - who does he think he is - God's equal?)*

19:8 The claim of Jesus' deity only served to accelerate Pilate's superstitious fears.

19:9 He went again into the judgment hall and asked Jesus, "Tell me, who are you really?" Jesus did not answer him.

19:10 Pilate said, "Why do you not answer me, do you not realize my position? I have the power to crucify or free you!"

19:11 Jesus said, "You have no authority over me, except what was given you from above. Therefore he *[Caiaphas, the High Priest]* **who handed me over to you has the greater sin.** *(exousia, out of I am)*

19:12 This motivated Pilate even more to make every effort to release him; but the Jews would not buy into it at all; they cried out, "If you even con-

sider to release this man you prove that you are not loyal to Caesar - this man's claim to royalty makes him Caesar's enemy!"

19:13 These words persuaded Pilate to go through with the procedures. He led Jesus outside and sat down in judgment in a place called the Stone Pavement, a decorated mosaic area in the court which was called Gabbatha in Hebrew which means an elevated platform.

19:14 This was still during the preparation for the Passover, about the 6th hour. He announced to the Jews, "Behold! Your king!" (*About the sixth hour, hōs hektē. Roman time, about 6 a.m. when Pilate rendered his final decision. Mark 15:25 notes that it was the third hour (Jewish time), which is 9 a.m. Roman time, when the crucifixion began. Why should John give Jewish time writing at the close of the first century when Jerusalem and the Jewish state passed away in A.D. 70? He is writing for Greek and Roman readers. See also John 20:19*)

19:15 But they cried out, "¹Lift him up! Lift him up! Crucify him!" Pilate said, "Shall I crucify your king?" The Chief priests answered, "We have no other king but Caeser!" (*The word, ¹airo means to lift up, to elevate. See John 12:32,33.*)

19:16 He then handed Jesus over to them to be crucified and they led him away.

19:17 Bearing the cross himself, Jesus went out from the Courtyard to the place called Skull; its Hebrew name was Golgotha.

19:18 There they crucified Jesus along with two others on either side of him.

19:19 Pilate wrote a placard and placed it on the cross. It read, "Jesus the Nazarene, the king of the Jews." (*Nazarite - "one separated" A name later given to Christians by the Jews, Acts 24:5*)

19:20 Many of the Jews who came up to the Passover feast from other nations could read this title since the place where he was crucified was near the city and it was written in Hebrew, Latin and Greek.

19:21 But the Jewish rulers and priests complained about this and requested that he changes the wording to read, "He said, I am the king of the Jews."

19:22 To which Pilate replied, "What I have written, I have written!"

19:23 The soldiers who crucified Jesus took his outer garments and divided it between the four of them; the inner garment was a seamless woven tunic. (*The four pieces of the outer garment would be the head gear, the sandals, the girdle, the tallith which was the outer garment with fringes.*)

19:24 They therefore discussed between themselves to rather not tear the inner garment but to cast lots for it to determine whose it shall be. This was the fulfilment of prophetic scripture, "They divided my outer garments among them and for my inner garment they cast lots." These very things predicted by David in Psalm 22:18, the soldiers unwittingly performed.

19:25 Standing by the cross were the three Mary's, the mother of Jesus, his aunt Mary the wife of Clopas and Mary of Magdala.

19:26 When Jesus saw his mother and the beloved disciple standing nearby, he said to her, "Ma'am, behold your son!"

19:27 Then he said to the disciple, "Behold your mother!" From that moment the disciple adopted her as his own mother. *(Canon Westcott remarks upon the four exclamations in this chapter - Behold the man! Behold your King! Behold your son! Behold your mother! as a remarkable picture of what Christ is, and what He reveals people to be.)*

19:28 With this Jesus, realizing that all things are now fully accomplished and that what was written was to be fulfilled, said, "I thirst!"

19:29 There was a jar filled with vinegar in which someone dipped a sponge attached to a branch of hyssop and lifted it to his mouth.

19:30 When Jesus had taken the vinegar he said, "It is finished!" He then bowed his head and handed over the spirit.

19:31 The Jews were keen to have the bodies removed from the cross before sunset when the Sabbath began, especially since this particular Sabbath would coincide with the first day of unleavened bread which was a 'great' day. Their preparation for the feast of unleavened bread and eating the Passover meal was in full swing. They approached Pilate therefore and requested that the bones of the victims be broken and that they might be lifted off the cross. *(To commemorate the unleavened bread that the Israelites ate when they left Egypt, they don't eat or even retain in their possession any "chametz" from midday of the day before Passover until the conclusion of the holiday. Chametz means leavened grain - any food or drink that contains even a trace of wheat, barley, rye, oats, spelt or their derivatives and wasn't guarded from leavening or fermentation. This includes bread, cake, cookies, cereal, pasta, and most alcoholic beverages. Ridding their homes of chametz is an intensive process. It involves a full-out spring-cleaning search-and-destroy mission during the weeks before Passover, and culminates with a search for chametz on the night before Passover, and then burning the chametz on the morning before the holiday.*

Instead of chametz, they eat matza - flat unleavened bread. It is a mitzvah to partake of matza on the two Seder Nights. During the rest of the holiday it is optional.

The highlight of Passover is the two "Seders," observed on the first two nights of the holiday. The first Seder is on Friday Evening, and the second Seder is on Saturday Evening, The Seder is a family oriented tradition and a ritual packed feast.

The focal points of the Seder are:

Eating matza.

Eating bitter herbs -- to commemorate the bitter slavery endured by the Israelites.

Drinking four cups of wine or grape juice - a royal drink to celebrate their newfound freedom.

The recitation of the Haggadah, a liturgy that describes in detail the story of the

Exodus from Egypt. The Haggadah is the fulfillment of the biblical obligation to recount to our children the story of the Exodus on the night of Passover.

19:32 The soldiers then broke the legs of the two men who were crucified with Jesus.

19:33 But when they saw that Jesus was already dead they did not break his legs.

19:34 One of the soldiers then pierced his side; blood and water flowed from the wound. *(The presence of these two elements was evidence that there had been heart rupture.)*

19:35 The one who witnessed these things has recorded their detail to convince the reader of their significance.

19:36 These things happened in fulfilment of that which was written prophetically, "No bone in the Pascal lamb shall be crushed." *[Ex 12:46 1500 - BC]*

19:37 Also another scripture which reads, "They shall gaze upon him whom they have pierced!" *[Zec 12:10]*

19:38 Then Joseph of Arimathea asked Pilate permission to remove the body of Jesus which Pilate was pleased to do. Joseph was a prominent leader, and a secret follower of Jesus, *(but here, while most of his close friends and followers forsook him, Joseph fearlessly offers to bury Jesus in his own rock-hewn tomb! See Matthew 27:60 He was a rich man and a counsellor of the great Sanhedrin, Luke 23:50. Mark emphasises the boldness of this act. Mark 15:43)*

19:39 Also Nicodemus, who was the one who approached Jesus in the shelter of the night in order not to be publicly associated with him, made a very bold announcement of his love for Jesus and brought expensive sweet-smelling spices; a mixture of myrrh and aloes which weighed about a hundred pounds.

19:40 Then Joseph and Nicodemus took Jesus body and prepared it for burial. And according to Jewish custom they wrapped the body in linen cloths together with the spices.

19:41 In the area where he was crucified was a garden with a new tomb which was never used before.

19:42 Since it was still during their preparation for the Sabbath the location of the tomb where Joseph and Nicodemus placed Jesus was conveniently close. *(The Hebrews reckoned two evenings, an earlier and a later. The former began midway between noon and sunset, or at three o'clock in the afternoon. The latter began at sunset, six o'clock. The reference here is to the earlier evening, though the time may have been well on toward the beginning of the later. The preparations had to be hurried because the Sabbath would begin at sunset - Vincent.)*

20:1 The first day of the Sabbaths, Maria from Magdala came to the tomb while it was still very early and saw that the stone was lifted out of the grave.

20:2 She left the tomb at once and ran to find Simon Peter and the other disciple whom Jesus was so fond of, and said to them, "They have taken the Lord out of the grave and we have no idea where they put him!" *(Mary fears a grave robbery. She did not suspect his resurrection.)*

20:3 So Peter and the other disciple immediately went to the tomb.

20:4 They were both running but the other brother out-ran Peter and arrived at the tomb first.

20:5 He stooped down and observed with careful attention the strips of linen cloth lying there, yet he did not enter. *(Seeing the grave cloths, he immediately knew that it wasn't a grave robbery!)*

20:6 Then Simon Peter also arrived and went straight into the tomb and took a long look at the grave cloths lying there.

20:7 He also noticed that the cloth that was wrapped around the head of Jesus, was not lying with the other strips of linen cloth, but neatly rolled up separately.

20:8 Then the other disciple who arrived there first also went in and he saw and was convinced! *(According to Luk 24:12 Peter went away "wondering" still.)*

20:9 It was as if they could not fully grasp that this was indeed what was predicted in scripture, that Jesus was [1]destined to rise up out of death. *(See Psalm 16:10 "For you will not leave my soul in Sheol; you will not let your Holy One see corruption." Destined; must happen - [1]dei. See Mark 8:31; Matthew 26:54; Luke 9:22; Luke 17:25; Luke 22:37; Luke 24:7, Luke 24:26,27, Luke 24:44, 46; John 3:14; John 12:34; Acts 1:16. Jesus emphasized the fact and the necessity of his resurrection which the disciples slowly perceived.)*

20:10 The disciples went away to [1]face their own thoughts. *([1]pros hautous - facing themselves.)*

20:11 But Maria remained facing the the tomb, weeping. Then she stooped down and [1]gazed into the tomb. *(The word, parakupto from para,close poximity and kupto to stoop down, bend forward, to view attentively with scrutiny.)*

20:12 She saw two angels dressed in dazzling white seated, one at the head and the other at the feet where Jesus' body had been lying.

20:13 They asked her, "Woman why are you weeping?" She said to them, "They took my Lord away and I do not know where they have put him."

20:14 As she said this she looked around *(as if she instinctively felt the presence of someone behind her)* and saw Jesus standing but did not immediately recognise him.

20:15 Jesus said to her, "Woman, why are you weeping? Who are you looking for? She thought he was the gardener and said, "Sir, if you have taken him away, please tell me where you put him so that I may fetch him!"

20:16 Jesus said to her, "Mariam!" she turned in her step and exclaimed, "Raboni!" which is Hebrew for, my Teacher!

20:17 "You'll have to let go of me, so that I may continue on to the Father. Go and tell my brothers that I am ascending to my Father and your Father; to my God and your God!" (*mē mou haptou, present middle imperative in prohibition with the genitive case, meaning "cease clinging to me!"*)

20:18 So Maria the Magdalene went to the disciples and announced to them, "I saw the Lord!" And she told them all that he told her.

20:19 That evening of the first day of the week, the disciples were gathered in a room with the doors locked because they were afraid of the Jews. Suddenly Jesus stepped into their midst and said, "Shalom!"(*The addition of tēi miāi sabbatōn proves that John is using Roman time, not Jewish, for here evening follows day instead of preceding it.*)

20:20 Then he showed them his scarred hands and side and having now seen the Lord for themselves, they were exceedingly glad!

20:21 Again he repeated his salutation and said, "Peace be unto you! Just as the Father has commissioned me so do I now send you!"

20:22 Having said this he [1]breathed an effusion of spirit upon them and said, "[1]Take Holy Spirit as your companion." (*Having breathed on them, [1]enephusēsen. First aorist active indicative of emphusaō, late verb, here only in N.T. though eleven times in the Septuagint and in the papyri. It was a symbolic act with the same word used in the Septuagint when God breathed the breath of life upon Adam (Gen 2:7). It occurs also in Ezek 37:9. See Christ's promise in Joh 16:23. The word [1]lambano, to take what is one's own, to take to one's self, to associate with one's self as companion. Jesus gives the disciples a foretaste of pentecost.*)

20:23 "If you [1]forgive someone's sins, they are [1]gone and forgotten. If you don't [2]let go, then you are [2]stuck with them." (*[1]aphiēmi, to let go, to divorce, to leave behind, to forgive; [2]krateō to seize. In the context of what has happened on the cross and here emphasized in the previous 3 verses, the basis of true forgiveness is the death and closure that Jesus brought to whatever it was that testified against us; his glorious resurrection and the companionship of Holy Spirit as the very breath of our zoe-life are the essence and authority of our commission which is to announce mankind's redeemed innocence!*)

20:24 But Thomas, the Twin, one of the Twelve, was not with them when Jesus came.

20:25 The other disciples told him that they have seen the Lord. But his response was, "I will never believe it unless I see his nail pierced hands and thrust my finger into the wounds and also my hand into his his side."

20:26 The next Sunday evening, Jesus again just showed up in their midst even though all the doors were locked and greeted them with, "Peace be unto you!" This time Thomas was with them.

20:27 Jesus immediately turned to Thomas and said to him, "Give me your finger and touch my hands so you that can see for yourself; and give me your hand and thrust it into my side! Replace your scepticism with persuasion!"

20:28 Without hesitation Thomas responded to Jesus with, "My Lord and my God!"

20:29 Jesus said to him, "You believe because you saw with your own eyes; blessed are those who believe even though they do not see!"

20:30 The truth is that Jesus did many more signs in front of his disciples' eyes than these ones recorded in this book.

20:31 But what is written here is enough evidence for the reader to be absolutely convinced that Jesus is the Christ, the son of God. And thus your belief will echo the zoe-life unveiled in his name.

21:1 Jesus also appeared to the disciples at the sea of Tiberias in the following incident:

21:2 Simon Peter and Thomas the twin, Nathaniel from Cana in Galilee, the Zebedee brothers and two of the other disciples were together.

21:3 It was Simon's idea to go fishing so they joined him and got into a boat and spend the night trying but caught nothing.

21:4 By daybreak Jesus was waiting for them at the shore but they did not recognize him.

21:5 Jesus asked them, "Lads, haven't you got anything to eat?" They said, "Nope!"

21:6 Then he told them to cast the net on the right side of the boat and they will definitely find some; so they did and took so many fish that they were unable to haul them in.

21:7 Then the disciple whom Jesus was so fond of said to Peter, "It is the Lord!" When Simon Peter heard that it was the Lord, he girded his outer garment around him since he was naked, and promptly jumped into the water.

21:8 The other disciples dragged the net full of fish with a little boat. They were only about 100 yards from the shore.

21:9 When they got out of the boat they were surprised to see a coal fire with fried fish and bread on it.

21:10 Jesus suggested that they also bring some of the fish they had just caught.

21:11 Simon Peter then joined them and pulled the net ashore; they counted 153 large fish, and the net didn't even tear!

21:12 Jesus then invited them to break their fast and feast together. By now they knew beyond doubt that it was the Lord and didn't even bother to ask him.

21:13 Jesus then took the bead and handed it to them and also the fish.

21:14 This was the third time Jesus appeared to the disciples since he rose from the dead.

21:15 After they had their breakfast Jesus asked Simon Peter, "Simon of Jonah, do you agape me more than any of the others?" He answered, "Surely Lord, you see how fond I am of you!" He said to him, "Show your love for me by feeding my little lambs."

21:16 He asked a second time, "Simon of Jonah, do you agape me?" He answered, "Of course Lord, you know that I dearly love you." He said, "Then shepherd my sheep."

21:17 He asked him a third time, "Simon of Jonah, are you very fond of me?" By now Peter was feeling a little uncomfortable that Jesus asked him a third time, "Do you dearly love me?" and he answered him, "Lord I cannot hide anything from you, and you know how fond I am of you!" And Jesus said to him, "Then nourish my sheep."

21:18 "You can mark my words, when you were younger you could choose what you wanted to wear and moved about freely wherever you wished; but there will come a time when someone else will dress you and take you where you do not want to go."

21:19 He pointed prophetically to Peter's martyrdom and death by which he would glorify God. And Jesus said to him, "Follow me."

21:20 Peter turned around and saw Jesus' beloved disciple following them; he was also the one who would lean against the breast of Jesus at the dinner table and asked, "Lord who will betray you?"

21:21 Seeing him Peter asked, "Lord, what about this man?"

21:22 Jesus said to him, "If I would rather have him remain while I am ¹going, should not concern you; just keep on following me. (The word ¹erchomai can mean coming or going - depends on context.)

21:23 So a rumor began amongst the followers that this disciple would not die. Yet Jesus didn't say that he wasn't going to die, he said, "If I wish that he remains while I am going should not concern you."

21:24 This is the very disciple who is bearing witness to all these things in this writing. We confirm that his testimony is true.

21:25 Were the vastness of the work and words of Jesus carefully detailed, the libraries of the world could not contain them. (See 20:30)

(In this final chapter and Epilogue to his book, John beautifully highlights a significant parallel, reflecting on their first encounter with Jesus, when, as business partners he and his brother James and Simon Peter toiled all night and had nothing to show for their efforts; here he portrays Peter taking the initiative to go back fishing to possibly help them deal with the extreme emotional tensions of the past days and also his disappointment with himself in denying Jesus three times. In John's account, Jesus again demonstrates dramatically how a greater grace dimension that outperforms their best efforts and intentions, eclipses their familiar world with its highs and lows. In Jesus' conversation with Peter, as Simon the son of Jonah, he deliberately calls him this name again to remind him of the significant moment when he discovered by revelation that in Jesus as the son of man, our physical identity is surpassed by a greater identity and birth, we are hewn out of the same rock; we share sonship because we have the same Father! This is the foundation of the ekklesia that Jesus builds. [Matthew 16.] Then instead of blaming Peter for denying him, Jesus deliberately reminds him of their friendship where their love for one another is reinforced three times; this love union will also be the basis of Peter's role in his Shepherd leadership of Jesus' flock. It is also interesting to note the names of Thomas, and Nathaniel in the account of the fishing episode; they, too, had their moments of doubt.)

ROMANS REVEALED

The Eagle Story

During our honeymoon in January, 1979, in the Blyderiver Canyons in Mpumalanga, South Africa, Lydia and I met a nature conservation officer who told us of a fascinating incident when they released a black eagle a week prior that had been in the Pretoria Zoo for ten years. She told us how excited they were when the bird finally arrived in its wooden crate. This was the day for this eagle to be freed. But their excitement soon turned to frustration when, after opening the cage, the bird refused to fly! Ten years of caged life seemed to have trapped its mind in an invisible enclosure! How could they get the eagle to realize that it was indeed free? No amount of prompting and prodding seemed to help. Then, after some hours the bird suddenly looked up, and in the distance they heard the call of another eagle; immediately the zoo-eagle took off in flight!

This dramatic story left a deep impression on my mind. I knew that in the light of Paul's revelation of the good news, we are left with one urgent priority, which is to announce to the nations with bold confidence the truth about their original identity and mirror-reflect the integrity of their redeemed innocence. No flying lessons are required when truth is realized!

This gives such clarity and content to the fact that Jesus came to the planet not to upgrade the cage of Judaism or any other religion by starting a new one called Christianity; but to be the incarnate voice of the likeness and image of God in human form! He came to reveal and redeem the image of God in us! His mission was to mirror the blueprint of our design, not as an example for us but of us! (Col 1:15, 2:9, 10).

In God's faith mankind is associated in Christ even before the foundation of the world. Jesus died humanity's death and when the stone was rolled away, we were raised together with him! Every human life is fully represented in him (Hosea 6:2).

If the gospel is not the voice of the free eagle, it is not the gospel.

Paul's Gospel

In this pivotal book, Paul immediately introduces himself and his intention: "My mandate and message is to announce the goodness of God to mankind. This message is what the scriptures are all about. It remains the central prophetic theme and content of inspired writing." (Rom 1:1, 2).

Scripture could never again be interpreted in any other way! The gospel of the success of the Cross gives content and context to scripture.

There is nothing to be ashamed of; this message unveils how God got it right to rescue man from the effect of what Adam did wrong! (Rom 1:16, 17)

The dynamic of the gospel is the revelation of God's faith as the only valid basis of our belief (from faith to faith). Paul quotes Habakkuk who prophetically introduced a new era when he realized that righteousness would be founded in what God believes and not in mankind's clumsy ability to obey the law.

From now on righteousness by God's faith defines life! (Hab 2:4, Rom 1:17, 3:27).

Instead of reading the curse when disaster strikes, Habakkuk realizes that the Promise out-dates performance as the basis to mankind's acquittal! Deuteronomy 28 would no longer be the motivation or the measure of right or wrong behavior! "Though the fig trees do not blossom, nor fruit be on the vines, the produce of the olive fail and the fields yield no food, the flock be cut off from the fold and there be no herd in the stalls, yet I will rejoice in the Lord, I will joy in the God of my salvation. God, the Lord, is my strength; he makes my feet like hinds' feet, he makes me tread upon my high places." (Hab 3:17-19 RSV).

From Romans chapters 1:18 to 3:20, Paul proceeds to give a graphic display of distorted human behavior. Being a Jew, and therefore to know the law, offers no real advantage since it offers no disguise or defense from sin. It is the same ugliness and deserves the same judgment. His triumphant statement in verses 16, 17 of chapter 1 and again reinforced in chapter 3:21-24, is set against this backdrop. The good news declares how the same condemned mankind in Adam is now freely acquitted by God's grace through the redemption that is unveiled in Christ Jesus.

He brings the argument of the ineffectiveness of the law to get a person to change their behavior, to a final crescendo in Chapter 7. He states in 7:1 that he is writing to those who know the law. They have first-hand experience therefore of the weakness of the rule to consistently govern a person's conduct.

The best the law could offer was to educate and confirm good intention; but the more powerful law, the law of sin introduced to mankind through one man's transgression, has to be challenged by a greater force than human willpower.

Because sin robbed mankind of their true identity and awakened in them all kinds of worse-than-animal-like conduct, a set of rules couldn't do it. The revelation of God's righteousness has to be far more effective and powerful than mankind's slavery to sin.

It is evident that because of mankind's corrupt behavior, we deserve nothing less than condemnation. Yet within this context the grace and mercy of God is revealed; not as mere tolerance from God's side to turn a blind eye and to put up with sin, but as God's triumphant act in Christ to cancel our guilt and to break sin's spell and dominion over us.

For salvation to be relevant it has to offer mankind a basis and reference from which their faith is to be launched. It has to offer a conclusion of greater implication than the stalemate condition they find themselves in under the dispensation of the law.

"My inner person agrees that the law is good and desires to obey its requirements yet my best intentions leave me powerless against the demands of sin in my body! Oh, wretched being that I am!"

Woe be to us but for the revelation of God's righteous intervention! The man Christ Jesus is the mediator of humanity. The judgment mankind rightfully deserved fell on him; he was made to be sin who knew no sin. "He was handed over because of our transgressions, and triumphantly raised because of our acquittal." (Rom 4:25).

Paul is convinced that whatever happened to the human race because of Adam's fall is far superseded in every possible proportion by the revelation of mankind's inclusion in the life, death and resurrection of Jesus Christ. He places the fall of Adam and every act of unrighteousness that followed against the one act of righteousness that God performed in Christ as proof of mankind's acquittal.

The revelation of righteousness by God's faith unveils how Jesus Christ represented and redeemed mankind. The etymological essence of the word, "righteousness" in its root form, diké, implies the idea of two parties finding likeness in each other; with no interference of any sense of blame, guilt or inferiority. The Hebrew word for righteousness is the word tzedek which refers to the wooden beam in a scale of balances. When Adam lost the glory of God (Hebrew, kabod, weight; the consciousness of God's likeness and image) the law proved that no amount of good works could balance the scale again. Grace reveals how God redeemed his image and likeness again in human form; now the scale is perfectly balanced! No wonder Jesus cried out on the cross, "It is finished!" *See commentary note on 2 Corinthians 6:14.*

This is the message that Paul says he owes the entire world!

"I proclaim Jesus Christ according to the revelation of the mystery which was concealed in silence in the sequence of timeless ages, but now is made publicly known, mirrored in prophetic scripture." ("Surely he was wounded by our transgressions; he was bruised by our iniquities. The chastisement that brought us peace was upon him and by his stripes we were healed." [Isa 53:4, 5]) And now the God of the ages has issued his mandate to make the mystery known in such a way that all the nations of the earth will discover the lifestyle that the hearing of faith ignites." (Rom 16:25, 26) Paul gives new definition to obedience when he calls it "the obedience of faith." Romans 1:5.

"The conclusion is clear: it took just one offense to condemn mankind; one act of righteousness declares the same mankind innocent. The disobedience of the one exhibits humanity as sinners, the obedience of another exhibits humanity as righteous. Romans 5:18, 19.

Just as all mankind became exceedingly sinful through one person's disobedience but did not know it until the law revealed it, so all mankind became exceedingly righteous through one act of righteousness but they do not know it until the gospel reveals it. The principle of faith is to see what God sees. God calls things that seem not to be as though they were. Romans 4:17.

While we look not at the things that the senses observe, we look at the revelation of the unseen as it is unveiled in our understanding through the mirror revelation of the Gospel of Christ. See 2 Corinthians 3:18; 2 Corinthians 4:18.

Romans 4:17 finds its context in Romans 1:17 and 10:17, "It is clear then that faith's source is found in the content of the message heard; the message is Christ. (We are God's audience; Jesus is God's language!)"

The incarnation is the voice of the free eagle.

(The beautifully illustrated Eagle Story is available on Amazon.com)

1:1 Paul, [5]passionately engaged by Jesus Christ, [1]identified in him to [2]represent him. My [3]mandate and [4]message is to announce the goodness of God to mankind. *(Mandate, the scope or horizon of my message, from [3]horitso, meaning marked out. The word, [2]apostelo, means an extension from him, a representative; [5]doulos, means slave from deo, to be bound or knitted together like a husband and wife; [1]kletos comes from kaleo, meaning called, to identify by name, to surname; and [4]eu + angellion, means well done announcement, good news, the official announcement of God's goodness.)*

1:2 This message is what the Scriptures are all about. It remains the central prophetic theme and content of inspired writing.

1:3 The son of God has his natural lineage from the seed of David; *(In Matthew 22:41-45 Jesus asked the Pharisees, "What do you think of the Christ? Whose son is he?" They said to him, "The son of David." He said to them, "How is it then that David, inspired by the Spirit, calls him Lord, saying, 'The Lord said to my Lord, Sit at my right hand, till I put your enemies under your feet'? If David thus calls him Lord, how is he his son?" Mat 22:41-45 "You must not call anyone here on earth Father, because you have only the one Father in heaven." [Mt 23:9]. "Yet there is for us only one God, the Father, who is the Creator of all things and for whom we live; and there is only one Lord, Jesus Christ, through whom all things were created and through whom we live." [1 Cor 8:6]. "For this reason I bow my knees before the Father, from whom every family in heaven and on earth receives its true name." [Eph 3:14, 15]. "... there is one God and Father of all people, who is Lord of all, works through all, and is in all." [Eph 4:6, 7].)*

1:4 however, his powerful resurrection from the dead by the Holy Spirit, [1]locates and confirms his being and sonship in God. *(The word, locates, comes from [1]apo + horizo, meaning to mark out beforehand, to define or locate, literally horizon. The same word is translated as mandate in verse 1. In Acts 13:32-33, Paul preaches the resurrection and quotes Psalms 2, "Today I have begotten you." Jesus locates us and confirms that we have our genesis in God! Peter understands that we were born anew in the resurrection of Christ. The relevance of the resurrection is the revelation of mankind's inclusion in Christ [see 1 Pet 1:3]. Hosea 6:2 is the only scripture that prophesies the third day resurrection, and here in this single dramatic prophesy, we are co-included in his resurrection! "After two days he will revive us, on the third day he will raise us up!" [RSV] This is the crux of the mystery of the Gospel! "Will the earth be brought forth in one day? Can a nation be born in a moment?" [Isa 66:8, 9].)*

1:5 The grace and commission we received from him, is to bring about a [1]faith-inspired lifestyle in all the nations. [2]His name is his claim on the human race. *(Paul immediately sets out to give new definition to the term, "obedience," no longer by law, but of faith. [1]Obedience, from upo + akoo, means to be under the influence of what is heard, accurate hearing; hearing from above. [2]Every family in heaven and on earth is identified in him (Eph 3:15).*

1:6 In Jesus Christ you individually discover [1]who you are. *(The word, [1]kaleo, means to call by name, to surname.)*

1:7 In addressing you, I address all in Rome. I am convinced of God's love for you; he [2]restored you to the harmony of your original design; you were made holy in Christ Jesus; no wonder then that you are [1]surnamed [2]Saints. His grace gift in Christ secures your total wellbeing. The Father of the Lord Jesus Christ is ours also; he is our God. *(The word, [1]kaleo, means called, identified by name, surname; [2]hagios, means saints, restored to the harmony of your original design; "He separated me from my mother's womb when he revealed his son in me, in order that I may declare him in the nations; immediately I did not consult with flesh and blood." [Gal 1:15, 16]. "From now on, therefore, we regard no one from a human point of view; even though we once knew Christ after the flesh, we regard him thus no longer." [2 Cor 5:16 RSV].)*

1:8 My greatest joy is to realize that your faith is announced throughout the entire world. The total cosmos is our audience.

1:9 I am completely engaged in my spirit in the gospel of God's son; constantly including you in my prayers; God is my witness.

1:10 Since I already feel so [1]connected to you I long to also see you face to face. *([1]To beseech, deomai, from deo to tie together, to be knitted together.)*

1:11 I really look forward to finally meet you in person, knowing that my spiritual [1]gift will benefit you greatly; it will cement and establish you in your faith. *(The word, [1]metadidomi, translates as the kind of giving where the giver is not distanced from the gift but wrapped up in it! The apostles, prophets, preachers, pastors, and teachers are gifts to the ekklesia to establish them in their faith and to present everyone in the full and mature stature of Christ [Eph 4:11-16]. There is such a vast difference between a gift and a reward! We are God's gifts to one another. What God now has in us is gift wrapped to the world. What we are in our individual expression is a gift and not a reward for personal diligence or achievement. These gifts were never meant to establish one above the other, or to become mere formal titles, but rather to identify specific and dynamic functions with one defined purpose, to bring everyone into the realization of the fullness of the measure of Christ in them!)*

1:12 And so we will be mutually refreshed in the [1]participation and reflection of our common faith. *(The word, [1]sumparakaleo, comes from sum, together; para, is a preposition indicating close proximity, a thing proceeding from a sphere of influence, with a suggestion of union of place of residence, to have sprung from its author and giver, originating from, denoting the point from which an action originates, intimate connection, and kaleo, meaning to identify by name, to surname.)*

1:13 Until now I have been prevented from coming to you, even though I have frequently desired to reap some harvest in you as much as I anticipate the full fruit of this gospel in all the nations.

1:14 I am so convinced of everyone's inclusion; I am [2]indebted both to the Greeks as well as those many [1]foreigners whose languages we do not even understand. I owe this message to everyone, it is not a matter of how literate and educated people are; the illiterate are equally included

in the benefit of the good news. *(The word, [1]barbaros, means one who speaks a strange and foreign language; [2]opheiletes, means to be indebted, obliges one to return something to someone that belongs to him or her in the first place.)*

1:15 Because of this compelling urgency I am so keen to preach to you Romans also.

1:16 I have no shame about sharing the good news of Christ with anyone; the powerful rescuing act of God persuades both Jew and Gentile alike.

1:17 Herein lies the secret of the power of the Gospel; there is no good news in it until the righteousness of God is revealed! The dynamic of the gospel is the revelation of God's faith as the only valid basis for our belief. The prophets wrote in advance about the fact that God believes that righteousness reveals the life of our design. "Righteousness by his *(God's)* **faith defines life."** *[Habakkuk 2:4]*

(The gospel is the revelation of the righteousness of God; it unveils how the Father, Son and Spirit succeeded to put mankind right with themselves. It is about what God did right, not what Adam did wrong. The good news reveals how God's righteousness rescued the life of our design and redeemed our innocence. Mankind's futile efforts to obey moral laws have failed them miserably - the good news shifts the emphasis away from mankind's failure and condemnation to highlight what it was that God accomplished in Jesus Christ on humanity's behalf! "Look away [from the law of works] unto Jesus; he is the Author and finisher of faith." [Hebrews 12:1]. The language of the old written code was, "Do in order to become! The language of the new is, "Be, because of what was done!" Instead of do, do, do, it's done, done, done! It is God's faith to begin with; it is from faith to faith, and not our good or bad behavior; we are not defined by our performance or circumstances. Paul refers here to Habakkuk 2:4, "The just shall live by his [God's] faith." Habakkuk sees a complete new basis to mankind's standing before God! Instead of reading the curse when disaster strikes, he realizes that the Promise out-dates performance as the basis to mankind's acquittal. Deuteronomy 28 would no longer be the motivation or measure of right or wrong behavior! Instead of righteousness as a reward to mankind's efforts to obey the law, Habakkuk celebrates God's righteousness based on God's belief, in the face of apparent disaster, represented in the evidence of all the curses mentioned in Deuteronomy 28! He sings, "Though the fig trees do not blossom, nor fruit be on the vines, the produce of the olive fails and the fields yield no food, the flock be cut off from the fold and there be no herd in the stalls, yet I will rejoice in the Lord, I will joy in the God of my salvation. God, the Lord, is my strength; he makes my feet like hinds' feet, he makes me tread upon my high places." [Habakkuk 3:17-19 RSV]. It is interesting to note that Habakkuk - chăbaqqûq, was possibly the son of the Shunammite woman and her husband who hosted the prophet Elisha. They could not have children, until Elisha declared that in a year's time she would embrace - chabaq - a child! When the child grew up to be a young man he died of sunstroke and Elisha stretched himself over the boy and mirror-embraced the dead child, face to face and the boy came back to life. Chabaqquq is a double embrace - it is the prophetic picture of our mirror-resurrection together with Christ! If anyone

knew that righteousness was not by works but by God's faith, it was Habakkuk!

The word righteousness comes from the Anglo Saxon word, "rightwiseness;" wise in that which is right. In Greek the word for righteousness is dikaiosune, from dikay, that which is right; it is a relationship word and refers to two parties finding likeness in each other. Righteousness points to harmony in relationship. See 2 Corinthians 6:14. Faith-righteousness has nothing in common with the pagan philosophies of karma and performance-based approval; they could never balance the scales or be evenly yoked together in any context. [The word heterozugeō, an unequal or different yoke; from the word, zugos, a yoke or a teaching; the yoke of a rabbi or philosopher represented their doctrine; from the Hebrew word, tzedek, the wooden beam in a scale of balances, which is the word for righteousness. It is also interesting to note that the Greek goddess of Justice is Dike [pronounced, dikay] and she is always pictured holding a scale of balances in her hand.] See also 2 Corinthians 6:15. In Colossians 2:9-10, "It is in Christ that God finds an accurate and complete expression of himself, in a human body! He mirrors our completeness and is the ultimate authority of our true identity.")

1:18 God's [1]passionate persuasion is uncovered from heavens perspective in sharp [2]contrast to the foolishness of [3]people who [4]suppress and conceal the truth about their redeemed innocence while they continue to embrace an [5]inferior reference of themselves. *(The righteousness of God that is endorsed in the heavens is so different to the counterfeit, earthly reference that blindfolds people in their own unrighteousness. The word often translated wrath, [1]orge, means desire - as a reaching forth or excitement of the mind, passion. The preposition [2]epi means over, above, across, against, continual influence upon; I translated it here as contrast. The word for the [3]human species, male or female is anthropos, from ana, upwards, and tropos, manner of life; character; in like manner. The word [4]katecho, to echo downwards is the opposite of anoche, to echo upward; see Romans 2:4 and 3:26. In Colossians 3:2 Paul encourages us to engage our thoughts with things above [God's belief], and not below [law of works]. The word [5]adikia, unrighteousness, is the opposite of dikay, two parties finding likeness in each other; thus, without harmony. The law reveals how guilty and sinful mankind is, while the gospel reveals how forgiven and restored to their original blueprint we are. See 2 Corinthians 4:4)*

1:19 God is not a stranger to anyone; whatever can be known of God is [1]evident in every human life. *(Jesus came to unveil God's likeness, not his "otherness". The word [1]phaneros from phaino, means to shine like light. Colossians 2:9,10 "It is in Christ that God finds an accurate and complete expression of himself, in a human body! Jesus mirrors our completeness." While the expanse cannot measure or define God, his exact likeness is displayed in human form. Jesus proves that human life is tailor-made for God! See also Ephesians 4:8)*

1:20 God is on display in creation; the very fabric of visible cosmos appeals to reason. It clearly bears witness to the ever present sustaining power and intelligence of the invisible God, leaving mankind without any valid excuse to ignore him. *(Psalms 19:1-4, "God's glory is on tour in the skies, God-craft on exhibit across the horizon. Madame Day holds classes every* *morning, Professor Night lectures each evening. Their words aren't heard, their voices aren't recorded, But their silence fills the earth: unspoken truth is spoken everywhere." — The Message)*

1:21 Yet mankind only knew him in a philosophical religious way, from a distance, and failed to give him credit as God. Their taking him for granted and lack of gratitude veiled him from them; they became absorbed in useless debates and discussions, which further darkened their understanding about themselves.

1:22 Their wise conclusions only proved folly.

1:23 Their losing sight of God, made them lose sight of who they really were. In their calculation the image and likeness of God became reduced to a corrupted and distorted pattern of themselves. Suddenly a person has more in common with "creepy crawlies" than with their original blueprint.

1:24 It seemed like God abandoned humanity to be swept along by the lusts of their own hearts to abuse and defile themselves. Their most personal possession, their own bodies, became worthless public property.

1:25 Truth suppressed *(v18)* became twisted truth. Instead of embracing their Maker as their authentic identity, they preferred the deception of a distorted image of their own making, religiously giving it their affection and worship. The true God is the blessed God of the ages. Hey! He is not defined by our devotion or indifference! *(And all this because they traded the true God for a fake god, and worshiped the god they made instead of the God who made them. Message)*

1:26 By being confused about their Maker they became confused about themselves; which led to all manner of sexual obsessions.

1:27 Men and women alike became inflamed with unnatural and perverted sexual attractions; [1]laboring with intense striving, pursuing the illusion of a [2]distorted image - only to receive within themselves an [3]inferior estimate of themselves. *(The word [1]katergazomai from kata, downward; also to emphasize intensity; and ergatsomai, to toil. Then he uses the word [2]aschēmosunē from aschēmōn, deformed, from a, negative or without and schema, form or pattern. The word [3]antimisthia from anti, against or opposite and [3]misthois, the wage of a hireling; translated here an inferior estimate; or a wage that leaves one disappointed. This word is only used again in 2 Corinthians 6:13)*

1:28 Their indifference veiled God from them.

1:29 Sin snowballs! It spreads like cancer, exhibiting its ugly symptoms in every possible form, from perverse sexual obsession, to every kind of atrocity. The problem with sin is that it never satisfies, leaving the victim miserably unfulfilled and constantly craving for more of the same deception: vileness, jealous anger, obsessed only with self. Life is cheap, murder doesn't matter; they are steeped in constant quarreling and wickedness, their conversation has become reduced to slanderous gossip.

1:30 No one is safe in their company; they think that by insulting people they can voice their hatred for God; proudly bragging about their latest inventions of filth. Sadly this often begins at home where children lose faith in their parents.

1:31 Parents abandoned their own [1]conscience (*[1]suneido, joint seeing, oneness of mind*) **and [2]divorce became an easy cop-out of their covenant agreement. Instead of cherishing one another with affection, they would make their children the victims of the merciless dilemma of their dispute.** (*The word [2]asunthetous, divorce, covenant break. These verses clearly point to where the rot starts, in broken homes where parents abandoned faith and preferred divorce.*)

1:32 It just doesn't make any sense, they started off knowing the [1]righteousness of God, yet by their lifestyle they flirt with death; it is almost as if sin has become a fashionable contest. (*[1]dikaioma, righteousness - not judgment, as some translations suggest!*

From verse 18 to 32 Paul paints the picture of the dilemma and darkness of the fallen mindset - where the distorted picture becomes the norm. This is the language of a law system, which defines people by their behavior rather than their design. He then concludes in 2:4 with this amazing statement to underline his conviction as recorded in 1:16,17 about the powerful rescuing act of God announced in the Gospel. "Do not underestimate God's kindness. The wealth of his benevolence and his resolute refusal to let go of us is because he continues to hear the echo of his likeness in us! Thus his patient passion is to shepherd everyone into a radical mind shift.)

2:1 A presumed knowledge of that which is right or wrong does not qualify you to judge anyone; especially if you do exactly the same stuff you notice other people do wrong. You effectively condemn yourself. No one is another person's judge.

2:2 God must judge all transgression, but your judging others does not make them any guiltier.

2:3 God is completely impartial in his judgment; you are not scoring any points or disguising your own sins by telling on others.

2:4 Do not [1]underestimate God's [2]kindness. The wealth of his [2]benevolence and his [3]resolute refusal to let go of us is because he continues to hear the echo of his likeness in us! Thus his [4]patient passion is to [5]shepherd everyone into a [6]radical mind shift. *(The word translated, underestimate is the word, [1]kataphroneō, from kata, down, and phroneo, to think, to form an opinion; thus a downcast mind, to despise or take for granted. It is the revelation of the goodness of God that leads us to [6]repentance; it is not our "repentance" that leads God to goodness! The word "repentance" is a fabricated word from the Latin word, penance, and to give religion more mileage the English word became re-penance! That is not what the Greek word means at all! The word, [6]metanoia, comes from meta, meaning together with, and nous, mind; thus, together with God's mind. This word suggests a [6]radical mind shift; it is to realize God's thoughts towards us. [See Isa 55:8-10] The word, [2]chrestos, kind, benevolent, from xeir, hand which is also root to the word xristos, to draw the hand over, to anoint, to measure; see also the Hebrew for Messiah, mashach, to draw the hand over, to measure! [Analytical Hebrew and Chaldee Lexicon, B Davidson.] In Jesus Christ, God has measured mankind innocent, he is the blueprint of our design! The word [3]anoches comes from ana, meaning upwards; ana also shows intensity and the word echo, to hold, or embrace, as in echo. He continues to hear the echo of his likeness in us! [See Rom 3:26.] The word, [4]makrothumias, means to be patient in bearing the offenses and injuries of others. Literally, passion that goes a long way; from the root word thuo, to slay a sacrifice. The word, [5]ago, means to lead as a shepherd leads his sheep.)*

2:5 A calloused heart that resists change accumulates cause to self-destruction, while God's righteous judgment is revealed in broad daylight. *(The gospel openly declares that God declared mankind innocent.)*

2:6 By resisting him you are on your own; your own deeds will judge you. *(Rejecting his goodness [v 4] keeps you snared in a lifestyle ruled by sin-consciousness and condemnation.)*

2:7 The quest of mankind is to be constant in that which is good, glorious and honorable and of imperishable value. We are eager to pursue the original blueprint-life of the [1]ages. *(The life of the ages, from [1]aionios, which is the most attractive life we could wish to live; it is the life of our design, yet it remains elusive outside the redemption that Christ achieved on our behalf. Not even the most sincere decision to live a blameless life under the law or any sincere philosophy could satisfy the heart hunger of humanity.)*

2:8 Yet there are those who ignore the truth through ²unbelief. *(The truth about their original identity as sons)* They continue to exist as mere ¹hirelings, motivated by a monthly wage *(rather than sonship)*. They believe in their failure and unrighteousness and are consumed by outbursts of anger and displeasure. *(The word, ¹eithea, comes from erithos, working as a hireling for wages; often translated, self-willed or contentious. The word, ²apeitheo, means to be not persuaded, without faith, often wrongly translated as disobedient.)*

2:9 Pressures from every side, like an ¹overcrowded room, *(or a cramped foot in an undersized shoe,)* is the experience of the soul of everyone who does what is worthless. The fact that the Jews are Jewish does not make their experience of evil any different from that of the Greeks. *(Symptoms of disease are the same in anyone; they are not a respecter of persons. The word, ¹stenochoria, means narrowness of room.)*

2:10 In sharp contrast to this, bliss, self-worth and total tranquillity is witnessed by everyone, both Jew and Greek, who finds expression in that which is good. We are tailor-made for good.

2:11 God does not judge people on face value.

2:12 Ruin and self-destruction are the inevitable results of sin, whether someone knows the law or not.

2:13 Righteousness is not a hearsay-thing, it is faith-inspired practical living, giving new definition to the law.

2:14 For even a pagan's natural instinct will confirm the law to be present in their conscience and though they have never even heard about Jewish laws. Thus they prove to be a law unto themselves.

2:15 The law is so much more than a mere written code; its presence in human conscience even in the absence of the written instruction is obvious, condemning or commending personal conduct.

2:16 Every hidden, conflicting thought will be disclosed in the daylight of God's scrutiny, based on the good news of Jesus Christ that I proclaim. *(The ineffectiveness of good intentions and self discipline to produce lasting change will be exposed as worthless in contrast to the impact of the message of Christ's death and resurrection as representing mankind's death and new birth as our ultimate reference to our redeemed identity and innocence.)*

2:17 Your Jewish identity does not make God your exclusive property,

2:18 even though you boast in the fact that you have the ¹documented desire of God ²published like an instruction manual in the law. *(The word, ¹dokimatso, comes from document, decree, approve; ²diaphero, from to carry through, to publish [Acts 13:49, the word was published throughout].)*

2:19 You promote yourself confidently as a guide for the blind, and a light bearer for those groping about in darkness.

2:20 You feel yourself so superior to the rest of the world that you promote yourself as the "kindergarten" teacher to the mindless, an instructor of infants, because you believe that in the law you have knowledge and truth all wrapped up in a nutshell.

2:21 However, the real question is not whether you are a good teacher; how good a student are you? What's the good of teaching against stealing when you yourself steal?

2:22 You speak against adultery while you cannot get your own mind off sexual sins. It just doesn't make sense does it? You say idolatry stinks yet you steal stuff from pagan shrines.

2:23 Your proud association with the law is ruined every time you dishonor God by dodging the doing bit.

2:24 This has been going on for hundreds of years; it is all recorded in scripture. No wonder the Gentiles think that your God is no better than any of their philosophies when it comes to living the life the law promotes.

2:25 The real value of circumcision is tested by your ability to keep the law. If you break the law you might as well not be circumcised.

2:26 The fact that you are circumcised does not distinguish you from the rest of the world; it does not give you super-human power to keep the commandments.

2:27 If it is not about who is circumcised or not, but rather who keeps the law or not, then in that case even uncircumcised people can judge the ones who claim to know it all and have it all! On the one hand you have those who feel naturally inclined to do what is right, yet none of them are circumcised, then you have the circumcised who know the letter of the law but fail to keep it.

2:28 So it is not about who you appear to be on the outside that makes you a real Jew, but who you really are on the inside.

2:29 For you to know who you are in your heart is the secret of your spirit identity; this is your true circumcision, it is not the literal outward appearance that distinguishes you. After all it is God's approval and not another's opinion that matters most. People see skin-deep; God knows the heart.

3:1 Having said all this, you might ask whether there is still any advantage in being Jewish? Is there any significance in circumcision?

3:2 Everything only finds its relevance and value in the original intention of God realized by faith.

3:3 The question is, how does someone's failure to believe God affect what God believes? Can their unbelief cancel God's faith? *(What we believe about God does not define him; God's faith defines us. See the RSV translation, "What if some were unfaithful? Does their faithlessness nullify the faithfulness of God? By no means!")*

3:4 God's word is not under threat! In fact if all of humanity fails, truth remains intact. Truth is defined in God; it is neither challenged nor vindicated by human experience. Contradiction does not intimidate or diminish the faith of God. Scripture records that God stands justified in his own word; it confirms that God's promise and purpose are not compromised through mankind's failure; neither is God's reputation threatened by our behavior. *(Truth does not become true by popular vote. It is already as true as it gets because God believes it; it is from faith to faith, says Paul [Rom 1:17]; there is no gospel in it until the righteousness of God is revealed; "we can do nothing against the truth!" [See 2 Cor 13:5 and 8]. David's sin did not cancel God's promise. "But my mercy I will not take from him" and "his house shall be made sure, and his kingdom for ever before me, and his throne shall be set up forever." [2 Sam 7:15-16].)*

3:5 We could argue then that God doesn't have a right to judge us, if our unrighteousness only emphasizes his righteousness.

3:6 This would make God an unfair judge of the world.

3:7 This almost sounds like I am saying that it is not really wrong to sin, if our cheating only serves to further contrast the truth of God.

3:8 Because of my emphasis on God's grace, some people slanderously make the assumption and accuse me that my teaching would give people a license to sin. "Let us do evil that good may come!" I strongly condemn such foolish talk! *"But if our wickedness advertises the goodness of God, do we feel that God is being unfair to punish us in return? (I'm using a human tit-for-tat argument.) Not a bit of it! What sort of a person would God be then to judge the world? It is like saying that if my lying throws into sharp relief the truth of God and, so to speak, enhances his reputation, then why should he repay me by judging me a sinner? Similarly, why not do evil that good may be, by contrast all the more conspicuous and valuable? (As a matter of fact, I am reported as urging this very thing, by some slanderously and others quite seriously! But, of course, such an argument is quite properly condemned." — Phillips Translation)*

3:9 It is common knowledge that sin holds the sway over both Jew and Greek alike. *(Just like disease would show the same symptoms regardless of someone's nationality.)*

3:10 Scripture records that within the context of the law, no-one succeeds to live a blameless life. *(Psalm 14:1-3, "To the choirmaster of David. The fool says in his heart, 'There is no God.' They are corrupt and they do abominable deeds, there is none that does good. The Lord looks down from heaven upon the children of men, to see if there are any that act wisely, that seek after God. They have all gone astray, they are all alike corrupt; there is none that does good, no, not one [RSV]." In Genesis 18, Abraham intercedes for Sodom and Gomorrah, "If there perhaps are 50 righteous people, will you save the city on their behalf?" He continues to negotiate with God, until he's down to, "perhaps ten?"..."there was none righteous, no not one ..." This argument is building up to the triumphant conclusion of the fact that there is indeed no distinction; the same people who fell short of the glory of God are now justified through God's work of grace in Christ. If mankind was 100% represented in Adam, then they are equally 100% represented in Christ! [Rom 3:21-24].)*

3:11 Because there seems to be no sincere craving and desire to know God there is no spiritual ¹insight. *(While a person remains casual and indifferent about God, their heart remain calloused; the word, ¹**suinemi**, means a joint-seeing.)*

3:12 Their distraction has bankrupted their lives; that goes for the mass of mankind, without any exception.

3:13 "When they open their mouth to speak they bury one another with destructive words. They snake each other with lies and corruption.

3:14 With sharp tongues they ¹cut one another to pieces, cursing and cheating; their every word is inspired by the ²wearisome effort to survive in a dog-eat- dog world. *(Taken direct from the Hebrew text in Psalm 10:7 in Hebrew, ¹**tok tok** from **tavek**, to cut to pieces. In Hebrew ²**amal** and **aven**, to exert oneself in wearisome effort.)*

3:15 Murder has become a regular ritual; without any regard for another's life.

3:16 Their path is littered with broken lives.

3:17 They have lost the art of friendship.

3:18 They have completely lost sight of God." *(3:13-18 are quotations from Psalm 10 and Psalm 14.)*

3:19 The fact that all these quotations are from Jewish writings, confirm that their law of moral conduct did not free them from the very same sins the rest of the world was trapped in. The entire human race is now confronted with the ¹righteousness of God. *(The word ¹**upodikos**, from **upo** under and **dikay**, two parties finding likeness in each other, the root of the word **dikaiosunay**, righteousness. See Romans 1:17; also 3:21 and Acts 17:31, Romans 4:25.)*

3:20 The law proves all of mankind equally guilty and confirms that their most sincere duty-driven decision and 'self-help' program within the confines of the flesh could not give them any sense of improved confidence in their standing before God.

3:21 We are now talking a complete different language: the gospel unveils what God did right not what we did wrong! Both the law and all the prophetic writings pointed to this moment! *(This brings me back to the theme of my ministry, chapter 1:1, 2, 5, 16, 17. There is no point in telling people how condemned they are! Tell them how loved they are! God's dealing with mankind is based on the fact that their conscience continues to bear witness to their original design. Romans 7:22.)*

3:22 Jesus is what God believes about you! In him the righteousness of God is on display in such a way [1]that everyone may be equally persuaded about what God believes about them, regardless of who they are; there is no distinction. *(The preposition, [1]eis, indicates a point reached in conclusion.)*

3:23 Humanity is in the same boat; their [1]distorted behavior is proof of a [2]lost [3]blueprint. *(The word sin, is the word [1]hamartia, from ha, negative or without and meros, portion or form, thus to be without your allotted portion or without form, pointing to a disorientated, distorted, bankrupt identity; the word meros, is the stem of morphe, as in 2 Corinthians 3:18 the word metamorphe, with form, which is the opposite of hamartia - without form. Sin is to live out of context with the blueprint of one's design; to behave out of tune with God's original harmony. See Deuteronomy 32:18, "You have forgotten the Rock that begot you and have gotten out of step with the God who danced with you!" Hebrew, khul or kheel, to dance. See Romans 9:33 in the Mirror! The word [2]hustereo, to fall short, to be inferior, [3]doxa, glory, blueprint, from dokeo, opinion or intent.)*

3:24 Jesus Christ is proof of God's grace gift; he redeemed the glory of God in human life; mankind condemned is now mankind justified! *(He proved that God did not make a mistake when he made you in his image and likeness! Sadly the evangelical world proclaimed verse 23 completely out of context! There is no good news in verse 23, the gospel is in verse 24! All fell short because of Adam; the same 'all' are equally declared innocent because of Christ! The law reveals what happened to mankind in Adam; grace reveals what happened to the same mankind in Christ. Their is no distinction - all have sinned and fallen short of the glory of God - now they are all justified freely as a gift through the redemption [the liberating action] of Jesus Christ!)*

3:25 Jesus exhibits God's mercy. In his blood conciliation God's faith persuades humankind of his righteousness and the fact that he has brought closure to the historic record of their sins. *(Not by demanding a sacrifice but providing the sacrifice of himself.)* Jesus is the unveiling of the Father's heart towards us. *(See note to Hebrews 8:12; also 1 John 2:2)*

3:26 All along God [1]refused to let go of mankind. At this very moment God's act of [2]righteousness is [3]pointing them to the evidence of their innocence, with Jesus as the [4]source of their faith. *(God's tolerance, [1]anoche, to echo upwards; God continued to hear the echo of his likeness in us. See Rom 2:4. In both these verses [25+26] Paul uses the word, [3]endeixis, where we get the word indicate from. It is also part of the root for the word translated as righteousness, [2]dikaiosune. To point out, to show, to convince with proof. Then follows, [4]ek pisteos iesou; ek, source or origin and iesou is in the Genitive case, the owner* *of faith is Jesus! He is both the source and substance of faith! Hebrews 11:1, 12:2)*

3:27 The law of faith cancels the law of works; which means there is suddenly nothing left for anyone to boast in. No one is superior to another. *(Bragging only makes sense if there is someone to compete with or impress. "While we compete with one another and compare ourselves with one another we are without understanding. [2 Corinthians 10:12]. "Through the righteousness of God we have received a faith of equal standing." [See 2 Peter 1:1 RSV] The OS (operating system) of the law of works is willpower; the OS of the law of faith is love. Galatians 5:6 Love sets faith in motion. The law presented one with choices; grace awakens belief! Willpower exhausts, love ignites! If choices could save us we would be our own Saviors! Willpower is the language of the law, love is the language of grace and it ignites faith that leads to romance; falling in love beats "making a decision to believe in love" by far! See Rom 7:19 Willpower has failed me; this is how embarrassing it is, the most diligent decision that I make to do good, disappoints.)*

3:28 This leaves us with only one logical conclusion, mankind is justified by God's faith and not by their ability to keep the law.

3:29 Which means that God is not the private property of the Jews but belongs equally to all the nations. *(While the law excludes the non-Jewish nations, faith includes us all on level terms.)*

3:30 There is only one God, he deals with everyone, circumcised or uncircumcised exclusively on the basis of faith.

3:31 No, faith does not re-write the rules; instead it confirms that the original life-quality meant for mankind as documented in the law, is again realized.

4:1 If we look at our father Abraham as an example and scrutinize his life, would you say that he discovered any reason for placing confidence in the flesh through personal contribution? *(What qualified Abraham to be the father of the multitudes of nations? The only part he played was his unwavering belief in God's faith in him.)*

4:2 If he felt that his friendship with God was a reward for good behavior, then surely he would have reason to recommend the recipe; yet it is plain to see that it was all God's initiative from start to finish!

4:3 Scripture is clear, "Abraham believed what God believed about him and that concluded his righteousness."

4:4 There is a large difference between a reward and a gift: if you have earned something through hard work, what you receive in return is your due and certainly not a gift.

4:5 It is clear then that someone who believes that God declares the ungodly innocent understands that it is faith and not our toil that accounts for righteousness.

4:6 David confirms this principle when he speaks of the blessedness of the one who discovers God's approval without any reference to something specific that they had done to qualify themselves.

4:7 Oh what [1]happy progress one makes with the weight of sin and guilt removed and one's slate wiped clean! *(The Hebrew word [1]ashar, blessed, means to advance, to make progress. [See Ps 32:1])*

4:8 "How blessed is the one who receives a [1]receipt instead of an invoice for their sins." *([1]logitzomai, to make a calculation to which there can only be one logical conclusion, to take an inventory.)*

4:9 Is this blessing restricted exclusively to the circumcised or extended also to the uncircumcised? Remember we are looking at Abraham as an example; his righteousness was founded on faith.

4:10 Did circumcision play any role in Abraham's standing before God? Certainly not; it is clear that God already calculated his faith as righteousness before he was circumcised. *(Righteousness is not a reward for good behavior.)*

4:11 Circumcision was introduced as a *(prophetic)* external seal to confirm the fact that Abraham's faith already resulted in righteousness. This qualifies him to be the father of all uncircumcised people who would believe as he did in the impartation of acquittal. *(The seal was not meant to be a distraction but rather a prophetic confirmation to righteousness by faith. Just like a receipt is only a reference to, and not the actual transaction.)*

4:12 At the same time he also represents as father all those for whom circumcision is not merely a skin deep religious ritual, but who walk in the footprints of his faith.

4:13 Righteousness by faith and not righteousness by law prompted the promise when God announced to Abraham that he would father those who would inherit the world. It is again a matter of embracing a gift rather than receiving a reward for keeping the law.

4:14 Faith would be emptied of its substance and the principle of promise would be meaningless if the law of personal performance was still in play to qualify the heirs. *(Faith is not in competition with the law. The life quality that faith reveals is consistent with mankind's original design and mirrors the very life the law promotes.)*

4:15 The law system is bound to bring about disappointment, regret and anger; if there is no law there is nothing to break; no contract, no breach.

4:16 Therefore since faith sponsors the gift of grace, the promise is equally secured for all the children. The law has no exclusive claim on anyone *(the reward system cannot match the gift principle).* Faith is our source, and that makes Abraham our father.

4:17 When God changed Abram's name to Abraham, he made a public statement that he would be the father of all nations. *(Genesis 17:5)* Here we see Abraham faced with God's faith; the kind of faith that resurrects the dead and calls things which are not *(visible yet)* as though they were. *(Note that most of Abram's ancestors were allready fathers by the time that they had turned 30 or 35; yet Terah was 70 years old before he had Abram; his name suggests that Terah acknowledged that he could not claim parenthood of this son, he was 'fathered from above'! [Gen 11:12-26] Now imagine how nervous Abram was when eventually he was 75 and still without child! That was when God met with him and added to his name the 'ha' of Jaweh's (Jehovah) own name! In Arabic the word raham means drizzling and lasting rain. The innumerable drops of water in a drizzling rain are like the stars mentioned in Gen 15:5 ("look toward heaven, and number the stars, if you are able to number them . . . so shall your seed be") now imagine those innumerable stars raining down upon the earth and each one becomes a grain of sand! So shall your seed be! Gen 22:17 ("I will indeed bless you, and I will multiply your descendants as the stars of heaven and as the sand which is on the seashore"). Abraham's identity, his name, was the echo of God's faith and his bold confession in the absence of Isaac. The name change, similar to that of Simon to Rock, reminds mankind to realize their original identity as sons of God, hewn out of the Rock [Deut 32:18, Isa 51:1, 2].)*

4:18 Faith gave substance to hope when everything seemed hopeless; the words, "so shall your seed be" conceived in him the faith of fatherhood. *(Abraham's case here pictures the hopelessness of fallen mankind, having lost their identity, and faced with the impossibility to redeem themselves.)*

4:19 Abraham's faith would have been nullified if he were to take his own age and the deadness of Sarah's womb into account. His hundred year old body and Sarah's barren womb did not distract him in the least! He finally knew that no contribution from their side could possibly assist God in fulfilling his promise!

4:20 While he had every reason to doubt the promise, he did not hesitate for a moment but instead empowered by faith confidence, he continued to communicate God's opinion. (*His name was his confession: in the Hebrew language, "Abraham" was not a mere familiar sounding name, but a meaningful sentence, a confession of faith authority, against the odds. He did not become embarrassed about his name; he did not change his name to "Abe" for short when there seemed to be no change in his circumstances. Every time he introduced himself or someone called him by his name, it was a bold declaration and repetition of God's promise, calling things that were not as though they were. I would imagine that Sarah spoke his name the most! In fact, every time they addressed one another they spoke the promise, "Mother of nations, kings of peoples shall come from you!" [Gen 17:5, 16]. Abraham, "the father of the multitudes.")*

4:21 Abraham's confidence was his ¹dress-code; he knew beyond doubt that the power of God to perform was equal to his promise. (*¹plerophoreo, from plero to be completely covered in every part, + phoreo, to wear garments or armor; traditionally translated to be completely persuaded. His faith was his visible identity and armor; he wore his persuasion like he would his daily garments.)*

4:22 The persuasion of God rubbed off on Abraham and became his personal conviction. This was the ¹basis of his righteousness. (*"Righteousness was ¹reckoned to him," this means that God's faith pointed Abraham to an invisible future where mankind's innocence and identity would be redeemed again. Greek, ¹logitsomai, logical conclusion.)*

4:23 Here is the good news: the recorded words, "It was reckoned to him" were not written for his sake alone.

4:24 Scripture was written with us in mind! The same conclusion is now equally relevant in our realizing the significance of Jesus' resurrection from the dead. (*By raising Jesus from the dead God proclaims his belief in our redeemed innocence. Isaac's birth from Sarah's barren womb prophetically declared the resurrection of Jesus from the tomb! Abraham's best efforts could not produce Isaac. Sarah's dead womb is a picture of the impossibility of the flesh to produce a child. This underlines mankind's inability to redeem themselves under the law of willpower. Jesus said, "Abraham saw my day!" Mankind's most extreme self-sacrifice offered in an attempt to win the favorable attention of thier deity could never match the sacrifice of God's Lamb to win the attention of humanity! When Isaac questioned his father about the sacrifice, Abraham announced, "Jaweh jireh!" Jaweh sees! And he lifted up his eyes and behold **behind him** was a ram caught in the thorn bush by its horns! Faith sees the future in past tense-mode! The resurrection is the ultimate proof and trophy of righteousness by God's faith. [See Rom 6:11] "Consider [logitsomai] yourself dead indeed," compared with 4:19, "Abraham considered [logitsomai] his own body dead." We can only study scripture in the context of Christ as representing the human race; God had us in mind all along [John 5:39].)*

4:25 Here is the equation: He was handed over ¹because of humanity's ²fallen condition; he was raised ¹because we were declared righteous! His resurrection is the official receipt to our acquittal. (*His cross = our sins, his* resurrection = our innocence! His death brought closure to our fallen condition; his resurrection is proof of our redeemed righteousness. Why was Jesus handed over to die? Because of, [1]*dia*, our transgressions. Why was he raised from the dead? Because of, [1]*dia*, our righteousness! His resurrection reveals our righteousness! If mankind was still guilty after Jesus died, his resurrection would be irrelevant! This explains Acts 10:28 and 2 Corinthians 5:14 and 16.

See Youngs Literal Translation, Rom 4:25 "who was delivered up because of our offences, and was raised up because of our being declared righteous."

The word [2]*paraptōma* speaks of humanity's fallen condition.

In Acts 17:31, Paul explains to the Greek philosophers that according to the Jewish prophetic word, "God had fixed a day on which he would judge the world in righteousness by a man whom he has appointed, and of this he has given proof to all mankind by raising him from the dead." God's declaration of your redeemed innocence is his most urgent invitation to you(manity) to encounter intimate oneness!

See also 1 Peter 1:10-12 "This salvation which you now know as your own, is the theme of the prophetic thought; this is what captured the prophets' attention for generations and became the object of their most diligent inquiry and scrutiny. They knew all along that mankind's salvation was a grace revelation, sustained in their prophetic utterance! (Salvation would never be by personal achievement or a reward to willpower-driven initiative! The law of works would never replace grace!)

1:11 In all of their conversation there was a constant quest to determine who the Messiah would be, and exactly when this will happen. They knew with certainty that it was the spirit of Christ within them pointing prophetically and giving testimony to the sufferings of the Christ and the subsequent glory. (Whatever glory was lost in Adam, would be redeemed again in Jesus Christ!)

1:12 It was revealed to them that this glorious grace message that they were communicating pointed to a specific day and person beyond their own horizon and generation; they saw you in their prophetic view! This heavenly announcement had you in mind all along! They proclaimed glad tidings to you in advance, in the Holy Spirit, commissioned from heaven; the angelic messengers themselves longed to gaze deeply into its complete fulfilment.")

5:1 [1]**Concluding then that our righteousness has absolutely nothing to do with our ability to keep moral laws but that it is the immediate result of what Jesus accomplished on mankind's behalf, gives context to** [2]**God's faith and finds expression in unhindered,** [3]**face to face** [4]**friendship with God! Jesus Christ is the head of this union!** *(In one sentence Paul sums up the previous four chapters. "Therefore, being justified by faith, we have peace with God through our Lord Jesus Christ." [KJV] The word* [1]*dikaiothentes is an Aorist participle, which translates, "having been justified by faith."* [2]*Paul's reference to our justification is the faith of God and not our own efforts to justify ourselves - see Romans 1:16,17 and Habakkuk 2:4. The preposition* [3]*pros means face to face; see John 1:1. The word,* [4]*eirene, means peace, to join; it refers to the "dove-tail" joint in carpentry. Peace is a place of unhindered enjoyment of friendship beyond guilt, suspicion, blame or inferiority.)*

5:2 Jesus is God's grace [1]**embrace of the entire human race. So here we are,** [2]**standing tall in the joyful bliss of our redeemed innocence! We are God's** [3]**dream come true! This was God's** [4]**idea all along!** *(To be welcomed with wide-open arms,* [1]*prosagoge echo. The words, 'by faith' are in brackets in the Greek text and are not supported by the best Greek manuscripts. Joy is not an occasional happy feeling; we are* [2]*positioned there,* [2]*histemi, in an immovable, unthreatened union! Hope,* [2]*elpis from elpo, to anticipate, usually with pleasure. The word* [4]*doxa, often translated, glory, is from dokeo, to form an idea, opinion.)*

5:3 Our blissful boasting in him remains uninterrupted in times of trouble; we know that pressure reveals patience. Tribulation does not have what it takes to nullify what hope knows we have!

5:4 Patience provides [1]**proof of every positive expectation.** *(*[1]*dokimos, proof. Thayer Definition: scrutinized and accepted, particularly of coins and money.)*

5:5 This kind of hope does not disappoint; the gift of the Holy Spirit completes our every expectation and ignites the love of God within us like an artesian well. *(ekxeo, to pour out. The Holy Spirit is an outpouring not an in-pouring! See John 7:37-39, also Titus 3:6)*

5:6 God's timing was absolutely perfect; humanity was at their weakest when Christ died their death. *(We were bankrupt in our efforts to save ourselves.)*

5:7 It is most unlikely that someone will die for another person, even if they are righteous; yet it is remotely possible that someone can brave such devotion that one would actually lay down one's own life in an effort to save the life of an extraordinary good person.

5:8 Herein is the extremity of God's love gift: mankind was rotten to the core when Christ died their death.

5:9 If God could love us that much when we were ungodly and guilty, how much more are we free to realize his love now that we are declared innocent by his blood? *(God does not love us more now that we are reconciled to him; we are now free to realize how much he loved us all along! [Col 2:14, Rom 4:25])*

5:10 Our hostility and indifference towards God did not reduce his love for us; he saw equal value in us when he exchanged the life of his son for ours. Now that the act of [1]reconciliation is complete, his life in us saves us from the gutter-most to the uttermost. *(Reconciliation, from [1]katalasso, meaning a mutual exchange of equal value. Thayer Definition: to exchange, as coins for others of equivalent value. "For if while we were enemies we were reconciled to God by the death of his Son, much more, now that we are reconciled, shall we be saved by his life." — RSV)*

5:11 Thus, our joyful boasting in God continues; Jesus Christ has made reconciliation a reality.

5:12 One person opened the door to sin. Sin introduced *(spiritual)* death. Both sin and *(spiritual)* death had a global impact. No one escaped its tyranny.

5:13 The law did not introduce sin; sin was just not pointed out yet.

5:14 In the mean time *(spiritual)* death dominated from Adam to Moses, *(2500 years before the law was given)* no one was excluded; even those whose transgression was different from Adam's. The fact is that Adam's offense set sin into motion, and its mark was globally transmitted and stained the entire human race.

5:15 The only similarity in the comparison between the offense and the gift, is that both Adam and Christ represent the masses; their single action therefore bears global consequence. The idea of death and separation that was introduced by one person's transgression is by far superseded by the grace gift lavished upon mankind in the one man Jesus Christ. *(But God's free gift immeasurably outweighs the transgression. For if through the transgression of the one individual the mass of mankind have died, infinitely greater is the generosity with which God's grace, and the gift given in his grace which found expression in the one man Jesus Christ, have been bestowed on the mass of mankind.— Weymouth, 1912)*

5:16 The difference between the two men is further emphasized in that judgment and condemnation followed a single offense, whereas the free gift of acquittal and righteousness follows innumerable sins.

5:17 If *(spiritual)* death saw the gap in one sin, and grabbed the opportunity to dominate mankind because of one person, how much more may we now seize the advantage to reign in righteousness in this life through that one act of Christ, who declared us innocent by his grace. Grace is out of all proportion in superiority to the transgression.

5:18 The conclusion is clear: it took just one offense to condemn mankind; one act of righteousness declares the same mankind innocent. *(The Phillips translation reads: "We see then, that as one act of sin exposed the whole race of men to condemnation, so one act of perfect righteousness presents all men freely acquitted in the sight of God!")*

5:19 The disobedience of the one [1]exhibits humanity as sinners; the obedience of another exhibits humanity as righteous. (¹*kathistemi, to cause to be, to set up, to exhibit. We were not made sinners by our own disobedience; neither were we made righteous by our own obedience.*)

5:20 The presence of the law made no difference, instead it merely highlighted the offense; but where sin increased, grace superseded it.

5:21 *(Spiritual)* death provided sin its platform and power to reign; now grace has taken over sovereignty through righteousness to introduce unthreatened life under the Lordship of Jesus Christ over us.

6:1 It is not possible to interpret grace as a cheap excuse to continue in sin. It sounds to some that we are saying, "Let's carry on sinning then so that grace may abound." *(In the previous chapter Paul expounds the heart of the gospel by giving us a glimpse of the far-reaching faith of God; even at the risk of being misunderstood by the legalistic mind he does not compromise the message.)*

6:2 How ridiculous is that! How can we be dead and alive to sin at the same time?

6:3 What are we saying then in baptism, if we are not declaring that we understand our union with Christ in his death?

6:4 Baptism pictures how we were co-buried together with Christ in his death; then it powerfully illustrates how in God's mind we were co-raised with Christ into a new lifestyle. *(Hos 6:2)*

6:5 We were like seeds planted together in the same soil, to be co-quickened to life. If we were included in his death we are equally included in his resurrection. *(2 Cor 5:14 - 17)*

6:6 We perceive that our old lifestyle was co-crucified together with him; this concludes that the vehicle that accommodated sin in us, was scrapped and rendered entirely useless. Our slavery to sin has come to an end.

6:7 If nothing else stops you from doing something wrong, death certainly does.

6:8 Faith sees us joined in his death and alive with him in his resurrection.

6:9 It is plain for all to see that death lost its dominion over Christ in his resurrection; he need not ever die again to prove a further point.

6:10 His appointment with death was [1]once-off. As far as sin is concerned, he is dead. The reason for his death was to take away the sin of the world; his life now exhibits our union with the life of God. *(The Lamb of God took away the sin of the world; [1]efapax, once and for all, a final testimony, used of what is so done to be of perpetual validity and never needs repetition. This is the final testimony of the fact that sin's power over us is destroyed. In Hebrews 9:26, "But Jesus did not have to suffer again and again since the fall (or since the foundation) of the world; the single sacrifice of himself in the fulfillment of history now reveals how he has brought sin to naught." "Christ died once, and faced our judgment! His second appearance (in his resurrection) has nothing to do with sin, but to reveal salvation unto all who eagerly embrace him [Heb 9:28].")*

6:11 This reasoning is equally relevant to you. [1]Calculate the cross; there can only be one logical conclusion: he died your death; that means you died to sin, and are now alive to God. Sin-consciousness can never again feature in your future! You are in Christ Jesus; his Lordship is the authority of this union. *(We are not being presumptuous to reason that we are in Christ! "[1]Reckon yourselves therefore dead to sin" The word, [1]logitsomai, means to make a calculation to which there can only be one logical conclusion. [See Eph 1:4 and 1 Cor 1:30].*

"From now on, think of it this way: Sin speaks a dead language that means nothing to you; God speaks your mother tongue, and you hang on every word. You are dead to sin and alive to God. That's what Jesus did." — The Message)

6:12 You are under no obligation to sin; it has no further rights to dominate your dead declared body. Therefore let it not entice you to obey its lusts. *(Your union with his death broke the association with sin [Col 3:3].)*

6:13 Do not let the members of your body lie around loose and unguarded in the vicinity of unrighteousness, where sin can seize it and use it as a destructive weapon against you; rather place yourself in [1]readiness to God, like someone resurrected from the dead and present your whole person as a weapon of righteousness. *(Thus you are reinforcing God's grace claim on mankind in Christ; [1]paristemi, to place in readiness, in the vicinity of.)*

6:14 Sin was your master while the law was your measure; now grace rules. *(The law revealed your slavery to sin, now grace reveals your freedom from it.)*

6:15 Being under grace and not under the law most certainly does not mean that you now have a license to sin.

6:16 As much as you once gave permission to sin to trap you in its spiral of spiritual death and enslave you to its dictates, the obedience that faith ignites now, introduces a new rule, rightness with God; to this we willingly yield ourselves. *(Righteousness represents everything that God restored us to — in Christ.)*

6:17 The content of teaching that your heart embraced has set a new [1]standard to become the [1]pattern of your life; the grace of God ended sin's dominance. *(The word, [1]tupos, means form, mold. The Doddrich translation translates it as, "the model of doctrine instructs you as in a mold.")*

6:18 Sin once called the shots; now righteousness rules.

6:19 I want to say it as plainly as possible: you willingly offered your faculties to obey sin, you stained your body with unclean acts and allowed lawlessness to gain supremacy in all of your conduct; in exactly the same way, I now encourage you to present your faculties and person to the supremacy of righteousness to find unrestricted expression in your lifestyle.

6:20 You were sins' slaves without any obligation to righteousness.

6:21 I know you are embarrassed now about the things you used to do with your body; I mean was it worth it? What reward or return did you get but spiritual death? Sin is a cul-de-sac. *(Sin is the worst thing you can ever do with your life!)*

6:22 Consider your life now; there are no outstanding debts; you owe sin nothing! A life bonded to God yields the sacred expression of his character, and completes in your experience [1]what life was always meant to be. *(Lit. The life of the ages, [1]aionios; traditionally translated, "and the end, eternal life".)*

6:23 **The reward of the law is death the gift of grace is life! The bottom line is this: sin employs you like a soldier for its cause and rewards you with death; God gifts you with the highest quality of life all wrapped up in Christ Jesus our Leader.** *(A soldier puts his life on the line and all he gets in the meantime is a meager ration of dried fish for his effort!* **opsonion**, *a soldier's wage, from* **opsarion**, *a piece of dried fish.)*

7:1 I write to you in the context of your acquaintance with the law; you would agree with me that laws are only relevant in this life.

7:2 A wife is only bound by law to her husband while he lives; any further legal claim he has on her ends with his death.

7:3 The law would call her an adulteress should she give herself to another man while the first husband is still alive. Yet, once he's dead, she is free to be another's wife.

7:4 The very same finality in principle is applicable to you, my brothers and sisters. In the body of Christ you died to the system of the law; your inclusion in his resurrection brought about a new union. Out of this marriage, *(faith)* now bears children unto God. *(The first marriage produced sin; righteousness is the child of the new union. In the previous chapter Paul deals with the fact that our inclusion in Christ in his death broke the association with sin; now he reveals that it also broke the association with the system of the law of works as a reference to righteousness.)*

7:5 At the time when the flesh ruled our lives, the subtle influences of sins which were ignited by the law, conceived actions within us that were consistent in character with their parent and produced spiritual death.

7:6 But now we are fully released from any further association with a life directed by the rule of the law, we are dead to that which once held us captive, free to be slaves to the newness of spirit-spontaneity rather than age old religious rituals, imitating the mere face value of the written code. *(The moment you exchange spontaneity with rules, you've lost the edge of romance.)*

7:7 The law in itself is not sinful; I am not suggesting that at all. Yet in pointing out sin, the law was in a sense the catalyst for sinful actions to manifest. Had the law not said, "Thou shalt not covet," I would not have had a problem with lust.

7:8 But the commandment triggered sin into action, suddenly an array of sinful appetites were awakened in me. The law broke sin's dormancy.

7:9 Without the law I was alive; the law was introduced, sin revived and I died.

7:10 Instead of being my guide to life, the commandment proved to be a death sentence.

7:11 Sin took advantage of the law and employed the commandment to seduce and murder me.

7:12 I stress again that the law as principle is holy and so is every individual commandment it contains; it consistently promotes that which is just and good.

7:13 How then could I accuse something that is that good to have killed me? I say again, it was not the law, but sin that caused my spiritual death.

The purpose of the law was to expose sin as the culprit. The individual commandment ultimately serves to show the exceeding extent of sin's effect on humanity.

7:14 We agree that the law is spiritual, but because I am [1]sold like a slave to sin, I am reduced to a mere carnal life. *(Spiritual death. The word, [1]pip-rasko comes from perao, meaning to transport into a distant land in order to sell as a slave. Sin is a foreign land.)*

7:15 This is how the sell-out to sin affects my life: I find myself doing things my conscience does not allow. My dilemma is that even though I sincerely desire to do that which is good, I don't, and the things I despise, I do.

7:16 It is obvious that my conscience sides with the law;

7:17 which confirms then that it is not really I who do these things but sin manifesting its symptoms in me. *(Sin is similar to a dormant virus that suddenly breaks out in very visible symptoms.)* It has taken my body hostage.

7:18 The total extent and ugliness of sin that inhabits me, reduced my life to good intentions that could not be followed through.

7:19 Willpower has failed me; this is how embarrassing it is, the most dili-gent decision that I make to do good, disappoints; the very evil I try to avoid, is what I do. *(If mere quality decisions could rescue mankind, the law would have been enough. Good intentions cannot save someone. The revelation of what happened to us in Christ's death is what brings faith into motion to liberate from within. Faith is not a decision we make to give God a chance, faith is realizing our inclusion in what happened on the Cross and in the resurrection of Christ! See Rom 3:27.)*

7:20 If I do the things I do not want to do, then it is clear that I am not evil, but that I host sin in my body against my will.

7:21 It has become a predictable principle; I desire to do well, but my mere desire cannot escape the evil presence that dictates my actions.

7:22 The real person that I am on the inside delights in the law of God. *(The law proves to be consistent with my inner make-up.)*

7:23 There is another law though, *(foreign to my design)* the law of sin, acti-vating and enrolling the members of my body as weapons of war against the law of my mind. I am held captive like a prisoner of war in my own body.

7:24 The situation is absolutely desperate for humankind; is there any-one who can deliver me from this death trap?

7:25 Thank God, this is exactly what he has done through Jesus Christ our Leader; he has come to our rescue! I am finally freed from this conflict between the law of my mind and the law of sin in my body. *(If I was left to myself, the best I could do was to try and serve the law of God with my mind, but at the same time continue to be enslaved to the law of sin in my body. Compromise could never suffice.)*

8:1 Now the decisive conclusion is this: in Christ, every bit of condemning evidence against us is cancelled. *("Who walk not after the flesh but after the spirit." This sentence was not in the original text, but later copied from verse 4. The person who added this most probably felt that the fact of Paul's declaration of mankind's innocence had to be made subject again to a person's conduct. Religion under the law felt more comfortable with the condition of personal contribution rather than the conclusion of what faith reveals. The "in Christ" revelation is key to God's dealing with mankind. It is the PIN-code of the Bible. [See 1 Cor 1:30 and Eph 1:4].)*

8:2 The law of the Spirit is the liberating force of life in Christ. This leaves me with no further obligation to the law of sin and death. Spirit has superseded the sin enslaved senses as the principle law of our lives. *(The law of the spirit is righteousness by faith vs the law of personal effort and self righteousness which produces condemnation and spiritual death which is the fruit of the DIY tree.)*

8:3 The law failed to be anything more than an instruction manual; it had no power to deliver us from the strong influence of sin holding us hostage in our own bodies. God disguised himself in his son in this very domain where sin ruled us, in flesh. The body he lived and conquered in was no different to ours. Thus sin's authority in the human body was condemned. *(Hebrews 4:15, As High Priest he fully identifies with us in the context of our frail human life. Having subjected it to close scrutiny, he proved that the human frame was master over sin. His sympathy with us is not to be seen as excusing weaknesses that are the result of a faulty design, but rather as a trophy to humanity. He is not an example for us but of us.)*

8:4 The righteousness promoted by the law is now realized in us. Our practical day-to-day life bears witness to spirit inspiration and not flesh domination.

8:5 Sin's symptoms are sponsored by the senses, a mind dominated by the sensual. Thoughts betray source; spirit life attracts spirit thoughts.

8:6 Thinking patterns are formed by reference, either the sensual appetites of the flesh and spiritual death, or zoe-life and total tranquillity flowing from a mind addicted to spirit *(faith)* **realities.**

8:7 A mind focused on flesh *(the sensual domain where sin held me captive)* **is distracted from God with no inclination to his life-laws. Flesh** *(self-righteousness)* **and spirit** *(faith righteousness)* **are opposing forces.** *(Flesh no longer defines you; faith does!)*

8:8 It is impossible for those immersed in flesh to at the same time accommodate themselves to the opinion, desire and interest of God.

8:9 But you are not ruled by a flesh-consciousness, *(law of works),* **but by a spirit-consciousness,** *(faith);* **God's Spirit is [1]at home in you. Anyone who does not see [2]themselves fully [1]clothed and identified in the Spirit of Christ, cannot be [2]themself.** *(If anyone does not embrace the Spirit of Christ,* *they are not themselves. The word [1]echo means to have in hand, to hold, in the sense of wearing like a garment, to possess in mind, to be closely joined to a person, and [2]hauto from heauto, reflexive relation, himself, herself, themselves. In James 1:24, "for they away from what the mirror reveals, and immediately forget what manner of person they are." Also in Romans 1:23, "Losing sight of God, made them lose sight of who they really were. In their calculation the image and likeness of God became reduced to a corrupted and distorted pattern of themselves." See also Luke 15:17, "The prodigal son came to himself ... ." [same word used here, [2]heauto].)*

8:10 The revelation of [1]Christ in you [1]declares that your body is as good as dead to sin's demands; sin cannot find any expression in a corpse. You co-died together with him. Yet your spirit is alive because of what righteousness reveals. *(The word traditionally translated, "if" [1]de ei, as in "if Christ is in you ..." can either be a condition or a conclusion, which makes a vast difference. [1]"If God be for us" (v 31) is most certainly a conclusion of the revelation of the Gospel; all of God's action in Christ confirms the fact that he is for us and not against us. Thus, [1]"because God is for us ... " in the same context this verse reveals that Christ is in us. See Galatians 1:16, "it pleased the Father to reveal his Son in me, in order that I might proclaim him in the nations." See also Romans 10:6-8, "Righteousness by faith says ... .")*

8:11 Our union with Christ further reveals that because the same Spirit that awakened the body of Jesus from the dead inhabits us, we equally participate in his resurrection. In the same act of authority whereby God raised Jesus from the dead, he co-restores your body to life by his indwelling Spirit. *(Your body need never again be an excuse for an inferior expression of the Christ life, just as it was reckoned dead in Christ's death, it is now reckoned alive in his resurrection.)*

8:12 We owe flesh nothing.

8:13 In the light of all this, to now continue to live under the sinful influences of the senses, is to reinstate the dominion of spiritual death. Instead, we are indebted to now exhibit the highest expression of life inspired by the Spirit. This life demonstrates zero tolerance to the habits and sinful patterns of the flesh.

8:14 The original life of the Father revealed in his son is the life the Spirit now [1]conducts within us. *(The word, [1]agoo, means to conduct or to lead as a shepherd leads his sheep.)*

8:15 Slavery is such a poor substitute for sonship! They are opposites; the one leads forcefully through fear while sonship responds fondly to Abba Father.

8:16 His Spirit resonates within our spirit to confirm the fact that we originate in God.

8:17 Because we are his offspring, we qualify to be heirs; God himself is our portion, we co-inherit with Christ. Since we were represented and included in his suffering we equally participate in the glory of his resurrection.

8:18 He has taken the sting out of our suffering; what seemed burdensome in this life becomes insignificant in comparison to the glory he reveals in us.

8:19 Our lives now represent the one event every creature anticipates with held breath, standing on tip-toe as it were to witness the unveiling of the sons of God. Can you hear the drum-roll?

8:20 Every creature suffered abuse through Adam's fall; they were discarded like a squeezed-out orange. Creation did not volunteer to fall prey to the effect of the fall. Yet within this stark setting, hope prevails.

8:21 All creation knows that the glorious liberty of the sons of God sets the stage for their own release from decay.

8:22 We sense the universal agony and pain recorded in history until this very moment.

8:23 We ourselves feel the grief echo of their groaning within us while we are ready to embrace the original blueprint also of our physical stature to the full consequence of sonship. What we already now participate in as first fruits of the spirit will bloom into a full gathering of the harvest. *(The glorified physical body [Mt 17]. Also the full realization of everything reconciled in Christ. In James 1:18, "It was his delightful resolve to give birth to us; we were conceived by the unveiled logic of God, the Word of truth." We lead the exhibition of his handiwork, like first fruits introducing the rest of the harvest he anticipates.)*

8:24 For what we already experience confirms our hope and continues to fuel our expectation for what we still cannot see. In the final visible completeness of the harvest, hope has fulfilled its function.

8:25 In the meantime our expectation takes us beyond visual confirmation into a place of patient contentment.

8:26 The Spirit also sighs within us with words too deep for articulation, assisting us in our prayers when we struggle to know how to pray properly. When we feel restricted in our flesh, he supersedes our clumsy efforts and hits bulls-eye every time. *(He continues to call things which seem nonexistent as though they were! [Rom 4:17]. He is never distracted, he only sees and celebrates perfection.)*

8:27 He who scrutinizes the heart understands the intention of the spirit. His [1]intercession for the saints is consistent with the blue-print purpose of God. *("I knew you even before I fashioned you in your mother's womb" [Jer 1:5]. "Then you will know, even as you have always been known." [1 Cor 13:12]. He knows us so much better than what we know ourselves. He intercedes for us, [1]entungchano, means to hit the target with an arrow or javelin. He is not trying to persuade God about us, he persuades us about the Father! He brings our conversation back to the point; the success of the cross.)*

8:28 Meanwhile we know that the love of God causes everything to mutually contribute to our advantage. His Master Plan is announced in our

original identity. *(Called according to his purpose, **kaleo**, meaning to surname, to identify by name.)*

8:29 He pre-designed and engineered us from the start to be jointly fashioned in the same mold and image of his son according to the exact blueprint of his thought. We see the original and intended pattern of our lives preserved in his Son. He is the firstborn from the same womb that reveals our genesis. He confirms that we are the invention of God. *(We were born anew when he was raised from the dead! [1 Peter 1:3] His resurrection co-reveals our common genesis as well as our redeemed innocence. [Rom 4:25 and Acts 17:31] No wonder then that he is not ashamed to call us his brethren! We share the same origin [Heb 2:11}, and, "In him we live and move and have our being, we are indeed his offspring!" [Acts 17:28].)*

8:30 Jesus reveals that we [1]pre-existed in God; he defines us. He justified us and also glorified us. He redeemed our innocence and restored the glory we lost in Adam. *(As in Romans 3:23, 24; [1]**prooritso**, pre-defined, like when an architect draws up a detailed plan; **kaleo**, to surname, identify by name.)*

8:31 All these things point to one conclusion, God is for us! Who can prevail against us?

8:32 The [1]gift of his son is the irrefutable evidence of God's heart towards us. He [2]held nothing in reserve; but freely and undeservedly [3]gave everything we could ever wish to have; this is what our [4]joint sonship is all about. *(The word [1]**paradidomi**, reflects the source of the gift, the very bosom of the Father. The word [1]**pheidomai**, means to treat leniently or sparingly. To show one's self gracious, kind, benevolent, is the word [3]**charizomai**. The word [4]**sun** (pronounced soon) suggests complete union. Everything we lost in Adam is again restored to us in Christ. Sin left mankind with an enormous shortfall; grace restores mankind to excellence! [Rom 3:21-24, 1Cor 2:7])*

8:33 God has [1]identified us, who can disqualify us? His [2]word is our origin. No-one can point a finger; he declared us innocent. *(The word [1]**kaleo**, means to identify by name, to surname. The word [2]**eklektos** suggests that we have our origin in God's thought; from **ek**, source, and **lego**, to communicate. He has placed us beyond the reach of blame and shame, guilt and gossip!)*

8:34 What further ground can there possibly be to condemn mankind? In his death he faced our judgment; in his resurrection he reveals our righteousness; the implications cannot be undone! He now occupies the highest seat of authority as the executive of our redemption in the throne room of God. *(See v 1, also Rom 4:25.)*

8:35 What will it take to distance us from the love of Christ? You name any potential calamity: intense pressure of the worst possible kind, cluster-phobia, persecution, destitution, loneliness, extreme exposure, life-threatening danger, or war?

8:36 Let me quote scripture to remind you, "Because of our association with you, we are reckoned as sheep to be slaughtered; we have been thoroughly slain on the day. "(*Psalm 44:22. See also Ephesians 2:5; 4:8,9; Hosea 6:2, "After two days he will revive us, on the third day he will raise us up! We have been co-crucified, co-raised and are now co-seated together with Christ!*)

8:37 On the contrary, in the thick of these things our triumph remains beyond dispute. His love has placed us above the reach of any onslaught.

8:38 This is my conviction; no threat whether it be in death or life; be it angelic beings, demon powers or political principalities, nothing known to us at this time, or even in the unknown future;

8:39 no dimension of any calculation in time or space, nor any device yet to be invented, has what it takes to separate us from the love of God demonstrated in Christ. Jesus is our ultimate authority.

9:1 What I am about to say is my honest persuasion; I am convinced beyond doubt of our inseperable union in Christ; my own conscience bears witness to this in the Holy Spirit.

9:2 In the light of mankind's inclusion and redeemed innocence, I feel such sorrow and painful longing for my fellow Jews. *(They are all equally included but they just do not see it!)*

9:3 If it could in any way profit them I would prefer myself to rather be excluded from the blessing of Christ. If my exclusion could possibly help them understand their inclusion, I would gladly offer my body as a sacrifice.

9:4 Sonship is the natural heritage of Israel; they historically witnessed the glory and covenants and the dramatic endorsement of the law; the prophetic rituals of worship and the Messianic promises belong to them.

9:5 They are the physical family of the Messiah. Yet he supersedes all our definitions; he is God, the [1]source of blessing and the ultimate announcement of everything good, for all ages. Amen! *(The word, [1]eulogetos, means blessed, from eulogeo, good word, good news, or "well done" announcement; normally translated, blessing. The Word of God reaches far beyond the boundaries of Israel, it includes every nation.)*

9:6 It is not as though their unbelief neutralized the Word of God in its effect; Israel is no longer restricted to a physical family and geographic location.

9:7 It is not the natural seed of Abraham that gives them their [1]identity, but Isaac, the faith-child. God said, "Your children's [1]identity is revealed in Isaac." *([Gen 21:12]; [1]kaleo, to surname, or to identify by name. Mankind's original identity was not preserved in the flesh, but in the Promise.)*

9:8 By this God clearly indicates that mankind's true spirit identity is revealed in faith and not in flesh. The Promise is the fuel of faith. *(The promise ignites faith. Faith gives substance to what hope sees.)*

9:9 Remember God's pledge, "In nine months time, Sarah shall have a son." *(Genesis 18:10, "according to the time of life, thus nine months; Galatians 4:4, Jesus is the fullness of time; the promise is a Person!)*

9:10 Rebecca and Isaac also conceived, consistent with the promise, to further prove the point of faith versus performance.

9:11 God spoke to Rebecca while the twins were still in the womb. Nothing distinguished them in terms of good looks or performance *(except the fact that the one would be born minutes before the other, which would give him preference according to human tradition)*. It was recorded to emphasize the principle of [1]faith-identity as the ultimate value above any preference according to the flesh. *(The word often translated as "election" is the word [1]ekloge, from ek, origin, source and lego from logos, the word, see Jhn 1:1,14. Faith nullifies any ground the flesh has to boast in. Rom 3:27)*

9:12 She was told, "the elder shall serve the younger."

9:13 We would say that Esau had the raw deal; he was disliked while Jacob was favored. *(And the Lord said to her, "Two nations are in your womb, and two peoples, born of you, shall be divided; the one shall be stronger than the other; the elder shall serve the younger." [Gen 25:23].*

The two come out of the same mold; yet they represent two types of people: one who understands his true identity by faith and one who seeks to identify himself after the flesh. Again, the law of performance versus the law of faith is emphasized in order to prepare the ground for the promise-principle. Mankind's salvation would be by promise and not by performance; i.e. it would not be a reward for good behavior. No one will be justified by the tree of the knowledge of good and evil; ponero, "evil," full of hardships, annoyances and labor!)

9:14 To say that God is unfair, is to miss the point.

9:15 Moses saw the glory of God's goodness; he saw God's mercy and the kindness of his compassion. *(Even when Israel deserved his absence he promised them his presence. Moses saw the glory and goodness of God, while he hid in the cleft of the rock. [Gen 33:18, 19]. Throughout scripture the Rock represents the blueprint of mankind's original identity [Isa 51:1, Deut 32:18, Mt 16:15-18].)*

9:16 God's mercy is not a reward for good behavior; it is not a wreath given to the fastest athlete.

9:17 God employed Pharaoh as a prophetic figure to demonstrate the drama of mankind's salvation from their slavery to an inferior identity. Scripture records God's conversation with Pharaoh, (Ex 9:16) "But to show you my power working in you, I raised you up so that my Name *(revealing mankind's authentic and original identity)* **might be declared throughout all the earth."** *(Mankind's identity is not in Pharaoh's claim or some political leader's influence, but in their Maker.)*

9:18 The same act of mercy that he willingly bestows on everyone, may bless the one and harden the heart of the other.

9:19 This just doesn't sound reasonable at all! What gives God the right then to still blame anyone? Who can resist his will?

9:20 Who can dispute with God? The mold dictates the shape. *(There is only one true mold of mankind's design: the image and likeness of God.)*

9:21 The Potter sets the pace; same Potter, same clay; one vessel understands its value and another not; one realizes that it is priceless, the other seems worthless to itself.

9:22 Their sense of worthlessness has labelled them for destruction, yet God's power and passion prevail in patient endurance. *(God is not schizophrenic, having to balance out a seemingly unstable character by creating a nice guy and a bad guy: one for blessing and one for wrath! He cannot be both the Author of light and darkness; there is in him no shadow of compromise or change; no inconsistency or distortion whatsoever! [Jas 1:17, 18]. Mankind deceive themselves* *when their knowledge of their true identity becomes blurred by the flesh. "They go away and immediately forget what manner of person they are."*

Paul's noble birth carried no further significance when he discovered his spirit identity revealed in Christ. The recorded history of Israel prepares the prophetic stage of God's dealing with universal mankind. Faith and not flesh would be the medium of God's dealing with man. Flesh reduces man to the senses and the soul realm, while faith's substance reveals mankind's true spirit identity. Truth ignites faith. His patience is shown in Pharaoh: "So get your livestock under roof, everything exposed in the open fields, people and animals, will die when the hail comes down." All of Pharaoh's servants who had respect for God's word got their workers and animals under cover as fast as they could, but those who didn't take God's word seriously left their workers and animals out in the field [Ex 9:19-21]. "For good news came to us just as to them; but the message which they heard did not benefit them, because it did not meet with faith in the hearers." [Heb 4:2 RSV])

9:23 He has set the stage to exhibit the wealth of his mercy upon the vessels of value. He desires to confirm in them his original intent. *(His glory,* **doxa,** *opinion, intent.)*

9:24 Being Jewish or Gentile no longer defines us; God's faith defines us. *(He "called" us;* **kaleo,** *to identify by name, to surname.)*

9:25 Hosea voiced the heart of God when he said, "I will call a people without identity, my people, and her who was unloved, my Darling." *(Even Esau whom you said that I hated. [See v 13]. It was common among the Hebrews to use the terms "love" and "hatred" in this comparative sense, where the former implied strong positive attachment, and the latter, not positive hatred, but merely a less love, or the withholding of the expressions of affection [compare Gen 29:30-31; Lk 14:26].)*

9:26 He prophesies that the very same people who were told that they are not God's people, will be told that they are indeed the children of the living God.

9:27 Isaiah weeps for Israel: "You might feel lost in the crowd, because your numbers equal the grains of the sand of the sea, but God does not abandon the individual." Numbers do not distract God's attention from the value of the one. *("Isaiah maintained this same emphasis: If each grain of sand on the seashore were numbered and the sum labelled 'chosen of God,' They'd be numbers still, not names; salvation comes by individual realization. God doesn't just count us; he calls us by name. Arithmetic is not his focus." — The Message)*

9:28 For his word will perfect his righteousness without delay; his word is poetry upon the earth. *(Jn 1:1, 14, Rom 1:16, 17.)*

9:29 The Lord of the ¹multitudes preserved for us a Seed, to rescue us from the destruction of Sodom and Gomorrah. *(From Hebrew, ¹tzaba, (tsabaoth), a mass of people. [See note on Rom 3:10] In Genesis 18, Abraham intercedes for Sodom and Gomorrah, "If there perhaps are 50 righteous people, will you save the city on their behalf?" He continues to negotiate with God, until* *he's down to "perhaps ten?" " ... there was none righteous, no not one ... ." The remnant represents the one Seed that would rescue the mass of humanity! In Romans 5:17, "one man's obedience and act of righteousness, surpasses the effect of a multitude of sins!" If (spiritual) death saw the gap in one sin, and grabbed the opportunity to dominate mankind in Adam, how much more may we now seize the advantage to reign in righteousness in this life through that one act of Christ, who declared us innocent by his grace. Grace is superior in authority to the transgression! The single grain of wheat did not abide alone! [See John 12:24] Romans 5:18-19 states, "The conclusion is clear: it took just one offense to condemn mankind; one act of righteousness declares the same mankind innocent! The disobedience of the one exhibits humanity as sinners; the obedience of another exhibits humanity as righteous!")*

9:30 This means that the nations that stood outside and excluded, the very Gentiles who did not pursue righteousness through religious discipline of any kind, have stumbled upon this treasure of faith.

9:31 Yet Israel who sought to achieve righteousness through keeping the law, based upon their own discipline and willpower, have failed to do so.

9:32 How did they fail? Faith seemed just too good to be true. They were more familiar and felt more comfortable with their own futile efforts than what they did with faith. Their faith identity *(reflected in Christ)* **was a stone of offense.**

9:33 The conclusion of the prophetic reference pointed towards the rock as the spirit identity of human life. In Messiah, God has placed his testimony of humanitiy's identity in front of their eyes, in Zion, the center of their religious focus, yet, blinded by their own efforts to justify themselves, they tripped over him. But those who recognized him by faith, as the Rock from which they were hewn, are freed from the shame of their sense of failure and inferiority. *(See Deuteronomy 32:18, "you have forgotten the Rock that birthed you...", and in Isaiah 51:1, "Look to the Rock from which you were hewn." It is only in him that humanity will discover what they are looking for. "Who is the son of man?" Mankind's physical identity is defined by their spiritual origin, the image and likeness of God, "I say you are Petros, you are Mr Rock, a chip of the old block! [See Matthew 16:13-19]. Mankind's origin and true identity is preserved and revealed again in the Rock of Ages. The term, "rock" in those days represented what we call the "hard drive" in computer language; the place where data is securely preserved for a long time. Rock fossils carry the oldest data and evidence of life.)*

10:1 God knows how my heart aches with deep and prayerful longing for Israel to realize their salvation.

10:2 I have been there myself. I know their zeal and devotion; their problem is not their passion, but their ignorance.

10:3 They are tirelessly busy with their own efforts to justify themselves while blatantly ignoring the fact that God already justified them in Christ.

10:4 Christ is the conclusion of the law, everything the law required of mankind was fulfilled in him; he thus represents the righteousness of the human race, based upon faith *(and not personal performance).*

10:5 Moses is the voice of the law; he says that a person's life is only justified in their doing what the law requires.

10:6 But faith finds its voice in something much closer to a person than their most disciplined effort to obey the law. Faith understands that Christ is no longer a distant promise; neither is he reduced to a mere historic hero. He is mankind's righteousness now! Christ is no longer hidden somewhere in the realm of heaven as a future hope. For the Jews to continue to ask God to send the Messiah is a waste of time! That is not the language of faith.

10:7 Faith knows that the Messiah is not roaming somewhere in the region of the dead. "Who will descend into the abyss to bring Christ back from the dead," is not the language of faith. *(Those who deny the resurrection of Christ would wish to send someone to go there and confirm their doubts, and bring back final proof that Jesus was not the Messiah. Faith announces a righteousness that reveals that humankind has indeed been co-raised together with Christ; the testimony of the risen Christ is confirmed in the heart and life of every believer.)*

10:8 Faith-righteousness announces that every definition of distance in time, space, or hostility has been cancelled. Faith says, "The Word is near you. It is as close to you as your voice and the conviction of your heart." We publicly announce this message *(because we are convinced that it belongs to everyone).*

10:9 Now your salvation is realized! Your own [1]words echo God's voice. The unveiling of the masterful act of Jesus forms the words in your mouth, inspired by the conviction in your heart that God indeed raised him from the dead. *(In his resurrection, God co-raised us [Hos 6:2]. His resurrection declares our innocence [Rom 4:25]. Salvation is not reduced to a recipe or a "sinners prayer" formula; it is the spontaneous inevitable conversation of a persuaded heart! To confess,* [1]*homologeo, homo, the same thing + logeo, to say)*

10:10 Heart-faith confirms the fact of mankind's righteousness and ignites the kind of conversation consistent with salvation. *(He restored us to blameless innocence! It is impossible not to boldly announce news of such global consequence [Isa 40:9].)*

10:11 Scripture declares that whosoever believes in Christ *(to be the fulfill-*

ment of the promise of God to redeem mankind) will ¹not be ashamed *(²hesitant)* to announce it. *([See Isa 28:16] These two Hebrew words, ²cush, to make haste, and [Isa 49:23] ¹bush, to be ashamed, look very similar and were obviously confused in some translations—the Greek from Hebrew translation. The Septuagint was the Scriptures Paul was familiar with and there the word was translated from the word ¹bush.)*

10:12 Nothing distinguishes the Jew from the Greek when it comes to the generosity of God. He responds with equal benevolence to everyone who sees themselves identified in him *(they realize that God defines them and not their cultural identity.)*

10:13 Salvation is to understand that every person's ¹true identity is revealed in Christ. *(Whosoever shall ¹call upon the Name of the Lord shall be saved; ¹epikaleomai, to entitle; to identify by name, to surname.)*

10:14 How is it possible to convince people of ¹their identity in him while they do not believe that he represents them? How will they believe if they remain ignorant about who they really are? How will they understand if the Good News of their inclusion is not announced? *(The word, ¹epikaleomai, traditionally translates as "to call upon," from **kaleo**, which literary means to surname, or to identify by name. This is also the root word in **ekklesia**, with **ek** being a preposition that denotes origin, and **kaleo**. In the context of Matthew 16 where Jesus introduces this word, he reveals that the son of man is indeed the son of God, "I say to you Simon, son of Jonah, you are **Petros** [Rock] and upon this **petra** I will build my **ekklesia**!" [See note on Rom 9:33].)*

10:15 What gives someone the urgency to declare these things? It is recorded in prophetic scripture, "How lovely on the mountains *(where the watchmen were stationed to witness the outcome of a war)* **are the feet of them leaping with the exciting news of victory. Because of their eyewitness encounter they are qualified to run with the Gospel of peace and announce the consequent glad tidings of good things that will benefit everyone."**

10:16 It is hard to imagine that there can yet be a people who struggle to hear and understand the good news. Isaiah says, "Lord, who has believed our report?"

10:17 It is clear then that faith's ¹source is found in the content of the message heard; the message is Christ. *(We are God's audience; Jesus is God's language! The Greek, ¹ek, is a preposition that denotes source or origin; thus, faith comes out of the word that reveals Christ. The word "Christ" appears in the best manuscripts. Herein lies the secret of the power of the gospel; there is no good news in it until the righteousness of God is revealed! [See Rom 1:17] The good news is the fact that the cross of Christ was a success. God rescued the life of our design; he redeemed our innocence. Mankind would never again be judged righteous or unrighteous by their own ability to obey moral laws! It is not about what someone must or must not do but about what Jesus has done! God now persuades everyone to believe what he knows to be true about them. [It is from faith to faith.] The prophets wrote in advance about the fact that God believes that righteousness unveils the* *life that he always had in mind for us. "Righteousness by his (God's) faith defines life." [Habakkuk 2:4].)*

10:18 Has God not given humanity a fair chance to hear? Psalm 19 says, "His words touch the entire world like the rays of the sun; nothing is hid from its heat; yes, truly their resonance resounded in all the earth, and their voice unto the ends of the earth."

10:19 I cannot understand how Israel could be so blind as to miss the Messiah in their midst. First it was Moses who predicted that God would provoke them to jealousy with a mass of people who are the nobodies in their estimation; a seemingly senseless bunch of people will steal the show to the disgust of Israel. *("They have stirred me to jealousy with what is no god; they have provoked me with their idols. So I will stir them to jealousy with those who are no people; I will provoke them with a foolish nation." [Deut 32:21 RSV])*

10:20 Then Isaiah in no uncertain terms hears God say, "I was stumbled upon by them who did not even bother to seek me, I became obvious to a people who did not pursue me."

10:21 "Yet My hands were continually hovering over Israel in broad daylight beckoning them, while their [1]unbelief and negative and [2]contradictory conversation caused them to blatantly ignore me." *(The word, [1]apetheo, (apathy) means refusal to believe; and [2]antilego means contradictory conversation. [See Isa 65:1, 2].)*

11:1 I want to make it clear that I am not saying that God rejected Israel, my own life bears witness to that, and I am as Jewish as you can get; you can trace me back to Benjamin and Abraham.

11:2 God did not push his people aside; his reference is his knowledge of them before they rejected him. Scripture accounts occasions where God had abundant reason to abandon Israel. Elijah hits out against them and lists their sins to persuade God to utterly cast them off. *(proginosko - to know in advance.)*

11:3 "Lord, they butchered your prophets, and undermined your provision through the sacrificial altar; I am the only one left and scared to death." *(1 Kings 19:14.)*

11:4 Yet God answers him in a completely different tone, "You are counting wrong, you are not alone; I have seven times a thousand on reserve who have not bowed the knee to Baal." *(They have not exchanged me for a foreign owner. Seven times a thousand refers to an innumerable amount and not to an exact 7000 people. The Hebrew word "Baal" means owner, husband or master [1 Kings 19:18].)*

11:5 Thus even in today's context, God's original word of grace has preserved a remnant of much larger proportion than what we can number. *(The word, ekloge, from ek, a preposition denoting source or origin, + logos, word or logic, thus translated as the "original word." Traditionally this is translated as "election.")*

11:6 Grace cannot suggest debt or obligation at the same time. The word grace can only mean what it says. The same argument goes for mankind's good works; if salvation or any advantage for that matter is to be obtained according to prescribed regulations of conduct, then that's it. No amount of grace can change the rules! Grace means grace and work means work.

11:7 The very thing Israel sought to obtain through their diligent labor they failed to get; yet those who embraced grace as God's original intent hit the bull's eye every time, leaving the rest groping around in the dark like blindfolded archers. *(eklego: the original reasoning, logic, word.)*

11:8 Isaiah said that God has given them a spirit of slumber, causing their eyes and ears not to function. This drowsiness seems to prevail even to this day. *(Unbelief and religious ritual are blindfolds. "And the Lord said, this people draw near to me with their mouth and honor me with their lips but remove their hearts and minds far from me, and their fear and reverence for me are a commandment of men that is learned by repetition ... ." [Isa 29:10, 13])*

11:9 David sees how the very table of blessing has become a stumbling block to them through their ignorance. The table of the Lord is the prophetic celebration of the sacrificed Lamb, where God himself provides redemption according to the promise; yet therein they were trapped and snared and they stumbled by their own unbelief. Now their only reward is the table they set for themselves. *([See Ps 69]. Commentary by John Gill: "... the table may be called an altar." 'You put unclean bread on my altar. And you* *say, 'How have we made it unclean?' By your saying, the table of the Lord is of no value [Mal 1:7].*

The sacrifices offered up upon "the table;" their meat offerings and drink offerings, and all others, likewise the laws concerning the differences of meats and indeed the whole ceremonial law which lay in meats and drinks and such like things; now the Jews are placing their justifying righteousness before God, in the observance of these rites and ceremonies, and imagining that by these sacrifices their sins are really expiated and atoned for; they neglected and submitted not to the righteousness of Christ, but went about to establish their own so that which should have led them to Christ became a handwriting of ordinances against them, and rendered Christ of no effect to them. Moreover, the sacred writings, which are full of spiritual food and divine refreshment, the prophecies of the Old Testament which clearly pointed out Christ, are not understood but misapplied by them, and proved a trap, a snare, and a stumbling block to them.)

11:10 This is the penalty of their disbelief; eyes that constantly fail to focus on the fact that Christ took their burdens and now their backs are still bending to the point of breaking under the strain of their own burdens.

11:11 Does this mean that the Jews are beyond redemption? Is their stumbling permanent? No! May it never be too late for them. Their failure emphasized the inclusion of the Gentile nations. May it only prove to be their wake-up call.

11:12 If their stumbling enriched the rest of the world and their lack empowered the Gentiles, how much more significant will their realizing their completeness be?

11:13 In my capacity as a representative of the good news to the Gentiles, I will speak in such a way that the clarity of my conclusion

11:14 will provoke my own flesh-and-blood family to jealousy. I know that my words will rescue many of them.

11:15 The Gentile nations realized their inclusion in Christ in a sense at the expense of the Jews; to now also embrace the Jews in the welcome of God is to raise them from the dead.

11:16 The seed sets the pace; it sanctifies what sprouts from it. Seed produces after its kind. If the invisible root is holy so are the visible branches.

11:17 And if some of the original branches were broken off, and you Gentiles like a wild olive were grafted in to partake of the same nourishing fatness of the roots,

11:18 then there is no cause for boasting against the ignorance of the Jews because you are now suddenly better off than they are. Remember, the roots sustain the branches, and not the other way round!

11:19 There is no point in thinking that in order to accommodate you, God had to first break off the Jewish branches.

11:20 Their unbelief was their loss; your faith is your gain.

11:21 God could do them no favors just because they were the natural branches; neither does God now owe you any special privileges.

11:22 Both God's goodness as well as his decisiveness are based on his integrity; unbelief is not tolerated, not in them, neither will it be tolerated in you. His favor is not to be taken for granted; instead, continue to embrace and appreciate his goodness with gratitude.

11:23 The moment Israel turns from their unbelief, God is ready to immediately graft them back into the tree.

11:24 You were cut out of the unfruitful olive tree and were grafted into the stock of the original tree. How much more will these natural branches be grafted again into their original identity.

11:25 Do not be ignorant then of the mystery of their temporal exclusion; their blindness opened your eyes to the fullness of God's plan for the whole world.

11:26 Once the nations realize the full extent of their inclusion, then all Israel shall also be saved. Just as it is written prophetically, "There shall come a Deliverer out of Zion; he shall turn ungodliness away from Jacob.

11:27 For this is my covenant with them that I shall take away their sins." (*"And as a Savior he will come to Zion, turning away sin from Jacob, says the Lord." [Isa 59:20] "And as for me, this is my agreement with them, says the Lord: my spirit which is on you, and my words which I have put in your mouth will not depart from your mouth, or from the mouth of your children, or from the mouth of your children's children, says the Lord, from now and for the ages to come." [Isa 59:21]*)

11:28 In your estimation they appear to be enemies of the gospel, but their Father's love for them has not changed. He knows their original worth.

11:29 For God's grace gifts and his persuasion of mankind's original identity are irrevocable. (*kaleo - to surname, to identify by name.*)

11:30 In days gone by, you did not believe God; yet in a sense Israel's unbelief opened the door for you to realize God's mercy.

11:31 Now you are returning the favor as it were; your testimony of his mercy extends an opportunity to them to turn from their unbelief and embrace mercy.

11:32 In God's calculation the mass of humanity is trapped in unbelief. This qualifies all mankind for his mercy.

11:33 I am overwhelmed by the limitless extent of the wealth of God's wisdom and the perfection of his knowledge. How we have failed to explore or fathom the conclusion of his resolve! In our clumsy efforts to find him, we have completely lost track of God.

11:34 Who inspired his thought? Who sat in council with him?

11:35 Is God indebted to anyone?

11:36 Everything originates in him; finds both its authentic expression and ultimate conclusion in him. His opinion rules the ages. We cannot but agree with our yes and awe. Amen.

12:1 Live consistent with [1]who you really are, inspired by the loving kindness of God. My [2]brothers, the most practical expression of worship is to [3]make your bodies available to him as a living sacrifice; this pleases him more than any religious routine. He desires to find visible, individual expression in your person. *(The word, [1]parakaleo, comes from para, a preposition indicating close proximity, a thing proceeding from a sphere of influence, with a suggestion of union of place of residence, to have sprung from its author and giver, originating from, denoting the point from which an action originates, intimate connection; and kaleo, meaning to identify by name, to surname. Jesus introduces the Holy Spirit in the same capacity: parakletos, meaning close companion, kinsman [John 14:16]. The word, [2]adelphos, comes from a, as a connective particle, and delphos, meaning womb. Commonly translated as brother. [See Heb 2:11] The word, [3]paristemi, means to exhibit, to present. In the context of the New Testament, the sacrificial system no longer involves dead animals, but living people. "You died in his death and are now alive to God" [Rom 6:11].)*

12:2 Do not allow [1]current religious tradition to mold you into its pattern of reasoning. Like an inspired artist, give attention to the detail of God's desire to find expression in you. Become acquainted with perfection. To [2]accommodate yourself to the delight and good pleasure of him will transform your thoughts afresh from within. *(The word, [1]aion, is traditionally translated as "do not be conformed to this world." Actually aion points to a period of time of specific influence. In the context of this writing, Paul refers to the religious traditional influence of his day. The word [2]euarestos, comes from eu, praiseworthy, well done + arestos, meaning to accommodate one's self to the opinions, desires, and interests of others.)*

12:3 His grace gift inspires me to say to you that your thinking must be consistent with everything that is within you according to the measure of faith that God has apportioned to every individual. [1]Let the revelation of redemption shape your thoughts. *(The word [1]sophroneo means a saved mind.)*

12:4 The parallel is clear. There are many different members in one body, yet not one competes with the other in function. Instead every individual member co-compliments the other.

12:5 In Christ, the many individuals are all part of the same body and members of one another.

12:6 Our gifts may differ in function, but his grace is the same. If it is your turn to prophesy, let faith and not a title be your inspiration.

12:7 The same goes for every aspect of ministry, whether it be serving or to give instruction,

12:8 or to just be there [1]alongside someone to remind them of their true identity; always let faith set the pace. You are [3]intertwined with your [2]gift, wrapped up in the same parcel. Lead with passion; minister mercy cheerfully. *([1]parakaleo, alongside, closest possible proximity of nearness; [2]metadidomi [see note on Rom 1:11], and [3]haplous from ha, a particle of union and* *pleko*, *to plait, braid or weave together. You cannot distance yourself from your giving! What God now has in us is gift wrapped to the world [Eph 4:11].)*

12:9 Love without any hidden agenda. Utterly detest evil; be glued to good.

12:10 Take tender care of one another with fondness and affection; esteem one another's unique value.

12:11 Do not allow any hesitation to interrupt the rhythm of your zeal; capture the moment; maintain the boiling-point intensity of spirit devotion to the Lord.

12:12 Delight yourself in the pleasure of [1]expectation; prayer prevails victoriously under pressure. *([1]elpis, to anticipate, usually with pleasure.)*

12:13 Purpose with resolve to treat strangers as saints; pursue and embrace them with fondness as friends on equal terms of fellowship. Make yourself useful in the most practical way possible.

12:14 Continue to speak well even if someone wants to take advantage of you; bless and do not blame when you feel exploited.

12:15 Do not merely act the role in someone else's gladness or grief; feel with them in genuine joy and compassion.

12:16 Esteem everyone with the same respect; no one is more important than the other. Associate yourself rather with the lowly than with the lofty. Do not distance yourself from others in your own mind. *("Take a real interest in ordinary people." — JB Phillips)*

12:17 Two wrongs do not make a right. Never retaliate; instead, cultivate the attitude to [1]anticipate only beauty and value in every person you encounter. *([1]pronoew, to know in advance.)*

12:18 You have within you what it takes to be everyone's friend, regardless of how they treat you. *(See Rom 1:16, 17. Also Mt 5:44, 45.)*

12:19 Do not bother yourselves to get even, dear ones. Do not let anger or irritation distract you; [1]that which we have in common with one another *(righteousness)* **must set the pace. Scripture confirms that the Lord himself is the [1]revealer of righteousness.** *([1]ekdikeo, from ek, a preposition denoting origin, and dikeo, two parties finding likeness in one another. That which originates in righteousness sets the pace in every relationship.)*

12:20 "If your enemy is hungry, feed him; if he is thirsty, give him something to drink." These acts of kindness will certainly rid your enemy of the dross in his mind and win him as a friend. *(A refiner would melt metal in a crucible and intensify the process by heaping coals of fire on it [Prov 25:21, 22]. This is good strategy; be sensitive to the needs of your enemies. God sees gold in every person. Hostility cannot hide our true value. He won us while we were hostile towards him [see also Rom 5:8, 10]. His kindness led us to repentance [Rom 2:4].)*

12:21 Do not let evil be an excuse for you to feel defeated, rather seize the opportunity to turn the situation into a victory for good.

13:1 Submit to the authorities with your whole heart. Any authority only has its relevance in God. God is a God of order.

13:2 To rebel against a God ordained structure of authority is a criminal offense.

13:3 Rulers are there to encourage good behavior and frighten off any evil intention.

13:4 They represent God's desire to protect you and to do you good. The sword they carry is not for decoration; they know how to use it against evil.

13:5 Do not let fear of punishment be your motivation, rather embrace a good conscience.

13:6 The taxes you pay is to show the government that you support what they represent on God's behalf.

13:7 Fulfill all your obligations to the government, whatever the tax is that they require of you. Give them their due honor and respect.

13:8 Remain debt free; the only thing we owe the world is our love. This is the essence of the law.

13:9 Love makes it impossible for you to commit adultery, or to kill someone, or to steal from someone, speak evil of anyone, or to covet anything that belongs to someone else. Your only option is to esteem a fellow human with equal value to yourself.

13:10 Everything love does is to the advantage of another; therefore, love is the most complete expression of what the law requires.

13:11 You must understand the urgency and context of time; it is most certainly now the hour to wake up at once out of the hypnotic state of slumber and unbelief. Salvation has come.

13:12 It was [1]night for long enough; the day has arrived. Cease immediately with any action associated with the darkness of ignorance. Clothe yourself in the radiance of light as a soldier would wear his full weaponry. *(The night is far spent, [1]prokopto, as a smith forges a piece of metal until he has hammered it into its maximum length.)*

13:13 Our lives exhibit the kind of conduct consistent with the day, in contrast to the [1]parade of the night of intoxicated licentiousness and lust, with all the quarrels and jealousy it ignites. *(The word, [1]komos, refers to a nocturnal and riotous procession of half drunken and frolicsome fellows who after supper parade through the streets with torches and music in honor of Bacchus or some other deity, and sing and play before houses of male and female friends; hence used generally to describe feasts and drinking parties that are protracted late into the night and indulge in revelry.)*

13:14 By being fully [1]clothed in Christ makes it impossible for the flesh to even imagine to find any further expression or fulfillment in lust. Jesus is Lord of your life. *([1]enduo, fully immersed in the consciousness of the Christ-life, as defining you.)*

14:1 [1]Welcome those who are young in their faith with warm hospitality. Avoid controversial conversation. (*[1]proslambano, to take somebody as one's companion.*)

14:2 One may feel free to eat anything, while another believes one should only eat vegetables.

14:3 By having faith to eat anything does not qualify you to judge the one who abstains; God doesn't treat the vegetarian any differently.

14:4 You are in no position to criticize the hospitality of God; he invited both to the same table and he is well capable to uphold and establish someone who still stumbles and seems weak in faith.

14:5 One person may see more religious importance in some days while another values every day the same. Let everyone come to the full conclusion of what the day means in their own understanding.

14:6 Whoever esteems the specific importance of a certain day does so to the Lord, so does he who values every day equally. One eats while another abstains; both honor God in gratitude.

14:7 No one can live or die in isolation; our life and death touch others.

14:8 Neither can our life or death distance us from him; we remain his property.

14:9 The death Jesus died and his resurrection and the conclusion of his life now in us is the only relevance of life and death.

14:10 What qualifies you to be your brother's judge? On what grounds do you condemn your brother? All of us stand in the footprint of Christ. (*We are equally represented in him.*)

14:11 The prophet recorded what he heard God say, "My own life is the guarantee of my conviction, says the Lord, every knee shall freely bow to me in worship, and every tongue shall spontaneously [1]speak from the same God-inspired source." (*[1]exomologeo, from ek, source, origin, homo, the same and logeo, to speak, thus to speak from the same source, the same inspired persuasion, to fullty agree! [Isa 45:23] This echoes what John heard in Revelation 5:13, "Then I heard the voice of everything created in heaven, upon earth, under the earth and in the sea, all living beings in the universe, and they were singing: "To him who sits upon the throne and to the Lamb, be praise and honor, glory and might, for timeless ages!" And in Colossians 1:15-17, "Now Christ is the visible expression of the invisible God. He existed before creation began, for it was through him that everything was made, whether spiritual or material, seen or unseen. Through him, and for him, also, were created power and dominion, ownership and authority. In fact, every single thing was created through, and for him. He is both the first principle and the upholding principle of the whole scheme of creation ... ." [Phillips] Colossians 1:20, "And God purposed through him to reconcile the universe to himself, making peace through his blood, which was shed upon the Cross, in order to reconcile to himself through him all things on earth and in heaven.*

[Weymouth Translation] In Ephesians 1:9, 10, "For God had allowed us to know the secret of his plan, and it is this: he purposed in his sovereign will that all human history shall be consummated in Christ, that everything that exists in heaven or earth shall find its perfection and fulfillment in him." [Phillips Translation])

14:12 Thus the logic of God will find its personal expression in every person.

14:13 There remains no further cause for judging anyone. Rather determine that you will not allow suspicion or prejudice to snare your brother into a trap.

14:14 I am completely persuaded that in the Lord Jesus nothing is unclean in itself; it only seems unclean in someone's own religious reasoning.

14:15 But to walk in love is more important than to feed your appetite with your favorite food. Much rather lose out on a meal than lose a brother for whom Christ died. I mean Jesus sacrificed his life; for you to sacrifice a meal is no big deal.

14:16 Do not let your right to eat bring shame on Christ.

14:17 God's royal dominion is not based on food and drink regulations, but righteousness, *(likeness)* friendship *(peace)* and joy in the Holy Spirit.

14:18 This is definitely a win-win situation; God is pleased and people respect you.

14:19 Pursue whatever promotes peace and mutual encouragement.

14:20 Do not let a diet issue undo the work that God has done in someone's life. All foods are good in essence; it only becomes evil if someone causes or takes offense.

14:21 For your brother's sake, in order not to offend or tempt his weakness, it is better to not eat meat or drink wine in his presence.

14:22 At the end of the day, it is your own belief that matters most before God; do what your heart approves of without allowing guilt to interfere with your joy.

14:23 Don't let doubt dictate what you eat; whatever is not prompted by faith is reduced to flesh, if faith does not inspire you; you miss the point.

15:1 We who are strong in faith are obliged to lift up those who are weak, to seek their advantage and not our own.

15:2 We are to please others and consider their good and benefit.

15:3 For Christ was not in it for himself, but for us. It is written about him, that he took the full blow of the reproach and insults directed at us.

15:4 Whatever was written about him includes and represents us. We take instruction and encouragement from his patience, while Scripture is our close companion to remind us of our true spiritual identity. We anticipate the future with delight.

15:5 God's patience and reflection of who we really are transmits in us like-mindedness toward one another according to the pattern of Christ Jesus.

15:6 The opinion of God, the Father of our Lord Jesus Christ, speaks one universal language in us inspired by the same passion.

15:7 This gives us all the more reason to embrace one another in friendship with the same warmth wherewith Christ embraced us into the welcome of God.

15:8 I am convinced that the ministry of Jesus Christ was confirmation to the circumcised Jews of the truth of God's promises to their fathers.

15:9 So also will the Gentile nations glorify God for his mercy towards them. David prophesied the resonance and echo of praise in the Gentile nations who would discover their true identity in his name. *(See also Ps 22:27)*

15:10 Again scripture reveals in Deuteronomy 32:43 that the Gentiles will join in celebration as they too are co-revealed as his people. *(See context of Deut 32)*

15:11 Yet again in Psalm 117:1 the Gentiles are exhorted to give God praise and to join in the universal applause of all the peoples of the earth.

15:12 The prophet Isaiah sees the root of Jesse who shall rise out of the ground where it was cut off, to reign over the Gentiles; he will win their trust. *(Isa 11:1,10)*

15:13 God who is the engineer of expectation fills you to the brim with tranquil delight. The dynamic of the Holy Spirit causes faith to exceed any possible hesitation in hope.

15:14 I am completely persuaded about you, my brothers, that you are able to mutually instruct one another in the full measure of the knowledge of everything that is good in you.

15:15 God's gift of grace is the motivation of my writing to you; I urge you to remember your [1]allotted portion in life. *(The word, [1]**meros**, means form or allotted portion; note the word translated as "sin" is **hameros**, which means to be* *without form, without your allotted portion. Every sin springs thus from someone's sense of unfulfillment and lack, due to ignorance concerning those things which rightfully belong to them, their true spiritual identity, their redeemed innocence, and their participating in the Divine nature which is their inheritance in Christ.)*

15:16 It is because of Jesus Christ that I am in the people business. I occupy this priestly office representing the goodness of God to [1]the masses of humanity persuading them to see how presentable and approved they are to God in the Holy Spirit. *(The word [1]ethnos, means the masses of non-Jewish people, gentiles)*

15:17 Because of who I am in Christ Jesus, I have taken a bold stand before God.

15:18 I could entertain you with all the details of my personal adventures, yet all I desire to communicate is how actively Christ worked through my words to grab the attention of the nations.

15:19 The message was confirmed in every sign and miracle in the power of the Holy Spirit. Thus, I went full circle from Jerusalem to Illyricum proclaiming the glad tidings of Christ in its most complete context. *(Taking Jerusalem as a center, Paul preached not only in Damascus and Arabia, but in Syria, in Asia Minor, in all of Greece, in the Grecian Islands, and in Thessaly and Macedonia. Illyricum was a country of Europe extending from the Adriatic Gulf to Pannonia; it extended from the river Arsia to the river Drinius thus including Liburnia on the west and Dalmatia on the east. It now forms part of Croatia, Bosnia, Istria, and Slavonia.)*

15:20 I have placed such fond value on the fact that I could pioneer the glad tidings in many of these areas without building on someone else's interpretation of Christ.

15:21 Isaiah prophesied that, "Those who have never been told about him, will be startled to see him clearly; even though they have never heard of him, they will understand his message." *(The message of truth speaks a global language. Paul says that the open statement of the truth, which is the Word made flesh in us in the mirror reflection of Christ, appeals to everyone's conscience [2 Cor 4:2]. "Our lives are letters known and read by all." [2 Cor 3:2])*

15:22 Now you know why it took me so long to finally get to you.

15:23 There seems to be no more room for pioneering work in these regions, after these many years I can finally fulfill my dream.

15:24 I purpose to journey all the way through Italy to Spain, but it is with great delight that I look forward to meeting with you first and enjoy a rich measure of fellowship that will again propel me onward.

15:25 I am on my way to Jerusalem to encourage the saints.

15:26 The believers in Greece, all the way from Macedonia as well as those in Achaia, have prepared a gift with great delight to bring relief to their Jewish brothers in Jerusalem who are struggling financially.

15:27 They feel indebted to them since they share freely in their spiritual wealth.

15:28 As soon as I have delivered their harvest officially, I will depart to Spain via you.

15:29 I know that my coming to you will be like a cargo ship [1]filled to the brim with the blessing of everything that the Gospel of Christ communicates. (*[1]pleroma means those things with which a ship is filled, freight, merchandise, etc.*)

15:30 Being co-identified with you as members of a godly family through our Lord Jesus Christ and feeling the same spiritual love-bond toward one another, we are prayer partners before God joined in urgent passion.

15:31 Labor fervently in prayer with me that I will be rescued from the unbelievers in Judea, and also that my service to the saints in Jerusalem will be favorably received.

15:32 Through the pleasure of God's purpose I will arrive in Rome in joy so that we may be mutually refreshed in one another's company.

15:33 God who sustains us in oneness and [1]peace is with every one of you. Amen. (*The word, [1]eirene, is "peace" from eiro, meaning to join like the "swallow tail" joint in carpentry, which is the strongest joint in carpentry.*)

The names of 37 individual believers are personally honored in this chapter of salutation. Seven home churches are also specifically mentioned, five in Rome and two in Corinth. Since Paul never visited Rome before, these people were all acquaintances, converts, fellow prisoners, or travel companions of his before they moved to Rome.

Since Prisca and Aquilla originally came from Rome (Acts 18:2, 26 and 1 Cor 16:19), they possibly purposefully returned there to start or strengthen the ekklesia together with a strong team of believers. Their strategy was to scatter several home-fellowships throughout the city. This is reflected in Paul's letter to the Corinthians where he says, "Our expectation is that as your faith increases, our field amongst you will be greatly enlarged so that we may preach the gospel also in lands beyond you." (2 Cor 10:15, 16)

16:1 I would like to introduce Phoebe to you, she is our sister and serves the ekklesia in Corinth located in the port of Cenchreae.

16:2 Welcome her with appropriate saintly hospitality in the Lord. Support her and her business in every possible way you can. I am one of many who have greatly benefitted from her care and practical help.

16:3 Warmly embrace Prisca and Aquilla, my business partners in the Lord.

16:4 They are respected in all the Gentile churches for their unselfish lives. They have risked their own necks for me.

16:5 Salute the ekklesia in their house. Give my dear friend Epaenetus a warm hug from me. He represents the whole of Asia to me since he was my first convert there.

16:6 Miriam must also be mentioned; I remember how relentlessly she exhausted herself for others.

16:7 Embrace my cousins Andronicus and June who were in prison with me. I hold them in high regard as ambassadors for Christ; they are my seniors in him.

16:8 Hug Amliatus, my lovely friend in the Lord.

16:9 Then there is Urbanos, my co-worker in Christ, as well as my dear friend Stachys.

16:10 Acknowledge Apelles, a true veteran in Christ; honor the household of believers in the home of Aristobulus.

16:11 Say a big hello to cousin Herodian; greet the believers in the Narcissus home.

16:12 Salute Tryphena and Tryphosa whose work in the Lord bears testimony to their diligence; also my dear friend Persis who works so tirelessly.

16:13 I also remember Rufus as an outstanding worker in the Lord, and salute his mother who has become a mother to me.

16:14 I embrace Asyncritus, Phlegon, Herman, Patrobas, Hermes and all the family in fellowship with them.

16:15 Warmly greet Philologus and Julia, Nereus and his sister, as well as Olympas and all the saints in their fellowship.

16:16 Our friendship is sacred. The ekklesia of Christ here in Corinth salutes you.

16:17 Consistent with who you really are my brothers, be alert to avoid anything that causes disunion or offense, contrary to the teaching that you have become acquainted with.

16:18 For there are those who are not addicted to our Lord Jesus Christ but, prompted rather by the hidden agenda of their own fleshly appetites, they use their clever manipulation of words and eloquent speech to deceive the emotionally unstable.

16:19 Your [1]obedience *(faith-focus)* has become known everywhere. I am so happy for you; still, I desire for you to be wisely and exclusively acquainted with that which is good and [2]innocent *(unmixed)* of evil. *(Paul's mission is to bring about the obedience prompted by faith [Rom 1:5, 16:26]. The word, [1]upoakouo, is translated as obedience or accurate hearing; and [2]akeraios as unmixed, innocent.)*

16:20 God who is the author of our peace shall quickly and utterly trample [1]Satan, doing it with your feet. Your victory is realized in the revelation of the grace of our Lord Jesus Christ, and echoed *(personalized)* in your amen. *(We are the body of Christ. God desires to demonstrate his reign of peace in us by confirming satan's defeat in our practical day to day experience. The defeat of [1]accusation is celebrated in what grace communicates. The word, [1]satanos, means accuser. The law of faith defeated the law of works!)*

16:21 Timothy my co-laborer greets you affectionately; also Luke, and Jason and Sosipater who are fellow Jews, salute you kindly.

16:22 I, Tertius, who wrote this epistle, acknowledge you in the Lord.

16:23 My host, Gaius, in whose house the church meets, sends you his greetings. Then there is Erastus, the city chief who greets you, so does Brother Quartos. *(See Acts 19:29: Gaius was a travel companion of Paul, and he also mentions him in 1 Cor 1:14.)*

16:24 The grace of our Lord Jesus Christ belongs to you.

16:25 I am not talking "hear-say-theory"; I own the gospel I proclaim! This is my message! I salute God who empowers you dynamically and establishes you to be strong and immovable in the face of contradiction. Jesus Christ is the disclosure of the very mystery that was concealed in silence before [1]time or human [2]history were recorded. *(Titus 1:2 This is the* *life of the [1]ages which was anticipated for generations; the life of our original design announced by the infallible resolve of God before [2]time or space existed. (Mankind's union with God is the original thought that inspired creation. The word, [1]aionios, speaks of ages. Paul speaks of God's mind made up about us, before the ages, which is a concept in which eternity is divided up into various periods, the shorter of which are comprehended in the longer. The word, [2]xronos, means a measured duration or length of time; kairos is a due, or specific moment of time. This was before the ages or any measure of calendar time existed, before the creation of the galaxies and constellations. There exists a greater dimension to eternity than what we are capable of defining within the confines of space and time! God's faith anticipated the exact moment of our redeemed union with him for all eternity!*

This life was made certain before eternal time. [BBE 1949, Bible in Basic English]

Paul's gospel does not merely proclaim Christ in history; he announces Christ unveiled in human life; Christ in you! Colossians 1:27)

16:26 The mystery mirrored in [1]prophetic scripture is now unveiled. The God of the ages determined to make this mystery known in such a way that all the nations of the earth will hear and realize the [2]lifestyle that faith ignites. *(This gospel breaks the silence of the ages and reveals how God succeeded to redeem his image and likeness in mankind. [1]Isa 53:4, 5. See note on verse 19. Faith inspires an [2]obedience of spontaneity beyond duty driven obligation.)*

16:27 Jesus Christ [1]uniquely [2]articulates the [3]wisdom of God; he is the [4]conclusion of the ages. *(Uniquely, [1]monos, alone, Jesus has no competition, this one man represents the entire human race; this is the mystery of the ages. 1 Cor 2:7 We voice words of wisdom that were hidden in silence for timeless ages; a mystery unfolding God's Masterful plan whereby God would redeem his glory in mankind. 2:8 Neither the politicians nor the theologians of the day had a clue about this mystery (of mankind's association in Christ); if they did, they would never have crucified the Lord whose death redeemed our glory!*

The word, [3]sophos, means clarity, wisdom. He forever broke the silence of the ages! The words, [4]eis aion, eis indicates a point reached in conclusion, thus the conclusion of the ages. He is the [2]doxa, opinion; the logos that was before time was; the Word that became flesh and dwells within us [Jn 1:1, 14]. The incarnation (Latin, in carne, in the body) is the final trophy of the eternal logos and doxa of God. (Col 1:15 In him the image and likeness of God is made visible in human life in order that every one may recognize their true origin in him. He is the firstborn of every creature. (What darkness veiled from us he unveiled. In him we clearly see the mirror reflection of our original life. The son of his love gives accurate evidence of his image in human form. God can never again be invisible!) Col 2:3 In Christ the complete treasure of all wisdom and knowledge is sourced. Col 2:9 It is in Christ that God finds an accurate and complete expression of himself, in a human body!

(While the expanse cannot measure or define God, his exact likeness is displayed in human form. Jesus proves that human life is tailor-made for God!)

Col 2:10 Jesus mirrors our completeness and [1]endorses our [2]true identity. He is "I am" in us. (Isn't it amazing that God packaged completeness in "I am," mirrored in you! Delay is outdated! The word, [1]arche, means chief in rank. The word, [2]exousia, is often translated as meaning authority; its components are, ek + eimi, originating out of "I am." The days are over where our lives were dictated to under the rule of the law of performance and an inferior identity. [See Col 1:19] The full measure of everything God has in mind for a person, indwells him.)

Paul's persuasion is firmly founded in his understanding of the success of the cross. In the economy of God, Jesus represents the human race. Every possible contradiction is filtered through this perspective.

In this letter Paul addresses several concerns regarding reports of divisions amongst the believers, a sexual scandal in their ranks and questions regarding marriage, diets and money.

In the first four chapters he takes his time to reinforce their faith in the finished work of the cross as the only valid reference to their lives.

In chapters 12 and 14, he brings clarity regarding the charismatic gifts.

Then he highlights the essence of the gospel in the most beautiful love poem in chapter 13. For many years this chapter was read and preached in a typical window-shopping frame of mind.

In Paul's gospel this mind-set is completely reversed; he proclaims that what God has done in Christ actually unveils the life of our design. Love celebrates the completeness of all that God has always had in mind for us. Love is not some prize one has to labor for; love mirrors who you are! What we perceived in prophetic glimpses is now concluded in completeness! (1 Cor 13:9, 10)

In chapter 15, he emphasizes that the resurrection revelation is the theme and conclusion of the message he preaches.

Then he concludes in chapter 16:14 with, "Agape is your genesis. Loving everyone around you is what you are all about." (Our love for one another is awakened by God's love for us.) And in verse 22, he makes this final powerful statement: "Anyone who prefers the law above grace remains under the curse mentality. Jesus Christ has come; grace is the authority of his Lordship; we are so fond of him! He is the Messiah the world has been waiting for. (The Aramaic word, maranatha, means, our Lord has come!)

1:1 My name is Paul, the ministry of Jesus Christ is the mandate of my life according to God's delightful purpose. Brother Sosthenes is my colleague. *([1]He was formerly the chief ruler of the synagogue at Corinth. [Acts 18:17])*

1:2 I address this writing to the [1]ekklesia of God in Corinth. You have been restored to the harmony of your original design, made holy in Christ Jesus; no wonder then that you are surnamed Saints. You are in association with all those who have discovered their true identity in Jesus Christ everywhere in every location; he is the head of this union; his name relates us to one another in a global family. *(Eph 3:15 " ... from whom every family in heaven and on earth is named." [1]Church, **ekklesia**, those who have discovered their original identity; from **ek**, source, origin + **kaleo**, to surname, identify by name.)*

1:3 Grace and peace is your portion from God who is our Father and from his executive, Jesus Christ. *(Grace and peace express the sum total of every beneficial purpose of God towards us. Paul brands his gospel with these words in order to distinguish the message of the revelation of the finished work of Christ as the basis to our faith from the law of Moses which restricted a person to their own efforts to justify themselves. It is a matter of grace vs reward and peace vs striving.)*

1:4 I am always so happy for you when I consider how greatly advantaged you are because of God's grace unveiled in Jesus Christ.

1:5 Your knowledge of Christ is based on so much more than hearsay; every aspect of your life gives eloquent expression to the rich reservoir of your union in him.

1:6 You certainly have the testimony of Christ evidenced in you. *(You possess full knowledge and give full expression because in you the evidence for the truth of Christ has found confirmation. — NEB)*

1:7 In [1]receiving the [2]revelation of Jesus Christ as the principal influence in your life *(his Lordship),* you prove that you lack nothing and that his grace gifts fully compliment you. *(This is in such contrast to those days when under-achievement was the rule; when you felt that you were never good enough and always lagging behind. Note: [1]**apekdechomai** is not "eagerly waiting for," but "eagerly accepting" or to welcome with hospitality; [2]**apokalupsis** is the unveiling, disclosure. I don't know why most translations always want to postpone what God has already unveiled!)*

1:8 He establishes you from start to finish; to stand [1]vindicated in your identity in the light of day as evidenced in the Lord Jesus Christ. *(The word, [1]**anegkletos**, from **ana**, upwards, **en**, in and **kaleo**, to identify by name. Jesus gives evidence to our original identity. Compare **anoche** from **ana** + **echo** in Rom 3:26)*

1:9 We are [1]surnamed by God, he is our true lineage; he is faithful and fully persuaded about our joint participation in the fellowship of sonship; we are included in everything that our Lord Jesus Christ and the Father enjoys. *(The word [1]**kaleo**, means to call or identify by name, to surname.)*

1:10 My dear fellow believers, because we are surnamed and identified in the name of our master Jesus Christ, I ¹urge you to speak with one voice, *(to say the same thing)* we share the same source as our reference; no division or any sense of distance is tolerated, which makes us a perfect match, accurately joined in the same thought and communicating the same resolve. *(The word, ¹parakaleo, is from para, a preposition indicating close proximity, a thing proceeding from a sphere of influence, with a suggestion of union of place of residence, to have sprung from its author and giver, originating from, denoting the point from which an action originates, intimate connection and kaleo, to surname.)*

1:11 Some of the believers in Chleo's fellowship told me about the controversy in your ranks; this is most disturbing!

1:12 What I was told is that you are divided into groups, where some side with Paul, others with Apollos, still others with Cephas, and even some who say, "we are the Messianic group!"

1:13 This is really ridiculous: can Christ be cut up into little relics? Was Paul crucified for you? Were you baptized into Paul's name?

1:14 Baptism is not my business or emphasis; I am glad that I only baptized Crispus and Gaius amongst you! *(Crispus was his neighbor and leader of the synagogue [see Acts 18:8]. Gaius resided at Corinth. Paul stayed with him when he wrote the Epistle to the Romans [Rom 16:23]; he was also a travel companion of Paul's [Acts 19:29].)*

1:15 I distance myself from the idea of employing baptism as a means of branding my ministry with my name! Somehow baptism has become a snare to some who wish to win members to their denomination!

1:16 O yes! Now I remember that I also baptized the family of Stephanus. *(In 1 Corinthians 16:15, the family (young and old) of Stephanus were the first converts in Achaia)*

1:17 My mandate was not about winning members for some 'Christian club' through baptism! I am commissioned to declare the good news without any strings attached; nothing to distract from the powerful effect of the revelation of the cross of Christ. *(The mystery of the cross is the revelation of mankind's inclusion in his death and resurrection [see 1 Cor 2:7].)*

1:18 To their own loss the message of the cross seems foolish to some; but to us who discover our salvation there, it is the dynamic of God.

1:19 Isaiah wrote: I will confuse the wisdom of the "so-called" wise and prove their experts wrong! *(Isa 29:14)*

1:20 God's wisdom *(revealed in the success of the cross)* puts the rest out of business! *(when it comes to real answers to the dilemma of mankind)* they have all closed shop; the philosophers, the academics, the smooth-talkers, the lot!

1:21 By suspicious scrutiny the sense-ruled world surveys the works of

God in creation and still do not recognize or acknowledge him; in sharp contrast to this, the foolishness of the message we proclaim brings God's work of redeeming his image in us into faith's focus. (*What we preach cancels every basis for boasting in personal contribution, which seems folly to the DIY systems of this world.*)

1:22 The Jews crave signs (*to confirm their doubts*) **while the Greeks revel in philosophical debate!** (*Both groups are addicted to the same soul realm.*)

1:23 The crucified Christ is the message we publicly proclaim, to the disgust of the Jews while the Greeks think we are wacky!

1:24 The dynamic of God's wisdom is the fact that both Jew and Greek are equally included and defined in Christ.

1:25 It seems so foolish that God should die mankind's death on the cross; it seems so weak of God to suffer such insult; yet their wisest schemes and most powerful display of genius cannot even begin to comprehend or compete with God in his weakest moment on the cross.

1:26 You might as well admit it, my friends; it was not your academic qualifications or your good looks or social connections that influenced God to represent you in Christ.

1:27 It is almost as if God deliberately handpicked the wacky of this world to embarrass the wise, the rejects to put to shame the noble.

1:28 The ones with no pedigree of any prominence, the "nobodies" in society, attracted God's initiative to unveil his blueprint opinion in order to redefine mankind. Thus he rendered any other social standard entirely irrelevant and inappropriate. (*Blueprint opinion, **eklegomai**, from ek, meaning origin, source, and **legomai** from **logos**, the logic of God; traditionally translated as "elect."*)

1:29 Every reason for someone's boasting in themselves dwindles into insignificance before God.

1:30 [1]Of God's doing are we in Christ. He is both the genesis and genius of our wisdom; a wisdom that reveals how righteous, sanctified and redeemed we already are in him. (*The preposition, [1]ek, always denotes origin, source. Mankind's association in Christ is God's doing. In God's economy, Christ represents us; what mankind could never achieve through personal discipline and willpower as taught in every religion, God's faith accomplished in Christ. Of his design we are in Christ; we are associated in oneness with him. Our wisdom is sourced in this union! Also, our righteousness and holiness originate from him. Holiness equals wholeness and harmony of a person's spirit, soul, and body. Our redemption is sanctioned in him. He redeemed our identity, our sanity, our health, our joy, our peace, our innocence, and our complete well-being! [See Eph 1:4]. The Knox Translation reads, "It is from him that we take our [1]origin."*)

1:31 He is our claim to fame. (*This is what Jeremiah meant when he wrote: "Let not the wise glory in their wisdom, let not the mighty glory in their might, let not* *the rich glory in their riches; but let the one who glories glory in this, that they understand and know me, that I am the Lord who practice steadfast love, justice, and righteousness in the earth; for in these things do I delight, says the Lord." Jeremiah 9:23, 24.)*

2:1 My intention in visiting you was not to engage with you in theological debate or to impress you with clever words guessing about the evidence of God.

2:2 The testimony of God is my only persuasion concerning you: Jesus Christ died your death on the cross! I can see you in no other light! *(For I determined to know nothing in you except Jesus Christ and him crucified.)*

2:3 I felt completely inadequate; you know that it was not my eloquent speech that persuaded you. I was so nervous that my whole body was trembling with stage fright!

2:4 My message was not with persuasive arguments based on secular wisdom, since my aim was ¹not to point people to me but rather to the powerful working of the Spirit in them. *(Thayer's Greek definition of ¹apodeiknumi is to point away from one's self. Previous translations of this word have often given the impression that the great, miracle-working man of God would steal the show and entertain the crowds! This was so unlike Jesus and Paul! Paul never writes about how many people he had healed and brought to faith, etc. His all-consuming concern was that the eyes of our understanding would be illuminated with the revelation of Christ in us.*

Note 2 Corinthians 10:10 [RSV], "For they say, 'His letters are weighty and strong, but his bodily presence is weak, and his speech of no account.'" Also, 2 Corinthians 11:6, "Even if I am unskilled in speaking, I am not in knowledge." — RSV)

2:5 Mankind's wise schemes of influence could never match the power of God as reference to your faith.

2:6 The words we speak resonate revelation wisdom in those who understand how perfectly redeemed they are in Christ, this wisdom supersedes every secular kind; suddenly what once seemed wise and good advice has become useless information. *(All popular programs towards improved moral behavior are now outdated. "Of God's doing are we in Christ. He is both the genesis and genius of our wisdom; a wisdom that reveals how righteous, sanctified, and redeemed we already are in him." In God's economy, Christ represents us; what mankind could never achieve through personal discipline and willpower as taught in every religion, God's faith accomplished in Christ [1 Cor 1:30].)*

2:7 We voice words of wisdom that were hidden in silence for timeless ages; a mystery unfolding God's Masterful plan whereby he would redeem his glory in human life.

2:8 Neither the politicians nor the theologians of the day had a clue about this mystery *(of mankind's association in Christ)*; if they did, they would never have crucified the Lord whose death redeemed our glory!

2:9 It is written: "What has been concealed for ages in a realm inaccessible to the senses; what no human eye could catch a glimpse of, nor their ear could even hear a whisper of, neither could the inquiring mind decipher the code of that mystery which God has already ¹fully arranged and was ready to reveal to ²those who love him." *(The exact detail of his plan to rescue his image and likeness in mankind was in place. How Jesus would represent humanity to die their death was the wisdom of God concealed. In the mind of God we were associated in Christ before the ages; this was according to God's eternal resolve. "The things that God has prepared" or* **¹hetoimatzo**, *from the oriental custom of before a king's journey sending people ahead to level the roads and make them passable. What seemed a cul-de-sac for the flesh is a royal highway for faith.*

The redemption of mankind was not to be the product of human philosophy or speculation. In Isaiah 64:4 the Hebrew word, **²ghaka**, *is used, which means to carve an image; to show by drawing or description, piercing, here translated as those who "wait upon the Lord." (In Isa 40:31, a different word is used for those who "wait" upon the Lord,* **kawa** *means to intertwine.) Paul writes in Greek when he quotes Isaiah and uses the phrase, "for those who love him." Thus, faith opens the horizon of love's mystery. It is a place where thoughts carve an impression; a place not accessible to the scrutiny of a suspicious academic or from religious guilt and a performance-based approach [see 1 Cor 3:20].)*

2:10 **These profound mysteries of God's eternal resolve are now thoroughly unveiled to us by his Spirit; nothing is hidden from him; he explores the innermost thoughts of God.**

2:11 **Just as a person's spirit knows their own thoughts beyond the public eye, even so the Spirit of God is our faith decoder to access the thoughts of God.** *(In modern technology it would be impossible to access information from a source that is not compatible with your device; or without a decoder.)*

2:12 **The Spirit proceeding from God unveils the gifts of his generosity. He has graced us with understanding so that we may know what he has always had in mind for us; this is so unlike the secular spirit of the wisdom of the world where everything has a price tag!** *(Christ is the unveiling of the mystery of God's wisdom: now we know how God redeemed our righteousness and our wholeness in Christ. In God's economy, Christ represents us; what mankind could never achieve through personal discipline and willpower as taught in every religion, God's faith accomplished in Christ. Of his design are we in Christ; we are associated in oneness with him. Our wisdom is sourced in this union! Also our righteousness and holiness originate from him.*

Holiness equals wholeness and harmony of someone's spirit, soul and body. Our redemption is sanctioned in him. He redeemed our identity, our sanity, our health, our joy, our peace, our innocence and our complete well-being! [See note on 1 Corinthians 1:30] Secular religion is the product of the spirit of this world where everything is performance based; only the heroes of the moment are acclaimed; the rest are reduced to spectators and audience.)

2:13 **The impact of our words are not confined to the familiar wisdom of the world taught by human experience and tradition, but communicated by seamless spirit resonance, ¹combining spirit with spirit.** *(The word* **sugkrinō**, *suggests a spirit compatibility; joint together fitly, compound, combine, to interpret, to compare: thus, a joining of spirit with spirit!)*

2:14 **The soulish person has no capacity to comprehend the language of**

the Spirit of God; spiritual things seem meaningless to them; they are incapable to discern that which can only be spiritually appreciated. *(A performance-based mind-set cannot access what grace communicates. It would be as impossible as trying to get airborne with a motor car. Law cannot compete with grace.)*

2:15 Those who are spiritually awakened are immediately compatible to discern all things from a spiritual *(grace)* perspective, while they themselves are free from anyone's critical scrutiny.

2:16 There is no other basis to teach from but to echo the mind of Christ; he is the Master mind personified within us!

3:1 This is ridiculous! Who am I talking to here? Are you mere spiritual infants stuck in the soul-ruled mode of the flesh, reduced to baby-talk? *(Cooing sentimental gibberish about who your favorite preacher is instead of discovering who you are in Christ!)*

3:2 I fed you with milk and now after all this time it seems that you have no appetite nor capacity for the meat of the gospel. While you remain on the milk diet of the soul-ruled realm of the flesh *(knowing Christ merely from a human point of view [see 2 Cor 5:16]),* you are unable to digest the meat message of what has been concluded and revealed in your union with Christ! *(There is a huge difference between seeing Christ historically and sentimentally and realizing the revelation of the Gospel. This is the mystery of grace: God reveals us in Christ. He associated us in Christ before time began. Jesus did not die as an individual. He died our death and we were raised together with him.)*

3:3 Your heated debates and divisions prove that you are completely missing the point of the Gospel! You behave like any other spiritually unenlightened person, religiously obsessed with petty party politics while missing the essence of the message.

3:4 Can you not see that it is not about Paul or Apollos or any teacher you wish to associate with? We are not here to play the one off against the other, in a desperate attempt to win your vote to join our "group." *(Acts 19:1)*

3:5 Both Apollos and I are on the same assignment: we are here for you, to influence your faith to discover yourself in Christ. Every individual is equally gifted in him. *(See verses 21 and 22)*

3:6 I have planted, by bringing the gospel to you in the first place, then Apollos watered the seed in his ministry to you; but God causes the Christ life to ignite and expand in you.

3:7 If all we succeeded to do was to attach you to us as individuals, then we have failed you; the one who plants is not more important than the one who waters; it is not about us, it is about you realizing God's work within you. *(Our ministry has only one objective: to reveal Christ in you! See Paul's urgency in Philippians 2:12, "not only in my presence but much more in my absence, discover the full extent of your own salvation: it is God working in you both to will and to do!" This "working out your own salvation" has nothing in common with the duty driven, willpower-restricted law of works system. It is discovering his working in you; energizing you with both the desire and capacity to give expression to him.)*

3:8 Our individual assignment does not place the one above the other; we have exactly the same mission; how we succeed or fail in that is to our own account.

3:9 We are co-employed by God. You are God's agricultural field; or in another context, you are his building and he is the architect and engineer of the life of your design.

3:10 His grace is the only reference for my skill; his gift qualifies me *(I did not earn my certificate as Master Builder at a university as a reward to my excellence!).* **The faith foundation that I have laid in your lives gives evidence to that. So let the next person take extra caution to build consistent with what grace communicates.** *(Grace alone defines and inspires New Testament ministry.)*

3:11 Jesus Christ is the only foundation; nothing that anyone else can possibly teach you can replace him.

3:12 Imagine the contrast in building materials, one builds with gold, silver and precious stones, while another uses wood, hay and stubble. *(By comparison, the teaching of the cross and its glorious effect in the believer's life is like building with gold, silver, and precious stones, whereas the wisdom of this world system based upon religious good works and not faith is like building with wood, hay, and stubble which is fuel for fire!)*

3:13 Everyone's work shall be tested in the scrutiny of real life; it shall be made apparent as in broad daylight just as gold is tested in fire: what you teach will either burn like stubble or shine like gold. *(The revelation of mankind's co-crucifixion and co-resurrection with Christ is the gold of the gospel!)*

3:14 If what you teach is based on the revelation of the success of the cross it will certainly be confirmed in the heat of contradiction.

3:15 Obviously to witness the fruit of one's labor go up in smoke would be devastating, even though you escape with your own life!

3:16 Realize that your life is God's building; his sanctuary, designed for his permanent abode. His Spirit inhabits you! *(He designed every cell in your body to accommodate and express him.)*

3:17 Just like fire would burn away the dross, any defilement of God's temple would be destroyed in order to preserve human life as his permanent sanctuary. *(See verse 15)*

3:18 Why fool yourself? What is esteemed as wise according to popular Jewish sentiment is folly. There is no compromise when it comes to wisdom; the only wisdom that matters is what God deems wise, even if it seems foolishness to the reasoning of typical religion. Much rather be ridiculed by religion than esteemed as wise by them. *(The dynamic of God's wisdom is the fact that both Jew and Greek are equally represented and defined in Christ. It seems so foolish that God should die mankind's death on the cross; it seems so weak of God to suffer such insult; yet mankind's wisest schemes and most powerful display of genius cannot even begin to comprehend or compete with God in his weakest moment on the cross [1 Cor 1:24-25]. [See also 1 Cor 1:30, 2:7, 8])*

3:19 God's wisdom proves the foolishness of secular wisdom. It is on record in scripture how God outwits the wise of this world. *(In The Message Translation, Job 5:13 reads, He catches the know-it-alls in their conspiracies - all that intricate intrigue swept out with the trash!)*

3:20 The Lord is familiar with the ²unsuccessful search for meaning in

mankind's empty [1]debates and dialogue. *(The word, [1]dialogismos, translates as soemone deliberating with themselves. Psalm 94:11 says, "The Lord knows the thoughts of a person; that they are vanity." The word, [2]maten, translates as fruitless, unsuccessful search.)*

3:21 Therefore no one has any reason to boast in themselves, as if they gained anything that does not already belong to them! For all things you wish to gain already belong to you! *([See 1 Corinthians 4:7] Thus says the Lord: "Let not the wise glory in their wisdom, let not the mighty glory in their might, let not the rich glory in their riches; but let the one who glories glory in this, that they understand and know me, that I am the Lord who practice steadfast love, justice, and righteousness in the earth; for in these things I delight, says the Lord." [Jeremiah 9:23, 24])*

3:22 You are not winning any competition by picking your favorite teacher amongst Paul, Apollos or Kefas; they all belong to you anyway. The world belongs to you! Life and death are yours; in what you now have in this present moment you already possess the future! *(Not even death can threaten what you have in life! See Romans 8:38, 39.)*

3:23 As much as Christ is inseparably God's own, you are the property of Christ. You are one with him. *(Jesus endorsed God's ownership of the human race. See Psalm 24:1, Matthew 13:44 and Luke 15 where all three parables celebrate ownership - you cannot be lost unless you belong!)*

4:1 This is how one should regard us *(so called, Apostles)*: **we are the** [1]**under-rowers of Captain Christ; responsible for the engine room as it were! We are entrusted with the administration of the mysteries of God.** *(The unveiling of the mystery of the gospel of mankind's association in Christ is the driving force of the Church. The word,* [1]*huperetes, means an under-rower, who was one who was in the trireme, quadrireme, or quinquereme galleys and rowed in one of the undermost benches; those who were the lowest ranked slaves and often the most invisible part of the whole operation. We are not hiding behind fancy titles or impressive CV's to try and win your applause or financial support. We are not here to impress you with us; our mandate is to impress you with how complete you are in Christ because of God's doing. [See 1 Cor 1:30, 2:6-9].)*

4:2 *(Our title might be unimpressive, but our job is most significant.)* **For this reason our ministry is of unquestionable integrity.**

4:3 **The authority of my ministry is not based upon your scrutiny of my life or even any cross examination by a human court. Neither is it by my own assumption;**

4:4 **even though I know of nothing against my conscience, I am not thereby acquitted. The point is not how self righteous I appear in my own eyes; the Lord's judgment is the only valid reference to our innocence.**

4:5 **Any judgment prior to the Lord's coming** *(prior to the cross)* **is out of context.** *(The days of performance-based judgment are over!)* **His coming illuminates all the hidden mysteries** *(concerning mankind's inclusion in the death and resurrection of Christ. [See 1 Cor 2:7, 8])* **and unveils the** [1]**deepest desire of the heart of a person. In his appearing** *(through the proclamation of this gospel [see 1 Cor 5:4])* **shall everyone be** [2]**commended by God.** *(Not contaminated by an inferior judgment;* [2]*apo means away from the influence of mankind's judgment.* [1]*He is the desire of all nations. All nations long for the redemption of their true identity and their true innocence. [See Hag 2:7; also 1 Cor 1:7 and 1 Cor 2:7.] We voice words of wisdom that was hidden in silence for timeless ages; a mystery unfolding God's Masterful plan whereby he would redeem his glory in mankind.)*

4:6 **I have deliberately applied this to myself and Apollos to show you the futility of hero-worshipping; to put us in a contest would be completely out of context of what I have written to you** *(Both Apollos and I are on the same assignment: we are here for you, to influence your faith to discover yourself in Christ. Every individual is equally gifted in him. [See 1 Cor 3:5] Therefore no one has any reason to boast in themselves, as if they gained anything that does not already belong to them! For all things you wish to gain already belongs to you! [See 1 Cor 3:21])*

4:7 **How can there possibly be any ground left for dispute or discrimination if there is nothing in us that we did not freely receive? Now if who you are and what you have is a gift and not a reward for good behavior, then boasting makes no sense.**

4:8 **You are already saturated, literally jam-packed to capacity; you can-**

not get any wealthier than what you are! You are royalty *(because of what happened to you in Christ)* not because of Apollos or Paul! Oh, that you might know this so that we may co-reign together with you! *(We are not ranked any differently because we taught you the good news! So do not try and make heroes of us while you reduce yourselves to mere supporters and spectators [see also 1 Cor 1:30 and 2 Cor 10:12]. Paul is re-enforcing the message of how complete we already are in Christ as our only reference. We are no longer striving towards completeness; we are living from completeness. The language of the Old Covenant was "towards;" the language of the New is "from!" The old said, "Do!" The new says, "Done!")*

4:9 If you really want to know, there is nothing glamorous about being an apostle! It seems to some that God has us on exhibition as it were, as clowns in the circus; the laughing stock of the religious world-system! We are the latest gossip in town. Even the angels frown upon us! And you want to idolize us, think again! We are not handing out autographs! Neither are we your latest brand of Christianity! We have a death-sentence hanging over our heads!

4:10 Because of Christ we are considered fools *(in the eyes of the religious society!)* Our foolishness serves only one purpose though: to prove to you that Christ is your wisdom. Our weakness serves to convince you of your source of strength in Christ; our ill repute in the eyes of popular opinion is to persuade you of your honored standing in Christ! *(Do not allow what we are suffering for you to distract you from realizing how wise, and strong, and honored you really are in Christ.)*

4:11 While writing this to you my life would seem such a contradiction! I mean here I am telling you how complete and without shortcoming you already are, and I can hardly remember when last I have had a decent meal! As I am writing this my mouth is dry with thirst, I'm stripped of my clothing; I have been beaten black and blue, and have nowhere to go.

4:12 I feel the fatigue from my physical labor. When people insult us we make sure that we speak well of them. We are harassed, but bear with it.

4:13 Hurtful rumors do the rounds but we find refuge and ¹comfort in our true identity. We are reckoned as ²scapegoats, the scum of society. This is what we are faced with on a daily basis. *(The word, ¹parakaleo, comes from para, a preposition indicating close proximity, with a suggestion of union, and kaleo, to identify by name, to surname. The Greeks used to apply the term ²katharmata as scapegoats, to victims sacrificed to make expiation for the people, and even to criminals who were maintained at the public expense, that on the outbreak of a pestilence or other calamity they might be offered as sacrifices to make expiation for the state.)*

4:14 My intention is not to embarrass you. I bring these things to your attention because you are my very dear children.

4:15 While you may have countless mentors supervising your lives, you do not have many fathers; for in Christ Jesus I have begotten you through the Gospel.

4:16 I therefore summon you urgently to mirror my message.

4:17 This is why I send my beloved son Timothy to you. He is rock-solid in his faith. He shall remind you of me and reinforce my specific message and emphasis in every place and every church I visit. *(Paul's emphasis is unique in the way he teaches the "in Christ-", and "the Christ in you-" and his finished work-message. "There is no other gospel in spite of the many so-called Christian products branded 'gospel.' If any hint of the law remains, it is not good news but merely religious people's ideas, distracting from the gospel of Christ." [See Gal 1:7] "This is the heart of the gospel that I proclaim; it began with an unveiling of sonship in me, freeing me to announce the same sonship in the masses of non-Jewish people. I felt no immediate urgency to compare notes with those who were familiar with Christ from a mere historic point of view." [Gal 1:16] The Greek text is quite clear, "It pleased the Father to reveal his son in me in order that I may proclaim him in the nations!" The words, **en emoi**, translate as "in me," and **en ethnos** translates as in the Gentile nations, or the masses of non Jewish people! Not "among" the Gentiles as most translations have it. Later when Barnabas is sent to investigate the conversion of the Greeks in Acts 11, instead of reporting his findings to HQ in Jerusalem, he immediately finds Paul, knowing that Paul's gospel is the revelation of the mystery of Christ in the nations [see Col 1:27]. No wonder then that those believers were the first to be called Christians, or Christ-like! For the Son of God, Jesus Christ, whom we proclaimed in you, Silvanus and Timothy and I, was not Yes and No; but in him it is always Yes. [2 Cor 1:19])*

4:18 I know some of you have the vaunted idea that my message and I will just vanish off the face of the earth! You cannot wish me away!

4:19 In the Lord's purpose I might show up sooner than what you think; then we will know if there is any dynamic in their inflated talk.

4:20 The kingdom of God *(the dominion of the Christ life)* is about an empowered life and not just a matter of quoting your favorite teacher or scripture!

4:21 Would you prefer it if I come to you with a whip-in-hand approach or with a loving, gentle spirit?

5:1 The sexual scandal in your ranks has become public news: someone is said to have slept with his stepmother. This kind of behavior is not even tolerated in society in general, let alone among believers!

5:2 And you are engaged in discussing doctrine and organizing denominations! *(Chapter 1:10-13)* This is heartbreaking! This shameful situation should have been dealt with in the most urgent manner by clearly distancing yourselves from such behavior and even going as far as disassociating yourselves from this person. *(In the first four chapters Paul makes it very clear that this gospel is not an excuse to disguise sin but to remove it! Anyone who suggests that grace is a license to sin is fuel for fire! [See 1 Cor 3:12-15])*

5:3 Even though I am not physically with you, my spirit is present in this reading of my letter; and I assure you as solemnly as if actually present in your gathering, that I have already concluded my verdict in the Name of the Lord Jesus Christ:

5:4 As you meet together and I meet with you in my spirit by the power of our Lord Jesus Christ present with us,

5:5 such a person is to be released from your midst and handed over to the [1]Accuser; let the accusation consume his flesh until the light of day, the revelation of Jesus Christ rise for him again to rescue his spirit from the deceit of his sin. *(Consider Paul's heart in 2 Cor 2:6-8, 10-11, For such a one this punishment by the majority is enough; so you should rather turn to forgive and comfort him, or he may be overwhelmed by excessive sorrow. So I beg you to reaffirm your love for him. Any one whom you forgive, I also forgive. What I have forgiven, if I have forgiven anything, has been for your sake in the presence of Christ, to keep Satan ([1]satanos, accuser) from gaining the advantage over us; for we are not ignorant of his designs.*

In Ephesians 4:26-27, he says, Even if you think you have a valid excuse, do not let anger dominate your day! If you don't deal with it immediately (in the light of the likeness of Christ in you) the sun sets for you and your day becomes one of lost opportunity where darkness employs anger to snare you into sin. Any sin that you tolerate is an open invitation to the [2]devil. Do not give him a platform to operate from. (The word, [2]diabolos, or devil, comes from dia + ballo, translated as because of the fall; a fallen mind-set).

5:6 By ignoring the presence of even a small amount of leaven the whole lump of dough will soon be permeated; thus all ground for boasting in how good things seemed to have been will be lost!

5:7 Because Christ our Paschal Lamb has already been sacrificed once and for all, the old leaven of sin-consciousness, which was upheld by the law, has already been thoroughly removed. On that basis alone are you able to now permanently rid yourselves of the old leaven-mind set of tolerating sin, which was our reasoning under the law-system! *(We are talking a brand new language: the new covenant is the new lump of dough without a trace of the leaven of the old system that was done away with in Christ. A mind-set introduced*

195

and sustained by the law! "In the very repetition of these ritual sacrifices the aware-ness of guilt is reinforced rather than removed." [Heb 10:3] The testimony of God is my only persuasion concerning you: Jesus Christ died your death on the cross! I can see you in no other light! "I have determined to know nothing amongst you except Jesus Christ and him crucified!" [1 Cor 2:2]

Hebrews 9:11-12 says, But now Christ has made his public appearance as High Priest of a perfect tabernacle. The good things that were predicted have arrived. This new tabernacle does not derive from its shadow type, the previous man-made one. It is the reality. (The restoration of God's original dwelling place in human life is again revealed!) As High Priest, his permission to enter the Holy Place was not secured by the blood of beasts. By his own blood he obtained access on behalf of the human race. Only one act was needed for him to enter the most sacred place of grace and there to institute a ransom of perpetual consequence.

[The perfection of the redemption he secured needs no further sacrifice. There are no outstanding debts; there is nothing we need do to add weight to what he has accomplished once and for all. The only possible priesthood activity we can now engage in is to continually bring a sacrifice of the fruit of our lips, giving thanks to his Name; no blood, just fruit, even our acts of self-sacrifice, giving of time and money, etcetera are all just the fruit of our constant gratitude!])

5:8 Our daily life is now the extension of the Passover celebration; feast-ing on sustained innocence! The old sin conscious-system, the leaven-mind set *(always anticipating and tolerating sin)***, is replaced with an un-derstanding of our unleavened innocence, just like when a diamond is** **¹scrutinized in the rays of the sun to confirm its flawless integrity.** *(The word, ¹elikrineia, translates as scrutinized in the rays of the sun.)*

5:9 When I wrote to you about not associating with fornicators,

5:10 I certainly did not mean that you should distance yourself from the people of the world! If you had to avoid contact with the immoral, the greedy, the thieves, and the idol worshippers *(those worshipping a distorted image of themselves)***, then you would have to leave the planet!**

5:11 What I am saying is that anyone who acts like a brother while he con-tinues his old typical lifestyle of fornication, greed, idolatry, abusing peo-ple, drunkenness, and stealing is obviously not sitting around the same table of fellowship with you!

5:12 It is none of my business to speak about the behavior of those out-side the church; we are giving a responsible opinion regarding the be-havior of those within our ranks.

5:13 We know God's judgment regarding the world *(the cross of Christ)***; but in this case I am saying that you have to deal decisively with the troublemakers in your midst!** *(The sinners were attracted to Jesus not because he introduced a compromised set of rules; something like, "it's all right to sin just don't get caught or, try and do it less!" Instead, he revealed in his person the mir-*

ror-reflection of their true origin, their original identity and the integrity of their innocence! They knew that the lie they lived as their identity had no power against the resonance of their own conscience. Jesus didn't say to the prostitute, "Go and sin less," he said to her, "Go and sin no more!" Jesus knew something about the life of our design that we had lost sight of! What he revealed, he also redeemed!)

6:1 It alarms me that you even consider to have law-people decide on disputes within your fellowship, while these so-called "judges" have no clue of the basis of our righteousness in Christ. *(Now keep Paul's introduction in mind from 1 Cor 1:2: I address this writing to the ekklesia of God in Corinth. You have been restored to the harmony of your original design; made holy in Christ Jesus; no wonder then that you are surnamed Saints. His name relates us to one another in a global family.)*

6:2 Having discovered how thoroughly God sanctified us in Christ *(1 Cor 1:30)*, we now represent the principle of righteous judgment wherewith the whole world is to be judged; how can we possibly shrink from deciding a trivial matters within our own ranks?

6:3 If the judgment we are entrusted with extends even into the spiritual realm where we are to judge angels, how much more relevant is our judgment now in deciding on day-to-day matters!

6:4 Since you are fully competent to judge such matters in the light of the gospel of grace, why bother to involve people who judge according to the standards of this world?

6:5 I mean this is most embarrassing! Are you expecting more justice from the world than from your own family? Is there not even one wise person in your midst that is able to settle in-house disputes?

6:6 Do you see how foolish it would be for brothers to sue one another and reduce justice to a system that is founded in unbelief. *(A system based on the law of works and personal performance and not faith in the finished work of the cross.)*

6:7 Even if one wins the case, it is a defeat for the church! Why not suffer wrong; it is a far greater victory if you rather be cheated and accept it joyfully, than what it would be to fight for the right to prove your point.

6:8 By allowing the wisdom of this world to be your judge nothing will change; the injustice and fraud will merely continue to spread like cancer in your ranks.

6:9 Do not be distracted into error; the typical lifestyle of unrighteousness has nothing in common with the kingdom of God. *(The kingdom of God is the dominion of the Christ-life.)*

6:10 People who continue to engage in prostitution, idolatry, adultery, sexual perversions, stealing, greed, drunkenness, abusiveness, and rage while they profess to be believers are deceiving themselves and have distanced themselves from the life of their design.

6:11 What you once were in terms of your lifestyle has radically changed! You have been cleansed, restored to total harmony *(holiness)* and made righteous. The name of the Lord Jesus declares your salvation; the Spirit of our God realizes salvation in you! *(1 Cor 1:30, 2:2)*

6:12 I am free to do what I want, but if what I do is inappropriate, I refrain from doing it and will not be snared by sudden notions.

6:13 Your appetite for food and sex does not define you. Your life is tailor-made for God; you fit him like a glove; he fulfills your deepest longings! *("You know the old saying, "First you eat to live, and then you live to eat?" Well, it may be true that the body is only a temporary thing, but that's no excuse for stuffing your body with food, or indulging it with sex. Since the Master honors you with a body, honor him with your body!" — The Message. "But you cannot say that our physical body was made for sexual promiscuity; it was made for God, and God is the answer to our deepest longings." — Phillips)*

6:14 God reveals in dramatic fashion the value he places on the human body by our joint resurrection with Jesus from the dead. *(Faith sees us joined in his death and alive with him in his resurrection. It is plain for all to see that death lost its dominion over Christ in his resurrection; he need not ever die again to prove a further point [Rom 6:8, 9].)*

6:15 This means that your bodies are co-members of his; which makes it absurd to even consider engaging his body in sexual promiscuity!

6:16 Sex involves so much more than two bodies joining together; scripture speaks of a sacred union of two lives becoming one. How can we reduce this sacred union to harlotry? *(There's more to sex than mere skin on skin. Sex is as much spiritual mystery as physical fact. — The Message)*

6:17 In our union with him we are one spirit with the Lord.

6:18 Flee fornication. Every sexual sin is a violation of the sacredness of the human body and scars the conscience of the individual like no other sin does. *(The best way to escape temptation is to remember who you are.)*

6:19 Do you not realize that your body by design is the sacred shrine of the spirit of God; he echoes God within you. Your body does not even belong to you in the first place.

6:20 You are bought and paid for, spirit, soul and body. All of you are his. Live your life conscious of the enormous price with which God has valued you. Your whole being belongs to him and exhibits him. You are his address; you are his real estate.

7:1 In your writing to me you asked questions about marriage.

7:2 *(The fact that I am not married does not mean that I am against marriage.)* Where a man is attached to his wife and she to him they are sexually secure.

7:3 Marriage provides the ideal environment for both husband and wife to mutually esteem one another.

7:4 The wife belongs to her husband and he belongs to her. Their bodies are no longer their own.

7:5 By mutual agreement they may decide to abstain from physical contact for a specific period of time for prayer and fasting; not for prolonged times since this might give occasion for temptation.

7:6 I am not making rules about marriage; this is simply my advice to you in response to your request.

7:7 I could recommend my own life to everyone; yet I am convinced that life is a gift whether you are single or married.

7:8 My advice to the unmarried as well as to those who have lost their partner: it might be to your best interest to remain single even as I am.

7:9 Again, I am not laying down a law; much rather face the challenges of marriage than be consumed with desire!

7:10 Concerning your questions about divorce, I am strongly opposed to the idea; and this is not merely my advice, this is the Lord's instruction.

7:11 If the wife leaves her husband she is not to get re-married; her only option would be to be reconciled to her husband. In that case the husband may not resist her.

7:12 The brother who asked about his unbelieving wife: my advice is to remain committed to her as long as she is prepared to remain with you. *(Unbelief: not believing the truth about themselves as revealed in the gospel of the grace of God [1 Cor 1:30].)*

7:13 The same goes for the lady with the unbelieving husband; if he is pleased to be with you then you have no reason to divorce him.

7:14 In principle the unbelieving husband is sanctified by his wife's faith, and the unbelieving wife, by her husband's faith. If that was not true then your children would be contaminated by the unbelieving partner; yet they are pure because of the one parent's faith. The individual's faith blesses the whole family. *(Faith does not exclude; God's faith includes!)*

7:15 Yet if the unbelieving partner desires to divorce, then let it be. Pursue peace rather than forced friendship.

7:16 To fake friendship is not worth it; not even for the sake of possibly winning your partner to the Lord!

7:17 God dealt with each one of us uniquely and individually and connected with us regardless of our circumstances. He defines and completes your life, not your partner or lack of one! I am not just saying this in response to your questions about your specific challenges; I am equally persuaded about this in principle in all the churches.

7:18 Circumcision or the lack of it does not [1]define you! In Christ your Jewish or Gentile heritage is irrelevant and can never again [1]label you. *(The word, [1]kaleo, means to identify by name; to surname.)*

7:19 You couldn't keep the commandments anyway, whether you were circumcised or not! *(So if circumcision did not contribute anything while you were seeking to be justified under the law, how can it possibly now advantage you in your understanding of righteousness by faith?)*

7:20 You are not what your career or job description say you are.

7:21 Even if you were the lowest ranked slave before, it makes no difference to the dignity of your true identity. I am not saying that you should not go for promotion; by all means take it if it comes your way. The point that I am making is that in Christ you are equally free, whether you are a slave or free in society, a boss or an employee.

7:22 Society might label you as a slave, but Christ reveals how free you really are. Then again you might be a so called, "free person" in society but in Christ you are a bond slave!

7:23 You are not for sale *(to the religious system of the law of works)*. The ransom God paid for your freedom now binds you to the lordship of his love. The sign over your life says, SOLD!

7:24 We belong to the same [1]household. Every individual originates from God and is [2]surnamed in him; this is our true lineage, [3]abide herein without compromise. *([1]Brothers, **adelphos**, meaning from the same womb. The word, [2]kaleo, means to surname, and [3]para, is a preposition indicating close proximity, a thing proceeding from a sphere of influence, with a suggestion of union of place of residence, to have sprung from its author and giver, originating from, denoting the point from which an action originates, intimate connection.)*

7:25 With regards to your question whether it was proper that the young unmarried people refrain from marriage because of the times we are facing, I have no specific direction from the Lord, but again you can trust my good advice! By the mercy of God I personally have no plans to get married!

7:26 Especially in these stressful times I would say that it is a good thing to remain single and unattached.

7:27 So my advice is, if you are already in a relationship with someone, don't quit; and if you are unattached, don't get involved.

7:28 It is certainly not wrong to get married. All I am saying is that marriage brings extra challenges in already difficult times.

7:29 The urgency of these times might demand mutual sacrifices from those who are married, such as sacrificing their time together for other priorities.

7:30 Even our most personal space for grief or joy is invaded; that leaves you with no time to indulge in your own interests and possessions. If you are in the process of buying something, buy as if you will never own it!

7:31 Do not lean too hard upon the fragile *(economic)* structures of this world; they are here today and gone tomorrow!

7:32 In my opinion the unmarried person lives an uncomplicated life; fully devoted to the Lord without any distractions;

7:33 while the married person is confronted with all the typical domestic challenges absorbing his attention in his commitment to his wife and her delights and demands.

7:34 The same goes for the ladies; the unmarried woman can give her undivided attention to the Lord without any emotional or physical marital obligations.

7:35 I really have your focused devotion to the Lord at heart and desire for you to live a beautiful life without any distractions that could possibly snare you.

7:36 If a man is engaged to a young girl and feels that he doesn't want to wait until she is older before they marry, let them go ahead and marry, there is nothing wrong with that!

7:37 Yet if he decides to rather wait, he is free to do as he has determined in his heart.

7:38 My personal conviction is to remain single, but I am not at all against marriage.

7:39 As long as the husband is alive, his wife is bound by law to remain with him; if he dies, then obviously she is free to marry another as she is led by the Lord.

7:40 Of course in my opinion she should not marry again.

(Obviously Paul's advice is typically that of a bachelor who has to feel justified in his decision to remain single! Lydia and I are now together for more than 40 years and certainly do not find our commitment to one another a distraction from the Lord at all! On the contrary it is the most recommendable wonderful life! — August, 2014)

Paul addresses the same issues he writes about here in Chapters 7 and 8 in his letter to Timothy, warning him against those who forbid marriage and enjoin abstinence from foods which God created to be received with thanksgiving by those who believe and know the truth. For everything created by God is good, and nothing is to be rejected if it is received with thanksgiving (1 Tim 4:3, 4). These issues were obviously controversial at the time.

8:1 You have also asked me questions about whether believers are free to eat food offered to idols. We are free to hold to our own convictions about what to eat and what not to eat; but ultimately it is not about who wins the diet debate, but about sincerely loving people.

8:2 Let love define your convictions and not mere head knowledge.

8:3 Loving God *(and your fellow human)* is so easy when you understand that he knows you! Let God's knowledge of you inspire your love for him and your fellow human.

8:4 By making a fuss about eating food offered to idols gives idols undue prominence; they are nothing so why make something out of nothing! We know that there is only one God and that he has no competition!

8:5 There is a lot of talk about other gods and demonic powers operating on earth as well as in the heavenly realm; obviously they seem to be empowered by people's belief in them and conversation about them; so there seem to be many gods "lording" it over people.

8:6 This does not make them competition to God; we know that for us there is only one God who is the source of all things; there is only one authority, the Lord Jesus Christ. All things exist because of him; we owe our very being to him. He alone gives context and reference to our lives.

8:7 However not everyone realizes this; there are some believers who are convinced that idols are real, so for them to hear that we say that it's okay to eat food offered to idols presents a massive problem to their conscience.

8:8 Your diet preference certainly does not improve your standing before God; whether you eat meat or not.

8:9 The point is not about how justified you feel in your freedom to eat what you like, but how considerate you are not to be a stumbling block to someone else.

8:10 If someone who looks up to you as an example sees you eat at a banquet in a temple where the meat has obviously been sacrificed to idols, your liberty might give occasion for this person to be snared into idol worship.

8:11 So your "superior knowledge" is actually causing the ruin of someone for whom Christ died. *(You are influencing someone to exchange his new found belief in the sacrifice of Christ to become involved again in pagan worship and the sacrifice of animals.)*

8:12 You might think you have a valid argument to justify your position, but in the process you are beating your brother's conscience black-and-blue without realizing that you are injuring the cause of Christ.

8:13 I will much rather abstain from eating meat all together than run the risk of offending my brother.

9:1-6 There seems to be different criteria whereby our ministries are judged; some apostles seem to have liberties that others don't; in terms of their diets, financial benefits, plus the luxury to be accompanied by their wives. Would the brothers of Jesus and Kefas be rated higher than Barnabas and I amongst you? What would you say qualifies my commission to you? The fact that I have had a face-to-face encounter with our Master Jesus Christ followed by the impact and fruit of my ministry to you can surely not count against me?

9:7 Imagine a soldier goes to war at his own expense! I mean how absurd! Yet it is almost taken for granted that Barnabas and I have to earn our own living not to burden the very people we established and daily feed in their faith!

9:8 Anyone who plants a vineyard eats its fruit for free; the shepherd likewise is not expected to pay for a drink of milk!

9:9 Or is this just my own idea? If you insist on scriptural evidence, even the law of Moses says that the ox treading out the grain shall not be muzzled!

9:10 If God so cares for the oxen imagine how much more he cares for you! Moses certainly had more than oxen in mind in writing this; the farmer would be wasting his time plowing his field without participating in the harvest. While the oxen were still treading out the corn the farmer joyfully anticipates the bread.

9:11 Spiritual seed also translates into a material harvest.

9:12 While others enjoy this privilege why would it seem wrong that we share the same? We have not taken any advantage of you; we would rather suffer lack than insisting on our rights and in the process cause you to be distracted from the gospel of Christ.

9:13 It is common knowledge that the people engaged in temple ministry eat what is sacrificed there.

9:14 The same principle goes for those who proclaim the Gospel; and this is not just someone's good idea it is endorsed by the Lord.

9:15 The reason for my writing about these issues is not to bring you under any kind of obligation; on the contrary, I want to be very clear about this, the fact that I do things differently by not expecting anyone to pay me for my ministry is to emphasize my urgency to remove any possible excuse from anyone's mind that I might have ulterior motives! I am dead serious about this Gospel!

9:16 I live to preach; it consumes my total being. Your money is not going to make any difference since this Gospel has my arm twisted and locked behind my back! *(anagke)* In fact, my life would be reduced to utter misery if it were not possible for me to preach the good news!

9:17 If this was a mere career choice, then surely you could hire or fire me! But I am not for sale; I am employed by the economy of persuasion!

9:18 So what's in it for me, you may ask? The pleasure of declaring the Gospel of Christ at no expense is priceless! No, I am not cheating anyone or myself by foregoing the rights I might have as a preacher.

9:19 So in a sense I am free from everyone's expectation or management; yet I have voluntarily enslaved myself to all people. This beats any other motivation to influence people.

9:20 I am like a Jew to the Jew to win them; I am disguised as a legalist to win those stuck under the law!

9:21 To the Gentiles who have no regard for Jewish sentiment, I became like one without any obligation to Jewish laws to win them! Don't get me wrong; I am not sinning to identify with the sinners! I am in the law of Christ! *(The agape law!)*

9:22 I am so persuaded about every person's inclusion in Christ that I desire to be everything I need to be in order to win everyone's understanding of their union with Christ. I do not present myself as super strong to the weak, but rather expose myself to their weakness in order to win them. I do not distance myself from anyone. My mission is to be exactly what is required of me in every possible situation to bring salvation to [1]every kind of person, whoever they are! *(Traditionally translated, "in order to save some;" I do not believe that this is what Paul is saying here! The word, [1]tis, can also suggest every single kind.)*

9:23 The gospel explains my lifestyle; it is so much more than a pulpit ministry to me. My life is inseparably joined to you in the fellowship of the good news!

9:24 Athletes run a race to win; their aim is to receive the prize not just to compete! This why I preach to persuade you and not just to entertain you! *(A soccer player can do magic with his footwork and ball skills, but it is no good if he cannot take the gap and score the goal!)*

9:25 The athlete knows how to draw from focused inner strength in order to win the crown; for them all their effort translates into a mere moment celebrated by a fading wreath of honor. For us to win your faith is of imperishable value!

9:26 I run with certain victory in my every step! I am not shadow boxing when I preach!

9:27 I deliberately compare myself to the sacrifice and dedication of a champion athlete; in similar fashion I would pummel my body and subdue it! I would deny myself many things in my pursuit to win your faith so that you will not have any excuse to reject my message. I want you, not your money! *(Paul is not saying this because he is worried about God's approval. It is his audience's approval that he is after: "becoming all things to all types of people in order to win every single one of them!" 1 Corinthians 9:12, we would rather suffer lack than insisting on our rights and in the process cause you to be distracted from the gospel of Christ. [See also Paul's urgency in Col 1:25-28])*

10:1 Now remember how the people of Israel were all delivered from slavery; the cloud of God's presence, protection, and provision included everyone equally. They were all miraculously led through the Red Sea on dry land and witnessed how their oppressors were completely defeated. *("These Egyptians whom you see today you will never see again!" [Ex 14:13]. Pharaoh was not to be blamed for their forty-year detour in the desert!)*

10:2 The cloud and sea was a type of baptism that they underwent to identify with the leadership of Moses. *(This was all a prophetic picture of Christ leading us out of bondage and slavery in his death and resurrection.)*

10:3 All of them daily partook of the same miraculous food.

10:4 They drank the same supernatural water from the Rock that accompanied them in all their travels; the Rock was the Messiah! *(Their experience was saturated in spirit dimension and the miraculous, yet they died through unbelief! The supernatural is not proof of faith! Their unbelief was rooted in their believing a lie about themselves. [Num 13:33]. Yet Christ was there even in their unbelief, the Rock accompanied them!)*

10:5 The vast majority of them completely disappointed God and died in the desert. *(Israel never entered into their inheritance! The desert was not their destiny! Hebrews 4:1 admonishes, "What a foolish thing it would be for us if we should now fail in a similar fashion to enter into the full consequences of our redemption." And in Hebrews 4:6, "They failed because of unbelief; they underestimated their deliverance and believed a lie about themselves;" and in Hebrews 2:3, "No one can afford to underestimate and be blasé about this final message, a salvation of such magnificent proportions! There is no alternative escape. Salvation as it is articulated in Christ is the message that God spoke from the beginning, and it was confirmed again and again by those who heard him. We cannot afford to delay the promise to a future event yet again.")*

10:6 We are clearly reminded not to follow their example; instead of feasting on God's merciful provision they had a craving appetite for evil.

10:7 Their idolatry snared them further! They were infatuated with a distorted pattern of themselves! *(This all started with them believing a lie about themselves [Num 13:33]. This was the same sin that snared Eve in paradise.)*

10:8 They became completely disorientated and indulged in sexual sins which killed countless thousands of them! *(What a foolish alternative to embracing and possessing the promise: Jesus redeemed the life of our design.)*

10:9 Remember also how Israel spoke against God and Moses and were snared by their own unbelief, suspiciously scrutinizing the Messiah who is the promise of God! *(They blamed God for what they brought upon themselves! [See Num 13:33 and Num 21:5, 6, 8] Even though God mercifully provided for them, they remained unfulfilled in their own miserable unbelief! Grumbling sets up the stage for the enemy to snare you! God's mercy prevailed in spite of their sins and here we see another dramatic prophetic picture of the judgment that was our due, taken by the scapegoat, Jesus. [Jn 3:14, 15; Gal 3:13; see notes in Mirror*

Translation on 2 Cor 5:21]. Jesus says in John 12:32, "When I am lifted up (on the cross), I will draw all judgment to me!")

10:10 Grumbling is a killer!

10:11 Now these prophetic pictures were written to alert us to the fact that they pointed to what we are now witnessing in the gospel; we are confronted with the completeness of everything that was promised!

10:12 If you reckon that you have it all together, make sure that you are standing strong *(in your true identity)* **when temptation strikes! How foolish it would be for us to now fall into the same unbelief that killed Israel!** *(They believed a lie about themselves [Num 13:33].)*

10:13 Your situation is not unique! Every human life faces contradictions! Here is the good news: God believes in your freedom! He has made it possible for you to triumph in every situation that you will ever encounter!

10:14 My ¹dearly loved friends! Escape into his image and likeness in you where the ²distorted image *(²idolatry)* **loses its attraction!** *(Dearly loved friends, translated as ¹agapetos; to know the agape love of God is to know our true identity! The word, agape, comes from agoo, meaning to lead as a shepherd guides his sheep, and pao, to rest, like in Psalm 23, "he leads me beside still waters where my soul is restored; by the waters of reflection my soul remembers who I am! Now I can face the valley of the shadow of death and fear no evil!")*

10:15 I appeal to your common sense! Do not underestimate what I am saying to you.

10:16 When we share a meal together we declare our association in Christ! Every time we drink from the same cup, we communicate the language of the covenant of grace, which is what our fellowship is all about. The wine we drink is our participation in what the blood of Christ represents. *(You know that you were ransomed from the futile ways inherited from your fathers, not with perishable things such as silver or gold, but with the precious blood of Christ, like that of a lamb without blemish or spot [1 Pet 1:18, 19]. He redeemed our original value and transparent innocence!)* **The bread we break celebrates our participation in the incarnation! The prophetic promise became flesh in his person; we are jointly declaring that in the revelation of our inclusion in his death and resurrection we are now the visible body of Christ.**

10:17 The single loaf of bread that we all partake of represents the fact that although there are many of us, there is only one Christ! By eating together from that one bread we are declaring that we are one body in Christ and that he is incarnated in each one of us! *(Our "many-ness" becomes "one-ness;" Christ doesn't become fragmented in us. Rather, we become unified in him. — The Message)*

10:18 Let us consider the context of the prophetic type of the sacrificial system of Israel; those who ate the sacrificed animals were partners in the same altar.

10:19 Now by this I am not saying that there is any magical power in a sacrifice made to an idol; an idol is nothing more than a mere figment of the imagination. The meat offered to an idol is just meat like any other barbecue!

10:20 The difference between Israel and the Gentile nations is in the prophetic type that Israel's sacrifices pointed to; a sacrifice offered to demons points to nothing and holds no advantage to you. I mean why would you associate with anything that reduces you to less than what you are! *(The only significance in the Jewish sacrificial system was in its pointing to the Messiah; both the promise and the person of the Messiah points to the redemption of mankind's original identity and innocence!)*

10:21 You cannot celebrate the Lord in one meal and then devote yourselves to pagan worship the next time you eat! Every time you drink and eat you ¹co-echo your union in Christ! *(In our every communion, even in our daily meals, we co-echo "I am!" To partake comes from ¹**metecho**; with **meta** meaning together with, and **echo** meaning to echo what God spoke to us in Christ; like the word **metanous**, NOT repentance (re-penance); but to co-know with God; to agree with God about you.)*

10:22 God is not in a tug of war with demons or our obsession with religious rituals! He has no competition. He is I am! *(Even the Jews, who continued their sacrificial rituals after Christ was sacrificed as God's Passover Lamb, were presenting their offerings to pagan gods and not to God! There remains no further spiritual relevance in the practice of Jewish rituals, including the Sabbaths and the annual feasts!)*

10:23 Everything is ¹endorsed in I am! Everything originates and ²concludes in I am. Now that the prophetic picture is completed in Christ, Jewish rituals can no longer be ³accommodated under the same roof. Christ is the relevance, not the historic ritual. *(Everything begins in I am. This comes from the Greek, **exesti,** from ¹**exousia,** which is **ek + eimi.** The word **ek** always denotes origin and **eimi,** I am. This word is often translated as "authority," or in this case, "endorsed;" traditional translations read, everything is "lawful." The word, ²**sumphero,** means to bear together, to conclude. The image and likeness of God revealed and redeemed in human form is the substance of the prophetic picture. The word, ³**oikodome,** comes from **oikos,** meaning dwelling or family and **dome,** meaning roof. Paul is urging the church to find their fellowship in the revelation of Christ and not in a mixture of Jewish and pagan religious rituals!)*

10:24 Even though I am free in my own persuasion, I do not pursue my freedom at someone else's expense! So even though we might feel perfectly justified in our own convictions, let each one of us consider how to benefit one another instead. *(The good news of what happened to every single person in Christ is all that matters!)*

10:25 Do not think twice about eating meat bought from the local market; why bother to ask questions about whether or not it was sacrificed at a Jewish or heathen temple. Such questions are completely irrelevant! To continue to live in a right or wrong consciousness is to injure yourself and others.

10:26 In Psalm 24:1, David declares categorically that the earth is the Lord's and the fullness thereof. *(That should settle your conscience once and for all about diet debates! In mankind's mind an animal is sacrificed to a demon or deity of choice but the Creator owns everything anyway and he needs no one's permission to endorse his ownership, neither is he influenced by what a person believes.)*

10:27 Should you get a personal invitation to a banquet hosted by unbelievers and you desire to go, then be at liberty to eat whatever they prepare. Please do not embarrass them by asking sensitive questions about whether the food was sacrificed to idols or not! Leave your religious sentiment behind and enjoy the feast!

10:28 However if someone specifically mentions to you that the meat was indeed sacrificed to idols, then for that person's conscience sake rather refrain from eating the item in question in order to avoid giving the impression that you approve of idol worship.

10:29 No, I am not compromising my freedom by being sensitive to someone else's conscience! *("But, except for these special cases, I'm not going to walk around on eggshells worrying about what small-minded people might say; I'm going to stride free and easy, knowing what our large-minded Master has already said." — The Message)*

10:30 Grace sets the pace in my conscience, not people's suspicious scrutiny. Every meal to me is a celebration of what grace reveals.

10:31 Live your life overwhelmed by God's [1]opinion of you! Your eating and drinking is certainly a constant reminder that you are his glory. Every meal proclaims the fact that the life of your design is redeemed again in Christ; salute life! *([1]Glory, doxa from dokeo, a good opinion)*

10:32 So live your life in freedom and wisdom. Thus the Jews, the Gentiles and the church will all witness the attraction of your life without taking any offense.

10:33 I am so persuaded about every person's inclusion in Christ that I desire to be everything I need to be in order to win everyone's understanding of their union with Christ; my mission is to be exactly what is required of me in every possible situation to bring salvation to every kind of person, whoever they are! I have no other agenda. *(See 1 Cor 9:22)*

11:1 Mirror me as I mirror Christ. *(Jesus is not an example for us but of us!)*

11:2 I commend you for ¹giving such attention to detail concerning the heart of the gospel that I communicate. *(The word, ¹paradidomi, comes from para, a preposition that indicates close proximity, sphere of influence, and the word, didomi, meaning to give to someone what already belongs to them)*

11:3-17 *(I skipped these verses since they are certainly not in the context of the gospel that Paul preached. Paul understood that when Jesus died, all died; he therefore no longer knew people from a human point of view [see 2 Cor 5:14,16]. He declares in Galatians 3:28 [RSV], "There is neither Jew nor Greek, there is neither slave nor free, there is neither male nor female; for you are all one in Christ Jesus." I had no liberty to translate these verses. These thoughts seem to have been added somehow by some church father to justify the tradition of the day where women had to show their submission to their husbands by wearing a head covering.*

My eldest son Renaldo once attended a church with Lydia and I where the women wore head coverings. One of the ladies brought a napkin and placed it on Lydia's head. Renaldo started giggling and when I asked him what was so funny, he said, "Dad, this is a crazy church, women are not allowed to show their hair but it's okay to show their breasts!" All around us there were mothers feeding their babies! This is Africa!)

11:18 My priority concern is that you are divided into different and distracting opinions when you gather as a church. Our focus is the nitty-gritty essence of the gospel. I believe in oneness not divisions.

11:19 The only advantage of any controversy is that the authentic becomes even more apparent in you.

11:20 What I heard is most disturbing: when you get together for a fellowship meal, instead of celebrating what the Lord's communion introduced,

11:21 some behave like gluttons while others are starving; then there are those who get wasted on the wine.

11:22 If you want to over indulge then do so in the privacy of your own homes! Why despise the assembly and insult the poor in the process! This is most disgusting! I am disappointed in you.

11:23 Let me remind you then what we are actually celebrating in our fellowship meal: The night in which the Lord Jesus was betrayed, he took bread

11:24 and gave thanks; breaking the bread into portions, he said, "¹Realize your association with my death, every time you eat, remember my body that was broken for you!" *(Meaning ¹take, grasp, lambamo, to take what is one's own, to associate with one's self.)*

11:25 He did exactly the same with the cup after supper and said, "This cup holds the wine of the New Covenant in my blood; you celebrate me every time you drink with this understanding!" *(From now on our meals are* *meaningful. We celebrate the fact that the incarnation reveals our redemption; the promise became a person.*

He redeemed our original value, identity, and innocence; he died our death and defines the life we now live. He fulfills the theme of scripture: the sufferings of the Messiah and the subsequent glory! [1 Pet 1:10, 11])

11:26 Your every meal makes the ¹mandate of his ²coming relevant and communicates the meaning of the New Covenant. *(Whether you eat or drink, you are declaring your joint inclusion in his death and resurrection, confirming your redeemed innocence. Some translations read, "until I come..." The word translated until is, ¹achri, from akmen, which means extremity, conclusion, the present time; Jesus is the conclusion of prophetic time! The word ²erchomai, to come is in the the Aorist Subjunctive Mood, elthe, which is similar to the Optative expressing a wish. The Mood of the Greek verb expresses the mode in which the idea of the verb is employed. Thus, we are communicating the desire to have all people realize the meaning of the New Covenant. See 2 Peter 1:19 "For us the appearing of the Messiah is no longer a future promise but a fulfilled reality. Now it is your turn to have more than a second-hand, hear-say testimony. Take my word as one would take a lamp at night; the day is about to dawn for you in your own understanding. When the morning star appears, you no longer need the lamp; this will happen shortly on the horizon of your own hearts.")*

11:27 So whoever does not value the meaning of the bread and the wine, keep themselves in condemnation.

11:28 To see oneself associated in Christ's death and declared innocent in his blood is the only worthy manner in which to examine one's own life in the context of the new covenant meal. *(Self examination according to the Old Covenant, i.e. Deuteronomy 28 is no longer relevant. "Examine yourselves to see whether you are holding to your faith, test yourselves, do you not realize that Jesus Christ is within you!" [2 Cor 13:5 — RSV])*

11:29 Anyone who partakes of this meal in an indifferent manner, either because of religious sentiment or merely being blasé about the meaning of the meal, eats and drinks judgment upon themselves! The human body of Jesus represents the judgment of every single human life; to fail to acknowledge this is to deliberately exclude yourself from the blessing of the New Covenant. *(Isaiah 53:3-8, He was despised and rejected by men; a man of sorrows, and acquainted with grief, and we esteemed him not. Surely he has borne our griefs and carried our sorrows; yet we esteemed him stricken, smitten by God, and afflicted. But he was wounded by our transgressions, he was bruised by our iniquities; upon him was the chastisement that made us whole, and with his stripes we are healed. All we like sheep have gone astray; we have turned every one to his own way; and the Lord has laid on him the iniquity of us all. Like a lamb that is led to the slaughter, and like a sheep that before its shearers is dumb, so he opened not his mouth. By oppression and judgment he was taken away; and as for his generation, who considered that he was cut off out of the land of the living, stricken for the transgression of my people? [RSV] No one can afford to underestimate what* *happened to us on the cross! To discern the Lord's body is to grasp what God's faith saw when Jesus died!)*

11:30 This is the reason why many of you are suffering unnecessarily with weaknesses and illnesses, and many have already died.

11:31   By judging that we indeed co-died in his death we are free from any kind of judgment! *(John 5:22, "The Father judges no one, but has given all judgment to the Son." [RSV] John 12:31-33, "Now is the judgment of this world, now shall the ruler of this world be cast out; and I, when I am lifted up from the earth, will draw all judgment to myself." He said this to show by what death he was to die.")*

11:32 By discerning the broken body of Christ we can only conclude that he was wounded by our transgressions and that indeed the chastisement that brought us peace was upon him. This is the instruction of the Lord; what foolishness it would be to continue to place yourself and the rest of the world under judgment when Jesus already took all judgment upon himself!

11:33 So when you come together to eat the covenant meal, embrace one another with utmost courtesy;

11:34 there is no point in getting together to see who can eat or drink the most! Eat at home if you are hungry; why turn a celebration into condemnation? *(Our feast celebrates the success of the cross and has nothing in common with a pagan banquet!*

The prophetic picture of the table was most significant! The priests had to daily place fresh bread on the table in the sanctuary. It was called Showbread, **lechem haPānīm,** *literally: "Face-bread; Bread of the Presence". The Hebrew word for presence means face to face! While Jesus spoke to the two disciples on their way to Emmaus in Luk 24, they did not recognize him, even though their hearts ignited while he was pointing to himself in scripture, explaining the prophetic promise of mankind's redemption, from Moses through the Psalms and the prophets. In Luke's interview, he pressed them for the detail; he wanted to know exactly at what point in their meeting with Jesus they recognized him in person! He writes in verse 28, "So they drew near to the village to which they were going and Jesus appeared to be going further..." Wow! Should Jesus not at this point have given them an opportunity to make a commitment or at least say a "sinners prayer"? Not even the best Rabbi could take them any further! Luke 24:29 "But they constrained him, saying, "Sir, stay with us, for it is toward evening and the day is now far spent." So he went in to stay with them." Luk 24:30 "When he was at table with them, he took the bread and blessed, and broke it, and gave it to them."*

Luk 24:31 "And their eyes were opened and they recognized him; and he vanished from their sight." Instead of disappointment, a great excitement arrested their hearts and they took off in the night desiring to tell the others back in Jerusalem! Nothing mobilizes one more than realizing the relevance of the revelation of the incarnation! They knew that Jesus could no longer be any more present in his person than what he is present in the Word incarnate in us!

The moment we discover Jesus in scripture as in a mirror, our hearts ignite and our very next meal becomes a celebration of the incarnation! "Every time you eat or drink, remember me!" Every meal celebrates the temple! Your body is God's address on planet earth! He does not dwell in buildings made by human hands. You will never again need to employ your willpower to diet and get into shape! Willpower is the language of the law! Love and value-consciousness ignites belief. The revelation of the truth sets you free to be free indeed! The days of fast food and junk-food are over! The Table is sacred and celebrates your body as the sanctuary of your redeemed life, the life of your authentic design! Sitting around the table is a feast of friendship and delightful conversation. Eat food that blesses the temple! Most diseases are diet-related! Study nutrition! We have this treasure in earthen vessels! The vessel takes its value from the treasure it holds!)

12:1 Spiritual manifestations are not to be confused with the spooky! Just because it is spirit dimension does not mean that you cannot understand what God's Spirit is saying to you.

12:2 Remember how, when you were still practicing pagan worship, you got carried away by dead and dumb idols into doing many weird things. *(Then you were snared by voiceless idols, now you are empowered by the voice God finds in ordinary people who amplify what he spoke to mankind in Christ.)*

12:3 Holy Spirit will never distract from Jesus or prompt anyone to dishonor Christ; Holy Spirit will always magnify the Lordship of Jesus! *(See John 16:13 But when she is come, the Spirit of truth, she will take you by the hand and guide you into the path of all truth. She will not draw attention to herself but will communicate and unveil everything she hears and discerns from a heavenly perspective about the things that is about to happen within you. John 16:14 Holy Spirit will endorse my opinion of you by taking that which is mine and interpreting it in you. See commentary notes in Mirror Bible.)*

12:4 There may be different manifestations of the grace gifts but they will not confuse, since the same Spirit is speaking.

12:5 Also ministries may appear to be different in their function but the same Lord endorses his purpose and management in everyone.

12:6 We might be doing things differently but we are drawing from the same source. God energizes each and everyone for their particular purpose.

12:7 Every expression of the Spirit is given to bring that which God accomplished in Christ [1]into full focus. *(The word, [1]sumphero, means to co-bear, bring together.)*

12:8 To one is given a word that clears the air and wisdom prevails; to another a word of knowledge, where something that could not be known in any other way comes to light! The same Spirit is the source.

12:9 Yet another person is inspired with a gift of faith in the same Spirit and another with gifts of healing of specific diseases in the same Spirit.

12:10 And to another the working of mighty acts of miracles, and to another enlightened speech *(prophecy)*; to another the ability to discern the difference between God's Spirit and a foreign spirit; to someone else the ability to communicate in many different languages; another has a gift to interpret these languages.

12:11 All these various gifts are inspired by the same Spirit who individually works in every person as Holy Spirit desires. *(See 1 Cor 14:1)*

12:12 The many members of the same body do not divide the oneness of the individual. The various gifts and workings of the Spirit of Christ find a beautiful similitude taken from the mutual dependence of the numerous parts of the human body. All the parts unite harmoniously into one whole. The Spirit of Christ is one Spirit; although their workings in each one of us may seem different there is no distraction from their oneness in us.

12:13 For in one spirit we are all immersed into one body; Jew and Gentile alike, whether we were slave or free is no longer relevant, we are all saturated in one spirit. We are drinking from the same fountain.

12:14 The individual member and its function do not define the body; the body gives context to the individual member. Your specific gifting does not define you; Christ defines you!

12:15 The different members co-compliment each other. The hand is not a more valid member of the body than the foot. How silly it would be for the foot to feel inferior to the hand simply because it does not look the same! They fulfill completely different roles but are equally part of the same body.

12:16 Should the ear say, "Because I am not the eye I am not part of the same body;" does that mean that the ear is right?

12:17 If the body was just one huge eye, then everything would be silent; if it was all ears, then how could it smell the fragrance of the flowers!

12:18 God engineered every individual part of the body according to his deliberate design.(The hearing ear and the seeing eye, the Lord has made them both. [Prov 20:12])

12:19 Our individual significance only finds context in relationship to others!

12:20 The sum total of the members equals one body.

12:21 The eye perceives and the hand touches; they do not compete for importance. The head will never make the feet feel inferior! In the body there is no sense of, "I am positioned higher than you and therefore I do not need you!"

12:22 The members are not rated in importance with how visible and prominent they seem to be. The less visible parts are indispensable; it is impossible for the body to function without them.

12:23 Those members that seem to be of lesser visible value deserve the greater and more personal care. There is so much more to a person than a pretty face!

12:24 God so structured the body that every single part is equally valued; the less visible parts are often treated with even greater honor and more specific care.

12:25 Because of the delicate interdependence of the various parts of the body it is natural that no schism can be tolerated; instead every member considers the other with affectionate care.

12:26 It is impossible for one part of the body to suffer injury without the rest of the body being immediately alerted to it; the pain of the one is the pain of all. In the same way the complete person is honored, not just the fingers that skillfully play the harp. Everyone is equally included in the same joy. *(This parallel explains perfectly mankind's inclusion in the horror of Christ's death and the glory of his resurrection; one has died for all, therefore all died! [2 Cor 5:14-17])*

12:27 You are the body of Christ; individually as much as you are his body corporately. Everyone of you mirrors him. [1]He defines your [2]form. The individual member does not give context to the body; the body gives context to the member. *("Members in particular" or individually comes from [1]ek, a preposition that always denotes origin and [2]**meros**, meaning a part or portion.)*

12:28 Wherever God places you in the body is to co-compliment the full function of the ekklesia. The seemingly most prominent and visible gifts are the apostolic, then the prophetic, the teachers, the workers of miracles, those gifted with healing various diseases. Then there are those who can fulfill any role required of them for the moment; they are the ones who can [1]stand in full support to assist any of the other gifts! The administrators are gifted to [2]manage the various functions of the ekklesia with great skill. Then there are those gifted in languages. *(The word, [1]antilepsis, means to lay hold of together; the word [2]**kubernesis** comes from **kubernao**, Latin for "to steer." No one is more important than the other! An apostle is not a title! To be "apostolic" simply explains that you are gifted with a specific function, which includes your commission to pioneer new frontiers as well as to take leadership initiative with wisdom and passion. A gift can never be mistaken with reward! Your gift does not define you; so don't let people call you Mr. Prophet! [See Eph 4:11]*

What God now has in us is gift wrapped to the world; some are commissioned to pioneer; others are gifted prophetically; some gifted as announcers of good news; some are shepherds with a real gift to care and nurture, and others have a gift to ignite instruction through revelation knowledge.

[Couriers, communicators, counselors and coaches —Rob Lacey]

Each expression of his gift is to fully equip and enable the saints for the work of the ministry so that they may mutually contribute in their specific function to give definition to the visible body of Christ [Eph 4:12].)

12:29 Everyone is not an apostle, or a prophet, or a teacher, or a miracle worker! *(Your gift does not exalt you above anyone else; it is clear then that there can be neither competition nor any ground for boasting. The gifts do not compete with the each other; instead each gift compliments the other.)*

12:30 All are not specifically gifted as healers. All do not necessarily speak in tongues. Are all equally accurate in their interpretation of what was said in a foreign tongue? *(The point is not how gifted you are in yourself, but how effective you are to equip others to discover themselves in the full stature of Christ.)*

12:31 While you are keen to discover which are your favorite gifts, allow me to introduce you to the *summum bonum* of life. This transcends all! *(**summum bonum** - the highest good - Latin)*

LOVE IS WHO YOU ARE!

13:1 Speaking in tongues is not the point; [1]love is. It is neither angelic eloquence, nor the mastery of human language that persuades. It doesn't matter how poetic, prophetic, or profound I may sound; my conversation is reduced to the hollow noise of clanging brass cymbals if love's echo is absent. (*The Greek word for the love of God is* [1]*agape from the word,* **agoo***, meaning to lead like a shepherd guides his sheep, and* **pao***, meaning to rest, i.e. "he leads me beside still waters." By the waters of reflection my soul remembers who I am. [Ps 23]. God's rest is established upon his image and likeness redeemed in us. Thus, to encounter agape is to remember who I am. Jesus the Savior of humankind rescued God's image and likeness in human form. The grace of God shines as bright as day making the salvation of humankind undeniably visible [Titus 2:11].*)

13:2 I could predict the future in detail and have a word of knowledge for everyone. I could possess amazing faith, and prove it by moving mountains! It doesn't make me any more important than anyone else. Love is who you are! You are not defined by your gift or deeds. (*Love gives context to faith. Moving mountains is not the point, love is.*)

13:3 Love is not about defending a point of view; even if I am prepared to give away everything I have and die a martyr's death; love does not have to prove itself by acts of supreme devotion or self sacrifice!

13:4 Love is large in being passionate about life and relentlessly patient in bearing the offenses and injuries of others with kindness. Love is completely content and strives for nothing. Love has no desire to make others feel inferior and has no need to sing its own praises.

13:5 Love is predictable and does not behave out of character. Love is not ambitious. Love is not [1]spiteful and gets no mileage out of another's mistakes. (*The word,* [1]*paroxuno, translates as spiteful, it has no sharp edges.*)

13:6 Love sees no joy in injustice. Love's delight is in everything that truth celebrates.

13:7 Love is a fortress where everyone feels protected rather than exposed! Love's persuasion is persistent! Love believes. Love never loses hope and always remains constant in contradiction.

13:8 Love never loses its altitude! (*The word,* **ekpipto***, means to lose height, to stop soaring.*) Prophecies will cease. (*Just like when a placenta is discarded after a baby is born.*) Tongues will pause. (*In order for that which was spoken in shadow-language to be fully interpreted.*) The quest for knowledge will be inappropriate when perfection is grasped.

13:9 What we perceived in prophetic glimpses

13:10 is now concluded in completeness!

13:11 When I was an [1]infant I spoke infant gibberish with the mind of an infant; my reasoning also was typical of an infant; how it all changed when I became a grown-up! I am an infant no more! (*The word,* [1]*nepios, means without any command of speech.*)

217

13:12 There was a time of [1]suspense, when everything we saw was merely mirrored in the prophetic word, like in an enigma; but then *(when I became an adult in the revelation of Christ)* I gaze face-to-face that I may know me, even as I have always been known! *(The word, [1]arti, comes from airo, meaning to keep in suspense. "I knew you before I formed you in your mother's womb!"[Jer 1:5])*

13:13 [1]Now persuasion and every pleasurable [2]expectation is [3]completed in agape. *(Here, in agape, my soul remembers who I am! Psalm 23)* Faith, hope and love are in [3]seamless union. Agape is the superlative of everything faith and [2]hope always knew to be true about me! Love defines my [3]eternal moment! *(Where the word, [1]nun, means now, at this very moment, arti, [v 12] means until now, a time of suspense; [2]elpis, means hope, pleasant expectation; and [3]meno, means to continue to be present. To continue in a seamless union)*

14:1 Be love driven in your pursuit of spiritual gifts; desire earnestly to speak with inspired revelation. *(The word, **prophetes**, translates as enlightened speech. In Greek writings, a **prophetes** is an interpreter of oracles or of other hidden things. In the context of scripture, Jesus is both the theme as well as the completeness of the prophetic word. The prophetic foretelling of the Old Testament pointed to Christ. [Lk 24:27, 44; Jn 5:39].*

In the New Testament the prophetic has its reference in the finished work of the cross more so than in the prediction of future events. The prophets who prophesied of the grace that was to be yours searched and inquired about this salvation; they inquired what person or time was indicated by the Spirit of Christ within them when predicting the sufferings of Christ and the subsequent glory. [1 Pet 1:10-11 RSV]

Hebrews 1:1 Throughout ancient times God spoke in many fragments and glimpses of prophetic thought to our fathers.

1:2 Now, the sum total of his conversation with us, has finally culminated in a son. In his sonship, God declares him the heir of all things. He is, after all, the author of the ages.

1:3 We have our beginning and our being in him. He is the force of the universe, sustaining everything that exists by the logic of his eternal utterance! Jesus is the radiant and flawless expression of the person of God. He makes the glorious intent of God visible and mirrors the character and every attribute of God in human form. This powerful final utterance of God is the vehicle that carries the weight of the universe. What he communicates is the central theme of everything that exists. The content of his message celebrates the fact that God took it upon himself to successfully cleanse and acquit humankind. The man Jesus is now his right hand of power, the executive authority seated in the boundless measure of his majesty. He occupies the highest seat of dominion to endorse our innocence! His throne is established upon our redeemed righteousness. ("Having accomplished purification of sins, he sat down ..." More than two thousand years ago the conversation that had begun before time was recorded—sustained in fragments of thought throughout the ages, whispered in prophetic language, chiseled in stone and inscribed in human conscience and memory—became a living person. Beyond the tablet of stone, the papyrus scroll or parchment roll, human life has become the articulate voice of God. Jesus is the crescendo of God's conversation with humankind; he gives context and content to the authentic thought. Everything that God had in mind for mankind is voiced in him. Jesus is God's language. His name defines his mission. As Savior of the world he truly redeemed the image and likeness of the invisible God and made him apparent again in human form, as in a mirror.)

The purpose of the prophetic, just like with every other ministry gift, is to encourage and edify the church with the success of the cross as its reference. In the instance recorded in Acts 11 where Agabus and his team foretold the famine that was to come, the new believers from Antioch immediately saw this as a brilliant strategy of the spirit to prepare provision for their Jewish friends in Judea. Antioch was the first community of believers to be called Christian, and they were non-Jewish; this might have caused distance between them and the Jewish church but here was their opportunity to take the initiative to break down any such barriers! "When your enemy is hungry, feed him!" [Rom 12:20]

Some modern day prophetic ministries have brought confusion rather than clarity and freedom by a wrong emphasis on the prophetic! Many sincere believers became addicted to the "prophetic" and began to attach more value to yet another future prediction than what they saw in the completed work of Christ! This became a snare and made the "prophetic" a type of Christian fortune telling! While knowledge about future happenings is exciting and also can be strategic, if it does not celebrate the finished work of Christ as its point of reference it becomes a distraction.

The most profound future information pales in significance in the light of what already happened to mankind in Christ! Religion thrives on two lies, distance and delay; Jesus cancelled both. Every possible definition of distance was cancelled on the cross. "Every valley shall be lifted up, and every mountain and hill be made low; every crooked place shall be made straight and every rough place smooth!" [Isa 40:4] Every excuse that anyone could have to feel separated from God was deleted in Christ.

The hour that was to come has come; Jesus is the fullness of time! God can never get any closer to mankind than what he already did in the incarnation. God cannot say more to the human race than what he did in Jesus.)

14:2 For the one who speaks in a strange tongue speaks intimate spirit mysteries between him and God but no one else can understand him.

14:3 But those who prophesy inspire their audience constructively and comfort them with ¹companionship and ²instruction. *(The word ¹parakaleo; to accompany; to affiliate; to associate; from **para**, a preposition indicating close proximity, a thing proceeding from a sphere of influence, with a suggestion of union of place of residence, to have sprung from its author and giver, originating from, denoting the point from which an action originates, intimate connection, and **kaleo**, to identify by name, to surname. Instruction is translated from ²paramutheo, from **para** and **muthos** from **mueo**, meaning to teach with narratives.)*

14:4 While speaking in tongues is primarily for personal edification, prophetic instruction inspires the church.

14:5 I am happy for all of you to speak in tongues, but I desire even more that each one of you will also speak revelation knowledge for the benefit of the whole church. So please do not speak in tongues in the church unless you can also interpret what you have just said.

14:6 Imagine how confusing it would be if I visit you and all I do is impress you with my spirituality by speaking in tongues; how could I possibly benefit you unless I speak with revelation insight and inspired prophetic instruction.

14:7 Any musical instrument like a flute or guitar would irritate the audience if all it did was repeating indistinct sounds without any melody. Play music that everyone will appreciate! *(The Greek word for harp is **kithara**.)*

14:8 If the bugle gives an uncertain sound, the soldiers will miss the moment to prepare themselves to advance in battle! *(Do you realize the importance of what I am saying? Do not misinterpret strategic instruction for personal edification.)*

14:9 Make every word count in order to bring maximum benefit to your audience; [1]weigh your words then you will not be wasting your breath! *(The words [1]eusemos logos translates as a well marked word.)*

14:10 In nature every voice vibrates with meaning; even animal and bird sounds are distinct and significant.

14:11 There is no point in having a conversation with someone if you do not understand the one another's language.

14:12 Let me make it very clear, while speaking in tongues has its personal benefits, do not make it the thing everybody wants to do! Then you miss the whole point of spiritual gifts! What is the value if a million people can speak in tongues but they are completely incapable of bringing a word of inspired instruction? Tongues are most certainly not a mark of spirituality! The greater blessing is not in getting the blessing but in being a blessing to others!

14:13 Do not even attempt to speak in tongues in the congregation if you are unable to also unfold and explain the meaning of what was said!

14:14 Why pray in tongues without understanding? Then there is no point in it.

14:15 Even in worship the two go hand in hand: I will pray with the spirit and continue with understanding; I will worship God in spiritual songs and then conclude by singing with inspired understanding! *(Remember Paul's introduction to the spiritual gifts in chapter 12:1, "Spiritual manifestations are not to be confused with the spooky! Just because it is spirit dimension does not mean that you cannot understand what God's Spirit is saying to you." Paul's passion is to make all men see what God saw when Jesus died and was raised; the spiritual gifts are not to add confusion but clarity to the gospel.)*

14:16 If all you do is speak blessings in tongues, how can anyone else in the same room, especially those who are completely ignorant of spiritual things, feel included and in agreement with what you are saying?

14:17 There is nothing wrong with your thanksgiving as such; it is just a pity that you should exclude someone in your immediate audience.

14:18 Am I against speaking in tongues? Not at all! I am so grateful to God that I speak in tongues; I do so perhaps more than all of you!

14:19 But when we gather together I would rather speak five words with my understanding in order to inspire someone with mutual [1]resonance than waste a thousand words in tongues. *(The word, [1]katecheo, is where the word catechism comes from, from **kata**, downward and echo, to hold or echo; thus, to resonate. Resonance instructs truth and defeats debate.)*

221

14:20 Brothers and sisters, the days of being children in our understanding of spiritual matters are over! Be innocent as ¹infants concerning evil but in ²understanding be perfectly articulate! *(The word, ¹nepios, translates as without the command of language, babyish, gibberish. The word Paul uses here for understanding is the word ²phren where we get the word diaphragm; it refers to an inner knowing, a deeper knowledge than mere academic consent.)*

14:21 In the law it is written, "In foreign tongues and strange sounds I will speak to this people, and still they will not understand," says the Lord. *(The law refers to the Old Covenant Scriptures, including the Psalms and the Prophets. In Isaiah 28:9-11, Isaiah writes: You say, "Who are you to lord it over us? We're not babies in diapers to be talked down to by such as you — 'Da, da, da, da, blah, blah, blah, blah. That's a good little girl, that's a good little boy.' But that's exactly how you will be addressed. God will speak to this people in baby talk, one syllable at a time — But they won't listen." — The Message.)*

By now you (Jews) should have been professors, able to teach the rest of the world, but you are still struggling with the ABC of God's language in Christ [Heb 5:12]. The difference between the prophetic shadow and the real is like that between milk and meat in your diet. You cannot live on baby food for the rest of your lives! [Heb 1:1-3] The revelation of righteousness is the meat of God's word. [Babes live on milk, "the prophetic shadow of the real, which was to come."]) So does everyone who is not ¹pierced in the ear of his heart by the revelation of Christ. [Romans 1:17, God's act of righteousness in Christ restored mankind to blameless innocence.] The word, ¹apeiros, translates as not pierced, tested by piercing.

Hebrews 5:14, This is the nourishment of the mature. They are those who have their faculties of perception trained as by gymnastic precision to distinguish the relevant from the irrelevant. (The mature are those who know the difference between the shadow and the substance; between the futility of the law of works and willpower to work righteousness, and righteousness revealed by the faith of God in the finished work of Christ.)

14:22 In a certain sense tongues are also a prophetic sign pointing towards the revelation of Christ; thus unbelievers are brought to faith.

(Acts 2:4-11 says it all: "And they were all filled with the Holy Spirit and began to speak in other tongues, as the Spirit gave them utterance.

Now there were dwelling in Jerusalem Jews, devout men from every nation under heaven. And at this sound the multitude came together, and they were bewildered, because each one heard them speaking in his own language. And they were amazed and wondered, saying, "Are not all these who are speaking Galileans?

And how is it that we hear, each of us in his own native language? Parthians and Medes and Elamites and residents of Mesopotamia, Judea and Cappadocia, Pontus and Asia, Phrygia and Pamphylia, Egypt and the parts of Libya belonging to Cyrene, and visitors from Rome, both Jews and proselytes, Cretans and Arabians, we hear them telling in our own tongues the mighty works of God." [RSV])

Prophetic instruction is often used specifically to edify the believers; *(but can also be used to convince an unbeliever, e.g., through a word of knowledge. [See Jn 4:18, 19, 29])*

14:23 If an unbeliever or someone completely ignorant of spiritual things happens to walk into one of your meetings while everyone is going off in tongues they will think that you are crazy and nothing will attract them to your faith.

14:24 However if all speak with inspired revelation, the newcomer will feel drawn by the message that brings conviction and light.

14:25 By witnessing the gift of the word of knowledge, where something that could not be known in any other way comes to light, the visitor will be struck with awe and acknowledge God in you and will yield himself to God in worship.

14:26 I would encourage you to conduct your meetings in such a way that everyone is mutually edified. Each one in turn may contribute in music, in a teaching; another may bring a tongue with a revelation and interpretation.

14:27 I want to be very clear on the issue of tongues and its practice in the assembly: if someone insists on speaking in tongues; keep it short, let it be only two or at the most three in turn, definitely not all three at the same time, and let one interpret what was said.

14:28 If there is no interpretation, let the one who wants to talk in tongues rather be quiet; he can have his own private conversation with God when he is alone.

14:29 Let only two or three prophets speak while the others weigh what was said.

14:30 If another picks up something that is not consistent with the revelation of the gospel, he should bring the conversation back to order while the first person be silent. *(Which is exactly what I have done with verses 34-38. I do not consider them legitimate scriptures from Paul.)*

14:31 The two or three people prophesying should take turns to speak; if more than one speaks at the same time the objective is lost and no one can gain any insight or encouragement from the prophetic word.

14:32 The spirit of the prophet is subject to the prophet.

14:33 Confusion is not of God; peace and harmony sets the pace in all the churches of the saints.

14:34-35 *(Women should shut up in church; they should know their place of submission just as they are taught in the law! If they need to know anything their husbands can instruct them at home; church is certainly not a place where women should voice their opinion; they also do not qualify to operate in any of the gifts of the spirit!*

Hee hee hee! This sounds like a grumpy old church father voicing his opinion!

This is certainly not consistent with Paul's revelation that in Christ there is neither male nor female! [See 2 Corintians 5:14,16, Galatians 3:28, also 1 Corinthians 11:3-17])

14:36-38 *(Now to add insult to injury, the same author of the previous verses lashes out against anyone who would not share his sentiment concerning women.)*

14:39 To conclude the tongues and prophecy debate; encourage prophecy with greater enthusiasm than tongues. However do not forbid tongues altogether,

14:40 but let it all happen with discretion and dignity!

15:1 Brothers and sisters, herewith a summary of the good news that I endorse; I announced to you with glad confidence how greatly advantaged you are in Christ; you immediately associated yourselves with this message in which you are now firmly established.

15:2 In this gospel you realized your salvation; the words I spoke echoed in your hearts; I now desire to reinforce your faith in order to erase any possible grounds for doubt.

15:3 I fully included you in the message I embrace with my whole being. Of first importance is the fact that the death that Jesus died for our sins was in exact fulfillment of the promise recorded in scripture. *(Isa 53:4, 5, Ps 22)*

15:4 Also his burial and third day resurrection were accurately foretold. *(Hos 6:2)*

15:5 Then there are the many eyewitnesses; Kefas, as well as all the other disciples who saw him after his resurrection.

15:6 He then appeared to more than five hundred followers of whom most are still alive at the time of this writing.

15:7 After that he was seen by James *(Jesus's brother; Gal 1:19)*, then again by all the apostles *(at the Mount of Olives.)*,

15:8 and finally he also appeared to me; certainly not as a reward for my spirituality or good behavior! It was like an unexpected traumatic birth. *(The word, **ektroma**, means out of trauma.)*

15:9 Because I persecuted the church of God, I cannot even begin to rate myself along with the apostles. I am the least of the least and unworthy to even be called an apostle.

15:10 While my own doing completely disqualified me; his doing now defines me. I am what I am by the grace of God. I am because he is! His grace was not wasted on me; instead I am inspired to labor beyond the point of exhaustion, more than anything I ever did under the law of performance; whatever it is that I accomplish now has grace written all over it. I take no credit for it.

15:11 Whether you came to faith through my preaching or someone else's is not important.

15:12 What is important though is that you understand the revelation of his resurrection. The resurrection of Christ from the dead is the theme of preaching; for some to say that he is not also raised within you is to miss the whole point of the message.

15:13 If our co-resurrection is not proclaimed then the resurrection of Jesus from the dead is no longer relevant.

15:14 If Christ is not raised from the dead there is nothing left for us to preach and nothing left for you to believe.

15:15 We would be misrepresenting God since we declared that he raised Christ from the dead; when in fact he did not, so it would be man's word against God's!

15:16 If there is no universal resurrection from the dead then there can be no individual resurrection from the dead; then Jesus did not really rise from the dead.

15:17 And if Jesus is still dead your faith has no relevance and you are still in your sins. *(In Paul's understanding the body of Christ on the cross was the document of humanity's guilt and the resurrection was the receipt of their acquittal [Col 2:14, 15 and Rom 4:25]. If humanity was still guilty after Jesus died, his resurrection would neither be possible nor relevant! This explains Acts 10:28 and 2 Cor 5:14 and 16. Acts 17:31 says, "because God had fixed a day on which he would judge the world in righteousness by a man whom he has appointed, and of this he has given assurance to all men by raising him from the dead.")*

15:18 No resurrection implies no hope for anyone beyond the grave; it makes no difference whether you believed that you were included in Christ's death or not.

15:19 If our hope in Christ was restricted to only benefit us in this life then imagine the severity of our disappointment if it all had to come to an abrupt end when we died.

15:20 However this very moment the risen Christ represents everyone who has ever died; exactly how the first fruit would represent the complete harvest.

15:21 The same humanity who died in a man was raised again in a man.

15:22 In Adam all died; in Christ all are made alive.

15:23 All are individually made alive in the order of Christ; he is the first fruit and in [1]his immediate presence we are personally revealed as his own. *(The word [1]parousia was often translated to mean the coming of the Lord; however, the two components of the word are, **para,** a preposition indicating close proximity, a thing proceeding from a sphere of influence, with a suggestion of union of place of residence, to have sprung from its author and giver, originating from, denoting the point from which an action originates, intimate connection; and **eimi,** I am: his immediate presence realized in me.)*

15:24 The complete conclusion in his work of redemption is celebrated in his yielding the full harvest of his reign to God the Father, having [1]brought to naught the law of works which supported every definition of dominion under the fall, including all [2]principalities, all [3]authority and every [4]dynamic influence in society. *(He brought to naught the law of works, [1]katargeo, from **kata,** meaning intensity, and **argos,** meaning labor; thus free from all self effort to attempt to improve what God has already perfected in Christ. All principalities, [2]arche, or chief ranks, i.e., kings, governors; this includes any governing system whereby one is ranked above the other on the basis of their performance or preference. All authority, [3]exousia, comes from **ek,** denoting origin and* *eimi, I am; in this case, because of what I can do I am defined by what I can do better than you; therefore, I have authority over you. Every dynamic influence in society, [4]dunamis, means power, in this case, willpower. Every government structure in society will be brought under the dominion of grace where the Christ life rules.*

The kingdom of God is the dominion of the Christ life in human form, where righteousness is based on who we are and not on what we do; who we are by God's doing and not who we are by our own doing; right being and not merely right acting. Where the law of works was duty and guilt driven; the law of faith is love driven. [Rom 3:27, Gal 5:6, 2 Cor 10:12] when they measure themselves by one another, and compare themselves with one another, they are without understanding.)

15:25 His dominion is destined to subdue all hostility and contradiction under his feet. *(The lowest part of the human body will equally share in this victory. "The Lord said to my Lord, Sit at my right hand until I make your enemies your footstool." [Ps 110:1] Jesus is Lord of Lords; in his victory mankind is restored to lordship; "I say you are gods, all of you are sons of the Most High" [Ps 82:6 RSV].)*

15:26 Resurrection life will finally triumph over every definition of death.

15:27 When David says in Psalm 8 that mankind is destined to reign over all things he obviously does not mean that humanity will also rule over their Maker. *(He has made mankind all but equal to himself, he crowned them with his own glory and dignity, and appointed them in a position of authority over all the works of his hands." [Hebrews 2:7 and Psalm 8:4-6; no angel can boast that.]*

Hebrews 2:8 God's intention was that mankind should rule the planet. He subjected everything without exception to their control. Yet, looking at the human race, it does not seem that way at all.

Hebrews 2:9 But what is apparent is Jesus ["but now God spoke to us in a son ..." Heb 1:1-3] Let us then consider him in such a way that we may clearly perceive what God is saying to mankind in him. In the death he suffered he descended for a brief moment below the lowest ranked angel in order to taste the death of the entire human race; and in doing so, to fulfill the grace of God and be crowned again as a man, representing all mankind with glory and highly esteemed honor.

Hebrews 2:10 He now towers in conspicuous prominence far above all things. He is both their author and their conclusion. He now summons every son of his, through a perfected salvation, to his own glory. The extent of the suffering he bore is the measure of the perfection of the salvation over which he presides. [The word, prepo, means to tower above in prominence. See also Heb 7:26]

Ephesians 4:8 Scripture confirms that he led us as trophies in his triumphant procession on high; he repossessed his gift [likeness] in mankind. [Eph 2:6, We are also elevated in his ascension to be equally welcome in the throne room of the heavenly realm where we are now seated together with him in his authority. Quote from the Hebrew text in Psalm 68:18; lakachta mattanoth baadam, thou hast taken gifts in human form, in Adam. [The gifts which Jesus Christ distributes to us he has received in us, in and by virtue of his incarnation. Commentary by Adam Clarke.]

Eph 4:9 The fact that he ascended confirms his victorious descent into the deepest pits of human despair. [In John 3:13: "No one has ascended into heaven but he who descended from heaven, even the son of man." All mankind originates from above; we are anouthen, from above. See Jas 1:17, 18.])

Ephesians 4:10 He now occupies the ultimate rank of authority from the lowest regions where he stooped down to rescue us to the highest authority in the heavens, having executed his mission to the full. (Fallen mankind is fully restored to the authority of the authentic life of their design. [Ps 139:8].)

15:28 In subduing all things under him the son himself in his own submission to the Father will confirm that God is all and in all. *(John 14:20, "In that day you will know that I am in my father and you in me and I in you." The day Jesus refers to here happened when he died and was raised again; the day for us dawns the moment we realize our co-inclusion in his death and resurrection.)*

15:29 *Now here's a novel idea: if someone died who didn't get baptized then you can baptize someone else in their stead. (That should convince God to raise that person from the dead one day; this way you don't have to worry about anything, just remember to charge a decent fee so that you can build an Olympic size pool in your church!)*

(There is no doubt that this passage was squeezed in here by some heretic church father; since the practice referred to only existed in some churches 200 years later and is in total contradiction to Paul's message; as were other practices that later evolved in churches, such as buying indulgences to shorten a deceased loved one's time in the church's idea of "purgatory!"

Here is Paul's take on baptism: *1 Cor 1:17, "My mandate was not about winning members for some "Christian club" through baptism! I am commissioned to declare the good news without any strings attached; nothing to distract from the powerful effect of the revelation of the cross of Christ." [The mystery of the cross is the revelation of mankind's inclusion in his death and resurrection. See 1 Cor 2:7])*

15:30 Why would we bother to constantly put ourselves in life threatening situations by preaching this gospel if it is all coming to nothing in the end anyway?

15:31 My passion for your joy in Christ Jesus our Lord puts my life at frequent risk. As [1]certain as I am of your salvation, so certain am I of the resurrection; therefore, I am more than confident to daily live dangerously close to death. *(This [1]ne is a particle of swearing. People swear or affirm by their objects of dearest affection and desire; our salvation and joy was Paul's dearest affection.)*

15:32 If I like many other prisoners had to fight wild beasts in the amphitheater of Ephesus, what would be my gain if the dead are not raised; then we might as well live by the philosophy, "let us eat and drink as much as we can today for tomorrow we die!"

15:33 Do not be distracted by a message that excludes the revelation of the resurrection; yielding yourselves to the persuasive conversation of others, their negative influence in your lives would be inevitable.

15:34 Awake to righteousness, and the distortion of sin will have no further effect on you. God is not confused. What a shame that anyone should exchange what God knows to be true about us to someone else's inferior opinion.

15:35 There might be many skeptics who would say, "How are the dead raised and what does the resurrected body look like?"

15:36 Think about it this way, a seed that is sown has to first die before it lives again.

15:37 And the plant that grows from the seed does not even resemble the grain that was sown. If you only know what wheat looks like in its seed form you might not be able to recognize its plant.

15:38 God has designed a unique body for every plant species.

15:39 The human body differs from the bodies of animals and so do the bodies of fish and birds differ from all other bodies.

15:40 There are celestial bodies as well as terrestrial bodies. The glory of the one differs from the other. There are skin-bodies and spirit-bodies. *(Our skin-bodies have a sell by date; our spirit-bodies are eternal. [2 Cor 5:1])*

15:41 The glory of the sun differs from the glory of the moon; *(while the one radiates light, the other reflects light.)* Also the stars differ from one another. Each one occupies its own unique place in space.

15:42 So also with the resurrection from the dead, the body that was sown into the earth decays, but the risen person is immortal.

15:43 It is sown in sadness but raised in honor; it is sown in frailty but raised in power.

15:44 It is sown as a physical body and raised as a spiritual body. The fact that there is a physical body confirms that there is also a spiritual body.

15:45 It is recorded in scripture how the first Adam became a living soul; the last Adam is a life radiating spirit. *(In partaking of resurrection life now, we radiate the Christ life. No wonder then that Peter's shadow healed people! Jesus is the last Adam; when he died mankind's Adamic reference died. Jesus is the head of the human race. Human life is not defined by Adam but defined in Christ.)*

15:46 Physical life is the platform for spiritual life.

15:47 Human life was reduced to slavery and the soul-ruled earthly realm through Adam's fall but is now awakened to lordship in the heavenly realm of spiritual realities through the knowledge of our co-resurrection with Christ. *([See Col 3:1-11.] We theologically created the idea of mankind being "sinful by nature" as if humans are flawed by design. In fact it is a distorted mind-*

set that we inherited from Adam that Jesus had to free us from. "Your indifferent mind-set alienated you from God into a lifestyle of annoyances, hardships, and labors, sponsored by the law of sin and death that lodged in your bodies hosting a foreign influence, foreign to your design; just like a virus that would attach itself to a person." Col 1:21 There is nothing wrong with our design or salvation, we were thinking wrong. [See Isa 55:8-11, Eph 4:17, 18 and also Eph 2:1-11.])

15:48 The reduced state of the individual left its mark on mankind as being earthly; now the redeemed state of mankind confirms their origin in God and marks their new heavenly life.

15:49 Just as we were once defined by the flesh *(our earthly image)* **we are now defined by our spirit** *(our heavenly)* **image.**

15:50 Flesh and blood has a sell-by date; the bodies you live in now will not last forever.

15:51 [1]Ponder this mystery, I want to show you something that you have never seen before: [2]no one will sleep; [3]we will all experience exactly the same change. *(In other words, [1]idou musterion, Look! A Mystery! And [2]pantes ou koimethesometha, means no one will sleep; and [3]pantes de allangesometha; everyone will be changed. See 1 Thessalonians 4:13-18*

If our hope in Christ was restricted to only benefit us in this life then imagine the severity of our disappointment if it all had to come to an abrupt end when we died. However this very moment the risen Christ represents everyone who has ever died; exactly like the first fruit would represent the complete harvest [1 Cor 15:19-22].

The same humanity who died in a man was raised again in a man. In Adam all died; in Christ all are made alive. [See 2 Cor 5:14] The love of Christ resonates within us and leaves us with only one conclusion: Jesus died humanity's death; therefore, in God's logic every individual simultaneously died. [See also Heb 9:27, 28] The same goes for everyone: a person dies only once and then faces judgment. Christ died once and faced the judgment of the entire human race! His second appearance has nothing to do with sin but to reveal salvation for all to lay a hold of him. He appeared as High Priest before the Throne of Justice once, with his own blood to atone for the sins of the whole world. In his resurrection he appeared as Savior of the world! Sin is no longer on the agenda for the Lamb of God has taken away the sin of the world! The same High Priest who atoned for mankind is now also their Advocate! [1 Cor 15:3-5, Rom 4:25, Acts 17:30, 31; 1 Jn 2:1])

15:52 This will happen in an instant, in a blink of the eye: the final trumpet will sound, then the dead shall be raised and we, who are still alive, shall be instantly changed into a different kind of body.

15:53 For this corruptible must be clothed with incorruption and this mortal must be clothed with immortality.

15:54 What was spoken in Isaiah 25:8 is finally realized even in our physical death: "Death is swallowed up in victory!"

15:55 O death where is your sting? O grave, where is your victory?

15:56 The sting of death is sin; the strength of sin is the law. *(It was sin that made death so frightening and law-code guilt that gave sin its leverage. — The Message)*

15:57 Your victory is not a maybe; because of the magnanimous doing of Jesus Christ, it is a given! *(But now in a single victorious stroke of Life, all three—sin, guilt, death—are gone, the gift of our Master, Jesus Christ. Thank God! — The Message)*

15:58 For this reason you can afford to be absolutely settled and rock-solid in faith's persuasion and always ready to go beyond where you would have gone before. Your doing now is inspired by your knowing that you are in him. If his resurrection is yours then his victory over sin and death is equally yours.

16:1 With regards your financial contributions to the saints, I have the following arrangement with all the churches in Galatia:

16:2 I encourage you to prepare your individual gifts in advance on a [1]week-by-week basis to whatever extent each one has prospered. This should be kept in treasury; this way there will be no delays or distractions regarding money matters when I visit you.

(Romans 15:25-27, "I am on my way to Jerusalem to encourage the saints. The believers in Greece, all the way from Macedonia as well as those in Achaia have prepared a gift with great delight to bring relief to their Jewish brothers and sisters in Jerusalem who are struggling financially. They feel indebted to them since they share freely in their spiritual wealth.

In Greek, "[1]On one of the Sabbaths." The Jews, however, used the word Sabbath to denote the week; the period of seven days [See Mt 28:1, Mk 16:9, Lk 18:12, Lk 24:1, Jn 20:1, and Jn 20:19; compare with Lev 23:15 and Deut 16:9.] Christians celebrate the first day of the week rather than the seventh in order to celebrate the resurrection of Jesus as the new beginning of every week.)

16:3 Upon my arrival I will endorse by letter those whom you delegate to take your grace gifts to Jerusalem.

16:4 Should there be any merit in my joining them, then they can travel with me.

16:5 It is my intent to visit you via a brief visit to the province of Macedonia. *(Northern Greece)*

16:6 I will probably stay for a while and might even spend the winter with you; then you can help me prepare for my next destination wherever that might be. Some of you may even join me!

16:7 Even though I am not far from you presently, I would prefer not to just see you now in passing but would rather enjoy an extended stay with you in the Lord's purpose. *(The trip from Ephesus to Corinth was merely across the Aegean Sea, and comparatively a short passage en-route to Macedonia. He eventually stayed three months. [See Acts 20:2, 3])*

16:8 I am presently in Ephesus and will not begin my journey before Pentecost. *(Which was in the latter part of spring.)*

16:9 A massive door of opportunity to establish a powerful and effective ministry in Ephesus has opened for me, but since there are also many who dispute this message, I do not want to leave here too soon. *(In Acts 19:9, 10: "but when some were stubborn and disbelieved, speaking evil of the Way before the congregation, he withdrew from them, taking the disciples with him, and dialogued daily in the school of Tyrannus. This continued for two years, so that all the residents of Asia heard the word of the Lord, both Jews and Greeks." Luke does not mention the size of the building but much can be said about the impact of the message! In Acts 19:20-22, "So the word of the Lord grew and prevailed mightily. Now after these events Paul resolved in the Spirit to pass through Macedonia and*

Achaia and go to Jerusalem, saying, 'After I have been there, I must also see Rome.' And having sent into Macedonia two of his helpers, Timothy and Erastus, he himself stayed in Asia for a while'" [RSV])

16:10 My colleague in ministry, Timothy, should arrive in Corinth shortly; ensure that he feels absolutely at home with you. *(In 1 Corinthians 4:17, "This is why I send my beloved son Timothy to you. He is rock-solid in his faith. He shall remind you of me and re-enforce my specific message and emphasis; (the way I teach the 'in Christ' and 'the Christ in you' and his finished work message) in every place and every church I visit.")*

16:11 No one should underrate him; honor him by providing for him and even accompanying him on his journey to join me again in Ephesus. I am eagerly anticipating to welcome him and his team on their arrival from you.

16:12 I strongly urged Apollos to join the team visiting you at present, but he did not feel at liberty to do so. I am sure that he will come in due time. *(Apparently Apollos had left Corinth in disgust over the strife there, which involved him and Paul. He had enough of partisan strife over preachers. [See Acts 19:1 and 1 Corinthians 1-4])*

16:13 Be wide awake and constant in your faith, courageous and invincible.

16:14 Agape is your genesis. Loving everyone around you is what you are all about. *(Our love for one another is awakened by God's love for us.)*

16:15 Here is my urgent appeal to you: take the household of Stephanos as an example; this family was my first fruit of Greece and have taken the initiative to position themselves in ministering to the needs of the saints.

16:16 Give yourselves in the same way to them and to everyone laboring tirelessly in team ministry.

16:17 I want you to know my delight in having Stephanus, Fortunatus and Achaius here with me in Ephesus! They certainly represent you and have made up for your absence!

16:18 Because of them I have such peace about you! They are a real credit to you.

16:19 The churches in all of Asia salute you; also Aquila and Priscilla and the church in their home greet you fondly in the Lord.

16:20 The whole church family sends you big hugs from here; greet one another with a sacred kiss.

16:21 This letter carries my personal signature.

16:22 Anyone who prefers the law above grace remains under the curse mentality. Jesus Christ has come; grace is the authority of his Lordship; we are so fond of him! He is the Messiah the world was waiting for. *(The Aramaic word, **maranatha**, means, our Lord has come!*

Instead of reading the curse when disaster strikes, Habakkuk realizes that the Promise out dates performance as the basis to mankind's acquittal! Deuteronomy 28 would no longer be the motivation or the measure of right or wrong behavior! "Though the fig tree do not blossom, nor fruit be on the vines, the produce of the olive fail and the fields yield no food, the flock be cut off from the fold and there be no herd in the stalls, yet I will rejoice in the Lord, I will joy in the God of my salvation. God, the Lord, is my strength; he makes my feet like hinds' feet, he makes me tread upon my high places." [Hab 3:17–19 RSV])

16:23 His grace is with you; you are highly favored!

16:24 My love is with you; our lives are intertwined in Christ Jesus. I salute him! Amen! Paul.

In defense of his personal integrity and the content of his message, Paul writes with utmost clarity and confidence in chapter 1:18, 19, "God's certainty is our persuasion; there is no maybe in him! The son of God, Jesus Christ whom I, Paul, Sylvanus, and Timothy boldly announced in you is God's ultimate yes to mankind; human life is associated in all that he is. In God's mind there exists not even a hint of hesitation about this!"

The two passages of scripture that impacted my own life and message perhaps more than anything else are recorded in this Epistle. They are 2 Corinthians 3:18, "Now we all with new understanding see ourselves in him as in a mirror; thus we are changed from an inferior mindset to the revealed opinion of our true Origin.".   Then there are these verses in 2 Corinthians 5:14-17, "The love of Christ resonates within us and leaves us with only one conclusion: Jesus died humanity's death; therefore, in God's logic every individual simultaneously died.

"Now if all were included in his death they were equally included in his resurrection. This unveiling of his love redefines human life! Whatever reference we could have of ourselves outside of our association with Christ is no longer relevant.

"This is radical! No label that could possibly previously define someone carries any further significance! Even our pet doctrines of Christ are redefined. Whatever we knew about him historically or sentimentally is challenged by this conclusion.

(By discovering Christ from God's point of view, we discover ourselves and every other human life from God's point of view!)

"Now whoever you thought you were before, in Christ you are a brand new person! The old ways of seeing yourself and everyone else are over. Look! The resurrection of Jesus has made everything new"

Scofield's Reference Bible notes the following on 2 Corinthians

DATE: A.D. 60; probably from Philippi, after the events of Acts 19:23 to 20:1-21.

THEME: This Epistle discloses the touching state of the great apostle at this time. It was one of physical weakness, weariness and pain. Also his emotional burdens. These were two kinds: solicitude for the maintenance of the churches in grace as against the law-teachers, and anguish of heart over the distrust felt toward him by Jews and Jewish Christians. The chilling doctrines of the "legalizers" were accompanied by detraction, and by denial of his apostleship.

It is evident that the really dangerous sect in Corinth was that which said, "and I of the Messiah" [1 Cor 1:12]. They rejected the new revelation through Paul of the doctrines of grace; grounding themselves, probably, on the kingdom teachings of our Lord as "a minister of circumcision" [Rom 15.8]; seemingly oblivious that a new dispensation had been introduced by Christ's death. This made necessary a defense of the origin and extent of Paul's apostolic message. — *Scofield's*)

1:1 I, Paul, am overwhelmed with the sense of God's commission on my life; Jesus Christ is the compelling urgency of my ministry. My brother Timothy and I address this writing to the [1]ekklesia of God in Corinth, including all the saints in the whole of Greece. (*Meaning [1]church; from the preposition* **ek,** *which always denotes origin, and* **kaleo,** *which means to identify by name; to surname.*)

1:2 The Lordship of Jesus the Messiah endorses the fact that you are the object of God's favor and friendship.

1:3 [1]Well done, God! You are the Father of our Master Jesus Christ; you are the Father of [2]compassion and the God in whom everyone is equally esteemed! (*The word,* [1]**eulogeo,** *is the well done announcement;* [2]**parakaleo,** *comes from* **para,** *a preposition indicating close proximity, a thing proceeding from a sphere of influence, with a suggestion of union of place of residence, to have sprung from its author and giver, originating from, denoting the point from which an action originates, intimate connection and* **kaleo,** *meaning to surname.*)

1:4 There is no contradiction of any proportion that we can possibly face that has what it takes to exasperate us or distance us from God. Our consciousness of his inseparable nearness immediately reinforces us to extend the same tangible [1]closeness to you in your difficult times, and together we snuggle up in the [1]comfort of his intimate embrace! (*Paul uses the word,* [1]**parakaleo,** *which comes from* **para,** *close proximity, and* **kaleo,** *to identify by name; often translated, to comfort.*)

1:5 This bliss and closeness we now participate in was made possible through the enormous [1]consequence of the sufferings of Christ. The overwhelming extent of his sufferings brought about this equally overwhelming sense of inseparable oneness! (*Paul uses* [1]**eis,** *which is a primary preposition indicating the point reached in conclusion. The theme of scripture is the sufferings of Christ and the subsequent glory. "This is why no form of suffering can interfere with my joy. Every suffering on your behalf is just another opportunity to reinforce that which might still be lacking [in your understanding] of the affliction of Christ on behalf of his body which is the church." [1 Pet 1:10 and Col 1:24]*

The inconvenience that Paul might be suffering on behalf of the believers is not to add to the sufferings of Christ—as though the sufferings of Christ on our behalf were insufficient, but it is to further emphasize and confirm the principle of unselfish love that constrains New Testament ministry.)

1:6 Our afflictions and testimony of his closeness in the midst of it all is to spark you with courage whenever you might be facing similar contradictions. We all participate in the same salvation and enjoy equal closeness!

1:7 We are so confident about you, knowing that there is nothing you could possibly face or suffer that can separate you from his nearness.

1:8 We want you to know that we are not exaggerating the extreme contradictions and sufferings we faced in Asia! We were weighed down with enormous persecution beyond any measure of endurance; we really thought that we were going to die!

1:9 We came to terms within ourselves with the fact that we were on death row; there was no escape except our belief that God could raise us from the dead.

1:10 In the resurrection of Jesus from the dead he already delivered us from death's greatest threat; now he continues to make our victory over death's claim a daily reality. We are confident that he will raise us again! *(See 2 Cor 11:24-28 and Acts 14:19.)*

1:11 We value your prayers! The more people partner with us in prayer the greater the gratitude shared in our testimony!

1:12 The testimony of our [1]conscience is the source of our joy! We are [2]intertwined together in [3]transparent innocence; there is no trace of a hidden agenda for the flesh to glory in. God's grace is our conversation in the world and is amplified in our oneness with you. Grace abounds! *(What we are able to see together gives me so much reason for boasting in our salvation! The word, [1]suneido, translates as conscience, joint-seeing; and [2]haplous comes from hama, a particle of union. The word, pleko, translates as to intertwine, and [3]heilikrine translates as scrutinized in the rays of the sun to prove its flawlessness.)*

1:13 There is nothing to be read between the lines but only that which you will be able to [1]recognize with [2]immediate resonance. I am convinced that you will see the full intent and conclusion of our testimony from start to finish, and that you will never find any reason to think otherwise! *(The word, [1]anaginosko, means to know again by recognition and repetition, and [2]epiginosko means to become fully acquainted with.)*

1:14 To some extent you have already understood that our joy is [1]mirrored in one another. The [2]day of the Lord Jesus Christ is no longer a distant promise but a fulfilled reality. *(The word, [1]kathaper, comes from kata, meaning according to and per, which is an enclitic particle significant of abundance and thoroughness which comes from the word, peiro, meaning to pierce. The use of the Latin enclitic relates to a word that throws an accent back onto the preceding word, which is here translated as mirrored.*

The "day of the Lord Jesus Christ," is [2]hemera, which is a specific and measured period. Eastern usage of this term differs from our western usage. Any part of a day is counted as a whole day, hence the expression, "three days and three nights," does not mean literally three whole days, but at least one whole day plus part of two other days.

The day of the Lord Jesus is the theme of scripture as in 1 Peter 1:10; this was what the prophets were studying and desiring to know. The content of their message always pointed to the day and the person where the promise of redemption would be realized. The sufferings of the Messiah would redeem and release the glory of God's image and likeness in human life; the glory that Adam lost on behalf of the human race, returns. In Acts 17:31, "In the resurrection, God gave proof to the redeemed innocence of mankind; the "day and the person" prophesied was fulfilled in Jesus." Jesus gives context to this day in John 14:20, "In that day you will know that I am in my Father and you in me and I in you.")

1:15 Looking forward to celebrate our mutual joy, my initial plan was to come to you first before going anywhere else. We wanted you to enjoy the double blessing of our visit.

1:16 We were really looking forward to seeing you again on our return from Macedonia and then to be escorted by you on our trip to Judea.

1:17 It is not our style to hesitate between two opinions. We have no desire to make promises that we cannot keep. When we said yes to you we did not mean, no!

1:18 God's certainty is our persuasion; there is no maybe in him!

1:19 The son of God, Jesus Christ, whom I, Paul, Sylvanus, and Timothy boldly announced in you is God's ultimate yes to mankind. Human life is associated in all that he is. In God's mind there exists not even a hint of hesitation about this!

1:20 In him the detail of every single promise of God is fulfilled; Jesus is God's yes to your total well being! In our union with him the Amen that echoes in us gives evidence to his glorious intent through us.

1:21 God himself endorses this union that we enjoy in Christ.

1:22 His personal signet signature is the official stamp that sanctions our integrity; the Spirit seals God's guarantee in our own hearts.

1:23 So God is my witness in this; I did not break my promise to you. The only reason I did not come to Corinth was to spare you the embarrassment.

1:24 I am not your faith-monitor! I am your co-worker and I am jealous for your joy! You stand on your own feet in your faith!

2:1 I came to the following conclusion that paying you another painful visit *(on my return trip)* would be of no advantage to you!

2:2 My visit would only put you in an awkward position; since you knew that you caused me grief, you would feel under obligation to cheer me up!

2:3 I wrote to you instead; not risking the embarrassment of facing you and then having to deal with sorrow when all I really desired from you was joy! I am convinced that my joy is also your joy!

2:4 There was nothing blasé about my writing. I was in tears with painful distress and deep-felt anguish, certainly not to upset you but that you would know the intensity of my love for you.

2:5 I am not exaggerating the issue by saying that the man whose behavior caused such alarm in me did not merely grieve me but in a sense everyone of you.

2:6 This person has been amply taxed by all.

2:7 It is due time now to offer him your forgiveness and closeness lest he be completely swamped with regret.

2:8 I implore you to make your love for him [1]very clear. *(The word, [1]kuroo, translates as officially; publicly confirm your love for him.)*

2:9   The intent and urgency of my first letter was to prove your loyalty to my ministry and message in its full context.

2:10 I am joined to you *(geographic distance does not separate us)*; your forgiveness is my forgiveness. The favor reflected in the face of Christ is our only valid reference to true forgiveness anyway.

2:11 The [2]agenda of any [1]accusation is to divide and dominate. We are not ignorant about that. *(The word [1]satanas means accuser and [2]nous refers to mind or strategy, agenda, schemes.)*

2:12 So instead of coming to you I went to Troas where again a great ministry opportunity in the good news of Christ was opened for me in the Lord. *(There is not a place on this planet that is not an open door for this gospel!)*

2:13 I expected to find Titus in Troas and was hoping to hear from him refreshing news concerning you. I felt so urgent to meet with Titus that I took leave from Troas and hastened on to look for him in Macedonia. *(See 2 Cor 7:4-8)*

2:14 I am overwhelmed with gratitude! Wherever my travels take me I am so aware that God leads us as trophies in his victory parade. What he knows to be true about us diffuses through us like a perfume of sweet aroma everywhere we go, celebrating the success of the cross. *(In ancient triumphs, abundance of perfumes and wreaths of sweet smelling flowers were used in victory celebrations.)*

2:15 We are a sweet savor of Christ to God evident in everyone we meet. The fragrance of Christ is recognized in all to salvation. The same gospel that announces the fragrant victory of Christ declares the odor of death; the [1]defeat of [2]destruction in everyone! *(This parade of victory is a public announcement of the defeat of the religious systems and structures based on the law of works. Just like it is in any public game where the victory celebration of the winning team is an embarrassment for the losing team. The death of evil is announced in resurrection life! The word,* **apollumi***, is derived from [1]***apo***, away from, and [2]***ollumi***, to destroy, to ruin.)*

2:16 The message we communicate is a fragrance with an immediate association; to darkness, it is the smell of doom *(the death of death)*; to life it is the familiar fragrance of life itself.

2:17 We are not competing with those who have added their [1]price tag to the gospel. Our conversation has its source in Christ; we communicate from the transparent innocence of a face to face encounter with God. *(The law of personal performance or [1]***kapeleuo***, meaning retail.)*

3:1 The days when I needed letters to endorse my authority are over! *(See Acts 9:2)* We are not in a competition showing off our credentials! Some insist on certificates; I do not see any relevance in it! Neither do I require a note of recommendation to you or from you.

3:2 Instead of an impressive certificate framed on my wall I have you framed in my heart! You are our Epistle written within us, an open letter speaking a global language; one that everyone can ¹read and recognize as their mother tongue! *(The word ¹anaginosko, from ana, upward and ginosko, to know upward; thus to draw knowledge from a higher reference; from above; to recognize; to read with recognition.)*

3:3 The fact that you are a Christ-Epistle shines as bright as day! This is what our ministry is all about. The Spirit of God is the living ink. Every trace of the Spirit's influence on the heart is what gives permanence to this conversation. We are not talking law-language here; this is more dynamic and permanent than letters chiseled in stone. This conversation is embroidered in your inner consciousness. *(It is the life of your design that grace echoes within you!)*

3:4 Because of what Christ has done, your lives are proof of our persuasion before God.

3:5 We have not ¹reached this conclusion by any merit of our own! Of God's doing are we made competent! *(The word, ¹logitsomai, means to reckon; making a calculation to which there can only be one logical conclusion.)*

3:6 It is God's signature in our spirit that authorizes New Testament ministry. We are not qualified by a legal document endorsed by a fellow human. The letter *(of the law)* is the administration of death; it is the Spirit *(of grace)* that quickens life.

3:7 Because of its prophetic purpose even the old administration of death, carved in stone evidenced a glimpse of glory; for a brief moment the face of Moses shone with such brilliance that the people of Israel could not even look at his face. The fact that the glory reflected in Moses was brief and fading confirmed that the ministry of the letter had a "sell by" date and that it was destined ¹to be brought to naught. *(It served merely to emphasize the failure of the flesh to access the glory that Adam had lost on humanity's behalf. The word, ¹katargeo, derives from kata, meaning intensity, and argos, meaning labor, denotes that the law of works would be rendered entirely useless; thus, the new arrangement would free us from all self effort to attempt to improve what God has already perfected in Christ. Consider the contrast in verse 18; from a mere glimpse of a veiled and fading glory to unveiled gazing into the face of glory as in a mirror and a transformed life radiating the same glory!)*

3:8 How much more radiant would the ministry of the Spirit be.

3:9 If the ministry of condemnation had a glimpse of glory, the glory that the ministry of righteousness now communicates is beyond comparison! *(There are two administrations: the one confirms mankind's guilt because of Adam;*

the other confirms mankind's innocence because of Christ! The one was upheld by the letter of the law; the other is sustained by the life of the Spirit. Mankind's standing before God is restored; righteousness by the merit of the cross far outweighs any attempt of the flesh to compete! Nothing that anyone can do can improve their standing before God!)

3:10 What seemed glorious and important at the time has been reduced to total obscurity and irrelevance.

3:11 The fragile and fading glory of the flesh is dwarfed into insignificance by the unfading glory of the Spirit! *(The ministry of the New Testament reveals oneness and permanence. In Christ the idea of distance and delay is cancelled.)*

3:12 Our every expectation is fulfilled; therefore, we speak with clarity and conviction! *(Every definition of veil is removed from our conversation! We have no hidden agenda! This is what we say as plainly as possible: the glory that Adam lost on humanity's behalf, Jesus redeemed! The image and likeness of God is no longer a future promise of possibilities and potential; it is our reality and reference now! See Col 1:27)*

3:13 What we say is so unlike Moses who had to keep Israel in suspense with a veiled face; they did not realize that this arrangement would never suffice to secure their standing before God. In essence the letters on stone confirmed their death. All that they could see was the futility of the law of works; how entirely useless their best attempts would be to match the life of their design. *(In Adam all people alike stood condemned; they did not realize it until the law revealed it. In Christ all are declared innocent; yet they do not know it until the Gospel reveals it. [Rom 10:17 and Rom 7:4-25])*

3:14 Since the time of Moses until this very day their minds remain calloused and veiled. They are kept in suspense without realizing that there is no glory left in the law: *(whatever glory there was, carried merely a fading, prophetic glimmer)* **reading the Old Covenant without understanding that Christ is the fulfilment of Scripture is a complete waste of time. Only in discovering our union with Christ is the veil removed and do we realize that the old system is [1]rendered entirely useless.** *(The word [1]katergeo comes from kata, meaning intensity, and argos, meaning labor, the law of works is rendered entirely useless; thus the new arrangement frees us from all self effort to attempt to improve what God has already perfected in Christ.)*

3:15 In the meantime nothing seems to have changed; the same veil continues to blindfold the hearts of people whenever Moses is read. *(Moses symbolizes the futility of self righteousness as the universal blindfold of the religious world. [John 1:17] Against the stark backdrop of the law; with Moses representing the condemned state of mankind, Jesus Christ unveils grace and truth! He is the life of our design redeemed in human form.)*

3:16 The moment anyone [1]returns to the Lord the veil is gone! *(The word, [1]epistrepho means to return to where we've wandered from; "we all like sheep have gone astray." Jesus is God unveiled in human form. [Col 1:15] See also Hebrews*

8:1, "The conclusion of all that has been said points us to an exceptional Person, who towers far above the rest in the highest office of heavenly greatness. He is the executive authority of the majesty of God. 8:2 The office he now occupies is the one which the Moses-model resembled prophetically. He ministers in the holiest place in God's true tabernacle of worship. Nothing of the old man-made structure can match its perfection. 8:10 Now, instead of documenting my laws on stone, I will chisel them into your mind and engrave them in your inner consciousness; it will no longer be a one-sided affair. I will be your God and you will be my people, not by compulsion but by mutual desire." See James 1:25, "Those who gaze into the mirror reflection of the face of their birth are captivated by the effect of a law that frees them from the obligation to the old written code that restricted them to their our own efforts and willpower. No distraction or contradiction can dim the impact of what they see in that mirror concerning the law of perfect liberty [the law of faith] that now frees them to get on with the act of living the life [of their original design]. They find a new spontaneous lifestyle; the poetry of practical living." [The law of perfect liberty is the image and likeness of God revealed in Christ, now redeemed in human life as in a mirror.])

3:17 The Lord and the Spirit are one; his Lordship sanctions our freedom. A freedom from rules chiselled in stone to the voice of our redeemed design echoing in our hearts!

3:18 The days of window-shopping are over! In him every face is [1]unveiled. In [2]gazing with wonder at the [5]blueprint of God displayed in human form, we suddenly realize that we are looking into a mirror, where every feature of his [3]image articulated in Christ is [2]reflected within us! The Spirit of the Lord engineers this radical [4]transformation; we are led [6]from an inferior [5]mind-set to the revealed [5]endorsement of our authentic identity. *(The word, [1]anakalupto; from ana, a preposition denoting upward, to return again, and kalupto, to uncover, unveil. The word, [2]katoptrizomai, means to gaze into a reflection, to mirror oneself. Paul uses [4]metamorphumetha as a present passive indicative from metamorpho; meta, together with, and morphe, form. [The word commonly translated sin, [1]hamartia, from ha, negative or without and meros, alloted portion or form; thus, a distorted form, which is the opposite of metamorphe; with form. The word meros is the stem of morphe.] The word, [3]eikon, translates as exact resemblance, image and likeness; eikon always assumes a prototype, that which it not merely resembles, but from that which it is drawn; [5]doxa, glory, translates as mind-set, or opinion from dokeo, authentic, blueprint-thought. Changed 'from glory to glory', apo doxes eis doxan; eis, a point reached in conclusion; [6]apo, away from, meaning away from the glory that previously defined us, i.e. our own achievements or disappointments, to the glory of our original design that now defines us. Two glories are mentioned earlier in this chapter, the veiled, fading kind represented by Moses, and the unveiled, unfading glory of God mirrored in the face of Christ. See also chapter 4:4 and 6. [Paul writes in Romans 1:17 about the unveiling of God's righteousness and then says it is from faith to faith. Here he does not use the word apo, away from, but the preposition, ek, which always denotes source or origin.] Two glories are mentioned in this chapter; the glory of the flesh, and the unfading glory of God's image and likeness* *redeemed in us. The fading glory represented in the dispensation of the law of Moses is immediately superseded by the unveiling of Christ in us! Some translations of this scripture reads, "we are being changed from glory to glory." This would suggest that change is gradual and will more than likely take a lifetime, which was the typical thinking that trapped Israel for forty years in the wilderness of unbelief! We cannot become more than what we already are in Christ. We do not grow more complete; we simply grow in the knowledge of our completeness! [See Colossians 3:10] We are not changed "from one degree of glory to another," or step by step. How long does it take the beautiful swan to awaken to the truth of its design? The ugly duckling was an illusion! Whatever it was that endorsed the 'ugly duckling' mindset, co-died together with Christ! In the death and resurrection of Jesus Christ, God did not redeem a compromised replica of you; he rescued the original, blueprint you, created in his radiant mirror likeness! Any other 'self' you're trying to find or esteem will disappoint! Reckon your 'DIY-law of works-self' dead, and your redeemed self co-raised and co-seated together with Christ! This is freedom indeed! Galatians 2:19,20; Romans 6:11)*

4:1 Since we are employed by the mercy of God, and not by our own qualifications, quitting is not an option.

4:2 We have renounced hidden agendas (*employing a little bit of the law in an attempt to "balance" out grace*); we have distanced ourselves from any obscure [1]craftiness to manipulate God's word to make it mean what it does not say! With truth on open display in us, we highly recommend our lives to every one's [2]conscience! Truth finds its most authentic and articulate expression in human life. This beats any doctrinal debate! (*It is our passion for all to see what is so completely obvious in the mirror of our redeemed likeness and innocence! The word translated craftiness, is the word* [1]*panourgia from* **pas** *and* **ergon,** *all manner of wearisome labor!* [2]*Conscience in Latin means to know together; in the Greek,* [2]**suneido,** *translates as joint seeing; which is the opposite of* **hades,** *not to see.*)

4:3 If our message seems vague to anyone, it is not because we are withholding something from certain people! It is just because some are so stubborn in their efforts to uphold an outdated system that they don't see it! They are all equally found in Christ but they prefer to remain lost in the cul-de-sac language of the law!

4:4 The survival and self-improvement programs of the [1]religious systems of this world veil the minds of the unbelievers; exploiting their ignorance about their true origin and their redeemed innocence. The veil of unbelief obstructs a person's view and keeps them from seeing what the light of the gospel so clearly reveals: the [2]glory of God is the image and likeness of our Maker redeemed in human form; this is what the gospel of Christ is all about. (*The god of this* [1]*aion, age, refers to the religious systems and governing structures of this world. The unbelief that neutralized Israel in the wilderness was the lie that they believed about themselves; "We are grasshoppers, and the 'enemy' is a giant beyond any proportion!" [Num 13:33, Josh 2:11, Heb 4:6] "They failed to possess the promise due to unbelief." The blueprint* [2]*doxa, glory of God, is what Adam lost on humanity's behalf. [See Eph 4:18]*)

4:5 Even though we recommend ourselves with great confidence, it is not with arrogance; we do not preach ourselves! We preach Christ Jesus the Lord; we are addicted to this gospel; employed by Jesus for your sakes.

4:6 The light source is founded in the same God who said, "Light, be!" And light shone out of darkness! He lit the lamp in our understanding so that we may clearly recognize the features of his likeness in the face of Jesus Christ reflected within us. (*The same God who bade light shine out of darkness has kindled a light in our hearts, whose shining is to make known his glory as he has revealed it in the features of Jesus Christ. — Knox Translation*)

4:7 And now, in the glow of this glorious light and with unveiled faces we discover this treasure where it was hidden all along, in these frail skin-suits made of clay. This is God's marvelous doing; we can take no credit for it! (*"The kingdom of heaven is like treasure hidden in an agricultural field, which a man found and covered up; then in his joy he goes and sells all that he has and buys the entire field." [Matthew 13:44]*)

4:8 We often feel completely hemmed in on every side but our inner space remains unrestricted; when there seems to be no way out, we escape within!

4:9 At times we are persecuted to the extreme but we are never abandoned. We are knocked down but not knocked out.

4:10 Wherever we go, whatever we encounter in our bodies, we bear witness within us of the fact that Jesus died our death; in this same body, we now exhibit his life. The fact that we co-died in his death confirms that we now co-live in his resurrection!

4:11 Our day-to-day experience continues to exhibit that even in the face of death, our association with the death Jesus already died remains the inspiration of his life made so clearly visible within us. This is in such contrast to the circumstances that we are often faced with.

4:12 Living aware of our co-crucifiction with Christ (*the thought of our mutual death*) in the face of death threatening circumstances [1]inspires life in you! (*The word, [1]energeo, translates as energy trigger.*)

4:13 We [1]echo the exact same spirit of faith David had when he wrote: "I believe and so I speak!" We too believe and so we speak! Our persuasion is our conversation. (*The word, [1]echo, means to hold or to embrace. Paul quotes David here in Psalm 116; sometimes one's soul wants to gallop away into distraction like a wild horse; David speaks to and reminds himself to, "Return, O my soul, to your rest; for the Lord has dealt bountifully with you!" [RSV] "I believe, and so I speak!" God's bountiful dealings with us in Christ is our only valid rest; Sabbath celebrates perfection! And remember God does not employ circumstances to teach us something! The finished work of Christ teaches us; his work on the cross rescued us!*)

4:14 This resurrection life we enjoy in Jesus fully includes you.

4:15 Whatever we go through in the gospel is to advantage you! We live for you! As grace abounds in more and more people so does the volume of gratitude in the accomplished mission of Jesus break through the sound barrier to exhibit the [1]heart dream of God. (*The word, [1]doxa, means glory, from dokeo, meaning intent opinion, the heart dream of God is his image and likeness redeemed in mankind.*)

4:16 We have much reason to be brave! There might be a lot of wear and tear on the outside; but don't be distracted by that! On the inside we are celebrating daily revival!

4:17 We are fully engaged in an exceedingly superior reality; the extent and weight of this glory makes any degree of suffering vanish into insignificance! The suffering is fleeting and ever so slight by comparison to the weight and enduring effect of this glory we participate in for all eternity. (*In Afrikaans: Ons is totaal oorweldig deur die verbysterende ewige dimensies van heerlikheid wat reeds ons deel is en nooit onderskep kan word deur hierdie kortstondige ligte verdukking nie.*)

4:18 We are not keeping any score of what seems so obvious to the senses on the surface; it is fleeting and irrelevant; it is the unseen eternal realm within us which has our full attention and captivates our gaze! *(See John 1:18 Until this moment God remained invisible to mankind; now the [1]authentic begotten Son, ([1]monogenes, begotten only of God) the blueprint of mankind's design who represents the innermost being of God, the Son who is in the bosom of the Father, brings him into full view! He is the [2]official authority qualified to announce God! He is our guide who accurately declares and interprets the invisible God within us. (Official guide, [2]eksegesato, from ek, preposition denoting source, and hegeomai, the strengthened form of ago, to lead as a shepherd leads his sheep; thus hegeomai means to be officially appointed in a position of authority.*

2 Cor 3:18 The days of window-shopping are over! In him every face is unveiled. In gazing with wonder at the blueprint likeness of God displayed in human form, we suddenly realize that we are looking at ourselves! Every feature of his image is mirrored in us! This is the most radical transformation engineered by the Spirit of the Lord; we are led from an inferior mind-set to the revealed endorsement of our authentic identity.)

5:1 Our ¹skin-bodies have a ²"sell by" date; our spirit-bodies are eternal. The same God who fashioned these skin-bodies in our mother's womb, engineered our spirit-bodies to be our permanent dwelling. *(The word, ¹skenos, reminds of the English word skin and translates, tabernacle. The word, ²kataluo means to be loosed because it has completed its function - like on a journey of travelers, when they halt to put up lodge for the night; the straps and packs of the beasts of burden are unbound and taken off or, more correctly, from the fact that a traveller's garments were tied up when they were on a journey to be loosed at its end.)*

5:2 Facing pressure times the way we often do, makes us sigh with longing to exchange our skin-suit with the permanent splendor of the heavenly-suit.

5:3 In the meantime, whatever challenges we are facing in the meat-box, we know that we shall never be found naked; since we are already fully clothed with our heavenly identity in Christ in our inner person!

5:4 We are not complaining about our bodies, even though we are often aware of its frailties; instead we yearn to be overwhelmed with life. We know that every evidence of death, even in our bodies, will dissolve into life!

5:5 God wired us this way; his Spirit already confirms within us the present evidence of eternity. We are eternal beings by design.

5:6 We are cheerfully courageous, knowing that our immediate address in our earthly bodies cannot distance us from the Lord, since we originate from him.

5:7 Faith is to our spirit what our senses are to our bodies; while the one engages with the fading and the fragile, the other celebrates perfection!

5:8 Our ¹confidence stems from ²knowing that even though it might feel at times that we are merely ⁴reduced to flesh, our ³greater reality is that we are ⁵entwined in the Lord. He is our permanent abode! *(The word, ¹tharreo, means confident courage; ²eudokeo, means well done opinion; ³mallon, means prefer or rather; and ⁴ekdemeo, from ek, is a preposition that always denotes origin or source and demeo from deo, to bind, to wind, to tie, to knit; originating out of the body (we were knitted together in our mother's womb). In severe affliction one feels at times reduce d to mere physical identity; but ²our persuasion is anchored in a greater ²opinion; the reality of our genesis in God and our union in him. The word, ⁵endemeo, means entwined, knitted together, tied in oneness. Yet at times it almost feels strange to be trapped in this body especially when we are exposed to such abuse and suffering; one longs to then do the exchange and relocate to our permanent address, where our hearts already are; in the immediate embrace of the Lord.)*

5:9 We are ¹completely engaged in the loveliness of that which is of exceedingly great value; whether we are ²in a physical union with our bodies or a ³spiritual union with our source; it makes no difference to God's esteem of us! We are highly favored by the Lord. *(The word, [1]philotimeo-mai, comes from phileo, meaning dear, fondness; timay, meaning value, esteem; and einai from eimi, I am. The word, [2]endemeo, means in union with, entwined; and [3]ekdemeo means tied to our source.)*

5:10 For we have all been [1]thoroughly scrutinized in the [2]judgment of Jesus. We are [3]taken care of and restored to the life of our design, regardless of what happened to us in our individual lives, whatever amazing or meaningless things we encountered in the body. *(See 5:14,16. We are mirrored in his life; his life reflects ours, not as an example for us but of us. See 2 Cor 3:18. The word, [1]phaneroo, means to render apparent; to openly declare; to manifest. Paul uses the aorist passive infinitive tense phanerothenai, not referring to a future event. The present infinitive expresses progressive or imperfective aspect. It pictures the action expressed by the verb as being in progress .The aorist infinitive however, does not express progressive aspect. It presents the action expressed by the verb as a completed unit with a beginning and end. The word, bematos, comes from [2]bayma, means footprint, also referring to a raised place mounted by steps, or a tribunal, the official seat of a judge The word, [3]komitzo, comes from kolumbos, meaning to tend, to take care of, to provide for, to carry off from harm. Paul's reference was not about how much abuse and affliction he suffered, neither was it the many good times he remembered that defined him; "I am what I am by the grace of God!" If we are still to be judged for good or bad deeds that we performed in the body, then the judgment that Jesus faced on humanity's behalf was irrelevant.)*

5:11 We persuade people in the [1]radiance of the Lord! His visible glory is mirrored in us! Our lives are transparent before God; we anticipate that you will witness the same transparency in your [2]conscience! *(The word, [2]suneido, translates as conscience, joint seeing. In 2 Corinthians 4:2, "with the open statement of the truth we commend ourselves to everyone's conscience." The word, phobe, speaks of dread terror and fear! I would prefer to use the word, [1]phoibe, which means radiant! Jesus is the express image of God, the radiance of his beauty! He has made the invisible God visible! He is the Father of lights with whom there is no shadow due to compromise; there is no dark side to God! Paul is not one day motivated by the terror of God and the next day by his love! See v14)*

5:12 We do not want you to pity us, but rather to be proud of us for your own sakes! We are not into window-dressing because we are not into window-shopping. Neither are we here to impress you with us but to impress you with you!

5:13 We are [1]blissfully out of our minds with pleasure before our Maker; he delights in our ecstasy. Our insane mode is between us and God; we promise to behave ourselves sane and sober before you! *(The word, [1]ekstase, is to be blissfully out of one's mind with pleasure!)*

5:14 The love of Christ [1]resonates within us and leaves us with only one conclusion: Jesus died humanity's death; therefore, in God's logic every individual simultaneously died. *(The word, [1]sunecho, from sun, meaning together with and echo, meaning to echo, to embrace, to hold, and thus translated, to resonate. Jesus didn't die 99% or for 99%. He died humanity's death 100%! If Paul had to compromise the last part of verse 14 to read: "one died for all therefore only those who follow the prescriptions to qualify, have also died," then he would have had to change the first half of the verse as well! Only the love of Christ can make a calculation of such enormous proportion! The religious mind would question the extremity of God's love and perhaps prefer to add a condition or two to a statement like that!)*

5:15 Now if all were included in his death they were equally included in his resurrection. This unveiling of his love redefines human life! Whatever reference we could have of ourselves outside of our association with Christ is no longer relevant.

5:16 This is radical and our most defining moment! No label that could possibly previously identify someone carries any further significance! Even our pet doctrines of Christ are redefined. Whatever we knew about him historically or sentimentally is challenged by this conclusion. *(By discovering Christ from God's point of view we discover ourselves and every other human life from God's point of view! Paul sees by revelation that what Jesus redeemed in every person brings absolute closure and death to any other reasoning and judgment we may have had of ourselves or anyone else for that matter! This is our 'metanoia' moment! "From now on therefore, we no longer know anyone according to the flesh, even though we once knew Christ from a human and religious point of view.")*

5:17 Now, in the light of your co-inclusion in his death and resurrection, whoever you thought you were before, in Christ you are a brand new person! The old ways of seeing yourself and everyone else are over. Acquaint yourself with the new! *(Just imagine this! Whoever a person was as a Jew, Greek, slave or freeman, Boer, Zulu, Xhosa, British, Indian, Muslim or American, Chinese, Japanese or Congolese; is now dead and gone! They all died when Jesus died! Remember we are not talking law language here! The 'If' in, "If anyone is in Christ" is not a condition, it is the conclusion of the revelation of the gospel! Mankind is in Christ by God's doing [1 Cor 1:30 and Eph 1:4]. The verses of 2 Corinthians 5:14-16 give context to verse 17! For so long we studied verse 17 on its own and interpreted the 'if' as a condition! Paul did not say, "If anyone is in Christ," he said "THEREFORE if anyone is in Christ ..." The "therefore" immediately includes verses 14 to 16! If God's faith sees everyone in Christ in his death, then they were certainly also in Christ in his resurrection. Jesus did not reveal a "potential" you, he revealed the truth about you so that you may know the truth about yourself and be free indeed! In the death and resurrection of Jesus Christ, God did not redeem a compromised replica of you; he rescued the original, blueprint you, created in his radiant mirror likeness! Any other 'self' you're trying to find or esteem will disappoint! Reckon your 'DIY-law of works-self' dead, and your redeemed self co-raised and co-seated together with Christ! This is freedom indeed! Galatians 2:19,20; Rom 6:11. See 1 Pet 1::3 We are reconnected with our original genesis through the resurrection of Jesus from the dead! This new birth endorses and celebrates the hope of the ages; God's eternal love dream concludes in life!)*

5:18 To now see everything as new is to simply see what God has al-

ways known in Christ; we are not debating human experience, opinion, or their contribution; this is 100% God's belief and his doing. In Jesus Christ, God [1]exchanged equivalent value to redeem us to himself. This act of reconciliation is the mandate of our ministry. *(The word, [1]katalasso, translates as reconciliation; a mutual exchange of equal value.)*

5:19 Our ministry declares that Jesus did not act independently of God. Christ is proof that God reconciled the total kosmos to himself. Deity and humanity embraced in Christ; the fallen state of mankind was deleted; their trespasses would no longer count against them! God has placed this message in us. He now announces his friendship with every individual from within us! *(God was in Christ, when he reconciled the world to himself. The incarnation did not separate the Father from the Son and the Spirit. In him dwells the fulness of God in a human body. Col 2:9. As a human person, Jesus felt the agony of fallen humanity on the cross when he echoed Psalm 22, "My God, my God, why have you forsaken me! Why are you so far from helping me, from the words of my groaning?" But then in verse 24, David declares triumphantly: "He has not despised or abhorred the affliction of the afflicted; and he has not hid his face from him, but has heard, when he cried to him.")*

5:20 The voice God has in Christ he now has in us; we are God's ambassadors. Our lives exhibit the urgency of God to [1]persuade everyone to realize the reconciliation of their redeemed identity. *(The word, [1]parakaleo, comes from para, a preposition indicating close proximity, a thing proceeding from a sphere of influence, with a suggestion of union of place of residence, to have sprung from its author and giver, originating from, denoting the point from which an action originates, intimate connection, and kaleo, to identify by name, to surname. In Luke 15:28, 31, His father pleaded with him, "My child, you are always with me, and all that I have is yours." "Be reconciled" could not be translated, "Become reconciled!" "Do in order to become" is the language of the Old Testament; the language of the New Testament is, "Be, because of what was done!"*

5:21 This is the divine exchange: he who knew no [1]sin embraced our distortion; he appeared to be without form; this was the mystery of God's prophetic [2]poetry. He was disguised in our distorted image and marred with our iniquities; he took our sorrows, our pain and our shame to his grave and [3]birthed his righteousness in us. He took our sins and we [3]became his innocence. *(The word sin, is the word [1]hamartia, from ha, negative or without and meros, portion or form, thus to be without your allotted portion or without form, pointing to a disorientated, distorted, bankrupt identity; the word meros, is the stem of morphe, as in 2 Corinthians 3:18 the word metamorphe, with form, which is the opposite of hamartia - without form. Sin is to live out of context with the blueprint of one's design; to behave out of tune with God's original harmony. The word, [2]poema, often translated "made" like in, "he was made to be sin." However, because of its context here I have translated poema to read prophetic poetry. As the scapegoat of the human race, he took on the distorted image of fallen mankind, he did not become a sinner, but the official representative of humanity's sin. Then Paul uses the word [3]ginomai, he birthed his righteousness in us since we were born anew in his resurrection from the dead. Hos 6:2, Eph 2:5, 1 Pet 1:3.*

Isaiah 52:10 "The Lord has bared his holy arm before the eyes of all the nations, and all the ends of the earth shall see the salvation of our God." Isaiah 52:14-15 "Just as many were astonished at you—so was he marred in his appearance, more than any human and his form beyond that of human semblance—so will he startle many nations. Kings will shut their mouths because of him; for what had not been told them, they will see and what they had not heard, they will understand." Isaiah 53:4-5 "Surely he has borne our griefs and carried our sorrows; yet we esteemed him stricken, smitten of God, and afflicted. But surely he was wounded by our transgressions; he was bruised by our iniquities; the chastisement of our peace was on him and by his stripes we ourselves are healed."

He was not bruised by God but by the very humanity he was about to redeem!

*You may ask, "But what about Isaiah 53:10!?" [It pleased the Lord to "crush" him!] Translators of the New Revised Standard Version say in their footnotes to this verse: "Meaning of Hebrew uncertain." The Septuagint [Greek version] of this verse, written 200 years before Jesus, by 70 Hebrew scholars [with access to many older manuscripts than what we have today,] have rendered the Hebrew text as follows: "and the Lord desires to purify him of the plague!" This can also be translated, "The Lord desires to cleanse his wounds! The word, **plege** means a wound."*

*Deuteronomy 32:5, 6 "They have corrupted themselves; they did not behave as his children, they have become a distorted generation of people, twisted out of their true pattern; they are a crooked and perverse generation." (Paul quotes this verse in Philippians 2:15.) Deuteronomy 32:18 "You were unmindful of the Rock that begot you and have forgotten the God who danced with you." (Hebrew, **khul** or **kheel**, to dance.)*

*Romans 8:29 "He pre-designed and engineered us from the start to be jointly fashioned in the same mold and image of his Son according to the exact blueprint of his thought. We see the original and intended pattern of our lives preserved in his Son. He is the firstborn from the same womb that reveals our genesis. He confirms that we are the idea and invention of God." (We were born anew when he was raised from the dead! [1 Peter 1:3] His resurrection co-reveals our common genesis as well as our redeemed innocence. [Romans 4:25 and Acts 17:31, 2 Timothy 1:9] No wonder then that he is not ashamed to call us his family! We indeed share the same origin [Hebrew 2:11}, and, "In him we live and move and have our being; we are indeed his offspring!" [Acts 17:28].) Romans 8:30 Jesus reveals that mankind pre-existed in God; he defines us. He justified us and also glorified us. He redeemed our innocence and restored the glory we lost in Adam. [Romans 3:23, 24: the word, **prohoritso**, means pre defined, like when an architect draws up a detailed plan; and the word, **kaleo**, to surname, identify by name.]*

Titus 2:11 "The grace of God shines as bright as day making the salvation of humankind undeniably visible.")

6:1 I want you to hear the urgency of our appeal: we are co-employed and implore you not to take God's grace for granted; what a waste it is to see less in grace than what God does! The danger is not to exaggerate what happened to mankind in Christ, but rather to underestimate it! *(Jesus did not warn his disciples not to see him in too many people, but certainly cautioned them not to miss him in the most unlikely! "How you treat the least is how you treat me." See 2 Cor 1:19, "The Son of God, Jesus Christ, whom I Paul, Sylvanus, and Timothy boldly announced in you, is God's ultimate yes to mankind. Human life is associated in all that he is. In God's mind there exists not even a hint of hesitation about this!")*

6:2 God declares that it is his [1]delight to do you good! "I have heard the [3]cry of the human race echo within [2]you *[Jesus; Ps 22:1]* and immediately [3]ran to your rescue." Now this is mankind's defining moment! See it for yourself! This is your time; this is your salvation! *(Already in the previous chapter Paul shares his own "from-now-on-therefore moment" in 2 Cor 5:16. Now he encourages us to come to the same conclusion. There is no need to wait any longer for that which was written to be fulfilled! God spoke of a specific time and person when he announced salvation. Jesus is the day of salvation [Jeshua] that Isaiah foretold. This day has fully come! Even though Isaiah spoke these words 700 years BC they were already recorded in the past tense! The Hebrew word, [1]ratson, means pleasure, delight, favor, goodwill, acceptance. The Greek word, [3]boētheō, from boao, a boisterous, most urgent cry for help, and theo, to run to the rescue. This is so typical of God; the Greek for God is theos, which is so similar to theo! God heard the cry of the human race echo in Christ. "My God my God, why have you forsaken me!" Ps 22:1, and in verse 24 he says, "For he has not despised nor distanced himself from the affliction of the afflicted; and he has not hid his face from him, but has heard, when he cried to him." Note the [2]singular, soi, thus pointing to the Messiah, the one who died for all, as in 2 Cor 5:14. Isaiah saw the human race fully represented in the one act of righteousness completed in the one man! [Isa 53:4,5.] See also Heb 4:16, For this reason we can approach the authoritative throne of grace with bold utterance. We are welcome there in his embrace, and are reinforced with immediate effect in times of trouble. (The word, boetheia, means to be reinforced, specifically a rope or chain for frapping a vessel in a storm.))*

6:3 See to it that you do not give offence or allow any kind of casual indifference to discredit this message.

6:4 In every circumstance we commend ourselves to be jointly positioned as [1]deacons of God; we co-exhibit incarnate grace, regardless of the degree of the contradictions that we might be facing. We remain constant in a fortress of patience, in situations of extreme pressure; even at times where it seems like we have our arms locked behind our backs and we feel squeezed into claustophobic spaces. *(The Greek word, [1]diakonos, from dia, a primary preposition denoting the channel of an act, and konos, dust; thus, we [1]co-exhibit incarnate grace.)*

6:5 In physical abuse; beaten up and bruised; caged in prison cells; often in chaotic circumstances; exasperating toil, with little sleep and nothing to eat!

6:6 While abiding constantly in bliss knowing what our innocence is founded in, we remain absolutely unmoved by any of these severe contradictions. We are in Christ; in Holy Spirit; in agape without a hint of hypocrisy.

6:7 We are sheltered in the word, entwined in unveiled truth, in the dynamic of God's power, because righteousness empowers us with every necessary weapon in our right and left hand to daily live undefeated by any of these onslaughts and contradictions! *(Righteousness by God's faith frees us from anything more we could do to prove or defend ourselves through our own efforts. See Habakkuk 2:4; 17-19 and Romans 1:17, also Hebrews 12:1.)*

6:8 Whether people esteem us or despise us; whether we are ridiculed or recognized, we may even be accused of misleading people we are in actual fact freeing people!

6:9 Some would say that we are vague and ambiguous and yet who we are is an open letter to everyone's conscience. Some would wish us dead; but hey, here we are, fully alive! *(2 Corinthians 4:2)*

6:10 Our joy exceeds any reason for sadness; to enrich countless others by far outweighs the expense. It may appear that we are empty handed, yet we have everything in a firm grasp!

6:11 Precious Corinthians! Our bold words flow from hearts where you are embraced in a wide-open space!

6:12 Any sense of inadequacy you might feel comes from having an inferior perception about yourselves; the gospel we communicate esteems you highly!

6:13 We invite you in the most affectionate terms to respond to us without hesitation or restraint. See yourselves [1]mirrored in the same boundless space. *(The word [1]antimisthia, means requital, or correspondence, which I translated here, "mirrored".)*

6:14 Faith-righteousness has nothing in common with the philosophies of karma and performance-based approval; they could never [1]balance the scales or be evenly yoked together in any context. *(The word [1]heterozugeō, an unequal or different yoke; from the word, zugos, a yoke or a teaching; the yoke of a rabbi or philosopher represented their doctrine; from the Hebrew word, tzedek, the wooden beam in a scale of balances, which is the word for righteousness. The Greek root word for righteousness is dike - interesting to note that the Greek goddess of Justice is Dike [pronounced, dikay] and she is always pictured holding a scale of balances in her hand.)*

6:15 There is no [1]symphony between the value that Christ reveals in people and the worthlessness that [2]Belial represents! Faith-righteousness and work based-righteousness are two opposites; they are conflicting systems that can never match. *(Paul uses the word [1]sumphonēsis from sun, denoting union and phonay, voice. Faith-righteousness is to know the truth about the redeemed life of your design; whereas a works based-righteousness is to believe a lie about yourself. The Hebrew word, [2]beliya'al literally means without profit; worthlessness. The etymology of this word has been variously given. The Talmud (Sanh. 111b) regards it as a compound word, made up of "beli" and "'ol" (without a yoke) which is very interesting in this context! Jesus says, "My yoke is easy and my burden is light!" Peterson renders it, "Walk with me and work with me--watch how I do it. Learn the unforced rhythms of grace. I won't lay anything heavy or ill-fitting on you. Keep company with me and you'll learn to live freely and lightly. Matthew 11:29,30. The Message)*

6:16 How can the tangible, physical address of the living God [1]compare with a phantom image that people host in their minds? Mankind is God's idea - we did not invent God or ourselves; he invented us! He said, "In you will I reside and move and have my being; we belong together; I am yours and you are mine!" *(Ezekiel 37:27 My dwelling place shall be with them; and I will be their God, and they shall be my people. The word, [1]sugkatathesis means, a putting together or joint deposit (of votes), hence approval, assent, agreement; you cannot vote for both systems, they are opposites!)*

6:17 "Consequently, escape the snare of these phantom ideas; do not reduce your horizon to become [1]attached to anything that is not equally [2]elevated. *(in your joint seatedness in heavenly places, in your co-resurrection and co-ascension with Christ. The word [1]haptomai means to fasten to oneself; to adhere to; to cling to. The word [2]akathartos, from ha, which is a negative particle, and kathairō, from kata, intensive and airo, to lift up. The same word is used in John 15 where it was translated, to "prune, or cut off" the branches that do not bear fruit; yet the word would rather mean to lift up those branches so that they may bear more fruit!)*

6:18 Then you will know the embrace of your Father and you will be my sons and daughters," says the Almighty.

7:1 Dearly beloved, these promises engage us with elevated thoughts and free us from the frustrating efforts of the flesh to compete with the innocence of the spirit in our divine devotion. *(Paul contrasts the futile efforts of the flesh to the spirit of grace, which is celebrated in the bliss of righteousness by faith.)*

7:2 You will have to admit it, we have judged no-one in an unworthy manner, or made anyone feel inferior, neither have we taken advantage of anyone.

7:3 There is no hint of condemnation in my message; I have always maintained that our hearts are joined with you in death and in life.

7:4 I am absolutely persuaded about you and take great pride in you; we are ¹seamlessly one; therefore my joy rises ²above all sense of ³claustrophobia ! *(The word, ¹parakaleo, comes from para, a preposition indicating close proximity, a thing proceeding from a sphere of influence, with a suggestion of union of place of residence, to have sprung from its author and giver, originating from, denoting the point from which an action originates, intimate connection; and kaleo, meaning to identify by name, to surname. The word ²epi, is a preposition of position, over or against. The word ³thlipsis means a pressing, to be under severe pressure; from thlibō, to crowd (literally or figuratively): - afflict, narrow, throng.)*

7:5 When we first arrived in Macedonia we had no chance to relax for a moment; we were literally thronged by trouble; we faced conflict on every side and felt deeply alarmed.

7:6 How wonderful it is to discover God's ¹comforting closeness when one feels like a bird that ²cannot rise in flight to escape the fowler; this time God's closeness was reinforced in the arrival of Titus! *(The word, ¹parakaleo, comes from para, a preposition indicating close proximity, and kaleo, meaning to identify by name, to surname. The word, ²tapeinos, means, not rising far from the ground.)*

7:7 Oh, and what a joy it was to hear personally from him how greatly encouraged he was by all of you! He told us how deeply you missed me and how you grieved with sincere concern for me. I immediately went from feeling a little sorry for myself into a happy-dance-mode!

7:8 For a brief moment I felt a little bad that I had perhaps saddened you with my previous letter yet I have no regrets now!

7:9 I rejoice in knowing that your sadness caused you to realize my sincere concern for you! The grief you felt brought God's heart into clear view and confirmed in you that I have always only had your best interest in mind!

7:10 To ¹anchor one's thoughts in God's thoughts when faced with difficult or painful experiences, brings escape from sorrow and leaves one with no ²regrets; but oh, what a dreadful contrast is the world system *(of the law of karma and works)* which adds ²regret upon sorrow! Whereas the one brings such immediate relief, the other seems to be an inescapable

deathtrap! *(The word [1]metanoia means to gather one's thoughts; in this context it means to realize God's thoughts. Sadly the Latin word, penance (repentance) became the popular English translation of metanoia. The word [2]metameletos, means with regret.)*

7:11 Consider how this very thing that caused you such initial grief has turned your attention to God! It revived an [1]immediate sense of urgency to [2]realize your position in grace; almost [3]like when your arm is twisted and locked behind your back, and your own efforts to clear or save yourselves were completely neutralized. You were greatly alarmed with an intense desire and burning zeal to [4]re-endorse the basis of your righteousness. And so in everything your blameless innocence is vindicated! *(The word [1]spoude suggests speed, immediate, urgent. The word [2]apologia means to answer with reason, to apologize, to defend one's case. The word [3]aganaktesis, from ago, to lead and anagke to bend the arm. The word [4]ekdikeo, is a compound word from ek, a preposition denoting origin, and dikeo, two parties finding likeness in one another; which is the basis of the word for righteousness, dikaios. That which originates in righteousness. See Romans 12:19, Do not bother yourselves to get even, dear ones. Do not let anger or irritation distract you; that which we have in common with one another (righteousness) must set the pace. Scripture confirms that the Lord himself is the revealer of righteousness. [ekdikeo])*

7:12 The object of my writing was not to debate the detail of who was wrong and who was wronged, but you, discovering the heart of God [1]mirrored in our urgent appeal to you. *(The word, [1]enopion, in the face or gaze of God.)*

7:13 We are so [1]inspired to know that you [1]are aquainted your true identity and are overjoyed by the way you have gladdened the heart of Titus; he is so happy and completely blessed and refreshed by all of you! *(The word, [1]parakaleo, comes from para, a preposition indicating close proximity, with a suggestion of union, originating from, and kaleo, meaning to identify by name, to surname. Jesus introduces the Holy Spirit in the same capacity: parakletos, meaning close companion, kinsman [John 14:16]).*

7:14 It is a wonderful thing to brag about one another and to know that we can never exaggerate the truth! Titus has confirmed our boasting about you!

7:15 He is absolutely overwhelmed with deep affection for you and reminded of the way you have accurately heard and the warm hospitality that all of you have shown him.

7:16 This pleases me so much! I am so proud of you!

8:1 Allow me to encourage you with the striking testimony of the grace of God evidenced in the churches of [1]Macedonia! *(The Romans had lacerated [1]Macedonia economically. (Livy, XLV. 30)[30] The churches in Macedonia included Philippi, Thessalonica and Berea.)*

8:2 Their mental mettle was [1]tested to the extreme; they found themselves squeezed into a very [2]narrow space. Yet, in the depth of their poverty, their ecstatic joy led them into extravagant generosity! They had discovered the conclusion of grace: no degree of poverty can separate us from our [3]seamless oneness with one another. Grace translates within us a wealth of liberality. *([1]Proof, dokimēi, a test proving the true character of metal. The word [2]thipsis from thlibo, to be thronged, hemmed into a very narrow space. The word [3]haplotes, from hama, which is a particle of union and pleko, braided; quality or state of unmixed motivation, without mental reservation, no hidden agenda, undivided heart.)*

8:3 I salute them for intentionally giving themselves beyond their means.

8:4 We had nothing to do with this - they were the ones who insisted with utmost sincerity and urgency that we mediate their [1]tangible grace-gift to their fellow saints. *(The word, [1]diakonos, deacon or minister from dia + konis literally through dust, translates here, tangible, practical or incarnate; this word commonly translates as ministry, service, running errands. I believe that the ultimate ministry is the expression of the heart of God in tangible human form, true New Testament deacon is a celebration of the incarnation.)*

8:5 No-one expected this from them! They simply demonstrated how completely sold out they were to the Lord and to us! This explains their generous giving! The delightful pleasure of God compelled them!

8:6 Inspired by their enthusiasm, we [1]prompted Titus to complete his initiative in this grace gift that you yourselves were keen to participate in! *(Here I have used the word prompted for [1]parkaleo, which literally means to draw from the source of your identity.)*

8:7 Now everything about you already shines with extravagant evidence of your faith, your conversation, your knowledge, your enthusiasm. All bear witness to the affection that we have awakened in you! This is your opportunity to now equally excel in the grace of giving! *(See 1 Corinthians 1:4, Every aspect of your life already gives eloquent expression to the rich reservoir of your union in him. 1:6 You certainly have the testimony of Christ evidenced in you.)*

8:8 I am not laying out rules on giving to bring you back into bondage and duty-driven legalism. Your sincere love, encouraged by the enthusiasm of fellow believers, is what distinguishes your giving *(from the old written code of tithing!)*

8:9 You are acquainted with what the grace of our Lord Jesus Christ communicates: He exchanged his riches for our poverty; the extremities of his identifying with our poverty became the reference to our wealth. Everything he has is ours. *(We are his wealth! See Matthew 13:44, "He sold all he* *had and bought the entire field;" in this parable Jesus persuades us that we are all he has!)*

8:10 Here is my advice: since you originally came up with the idea a year ago,

8:11 it can only be to your own advantage if you would now also complete your willingness by reaching into your resources and giving liberally according to your means.

8:12 The willingness of heart is matched by what someone is able to give! I mean it is one thing to be willing to give a million dollars, but if you haven't got a million dollars then at least give the $10 you do have!

8:13 I am not suggesting that others must be eased at your expense.

8:14 The idea is that everyone should always have enough; your abundance can now bring immediate relief to them and vica versa.

8:15 The principle of "share and share alike" is as old as the Scriptures! *(See Exodus 16:18)*

8:16 I thank God for Titus; he feels entrusted with an equal urgency about you.

8:17 He readily responded to our prompting and immediately volunteered to go.

8:18 A brother who is very gifted in the gospel and popular with every church will accompany Titus.

8:19 He was also [1]handpicked by all the churches to join us on this journey of grace in the administration of the gifts to the glory of the Lord. We know that this will meet with your approval since it is what you really wanted to do all along. *(The word [1]cheirotoneo means to handpick or to vote by a show of hands. See 1 Corintians 16:3)*

8:20 We understand how sensitive money matters are and have taken the utmost precaution to secure the transparency of the administration of your bountiful gift.

8:21 We [1]anticipate this to be a [2]beautiful testimony to the Lord and to everyone. *(The word [1]pronoeo means to know in advance, to anticipate; the word [2]kalon means beautiful.)*

8:22 Along with these two men we are also sending a brother in whom we have great confidence; he has often proven himself trustworthy in many different situations and is now even more eager than ever since he knows how urgent we feel about you.

8:23 As for Titus, he is my close companion and represents my heart to you. The brothers who accompany him are commissioned by the churches to the glory of Christ.

8:24 Give these churches proof of your love and confirm the good reason we have to be proud of you.

9:1 Our commitment to administer this relief fund to assist our fellow saints is obvious. It shouldn't even be necessary for me to write to you about this.

9:2 When I witnessed your enthusiasm a year ago, I bragged about you before the churches in Macedonia and your zeal greatly inspired many of them.

9:3 So now I am sending these brothers in response to your readiness to confirm our boasting about you.

9:4 I just want to make sure that should some of the Macedonians perhaps join me when I visit you that it won't turn out to your and our embarrassment!

9:5 This is the reason why I have recruited this team, to go in advance and give you the necessary time to arrange for the blessing that you have promised. I want it to remain the blessing that you originally intended and not something that you now feel pressurized to give!

9:6 We are all familiar with the natural law that says, "Stingy sowing will always reflect in the harvest; so does liberal sowing!"

9:7 Every individual must [1]thoroughly think this through in their own heart, not with thoughts of possible regret or out of a legalistic sense of duty! The agape-love of God inspires extravagance of [2]hilarious proportions! *(The word [1]proaireomai means to take full inventory; the Greek word [2]hilaros is from the root word hileos which means cheerful, attractive.)*

9:8 It is impossible to exaggerate the [1]dimensions and detail of the grace of God! Plunge into the [2]extravagance of grace where he exhibits the extreme [3]dynamics of his bountiful dealing with us! We are already advantaged [2]far beyond any calculation of personal merit to be completely [4]self sufficient at all times in every possible situation that we might face! The overflow thereof amply supplies the needs of others in many creative ways to do good! *(In Paul's estimate, grace cannot be exaggerated! He bursts forth in eloquent grace language in an attempt to explain the extremities of God's goodness. He strings together one superlative after the other in order to reinforce the all-inclusive and conclusive work of grace evidenced within us! With the word [3]dunatei, he speaks of the powerful dynamic of God, which is a word and a late tense that Paul invents from the word dunamos! Only he uses it and repeats it 3 times in his Epistles. In the words, [1]pasan charin, Paul includes every detailed aspect of grace; then he uses the verb, [2]perisseuo which means to exceed some number, measure, rank or need; to go over the limits, beyond and above, more than is necessary. Paul employs this verb in the Aorist Infinitive tense, perisseusai, which indicates prior completion of an action in relationship to a point in time. Greek infinitives could have either a present or aorist form. The contrast between the two forms have nothing to do with time. It is a difference of aspect. The present infinitive was used to express progressive or imperfective aspect. It pictures the action expressed by the verb as being in progress. The aorist infinitive however does not express progressive aspect. It presents the action expressed by the verb as a completed unit with a beginning and end. This is an important point since many translations of this verse suggests that God's ability to make all grace abound towards us can only be in response to something we must first do in order to trigger God into action! Our doing good is simply the overflow of his good work within us! The word ⁴autarkes, is translated self sufficient; it is the feeling you have when you are completely satisfied with yourself. This word is only used here, in Philippians 4:11 and in 1Timothy 6:6. The use of this word shows Paul's acquaintance with Stoicism. He takes this word from Greek philosophy and applies it to the revelation of the completeness of the life of our design restored in us! Paul lived his life in touch with this place within himself. He discovered that the same I am-ness that Jesus walked in, was mirrored in him! I am what I am by the grace of God!)*

9:9 Here is David's take on liberal and extravagant giving: in Psalm 112:9 he says, "He has distributed freely, he has given to the poor; his righteousness consistently triumphs even in challenging times."

9:10 The inventor of seed and bread is also the one who supplies and multiplies your resources and increases the harvest of your righteousness! *(Here Paul reminds them of Isa 55:10 & 11 "For as the rain and the snow come down from heaven, and return not but water the earth, making it bring forth and sprout, giving seed to the sower and bread to the eater, so shall my word be that goes forth from my mouth; it shall not return to me empty, but accomplish that which I purpose, and prosper in the thing for which I sent it.)*

9:11 You are mutually enriched in every possible sense of the word and ¹inseparably joined to one another in an undivided heart, without any hidden agenda. And together we, the conduit of your gifts, will set the stage for a joyous grace celebration to God! *(The word ¹haplotes, from hama, which is a particle of union and pleko, braided or entwined, suggests an undivided heart.)*

9:12 This is such a win-win situation: not only are the saints endorsed in their "I am-ness" through this most practical translation of your generosity, but it also causes an abundant overflow of great gratitude to God as the testimony of his goodness finds tangible expression in your gifts!

9:13 And so the ripple effect continues! The gospel you communicate has found a very articulate voice in your giving and produces a rich harvest of glory to God. Your union with them further communicates the all-inclusive nature of the ¹koinonia we all participate in. *(The word ¹koinonia means to participate in, to fellowship.)*

9:14 Can you imagine how your abundant generosity to them has tied them to you with deep affection in their prayers for you!

9:15 Gratitude is the language of grace! Your giving has given a voice to his gift, beyond words!

10:1 So here I am, Paul, somewhat shy when I am face to face with you, but, according to some rumors, my courage borders on arrogance in my absence. I ¹address you from this place where there is no distance; our authentic identity is referenced in gentleness and ²Christlikeness. (The word, ¹parakaleo, comes from para, a preposition indicating close proximity, a thing proceeding from a sphere of influence, and kaleo, meaning to identify by name, to surname. The word ²epeikeia, from epi, continual influence upon, and eiko, to be like, to resemble.)

10:2 I am ¹cautious not to come across arrogantly when I am ²present with you. Yet I am extremely confident before those who accuse me of conducting myself in a mere carnal manner. (The word ¹deomai, to desire, from deo, to bind; the word ²pareimi refers to the closest proximity of the source of my I am-ness.)

10:3 The fact that we are living in a physical world in human bodies of flesh does not mean that we engage ourselves in a combat dictated to by the typical "tit-for-tat" strategies of the politics of the day.

10:4 The dynamic of our strategy is revealed in God's ability to disengage mindsets and perceptions that have held people captive in pseudo fortresses for centuries!

10:5 Every lofty idea and argument positioned against the knowledge of God is cast down and exposed to be a mere invention of our own imagination. We arrest every thought that could possibly trigger an opposing threat to our redeemed identity and innocence at spear point! The caliber of our weapon is empowered by the revelation of the ultimate consequence of the obedience of Christ. (The obedience of Christ dwarfs the effect of the disobedience of Adam into insignificance! See Romans 5:12-21.)

10:6 Our ears are fine tuned to ¹echo the voice of ³likeness that resonates within us. We are ²acquainted with the articulate detail of the ⁴authentic language of our origin. (The word ¹echo, means to hold or embrace; the word ²hetoimos, is from an old noun heteos (fitness) which means adjusted, ready, prepared. The word ³ekdikeō from ek, denoting origin + dike, two parties finding likeness in each other. The word ⁴parakoē from para, originating from, + akouo, to hear.)

10:7 Do you form your perceptions on mere face value? No one has a secret advantage in his or her claim of Christ; think again: each one belongs equally to him, despite appearances or whether they realize it or not!

10:8 There is nothing superior in my confidence in who I am! God's gift to you wrapped up in me is not to intimidate you but to edify you!

10:9 The intention of my letters is not to daunt you with eloquent words!

10:10 Some are of the opinion that my letters are forceful, but my physical appearance is feeble and I am not much of a public speaker.

10:11 I assure you that the words my epistles communicate in my absence, are confirmed in my day to day lifestyle.

10:12 We are not contesting with those who desire to commend themselves! While they compete and compare with one another they completely miss the point; they fail to ¹comprehend our joint I am-ness! *(The word, ¹sunieimi is to fully comprehend, from sun, a preposition denoting union, and eimi, I am.)*

10:13 Why boast in something you can take absolutely no credit for! The only valid measure that defines our lives and explains why we have ¹arrived on your doorstep with the gospel, is the one with which God has measured us in Christ. *(One cannot measure temperature with a ruler. The word ¹ephikneomai, from epi, continual influence upon, and hēkō, to have come, to have arrived, to be present. See Romans 6:14, Sin was your master while the law was your measure; now grace rules. [The law revealed your slavery to sin; now grace reveals your freedom from it.] Also Romans 3:27 The law of faith cancels the law of works, which means there is suddenly nothing left for mankind to boast in. No one is superior to another. Bragging only makes sense if there is someone to compete with or impress. "Through the righteousness of God we have received a faith of equal standing." See 2 Pet 1:1 RSV The OS (operating system) of the law of works is willpower; the OS of the law of faith is love. Gal 5:6 Love sets faith in motion. The law presented mankind with choices; grace awakens belief! Willpower exhausts, love ignites! If choices could save us we would be our own Saviors! Willpower is the language of the law, love is the language of grace and it ignites faith that leads to romance; falling in love beats "making a decision to believe in love"! See Rom 7:19)*

10:14 Our ministry to you is proof that there are no geographic limitations that could possibly exclude you from the gospel of Jesus Christ!

10:15 We are not competing with others for your membership; our vision for you is to see your faith mature into a full harvest; this is our standard rule, we have no other expectation! To the same degree that your faith matures, our field among you is greatly increased!

10:16 You become the extension of our sphere of influence as we together reach neighbouring regions beyond yourselves. The gospel is the key role-player here, not hidden agendas of man-made ministries!

10:17 So if you desire to boast about anything boast in the Lord! *(Even as Jeremiah writes in Jer 9:23 & 24 "The LORD says: "Let not the wise glory in their wisdom, let not the mighty glory in their might, let not the rich glory in their riches; but let the one who who glories glory in this, that they understand and know me, that I am the LORD who practice steadfast love, justice, and righteousness in the earth; for in these things I delight, says the LORD.")*

10:18 The true ¹recipe for authentic ministry is not in clever marketing schemes; let the Lord promote you, he beats the best! *(The word ¹dokimos means test, proof, accepted, particularly of coins and money.)*

11:1 This might sound a little foolish, but please bear with me!

11:2 I feel a divine jealousy for you! I have as it were been the groomsman who wooed you to belong solely to your one husband and presented you as a pure bride to Christ.

11:3 I am concerned for you that that you might [1]pine away through the [2]illusion of separation from Christ and that, just like Eve, you might become [3]blurry-eyed and [4]deceived into believing a lie about yourselves. The temptation was to exchange the truth about our completeness *(I am)* with the idea of incompleteness *(I am not)* and shame; thinking that perfection required your toil and all manner of wearisome labor! *(The word, [1]phteiro, means to pine or waste away, to whither. Any idea of separation causes one to whither away in loneliness! The word [2]haplotes from hama, a particle of union, and pleko, to braid or plait together; sometimes translated, simplicity or unmixed. The Greek word, [3]ophis is translated serpent and comes from optomai, to gaze, in this case, to present a visual idea through illusion. The word [4]exapataō from ek, source + apateo, apathy is the source of deception, to be without faith, believing a lie about yourself! Heb 4:6 Israel died in the wilderness because of their unbelief. [Both Adam and Israel believed a lie about themselves. Num 13:33, Josh 2:11, 2 Cor 4:4.] The word [5]panourgia, from the words, pas, all, and ergon, work or toil, where your complete existence is reduced to wearisome labor. This word is often translated, cunning or craftiness. See also 2 Cor 4:2 "We have renounced hidden agendas [employing a little bit of the law in an attempt to "balance" out grace]; we have distanced ourselves from any obscure craftiness to manipulate God's word to make it mean what it does not say!")*

11:4 You will know by the echo within you whether the Jesus someone else preaches is the same Jesus we proclaim to you. You will recognize the same spirit; if it is a different spirit, it is not the same gospel! Why would you politely put up with deception, even if it comes packaged in prominent names and titles!

11:5 I am not inferior by any calculation to those apostles so highly ranked in your estimate!

11:6 I am not here to entertain you with my public speaking skills, or to impress you with [1]me, but to impress you with you! It is not in the plausible sounding words of my conversation, it is in what I know to be true about you. This is clearly evident in all of our dealings with you. *(See 1Cor 2:4 "My message was not with persuasive arguments based on secular wisdom, since my aim was not to point people to me but rather to the powerful working of the Spirit in them." Thayer's Greek definition of [1]apodeiknumi is to point away from oneself. Previous translations of this word have often given the impression that the great, miracle-working man of God would steal the show and entertain the crowds! This was so unlike Jesus and Paul! Paul never writes about how many people he had healed and brought to faith, etc. His all-consuming concern was that the eyes of our understanding would be illuminated with the revelation of our own salvation. Note 2 Corinthians 10:10 [RSV], "For they say, 'Paul's letters are weighty and strong, but his bodily presence is weak, and his speech of no account.'")*

11:7 Something doesn't seem to match here – am I humbling myself in order to elevate you by not putting a price tag on my preaching of God's gospel? Am I presenting a distorted picture?

11:8 It seems to me that you are taking it for granted that other churches sponsored my ministry to you!

11:9 Even while I was with you I did not burden you with my personal needs, but received provision from my Macedonian friends. I have no intent to ever be a burden to you!

11:10 The integrity of my ministry is [1]endorsed by Christ in me and not by human opinion; the same goes for my confident joy even in the regions of Achaia! *(The word [1]sphragizō, to set a mark upon by the impress of a seal or a stamp. Achaia was that part of Greece of which Corinth was the capital.)*

11:11 How is it possible for you to think that I do not love you? God knows my heart!

11:12 The way I do things exposes the agendas of others who claim that we are in the same team!

11:13 They are obviously operating under the deceitful disguise of an apostleship with a hidden agenda! They are certainly not apostles of Christ.

11:14 It shouldn't be a surprise since the [1]Accuser often comes camouflaged as a bearer of light! *(The word [1]satanos means the accuser. The dispensation of the law is the ministry of accusation.)*

11:15 Therefore it is no big deal if his associates in ministry would claim to also teach righteousness under the disguise of grace, while their message clearly promotes a righteousness based on their own works *(and not upon the finished work of Christ!)*

11:16 Let me put it to you plainly, if I am already behaving foolishly in your opinion, would you please bear with me in the foolishness of my boasting!

11:17 I am not saying, "the Lord says!" but allow me to say a few foolish things in my own defense!

11:18 Since there are so many who are boasting according to the flesh, I might as well enroll in the competition!

11:19 Your wisdom certainly equips you to grin and bear with the foolishness of others!

11:20 The ability to perceive things from an elevated place of wisdom already gives you the advantage to bear with their insults. Their intent is obvious: all they wish to achieve is to bring you back into the bondage of their own Jewish legalism. They wish to abuse and devour you; their apparent attempts to raise themselves to your level are only to slap you in the face.

11:21 Since Timothy and I did not take any part in their bravado at the time, it perhaps appeared to you as a weakness on our part. I know this might not make sense to you, but whatever extreme measures they pride themselves in, I can match!

11:22 Every possible advantage they claim through their natural lineage, whether it be their Hebrew language, their Jewish identity or their connection to the patriarch Abraham himself, I can equal that!

11:23 If you want to compare notes, I eclipse their claims as ministers of Christ. I speak from personal experience; none of them could compete with me when it comes to the extremities of wearisome labors endured: I was beaten up many times, frequently jailed, often face to face with death.

11:24 To be more specific, I received the infamous forty lashes less one, five times from the Jews!

11:25 Three times the Romans beat me up with sticks; once I was stoned and left for dead! Three times on my journeys I have been shipwrecked. I have been adrift at sea for a night and a day.

11:26 My frequent travels have kept me on the road more than most people I know; I faced flooded rivers, I was attacked by robbers and encountered life threatening dangers from both Jew and Gentile. Everywhere I turned I was confronted with great danger, whether in the city, countryside or at sea. It seemed that there was no safe place left for me on the planet! Even amongst fellow Christians I was snared into controversy and betrayal!

11:27 I was often extremely exhausted with a burdensome workload. The list goes on and on: I had many a sleepless night; I was frequently forced to fast since I had nothing to eat or drink; I suffered extreme exposure in bitterly cold conditions with nothing warm to wear.

11:28 Beside the many external challenges I face daily, I continuously care for the churches in every place with all my heart.

11:29 Don't talk to me about weaknesses and scandalous insults! I have been there and bought the T-shirt! The scandal of the cross ignites me with fervor!

11:30 My frailties are my claim to fame!

11:31 God, the Father of our Lord Jesus Christ, has the full panorama of my life and testimony. In Jesus the ages conclude in beautiful logic! He is the ultimate reason of the universe! (The word [1]eulogētos often translated, blessing, is from eu, beautiful or well done, and logos, word, thought or logic.)

11:32 O yes, and here is another bit of adventure: while in Damascus the governer under King Aretas set up a military guard in the city of Damascenes to hunt me down and arrest me.

11:33 I escaped through a window in the city wall, having been let down in a basket! (Acts 9:25)

12:1 It would be inappropriate for me to boast about anything as though I achieved it by my own doing! My confident persuasion in what I have received by revelation of the Lord is not to be confused with arrogance!

12:2 I know of an encounter in Christ fourteen years ago, where a person was translated into the third heaven.

12:3 Only God knows whether it was in or out of the body; it does not really matter to me!

12:4 This person was caught up into paradise! There he heard words that could not be articulated into language; he understood a conversation that did not [1]originate in human thought! *(The word [1]exousia, has two components, ek, a preposition pointing to the origin of something, and eimi, I am, in this case Paul refers to who I am as a human being.)*

12:5 Of this encounter I will confidently boast because it has nothing to do with anything that I did to promote myself! I would rather glory in that which emphasizes my failure to get it right by myself! Divine revelation is a gift, not a reward!

12:6 Even though I have legitimate reasons to boast, I prefer not to. My life speaks for itself and I have nothing to hide! *(See also 1 Corinthians 4:10-14 and 2 Corinthians 6:4-8)*

12:7 In sharp contrast to these spiritual revelations, the physical pain that I suffered and my severe discomfort momentarily distracted me. It was as if the old mindset of accusation *(Satan)* persuaded me that this affliction was actually God's way of keeping me humble. *(Note that it was not a messenger from God, but from Satan! The word, satanos means accuser! By these revelations of extreme proportions and consequence Paul understood that we are indeed co-seated together with Christ in heavenly places. In his resurrection he already elevated us beyond any claim of accusation. See Hosea 6:2 and Ephesians 2:5,6. We cannot get any more elevated into the bliss of our redeemed innocence than discovering our joint-seatedness with Christ in the throne room! Colossians 3:1-3)*

12:8 I almost believed this lie and even implored the Lord three times to remove the thorn from my flesh.

12:9 Finally it dawned on me that grace is God's language; he doesn't speak "thorn-langauge"! He said to me, "My grace [1]elevates you, to be fully content." And now, instead of being overwhelmed with a sense of my own weakness, he overwhelms me with an awareness of his strength! Oh what [2]bliss to rejoice in the fact that in the midst of my frailties I encounter the dynamic of the grace of God to be my [3]habitation! *(The word [1]arkeo, content, stems from the word airo which means to elevate. The word [2]hedista from hedeos, means pleasure. The word [3]episkenoo has two components: epi, continual influence upon and skenoo, to encamp, to reside in a tent; the noun, skenos reminds of the English word skin! Paul suggests that God's grace fits you like a skin! One feels most at home in the consciousness of his grace!)*

12:10 I now enjoy a [1]delightfully different frame of mind when I encounter things that would normally make me feel frail, whether it be from insults or when I am in situations where [2]I'm forced to do things with my arms twisted behind my back; whether I am persecuted or feel squeezed into [3]claustrophobic spaces. Because of Christ, every time that I encounter weakness I escape into the strength of my [4]I am-ness! *(The word, [1]eudokeo is a compound word from, **eu**, well done, beautiful, and **dokeo**, to form an opinion. The word [2]anagkē to bend the arm like when your arm is locked behind your back, where your own efforts to clear or save yourself are completely neutralized. The word [3]stenochōria, means a narrowness of place. The word [4]eimi, is the verb, I am.)*

12:11 It is not my style to talk so much about myself, but here I am foolishly defending my reputation against your esteemed Apostles! Hey, I was hoping that you would rather defend me!

12:12 All the signs that confirmed my commission and apostleship were evidenced in you. These signs and miracles and mighty works consistently accompany my ministry.

12:13 How can you possibly feel neglected? The only way in which you were treated differently from the other churches is that I did not burden you with any financial obligations to me.

12:14 This will be my third visit to you and again I have no intent to burden you in any way! Your money cannot enrich me but your friendship surely does! It is the parent's job to look after their children and not the other way around!

12:15 It is my pleasure to go to any expense, even to the extreme of bankrupting myself for your sakes! Yet it seems to me that the more I show my love the less I am loved!

12:16 Did I have a hidden agenda, tricking you with guile?

12:17 Did anyone that I sent to serve you perhaps abuse you?

12:18 I entreated Titus to encourage you in our [1]joint-affiliation and co-assigned our brother *(Luke)* with him; did Titus take any advantage of you? Did we not conduct ourselves in the same spirit and leave the same impression? *(The word, [1]parakaleo, comes from **para**, a preposition indicating close proximity, with a suggestion of union, originating from, and **kaleo**, meaning to identify by name, to surname. Jesus introduces the Holy Spirit in the same capacity: **parakletos**, meaning close companion, kinsman [John 14:16].*

12:19 My intent is not to justify myself at your expense! God knows that our sincere desire in everything we say is to edify you in Christ, dearly beloved!

12:20 I do not desire that my coming to you will disappoint any of your or my expectations! Contentious debates, petty jealousies, flaring emotions, divisions, bad-mouthing, rumorous gossip, inflated selfish ambitions and disharmony can certainly not be justified and should not be allowed to replace the rich and edifying fellowship which we can anticipate.

12:21 I certainly have no desire to be humiliated again facing the same old mindsets and sins of imorality, adultery and licentiousness ! This will break my heart! God knows.

13:1 In getting ready to visit you now for the third time, I am reminded of the scripture that says that at the mouth of two or three witnesses every word shall be established.

13:2 I addressed this issue during my second visit and do so again now, in my absence, with this letter: when I arrive I will not tolerate the stubborn attitude of those who wish to continue in their [1]old distorted deeds. *(The word, [1]prohamartia, translate, old sins or previous sins, from pro, previous, and the word ha, without and meros, alloted portion or form; suggesting the distorted patterns of judgments we have had of ourselves, thus justifying the lies that we believed about ourselves and one another.)*

13:3 The frailties that I testify to in myself, do not distract from the powerful impact that the word of Christ in me, has in you! This should be enough proof to you of the integrity of my ministry!

13:4 It seems such a paradox when one considers the frailty of Christ's frame, how he suffered such a dreadful death on the cross, compared to the power of God so evident in him as his source of life. Our own lives often mirror the same contrasting paradox that we have witnessed in Christ, where our times of weakness become a platform for the power of God to be displayed as the secret source of the life we participate in together with Christ, to encourage you!

13:5 I implore you to [1]examine faith for yourselves in order to test what it is that you really believe. Faith is so much more than the mere veneer of a superstitious belief in a historic Christ; faith is about realizing Jesus Christ in you, in the midst of contradiction! Just [2]as ore is placed into a crucible, where the dross is separated from the gold in a furnace, come to the conclusion for yourselves of his indwelling! Should it appear to you that Christ is absent in your life, look again, you have obviously done the test wrong! *(You cannot measure temperature with a ruler! Paul uses the word, [1]peiratzo, to examine closely, from peira, to pierce; a test to determine the hidden value of something; also from the word peras, which speaks of extremity or the furthest boundary. Faith is not a veneer to cover up potential depression or disappointment when faced with trying times! Note that Paul is not speaking about you putting your beliefs to the test; but you testing the faith for yourself! There is only one valid faith, not what we believe about God or about ourselves, but what God believes about us! Paul wants you to discover for yourselves what God believes about you. God is persuaded about Christ indwelling you, now he wants you to be equally persuaded! Then he uses the word, [2]dokimatzo, as in the testing of metals. Self examination has nothing to do with finding hidden sins and flaws in you; it is all about realizing Christ in you! The object of the furnace is not to reveal the dross, but the gold! Christ himself is the proof of faith, he is the substance of things hoped for, the evidence of things not seen. Hebrews 11:1. The test of truth is foolproof! See verse 8. Truth is not threatened by our scrutiny! See also 2 Corinthians 4:18 We are not keeping any score of what seems so obvious to the senses on the surface, it is fleeting and irrelevant; it is the unseen eternal realm within us that has our full attention and captivates our gaze! 2 Corinthians 4:7 We have discovered* *this treasure where it was hidden all along, in these frail skin-suits made of clay. 1 Corinthians 1:6 You certainly have the testimony of Christ evidenced in you. [You possess full knowledge and give full expression because in you the evidence for the truth of Christ has found confirmation. — NEB])*

13:6 I really hope that in your discovery of Christ indwelling you, you will realize that we ourselves are equally found to have passed the test!

13:7 My sincere prayer is that, even if you cannot see us as meeting the requirements in your estimate, you do not use our apparent failure as an excuse to disqualify yourselves!

13:8 Truth does not become true by popular vote! It is already true without our permission! Therefore truth is not defined by our behavior. Nothing we do distracts from what truth really is. Truth triumphs inspite of what people think or do! *(The truth about you has its ultimate reference in Jesus. Ephesians 4:21)*

13:9 We rejoice in the fact that our weakness serves to prove you strong! We pray that you will find all the evidence you need to persuade yourself of your own perfection!

13:10 Somehow it seems better for me to write my thoughts to you; I think that was I physically present with you now, I might have been more abrupt! Yet [1]who I am in the Lord is a gift to you; I only wish to edify you; there is nothing in me that could possibly do you any harm. *(The word [1]exousia, from ek, source, and eimi, I am, is often translated, authority. Thus it would read, "according to the authority which the Lord has given me to build you up and not to disappoint you.)*

13:11 And now, dear Friends, we wish you joy; to be fully established, living your lives [1]within the immediate proximity of your true identity; with your minds made up about the fact that we are one, fitly joined together in perfect harmony; and knowing that God is your constant companion and that he himself is the source of love and peace. *(The word, [1]parakaleo, comes from para, a preposition indicating close proximity, a thing proceeding from a sphere of influence, with a suggestion of union of place of residence, to have sprung from its author and giver, originating from, denoting the point from which an action originates, intimate connection; and kaleo, meaning to identify by name, to surname.)*

13:12 Embrace one another with godly affection.

13:13 All the saints enfold you in their hearts!

13:14 The grace of the Lord Jesus Christ and the love of God and the fellowship of the Holy Spirit abide with all of you!

In this amazing book, Paul endorses the gospel he owns and proclaims as a gift by the revelation of Christ within him.

Gal 1:12 This message is not invented by a man; my source was not my formal religious education; I received it by the revelation of Jesus Christ.

Gal 1:15-16 God's eternal love dream separated me from my mother's womb; his grace became my identity. This is the heart of the gospel that I proclaim; it began with an unveiling of sonship in me, freeing me to announce the same sonship in the masses of non-Jewish people. I felt no immediate urgency to compare notes with those who were familiar with Christ from a mere historic point of view.

Paul contrasts the futility of the law of works in its clumsy effort to improve human behavior with the amazing revelation of the life of our design redeemed in us, in Christ! He uses the words, "law," "flesh" and "works" vs. grace, "spirit" and "faith" to give reference to the dynamic of the success of the cross.

The promise is concluded in the person of Christ; unveiled in human life!

Gal 3:21 No, the law does not oppose God's promise; it emphasizes the desperate need for a Redeemer to release righteousness in mankind as their life; something the law would certainly not be capable of! Had it been possible for the human race to be justified by the law, the promise would be unnecessary.

Gal 3:22 Scripture concludes that all mankind without exception are in the same predicament; they are imprisoned to sin. Now faith brings the promise of immediate release within everyone's reach! Jesus Christ makes it possible for all to believe what God believes concerning their righteousness and restored innocence.

Gal 4:5 Jesus' mandate was to rescue the human race from the regime of the law of performance and announce the revelation of their true sonship in God.

Gal 4:6 To seal our sonship God has commissioned the Spirit of sonship to resonate the Abba echo in our hearts; and now, in our innermost being we recognize him as our true and very dear Father.

Gal 5:1 Christ defines your faith; he is your freedom from anything the law could never free you of! Find your firm footing in this freedom. Do not let religion trip you up again and harness you to a system of rules and obligations!

Gal 5:6 Love sets faith in motion. *(It is easy for love to believe!)*

1:1 My name is Paul, my ministry and message are neither accredited to a theological education, nor am I sponsored by a religious institution. I am sanctioned by Jesus the Messiah and God the Father who raised him from the dead. *(Apostle, compelled to go, commissioned. [2 Cor. 5:14, 20 and Rom. 1:5] Rather than a title, apostleship defines the compelling urgency that prompts the spreading of the gospel. The resurrection revelation inspires the commission. Paul saw that mankind was co-raised together with Christ [Hos 6:2 and Eph 2:5, 6])*

1:2 I and my team of fellow believers here in Rome address this letter to all the churches in Galatia.

1:3 We greet you with grace and the peace that comes from knowing God as your Father, and Jesus who heads up the Christ-life. *(Jesus is Lord of the Christ-life; the life of our design unveiled.)*

1:4 Grace and peace have their reference in the fact that Jesus gave himself as the scapegoat for our sins and plucked us out from the ¹evil of this present religious age that encroached on us. This was exactly what the Father had planned in his love for mankind. *(The word, ¹poneros, means full of labors, hardships and annoyances; the fruit of the tree of the knowledge of good and labor "poneros"!)*

1:5 His glorious reputation is ageless; it extends beyond all times and seasons. We salute him with our amen! *(Nothing that religion communicates in any age or context can match him.)*

1:6 I am amazed that you can so easily be fooled into swapping the Gospel for a gimmick! The Gospel reveals the integrity of your original identity rescued in Christ; the gimmick is a conglomeration of grace and legalism. This mixture boils down to a do-it-yourself plan of salvation. *(Which is a recipe for disaster.)*

1:7 There is no other gospel in spite of the many so-called Christian products branded "gospel." If any hint of the law remains, it is not good news but merely religious people's ideas, detracting from the gospel of Christ. *(Some seek to unsettle your minds by perverting the Gospel to accommodate their own opinion.)*

1:8 I and any of my team would stand equally disqualified, even if we claim to have had an angelic visitation, if what we preach were to stray ever so slightly from the Gospel of the finished work of Christ.

1:9 Let me be blatant and clear about this: any gospel that does not emphasize the success of the cross is counterfeit and produces nothing but the curse!

1:10 *(In sharp contrast to the time when I needed letters of authority from the religious institutions of the day, endorsing my mission)* God is my complete persuasion. I answer to him alone, not anyone else. Christ employs me; I am addicted to his grace. Popular religious opinion will not influence me to compromise my message. *(What is the point of an impressive CV, when your Maker is not even asking for it?)*

1:11 I want to make it very clear to you my friends that the message I proclaim is not mere speculation or the product of religious debate.

1:12 This message is not invented by any person; my source was not my formal religious education; I received it by the revelation of Jesus Christ. *(Even though we once knew Christ from a human point of view, we know him thus no longer. [2 Corinthians 5:16])*

1:13 Everyone knows what a zealous Jew I was when I savagely persecuted God's church.

1:14 And how I progressed in the Jewish faith beyond many of my peers in my excessive eagerness to preserve the traditions of my ancestors.

1:15 God's eternal [1]love dream separated me from my mother's womb; his grace became my [2]identity. *(The word, [1]eudokeo, means his beautiful intention; the well done opinion. [My mother's womb, my natural lineage and identity as son of Benjamin.] The word, [2]kaleo, means to surname, to summon by name.)*

1:16 This is the heart of the gospel that I proclaim; it began with an unveiling of his Son [1]in me, freeing me to announce the same sonship [2]in the masses of non-Jewish people. I felt no immediate urgency to compare notes with those who were familiar with Christ from a mere historic point of view. *(The Greek text is quite clear: "It pleased the Father to reveal his Son in me in order that I may proclaim him in the nations!" The words, en emoi, translate as "in me," and en ethnos translate as in the Gentile nations, or the masses of non Jewish people! Not "among" the Gentiles as most translations have it. Later, when Barnabas is sent to investigate the conversion of the Greeks in Acts 11, instead of reporting his findings to HQ in Jerusalem, he immediately finds Paul, knowing that Paul's gospel is the revelation of the mystery of Christ in the nations [see Col 1:27]. No wonder then that those believers were the first to be called Christians, or Christ-like!)*

Jesus Christ confirms that the son of man is the son of God. "Call no man your father on earth, for you have one Father who is in heaven." [Mt 23:9] Paul reminds the Greek philosophers in Acts 17 that we live and move and have our being in God; humankind is indeed the offspring of God. He is quoting from their own writings, Epimenedes 600 BC and Aratus, 300 BC. The incorruptible seed of sonship is as much present in every person as the seed is already in all soil, even in the desert, waiting for the rain to awaken and ignite its life!

"For as the rain and the snow come down from heaven and water the earth, making it bring forth and sprout, so shall my word be that proceeds from my mouth, it shall not disappoint my purpose, it shall saturate the soil and cause it to bring forth and sprout. Instead of the thorn the cyprus and instead of the brier the myrtle!" [Isa 55:8-11, 13]

In Matthew 13:44, Jesus says that the kingdom of heaven is like a treasure hidden in an agricultural field! There is more to the field than what meets the eye!

In 2 Corinthians 4:4, 7 Paul says that we have this treasure in earthen vessels! But the god of this world has blindfolded our minds through unbelief [believing a lie about ourselves, Num 13:33] to keep us from seeing the light of the gospel revealing the glory of God in the face of Christ who is the image of God, as in a mirror!

When Jesus speaks of the sinner he speaks of him as the lost sheep, coin, or son. [Lk 15] You cannot be lost unless you belong! The inscription and image did not disappear from the coin when it was lost. How can we praise God and with the same mouth curse a person made in his image? [James 3:9 and Luke 20:20-26] Mankind has forgotten what manner of people they are by design; we are the image and likeness bearer of our Maker; this is exactly what Jesus came to reveal and redeem.

We may now behold him with unveiled faces as in a mirror and be immediately transformed [in our understanding] into his likeness. From the glory [opinion] of the flesh to the glory [opinion] of God. Legalistic religion kept the veil in place; the proclaiming of the liberating truth of the Good News, removes the veil! The "ugly duckling" didn't need a face-lift or lessons on how to fake the swan life! It only needed to know the truth about itself to be free indeed.)

1:17 This is radical! I deliberately distanced myself from Jerusalem and the disciples of Jesus. I landed up in Arabia before I returned again to Damascus. *(The weight of this revelation left me no choice; instead of finding out more about Christ in history, I desire to discover him more in me! [See also 2 Cor 5:16])*

1:18 Then three years later I ventured into Jerusalem, specifically to meet with ¹Kefas. I ended up staying with him for two weeks. *(In ¹Aramaic the word "rock" is **kefas**, and in Greek it is **petros**. Here Paul calls Peter Kefas in order to emphasize the meaning of his name rather than the familiar sound of Peter. Jesus said that the revelation of mankind's true identity and origin is the rock foundation of the **ekklesia**, lit. original identity from **ek**, the preposition denoting origin and **kaleo**, to surname. [Mt 16:13-18; see also Isa 51:1; Deut 32:18; 1 Peter 2:5 and 1 Kings 6:7])*

1:19 During this time I did not see any of the other apostles except James, the younger brother of Jesus. *(Saul (Paul), Peter (Kefas) and James shared a vital revelation; all three of them discovered their original identity beyond their natural birth: "Simon son of Jonah, flesh and blood did not reveal to you that I, the son of man, am the Christ, the Son of God; now that you know who I am, allow me to introduce you to you! I say that you are Rock, a chip of the old block. [Mt 16:17, 18]*

During the three years of Jesus's ministry none of his brothers believed in him. [Jn 7:5] But in 1 Corinthians 15:7, Paul specifically mentions the fact that Jesus also appeared to James after his resurrection. Suddenly it dawns on James that the Father of light birthed mankind by the eternal Word of truth; the word that became flesh and died humanity's death and who co-raised humankind into newness of life in his resurrection. If anyone hears this word they see the face of their birth as in a mirror! As Peter later admitted "We were born anew when Jesus was raised from the dead!" [1 Pet 1:3] The word that was before time was is our genesis. [Jas 1:17, 18, 23, 24])

1:20 I'm not writing this to trick you into anything; this is really how I started off preaching this gospel.

1:21 After my brief visit to Jerusalem, I travelled the regions of Syria and Cilicia.

1:22 None of the Judean Christian churches knew me face to face.

1:23 They only heard the rumor that the fierce opponent of their cause was now proclaiming the very Gospel he once endeavored to eradicate.

1:24 Consequently they recognized God's approval of my life and acknowledged God in me.

2:1 It was fourteen years since that first visit that I went on a special mission to Jerusalem with Barnabas; we deliberately took Titus with us; *(... since he was one of our first fruits in Greece. Remember Barnabas was sent by HQ in Jerusalem to investigate the rumor of Greek converts; instead of returning to Jerusalem to give feedback to the senior Apostles, he went to fetch Paul, knowing his gift as a teacher and revelation of the mystery of Christ in you. [Col 1:26 and Acts 11:25,26])*

2:2 I especially wanted the most senior leadership of the church to hear what I teach in the Gentile nations as my revelation and specific emphasis of the Gospel. We decided to meet in private to avoid any possible public controversy. In this way they could best judge for themselves whether, according to their opinion, my ministry had credibility or not.

2:3 Our Greek companion, Titus, survived the circumcision scrutiny and wasn't forced to go for the cut!

2:4 Some disguised Jewish "brothers" secretly sneaked in on us to spy out whether he was circumcised or not! Our liberty in Christ offended them; these spies had one agenda; to enslave us to their legalistic bondage!

2:5 We want you to know that we are sold out to keep the Gospel undiluted for your sakes; had we compromised the message ever so slightly to accommodate their opinion, the whole Gentile world would have felt cheated! We see such a future for the pure gospel in you.

2:6 The high ranked leaders had nothing to add to my message. I must say that their seniority did not intimidate me in the least. God does not judge people on face value. *(The important ones and the unimportant ones are equally esteemed and loved by him. [2 Cor 5:14, 16])*

2:7 From what I shared with them they acknowledged the accuracy of my message and felt that while Peter's ministry was more directed to the Jews, mine is tailor-made for the Gentile world!

2:8 They acknowledged that as much as Peter's ministry was sanctioned by God to preach to the Jews, my assignment was to evangelize the Gentiles.

2:9 The so-called pillars of the church, James *(the Lord's brother [Gal 1:19])*, Kefas, and John acknowledged my gift in the revelation of the message of grace, and extended their blessing on my work by giving us the right hand of fellowship. While they concentrated on converting the Jews I was recognized as the one with a message for the Gentiles.

2:10 Their only request was that we give something to the poor amongst them which we were keen to do since we already came prepared with gifts. *(Acts 11:29, 30)*

2:11 But when Kefas in turn visited Antioch I had to take him to task for his hypocrisy.

2:12 His fellowship with the Greek believers seemed so sincere, he even ate with them until James's group arrived from Jerusalem. Then his loyalty to the law showed its true colors! His pretence was an embarrassment!

2:13 Because of his senior position, the other Jewish believers were swept along with his hypocrisy; they even seduced Barnabas! What a shame!

2:14 Their interpretation of the Gospel was clearly compromised. I confronted Peter publicly about this. "Behind your colleagues' backs you pretend to live just like a Gentile as if your Jewish customs were no longer relevant; now suddenly you're imposing out-dated Jewish rules on these Gentile believers, to impress your Jewish friends!"

2:15 Sin is not a respecter of persons! Sin is sin whether you're Jew or Gentile.

2:16 As Jews we should be the first to know that no one will achieve a blameless standing before God through personal performance according to the requirements of the Law. [1]What Jesus Christ believes concerning our innocence matters most; he is persuaded that he did enough to declare mankind righteous. Our best intentions to do good cannot add any weight to our righteousness. Righteousness is not a reward for our good behavior. As Jewish believers we know this! We have no advantage over any other person. Jew and Gentile alike were equally guilty, now we are equally justified because of Jesus and for no other reason! *(Paul uses the [1]objective genitive - "faith of." "He is the author and finisher of faith; he is both the origin and conclusion of faith" [Heb. 12:2]; "from faith to faith" [Rom 1:17]. It is God's persuasion in the merit of his Son's achievement that awakens faith in mankind.")*

2:17 However, if in our quest to discover righteousness by faith in what Christ did for us, we find that it is still possible to stumble; do not now label yourself a sinner yet again! The fact that you sinned does not cancel the cross of Christ and gives you no reason to abandon justification by faith as if Christ is to be blamed for your distraction! That would be absurd! *(Now all of a sudden you want to keep the law again to further add to your righteousness as if Christ did not achieve enough. Do not let your experience deceive you to invent a new doctrine.)*

2:18 Only a con artist will try to be a law-person and a grace-person at the same time!

2:19 My co-crucifixion with Christ is valid! I am not making this up. In his death I died to the old system of trying to please God with my own good behavior! God made me alive together with Christ. How can any human effort improve on this! *(Hos 6:2 and Eph 2:5)*

2:20 The terms, co-crucified and co-alive define me now. Christ in me and I in him! *(Jn 14:20)* His sacrificial love is evidence of his persuasion of my righteousness! *(The life that I now live in the flesh I live by the faith of the Son of God. He believes in my innocence!)*

2:21 It is an insult to the grace of God to prefer Moses to Jesus! If the law could justify you then Jesus wasted his time dying your death! *(That would reduce salvation to a ludicrous contest between your obedience and the obedience of Christ! [Rom 5:19])*

3:1   Galatians! Galatians! Have you completely lost your common sense? Can't you see how the law bewitched you and blurred your vision to distort the revelation of what the cross of Christ accomplished in you? This was so clearly predicted in scripture. How can you not be persuaded by the truth? *(He did not die as an individual, he died your death! [Isa 53:4, 5])*

3:2   Please would you reason with me on this one issue; on what basis did you receive the Holy Spirit? Are we talking gift or reward here? What kind of message ignites faith? What a condemned sinner and failure you are as revealed in the law, or what God believes to be true about you as revealed in the Gospel. Let's not confuse Law with Grace.

3:3   Can you see how stupid it would be to start in the spirit *(believing in the success of the cross)* and then for some crazy reason to switch modes back to DIY again! As if your own works could add anything to what God has already done in Christ. ([DIY - Do It Yourself.] *It would be suicidal! It's like deliberately jumping out of the boat to try and swim across the ocean! There are two trees: the DIY tree or the Life tree. They represent two laws or systems: the law of works and the law of faith; the one represents what you have to do in order to become. The true tree reveals who you are by your redeemed design. Because of the Calvary-tree we are free to be! Spirit = faith; flesh = works)*

3:4   Remember how you felt when you first encountered faith; are you prepared to exchange that for religious sentiment? All the ground you've gained would be lost. *(The law does not complete faith, it nullifies it.)*

3:5   Would you accredit what you have received from God to something you did or something you have heard? Did God reward you for your high moral standards when he worked extravagant miracles in you and lavished his Spirit upon you; or did it perhaps have anything to do with the content of the revelation of the message of grace that you have heard? Faith is the source of God's action on mankind's behalf; our hearing is the conduit of what God's faith reveals.

3:6   Abraham had no other claim to righteousness but simply believing what God declared concerning him! Isaac confirmed God's faith, not Abraham's efforts. This is all we have in common with Abraham. *(Righteousness reveals God's faith as responsible for mankind's salvation in direct contrast to their doing it themselves by keeping moral laws!)*

3:7   The conclusion is clear; faith and not flesh relates us to Abraham! *(Grace rather than law is our true lineage. Ishmael represents so much more than the Muslim religion. Ishmael represents the clumsy effort of the flesh to compete with faith; the preaching of a mixed message of law and grace.)*

3:8 Scripture records prophetically that the mass of non-Jewish nations would be justified by faith and not by keeping moral laws. This announcement by God over Abraham is the gospel in advance. God saw every nation included in the same principle of the faith that Abraham pioneered. "In you all the nations of the earth are equally represented in the blessing of faith." *([Gen 22:17] I will indeed bless you, and I will multiply your seed as the stars of heaven and as the sand which is on the seashore. And your seed shall possess the gate of their enemies, Gen 22:18 and by your seed shall all the nations of the earth bless themselves. Righteousness by faith is the revelation of the gospel; [Rom 1:17 and Hab 2:4] "the just shall live by his (God's) faith" Righteousness by faith defines your life!)*

3:9 As did Abraham so do we now find our source in the blessing of faith.

3:10 In clear contrast to faith, the law is the authority of the curse. As it is written, "Everyone who fails to perform the detailed requirements of the law, even in the least, is condemned." *(Deut 27:26)*

3:11 Habakkuk confirms conclusively that righteousness by God's faith is the only basis to life; this terminates any possible justification before God based on moral behavior. *(Hab 2:4, 3:17-19)*

3:12 Law and faith have nothing in common! Law measures a person's doing and experience as defining their life. *(Faith measures God's doing in redeeming his design in us, as defining our lives.)*

3:13 Christ redeemed us from the curse as consequence of our failure to keep the law. In his cross he concentrated the total curse of the human race upon himself. In his abandoning himself to death, he absorbed and dissolved the horror of the curse in his own person. Scripture declares that anyone hanging on a tree embodies the curse. *(Deut 21:23)*

3:14 This act of Christ released [1]the blessing of Abraham upon the [2]Gentiles! Now we are free to receive [1]the blessing of the Spirit. *([1]Righteousness by God's faith in the achievement of Christ, and not as a reward for our behavior. In the obedience of Christ Deuteronomy 28 is out-dated! [Rom 5:19, Eph 1:3] [2]The mass of non-Jewish nations.)*

3:15 We are familiar with the fact that in civil affairs a testament, once endorsed, is authoritative and cannot be tampered with at a later stage.

3:16 It is on record that the promise *(of the blessing of righteousness by God's faith)* **was made to Abraham and to his seed, singular,** *(thus excluding his effort to produce Ishmael.)* **Isaac, the child of promise and not of the flesh mirrors the Messiah.**

3:17 This is my reasoning: God endorsed the covenant of promise in Christ 430 years before the law was given. The law did not later replace the promise! *(God's means of justifying humanity would always be by faith in his promise and never by their own ability to keep moral laws.)*

3:18 The law and the promise are not compatible; the one system nullifies the other. God gifts Abraham with heir-ship by promise *(and not by reward for his behavior.)*

3:19 So what is the use of the law then? It was an intermediary arrangement to make people aware of the extent of their wrong doings and at the same time point them to the promise of a Redeemer, the Messianic seed!

It was given by angelic beings to Moses as the middleman.

3:20 With Abraham there was no middleman; it was just God! (*The Mosaic law required mediators [the Levitical priesthood] because it was an arrangement whereby mankind had a part and God had a part. Mankind's part was to obey the commandments and God's part was to bless. God's covenant with Abraham was a grace covenant pointing to the man Jesus Christ, in whom God himself would fulfil mankind's part and therefore needed no mediator apart from himself. See Heb 6:17*

A dear friend, Melissa Perez says, In the incarnation Jesus fulfills both the proposal and the "I do!")

3:21 No, the law does not oppose God's promise; it emphasizes the desperate need for a Redeemer to release righteousness in mankind as their life; something the law would certainly be incapable of! Had it been possible for a person to be justified by the law, the promise would be unnecessary. (*"For if any kind of rule-keeping had power to create life in us, we would certainly have gotten it by this time." — The Message.*

Romans 5:6 "God's timing was absolutely perfect; humanity was at their weakest when Christ died their death — we were bankrupt in our efforts to save ourselves.")

3:22 Scripture concludes that all men without exception are in the same predicament; they are imprisoned to sin; now faith brings the promise of immediate release within everyone's reach! Jesus Christ makes it possible for all to believe what God believes concerning their righteousness and restored innocence. (*Jesus is the embodiment of God's faith in mankind. The righteousness of God is now on display in such a way that all may believe, regardless of who they are, there is no distinction. The same mass of mankind that was once reduced to an inferior identity through their sin, is now gifted with acquittal on the basis of the ransom paid by Jesus Christ for their liberation. [Rom 3:22-24]*)

3:23 We were confined to the law, kept in custody to its constraining influence until the revelation of faith would come to our rescue!

3:24 The law was acting just like a slave appointed to be the guardian of his master's children, until they would be of age to go to the proper school of Christ to find in faith their righteousness revealed and endorsed.

3:25 Now that we have arrived at our destination, the prophetic road signs and pointers are of no further use. Faith replaced the Custodian. Now that faith has come the law is no longer relevant.

3:26 What Jesus Christ believes to be true about you is the final confirmation of mankind's redeemed sonship. His faith is the only valid reference to your belief!

3:27 Whoever is immersed in Christ is fully clothed with him! He is your brand new wardrobe confirming your sonship! (*From now on the diaper days are over! "Our own righteousness by doing the law compares to filthy rags!" [Isa 64:6]*)

3:28 Nothing resembles your previous identity as Jew or Gentile, bond or free, male or female, Billabong or Gucci, now you are all defined in oneness with Christ! He is your significance and makes you stand out!

3:29 Since Christ is the seed of promise, it is only in our realizing our union with him *(in the incarnation)* that we are equally related to Abraham and heirs of the promise. Faith and not flesh relates us to Abraham. *(We inherit his righteousness by the same faith!)*

4:1 Infant heirs have no more say than a slave, even though they own everything! *(The best deal the law could possibly broker confirmed mankind's slavery to sin.)*

4:2 He would remain under domestic supervision and house rules until the date fixed by his father for his official graduation to the status of son-ship.

4:3 This is exactly how it was with us; we were kidnapped as it were into infancy and confined to that state through the law. *(An inferior mind-set as a result of Adam's fall.)*

4:4 But then the day dawned; the most complete culmination of time! *(Everything predicted was concluded in Christ!)* The son arrived, commissioned by the Father; his legal passport to the planet was his mother's womb. In a human body exactly like ours he lived his life subject to the same scrutiny of the law.

4:5 His mandate was to rescue the human race from the regime of the law of performance and announce the revelation of their true sonship in God. *(Now our true state of sonship is again realized! [Jn 1:12; see Jn 1:11-14] "It was not as though he arrived on a foreign planet, he came to his own, yet his own did not recognize him. [Ps 24:1] But to everyone who realizes their association in him, convinced that he is their original life, in them he confirms that we are his offspring. These are they who discover their genesis in God beyond their natural conception! Man began in God. We are not the invention of our parents! Suddenly the invisible eternal Word takes on visible form! The Incarnation! In him, in us! The most accurate tangible display of God's eternal thought finds expression in human life! The Word became a human being; we are his address; he resides in us! He captivates our gaze! The glory we see there is not a religious replica; he is the authentic* **monogenes** *begotten only of God. In him we recognize our true beginning. The Glory that Adam lost, returns! In fullness! Only Grace can communicate truth in such complete context!)*

4:6 To seal our sonship God has commissioned the Spirit of sonship to resonate the Abba echo in our hearts; and now, in our innermost being we recognize him as our true and very dear Father. *(The original life of the Father revealed in his Son is the life the Spirit now conducts within us. [Rom 8:14] Slavery is such a poor substitute for sonship! They are opposites; the one leads forcefully through fear; sonship responds fondly to Abba Father. [Rom 8:15] His Spirit resonates within our spirit to confirm the fact that we originate in God. [Rom 8:16] Because we are his offspring, we qualify to be his heirs, God himself is our portion, we co-inherit with Christ.[Rom 8:17])*

4:7 Can you see how foolish it would be for a son to continue to live his life with a slave mentality? Your sonship qualifies you to immediately participate in all the wealth of God's inheritance which is yours because of Christ. *(Legalism in its every disguise contradicts sonship! Sonship is not for sale!)*

4:8 What really amazes me is how gullible you Gentile believers are to get yourselves all tangled up again in oppressive Jewish rites! I mean you know all about your BC days of slavery to imaginary gods under your pagan beliefs.

4:9 In the meantime, you have come to know the real God; *(quite unlike the god of your imagination)* what is most significant however, is to discover that he knew you all along! After all, how could you possibly feel attracted again to the pathetic principles of religious deception? It does not matter in what disguise legalism comes, whether pagan or Jewish, it brings the same bondage.

4:10 All of a sudden there are special days, months, seasonal, and annual festivities that are scrupulously celebrated; this is nothing more than superstitious religious sentiment.

4:11 I am alarmed that all my passion seems wasted on you!

4:12 I urge you to imitate me *(in my conviction about the fact that Jewish customs and their shadow-sentiments are out-dated!).* **We are exactly in the same boat, it is really not about me; it is about you!** *(Our Jewish or Gentile background makes absolutely no difference! I'm not into winning or losing votes for my ministry or me! It's this Gospel that is my concern and urgency!)*

4:13 I have never compromised the Gospel, from the first day I met you, even though I was physically challenged at the time it did not distract from the message.

4:14 Remember how hospitable and sensitive you were towards me in spite of my frail condition! Instead of feeling embarrassed or repelled you treated me like an angel with the same courtesy you would have shown Christ Jesus.

4:15 At that time you were so overwhelmed with gratitude towards me that you would have gladly given me what is most precious to you, even your own eyes, to give me relief for my discomfort. What tenderness of affection you showed!

4:16 Alas! How is it possible that the same truth that then bonded you to me now turns me into your enemy?

4:17 The people who make me out to be your enemy do that to your disadvantage: they are very eager to isolate you from me, so that your zeal for their Jewish sentiments will boost their religious ego! *(Can you not see it; the Law and its followers do not like you for you; their only desire is for themselves!)*

4:18 If you want to be zealous for the best possible cause, be zealous for grace. You are fooling yourselves to be nice to me when I'm with you but zealous for them behind my back! It is not about me, I am jealous for you! It is the message that matters most, not someone's private agenda!

4:19 My darling little children, my jealousy for you compares to a mother over her newly born! I gave birth to you once through my gospel; now I feel those same labor pains all over again. I travail for the full realization of Christ to be [1]formed within in you! *(The word, [1]morpho, means to mold, from **meros**, form or portion; note the word translated, sin, **hameros**, to be without form or without your allotted portion; **metamorpho**, together with form.)*

4:20 I long to be with you right now; I want you to hear the urgency in my voice! I wish I could convince you that the law is a cul-de-sac! *(Any effort of your own to add to what God has already perfected in you in Christ is a waste of time! It is like trying to re-invent the wheel.)*

4:21 Since you are so intrigued by the law, please understand its prophetic message:

4:22 The law records the fact that Abraham had two sons: one by a slave girl, the other by a free woman.

4:23 The one is produced by the flesh *(the DIY-tree)*, the other by faith *(the promise)*.

4:24 There is a parallel meaning in the story of the two sons: they represent two systems, works and grace.

4:25 Sinai is an Arabian rocky mountain named after Hagar, *(outside the land of promise)*. Its association with the law of Moses mirrors Jerusalem as the capital of Jewish legalism. Hagar is the mother of the law of works.

4:26 But the mother from above, the true mother of mankind is grace, the free Jerusalem; she is the mother of the promise.

4:27 For it is written, "Rejoice oh childless one! Erupt in jubilee! For though you have never known travail before, your children will greatly outnumber her who was married! *(to the law)*

4:28 We resemble Isaac: we are begotten of faith, the promise is our parent.

4:29 Just as when the flesh child persecuted the faith child, so now these Jerusalem Jews in their Christian disguise seek to harass you;

4:30 however, scripture is clear: "Expel the slave mother and her son; the slave son cannot inherit with the free son." *(In exactly the same way, rid your minds radically from the slave mother and child mentality. Light dispels darkness effortlessly.)*

4:31 Realize whose children we are my brothers and sisters: we are not children of the slave-mother, the law, but children of the free mother; we are begotten of grace!

5:1 Christ defines your faith; he is your freedom from anything from which the law could never free you! Find your firm footing in this freedom. Do not let religion trip you up again and harness you to a system of rules and obligations! *(In this parallel, Christ represents Sarah, the faith-mother who birthed you in the resurrection. The rock-hewn tomb represents Sarah's dead womb! [1 Pet 1:3])*

5:2 I, Paul, am of the opinion, and you can quote me: If you would again consider circumcision as necessary to improve your standing before God, then you make Christ of no relevance to yourselves. Then you might as well delete him from your life altogether! *(By still holding on to any Jewish sentiment like keeping the Sabbath, etc, has the same effect.)*

5:3 I will state it categorically, that if you endorse circumcision, you are immediately obliged to keep the whole law! *(In for a penny, in for a pound!)*

5:4 Law-righteousness has nothing in common with grace-righteousness; they are opposites. As impossible as it is for anyone to travel in two opposite directions at the same time, equally irrelevant Christ becomes to anyone who continues to pursue righteousness under the law.

5:5 Our minds are made up; there is absolutely no advantage for anyone to pursue righteousness in the flesh; righteousness is a spirit dimension reality and can only be grasped by faith. What God believes is our exclusive reference. *(Any other basis for righteousness leaves mankind falling hopelessly short.)*

5:6 God believes that we are fully represented in Christ which takes circumcision or any contribution of the flesh out of the equation. Love sets faith in motion. *(It is easy for love to believe!)*

5:7 You started off like an athlete on a mission, who distracted you? You seemed so completely persuaded about the truth!

5:8 God is not confused about you. He surnamed you!

5:9 It is impossible to hide the effect of the smallest amount of yeast; the process of fermentation is immediately triggered. *(A little bit of legalism corrupts a person's whole life.)*

5:10 In spite of the interference of those "law-loving" people, I remain convinced about our like-mindedness in the Lord. It does not matter what high profile position anyone may occupy, do not let their title disturb you! The very law they promote will be their judgment! *(The fermentation process is unavoidable when you host a legalistic mind-set.)*

5:11 Would I compromise the message of the cross and preach circumcision just to avoid persecution! How insane would that be? *(This whole matter boils down to thinking that justification is the result of something we still have to do, or knowing that it is the result of something that God has already done!)*

5:12 These people who are so keen to cut off things should cut off their legalistic influence in your lives altogether!

5:13 Your redeemed identity defines your freedom, my brothers! But freedom does not mean that you are now free to again employ the law. On the contrary, your freedom finds its most complete expression in a love that serves one another! As free as you are to the law, so enslaved you are now to love! *(You are at last free to live the life of your original design.)*

5:14 Love already completes the law: this is the nitty-gritty of the law; to value your fellow human as equal to yourself. *(Which was again and again proved to be completely impossible to achieve by employing the DIY tree-principle.)*

5:15 The best efforts under the legalistic mind-set sooner or later ended up in strife: back-biting, tearing one another apart, devouring and consuming one another. *(It gets ugly! See how divorce destroyed love dreams; ex-business partners fighting one another in court; consider how worthless life becomes in war!)*

5:16 I conclude: let spirit be the dominant influence in your daily walk and see how it defeats the cravings of flesh. *(Spirit is satisfied by the love law, the revelation of grace; flesh craves to prove and gratify itself by the DIY law. Faith defeats flesh.)*

5:17 While the law of works still features in your mind, it is a catalyst to disaster: you are caught in the middle of a war zone, wanting to do the things that you desire by design, but finding the flesh in strong resistance to what the spirit desires: *(The two trees, the flesh and the spirit, represent two opposing forces of influence, two separate mind-sets, external to the real person; but whilst hosted, like a virus, its influence becomes unavoidable and very visible.)*

5:18 Those who are led by the spirit *(of faith)* are free from the law *(of personal performance. [See 3:3])*

5:19 The influence of the flesh is obvious: wherever a legalistic judgmental attitude prevails, sexual sins are rampant! Anything goes: adultery, filth, and outrageous licentiousness;

5:20 *(The DIY lifestyle is driven by self effort and selfishness. A legalistic mind-set, the flesh, sponsors typical behavior that expresses itself in very visible symptoms:)* such as idolatry, which is worshipping a distorted image of oneself, drugs, hatred, constant conflict, jealous suspicion, violent outbursts of rage, everyone for himself in a cut-throat competitive world, trampling on others to get to the top, dissension, heresy, and manipulating people's minds with false teachings. *(The flesh is not your "lower nature;" it is the mind-set of fallen mankind trying to follow the life of their design as witnessed in everyone's conscience, by sheer willpower, independent of God.)*

5:21 Consumed with envious self pity, murder, drunken stupor, intoxicated licentiousness and lust, with all the quarrels and jealousy it ignites. As I have stated before: those who are practicing this kind of lifestyle have nothing in common with the Kingdom of God. *(The authority of the Christ-life opposes and defeats the dominance of the flesh.)*

5:22 The Spirit finds expression in love, joy, peace, endurance, kindness *(usefulness, obliging)*, goodness, faith, gentleness, self control *(spirit strength)*.

(In total contrast to the tree of the knowledge of good and evil, the tree of life bears fruit effortlessly consistent with the life of our original design!)

5:23 Legalism can neither match nor contradict this. There is no law against love! *(Love does not compete with law; love is extravagant in its exhibition of the Christ life.)*

5:24 Those who understand that their righteousness is of Christ and that it does not come as a reward for their ability to keep the law, have discovered that their flesh with its dictates and lusts were co-crucified with Christ. *(Gal 2:20; see also Gal 5:18)*

5:25 Because faith defines us and not flesh, we take our lead from the Spirit in our daily conduct. There is an authority in our step; we are marching in rank like soldiers! *(The Christ life is the dominant authority in the universe!)*

5:26 Quit your efforts to try and impress one another. The law of works reduces your life to envious comparison and petty competition, while love only always seeks the advantage of the other! *(This means total freedom from any external law!)*

6:1 Brothers and sisters, if it seems that someone continues to [1]anticipate their next [2]failure *(by carrying just too much load, see verse 2)*, from your position in faith restore such a person in a spirit of courtesy and grace, keeping your own attitude in check; a legalistic approach would want to suspiciously probe into problems. *(The word, [1]prolambano, means to anticipate, take in advance; [2]paraptoma, comes from para, close proximity, proceeding from a sphere of influence, and pipto, means to lose height, stop flying, to fail. Remember you represent grace not law.)*

6:2 The law of the Christ-life distinguishes your spirituality; taking the weight off someone's shoulder is fulfilling the law of Christ. *(The message of grace removes all law-related burdens such as guilt, suspicion, inferiority, shame and a sin-consciousness.)*

6:3 Anyone who imagines to be someone they are not, lives a lie. *(The law system sponsors pretence; grace reveals your true identity redeemed in Christ.)*

6:4 Now, without the pressure of pretence, you are free to give expression to your individual self and not some phony life you're trying to fake. Evaluate your own conduct in such a way that you do not need another's approval to confirm your joy.

6:5 Everyone ultimately lives their own life. *(even though we share our lives with one another)*

6:6 Both student and teacher draw from the same source; they equally participate in every good thing. The word they share echoes its distinct resonance within them.

6:7 Show-business does not deceive God! Do not be led astray and then pull your nose up at God, as if it was God who let you down. The harvest always reveals the seed.

6:8 The flesh cannot compete with the spirit; just like with Adam, the fruit of the DIY tree still produces death, while faith produces the spirit fruit of the life of the ages, the God-kind of life.

6:9 Every good deed has a predictable harvest. Let's not get discouraged in the in-between times. *(Make sure your good deeds are love-driven rather than duty-driven. Faith works by love, duty by willpower)*

6:10 Let us take advantage of every opportunity to be a blessing to everyone we meet, without neglecting our fellow faith family.

6:11 To raise the urgency in my voice, I will write the following in my own hand and in large letters:

6:12 Those who urge you to be circumcised are only trying to avoid persecution for the cross of Christ. They prefer to be popular with their fellow Jewish colleagues and thus compromise the message of the cross. To them it is only the outward sign in the flesh that matters.

6:13 It is not even so much for the law that they are concerned, they just want to boast in your flesh, as a sign that they successfully recruited you for their cause.

6:14 May my boasting be in nothing but the cross of our Lord Jesus Christ, through whom the world has been crucified to me and I to the world. The religious-systems and applause of this world have no appeal to me. As far as they are concerned, I am like a dead person.

6:15 The new creation in Christ steals the show; not whether someone is circumcised or not! *(God associated us in Christ; when he died we died, when he was raised we were raised together with him in newness of life)*

6:16 Our union with Christ sets the pace and makes us the true Israel, not whether we are Jew or Gentile, circumcised or not! Oh, what peace we discover in his mercy! This rule is the new law we submit ourselves to as the principle of our daily walk!

6:17 I will not be troubled anymore. I already bear enough scars in my body that brand me as being under the ownership of Jesus. *(Those scars that I carry from being persecuted for this Gospel are more significant to me than the scar of circumcision!)*

6:18 Brothers and sisters, may the revelation of the grace of our Lord Jesus Christ be the rule of your spirit.

Amen

In poetic articulation Paul unfolds the message of the mystery of Christ as representing humanity. He is absolutely passionate in his prayers and desires for everyone to see how completely associated they are in Christ. God found us in Christ before he lost us in Adam.

Eph 1:10 In the economy of the fullness of time, everything culminates in Christ; all that is in heaven and all that is on earth is reconciled in him.

He sees heaven not as a distant goal for us to strive towards, but how completely God has already lavished upon us every blessing heaven has in Christ. This is our point of departure! We are co-raised and co-seated together with Christ in heavenly places to begin with! Long before anyone but God believed it we were made alive together with Christ; "I desire that you know by revelation what he has known about you all along! I pray that your thoughts will be flooded with light and inspired insight."

Eph 2:10 We are engineered by his design; he molded and manufactured us in Christ. We are his workmanship, his poetry. We are fully fit to do good, equipped to give attractive evidence of his likeness in us in everything we do.

Eph 3:4 In reading these words you will perceive my insight into the mystery of Christ.

Eph 3:20 We celebrate him who supercharges us powerfully from within. Our biggest request or most amazing dream cannot match the extravagant proportion of his thoughts towards us.

Eph 4:7 The gift of Christ gives dimension to grace and defines our individual value.

Eph 4:23 Be renewed in your innermost mind! It will cause you to be completely reprogrammed in the way you think about yourself!

Eph 4:15 Love gives truth its voice. The conversation that truth inspires creates the atmosphere wherein growth is both spontaneous and inevitable. The whole person is addressed in Christ who is the head of the body; he is the conclusion of God's communication with mankind.

Eph 4:16 From him flows the original composition and detail of our design. Like words entwined in poetry, they connect layer upon layer to complete the harmony, following the rhythm of his thoughts like footprints. Meanwhile the body thrives and pulsates with the energy of love. Each individual expression finds its complete measure there.

Eph 4:21 It is not possible to study Christ in any other context; he is the incarnation; hear him resonate within you! The truth about you has its ultimate reference in Jesus.

He did not come to introduce a new compromised set of rules; he is not an example for us but of us!

Eph 5:14 This is the message of light; Christ awakens you from your intoxicated slumber and resurrects you out of the death trap of enslaved thought patterns.

1:1 Paul, employed by the delightful resolve of God and commissioned to represent Jesus Christ to the saints in Ephesus and also to every believer in Christ Jesus.

1:2 I greet you with the grace and peace that proceed from God the Father and the Lord Jesus Christ.

1:3 Let's celebrate God! He lavished every blessing heaven has upon us in Christ!

1:4 He associated us in Christ before [1]the fall of the world! Jesus is God's mind made up about us! He always knew in his love that he would present us again [2]face-to-face before him in blameless innocence. *(The implications of the fall are completely cancelled. Paul uses the word, [1]katabalo, meaning "to fall away, to put in a lower place," instead of themelios, meaning "foundation" [see 2:20]; thus, translated "the fall of the world," instead of "the foundation of the world." God found us in Christ before he lost us in Adam! We are presented in blameless innocence before him! The word, [2]katenopion, suggests the closest possible proximity, face-to-face!)*

1:5 He is the architect of our design; his heart dream realized our [1]coming of age in Christ. *(Adoption here is not what it means in our Western society. It is a coming of age, like the typical Jewish Barmitsva. See Galatians 4:1-6, " ... and to seal our sonship the spirit of his Son echoes Abba Father in our hearts." This is [1]huiothesia.)*

1:6 His grace-plan is to be celebrated: he greatly endeared us and highly favored us in Christ. His love for his Son is his love for us.

1:7 Since we are *(fully represented)* in him, his blood is the ransom that secures our redemption. His forgiving our sins measures the wealth of his grace.

1:8 This grace shown towards us communicates a wisdom and discernment of our worth that completely surpasses any definition.

1:9 The secret is out! His cherished love dream now unfolds in front of our very eyes.

1:10 In the [1]economy of the fullness of time, everything culminates in Christ. All that is in heaven and all that is on earth is reconciled in him. *(The word,[1]oikonomia, translates as administration. "All human history shall be consummated in Christ, everything that exists in heaven or earth shall find its perfection and fulfillment in him." — Phillips. "All that is in heaven, all that is on earth, summed up in him!" — Knox)*

1:11 This is how we fit into God's picture: Christ is the measure of our portion, we are in him, invented and defined in him. God's blueprint intention is on exhibition in us. Everything he accomplishes is inspired by the energy and intent of his affection. *(See Romans 8:29, "He engineered us from the start to fit the mold of sonship and likeness according to the exact blueprint of his design. We see the original and intended shape of our lives preserved* *in his Son; he is the firstborn from the same womb that reveals our genesis. He confirms that we are the invention of God.")*

1:12 It was our initial privilege *(as Jews)* to cherish the Messianic hope; our lives in Christ were destined to prophetically promote the celebration of his [1]**glorious plan with mankind** *([1]doxa, intention, opinion.)*

1:13 Now you *(Gentiles)* also have discovered yourselves to be equally included in him having witnessed [1]the unveiled [2]logic of God. What exciting news! Your salvation is publicly announced. Consistent with the promise of God, the Holy Spirit gives guarantee to the fact of your faith, like the stamp of a signet ring that certifies a document. You are in him! *([1]The Word, logic, from **logos**, of truth. The word, [2]**alethea**, comes from a + lanthano, meaning not hidden.)*

1:14 The Holy Spirit is our [1]tangible link to the inheritance that was ransomed and preserved for us. God's glorious plan for mankind is the theme of our celebration. *([1]Guarantee, or earnest comes from **arabon**, a Hebrew word meaning to braid, as two parties intertwine by giving something as surety and pledge. The pledge represents the full transaction. The legal document or title deed represents the complete value of the transaction. Like a wedding ring represents the marriage.)*

1:15 I am sure you can appreciate how the news of your faith and love greatly inspires me.

1:16 I am so happy for you; my thoughts and prayers are full of you.

1:17 I desire that you will draw directly from the source; that the God of our Lord Jesus Christ, the Father of glory ignites the spirit of wisdom and of revelation in you in the unveiling of his [1]Master Plan. I desire that you know by revelation what he has known about you all along! *([1]His intent, doxa, glory.)*

1:18 I pray that your thoughts will be flooded with light and inspired insight; that you will clearly picture his intent in identifying you in him so that you may know how precious you are to him. The saints are his treasure and the glorious trophy of his portion! *(We are God's assets and the measure of his wealth!)*

1:19 I pray that you will understand beyond all comparison the magnitude of his mighty power at work [1]in us who believe. Faith reveals how enormously advantaged we are in Christ. *(The preposition [1]**eis**, speaks of a point reached in conclusion)*

1:20 It is the same dynamic energy that he unleashed in Christ when he raised him from the dead and forever established him in the power of his own right hand in the realm of the heavens.

1:21 Infinitely above all the combined forces of rule, authority, dominion or governments; he is ranked superior to any name that could ever be given to anyone of this age or any age still to come in the eternal future.

1:22 I want you to see this: he subjected all these powers under his feet. He towers head and shoulders above everything. He is the head;

1:23 the ¹church is his body. The completeness of his being that fills all in all resides in us! God cannot make himself more visible or exhibit himself more accurately. *(The word, ¹ekklesia, comes from ek, a preposition always denoting origin, and klesia from kaleo, to identify by name, to surname; thus the "church" is his redeemed image and likeness in human form.)*

2:1 Picture where God found us. We were in a death trap of an inferior lifestyle, constantly living below the ¹blueprint measure of our lives. *(The word sin, is the word ¹hamartia, from ha, negative or without and meros, portion or form, thus to be without your allotted portion or without form, pointing to a disorientated, distorted, bankrupt identity; the word meros, is the stem of morphe, as in 2 Corinthians 3:18 the word metamorphe, with form, which is the opposite of hamartia - without form. Sin is to live out of context with the blueprint of one's design; to behave out of tune with God's original harmony. See Deuteronomy 32:18, "You have forgotten the Rock that begot you and have gotten out of step with the God who danced with you!" Hebrew, khul or kheel, to dance.)*

2:2 We were all part of a common pattern, swept along under a powerful invisible influence, a spirit-energy that adopted us as sons to its dictates through unbelief.

2:3 Throughout that time everyone of us were warped and corrupted in our conduct; snared in a jumble of forbidden lusts, driven by the desires of the senses, completely engaged in an expression of a life ruled by mind games; it was as if a twisted passion parented a universal breed of people.

2:4 None of this could distract from the extravagant love of God; he continued to love us with the exact same intensity.

2:5 This is how grace rescued us: sin left us dead towards God, like spiritual corpses; yet in that state of deadness and indifference, God co-quickened us together with Christ. Sin proved how dead we were *(the law confirmed it!)* **Grace reveals how alive we now are** *(the gospel announces it!)* **Before anyone but God believed it, he made us alive together with him and raised us up together with him.** *(We had no contribution to our salvation! God's master-plan unfolded in the mystery of the gospel declaring our joint inclusion in Christ's death and resurrection; God found us in Christ before he lost us in Adam! [Eph 1:4] In the economy of God, when Jesus died we died. God saw us in Christ, in his death and resurrection before we saw ourselves there! He declared our co-resurrection with Christ 800 BC [Hos 6:2]!)*

2:6 *(As much as we were co-included in his death,)* **we are co-included in his resurrection. We are also elevated in his ascension to be equally present in the throne room of the heavenly realm where we are co-seated with him in his executive authority. We are fully represented in Christ Jesus.** *(Our joint position in Christ defines us; this can never again be a distant goal to reach through religious devotion or striving, but our immediate reference. Col 3:1-3)*

2:7 *(In a single triumphant act of righteousness God saved us from the "guttermost" to the uttermost. Here we are now, revealed in Christ in the highest possible position of bliss! If mankind's sad history could not distract from the extravagant love of God,)* **imagine how God is now able for timeless perpetuity** *(the eternal future)* **to exhibit the trophy of the wealth of his grace demonstrated in his kindness towards us in Christ Jesus. Grace exhibits excessive evidence of the success of the cross.**

2:8 Your salvation is not a reward for good behavior! It was a grace thing from start to finish; you had no hand in it. Even the gift to believe simply reflects his faith! *(By grace you are! Saved by the gift of faith; grace reveals who we are and the faith of God persuades us of it! You did not invent faith; it was God's faith to begin with! It is from faith to faith, [Rom 1:17] He is both the source and conclusion of faith. [Heb 12:2])*

2:9 If this could be accomplished through any action of yours then there would be ground for boasting.

2:10 We are engineered by his design; he molded and manufactured us in Christ. We are his workmanship, his [1]poetry. *(God finds inspired expression of Christ in us. The Greek word for workmanship is [1]poeima.)* We are [2]fully fit to do good, equipped to give attractive evidence of his likeness in us in everything we do. *(God has done everything possible to find spontaneous and effortless expression of his character in us in our everyday lifestyle. The word, [2]proetoimatso, translates a notion that God has prepared a highway for us to lead us out like kings, just like the Oriental custom, where people would go before a king to level the roads to make it possible for the king to journey with ease and comfort. [Isa 40:3-5])*

2:11 Remember where you came from; *(not only were you spiritually dead but)* it wasn't long ago when you were still classified as non-Jewish, judging on the surface you had nothing that linked you to them. They sneered at you because you didn't share their distinguishing mark of circumcision, which was their claim to fame!

2:12 During that time you were distanced from the Messianic hope; you had nothing in common with Israel. You felt foreign to the covenants of prophetic promise, living a life with nothing to look forward to in a world where God seemed absent.

2:13 But now, wow! Everything has changed; you have discovered yourselves to be located in Christ. What once seemed so distant is now so near; his blood reveals your redeemed innocence and authentic genesis.

2:14 It is in him that we are one and at peace with everyone; he dissolved every definition of division. *(What we know will put war and divorce out of business!)*

2:15 In his incarnation, he rendered the entire Jewish system of ceremonial laws and regulations useless as a measure to justify human life and conduct. In that he died humanity's death all grounds for tension and hostility were entirely removed. The peace he proclaims reveals one new human race, created and defined in Christ, instead of two groups of people separated by their ethnic identity and differences.

2:16 Both parties are fully represented and equally reconciled to God in one human body through the cross. He reinstated the former harmony; all opposing elements were thus utterly defeated.

2:17 On that basis he made his public appearance, proclaiming the good news of peace to the entire human race; both those who felt left out in the cold *(as far as the promises and covenants were concerned)*, as well as to those who were near all along *(because of their Jewish identity)*.

2:18 Because of Christ both Jew and Gentile now enjoy equal access to the Father in one Spirit.

2:19 The conclusion is clear; you are no longer frowned upon as a foreigner; you are where you belong and part of an intimate family.

2:20 Your lives now give tangible definition to the spiritual structure, having been built into it by God upon the foundation that the prophets and apostles proclaimed. The first evidence of this building was Jesus Christ himself being the chief cornerstone. *(He is the visible testimony to the restored image and likeness of God in human form.)*

2:21 In him everyone of us are like [1]living Lego blocks fitted together of the same fabric *([1]conversation)*, giving ever [2]increasing articulation to a global mobile [3]sanctuary intertwined in the Lord. *(The word, [1]sunarmologeo, come from sun, meaning union, harmo meaning harmony, and logeo meaning conversation. The word, [2]auxano, means expanding with growth. The word, [3]naos, is translated as the most sacred dwelling space.)*

2:22 In him you are co-constructed together as God's permanent spiritual residence. You are God's address!

3:1 My ministry is not measured by the size of my prison cell. I am confined by his grace; Christ Jesus is the prison keeper. You are why I am here. *(Grace measures my ministry; this prison cell cannot hide my message from you!)*

3:2 It is common knowledge that I have been entrusted with a message that reveals how included you Gentiles are in the grace gift of God.

3:3 You must have heard how this mystery was revealed to me, in a dramatic disclosure that broke the silence of a long kept secret. I have previously written briefly about this.

3:4 In [1]reading these words you will perceive my [2]insight into the mystery of Christ. *(The word, [1]anaginosko, suggests an upward knowledge; to know again, to recognize, to read with recognition. Insight, [2]sunesis, from sun + eimi, together "I am", a flowing together like two rivers.)*

3:5 In no previous generation has there been a more comprehensive and detailed understanding *(of the full consequence of grace)* as it has now been uncovered in the Spirit to his ambassadors who brought the prophetic promise into full view! Mankind *(the sons of men)* may now realize that the prophetic word is fulfilled in them! Everything the prophets saw is now declared! Both the prophets *(who saw this in advance)* and the apostles *(who now proclaim this)* are sanctioned in Christ.

3:6 The essence of what I see reveals the fact that the multitude of humanity are joint participants in the same inheritance. *(together with Israel)* We are all part of one and the same body in Christ. The Good news is that God's promise is equally relevant and applicable to all.

3:7 This Gospel defines my ministry; I am supercharged by the gift of his grace!

3:8 I am the lowest ranked saint by far and qualified purely by his grace to declare this unexplored treasure of Christ in the nations. *(My claim to fame emphasizes the fact that grace is a gift and certainly not a reward for good behavior.)*

3:9 The mandate of my message is to make all men see. The unveiling of this eternal secret is to bring into public view an association that has always been hidden in God; Jesus Christ is the blueprint of creation. *(Eph 1:4)*

3:10 Every invisible authority and government in the arena of the heavenlies now witnesses the display of the wisdom of God. The church acts like a prism that disperses the varied magnitude of God in human form.

3:11 In Jesus Christ our Master, the timeless [1]prophetic thought of God is [2]poetically realized. *(Pre-determined, prophetic thought, from the prophetic significance of the face-bread in the temple, [1]prothesis which is the Greek word for the show bread. The Hebrew word is lechem paniym, face bread, or bread of the presence. Poetry, from poieo, to fashion.)*

3:12 His faith in us gives our lives integrity. We echo and articulate the [1]original conversation publicly. He is our platform to a global audience. *(The word [1]parrhesia, from para, a preposition indicating close proximity, a thing proceeding from a sphere of influence, with a suggestion of union of place of residence, to have sprung from its author and giver, originating from, denoting the point from which an action originates, intimate connection; and rhesia, conversation. In him we express ourselves freely and openly.)*

3:13 You have no reason to feel embarrassed or responsible because of what I am suffering; rather feel honored!

3:14 Overwhelmed by what grace communicates, I bow my knees in awe before the Father.

3:15 Every family in heaven and on earth originates in him; his is mankind's family name and he remains the authentic identity of every nation.

3:16 I desire for you to realize what the Father has always envisaged for you, so that you may know the magnitude of his [1]intent and be dynamically reinforced in your inner being by the Spirit of God. *(The word, [1]doxa, opinion or intent.)*

3:17 This will ignite your faith to fully grasp the reality of the indwelling Christ. You are rooted and founded in love. Love is your invisible inner source, just like the root system of a tree and the foundation of a building. *(The dimensions of your inner person exceed any other capacity that could possibly define you.)*

3:18 Love is your reservoir of super human [1]strength which [2]causes you to see everyone equally sanctified in the context of the limitless extent of love's breadth and length and the extremities of its dimensions in depth and height. *(The word, [1]exischuo means to be entirely competent, to be empowered to [2]comprehend. The word [2]katalambano, kata, strengthened form; with lambano, to grasp, thus to entirely grasp, means to come to terms with, to make one's own. Rom 12:13 Purpose with resolve to treat strangers as saints; pursue and embrace them with fondness as friends on equal terms of fellowship. Rom 12:16 Esteem everyone with the same respect; no one is more important than the other. Associate yourself rather with the lowly than with the lofty. Do not distance yourself from others in your own mind. ["Take a real interest in ordinary people." — JB Phillips] In the breadth and length we see the horizontal extent of the love of Christ: the complete inclusion of the human race. 2 Cor 5:14,16. The depth of his love reveals how his love rescued us from the deepest pits of hellish despair and led us as trophies in his triumphant procession on high. Eph 2:5,6, Eph 4:8-10, Col 3:1-4)*

3:19 I desire for you to become intimately acquainted with the love of Christ on the deepest possible level; far beyond the reach of a mere academic, intellectual grasp. Within the scope of this equation God finds the ultimate expression of himself in you. *(So that you may be filled with all the fullness of God! Awaken to the consciousness of his closeness! Separation is an illusion! Oneness was God's idea all along! He desires to express himself through* *your touch, your voice, your presence; he is so happy to dwell in you! There is no place in the universe where he would rather be!)*

3:20 We celebrate him who supercharges us powerfully from within. Our biggest request or most amazing dream cannot match the extravagant proportion of his thoughts towards us. *(Now to him that is able to do exceeding abundantly above all that we ask or think, according to the power that works in us...KJV)*

3:21 He is both the author and conclusion of the glory on display in the ¹ekklesia, mirrored in Christ Jesus. The encore continues throughout every generation, not only in this age but also in the countless ages to come. Amen! *(The word, ¹ekklesia, often translated church, comes from ek, a preposition always denoting origin, and **klesia** from **kaleo**, to identify by name, to surname; the ekklesia is the expression of his image and likeness redeemed in human life.)*

4:1 The fact that I am in prison does not in the least diminish my awareness of my "in-Christ-ness!" My complete existence is defined and confined in him. Let the detail of your day-to-day life ³flow from the consciousness of your true ²identity and ³worth as defined in him. *(Paul writing from prison, but seeing himself co-seated together with Christ in heavenly places! Eph 2:6. No distraction or contradiction can reduce his life to any other reality. "Walking worthy of your calling" I have replaced with, "Let the detail of your day-to-day life flow from the consciousness of your true identity and worth as defined in him. The word ¹**parakaleo**, inspired from within to live the life of your design. Your calling or vocation, from ²**kaleo**, to surname, to identify by name. To ³walk worthy, **axios**, meaning having the weight of another thing of like value, worth as much.)*

4:2 Meekness and tenderness are the fabric of your make-up; this enables you to show compassion even in seemingly impossible situations, eagerly bearing with one another in an environment where love rules.

4:3 Being vigilant to guard your oneness of spirit. We are prisoners of peace. We confirm the fact that there is only one body; also that there is only one Spirit.

4:4 We are identified in one expectation *(hope)*; there is no plan B. We bear the same ¹surname. *(Called, ¹kaleo, to identify by name, to surname.)*

4:5 We are employed by the same Boss; we share the same faith, and our baptism says the same thing. *(There is only one faith! Not what we believe about God but what God believes about us! Baptism declares that we are equally included in the death and resurrection of Jesus. Our faith does not invent God; his faith defines us!)*

4:6 There is only one God. He remains the ultimate Father of the universe. We are because he is. He is present in all; he is above all, through all and in all. *(He is not far from each one of us; in him we live and move and have our being. We are indeed his offspring. [Acts 17:24-28])*

4:7 The gift of Christ gives dimension to grace and defines our individual value. *(Grace was given to each one of us according to the measure of the gift of Christ. One measure, one worth! Our worth is defined by his gift not by a reward for our behavior.)*

4:8 Scripture confirms that he led us as trophies in his triumphant procession on high; he ¹repossessed his gift *(likeness)* in human form. *(See Ephesians 2:6, We are also elevated in his ascension to be equally welcome in the throne room of the heavenly realm where we are now seated together with him in his authority. Quote from the Hebrew text, Ps 68:18, ¹**lakachta mattanoth baadam**, you have taken gifts in human form, in Adam. [The gifts which Jesus Christ distributes to us he has received in us, in and by virtue of his incarnation. Commentary by Adam Clarke.] We were born anew in his resurrection. 1 Pet 1:3, Hos 6:2.)*

4:9 The fact that he ascended confirms his victorious descent into the deepest pits of human despair. *(See John 3:13, "No one has ascended into* *heaven but he who ¹descended from heaven, even the son of man." All mankind originate from above; we are ¹anouthen, from above [see Jas 1:17, 18].)*

4:10 He now occupies the ultimate rank of authority from the lowest regions where he stooped down to rescue us to the highest authority in the heavens, having executed his mission to the full. *(Fallen mankind is fully restored to the authority of the authentic life of their design. [Ps 139:8].)*

4:11 What God has in us is gift wrapped to the world: some are commissioned to pioneer, others are gifted prophetically, some as announcers of good news, some as shepherds with a real gift to care and nurture, and others have a gift to ignite instruction through revelation knowledge. *(Couriers, communicators, counsellors and coaches. — Rob Lacey)*

4:12 Each expression of his gift is to fully equip and enable the saints for the work of the ministry so that they may mutually contribute in their specific function to give definition to the visible body of Christ.

4:13 The purpose of these ministry gifts is to present everyone on par and in oneness of faith; believing exactly what the Son of God believes and knowing accurately what he knows concerning us. Standing face-to-face in equal stature to the measure of the ¹completeness of Christ. *(The word, ¹pleroma, means a life filled to the brim with Christ, like a freight ship carrying its cargo.)*

4:14 The most dangerous life you can live is an ignorant one. You're left like an infant on a ship out of control in the waves and winds of the storms of life. The fall of the dice dictates while the deceptive teachings of men and their distracting tricks entertain.

4:15 ¹Love gives truth its voice. The conversation that ²truth inspires creates the atmosphere wherein growth is both spontaneous and inevitable. The whole person is addressed in Christ who is the head of the body; he is the conclusion of God's communication with mankind. *("Speaking the truth in love" is not only the preferred attitude in our every conversation, but the only option; where truth gives integrity to love, and love gives attraction to truth. Love, ¹agape, comes from **ago**, to lead as a shepherd leads his sheep, and **pao**, to rest. God's rest celebrates our perfection; **agape** is to see the same value that God sees in every person. ²Truth as it is mirrored in Christ [v 21].)*

4:16 ¹From him flows the original composition and detail of our design like words entwined in poetry, *(¹like a conductor of music, ¹epichoregeo)* they connect layer upon layer to complete the harmony, following the rhythm of his thoughts like footprints. Meanwhile the body thrives and pulsates with the energy of love. Each individual expression finds its complete measure there. *(The church is not a dismembered, dysfunctional body, but a fully functional, coordinated lover of people." — Rob Lacey)*

4:17 My most urgent appeal to you in the Lord is this: you have nothing in common with the folly of the empty-minded ¹masses; the days of conducting your lives and affairs in a meaningless way are over! *(The Gentiles, ¹ethnos, the masses of people who are walking in the vanity of their minds.)*

4:18 The life of their design seems foreign to them because their minds are darkened through a hardened heart ruled by ignorance. They are blinded by the illusion of the senses as their only reference, stubbornly wearing a blindfold in broad daylight. *(Hardness of heart is the result of a darkened understanding; a mind veiled through unbelief. [See 2 Cor 4:4])*

4:19 Having become conditioned to a life distanced from God; they are calloused in spirit, and are lust and greed driven; they have completely abandoned themselves to outrageous shameless living. *(See Rom 1:19-23)*

4:20 Of what total contrast is Christ!

4:21 It is not possible to study Christ in any other context; he is the incarnation, hear him resonate within you! The truth about you has its ultimate reference in Jesus. *("The truth as it is in Christ." He did not come to introduce a new compromised set of rules; he is not an example for us but of us!)*

4:22 Now you are free to strip off that old identity like a filthy worn-out garment. Lust corrupted you and cheated you into wearing it. *(Just like an actor who wore a cloak for a specific role he had to interpret; the fake identity is no longer appropriate!)*

4:23 Be renewed in your innermost mind. *(Ponder the truth about you, as it is displayed in Christ; begin with the fact of your co-seatedness.)* this will cause you to be completely re-programmed in the way you think about yourself! *Notice that Paul does not say, "Renew your minds!" This transformation happens in the spirit of your mind, awakened by truth on a much deeper level than a mere intellectual or academic consent. We often thought that we had to get information to drop from the head to the heart; but it is the other way around! Jesus says in John 7:37, "When you believe that I am what the scriptures are all about, then you will discover that you are what I am all about, and rivers of living waters will gush out of your innermost being! The spirit of mankind was never contaminated; just like the watermark in a paper note. The lost coin never lost its original inscription and image [see also James 3:9]; it was the mind that was veiled by darkness; we were darkened in our understanding! Our thoughts were reduced to the soul realm reference, knowing ourselves, and one another merely after the flesh. Isa 55:8-11 There is nothing wrong with our design or our redemption; we were thinking wrong! In order for our thoughts to be rescued from the dominion of darkness, Jesus as the incarnate image and likeness of God, has gone into our darkest hellish nightmare, and faced our cruelest judgment and fears, and died our death! This is the mystery that was hidden for ages and generations, for our glorification! We were co-crucified, to bring absolute closure to every reference we have had of ourselves as a result of Adam's fall! And while we were dead in our sins and trespasses, God co-quickened us and co-raised us, and co-seated us in Christ! Now, we all with unveiled faces may behold the glory of the Lord as in a mirror! And be radically transformed in our thinking in order to rediscover his image and likeness fully redeemed in us!)*

4:24 Immerse yourself into this God-shaped new person from above! You are created in the image and likeness of God. This is what righteousness and true holiness are all about.

4:25 Faking it and lying to one another was part of the old life; now truth remains the constant inspiration in your every conversation. We are related to one another like different parts in the same body. *(Which means that cheating one another would be cheating yourself! Truth only finds context in Christ [v 21])*

4:26 Even if you think you have a valid excuse, do not let anger dominate your day! If you don't deal with it immediately *(in the light of the likeness of Christ in you)* the sun sets for you and your day becomes one of lost opportunity where darkness employs anger to snare you into sin.

4:27 Any sin that you tolerate is an open invitation to the devil. Do not give him a platform to operate from.

4:28 If you were a thief before, you are one no more. Find an honest job where the fruit of your labor can be a blessing to others!

4:29 Instead of cheap talk, your mouth is now a fountain of grace, giving encouragement and inspiration to everyone within earshot.

4:30 The Holy Spirit is your signet ring from God to confirm that you are redeemed to live your life in the light of day; any conduct that belongs to the night grieves him.

4:31 Take up the strongest possible position against every form of distorted behavior in your own life. Do not allow yourself to be spiteful; outbursts of violent emotion and rage do not become you. You don't have to shout in order to make your point. People must feel safe in your conversation; therefore, slander and hurtful words *(blasphemy)* are out!

4:32 Be inspired by kindness and compassion; your forgiving one another when you might feel irritated and frustrated demonstrates the way God graciously treated us in Christ.

5:1 Mirror God; you are his offspring. *(2 Cor 3:18.)*

5:2 This is how: let the love of Christ be your life; remember how he abandoned himself to us. His love is contagious, not reluctant but extravagant. Sacrificial love pleases God like the sweet aroma of worship. *(Resembling the holy anointing oil and the pure fragrant incense of spices, the work of a perfumer, to be burnt on the golden altar of incense in the inner court of the tent of meeting. [Ex 37:25-29])*

5:3 Love has nothing in common with lust, immoral acts, or greed. The absence of these motives even in the way you talk sets a standard of excellence.

5:4 Any [1]distorted language, sarcasm, or below the belt jokes are uncalled for; much rather let gratitude grace your conversation. *(The word, [1]morologia, means disfigured, exaggerated speech.)*

5:5 The Christ-life gives distinct definition to the kingdom of God. You cannot live a double-standard life. Abusing people through adultery, lust, and greed is like worshipping a distorted image of yourself, which is what idolatry is all about.

5:6 Avoid any association with those who employ hollow words to entice you; [1]unbelief only produces a breed of people that distorts the pattern of their design as image bearers of God; this certainly does not [2]please God. *(The phrase, [1]uious tes apeitheias, translates as unbelief produces a breed of people; not sons of disobedience as most translations read here! The word, [2]orge, means excitement of mind, from the word, **oregomai**, meaning to stretch one's self out in order to touch or to grasp something, to reach after or desire something.)*

5:7 Do not allow their unbelief to include you in their company.

5:8 You were there once, trapped in the same darkness, but now you are light; your life confirms that light rules.

5:9 The spiritual harvest of light is evident in all that is excellent, innocent, and of impeccable integrity.

5:10 This gives certain evidence to the life of God's delight.

5:11 Do not tolerate anything in your life that associates you with darkness; there is no profit in it for you. Let light dispel any residue of darkness in you.

5:12 By gossiping about shameful acts that people do in secret, you are giving those things undue mileage.

5:13 Darkness loses its grip upon that which light manifests. Light displaces darkness.

5:14 This is the message of light; Christ awakens you from your intoxicated slumber and resurrects you out of the death trap of enslaved thought patterns.

5:15 Take accurate stock of your life; wise conduct defeats foolishness.

5:16 Wisdom converts time into opportunity and frees your day from slog.

5:17 Make his master plan your meditation.

5:18 While wine offers no lasting escape from the evil of the day, spirit certainly does! Indulge in spirit intoxication!

5:19 Speak psalms to one another; burst out in spontaneous celebration songs and spirit-inspired resonance. In your heart do not let the music stop; continue to touch the Lord with whispers of worship.

5:20 Because you are identified in the Name of Jesus Christ, you can afford to always overflow in gratitude to the Father, [1]in spite of everything that happens to you. You are not under circumstances but above circumstances because you are in him! (*The word, [1]huper, translates as, in spite of, over and above, beyond the reach of circumstances. We are not grateful "for" everything like in many other translations, but inspite of everything!*)

5:21 Inspired by the selfless consideration you witnessed in Christ, show perfect courtesy to one another. (*The way he abandoned himself to the will of God and to us [verse 2]. See Colossians 1:24, This is why no form of suffering can interfere with my joy. Every suffering on your behalf is just another opportunity to reinforce that which might still be lacking (in your understanding) of the affliction of Christ on behalf of his body which is the church. (The inconvenience that Paul might be suffering on behalf of the believers is not to add to the sufferings of Christ—as though the sufferings of Christ on our behalf were insufficient but it is to further emphasize and confirm the principle of unselfish love that constrains New Testament ministry.)*)

5:22 (*Marriage is a portrait of this mutual yielding to one another.*) Wives give yourselves fully to your husbands as you would to the Lord. (*Remember verse 2: love is contagious, not reluctant but extravagant. Sacrificial love pleases God like the sweet aroma of worship.*)

5:23 In the same way that Christ gives salvation, security and completeness to the church as the head does to the body, the husband is all of that to his wife.

5:24 The church enjoys the full advantage of the complete package of salvation, by yielding themselves fully to Christ; even so the wife enjoys every benefit her husband represents in her abandonment to him.

5:25 The husband loving his wife pictures the parallel of Christ loving the church completely, and his unreserved giving of himself to us. (*This is what marriage is all about; it celebrates love's initiative, whether coming from the husband or the wife. This awakens a different level of commitment beyond any sense of duty or guilt.*)

5:26 Christ is the voice of God's language, immersed in this conversation, his love words bathe us and remove from us every stain of sin.

5:27 This intimate language presents the church *(his restored image and likeness)* **to himself, to his delightful approval without any distraction or reminder of a blemished past; no wrinkle or scar of sin's abuse remains; she stands before him in immaculate innocence.** *(1 Kings 6:7)*

5:28 *(A man could go through many disciplines in life to make himself look good financially or even go to great expense to win the applause of others; he could diligently workout in the gym and trim his body to perfection,)* **but the most valuable thing a man can do to himself is to love his wife.**

5:29 **Consider how abnormal it would be for a man to abhor and detest his own body; the opposite is true! You would much rather pamper and fuss over your bodies.** *(It's all you've got. You can't trade it in for a new one so take good care of it. Watch what you feed it, how you exercise it, and gently nurse it when it is in pain.)* **Now get the message, you are the body of Christ; he does not merely tolerate you politely, he delights himself in you! He wants to pamper you and take good care of you!**

5:30 **We are his flesh and bone body; bearing his image and likeness. We give tangible expression of him.**

5:31 **Marriage reflects this union: a man would separate himself from his own parents to be glued to his wife; thus two separate people are now merged into one new identity.** *(In the same way he elevated us from our natural birth as our only identity to an understanding of our origin in him. This he confirmed again in our new birth, his resurrection, and our subsequent restored joint position together with him in heavenly places. Thus, he brought about a new union of intimate oneness; God and humanity revealed again in one person.)*

5:32 **The secret of a successful marriage is reflected in this inseparable union between Christ and the church, as God's redeemed image and likeness in mankind.** *(This union ultimately defines both marriage and church.)*

5:33 **In conclusion then, no one has any excuse to love his wife less than what he loves himself; at the same time every wife is now free and fully empowered to honor her husband in the same context and devotion as the church would respond to the love initiative of Christ.** *(We love him because he first loved us! [1 Jn 4:19])*

6:1 *(This mutual yielding to one another continues in every social relationship we engage in and extends the attractive display of the Christ life, beginning at home, cradled in the warm embrace of loving parents;)* **the way children respond to their parents give evidence to their righteousness in the Lord.** *(In essence the term righteousness speaks of two parties esteeming likeness in one another.)*

6:2 The first commandment that includes an immediate and long term incentive is in reference to children honoring their father and mother.

6:3 Both quality and duration of life on earth is impacted by the way children relate to their parents. *(Length of life is meaningless outside of close-ness in relationship.)*

6:4 Fathers, your role is not to exasperate your children *(by giving them burdens and tasks too heavy to bear).* **You are rather to awaken their minds in an environment conducive to draw on every virtue that is in them in the Lord.**

6:5 The next level of relationship equally implicated includes the heart attitude of a slave towards their owner; because of your devotion to Christ, you are now able to give your boss the same undivided, sincere respect and devotion. *(Remember we are talking practical church; the Christ-life celebrates love's initiative in transforming society!)*

6:6 This is not a matter of merely trying to put up a front in order to im-press your boss; you are in essence slaves of Christ, addicted to the desire of God to find expression in you; now slave life becomes the Christ life. *(The so-called "low life" now mirrors the highest life.)*

6:7 However menial the task, put your heart and mind into it as you would to the Lord; he is your real boss, no-one else.

6:8 It is a well known fact that it is impossible for good deeds to go un-noticed. It makes no difference whether someone is free or a slave; every single good deed equally enjoys the favorable attention of the Lord. *(We already enjoy Gods favorable attention before we have done anything to deserve it. Our good works are now an expression of that and not an attempt to win his ap-proval.)*

6:9 If you're the boss, love's initiative applies to you on exactly the same terms; the way you treat your slaves with respect rather than threats, even when they do stupid things clears the air immediately. Take it from your heavenly Master; he does not judge people or circumstances on face val-ue.

6:10 In conclusion and with reference to the theme and context of this writing, I encourage you to realize your strength in the Master; your union with him is your limitless resource. *(Remember my prayer for you at the outset of this letter to the Ephesians: 1:19 I pray that you will understand beyond all comparison the magnitude of his mighty power towards us who believe. Faith reveals how enormously advantaged we are in Christ. Eph 1:20 It is the same dynamic energy that he unleashed in Christ when he raised him from the* *dead and forever established him in the power of his own right hand in the realm of the heavens. Eph 1:21 Infinitely above all the combined forces of rule, authority, dominion, or governments; he is ranked superior to any name that could ever be given to anyone of this age or any age still to come in the eternal future. Eph 1:22-23 I want you to see this: he subjected all these powers under his feet. He towers head and shoulders above everything. He is the head; the church (his redeemed image and likeness in mankind) is his body. The completeness of his being that fills all in all resides in us! God cannot make himself more visible or exhibit himself more accurately.)*

6:11 Fully immerse yourself in the detail and significance of every individual part of the armor of God. *(Acquaint yourself with all that God's victory in Christ represents.)* **Just like every aspect in a soldier's armor significantly completes their battle uniform to best equip them to face every ¹method and strategy that an ²enemy could possibly employ against them.** *(The word, ¹methodeia, means strategy; ²diabolos, comes from dia, because of, and ballo, cast down; thus referring to the fall of mankind or the fallen mindset of mankind, often translated devil, the accuser. [See 1 Cor 15:47] Human life was reduced to slavery and the soul-ruled earthly realm through Adam's fall but is now awakened to lordship in the heavenly realm of spiritual realities through the knowledge of our co-resurrection with Christ. [See Col 3:1-11] We theologically created the idea of a person being "sinful by nature" as if humans are flawed by design. In fact it is a distorted mindset that we inherited from Adam that Jesus had to free us from. Peter says that we were redeemed from the futile ways we inherited from our fathers. [1 Pet 1:18] "Your indifferent mindset alienated you from God into a lifestyle of annoyances, hardships, and labors, sponsored by the law of sin and death that lodged in your bodies hosting a foreign influence, foreign to your design; just like a virus that would attach itself to a person." Col 1:21. There is nothing wrong with our design or salvation, we were thinking wrong. [See Isa 55:8-11, Eph 4:17, 18 and also Eph 2:1-11.])*

6:12 People are not the enemy, *(whether they be husbands, wives, children, or parents, slaves, or bosses. They might host hostile, law inspired thought patterns through their unbelief or ignorance but)* **to target one another is to engage in the wrong combat. We represent the authority of the victory of Christ in the spiritual realm. We are positioned there** *(in Christ)***; we ¹target the mind games and ²structures of darkness, religious thought patterns, governing and conditioning human behavior.** *(The word, ¹pros, towards, in this context, means to advance, forward march, no retreat. The word, ²poneros, , is often translated as evil; this word actually means to be full of annoyances, hardships and labor, which is exactly what the DIY law-system of works produce!*

[See 1 Cor 15:24] The complete conclusion in his work of redemption is celebrated in his yielding the full harvest of his reign to God the Father, having ¹brought to naught the law of works which supported every definition of dominion under the fall, including all ²principalities, all ³authority and every ⁴dynamic influence in society. He brought to naught the law of works, from the word, ¹katargeo, from kata, meaning intensity, and argos, meaning labor; thus free from all self effort to attempt to improve what God has already perfected in Christ. All principalities,

2arche, or chief ranks, i.e., kings, governors; this includes any governing system whereby one is ranked above the other on the basis of their performance or preference. All authority, 3exousia, comes from ek, denoting origin and eimi, "I am;" in this case, because of what I can do, I am defined by what I can do better than you; therefore, I have authority over you. Every dynamic influence in society, 4dunamis, means power, in this case, willpower. Every government structure in society will be brought under the dominion of grace where the Christ life rules. The kingdom of God is the dominion of the Christ-life in human life, where righteousness is based on who we are and not on what we do; who we are by God's doing and not who we are by our own doing; right being and not merely right acting. Where the law of works was duty and guilt driven, the law of faith is love driven; [Rom 3:27, Gal 5:6, 2 Cor 10:12], when they measure themselves by one another, and compare themselves with one another, they are without understanding.)

6:13 It is most important therefore to acquaint yourself with every aspect of God's armor. You are fully fit to powerfully defeat any onslaught or contradiction on any day of confrontation, triumphantly standing your ground. The days where the law of 1hardships, annoyances and labor dictated your life are over! *(God's armor represents his reputation; his victory defines you. The word, 1poneros, means full of hardships, annoyances, and labor; traditionally translated evil. [See 1 Cor 15:48] The reduced state of the individual left its mark on mankind as being earthly; now the redeemed state of mankind confirms their origin in God and marks their new heavenly life. [1 Cor 15:49] Just as the flesh (our earthly image) once defined us we are now defined by our spirit [our heavenly] image.)*

6:14 Take your position: you have the truth *(of who you are in Christ)* **wrapped around your hips like a soldier's belt, holding the complete body armor together.** *(Know that your loins are protected from all manner of lust, gluttony and sexual sins.)* **Righteousness covers your heart like a bulletproof breastplate.**

6:15 You wear your eagerness and passion to communicate the good news like soldier's shoes. Announce peace; the battle has already been fought and won! *(Isa 52:7 How beautiful upon the mountains are the feet of him who brings good tidings, who publishes peace, who brings good tidings of good, who publishes salvation. Picture the body language of the messengers returning from the battlefield with the glad tidings of victory!)*

6:16 It is most important to engage your faith as a 1man-size shield that covers your whole person and empowers you to extinguish the flame in every arrow of contradiction that you might face. The only visible part of you is your faith! *(The word, 1thureos means a door-size shield. To co-believe with God protects your whole person, body, soul and spirit. See 2 Cor 5:7)*

6:17 Pondering redemption realities is your headgear that protects your mind; inspired thoughts give voice to God's word—this is your spiritual sword.

6:18 Prayer is an ongoing conversation; praying in the spirit includes every form of prayer, whether it be a prayer of request or a prayer of

thanksgiving, or worship or interceding for all to realize their saintly innocence. Oh, and remember, you do not have to do all the talking! Always be attentive to the voice of the Spirit. *(Prayer is so much more than a one-way conversation.)*

6:19 My most urgent request is for clarity of utterance every time I open my mouth to speak. I desire that my words will be gifted with inspiration, boldly articulating the mystery of the gospel.

6:20 I am an ambassador in bonds, chained to this task of confidently communicating the revelation of the Gospel with the accuracy it deserves.

6:21 I know this is not much of a newsletter. My urgency is not to talk about myself, but my dear friend and faithful helper Tychicus, will fill you in on the detail. *(He is also the scribe of this letter.)*

6:22 That is really why I sent him to you, that you may be well informed about our affairs and see yourselves fully identified with us.

6:23 My prayer for you is a relationship with one another of happy harmony, and love-entwined faith flowing from God the Father and the Lord Jesus Christ.

6:24 Grace greetings to all of you who share our undivided passion for our Master, Jesus Christ. He is echoed in your amen.

(Thoughts on spiritual warfare: Speak tenderly to Jerusalem; and cry to her, that her warfare is accomplished, that her iniquity is pardoned! [Isa 40:2]

The Message translation: " ... the slate wiped clean, that old arrest warrant canceled and nailed to Christ's Cross. He stripped all the spiritual tyrants in the universe of their sham authority at the Cross and marched them naked through the streets." [Col 2:14, 15])

Spiritual warfare teachings are a popular distraction that many modern-day churches engage in! It preaches a defeated devil back into business! Pharaoh was taken out of the equation when Israel was delivered out of Egypt! They then became their own worst enemy by continuing to believe a lie about themselves! [See Num 13:33 and Josh 2:11]

James says that a double-minded person deceives themselves!

Neither Jesus or anyone of the Acts church ever marched around towns to bind so-called "strong men" or poured oil over buildings or places!

Any teaching that distracts from the success of the cross is a waste of time to pursue. The only possible way we can delay the glory that follows the cross is by underestimating what happened there when Jesus died and cried: "It is finished!"

Jesus, grilled by the Pharisees on when the kingdom of God would come, answered; "The kingdom of God doesn't come by counting the days on the calendar." [The Message.] - The kingdom of God is within you! Luke 17:20.)

The kingdom of God is the authority of the Christ life, the life of our design redeemed to reign in the most attractive practical lifestyle. The world is a ready audience. Your life is the message; Christ is your life!)

Paul, Silas, Timothy and Luke visited Philippe and founded the first church in Europe on Paul's second missionary journey around A.D. 50 (Acts 16:11-40)

This letter was written in about 61 A.D. from Rome while Paul was under house arrest.

He writes from a place of strength and joy to encourage his dear friends in Philippi, who were also facing many contradictions.

Phil 1:20 My immediate circumstances do not distract from my message! I am convinced that our conversation now and always will continue to give accurate account of the magnificence of Christ. The message is incarnate in me; whether I live or die, it makes no difference.

Phil 1:21 Christ defines my life; death cannot threaten or diminish that.

Phil 2:12 "Not only in my presence but much more in my absence..." Paul knew that he would be more present in his message than in his person! Ministry success is not measured by how many partners you can congregate, but how absent you can preach yourself!

Phil 3:1 The conclusion of your faith is extreme gladness in the Lord. He is your constant reference to bliss! I am not just saying this to be repetitive; joy is your fortress! There is no safer place to be, but to be ecstatically happy!

Paul encourages them not to allow religion to distract from the delight of romance.

Phil 3:7 The sum total of my religious pedigree and sincere devotion amounts to zero! What we have been gifted with in Christ has reduced what once seemed so important, to meaningless information. To esteem the law is to your loss! Faith is your profit.

Phil 3:8 In fact, I have come to the conclusion that every association I have had with that which defined me before as a devout Jew, is by far eclipsed by what I have gained in knowing the Messiah. Jesus Christ and his masterful redemption define me now. Religion is like dog pooh; and it stinks, avoid stepping in it!

Phil 4:4 Joy is not a luxury option; joy is your constant! Your union in the Lord is your permanent source of delight; so I might as well say it again, rejoice in the Lord always!

Phil 4:6 Let no anxiety about anything [1]distract you!

Phil 4:11 I have discovered my "I am-ness" and found that I am fully [1]self sufficient, whatever the circumstance. (*Self sufficient,* [1]***autarkes,*** *self complacent, the feeling you have when you are completely satisfied with yourself.*)

Phil 4:13 In every situation I am strong in the one who empowers me from within to be who I am! (*Paul lived his life in touch with this place within himself. He discovered that the same I am-ness that Jesus walked in, was mirrored in him! I am what I am by the grace of God! 1 Cor 15:10*)

1:1 Paul and Timothy address all the saints in Christ Jesus in Philippi, including your leadership team, both the ¹overseers and the ²deacons. *(Overseer, ¹episkopos, from epi, indicating continues influence upon, and skopos, "scope" to see the overall picture, ²diakonos, from diako, to run errands, to pursue; see Phil 3:14.)*

1:2 The Father's favor joins our lives inseparably in the Lordship of Jesus Christ.

1:3 The thought of you always inspires me with joy and gratitude to God.

1:4 Praying for you is certainly not a job it is more like poetry; I joyfully anticipate the outcome of my prayers for you!

1:5 Our blissful participation in everything that the gospel communicates does not age. The freshness of our first encounter continues to this very day.

1:6 I possess an inward certainty about you, confident that he who is the ¹initiator of the good work within you is also the one who executes its completeness as mirrored in Jesus Christ, who is the light of day. He is the fullness of time. *(Initiator, ¹enarche, to rehearse from the beginning. See Eccl 3:15, "that which has been is now; and that which is to be has already been!")*

1:7 I am not being presumptuous to be this persuaded about you. In the context of our redeemed innocence I cannot think of you any differently; I have you in my heart! Your committed friendship in my imprisonment is of great encouragement to me in our combined defense and confirmation of the gospel. We are in this together! We are joint participants in the same grace. My grace is your grace.

1:8 God knows my intense longing for you! It is with the tender affections of Jesus Christ!

1:9 It is my desire for each one of you, that the realization of ¹love's completeness in you will increasingly burst through all boundaries, and that every sphere of your relationship with others will be greatly impacted by your intimate acquaintance with love. *(The word ¹agape is a compound word from ago, which means to lead as a shepherd leads his sheep, and pao, which means rest! His love leads me into his rest; into the full realization of his finished work! Agape is Psalm 23 in one word. "By the waters of reflection my soul remembers who I am.")*

1:10 I urge you to examine this agape-love with the utmost scrutiny, just like when a diamond is viewed in the full sunlight to prove its flawless perfection. I dare you to take love to its ultimate conclusion! There is no offence in love, as evidenced in Jesus Christ who is the light of day. *(If the diamond is flawless to begin with, every possible test will prove its perfection; how someone might respond to love's initiative is not the point, love's ultimate test was concluded on the cross. Truth does not become true by popular vote; someone's ignorance or indifference cannot change the truth.)*

1:11 You have been fully furnished with the harvest of your redeemed innocence and righteousness which Jesus Christ labored for! This is what the glorious intent of God is all about! Celebrate him!

1:12 I wish to encourage you dear friends that the opposition that I face, which was meant to defeat the gospel has only served to advance it!

1:13 The prison has become my pulpit! All the soldiers in the Governor's guard and everyone involved in the palace have learnt about my message. They know that I am not their prisoner but that I am enclosed in Christ.

1:14 My imprisonment has also persuaded many believers in the Lord to speak the word with fearless courage.

1:15 Some slander the message and others speak with passion and delightful certainty.

1:16 There are those who wish to get mileage out of my predicament for their own agenda.

1:17 Others again are completely love inspired and in full support with me in my defense of the gospel!

1:18 I am thrilled! Christ is the topic of conversation everywhere! Even the negative publicity continues to advertise him!

1:19 I can just see how the Spirit of Jesus Christ, like a ¹conductor of music takes all of this together with your prayers and turn it into a concert that celebrates salvation! *(The word, ¹epichoregeo, comes from epi, a preposition of position, over, in charge, + chorus, choir, orchestra, or dance + ago, meaning to lead as a shepherd leads his sheep; thus, the leader of a dance or the conductor of music.)*

1:20 My ¹thoughts are not trapped in my head! They roam free in expectation that I will not be ashamed by any contradiction! My ²immediate circumstances do not distract from my message! I am convinced that our ²conversation now and always will continue to give accurate account of the magnificence of Christ. The message is incarnate in me; whether I live or die, it makes no difference. *(The word, ¹apokaradokia is a compound word with 3 parts, apo, away from, kara, head and dokeo, thought. The word ²parrhesia, from para, a preposition indicating close proximity, a thing proceeding from a sphere of influence, with a suggestion of union of place of residence, to have sprung from its author and giver, originating from, denoting the point from which an action originates, intimate connection; and rhesia, conversation.)*

1:21 Christ defines my life; death cannot threaten or diminish that.

1:22 To be alive now is to feast on the harvest of your faith! I cannot tell when I shall lift up the anchor of the flesh and sail away! It doesn't really matter to me. *(The word, ¹aihreomai, from airo, to lift the anchor and sail away.)*

1:23 I am often torn between these two thoughts. I have this strong yearning to step out of the confines of this body into the immediate embrace of Christ! Can you imagine the awesomeness of that!

1:24 Yet this gospel has my [1]arm twisted and locked behind my back; I am therefore determined to remain in the body for your sakes. *(The word, [1]anagke, suggests to have the arm twisted and locked behind one's back. See 1 Cor 9:16.)*

1:25 I am certain that my time with you will inspire the happy progress of your pioneering faith!

1:26 The joy of our union in Christ knows no limits! We have so much reason to celebrate! I can just imagine the eruptions of bliss should I be there with you right now in person!

1:27 The [1]one essential thing that would fully engage the focus of your earthly citizenship is the fact that your daily conduct communicates [2]like value and gives context to the gospel of Christ! So whether I am present with you to witness your steadfastness with my own eyes, or absent, our spiritual [3]union and single mindedness will be equally evident. *(The word [1]monon, points to that which is singled out as most essential; the word [2]axios, means, having the weight of another thing of like value, worth as much. Psyche, Greek, pshuche, suggests consciousness, mental attitude, awareness. Paul desires to express an inseparable togetherness; [3]sunathleo, athletic contest. Bicycle racing uses the term peloton; where the riders are strongest and fastest when they ride in the so-called "peloton", which is a densely packed group of riders, sheltering in each others' draft. In a mass-start race, most of the competitors usually end up in one large peloton for most of the race. The word is French, from a term that means rolled up in a ball.)*

1:28 Your brave fearlessness in the face of every kind of obstacle is a sure sign to those who oppose you that their efforts are futile. Your triumphant attitude makes salvation even more apparent. *(There is no counterfeit; God has no competition! Religion's self-help programs of salvation do not threaten him!)*

1:29 Because of the grace that you are gifted with in Christ, whatever you might suffer on behalf of him can never distract from what faith knows to be true about you!

1:30 Our faith is on exhibit in the same public [1]arena; we are not spectators of one another's endurance, but co-witnesses thereof. We mirror one another triumphantly. *(The word, [1]agon, refers to the place of contest, the arena or stadium.)*

2:1 In Christ our [1]association is most intimate; we [2]articulate his love story; entwined in spirit communion and tender affections. *(The word [1]parakaleo, from para, a preposition indicating close proximity, a thing proceeding from a sphere of influence, with a suggestion of union of place of residence, to sprung from its author and giver, originating from, denoting the point from which an action originates, intimate connection, and kaleo, to identify by name, to surname. The word [2]paramuthion, is from para + muthos, a myth or tale, a story of instruction, told in heart to heart language.)*

2:2 Your Christ mindedness completes my delight! You co-echo the same agape; we are soul mates, resonating the same thoughts.

2:3 No hidden agenda with a compromised mixture of leaven or empty philosophical flattery can match a mind that genuinely values others above oneself

2:4 To discover your own completeness in Christ frees you to turn your attention away from yourself to others!

2:5 The way Jesus saw himself is the only valid way to see yourself!

2:6 His being God's equal in form and likeness was official; his sonship did not steal the limelight from his Father! Neither did his humanity distract from the deity of God!

2:7 His mission however, was not to prove his deity but to embrace our humanity. Emptied of his reputation as God, he fully embraced our physical human form; born in our resemblance he identified himself as the servant of the human race. His love enslaved him to us!

2:8 And so we have the drama of the cross in context: the man Jesus Christ who is fully God, becomes fully man to the extent of willingly dying humanity's death at the hands of his own creation. He embraced the curse and shame of the lowest kind in dying a criminal's death.

2:9 From this place of utter humiliation, God exalted him to the highest rank. God graced Jesus with a Name that is far [1]above as well as equally representative of every other name; *(The word, [1]uper, means above, also instead, or for the sake of). The name of Jesus endorses his mission as fully accomplished! He is the Savior of the world! Titus 2:11 The grace of God shines as bright as day making the salvation of humankind undeniably visible. [Clarence Jordan translates this, "For God's undeserved kindness has burst in upon us, bringing a new lease on life for all mankind."] See also Eph 3:15, Every family in heaven and on earth originates in him; his is mankind's family name and he remains the authentic identity of every nation.)*

2:10 What his name unveils will persuade every creature of their redemption! Every knee in heaven and upon the earth and under the earth shall bow in spontaneous worship!

2:11 Also every tongue will voice and resonate the same devotion to his unquestionable Lordship as the Redeemer of life! Jesus Christ has glorified God as the Father of creation! This is the ultimate conclusion of the Father's [1]intent! *(The word [1]doxa, intent, opinion, often translated, glory. Rev 5:13 And I heard every creature in heaven and on earth and under the earth and in the sea, and all therein, saying, "To him who sits upon the throne and to the Lamb be blessing and honor and glory and might for ever and ever!")*

2:12 Considering this amazing outcome of what our faith sees and celebrates I strongly urge you my darling friends to continue to have your [1]ears tuned to that which inspires your conduct to give full expression to the detail of your own salvation in a most personal and practical way. See salvation in its earth shattering awesome and ultimate conclusion. I know that my personal presence encourages you greatly but now I want you to realize an inspiration in my absence that supersedes anything you've known before. This would mean that even if you were never to see my face again or receive another Epistle from me, it will make no difference at all to your faith! *(The success of Paul's ministry was not to enslave people to him but to his gospel! He knew that he would be more present in his message than in his person! Ministry success is not measured by how many partners you can congregate, but by how absent you can preach yourself! The word often translated, obedience, is the word [1]upoakoo, to be under the inspired influence of what you hear.)*

2:13 Discover God himself as your inexhaustible inner source; he ignites you with both the desire and energy that matches his own delight!

2:14 Your entire life is a poem; any undercurrent murmuring or argumentative debating would be completely out of place! Do not let such issues disrupt the rhythm of your conversation.

2:15 Your flawless innocence radiates attraction as beacons of light in the midst of a people who have forgotten their true sonship and whose lives have become distorted and perverse. *(In this verse Paul quotes Deut 32:5 from the Greek Septuagint translation of the Hebrew text, with reference to Deut 32:4,5 &18. In context God's perfect workmanship as Father of mankind is forgotten; people have become "crooked and perverse" twisted and distorted out of their true pattern of sonship. Deut 32:18 says, you have forgotten the Rock that begot you and have gotten out of step with the God who [1]danced with you! Hebrew, [1]khul or kheel.)*

2:16 Your lives [1]echo-exhibit the [2]logic of the message of life. You are positioned like the stars in the night sky, superimposed and radiating light, which shining pierces the darkness. Thus you [3]confirm the day of the Lord and [3]complete my joy! You are my wreath of honor and [3]proof that I did not run my race in vain. *(The word, [1]epecho, is from epi, to superimpose, and echo, to hold, echo resonance. The word of life, [2]logos, it embodies a conception or idea, thought, logic. The preposition [3]eis, suggests a point reached in conclusion. See Col 1:29 Your completeness in Christ is not a remote goal, but your immediate reference! My labor now exceeds any zeal that I previously knew under the duty-driven law of willpower. I am laboring beyond the point of exhaustion, striving with intense resolve with all the energy that he mightily inspires within me.)*

2:17 I want you to see my ministry to you as wine poured out upon the altar of your faith. I rejoice in the thought that we drink from the same source and therefore celebrate a mutual joy!

2:18 Whatever you may suffer only concludes in joy! *(Joy is a bold declaration, in the face of severe danger and suffering, that contradiction does not define us or have the final say in our lives. We know that whether we live or die, our message is unstoppable and that it is conquering the world.)*

2:19 I trust the Lord that I will be able to send Timothy to you soon; this will be to me as if I am there personally with you!

2:20 I have no one here that share my heart more fully; I know that he will take care of you with utmost concern.

2:21 Sadly there are many in ministry with a selfish agenda

2:22 I do not need to tell you anything about Timothy because you already know his worth! We have labored together in the gospel in the closest possible association; we are like father and son in joint partnership.

2:23 I would like to send him to you immediately, but I am just waiting to see how things here turn out for me.

2:24 I obviously would be very keen to join him shortly! I trust in the Lord for a positive outcome in my trial.

2:25 I feel urgent about sending Epaphrodites to you immediately; he is my brother, fellow worker and co-campaigner. You initially sent him to help me and now I am returning the favor!

2:26 He longs for you and really misses you. He felt quite distressed when he heard of your concern for him when he was so sick.

2:27 He nearly died but thank God for his mercy, not just for Epaphroditus' sake but for ours also! I cannot imagine the grief we would have suffered had we lost him!

2:28 I am sending him to you without delay; knowing what joy he will be to you is already such a comfort to me!

2:29 The immense value of his life is to be celebrated with a massive bliss-party when he arrives! Oh the joy to love one another in the Lord!

2:30 I so honor his total commitment to the work of Christ; he had no problem to risk his life to serve me on your behalf!

3:1 The conclusion of your faith is extreme gladness in the Lord. He is your constant reference to bliss! I am not just saying this to be repetitive; joy is your fortress! There is no safer place to be, but to be ecstatically happy!

3:2 The circumcision party are the enemies of your faith and freedom! They work with an evil agenda! Be on your guard for them just like you would avoid a vicious hound on the loose! They have their knives in for you!

3:3 We give "circumcision" its true spiritual meaning! Our worship is not defined by anything external that would even remotely resemble the law of works and religious rituals! We worship God in the certainty of our redeemed innocence and rejoice in the finished work of Jesus Christ. Faith-righteousness gives substance to spiritual worship; the flesh occupies the religious mind with its own futile efforts to attain to righteousness. I am convinced that circumcision or any work of the law can add nothing to the righteousness that Jesus secured on our behalf.

3:4 I have more reason than anyone else to rely on my years of diligent and most sincere devotion to Jewish sentiment and rituals. If gaining God's approval had anything to do with striving and personal effort I would beat the best in the business! My pedigree is obvious:

3:5 I received the famous cut when I was 8 days old, exactly as the law prescribed. I am Israeli by birth; the head of my tribe is Benjamin. I am a Hebrew of the Hebrews! In my observance of the law I belonged to the strictest party; I was proud to be a Pharisee. *(Rachel was the darling wife of Jacob; she died while giving birth to Benjamin; also the two tribes that did not revolt were Benjamin and Judah. By saying that he is a Hebrew of the Hebrews Paul emphasises that his lineage from both parents side was not mixed with any Gentile blood.)*

3:6 The extremities of my fervor was demonstrated in the way I fiercely opposed and persecuted anyone who identified themselves in Christ. *(The so-called ekklesia.)* If keeping the law and these credentials could possibly have given me a blameless standing before God, I had it made!

3:7 The sum total of my religious pedigree and sincere devotion amounts to zero! What we have been gifted with in Christ has reduced what once seemed so important, to meaningless information. To esteem the law is to your loss! Faith is your profit.

3:8 In fact, I have come to the conclusion that every association I have had with that which defined me before as a devout Jew, is by far eclipsed by what I have gained in knowing the Messiah. Jesus Christ and his masterful redemption define me now. Religion is like dog pooh; and it stinks, avoid stepping in it!

3:9 So here I am; found in Christ! I was looking in the wrong place all along! My own duty- and guilt-driven religious endeavor snared me in the cul-de-sac maize of self-righteousness, sponsored by the law of works! The faith of Christ reveals my identity; righteousness defines who God believes that I really am. This righteousness is sourced in God and endorses the authority of faith. *(Faith is a fairy tale if Jesus is not the substance of it!)*

3:10 Oh to comprehend the dynamic of his resurrection! His resurrection is evidence of our righteousness! In the revelation of God's economy of inclusion, I actually co-suffered with him and co-died together with Christ! *(Because I was already fully represented in his sufferings, his death and resurrection, I am greatly inspired when faced with contradictions now!)*

3:11 When confronted with death, I actually come [1]face to face with my own resurrection! *(The word [1]katantao, from kata + anti, to come to a place over against, opposite another, face to face. 1 Cor 15:18 No resurrection implies no hope for anyone beyond the grave; it makes no difference whether you believed that you were included in Christ's death or not. 1 Cor 15:19 If our hope in Christ was restricted to only benefit us in this life then imagine the severity of our disappointment if it all had to come to an abrupt end when we died. 1 Cor 15:20 However this very moment the risen Christ represents everyone who has ever died; exactly like how the first fruit would represent the complete harvest. 1 Cor 15:21 The same humanity who died in a man was raised again in a man. 1 Cor 15:22 In Adam all died; in Christ all are made alive.)*

3:12 There may be blurry edges to my [1]comprehending the full scope of resurrection life beyond the grave; but I pursue the complete conclusion of co-comprehending and [2]fully grasping exactly that which Jesus Christ knew all along about me when he died my death; and to see me in his faith where I am so perfectly included when he rescued and raised me out of the grasp of death! *(The word, [1]lambano, means to comprehend, to grasp, to identify with. 1 Cor 13:12 To know even as I have always been known! The word [2]katalambano, from kata, which here strengthens the verb lambano, thus to entirely grasp; to come to terms with, to make one's own. The KJV reads, "that I may apprehend that for which also I am apprehended of by Christ Jesus.")*

3:13 I am not boasting about this new found righteousness as if I came up with the idea; on the contrary, I have distanced myself from everything the DIY-system of the law of works and willpower previously represented in my reference; now I am fully engaged with that which the prophetic pointed to. Christ is what we were reaching for all along! Here he is [1]in our face; within our immediate grasp! *(The DIY-system, is the fruit of the 'do it yourself-tree'. The word [1]emprosthen, from en, in, and pros, that which is right in front of me!)*

3:14 I have the prize of mankind's redeemed innocence in full view; just like a champion athlete in the public games I refuse to be distracted by anything else. God has [1]invited us in Christ, to lift up our eyes and realize our identity in him. *(The word, [1]klesis, invitation, from kaleo, to surname, to identify by name. While the law engages one with that which is below, faith captivates our gaze to only see that which is above, where we are co-seated together with Christ in heavenly places! We are identified in him. Col 3:1)*

3:15 We who have discovered our perfect righteousness have our thoughts anchored in Christ. If you still see yourself as imperfect, God will reveal to you that you are wasting your time to imagine that you can become more accepted and righteous than what you already are!

3:16 So then, let the message of grace set the pace. *(The law is a detour leading nowhere!)*

3:17 You are free to mimic me as we together impact the lives of many others to follow in our footsteps.

3:18 As you know I am often moved to tears talking about these things; I am so passionate about the revelation of mankind's redeemed innocence that it makes no sense to me that there can still be people who oppose this message. Many are openly hostile and indifferent to the cross of Christ.

3:19 Do they not realize that the DIY law-system leads to self-destruction? All their devotion to the god of their religious appetites, endorses their shame; yet they seem to have no problem with it since their minds are seared with [1]sin-consciousness. *("[1]Earthly things" in this case refers to the fallen mindset ruled by a sin-consciousness. See Col 3:1-3, Heb 10:1, 19-22)*

3:20 Our [1]citizenship is referenced in our joint position with Christ in heavenly places! Heaven is not our goal it is our [2]starting point! Our understanding is [3]sourced in a Savior; we [4]fully embrace the Lord Jesus Christ! *(The word, [1]politeuma, common wealth, our social identity. The word [2]uparcho, means to make a beginning, starting point. The word translated source is the word, [3]ek. To fully embrace, [4]apekdechomai, from apo, away from [that which defined me before] and ek, out of, source; and dechomai, to take into ones hands to accept whole heartedly, to fully embrace)*

3:21 The salvation that Jesus is the author of, re-fashions these bodies of clay and elevates us to fully participate in the same pattern of his heavenly glory! The severe contradiction that we might often face in the frailty of the flesh, is by far surpassed by the glorious splendor displayed in his human body raised from the dead; according to the working of God's dynamic power he imprints the mirror pattern of his likeness in us. Thus he subdues all things to himself. *(Paul's quest to fully comprehend the power of the resurrection (3:10) is consistent with his prayer in Eph 1:19 I pray that you will understand beyond all comparison the magnitude of his mighty power at work [1]in us who believe. Faith reveals how enormously advantaged we are in Christ. [The preposition [1]eis, speaks of a point reached in conclusion.] Eph 1:20 It is the same dynamic energy which God unleashed in Christ when he raised him from the dead and forever established him in the power of his own right hand in the realm of the heavens. Eph 1:21 Infinitely above all the combined forces of rule, authority, dominion, or governments; he is ranked superior to any name that could ever be given to anyone of this age or any age still to come in the eternal future. Eph 1:22 I want you to see this: he subjected all these powers under his feet. He towers head and shoulders above everything. He is the head; Eph 1:23 the [1]church is his body. The* *completeness of his being that fills all in all resides in us! God cannot make himself more visible or exhibit himself more accurately. [The word, [1]ekklesia, comes from ek, a preposition always denoting origin, and klesia from kaleo, to identify by name, to surname; thus the "church" is his redeemed image and likeness in mankind.]*

See again Phil 2:6 His being God's equal in form and likeness was official; his sonship did not steal the limelight from his Father! Neither did his humanity distract from the deity of God! Phil 2:7 His mission however, was not to prove his deity but to embrace our humanity. He emptied himself into a physical human form; born in our resemblance he identified himself as the servant of the human race. His love enslaved him to us! Phil 2:8 And so we have the drama of the cross in context: the man Jesus Christ who is fully God, becomes fully man to the extent of willingly dying humanity's death at the hands of his own creation. He embraced the curse and shame of the lowest kind in dying a criminal's death. Phil 2:9 From this place of utter humiliation, God exalted him to the highest rank. God graced Jesus with a Name that is far [1]above as well as equally representative of every other name; [The word, [1]uper, means above, also instead, or for the sake of. The name of Jesus endorses his mission as fully accomplished! He is the Savior of the world! See also Eph 3:15, Every family in heaven and on earth originates in him; his is mankind's family name and he remains the authentic identity of every nation.] Phil 2:10 What his name unveils will persuade every creature of their redemption! Every knee in heaven and upon the earth and under the earth shall bow in spontaneous worship! Eph 4:8 Scripture confirms that he led us as trophies in his triumphant procession on high; he [1]repossessed his gift (likeness) in mankind. (See Ephesians 2:6, We are also elevated in his ascension to be equally welcome in the throne room of the heavenly realm where we are now seated together with him in his authority. Quote from the Hebrew text, Ps 68:18, [1]lakachta mattanoth baadam, thou hast taken gifts in human form, in Adam. [The gifts which Jesus Christ distributes to us he has received in us, in and by virtue of his incarnation. Commentary by Adam Clarke.] We were born anew in his resurrection. 1 Pet 1:3, Hos 6:2))

4:1 Now in the light of all this, I am sure that you can appreciate what enormous delight you are to me! My precious friends and brethren, you are my trophy and my joy! Just as you have been doing, continue to stand immovably strong in the Lord!

4:2 Your [1]source defines you by name! Dear [2]Eodias and [3]Syntyche, let me remind you of the meanings of your names! Engage your thoughts to follow the direct and easy way of grace; thus you will together fulfill your mission in the Lord without distraction. *(The word, [1]parakaleo, comes from **para**, a preposition indicating close proximity, a thing proceeding from a sphere of influence, with a suggestion of union of place of residence, to have sprung from its author and giver, originating from, denoting the point from which an action originates, intimate connection; and **kaleo**, meaning to identify by name, to surname. The word [2]eudias, from **eu**, good, and **odos**, a road, thus a prosperous and expeditious journey, to lead by a direct and easy way; [3]suntuche, from **sun**, together with, and **tugchanō**, to hit the mark; of one discharging a javelin or arrow)*

4:3 Suzegos, you are the meaning of your name to me; my trustworthy yoke fellow! Associate yourself closely with these ladies who have been my fellow athletes in the gospel! Also Clement as well as all my other colleagues I have their names on record in the book of life! *(Paul has all his friends names on record! [See Romans 16:1-23] Zoe life as defined in Christ has given such rich meaning to proper names. **Suzugos**, meaning yokefellow. At Philippi, women were the first hearers of the Gospel, and Lydia the first convert. Acts 16:13-15. **Clement**, clear skies, bright and sunny weather. Paul whose own name was changed from, **Sheol**, meaning dark underworld, to **Pao**, rest, appreciates the meaning of proper names. He calls Peter, Kefas which is the Aramaic for petros, to deliberately steer away from the more familiar sound of Petros, thus he specifically emphasizes the meaning of his name. The rock foundation of God's ekklesia. In Mat 16 Jesus identifies Simon, the son of Jonah by a new name, Petros; and upon this revelation, that the son of man is the son of God the ekklesia is built!)*

4:4 Joy is not a luxury option; joy is your constant! Your union in the Lord is your permanent source of delight; so I might as well say it again, rejoice in the Lord always!

4:5 Show perfect [1]courtesy towards all people! The Lord is not nearer to some than what he is to others! *(Courtesy, [1]epieikes, from **epi**, indicating continues influence upon, and **eikos**, reasonable, courteous. This is exactly Paul's attitude towards the idol worshipping Greek philosophers in Acts 17:27,28. See also Titus 3:3. Your joy makes the gospel visible! Every definition of distance is cancelled!)*

4:6 Let no anxiety about anything [1]distract you! Rather translate moments into prayerful worship, and soak your requests in gratitude before God! *(The word [1]merimnao, anxiety, through the idea of distraction, from **meritzo**, to divide. Your requests do not surprise God; he knows your* *thoughts from afar and is acquainted with all your ways; yet he delights in your conversation and childlike trust! Song of Songs 2:14; Mat 6:8)*

4:7 And in this place of worship and gratitude you will witness how the peace of God within you echoes the awareness of your oneness in Christ Jesus beyond the reach of any thought that could possibly unsettle you. *(uperecho)* **Just like the ¹sentry guard secures a city, watching out in advance for the first signs of any possible threat, your hearts deepest feelings and the tranquility of your thoughts are fully guarded there.** *(This peace is not measured by external circumstances, it is residing deeply in the innermost parts of your being. We are not talking about a fragile sense of peace that can easily be disturbed; one that we have to fabricate ourselves; this is God's peace; the peace that God himself enjoys!)*

4:8 Now let this be your conclusive ¹reasoning: consider that which is ²true about everyone as evidenced in Christ. Live ³overwhelmed by God's opinion of you! Acquaint yourselves with the revelation of ⁴righteousness; realize God's likeness in you. Make it your business to declare mankind's redeemed ⁵innocence. Think ⁶friendship. Discover how ⁷famous everyone is in the light of the gospel; mankind is in God's limelight! Ponder how ⁸elevated you are in Christ. Study ⁹stories that celebrate life. *(See Col 3:3, "Engage your thoughts with throne room realities where we are co-seated together with Christ!" The word ¹logitsomai suggests a logical reasoning by taking everything into account; ²alethes, means that which was hidden, but is now uncovered; In Eph 3:21 Paul speaks about the truth as it is embodied in Jesus. The word overwhelmed is, ³semnos, from sebomai, to revere, to adore. The word for righteousness is ⁴dikaios, from dikay, two parties finding likeness in each other, where there is no sense of inferiority, suspicion, blame, regret or pressure to perform. The gospel is the revelation of the righteousness of God; it declares how God succeeded to put mankind right with him. It is about what God did right, not what Adam did wrong. See Rom 1:17. The word ⁵hagnos speaks of blameless innocence. The word ⁶prophileo, is exactly what it says, pro-friendship. The English word for famous is derived from the Greek word ⁷euphemos, from eu, well done, good and phemos; it means to be in the lime light, from phao, to shine; Jesus said, "you are the light of the world." Just like a city set on a hill, your light cannot be hid. The word ⁸arete, is often translated, virtue, from airo, to raise up, to elevate; ⁹epainos, commendable, praise worthy, from epi, indicating continual influence upon, and ainos, story.)*

4:9 These things are consistent with all that I teach and live; you can confidently practice what you hear and see in me. The peace that inevitably follows this lifestyle is more than a fuzzy feeling; this is God himself endorsing our oneness.

4:10 I am so happy in the Lord that after all this time you have shown such revived concern in my well-being. It is refreshing to know your support, even though you did not recently have the opportunity to express it.

4:11 Hey, don't get me wrong, I am not hinting for funding! I have discovered my "I am-ness" and found that I am fully ¹self sufficient, whatever

the circumstance. *(Self sufficient, [1]autarkes, self complacent, the feeling you have when you are completely satisfied with yourself.)*

4:12 I am not defined by abuse or abundance! It might be a different day and a different place, but the secret remains the same; whether I am facing a feast or a fast, a fountain or famine. *(Abundance is not a sign of God's goodness; neither is lack a sign of his absence! "Righteousness by his (God's) faith defines life." The good news is the fact that the Cross of Christ was a success. God rescued the life of our design; he redeemed our innocence. Mankind would never again be judged righteous or unrighteous by their own ability to obey moral laws! It is not about what someone must or must not do but about what Jesus has done! It is from faith to faith, and not a person's good or bad behavior or circumstances interpreted as a blessing or a curse [Hab 2:4]. Instead of reading the curse when disaster strikes, Habakkuk realizes that the Promise out-dates performance as the basis to mankind's acquittal. Deuteronomy 28 would no longer be the motivation or the measure of right or wrong behavior! "Though the fig trees do not blossom, nor fruit be on the vines, the produce of the olive fail and the fields yield no food, the flock be cut off from the fold and there be no herd in the stalls, yet I will rejoice in the Lord, I will joy in the God of my salvation. God, the Lord, is my strength; he makes my feet like hinds' feet, he makes me tread upon my high places [Hab 3:17-19 RSV]. "Look away [from the law of works] unto Jesus; he is the Author and finisher of faith." [Heb 12:1]. See Rom 1:17.)*

4:13 In every situation I am strong in the one who empowers me from within to be who I am! *(Paul lived his life in touch with this place within himself. He discovered that the same I am-ness that Jesus walked in, was mirrored in him! I am what I am by the grace of God! Christ in me, mirrors Christ in you! Phil 2:12, "Not only in my presence but much more in my absence! Col 1:27 In us God desires to exhibit the priceless treasure of Christ's indwelling; every nation will recognize him as in a mirror! The unveiling of Christ in human life completes mankind's every expectation. He is not hiding in history, or in outer space nor in the future, neither in the pages of scripture, he is merely mirrored there to be unveiled within you. [Mt 13:44, Gal 1:15, 16.]*

4:14 Now I am not saying that I did not need or appreciate your help! Your joint participation in my difficult times was like beautiful poetry to me!

4:15 You and I know very well that your initial encounter with the gospel inspired you to partner with me in the wonderful rythm of giving and receiving. Your generosity then financed my trip in and out of Macedonia! No other church did what you did. *(Paul visited Thessalonica and Berea, about 12 years before this epistle was written. Acts 17: 1-14.)*

4:16 You also helped me several times in Thessalonica.

4:17 I am not reminding you of your gifts for any other reason but to encourage you to realize the abundant harvest in the word that you are a living epistle of. *(Greek, the fruit of "your word.")*

4:18 This letter is my official [1]receipt to you, proving that my capacity is filled to the brim! I am bursting at the seams indulging in your gifts that

Epaphrodites brought! Your generosity celebrates God's pleasure like a sweet perfume poured out on the altar of your love for me. *(The word* [1]*apecho here is used as a commercial term meaning to receive a sum in full and give a receipt for it. From* **apo** *and* **echo**, *to hold; in this context the preposition* **apo** *with the accusative denotes correspondence of the contents to the capacity; of the possession to the desire. J.B. Lightfoot)*

4:19 My God shall also abundantly fill every nook and cranny to overflowing in all areas of your lives. The wealth of his dream come true in Christ Jesus measures his generosity towards you!

4:20 For countless ages upon ages God will be celebrated as our Father. We are his glory! Most certainly!

4:21 Embrace every saint in Christ Jesus on our behalf; the brethern with me embrace you!

4:22 All the saints, especially those within the household of Caesar greet you dearly!

4:23 The grace that Jesus Christ embodies embraces you in your spirit.

In this marvelous work, Paul continues to eloquently celebrate the perfection of God's work in Christ in redeeming his likeness in us. His aim is to make the mystery of the gospel known in its most accurate context; the unveiling of Christ in us completes our every expectation. Paul sees the whole world as his audience! He has no other agenda but to reveal Christ in the nations!

Col 1:28 This is the essence and focus of our message; we awaken every person's mind, instructing every individual by bringing them into full understanding *(flawless clarity)* in order that we may prove *(present)* everyone perfect in Christ.

Col 1:15 In him the image and likeness of God is made visible in human life; in order that every one may recognize their true origin in him; he is the firstborn of every creature. *(What darkness veiled from us he unveiled. In him we clearly see the mirror reflection of our original life. The son of his love gives accurate evidence of his image in human form. God can never again be invisible!)*

Col 2:9-10 Christ reveals that there is no place in the universe where God would rather be; his fullness physically resides in Christ! Jesus proves that human life is tailor-made for God! Jesus Christ mirrors our completeness; he is I am in us.

Any teaching that leaves you with a sense of lack and imperfection rather than completeness is a distraction from the truth.

Col 2:16 Do not let anyone therefore bring a restriction to your freedom by reviving religious rules and regulations pertaining to eating and drinking; all Jewish festivals, new moons, and Sabbaths have come to an end in Christ!

The religious facade that disguised the law of works as a means of defining a person's life, was openly defeated. The success of the Cross will never be silenced!

Col 3:1 Since you are in fact raised together with Christ, relocate yourselves mentally; engage your thoughts with throne room realities!

Col 4:4 My sincere desire is that my message will accurately unveil the mystery of Christ in its most complete context. You! This is the mission of my life! *(Eph 3:9)*

1:1 My name is Paul. My colleague, Timothy, and I are together in this mission ordained by the purpose of God, representing the ministry of Jesus Christ.

1:2 We greet you with grace, which is the blessing of his favor and friendship; and honor you who are in Colossae as saints and brothers included in Christ. God is our Father and Jesus Christ our Master.

1:3 Every time we pray for you we thank God for you. Together with our Lord Jesus Christ we enjoy a common origin in the Father.

1:4 The reports of your belief in Christ Jesus and your love for every devote follower inspires us.

1:5 Heaven *(the spiritual realm)* is the limitless reservoir of your expectation. The announcement of the goodness of God is not far-fetched or too good to be true. The word you heard is absolutely true!

1:6 This word resonates within you and its appeal is prevailing in the whole world. The harvest is evident everywhere and gaining ground; as also witnessed in your own experience from the moment you heard and understood the true implication and the relevance of his grace. *("My greatest joy is to realize that your faith is announced throughout the entire world. The total cosmos is our audience!" [Rom 1:8] Paul always sees the larger audience when he addresses the individual.)*

1:7 Your experience is consistent with the teaching you received from our dear co-worker Epafras. He is passionate about your well being in Christ.

1:8 He told us how much you love us in the spirit;

1:9 and so we have become inseparably linked to you. Our constant desire for you is that you might be overwhelmed with the knowledge of God's dream for your lives. We pray that the pattern of his wisdom and thoughts will fall into place for you in all [1]spiritual understanding. *(The word, [1]sunieimi, means a joining together as of two streams; a fusion of thought.)*

1:10 Go on a [1]walkabout tour to explore the extent of the land that is yours under his Lordship. Now you can conduct yourselves appropriately towards him, pleasing him in every harvest of good works that you bear. Meanwhile, you continue to increase in your intimate acquaintance with that which God knows to be true about you. This results in the most attractive and fulfilled life possible. *(The word, [1]peripateo, means to walk about everywhere. The knowledge of God is not our perception of him, but his knowledge of us; to know even as we have always been known. [Jer 1:5, 1 Cor 13:12])*

1:11 You are empowered in the dynamic of God's strength; [1]his mind is made up about you! He enables you to be strong in endurance and steadfastness with joy. *(His glorious power, or [1]doxa, comes from dokeo, to recognize for what it really is, true opinion; God's intention—his mind made up.)*

1:12 We are grateful to the Father who qualified us to participate in the complete portion of the inheritance of the [1]saints in the light. *(The light of the Gospel reveals what God accomplished to transform the sinner into a saint; from* **hagos***, an awful thing to* [1]**hagios***, a consecrated object: "call no-one unholy or unclean." [Acts 10:28])*

1:13 He rescued us from the [1]**dominion of darkness** *(the sense-ruled world, dominated by the law of performance)* **and relocated us into the kingdom where the love of his son rules.** *(Darkness is not a force, it is the absence of light. [See Eph 4:18] A darkened understanding veiled the truth of our redeemed design from us. 2 Cor 4:4. What "empowered" darkness was the lie that we believed about ourselves! The word,* [1]**exousia***, sometimes translated authority, is from* **ek***, origin or source, and* **eimi***, I am. Thus, I was confused about who I am until the day that I heard and understood the grace of God in truth, as in a mirror. See 2 Corinthians 3:18, John 1:12.)*

1:14 In God's mind mankind is associated in Christ; in his blood sacrifice we were ransomed; our redemption was secured; our [1]**sins were completely done away with.** *(The word sin, is the word* [1]**hamartia***, from* **ha***, negative or without and* **meros***, portion or form, thus to be without your allotted portion or without form, pointing to a disorientated, distorted, bankrupt identity; the word* **meros***, is the stem of* **morphe***, as in 2 Corinthians 3:18 the word* **metamorphe***, with form, which is the opposite of* **hamartia** *- without form. Sin is to live out of context with the blueprint of one's design; to behave out of tune with God's original harmony. See Deuteronomy 32:18, "You have forgotten the Rock that begot you and have gotten out of step with the God who danced with you!" Hebrew,* **khul** *or* **kheel***, to dance. Sin distorts the life of our design. Jesus reveals and redeemed our true form.)*

1:15 In him the image and likeness of God is made visible in human life in order that every one may recognize their true origin in him. He is the firstborn of every creature. *(What darkness veiled from us he unveiled. In him we clearly see the mirror reflection of our original life. The son of his love gives accurate evidence of his image in human form. God can never again be invisible!)*

1:16 Everything that is begins in him whether in the heavenly realm or upon the earth, visible or invisible, every order of justice and every level of authority, be it kingdoms or governments, principalities or jurisdictions; all things were created by him and for him.

1:17 He is the initiator of all things therefore everything finds its relevance and its true pattern only in him.

1:18 The ekklesia *(church)* **is the visible expression** *(body)* **of which Jesus is the head. He is the principle rank of authority who leads the triumphant procession of our new birth out of the region of the dead. His preeminent rank is beyond threat.** *(" ... leading the resurrection parade" —The Message)*

1:19 The full measure of everything God has in mind for mankind indwells him. *("So spacious is he, so roomy, that everything of God finds its proper place in him without crowding." — The Message)*

1:20 He initiated the reconciliation of all things to himself. Through the blood of the cross God restored the original harmony. His reign of peace now extends to every visible thing upon the earth as well as those invisible things which are in the [1]heavenly realm. *(The heavens, [1]ouranos, a place of elevation, from **oros**, a mountain, from **airo**, to lift, to raise, to elevate, "Not only that, but all the broken and dislocated pieces of the universe, people and things, animals and atoms, get properly fixed and fit together in vibrant harmonies, all because of his death." — The Message.)*

1:21 Your indifferent mindset alienated you from God into a lifestyle of annoyances, hardships, and labors. Yet he has now fully [2]reconciled and restored you to your original design. *(The word, [1]poneros, means annoyances, hardships, and labors, often translated as evil. [See Septuagint: tree of knowledge of good and hard labor!] To reconcile: [2]apokatallasso, fully restored to the original value. [In Thayer Definition: to change, exchange, as coins for others of equivalent value.])*

1:22 He accomplished this in dying our death in a human body; he fully represented us in order to fully present us again in blameless innocence, face-to-face with God; with no sense of guilt, suspicion, regret, or accusation; all charges against us are officially cancelled.

1:23 Remain under the influence of what your faith knows to be true about you, firmly consolidated in the foundation of your belief so that nothing can distract you from the expectation of the Gospel; a hope that is consistent with what you have heard. Just as I, Paul, am in the ministry to proclaim the one and only message that rings true with resonance in all of creation under heaven. *(The dimension of the invisible spiritual realm. "You stay grounded and steady in that bond of trust, constantly tuned in to the Message, careful not to be distracted or diverted. There is no other Message—just this one. Every creature under heaven gets this same Message. I, Paul, am a messenger of this Message." —The Message.)*

1:24 This is why no form of suffering can interfere with my joy. Every suffering on your behalf is just another opportunity to reinforce that which might still be lacking *(in your understanding)* of the affliction of Christ on behalf of his body which is the church. *(The inconvenience that Paul might be suffering on behalf of the believers is not to add to the sufferings of Christ—as though the sufferings of Christ on our behalf were insufficient but it is to further emphasize and confirm the principle of unselfish love that constrains New Testament ministry.)*

1:25 I am an administrator in God's economy; my mission is to make his word known to you with utmost clarity.

1:26 The element of prophetic mystery was concealed for ages and generations but is now fully realized in our redeemed innocence.

1:27 In us God desires to exhibit the priceless treasure of Christ's indwelling; every nation will recognize him as in a mirror! The unveiling of Christ in you exceeds your every expectation! *(He is not hiding in* *history, or in outer space nor in the future, neither in the pages of scripture, he is merely mirrored there to be unveiled within you. Mt 13:44, Gal 1:15, 16)*

1:28 This is the essence and focus of our message; we [1]awaken everyone's mind, instructing every individual by bringing them into [2]full understanding *(flawless clarity)* **in order that we may [3]prove** *(present)* **everyone [4]perfect in Christ.** *(Translating [1]vous + tithemi as to re-align every mind with God's mind. The word, [2]sophos, comes from sophes meaning clear, clarity. The word, [3]paristano, comes from para, sphere of influence, closest possible association, and histemi, meaning to stand, to exhibit with evidence. The word, [4]teleios, means perfect, without shortcoming and fully efficient.)*

1:29 [1]Your completeness in Christ is not a remote goal, but your immediate reference! My labor now exceeds any zeal that I previously knew under the duty-driven law of willpower. I am laboring beyond the point of exhaustion, striving with intense resolve with all the energy that he mightily inspires within me. *([1]eis, a point reached in conclusion.)*

2:1 Picture this: The stage is set; the game is on! And you are more than a mere spectator. We are ¹standing opposite each other in the ²arena like two athletes of exactly the same stature: the contest is to display Christ in you to the extent that all of you as well as those in Laodicea may witness what I know face-to-face and not just by hearsay! *(Christ is not more in Paul than what he is in his audience! The KJV reads, "What ¹great ²conflict!" The word, ¹**helikos**, from Thayers Definition translates "as tall as; as old as; equal comrades. Two contestants weighing the exact same weight as well as being athletes of the exact same age." And arena or contest, ²**agon**, in Thayers Definition is "an assembly met to see games within the arena or stadium.")*

2:2 The ¹mandate of my ministry is for everyone's heart to be awakened to their true identity, ²intertwined in love's tapestry. This will launch you into a life of knowing the wealth of every ³conclusion and joint witness hidden within the mystery of God who fathered us and co-revealed us in Christ. *(The word, ¹**parakaleo**, is often translated as comfort from **para**, a preposition indicating close proximity, a thing proceeding from a sphere of influence, with a suggestion of union of place of residence, to have sprung from its author and giver, originating from, denoting the point from which an action originates, intimate connection; and **kaleo**, to surname, to identify by name, to call by name. The phrase, ²**sumbibatzo en agape**, means intertwined in love's tapestry; and the word, ³**suniemi**, means joint seeing or understanding.)*

2:3 Everything that could possibly define our wealth is ¹hidden in Christ. In this place of our union in him the complete ²treasure of all wisdom and knowledge is sourced. *(The word, ¹**apokriphos**, translates from **apo**, away from and **krupto**, to conceal, to keep secret. The word, ²**thesaurus**, means treasure; the place in which precious things are collected and laid up; from **tithemi**, to place and **theo**, God, the ultimate capacity of all things. Christ is the context of all wisdom and knowledge.)*

2:4 I want to say it with such clarity that no one will be able to lead you to an inferior conclusion by bending your mind with clever words. *(Any message that would divert from the revelation of the mystery of Christ in you is founded in error.)*

2:5 My physical absence does not distance me from you spiritually. I rejoice to witness that your disciplined and practical lifestyle does not distract from the simplicity of your faith and confidence in Christ.

2:6 Your daily walk is no different from that initial embrace when you first understood your divine association in him. *(As you have received Christ, so walk in him.)*

2:7 Just like the roots of a tree, draw your sustenance and strength from him. Like a building rising up out of its foundation your life makes the full stature of Christ visible; standing tall in his shoes, firm in your faith posture. The language of gratitude that overflows from your lips reflects the exact impression of what you were taught.

2:8 Make sure that you become no one's victim through empty philosophical intellectualism and meaningless speculations, molded in traditions and repetitions according to mankind's cosmic codes and superstitions and not consistent with Christ. (*Any teaching that leaves you with a sense of lack and imperfection rather than completeness is a distraction from the truth.*)

2:9 It is in Christ that God finds an accurate and complete expression of himself, in a human body! (*While the expanse cannot measure or define God, his exact likeness is displayed in human form. Jesus proves that human life is tailor-made for God!*)

2:10 Jesus mirrors our completeness and [1]endorses our [2]true identity. He is "I am" in us. (*God packaged completeness in "I am," mirrored in you! Delay is outdated! We are not dealing with "I used to be", or "I'm striving to be"; we are celebrating, I am"! The word, [1]arche, means chief in rank. The word, [2]exousia, is often translated as meaning authority; its components are, ek + eimi, originating out of "I am." The days are over where our lives were dictated to under the rule of the law of performance and an inferior identity. [See Col 1:19] The full measure of everything God has in mind for mankind indwells him.*

"Your own completeness is only realized in him." — Phillips Translation.)

2:11 You were in Christ when he died which means that his death represents your true circumcision. Sin's authority in the human body was stripped off you in him dying your death.

2:12 In the same parallel (*your co-circumcision in his death*) **your co-burial and joint-resurrection is now demonstrated in baptism; your co-inclusion in Christ is what God's faith knew when he powerfully raised him from the dead.** (*Hos 6:2*)

2:13 You were once spiritually dead, as confirmed in your constant failure; being bound to a lifestyle ruled by the [1]distorted desires of the flesh, but now God has made you alive together with him, having forgiven you all your [2]trespasses. (*[1]The uncircumcision of the flesh, i.e., in the Greek, a life controlled by the sexual organs. The word, [2]paraptoma, comes from, para, close proximity, sphere of influence and pipto, to stop flying, from petomai, to fly; thus, to fall from flight or to lose altitude.*)

2:14 His body nailed to the cross hung there as the document of mankind's guilt; in dying our death he [1]deleted the detailed [2]hand-written [3]record of Adam's fall. Every [1]stain that sin left on our conscience was fully blotted out. (*The word, [1]exaleipho, comes from ek, out of, and aleipho, with a, as a particle of union, and liparos, to grease, to leave a stain; guilt was like a grease stain upon the conscience of fallen mankind. The word, [2]cheirographon, translates as hand-written. The word, [3]dogma, comes from dokeo, a thought pattern; thus thought patterns engraved by human experience of constant failure to do what the law required. In his personal handwriting mankind endorsed their own death sentence. The hands of fallen mankind struck the body of Jesus with the blows of their religious hatred and fury when they nailed his bloodied body to the tree; they did not realize that in the mystery of God's economy, Jesus was the scapegoat* *of the entire human race! [Isaiah 53:4, 5] "The slate wiped clean, that old arrest warrant canceled and nailed to Christ's Cross." —The Message)*

2:15 His brilliant victory made a public ¹spectacle of every ²rule and ³authority empowered by the fall of Adam. The ⁴voice of the cross will never be silenced! *(The horror of the Cross is now the eternal trophy of God's triumph over sin! The cross stripped religion of its authority to manipulate mankind with guilt. Every accusation lost its power to continue to blackmail the human race. The word, ¹apekduomai, is translated from apo, away from, and ekduo, to be stripped of clothing; the religious facade that disguised the law of works as a means of defining a person's life, was openly defeated. The dominance of the tree of the knowledge of good and evil [poneros, hard work and labor] was ended. The word, ¹deikmatizo, means to exhibit in public. The word, ⁴parresia, comes from pas, all and rheo, outspokenness, pouring forth speech.*

"He stripped all the spiritual tyrants in the universe of their sham authority at the Cross and marched them naked through the streets." — The Message

See commentary for 1 Corinthians 15:24, The complete conclusion in his work of redemption is celebrated in his yielding the full harvest of his reign to God the Father, having ¹brought to naught the law of works which supported every definition of dominion under the fall, including all ²principalities, all ³authority and every ⁴dynamic influence in society. [He brought to naught the law of works, ¹katargeo, from kata, meaning intensity, and argos, meaning labor; thus free from all self effort to attempt to improve what God has already perfected in Christ. All principalities, ²arche, or chief ranks, i.e., kings, governors; this includes any governing system whereby one is ranked above the other on the basis of their performance or preference. All authority, ³exousia, comes from ek, denoting origin and eimi, I am; in this case, because of what I can do I am defined by what I can do better than you; therefore, I have authority over you. Every dynamic influence in society, ⁴dunamis, means power, in this case, willpower. Every government structure in society will be brought under the dominion of grace where the Christ life rules.]

In 1 Corinthians 2:7-8, We voice words of wisdom that was hidden in silence for timeless ages; a mystery unfolding God's Masterful plan whereby he would redeem his glory in mankind. Neither the politicians nor the theologians of the day had a clue about this mystery [of mankind's association in Christ]; if they did, they would never have crucified the Lord whose death redeemed our glory!)

2:16 Do not let anyone therefore bring a restriction to your freedom by reviving religious rules and regulations pertaining to eating and drinking; all Jewish festivals, new moons, and Sabbaths have come to an end in Christ! *(Their relevance only served to remind of the promise of Christ on an annual, monthly, and weekly basis. They carried the promise like a placenta would hold the unborn child, but became obsolete as soon as the child was born.)*

2:17 These things were only prophetic shadows; Christ is the substance.

2:18 A religious mentality of voluntary humility and obsession with pious observances of angels will bring you no further reward. So do not let anyone who tries to act as an umpire of your devotion insist on his own

opinion, confined to a mind inflated by the sensational and spooky; his so called visions are just a puff of hot air. *(In his judgment he fails to correctly interpret the legal implications of the Cross.)*

"Don't tolerate people who try to run your life, ordering you to bow and scrape, [in order to improve your standing before God], insisting that you join their obsession with angels and that you seek out visions. They're a lot of hot air, that's all they are." — *The Message.*

2:19 Such religious jargon is completely out of rhythm with the head. You are directly connected to Christ who like a ¹choir conductor draws out the music in everyone like a tapestry of art that intertwines in harmony to reveal the full stature of divine inspiration. *(Which is Christ in you. The word, ¹epichoregeo, is choir director. [See 2 Pet 1:11] Thus, the great Conductor of music will draw your life into the full volume of the harmony of the ages.)*

2:20 If it is true that you were included in Christ's death, then the religious systems of this world with its rules and regulations no longer apply to you. What further relevance would there be for you to continue to live under the influence of mankind's doctrines and ideas?

2:21 Things like: "Do not associate with this one!" or "Do not taste that!" or "Do not even touch this with your finger!"

2:22 These instructions are of no permanent value in any case since they refer to things that perish after it is consumed, thus they leave no lasting impact in your life. So do not let man-made menus cause you to major on minors. *(Jesus said it is not what goes into the mouth that matters, but what comes out of the heart!)*

2:23 Religious tradition appears to be very devout and its followers seem to be so humble and holy in their strict observance of rules that seek to control the behavior of the body. The only problem with this is that the flesh is never permanently satisfied. *(The Message translates verses 19-23 as: "They're completely out of touch with the source of life, Christ, who puts us together in one piece, whose very breath and blood flow through us. He is the Head and we are the body. We can grow up healthy in God only as he nourishes us. So, then, if with Christ you've put all that pretentious and infantile religion behind you, why do you let yourselves be bullied by it? "Don't touch this! Don't taste that! Don't go near this!" Do you think things that are here today and gone tomorrow are worth that kind of attention? Such things sound impressive if said in a deep enough voice. They even give the illusion of being pious and humble and ascetic.)*

3:1 See yourselves co-raised with Christ! Now ponder with persuasion the consequence of your co-inclusion in him. Relocate yourselves mentally! Engage your thoughts with throne room realities where you are co-seated with Christ in the executive authority of God's right hand.

3:2 Becoming affectionately acquainted with throne room thoughts will keep you from being distracted again by the earthly *(soul-ruled)* realm. *("Set your minds upon the things that are above and not upon the things below!" RSV. Also note Romans 1:18, where the word **katecho** is used - to echo downwards is the opposite to **anoche**, to echo upwards - Romans 2:4 and Romans 3:26. Also 2 Corinthians 4:18 "We are not keeping any score of what seems so obvious to the senses in the natural realm, it is fleeting and irrelevant. It is the unseen, eternal realm within us which has our full attention and captivates our gaze!" A renewed mind conquers the space previously occupied by worthless pursuits and habits.)*

3:3 Your union with his death broke the association with that world; see yourselves located in a fortress where your life is hidden with Christ in God! *("In that day you will know that I am in my father, and you in me and I in you." [Jn 14:20] Occupy your mind with this new order of life; you died when Jesus died, whatever defined you before defines you no more. Christ, in whom the fullness of deity dwells, defines you now! The word, "hidden" can also be translated, secret; the secret of your life is your union with Christ in God! [See Col 2:9, 10] "Risen, then, with Christ you must lift your thoughts above where Christ now sits at the right hand of God, you must be heavenly minded; not earthly minded, you have undergone death, and your life is hidden away now with Christ in God. Christ is your life, when he is made manifest you are made manifest in his glory." — Knox Translation)*

3:4 The exact life on exhibit in Christ is now repeated in us. We are being ¹co-revealed in the same bliss; we are joined in oneness with him, just as his life reveals you, your life reveals him! *(This verse was often translated to again delay the revelation of Christ to a future event! The word, ¹**otan**, often translated as "when" is better translated as "every time." Thus, "Every time Christ is revealed we are being co-revealed in his glory." According to Walter Bauer Lexicon, **otan** is often used of an action that is repeated. Paul declares our joint-glorification in Christ! We are co-revealed in the same bliss. [See 1 Cor 2:7-8, Rom 3:23-24, Rom 8:30, 2 Pet 1:3.] In him we live and move and have our being; in us he lives and moves and has his being! [Acts 17:28])*

3:5 Consider the members of your body as dead and buried towards everything related to the porn industry, sensual uncleanness, longing for forbidden things, lust and greed, which are just another form of idol worship. *(Idol worship is worshipping a distorted image of yourself!)*

3:6 These distorted expressions are in total contradiction to God's design and desire for your life. *(The sentence, "upon the sons of unbelief" was added later in some manuscripts.)*

3:7 We were all once swept along into a lifestyle of lust and greed.

3:8 But now, because you realize that you co-died and were co-raised together with Christ, you can flush your thoughts with truth! Permanently put these things behind you: things such as violent outbursts of rage, depression, all manner of wickedness, slander *(any attempt to belittle someone else and to cause someone to receive a bad reputation, blasphemos)*, and every form of irregular conversation. *(The lifelong association with sin is broken; the dominion of the character of God is revealed again in ordinary life.)*

3:9 That old life was a lie, foreign to our design! Those garments of disguise are now thoroughly stripped off us in our understanding of our union with Christ in his death and resurrection. We are no longer obliged to live under the identity and rule of the robes we wore before, neither are we cheating anyone through false pretensions. *(The garments an actor would wear define his part in the play but cannot define him.)*

3:10 We stand fully identified in the new creation renewed in knowledge according to the pattern of the exact image of our Creator.

3:11 The revelation of Christ in us gives identity to the individual beyond anything anyone could ever be as a Greek or a Jew, American or African, foreigner or famous, male or female, king or pawn. From now on everyone is defined by Christ; everyone is represented in Christ. *(In seeing him not just recorded in history but revealed in us, we discover the face of our birth as in a mirror! [Jas 1:18])*

3:12 You are the product of God's love; he restored you to his original thought. You belong to him exclusively. It is like changing garments. Now that you have gotten rid of the old, clothe yourselves with inner compassion, kindness, humility, gentleness and patience, *(Just like you were once identified by your apparel, the characteristics of these qualities define you now.)*

3:13 upholding one another in positive expectation. If anyone finds fault with another, restore that person to favor, remembering how the Lord's forgiveness has transformed our lives.

3:14 Wear love like a uniform; this is what completes the picture of our oneness.

3:15 Appoint the peace of Christ as umpire in your hearts. We are all identified in the same person; there is only one body. We are born to be a blessing and exhibit his benevolence.

3:16 Christ is the language of God's logic. Let his message sink into you with unlimited vocabulary, taking wisdom to its most complete conclusion. This makes your fellowship an environment of instruction in an atmosphere of music. Every lesson is a reminder, echoing in every song you sing, whether it be a psalm *(raving about God in praise and worship accompanied by musical instruments)* or a hymn *(a testimony song)* or a song in the spirit *(a new spontaneous prophetic song)*. Grace fuels your heart with inspired music to the Lord.

3:17 Your every conversation and the detail of your daily conduct reflect him; his name and lordship define your lives and inspire your deep gratitude to God the Father for his grace.

3:18 His peace is the umpire of your every relationship, especially in the family! Wives, place yourselves in the intimate care of your husbands, acknowledging the lordship of Christ in them.

3:19 Husbands, love your wives tenderly. Do not exasperate them.

3:20 Children, you display the Christ-life in the way you respond to your parents, keep them glowing with joy, they reflect God's delight in you. *("Parents, don't come down too hard on your children or you'll crush their spirits." — The Message.)*

3:21 Parents are responsible for the atmosphere at home; avoid vibes that dampen the child's spirit.

3:22 If you are employed by someone, even having to work like a slave, remember your hearts are intertwined in devotion to God. Don't just look busy when you are being watched, show the same diligence behind your bosses back.

3:23 Whatever you do, picture Christ in the person you are doing it for; it makes such a difference when you put your heart into it.

3:24 God is no-one's debtor; you are employed under the Lordship of Christ.

3:25 To live contrary to the life of your design is to injure yourself; your job description does not define you, it doesn't matter who you are. Unrighteousness carries its own consequence and it is not a respecter of persons.

4:1 If you are the boss, treat those who work for you in the light of their equality in Christ; he treats you like that and he is the big Boss in the spiritual realm. *(This verse concludes the thought in 3:25 and should rather be part of the previous chapter. Paul did not write in chapters and verses.)*

4:2 Persist in prevailing prayer. Be attentive and sensitive *(to the voice of the Spirit; do not be over-occupied with prayers for yourself and your own needs)* Grace and gratitude is the language of prayer.

4:3 At the same time remember me in your prayers. Pray that what God has in me would impact many with the revelation of the mystery of Christ far beyond the walls of this prison cell. The confines of this prison do not measure my ministry; the message of the mystery of Christ in me does. *(Col 1:25-29)*

4:4 My sincere desire is that my message will accurately unveil the mystery of Christ in its most complete context. You! This is the mission of my life! **(***Eph 3:9***)**

4:5 Do not spoil your chances to touch others with the word through a lack of wisdom. Even though they may seem to be "outside," your attitude towards them will reveal to them how "inside" they in fact are. Redeem the time by making the most of every opportunity. *(Time only finds its relevance in redemption-realities.)*

4:6 Season your conversation with grace. This remains the most attractive and appropriate option to respond in every situation.

4:7 Tychicus will tell you all the news about me. He is my colleague and such a lovely brother whose ministry is distinguished by integrity.

4:8 I commissioned him to come to you in this capacity, to cross-pollinate between us, so that you may also be encouraged and comforted by him.

4:9 Onesimus, who originally comes from your area, will join him. He is a beloved and faithful brother. They will represent us with you.

4:10 Aristarchus, my fellow prisoner, greets you warmly; so does Mark, the son of Barnabas's sister. Remember I told you to give him a special welcome when he comes to you.

4:11 Then there is also Jesus, some call him Justus. These three brethren, originally Jews by faith, are my close companions and co-laborers for the Kingdom of God.

4:12 Epahras, who is also fruit of your ministry, salutes you. What a diligent worker of Christ he is, always laboring on your behalf with great intensity in his prayers. His desire for you is to stand strong in the full accomplishment of Christ and to be fully persuaded in God's purpose for your lives.

4:13 I can tell you that he has a real passion for your welfare, as well as for the believers in Laodicea and Hierapolis.

4:14 The dear doctor Luke greets you and so does Demas.

4:15 Please extend our greetings to the brethren in Laodicea and also to Nymphas and the church in her house.

4:16 Make sure that the church at Laodicea also gets the opportunity to read this epistle and that you again read the letter I wrote to them.

4:17 Archippus, I want you to be diligent to fulfill the ministry you have received in the Lord.

4:18 I, Paul, write this greeting with my own hand. You must remember my bonds. God's grace is yours.

This letter to the Thessalonians was probably the first of Paul's letters. It is not possible to say exactly when Paul appeared before Gallio, but Acts 18:12–18 suggests that this happened shortly after Gallio assumed office, probably towards the end of Paul's eighteen months in the city. It is likely that 1 Thessalonians was written shortly after Paul's arrival in Corinth. It may therefore be dated in the early part of 51 or 50 if the earlier dating of Gallio's assumption of office is preferred, making it the first written book in the New Testament.

Macedonia was organized as a Roman province in 146 B.C. Thessalonica was made the seat of government and was fondly called the Mother of all Macedon. Thessalonica, named after the stepsister of Alexander the Great, may have had as many as 200 000 people in Paul's day. It stood on the Via Egnatia, the Roman highway to the East and proved a very strategic location for a church. Also ideally situated for trade, Thessalonica attracted a community of Jews, which Luke notices by his reference to the synagogue Acts17:1

The following verses sum up Paul's heart toward the Thessalonians: For our appeal to you was from a place of union, a place of seamless oneness where distance or any definition of distraction of subtle hidden agendas were eliminated! *(The word, [1]parakaleo, comes from para, a preposition indicating close proximity, a thing proceeding from a sphere of influence, with a suggestion of union of place of residence, to have sprung from its author and giver, originating from, denoting the point from which an action originates, intimate connection; and kaleo, meaning to identify by name, to surname.)* In God's [1]esteem of us, we were entrusted with this wonderful announcement: the gospel! Our conversation is prompted by God's approval of us which might not be very popular with the typical religious mindset! *(The word [1]dokimatso, is from the word dokeo, to form an opinion, to estimate.)* Come on, you should know better than that! How could you possibly suspect us of setting you up with [1]smooth talk when all we were really after was your money and your vote? God knows that we would never disadvantage you. *(The Gospel does not flatter the religious ear because there is no ground left for boasting in personal achievement! Gift-language disarms reward-language! The word, [1]kolakeia means flattery.)* We were not even fishing for compliments from you or anyone else for that matter! We would never "pull rank" on you as commissioners of Christ! Instead we were fostering you with the tender care of a mother nursing her children. It is with this same motherly affection that we yearn for you and were delighted to present you God's gospel gift wrapped in us, since you are so very dear to us! 1 Thessalonians 2:3-8

1:1 Paul, Silvanus and Timothy greet the church in the region of Thessalonica with grace and peace from God our Father and the Lord Jesus Christ. *(The [1]ekklesia, or church, is those who discovered their original identity redeemed in Christ. From ek, origin and kaleo, to surname, to identify by name. The mission of Jesus through his church is to persuade the world of their true sonship: the son of man is the son of God! Matthew 16:13-18)*

1:2 You feature so prominently in our prayers and conversation which is always marked with the gentle cheerfulness of a grateful heart to God.

1:3 We fondly remember the testimony of your faith which is so evident in your day to day lives in your love labor, even through many difficult times, and the cheerful constancy of the very hope that our Lord Jesus Christ personifies, in whom we enjoy the immediate presence of our Papa God. *(In sharp contrast to a duty-and guilt driven rule, Paul mentions their faith inspired work and their love inspired labor. Paul understands that love ignites faith. Galatians 5:6)*

1:4 Beloved friends, you have come to understand that you are [1]God's idea to begin with! *(The word [1]ekloge has traditionally been translated and interpreted as election, which led to the illusion that some are in and some are out, by God's intent! However, the preposition ek, always denotes source or origin and lego points to the authentic thought, the logos that John refers to in John 1:1 &14.)*

1:5 Our [1]gospel [2]birthed in you so much more than mere intellectual reasoning; your encounter bore witness to the dynamic of the Holy Spirit as you became thoroughly [3]permeated with [1]the well done announcement and [4]perceived within yourselves the full impact of our immediate influence. *(The gospel, [1]euaggellion, is the well done announcement. The word [2]ginomai, means to cause to be, to become. The word [3]plerophoria means to be permeated. The word [4]eido means to see, to perceive. See Titus 3:5)*

1:6 In [1]embracing the word as your own, even in the midst of great contradiction, the [2]mirror likeness of the Lord reflected in us was ignited in you with the joy of the Holy Spirit! *(The word [1]dechomai means to to receive favorably, give ear to, embrace, make one's own, approve. The word [2]mimetes, means to imitate or mirror.)*

1:7 And so the story unfolds; your lives came to be the very mirror, modeling the Christ life and endorsing the faith of everyone throughout Macedonia and Achaia.

1:8 The word of the Lord found such an articulate voice in you and resounded forth to reach regions far beyond you! Not only in your immediate provinces, but in every place your faith concludes in a face to face encounter with God! You are the message! We need not say anything! *(The Greek preposition pros, indicates direction, forward to; that is toward the destination of the relation. Face-to-face is the conclusion.)*

1:9 Others from these provinces testify of this; they recall how our visit to you has greatly influenced your lives to return to God and now, instead of being absorbed by the imaginary illusions of idolatry you are engaged with God unveiled in real life!

1:10 And all along you remain focused on the son of God who reveals our joint-origin in the heavenlies. He endorsed our redeemed innocence in his resurrection! He has [1]drawn us to himself and rescued us from every definition of judgment! *(The word [1]rhuomai, means to draw to oneself, to rescue, to deliver.)*

2:1 I am sure that the ¹content of the gospel is clear to you ever since our first contact with you dear friends. *(The word ¹kenos, empty, means that our visit was not in vain.)*

2:2 As you know, the many things we suffered before, and even the way we were abused in Philippi, did not intimidate or distract us in any way. We were very bold in our God to communicate the news of what he has so wonderfully accomplished in Christ, in the face of much contradiction. *(The Greek word for the good news is the word ¹euangelion, which is the well done announcement! It is the news of what God has so wonderfully accomplished! The gospel is a declaration. We have made it an 'if-then' proposition. But the 'if-then' proposition is a catch 22 situation; which is a 'no-win' dilemma or paradox. Often these situations are such that solving one part of a problem only creates another, which ultimately leads back to the original problem. A situation in which a desired outcome or solution is impossible to attain because of a set of inherently illogical rules or conditions. For so long evangelism has been beg, coerce, bribe or scare, now it is no longer telling people what they must do but what God has done and believes about them!)*

2:3 For our appeal to you was from a place of union, a place of seamless oneness where distance or any definition of distraction of subtle hidden agendas were eliminated! *(The word, ¹parakaleo, comes from para, a preposition indicating close proximity, a thing proceeding from a sphere of influence, with a suggestion of union of place of residence, to have sprung from its author and giver, originating from, denoting the point from which an action originates, intimate connection; and kaleo, meaning to identify by name, to surname.)*

2:4 In God's ¹esteem of us, we were entrusted with this wonderful announcement: the gospel! Our conversation is prompted by God's approval of us which might not be very popular with the typical religious mindset! *(The word ¹dokimatso, is from the word dokeo, to form an opinion, to estimate.)*

2:5 Come on, you should know better than that! How could you possibly suspect us of setting you up with ¹smooth talk when all we were really after was your money and your vote? God knows that we would never disadvantage you. *(The Gospel does not flatter the religious ear because there is no ground left for boasting in personal achievement! Gift-language disarms reward-language! The word, ¹kolakeia means flattery.)*

2:6 We were not even fishing for compliments from you or anyone else for that matter! We would never "pull rank" on you as commissioners of Christ!

2:7 Instead we were fostering you with the tender care of a mother nursing her children.

2:8 It is with this same motherly affection that we yearn for you and were delighted to present you God's gospel gift wrapped in us, since you are so very dear to us! *(The word, ¹metadidomi, translates as the kind of giving where the giver is not distanced from the gift but wrapped up in it! The apostles,* *prophets, preachers, pastors, and teachers are gifts to the ekklesia to establish them in their faith and to present everyone in the full and mature stature of Christ [Eph 4:11-16]. There is such a vast difference between a gift and a reward! We are God's gifts to one another. What God now has in us is gift wrapped to the world. What we are in our individual expression is a gift and not a reward for personal diligence or achievement. These gifts were never meant to establish one above the other, or to become mere formal titles, but rather to identify specific and dynamic functions with one defined purpose, to bring everyone into the realization of the fullness of the measure of Christ in them!)*

2:9 I don't have to remind you to what extreme extents we were prepared to go in our efforts to bring you God's gospel at no expense to you at all! We kept going night and day, both teaching you as well as actively trading in the marketplace!

2:10 We behaved with utmost integrity and courtesy; making absolutely sure that we gave no offense to disappoint your faith. We have noting to hide! God knows we had no ulterior motives.

2:11 Just like a father would instruct his children, so we engaged ourselves with you to remind you of your origin in God,

2:12 ¹inspiring you to live in the ²daily awareness of your true value and ³identity. In God's opinion you are royalty. *(The word ¹paramutheomai, inspired from within to live the life of your design. To ²walk worthy, axios; having the weight of another thing of like value, to be worth as much. ³Your calling or vocation, from kaleo, to ²surname, to identify by name.)*

2:13 The way in which you joined yourselves to the word that we taught is such a constant source of gratitude to us; you immediately knew that this was not mere human opinion, but you took a hold of our message as the very logic of God, and so the truth energizes you from within, endorsing your faith.

2:14 You mirror those who have likewise discovered their original identity in Christ as God's ¹ekklesia in Judea. You suffered persecution from your own people just as they did from the Jews. *(The traditions and cultures that defined people historically are challenged by the ¹church, the ekklesia of God which is the revelation of the original identity of humanity now declared and redeemed in Christ.)*

2:15 They killed their own prophets as well as their Messiah, the Lord Jesus, and drove us out of their midst as if they were doing God a favor! Instead they have become enemies of the entire human race!

2:16 They sought to ¹intimidate us in order to dwarf our message into insignificance, hoping to prevent us from declaring to the nations their salvation. Their ²distorted behavior has come full circle! They have proved to themselves to be their own worst enemy. Their ³passion to oppose the message has become their judgment! *(¹kōluō , to prevent, from kolatzo, to dwarf. The word sin, is the word ²hamartia, from ha, negative or without and* *meros, portion or form, thus to be without your allotted portion or without form, pointing to a disorientated, distorted, bankrupt identity; the word* **meros***, is the stem of* **morphe***, as in 2 Corinthians 3:18 the word* **metamorphe***, with form, which is the opposite of* **hamartia** *- without form. Sin is to live out of context with the blueprint of one's design; to behave out of tune with God's original harmony. See Deuteronomy 32:18, "You have forgotten the Rock that begot you and have gotten out of step with the God who danced with you!" Hebrew,* **khul** *or* **kheel***, to dance. By killing their own prophets and their Messiah and now seeking to prevent the spreading of the gospel to the nations, they are opposing the very promise of their patriarch Abraham in whom God has blessed all the nations of the earth! The word* [3]**orge***, associated with wrath or punishment is from* **oregomai***, to stretch oneself, to reach out, to long for, to desire, to experience the excitement of the mind.)*

2:17 We were only briefly separated from you in person but never in our hearts. This has caused us to yearn with greater expectancy to see you face to face again!

2:18 On two occasions I was restrained from coming to you. *(Luke mentions two occasions when they were restrained by the Spirit of Jesus and the Holy Spirit not to go into an area for their own safety, Acts 16:6, Acts 16:7. Maybe the mention of Satan here in 1 Thessolonians 2:18 was in reference to the messenger of Satanos who frustrated Paul with the "thorn in the flesh" he mentions in 2 Corinthians 12 before he learned to deal with a defeated devil by the understanding of his sufficiency and authority in grace! The thorns on Jesus' head broke the curse associated with the thorn in the flesh! I am also of the opinion that maybe the reference to Satan was added later when it became a popular excuse to blame the devil when things did not seem to go according to plan.)*

2:19 We expect nothing less in the context of the gospel than you enjoying a face to face encounter in the [1]immediate presence of our Lord Jesus Christ! This is our delight and wreath of honor! *(The word* [1]**parousia** *speaks of the immediate presence of the Lord! From* **para***, a preposition indicating close proximity, a thing proceeding from a sphere of influence, with a suggestion of union of place of residence, to have sprung from its author and giver, originating from, denoting the point from which an action originates, intimate connection; and* **eimi***, I am! There is not even a hint of judgment or punishment in this word! Please do not believe everything you read in Strongs! "G3952 parousia from the present participle of G3918; a being near, that is, advent; often, return; specifically of Christ to punish Jerusalem, or finally the wicked."!!??)*

2:20 You are our trophy and joy!

3:1 We could not bear being separated from you and since it did not seem possible for me to visit you personally any time soon, we determined to send Timothy to you in the meantime whilst I remained behind in Athens.

3:2 He is such a dear brother and minister of God; my colleague in the good news of what Christ accomplished. His mission was to strengthen you and to establish you in your spirit identity and belief.

3:3 He was to make sure that none of you is shaken by these pressure times that somehow inevitably seem to lie in our way.

3:4 When we were with you, we told you that we were to often face fierce contradictions, just as you have indeed witnessed it for yourselves! (*The religious and traditional systems of this world will always feel threatened by what the gospel communicates, since your freedom means that they can no longer abuse you with fear and sin-consciousness.*)

3:5 It was most urgent then for me to get first-hand feedback from Timothy regarding your faith, since I know how temptation would scrutinize you and attempt to nullify what we have labored for in you.

3:6 So you can imagine how the wonderful news of your faith and love blessed us! Timothy returned with the happy tidings of how affectionately you remember me and also long to see me, even as I yearn for you.

3:7 We share such a constant bond in our oneness in Christ. Your faith greatly impacts and comforts us in our affliction and hard times.

3:8 Your strong standing in the Lord gives us such zest for life.

3:9 We cannot thank God enough for you! We dance with delight before him because of you!

3:10 You are constantly in our prayers, night and day; oh, how we long to see you face to face and thoroughly establish you in every area of your faith.

3:11 The God and Father of our Lord Jesus Christ will himself make a way for us to visit you.

3:12 We can already see how the Lord causes the love we have for you to dynamically impact each of you and burst its banks to flood the entire world!

3:13 The ¹dominion of the Christ life establishes you in blameless innocence before our God and Father in the constant awareness of his presence in our mutual togetherness with all the saints! (*The subject of the sentence is the Lord Jesus Christ from the previous verse. His lordship endorses the reign of the Christ life in us.*)

4:1 Finally then friends, we would earnestly implore you to mirror the walk which we share in this bond of oneness in the Lord Jesus. Live your lives fully in the delight of God.

4:2 For you are acquainted with the fact that Jesus Christ is the [1]source of our message. (*The word [1]paraggelia, from para, a preposition indicating close proximity, a thing proceeding from a sphere of influence, with a suggestion of union of place of residence, to have sprung from its author and giver, originating from, denoting the point from which an action originates, intimate connection; and angellos, to announce*

4:3 The resolve of God declares you innocent; this announcement frees you from fornication. (*The resolve of God is declared in his accomplished redemption of the life of our design in Christ. Fornication is a form of idolatry, which is to be engaged with a distorted image of yourself. It is to be obsessed with something that you feel you must have in order to complete you. Just like Eve was attracted to eat the fruit of the "I-am-not-tree".*)

4:4 Everyone of you should take ownership of your bodies with utmost care. The vessel takes its [1]value from the treasure it holds. (*The word [1]timay means a valuing by which the price is fixed. See 2 Corinthians 4:7*)

4:5 Lusting after things with an all-consuming longing is typical of people who do not know how complete they already are in God.

4:6 In all of your dealings with one another, whether in business or the mere day-to-day domestic and social matters, live [1]from the persuasion of your mutual likeness, just as we have given testimony to and instructed you in the revelation of the Lord's righteousness. (*The word [1]ekdike is traditionally, sadly, often associated with judgment and punishment! However the two components of this word are the preposition ek, which always points to source or origin, and dike, which means two parties finding likeness in each other. This is also the root of the word for righteousness, dikaiosune. The revelation of Paul's gospel declares how God succeeded in Christ to cancel all grounds for separation, hostility, inferiority and condemnation and how God's faith redeemed our blameless oneness. See Romans 1:17. The gospel is the happy announcement of the finished work of Christ and not a new compromised set of rules! Many traditional translations and interpretations do not distinguish between the deadly duty-driven law of self-effort and the life giving love-driven law of faith! Romans 3:27*)

4:7 By design God has [1]defined us as pure and not unclean. (*The word [1]kaleo means to surname, to identify by name.*)

4:8 This is not to be regarded lightly as mere good advice, since God has given us his Holy Spirit endorsing our holiness unto him, just as he has separated himself unto us!

4:9 I need not even write to you about your fondness for one another since the love of God is best taught by him within!

4:10 I know your affection for your fellow family throughout Macedonia. From this place of our close union in our [1]common origin we anticipate the ever [2]increasing impact of love's irresistible impression. *(Our common origin, [1]parakaleo; The word, [2]perisseuo means to super-abound.)*

4:11 Cultivate the [1]highest esteem for that which is of value and honor; [2]cease from striving; mind your own business and give whatever you do your personal touch! These practical instructions are all part and parcel of the same [3]source as our constant sphere of influence. *(The beautiful word [1]philotemeomai, means to have a fondness for value and honor. The word [2]hesuchatzo means to rest and to cease from striving. See commentary note on the word [3]paraggelia in verse 2)*

4:12 Always maintain a good attitude towards those who still see themselves as outside of your company; do not hint for favors, echo completeness.

4:13 I do not want you to be ignorant concerning those who seem to be fast asleep in their indifference and unbelief. There is no need for you to grieve as if they are beyond hope! *(See 1 Cor 15:51 [1]Ponder this mystery, I want to show you something that you have never seen before: [2]everyone will awaken out of sleep; we will [3]all experience exactly the same change. (In other words, [1]idou musterion, Look! A Mystery! And [2]pantes ou koimethesometha, means no one will sleep; and [3]pantes de allangesometha; everyone will be changed.)*

4:14 We believe that Jesus died and rose again, and that he fully represents and includes even those who have not awoken unto him yet. God will [1]lead them to realize that they are in Jesus. *(The word [1]ago means to lead as a shepherd leads his sheep. See 1 Corinthians 1:30, Ephesians 1:4.)*

4:15 We give voice to the word of the Lord; we are God's wake-up call to them that are asleep! We are exhibiting the [1]immediate tangible presence of the Lord and shall not [2]exclude them! *(The word [1]parousia means immediate presence. See my comment in 1 Thessalonians 2:19. See the use of the word [2]phthanō, to prevent, to hinder or exclude, also in 2 Corinthians 10:14, Our ministry to you is proof that there are no geographic limitations which could possibly exclude you from the gospel of Jesus Christ! See also 1 Thessalonians 3:12, "We can already see how the Lord causes the love we have for you to dynamically impact each of you and burst its banks to flood the entire world!" The people who dwelt in darkness have seen a great light! The true light that enlightens everyone has come! And the glory of the Lord shall be revealed and all flesh shall see it together!)*

4:16 The Lord will personally step out of the invisible heavenly realm into our immediate visible horizon with an inciting shout, announcing his triumphant reign in the trumpet-like billowing voice of God; and even the dead will rise from their sleep, since they too are included in Christ!

4:17 In the wake of their arising we will all be gathered into a large dense multitude of an innumerable throng of people, united as one, like the particles of water in a cloud, and we will encounter the Lord in the very air we breathe and so shall we continually celebrate our I-am-ness in our union with him. *(This is the moment that redemption declares, where Deity and humanity are married. The Bride and her Groom are united!)*

4:18 The fact that we are all deeply connected in the same source of our 'beingness' causes us to be constantly engaged in this conversation with one another.

5:1 I do not need to speculate about [1]specific prophetic moments or even mention [2]significant dates. *(The word [1]xronos, speaks of a specific space or portion of time, an individual opportunity, or season; [2]kairos, a fixed and definite time, the decisive epoch waited for.)*

5:2 You know for yourselves from experience how the day of the Lord suddenly dawns like a thief in the night! *(Acts 9:3 Now as he journeyed he approached Damascus, and suddenly a light from heaven flashed about him. 2 Corinthians 4:6 For it is the God who said, "Let light shine out of darkness," who has shone in our hearts to give the light of the knowledge of the glory of God in the face of Christ. Isa 9:2 The people who walked in darkness have seen a great light; those who dwelt in a land of deep darkness, on them has light shined. Joh 1:9 A new day for humanity has come. The authentic light of life that illuminates everyone was about to dawn in the world!)*

5:3 The systems of this world of darkness and unbelief, which held the masses under their pseudo-sway of make-belief peace and security shall suddenly be broken into, like travail upon a woman with child, and none of their captives shall remain under their claim! *(The gates of Hades shall not prevail!)*

5:4 You are no longer in darkness; there are no daunting surprises waiting for you like a thief in the night!

5:5 All of you are begotten of light, the Day of the Lord is your true parent! Neither night nor darkness have any claim on you!

5:6 Live alert and you will not become intoxicated by the indifference of others.

5:7 Sleeping and drunkenness are typical things people do at night, but now the day of the Lord has dawned within us and has put an end to the slumbering effect and intoxication of the practices of darkness.

5:8 So let us clothe ourselves with day-garments, protecting our sober seeing by having our hearts fully guarded by the breastplate of love-inspired faith, and having our minds encircled, like a helmet, with an expectation which is consistent with what salvation declares!

5:9 For God did not set us up for disappointment; he is not teasing us with [1]desires that we desperately reach for but cannot attain to! He has brought us to a place where we are surrounded by the poetry of what salvation communicates in the lordship of Jesus Christ. *(The word often translated, wrath, is the word [1]orge, from oregomai which means to stretch oneself out with strong and passionate desire.)*

5:10 The fact that he died our death is equally valid to those who are awake to its effect or still fast asleep in their indifference to it; we are together destined to live in the [1]closest possible association with him! *(The word [1]hama is a particle of union denoting close association.)*

5:11 Continue, as you so eloquently do, to edify one another by cultivating the environment of your [1]close association in your joint-genesis. *(The word [1]parakaleo is here translated as our joint-genesis)*

5:12 We also entreat you as our fellow family, birthed from the same womb, that you recognize those whose toil is evidenced in you; those who are appointed to be your guides in the Lord and who re-align your thinking.

5:13 You can confidently lavish your esteem and extravagant love upon them because of your immense appreciation for their work! Be at peace within yourselves, joined into oneness, into a place of union, which cannot be disturbed.

5:14 And we remind you of our joint-genesis as our point of reference for you to re-align the thinking of those who seem to have lost life's rhythm; encourage the fainthearted; be the sounding board to them who feel weak; be super patient with one and all!

5:15 No-one is to requite evil with evil, regardless of how much someone may seem to deserve retaliation! Never allow the old "law and judgment language" to influence you again! At all times, under all circumstances, let that which is good set the pace in your dealing with every single person, both those who are "in" as well as the so-called "outsiders"! *(If we are to treat offenders like that, how could we possibly reason that God is about to strike the world with 'punishment' like a "thief in the night"? Are we to be more tolerant than God?)*

5:16 Be cheerfully happy at all times!

5:17 Constantly engage your thoughts in worshipful prayer.

5:18 Your gratitude is not based on anything fragile or fading, but secured in the fact that God's purpose for you was concluded in Christ Jesus.

5:19 Do not suffocate the flame of the Spirit within you.

5:20 The prophetic word is not to be underestimated.

5:21 Test everything like one would test gold to determine its true value, then treasure that which is precious with great care.

5:22 Distance yourselves immediately from every practice remotely related to the fruit of the "I-am-not-tree", which is the typical exhausting [1]law of works system. *(The tree of the knowledge of good and evil [[1]poneros] represents mankind's lost sense of identity and righteousness, where the universal pursuit of humanity would now be their constant effort to achieve righteousness by means of their own works. This inevitably leads to disappointment where shame replaces innocence, and union and fellowship are lost. The word evil, **poneros**, suggests being full of hardships, labors and annoyances.)*

5:23 There, away from any effort of your own, discover how the God of perfect [1]peace, who fused you skillfully into oneness - just like a master craftsman would dovetail a carpentry joint - has personally perfected and sanctified the entire harmony of your being without your help! He has restored the detailed default settings. You were re-booted to fully participate in the life of your design, in your spirit, soul and body in blameless innocence in the [2]immediate presence of our Lord Jesus Christ. *(It is not in my "I-used-to-be-ness" or "I'm-trying-to-become-ness", but in my "I-am-ness!" The word [1]eirene, translated peace, refers to the dove-tail joint in carpentery. The word [2]parousia, suggests immediate presence; see my comment on 1 Thessalonians 2:19.)*

5:23 There, away from any effort of your own, discover how the God of perfect [1]peace, who fused you skillfully into oneness - just like a master craftsman would dovetail a carpentry joint - has personally perfected and sanctified the entire harmony of your being without your help! He has restored the detailed default settings. You were re-booted to fully participate in the life of your design, in your spirit, soul and body in blameless innocence in the [2]immediate presence of our Lord Jesus Christ. *(It is not in my "I-was-ness" or "I-used-to-be-ness" or "I'm-trying-to-become-ness", but in my "I-am-ness!" The word [1]eirene, translated peace, refers to the dove-tail joint in carpentery. The word [2]parousia, suggests immediate presence; see my comment on 1 Thessalonians 2:19.)*

5:24 You are defined by the faith of God; you are his poetry!

5:25 Our precious family, continue to include us in your prayers.

5:26 Embrace one another with generous fondness!

5:27 I hereby solemnly implore you by the Lord's authority that this Epistle is read to everyone in every church! *(This was Paul's very first Epistle to the churches)*

5:28 The grace of our Lord Jesus is your constant companion. Amen! *(This first of Paul's Epistles was written from Athens)*

Timothy is one of Paul's first disciples. His mother was a Jewess and a believer, and his father a Greek."

Paul wrote to Timothy from prison in Rome. This is his last writing, as he suffered martyrdom shortly thereafter; the tone of this letter is quite emotional and personal in character.

His love for Timothy is obvious: "As my close associate and travel companion, you fully participate in everything that my teaching and life proclaims; you share my resolve, my belief, my fortitude, my love, my perseverance." 2 Timothy 3:10.

Paul says about Timothy in Philippians 2:19 "I trust the Lord that I will be able to send Timothy to you soon, this will be to me as if I am there personally with you!"

"I am reminded of your tears and my heart takes such joyful courage at the thought of being with you soon. I rejoice in the pure faith that I see in you. Remember that you are the third generation of a strong lineage of faith. The same unwavering persuasion that indwelt your grandmother Lois also resides in your mother Eunice and is now abundantly evident in you. This gives me all the more reason to remind you to fan the flame of God's grace gift within you into a blazing hot fire. Your life and ministry mirrors mine; I endorsed the gift of God's boldness within you when I laid my hands on you. Become fully acquainted with his gift in you, there is nothing timid about it; the dynamic of a mind liberated in the spirit of love is fearless and unstoppable. Do not let my imprisonment make you feel embarrassed about the testimony of Christ or your association with me! We are partners in the afflictions of the gospel and also in the intensity of God's power! We experience a constant download of power in the midst of affliction!" 2 Timothy 1:4-8.

He reminds Timothy that, "Everything that grace pointed to is now realized in Jesus Christ and brought into clear view through the gospel: Jesus is what grace reveals. He took death out of the equation and re-defines life; this is good news indeed! Grace is my commission; it is my job and joy to proclaim this message and guide the nations into a full understanding of the love initiative of God." 2 Timothy 1:10,11.

He encourages him to, "See the future of this gospel in everyone you influence; their persuasion is also their competence to instruct others in the same revelation." 2 Timothy 2:2.

"Avoid foolish questions that do not educate anyone but only breed quarrels. In your position as someone completely dedicated to the Lord there is no virtue in winning an argument but losing the person! I would much rather have you exhibit a sensitive courtesy towards all people; skillfully educate them and keep your cool under pressure. Your gentle way of instructing those who oppose you will inevitably lead them to see what God believes concerning them and give them the best possible chance to acknowledge the truth." 2 Timothy 2:23-25.

1:1 The amazing news of [1]announcing this life which is unveiled in Christ Jesus is what my ministry is all about! The promise is a Person! I, Paul, am a man on a [2]mission; God's [3]delightful desire sponsors me! *(The word [1]epangelia means the promise, announcement; [2]apostelo, a man with a mission; [3]thelema, delightful desire.)*

1:2 Dear Timothy, you are my son in everything that grace, mercy and peace communicate. This life has only one reference: God is our Father and Jesus is our Master and brother; the Christ life rules!

1:3 I love the [1]constant [2]thought of you; I am aware of our union in Christ 24/7. [3]Prayer is such a permanent thing when we discover God's [4]grace-echo in our [5]worship! Our [6]conscience celebrates our [7]pre-creation [8]innocence before God! *(The word [1]adialeiptos, means without interruption; [2]mneia, remembrance; [3]deeisis, prayer; [3]charin echo, grace echo, sometimes translated as thanksgiving; [5]latreuo, to worship without obligation, not under compulsion; [6]suneido, conscience, to see together [with God]; [7]progonos, before birth; [8]katharos, innocence, clean, pure. We celebrate an innocence that pre-dates Adam's fall! We have allowed an illegitimate sin-consciousness to prevail in our theologies and worship! The prodigal son's father had no reference to, or remembrance of past sins; imagine how that would spoil the party!)*

1:4 I am reminded of your tears and my heart takes such joyful courage at the thought of being with you soon.

1:5 I rejoice in the pure faith that I see in you. Remember that you are the third generation of a strong lineage of faith. The same unwavering persuasion that indwelt your grandmother Lois also resides in your mother Eunice and is now abundantly evident in you.

1:6 This gives me all the more reason to remind you to fan the flame of God's grace gift within you into a blazing hot fire. Your life and ministry mirrors mine; I endorsed the gift of God's boldness within you when I laid my hands on you.

1:7 Become fully acquainted with his gift in you, there is nothing timid about it; the dynamic of a [1]mind liberated in the spirit of love is fearless and unstoppable. *(The word [1]sophronismos means a saved mind, a mind saved from tolerating inferior thoughts. Isa 55:8-11)*

1:8 Do not let my imprisonment make you feel embarrassed about the [1]testimony of Christ or your association with me! We are partners in the afflictions of the gospel and also in the [2]intensity of God's power! We experience a constant [2]download of power in the midst of affliction! *(The [1]testimony of Christ is what gives us great liberty. Jesus and his finished work is God's testimony of our redeemed innocence. [2]kata, down, also to emphasize intensity.)*

1:9 He rescued the [1]integrity of our original [2]design and revealed that we have always been his own from the beginning, even [3]before time was. This has nothing to do with anything we did to qualify or disqualify ourselves. We are not talking religious good works or karma here. Jesus unveils grace to be the [4]eternal intent of God! Grace celebrates our pre-creation innocence and now declares our redeemed union with God in Christ Jesus. *(The word [1]hagios, means holiness, purity, integrity; hagios + kaleo is often translated, holy calling; [2]kaleo means to identify by name, to surname; [3]pro xronos aionios; pro, before; xronos, means a measured duration or length of time; aionios, speaks of ages. Paul speaks of God's mind made up about us, before the ages, which is a concept in which eternity is divided up into various periods, the shorter of which are comprehended in the longer; this was before calendar time existed, before the creation of the galaxies and constellations. [kairos is a due, or specific moment of time.] What happened to us in Christ is according to God's eternal purpose ([4]prothesis), which he has shown in every prophetic pointer and shadow; in the Hebrew tradition the showbread (prothesis) pointed to the true bread from heaven, the authentic word that proceeded from the mouth of God - Jesus, the incarnate word - sustaining the life of our design. See Heb 9:2 The first tented area was called the Holy Place; the only light here came from the lamp-stand illuminating the table upon which the showbread - prothesis - was presented. The Hebrew word is lechem paniym, face bread, or bread of the presence. The lampstand was a beautifully crafted golden chandelier portraying budding and blossoming almond branches. Remember that this is also what Jeremiah saw in Jer 1:12, when God said, "I am awake over my word to perform it." The same Hebrew word is used here, shaqad, the almond was called the 'awake tree', because it blossomed first, while the other trees were still in their winter sleep. The showbread pointed towards the daily sustenance of life in the flesh as the ultimate tabernacle of God, realized in the account of Jesus with the two from Emmaus. Their hearts were burning with resonance and faith while he opened the scriptures to them, and then around the table their eyes were opened to recognize him as the fulfillment of scripture, their true meal incarnated: Luke 24:27-31; Mankind shall not live by bread alone, but by the authentic thought of God, the Word proceeding from his mouth, the original intent, his image and likeness incarnated, revealed and redeemed in human life.*

Titus 1:2 This is the life of the ages that was anticipated for generations; the life of our original design announced by the infallible resolve of God before time or space existed. [Mankind's union with God is the original thought that inspired creation. There exists a greater dimension to eternity than what we are capable of defining within the confines of space and time! God's faith anticipated the exact moment of our redeemed union with him for all eternity!

This life was made certain before eternal time. [BBE 1949, Bible in Basic English])

1:10 Everything that grace pointed to is now realized in Jesus Christ and brought into clear view through the gospel: Jesus is what grace reveals. He took death out of the equation and re-defines life; this is good news indeed!

1:11 Grace is my commission; it is my job and joy to proclaim this message and guide the nations into a full understanding of the love initiative of God.

1:12 What I suffer because of this does not frighten me at all; faith has

made him so [1]apparent. I am absolutely persuaded that I am safe in him. We are no longer looking for a future event, or another day, the day has come! Death is not Doomsday; nothing can interrupt what he has done! *(Greek, [1]eido, Latin, video, to see, to know)*

1:13 Your conversation echoes what you have heard from me; you articulate the exact [1]drift of my thought. We are fully embraced in the same persuasion of love, immersed in Christ Jesus. *(The word [1]para, is a preposition indicating close proximity, a thing proceeding from a sphere of influence, with a suggestion of union of place of residence, to have sprung from its author and giver, originating from, denoting the point from which an action originates, intimate connection.)*

1:14 This priceless treasure is placed in your custody by the Holy Spirit who inhabits us.

1:15 I'm sure that you have heard by now that everyone in the province of Asia deserted me because of my chains, even Phygellus and Hermogenes.

1:16 Onesiphorus and his family have been a real gift from the Lord and a great encouragement to me. They have often taken tender care of me. The fact that I was jailed did not intimidate them at all.

1:17 When he was in Rome he immediately searched for me until he found me.

1:18 His visit meant so much to me that day in Rome; he made God's mercy tangible! No one knows better than you what a blessing he has been to us in Ephesus!

2:1 Timothy my son, grace is the source of your strength. It is so much more than a doctrine, it is the person of Jesus Christ; he embodies what grace reveals.

2:2 What you have learned from me is not a theory; you have witnessed ample evidence that confirms the integrity of my message. See the future of this gospel in everyone you influence; their persuasion is also their competence to instruct others in the same revelation. *(See Titus 1:9)*

2:3 Picture yourself as a soldier who endures hardship for the cause of Christ.

2:4 A soldier does not get himself distracted by civilian pursuits; he fully engages himself with the job at hand.

2:5 An athlete stands no chance of winning the trophy if he cheats in his training.

2:6 A farmer understands how much hard work goes into a harvest. *(In all three examples, Paul reminds Timothy that our aim is to win the world with the gospel; the world is the trophy and the harvest of the cross; this is the motivation of our ministry.)*

2:7 Ponder my words; the Lord will give you insight which will inspire you in every contradiction that you face.

2:8 Make my gospel emphasis the focus of your thoughts: Jesus Christ is the seed of David, he is the promised Messiah; his resurrection from the dead is the proof. *(It is the evidence that he completed the salvation of mankind by defeating death. Hosea 6:2, Ephesians 2:5, Romans 4:25, Acts 17:31)*

2:9 I might be in bonds, but the word of God is not. *(It might seem to some that my suffering contradicts what I preach, but it cannot! My ministry is measured by the word not by my circumstances. See Colossians 1:24)*

2:10 This gives me more than enough reason not to quit. I desire for everyone to discover the fact that the life of their ¹design is redeemed in Christ Jesus; this is the timeless intent of God. *(The word ¹eklegomai, ek, source, origin, and legomai from logos, word, thus the life of our design.)*

2:11 The logic of God endorses our faith: we were included in his death and are therefore equally included in his resurrection.

2:12 Sufferings do not distract us; neither do they contradict our joint position with him in the throne room, the Christ-life rules. If we ¹contradict ourselves *(behave unlike ourselves),* he will contradict us and prove us wrong! *(The word ¹arneomai means to contradict.)*

2:13 Our unbelief does not change what God believes; he cannot contradict himself! *(See Rom 3:3,4 What we believe about God does not define him; God's faith defines us. God cannot be untrue to himself!)*

2:14 Gently remind your audience always of these things which focus on the fact that the life of your design is redeemed in Christ Jesus, because we were included in his death and are therefore equally included in his resurrection. This the foundation of our faith and cannot be contradicted by any persecution, because God cannot be untrue to himself! Let your testimony in your face to face encounter with the Lord, speak for itself! You don't need to engage in a war of words to desperately try and defend doctrines and perceptions! Instead of proving profitable, these debates are catastrophic to the faith of your students! To mix two systems will certainly confuse your audience! *(See verse 10, 11 and 2 Corinthians 5:14 & 15)*

2:15 ¹Without any delay ²live your life from a place where you are familiar with the complete approval of God; you do not need to apologize for the fact that your experience might be a contradiction to your faith! What God believes about you needs no defense! There is such an immediate authority in ³clarity! Truth triumphs over every contradiction! It makes a clear-cut division between light and darkness; the word of truth shows distinctly that the duty-driven law of works and annoyances and the love-driven law of perfect liberty have nothing in common! *(The word ¹spoudazō means to use speed, to be prompt, immediately. The word ²paristemi from para, a preposition indicating close proximity, a thing proceeding from a sphere of influence, with a suggestion of union of place of residence, to have sprung from its author and giver, originating from, denoting the point from which an action originates, intimate connection; and istemi, to position. The word ²alētheia means not concealed, truth, clarity.)*

2:16 Do not engage in any conversation that may sound pious but carries no content; it only leads to lengthy and meaningless ungodly debates.

2:17 Their conversation consumes like ¹gangrene; Hymenaeus and Philetus are typical examples. *(Greek, gaggraina, Gangarine.)*

2:18 They have completely lost track of the truth by arguing that the resurrection of Christ has no further relevance. Any teaching that distracts from humanity's joint-inclusion in Jesus' resurrection turns belief upside down! *(See verses 8 & 11. The inclusion of mankind in the death and resurrection of Christ is the focal point of the gospel! 1 Corinthians 2:8 Neither the politicians nor the theologians of the day had a clue about this mystery [of mankind's association in Christ]; if they did, they would never have crucified the Lord whose death redeemed our glory!)*

2:19 The foundation of what God believes about you stands immovable and beyond dispute regardless of human opinion or contradiction! The inscription and impression made by the signet ring of God is his signature in your innermost being; he knows you as his own. Let everyone see themselves defined by the name of Christ and depart from everything which does not reveal likeness.

2:20 Even in mega-rich households there are not only vessels of gold and silver but also of wood and clay; a vessel's usefulness defines its true value. Even though their functions differ, each vessel is equally important.

2:21 Realize your individual value and stop discrediting yourself! You are indispensable for your Master's use; he knows exactly what he has in you; be ready for any good work! *(See 2:12 If we contradict ourselves [behave unlike ourselves], he will contradict us and prove us wrong! Also 2:13 Our unbelief does not change what God believes; he cannot be untrue to himself!)*

2:22 The best way to escape the snare and distractions of youthful lusts, which are often typified by an all consuming longing for forbidden pleasures, is to pursue and engage your life actively in everything that celebrates your redeemed oneness. Instead of a sin-consciousness, cultivate a righteousness-consciousness. Become addicted to the adventures of faith; let the agape-love of God romance you into his rest where you cease from striving and bask in completeness. Feast on peace, celebrate your joint togetherness with everyone who has mutually discovered their original identity in the Lord. Live your life from this place of innocence, from your heart.

2:23 Avoid foolish questions that do not educate anyone but only breed quarrels.

2:24 In your position as someone completely dedicated to the Lord there is no virtue in winning an argument but losing the person! I would much rather have you exhibit a sensitive courtesy towards all people; skillfully educate them and keep your cool under pressure.

2:25 Your gentle way of instructing those who oppose you will inevitably lead them to see what God believes concerning them and give them the best possible chance to acknowledge the truth.

2:26 And so they will escape the intoxicating influence of the fallen mindset and the enslaving dictates of the devil.

3:1 Know also that there will be days where the ¹extremities of people's fallen mindsets will be very obvious; where the ²gulf between heavenly grace-thinking and earthly legalism-thinking will be most pronounced. *(The word ¹escahtos, extreme, is the superlative form of the word echo, to hold or to resonate. The "last days" doctrine - eschatology, is associated with this word. The word ²chalepos from chalao means to loosen, to slacken, to let down from a higher place to a lower. From 'I am' to 'I am not'; from finished to unfinished; from gift to reward; from love to judgment.)*

3:2 For people will be absorbed with their own selfish ambitions; in love with money and the illusion of how it could make their dreams come true; living a lie of pretence and vanity; loving the limelight; engaged in hurtful gossip and indifferent to their parents; taking everything for granted; ungrateful and having no genuine regard for that which is sacred.

3:3 Typically calloused and without affection; unforgiving, displaying the characteristic of an accusing diabolical mindset, they are without self-control; savage and cynical!

3:4 They easily betray friendship; are typically impulsive, living in pretence like a fire that is all smoke and no flame! Addicted to sensual pleasures but averse to God!

3:5 Their make-belief devotion denies the very dynamic of God! Avoid their hypocrisy!

3:6 They sneak into the homes of vulnerable women like wolves in sheep's clothing, and under the pretence of "ministry" they shepherd them into snares of exaggerated longings and the intoxicating lies of law-language!

3:7 These women are like sitting ducks, they never seem to learn. They fall for anything that remotely sounds like a "Bible-study" and fail to tell the difference between "window-shopping" the promises and "mirror-gazing" the truth!

3:8 These guys, with their deadly legalistic Jewish agendas, seem to be on par with the two Egyptian magicians, Jannes and Jambres, who tried their best tricks to compete with Moses! The supernatural is not proof of faith! These people oppose the truth *(of grace)*; their minds are fully engaged in selling their religious self-help programs, and they stubbornly refuse to acknowledge what God believes about them. *(Remember Israel died in the wilderness because of unbelief, which was believing a lie about themselves, not because of a lack of the supernatural! Numbers 13:33, Joshua 2:11)*

3:9 Enough is ¹enough! Their self-help systems are exhausted; their folly shall be on exhibit for all to realize, just like Jannes and Jambres! *(See Rom 13:12 It was ¹night for long enough; the day has arrived. Cease immediately with any action associated with the darkness of ignorance. Clothe yourself in the radiance of light [the night is far spent, ¹prokopto, as a blacksmith forges a piece of metal until he has hammered it into its maximum length.])*

3:10 As my close associate and travel companion, you fully participate in everything that my teaching and life proclaims; you share my resolve, my belief, my fortitude, my love, my perseverance.

3:11 You have witnessed the persecutions and hardships that I endured in Antioch, Iconium and Lystra; at anytime I could have been swept away by these, but the Lord dramatically rescued me out of every single situation!

3:12 Somehow, everyone who determines to live a life entwined in [1]beauty and worship in Christ Jesus will be persecuted. (The word [1]eusebos, from eu, good, well done, and sebomai, to adore, revere, worship, is born as the fruit of euaggelion, the well done announcement, the good of the good news! The spontaneity of such worship often seems to offend those engaged in a system controlled by the legalistic rituals of institutional religion.)

3:13 People who are trapped in the mindset of [1]hardships, labors and annoyances will continue to desperately try to get mileage out of a dead and redundant system. The [2]lie that they believe is the very currency in which they trade. (The word, [1]poneros, means hardships labors and annoyances. [2]Deceived and deceiving.)

3:14 In sharp contrast to this deceptive duty-driven system, continue to fully engage yourself in the certainty of what you have learned, knowing the integrity of your source.

3:15 The sacred scriptures that you were raised with from your mother's womb dynamically pointed you to the [1]explicit clarity of salvation! God's [2]belief was always wrapped up in Christ Jesus! (The Greek word for wisdom, [1]sophos, from saphe, that which is clear. The words [2]tes pisteos are in the genetive case which points to ownership, belonging to. "Righteousness by his (God's) faith defines life." [Habakkuk 2:4; 3:17-19]. Instead of reading the curse when disaster strikes, Habakkuk realizes that the Promise out-dates performance as the basis to mankind's acquittal).

3:16 Jesus Christ and his work of salvation is the theme of scripture. The [1]value of [2]scripture in its most complete context is always found in [3]God's prophetic voice inspiring a [4]thorough education in the revelation of righteousness! This is what carries the [3]breath of God and gives substance and [5]proof to accurately [7]gauge what is being [6]taught. (Humanity's righteousness, lost in Adam would be redeemed again in Christ. The breath of God, meaning [3]the words that proceed from his mouth, [4]educates us in the understanding of our original identity, likeness and innocence. The teaching of righteousness gives significance to scripture. "You search the scriptures, because you think that in them you have eternal life; and it is they that bear witness to me; yet you refuse to come to me that you may have life. John 5:39 ,40. The promise will become a Person, and in his death he would be the Lamb of God laying down his life to die humanity's death. Throughout the writings of Moses and the prophets and the psalms, God speaks in Messianic language, revealing his resolve to redeem his image and likeness in human form. "And beginning with Moses and all the prophets, *he interpreted to them in all the scriptures the things concerning himself." Luke 24:27 "They said to each other, did not our hearts burn within us while he talked to us on the road, while he opened to us the scriptures?" Luk 24:32 "Then he said to them, these are my words which I spoke to you, while I was still with you, that everything written about me in the law of Moses and the prophets and the psalms must be fulfilled. Then he opened their minds to understand the scriptures, and said to them, Thus it is written, that the Christ should suffer and on the third day rise from the dead" Luk 24:44-46*

"Ask a sign of the LORD your God; let it be deep as Sheol or high as heaven. But you would not, therefore the Lord himself will give you a sign. Behold, a young woman shall conceive and bear a son, and shall call his name Immanuel." Isa 7:11-14. "For unto us a child is born, to us a son is given; and the government will be upon his shoulder, and his name will be called Wonderful Counselor, Mighty God, Everlasting Father, Prince of Peace. Of the increase of his government and of peace there will be no end." Isaiah 9:6,7. See also Psalm 22 and Isaiah 53. In his resurrection on the third day, God would co-quicken humankind and co-raise us together with him! Hosea 6:2, Ephesians 2:5. Human life will again be the tabernacle of God! "Destroy this temple, and in three days I will raise it up." John 2:19. "For as Jonah was three days and three nights in the belly of the whale, so will the son of man be three days and three nights in the heart of the earth. " Mathew 12:40. "On the third day Esther put on her royal robes and stood in the inner court of the king's palace, opposite the king's hall. The king was sitting on his royal throne inside the palace opposite the entrance to the palace; and when the king saw Queen Esther standing in the court, she found favor in his sight and he held out to Esther the golden scepter that was in his hand. Then Esther approached and touched the top of the scepter." Esther 5:1,2

*In many fragments of prophetic thought, God would [1]heap up the evidence as [5]proof of his purpose to raise fallen mankind up to be [7]co-elevated with him, standing tall like a mountain-monument! The little stone that was cut out by no human hand is destined to strike that image of vanity and piety on its feet of iron and clay, to remove every trace of the substitute, man-made self-image with its glorious head of golden glitter and its silvery bust and bronze body. The stone will become in its place a Rock that fills the whole earth; the true image and likeness of God, restored and revealed in ordinary human life. (Dan 2:32-35) "And the ends of the earth shall remember and return to the Lord!" Psalm 22:27; "The prophets who prophesied of the grace that was to be yours, searched and inquired about this salvation; they inquired what person or time was indicated by the Spirit of Christ within them when predicting the sufferings of Christ and the subsequent glory." 1 Peter 1:10,11 See also Romans 4:25 "Our sins [1]resulted in his death; our redeemed righteousness resulted in his resurrection." His resurrection is the receipt for our acquittal. This is one of the most important statements in the entire Bible. Why was Jesus handed over to die? Because of, **dia**, our sins. Why was he raised from the dead? Because of, **dia**, we were justified! His resurrection reveals our righteousness! Here is the equation: his cross = our sins; his resurrection = our innocence! If we were still guilty after Jesus died, his resurrection would neither be possible nor relevant! This explains Acts 10:28 and 2 Cor 5:14 and 16. Paul proclaims to a group of idol wor-*

shipping Greek philosophers, in Acts 17:31, that because human life is the offspring of God, and in the light of what happened to mankind in Christ, God now urgently implores all of mankind everywhere to awaken in their understanding "because God had fixed a day on which he would judge the world righteous by a man whom he has appointed, and of this he has given proof to all mankind by raising him from the dead!" The resurrection of Jesus from the dead and mankind's mystical union with him in God's economy, the gospel announces our redeemed identity and innocence! This is what the teaching of righteousness is all about!

The following words are highlighted: [1]***ōphelimos**, valuable, profitable, from* **ophellō***, to heap up, to accumulate benefit;* [2]**pasa graphe***, scripture in completeness, context;* [3]**theopneustos** *, God-breathed, Divine inspiration;* [4]**pros paideian ten en dikaiosune***, for the purpose of a thorough education in the revelation of righteousness;* [5]**elegchos***, proof, evidence;* [6]**didaskalia***, teaching, instruction;* [7]**epanorthosis***, from* **epi***, continual influence upon,* **ana,** *upwards, and* **orthos** *from* **oros***, a mountain from* **airo***, to lift, to elevate, and* **ornis***, a bird, see Isaiah 40:3-5, & 31*

3:17 Being thoroughly schooled in the word of righteousness will equip you to be fully refreshed in sparkling newness of life, giving you a fresh start to tackle every relevant and good task with renewed inspiration.

4:1 I give testimony to this word as one standing face to face with God and the Lord Jesus Christ, who is about to be equally visible to those who have died as well as those who are still alive; the dominion of the Christ-life has the final say.

4:2 Broadcast the word on every occasion, even when it doesn't seem to be convenient; give evidence to this message; value every individual in your audience highly; esteem people's authentic identity passionately; teach tirelessly!

4:3 There will be times when people will not relate to their [1]inner resonance, when it comes to discerning [2]sound instruction! Instead they would prefer the familiar language of the [3]fallen mindset and [4]desperately chase after titles and teachers who [5]entertain rather than educate; they would [6]accumulate for themselves libraries of information without any revelation! *(I have translated [1]anechomai, our inner-resonance; from ana, upward and echo, to hold, to resonate, which suggests an upward echo. Our minds are redeemed to engage with the resonance of our inner witness - we are co-seated together with Christ in heavenly places - which is contrasted with a mindset engaged with the fallen soul realm below; from [3]kata, downward. See Colossians 3:1,2 "Set your minds upon the things that are above and not upon the things below!" Also note Romans 1:18, where the word katecho is used - to echo downwards, to suppress is the opposite to anoche, to echo upwards - Romans 2:4 and Romans 3:26. Also 2 Corinthians 4:18 We are not keeping any score of what seems so obvious to the senses in the natural realm, it is fleeting and irrelevant. It is the unseen, eternal realm within us which has our full attention and captivates our gaze! A renewed mind conquers the space previously occupied by worthless pursuits and habits. The word [2]hugiaino, means sound, healthy, wholesome; the word [4]epithumia, means constant cravings, panting after in hot pursuit; [6]episōreuō means to heap up, to accumulate in piles; [5]knetho from knao, means to tickle the ear; it suggests to be entertained rather than educated! Seneca, a famos Greek philosopher in Paul's days, uses this word and says: "Some come to hear, not to learn, just as we go to the theater, for pleasure, to delight our ears with the speaking or the voice or the plays".)*

4:4 In their pursuit they would exchange the truth for man-made fictions and fables as their source of reference!

4:5 But you be vigilant in all things, don't allow the devastating things that you suffer to get to you! Continue in the full persuasion of your ministry as herald of the good news; you cannot have a more poetic job description!

4:6 So here I am, my life is poured out as a wine offering on the altar of ministry; I am ready to go! *(See also Philippians 2:17,18 "I want you to see my ministry to you as wine poured out upon the altar of your faith. I rejoice in the thought that we drink from the same source and therefore celebrate a mutual joy! Whatever you may suffer only concludes in joy! - Joy is a bold declaration, in the face of severe danger and suffering, that contradiction does not define us or have the final say in our lives. We know that whether we live or die, our message is unstoppable and that it is conquering the world.)*

4:7 Like a champion athlete I have run my race and completed the course; I have carefully ¹attended to the faith! (*The word ¹tereo means to attend carefully, to guard.*)

4:8 My wreath of righteousness awaits me as testimony to the Lord's righteous judgment. He will crown me in that day, the moment I step out of this body. I will not be the only one receiving a wreath of honor; everyone, ¹loving the brilliance of his appearing will be jointly crowned! (*In seeing him, everyone will see themselves, mirrored in him. The word ¹agape, from ago, to lead as a Shepherd leads his sheep, and pao, to rest. By the waters of reflection, my soul remembers who I am! Psalms 23:2,3. Note the 1st verse of chapter 4. See also 1 Corinthians 15:49-54 "The reduced state of the individual left its mark on mankind as being earthly; now the redeemed state of mankind confirms their origin in God and marks their new heavenly life. Just as we were once defined by the flesh (our earthly image) we are now defined by our spirit (our heavenly) image. Flesh and blood has a sell-by date; the bodies you live in now will not last forever. Ponder this mystery, I want to show you something that you have never seen before: everyone will awaken out of sleep; we will all experience exactly the same change. This will happen in an instant, in a blink of the eye: the final trumpet will sound, then the dead shall be raised and we, who are still alive, shall be instantly changed into a different kind of body. For this corruptible must be clothed with incorruption and this mortal must be clothed with immortality." Also 1 Thessalonians 4:14-18 "We believe that Jesus died and rose again, and that he fully represents and includes even those who have not awoken unto him yet. God will ¹lead them to realize that they are in Jesus. (The word ¹ago means to lead as a shepherd leads his sheep.) We give voice to the word of the Lord, we are God's wake-up call to them that are asleep! We are exhibiting the ¹immediate tangible presence of the Lord and shall not ²exclude those who are asleep! (The word ¹parousia means immediate presence. See the use of the word ²phthanō, to prevent, to hinder or exclude. The true light that enlightens everyone has come! And the glory of the Lord shall be revealed and all flesh shall see it together!) The Lord will personally step out of the invisible heavenly realm into our immediate visible horizon with an inciting shout, announcing his triumphant reign in the trumpet-like billowing voice of God; and even the dead will rise from their sleep! In the wake of their arising we will all be gathered into a large dense multitude of an innumerable throng of people, united as one, like the particles of water in a cloud, and we will encounter the Lord in the very air we breathe and so shall we continually celebrate our I-am-ness in our union with him. (This is the moment that redemption declares, where Deity and humanity are married. The Bride and her Groom are united!)The fact that we are all deeply connected in the same source of our 'beingness' causes us to be constantly engaged in this conversation with one another.*

Also Hebrews 12:1 "So now the stage is set for us: all these faith-heroes cheer us on, as it were, like a great multitude of spectators in the amphitheater. This is our moment. As with an athlete who is determined to win, it would be silly to carry any baggage of the old law-system that would weigh one down. Make sure you do not get your feet clogged up with sin-consciousness. Become absolutely streamlined in faith. Run the race of your spiritual life with total persuasion, persuaded in the success of the cross. 12:2 Look away from the shadow dispensation of the law and the prophets and fix your eyes upon Jesus. He is the fountainhead and conclusion of faith. He saw the joy (of mankind's salvation) when he braved the cross and despised the shame of it. As the executive authority of God (the right hand of the Throne of God) he now occupies the highest seat of dominion to endorse our innocence!" (Having accomplished purification of sins, he sat down. [Heb 1:3, Isa 53:11])

4:9 I really need you with me right now; would you get over here as quick as you can!

4:10 Demas abandoned me and left for Thessalonica; he has fallen in love with the current mindset of this philosophical religious age. Crescens is in Galatia province, Titus in Dalmatia.

4:11 Luke is the only one here with me. Make sure to bring Mark with you; he will be a great help in ministry.

4:12 I'm sending Tychicus to Ephesus.

4:13 Bring my winter coat that I left in Troas with Carpus; also the books and [1]parchments. *(The word [1]membranas, means skin, membrane, or parchment. Dressed skins were among the earliest materials for writing, and were in common use before the art of making paper from rags was discovered. These "parchments" seem to have been something different from "books," and probably refer to some of his own writings. They may have contained notes, memorandums, journals, or unfinished letters.)*

4:14 Alexander the coppersmith has been a real pain in the butt! Is it not wonderful though to know that the Lord's work on the cross even includes him! He is equally forgiven. *(He will be rewarded according to his [the Lord's] work!)*

4:15 I do warn you however to be on the lookout for him, since he has greatly opposed our message.

4:16 No one dared associate themselves with me during my preliminary hearing, instead they all scattered; I hold nothing against them!

4:17 Throughout my trial, I was so aware of the Lord's tangible presence; he strengthened me with dynamic boldness and assured me that my life will be an accurate conduit of the message articulated in its most complete context, for all the nations to hear! And I was snatched from the very jaws of the lion!

4:18 I am so persuaded that the same Lord who delivered me out of the Lion's jaws, also safeguards me from getting snared by the subtle attempts of the [1]law-guys to break in on the effortless rhythm of grace that I am addicted to! Our salvation celebrates his heavenly kingdom. We live our lives from a dominion far superior to the systems of the world; there is no fading to the glory of his kingdom! His eternal intent spans the ages! *(The words, [1]poneros ergon, refer to the law of works, hardships and annoyances.)*

4:19 Give Priscilla and Aquila a big hug from me! Also the family of Onesiphorus.

4:20 Erastus stayed behind in Corinth. I had to leave Trophimus in Miletus since he was sick.

4:21 Make sure you get here before winter. Eubulus, Pudens, Linus, Claudia, and all your friends send their greetings.

4:22 May your spirit continuously encounter his Lordship and grace.

Paul reminds Titus that mankind's union with God is the original thought that inspired creation. My mission is to persuade people of their origin in God; by bringing them into a complete understanding of the truth as the only valid reference to meaningful devotion.

Tit 2:11 The grace of God shines as bright as day making the salvation of humankind undeniably visible.

The following verses are some of the most profound in Paul's writings:

Tit 3:2 Gossip is out! Never have anything bad to say about anyone! You do not have to win every argument. Instead, avoid quarreling, be appropriate, always show perfect courtesy to one and all.

Tit 3:3 Do not be harsh on others. Remember that we, too, were typically foolish. We were stubborn and indifferent to spiritual things. Our addiction to the sensual and sexual kept us running around in circles. We were engaged in malice and spiteful jealousies. We were bored and lonely, often utterly disliking ourselves and hating one another!

Tit 3:4 But then, oh happy day! It was the generosity of God and his fondness for mankind that dawned on us like a shaft of light. Our days of darkness were over! Light shone everywhere, and we became aware: God rescued the human race!

1:1 Paul the bondman of God, on assignment by Jesus Christ; my mission is to persuade people of their ¹origin in God; by bringing them into a complete understanding of the truth as the only valid reference to ²meaningful devotion. *(The word traditionally translated as 'elect' is ¹eklego; ek is a preposition that always denotes origin or source and **lego,** is the word or the logic of God as in Jhn 1:1, "To go back to the very beginning is to find the Word already present there. The Logic of God defines the only possible place where humankind can trace their genesis." ²**eusebeia,** beautiful worship, adoration.)*

1:2 This is the life of the ¹ages which was anticipated for generations; the life of our original design announced by the infallible resolve of God before ²time or space existed. *(Mankind's union with God is the original thought that inspired creation. The word, ¹**aionios,** speaks of ages. Paul speaks of God's mind made up about us, before the ages, which is a concept in which eternity is divided up into various periods, the shorter of which are comprehended in the longer. The word, ²**xronos,** means a measured duration or length of time; **kairos** is a due, or specific moment of time. This was before the ages or any measure of calendar time existed, before the creation of the galaxies and constellations. There exists a greater dimension to eternity than what we are capable of defining within the confines of space and time! God's faith anticipated the exact moment of our redeemed union with him for all eternity!*

This life was made certain before eternal time. [BBE 1949, Bible in Basic English]

Hebrews 13:8 Take your lead from Jesus. He is your reference to the most complete life. In him yesterday is confirmed today and today mirrors tomorrow. What God spoke to us in Christ is as relevant now as it was in the prophetic past and will always be in the eternal future! [Jesus is the same yesterday, today, and forever; there is a history to our salvation that carries more authority and relevance than anything that ever happened in our past, or anything present in time or still to happen in the future. Imagine the enormity of eternity in his sameness before time was; and we were there in him all along! See Rom 8:34 What further ground can there possibly be to condemn mankind? In his death he faced our judgment; in his resurrection he declares our innocence; the implications cannot be undone! He now occupies the highest seat of authority as the executive of our redemption in the throne room of God. See Rom 8: 1, also Rom 4:25. The heavens declare his glory, night to night exhibits the giant solar testimony that is mathematically precise, revealing that God knew before time was the exact moment he would enter our history as a man, and the exact moment the Messiah would expire on the cross and be raised again from the dead!])

1:3 My message announces the completeness of time; God's eternal moment realized the logic of our salvation. *(But then the day dawned; the most complete culmination of time! [Gal 4:4] Everything predicted was concluded in Christ!*

John 1:14 Suddenly the invisible eternal Word takes on visible form! The Incarnation! In him, and now confirmed in us! The most accurate tangible display of God's eternal thought finds expression in human life! The Word became a human being; we are his address; he resides in us! He captivates our gaze!

Hebrews 1:1 Throughout ancient times God spoke in many fragments and glimpses of prophetic thought to our fathers. 1:2 Now, the sum total of this conversation with us, has finally culminated in a son. In his sonship, God declares him heir of all things. He is, after all, the author of the ages.

Hebrews 1:3 We have our beginning and our being in him. He is the force of the universe, sustaining everything that exists by the logic of his eternal utterance! Jesus is the radiant and flawless expression of the person of God. He makes the glorious intent of God visible and mirrors the ¹character and every attribute of God in human form. This powerful final utterance of God is the vehicle that carries the weight of the universe. What he communicates is the central theme of everything that exists. The content of his message celebrates the fact that God took it upon himself to successfully cleanse and acquit humankind. The man Jesus is now his right hand of power, the executive authority seated in the boundless measure of his majesty. He occupies the highest seat of dominion to endorse our innocence! His throne is established upon our redeemed righteousness. ["Having accomplished purification of sins, he sat down ..." More than two thousand years ago the conversation that had begun before time was recorded — sustained in fragments of thought throughout the ages, whispered in prophetic language, chiseled in stone and inscribed in human conscience and memory — became a man. Beyond the tablet of stone, the papyrus scroll or parchment roll, human life has become the articulate voice of God. Jesus is the crescendo of God's conversation with humankind; he gives context and content to the authentic thought. Everything that God had in mind for mankind is voiced in him. Jesus is God's language. His name defines his mission. As Savior of the world he truly redeemed the image and likeness of the invisible God and made him apparent again in human form, as in a mirror.])

1:4 Titus, you really are like a son to me in our mutual faith. The Father's favor, compassion, and tranquillity is yours; this is what our Master Jesus Christ restored us to through his great act of salvation.

1:5 There is still some unfinished business in Crete; I would like you to give it your undivided attention by appointing a leadership team in every city exactly as I have instructed you.

1:6 Here are some practical guidelines: appoint people with unquestionable integrity; consider what kind of husband and father your potential leader is. He must obviously be a man who is completely devoted to his wife and whose children are steadfast and are not troublemakers or unruly.

1:7 An overseer must be above reproach; if he has a bad reputation in the community you do not want him to be part of your leadership team! A leader administrates God's economy and must therefore be a competent manager of God's business. A person with his own selfish agenda, or one who loses his temper easily, or someone that is known to over indulge in food or wine, or a bully, or greedy for money is certainly not a candidate.

1:8 He must be ¹fond of strangers and able to make people feel immediately at home. Your leader must be a ²caring person and one who shows

³unselfish devotion to the welfare of others. Someone ³sober-minded, whose thought-life is sorted out; one who walks in the ⁴revelation of the finished work of Christ; a man of ⁵mercy and who is strong in spirit. *(The word, ¹philoxenos, means fond of strangers. The word, ²philagathos, translates as benevolent, good, kind, humane, generous, liberal, benign, philanthropic, altruistic. The word, ³sophrone, means a saved mind. The word, ⁴dikaion, translates as righteousness, the revelation of the finished work of Christ, and the word, ⁵hosios, is translated as mercy as in Acts 13:44, which is a quote from Isaiah 55:3 from the Hebrew word, ghesed, for mercy)*

1:9 The overseer ¹mirrors the persuasion of the word he was taught and is competent to instruct with accuracy and to entreat and convince those who oppose the message. *(The word, ¹antechomai, comes from anti meaning against, standing opposite, and echo; thus one who mirrors the word.)*

1:10 There are many who engage in worthless debates about their Jewish sentiments and playing mind-games in order to snare new believers into legalism.

1:11 By entreating and persuading them with wisdom, their influence will be silenced. The rot must be stopped since they have already confused entire families with their teachings and robbed them financially in the process.

1:12 According to one of their own so called "enlightened" leaders, the Cretans are known to be phony, lazy gluttons, and savage brutes.

1:13 This gives all the more reason that they need distinguished leaders who are capable of rebuking such behavior sharply and establish them in robust faith. *(We are not here to merely comment on people's behavioral trends; we are here to declare people free to live the life of their redeemed design! Faith sees that old life co-crucified with Christ and the new resurrected life emerge victoriously. Faith is not a "mickey-mouse" cover-up for sin; faith defeats sin.)*

1:14 Admonish them not to pay any attention to Jewish fiction and their man-made rules and regulations which achieve exactly the ¹opposite to what truth promotes. *(The word, ¹apostrepho, means to reverse).*

1:15 The truth proves everything to be pure but to those who are contaminated with unbelief in their minds and conscience everything seems to be equally stained with impurity. *(Unbelief is to believe a lie about yourselves. [Num 13:33 and 2 Cor 4:4])*

1:16 They might even pretend that they know God by saying a few nice clichés, but when it comes to real life the veneer cracks and the stench is nauseating; the effects of unbelief cannot be camouflaged.

2:1 Your message is in its own class; you instruct with distinction!

2:2 Encourage the senior men to be established in their [1]"I am-ness"; [2]focused in their faith; to be [3]distinguished with a [4]mind established in redemption realities and [5]comprehensive in their belief, their [6]love, and in their [7]fortitude. (*[1]"I am-ness" from **eimi**, I am; often translated, "to be". The word, [2]**nephalios**, means sober, focused, not to compromise their belief with Jewish sentiment; [3]**semnos**, means eminent, distinguished; [4]**sophron**, means a saved mind; [5]**hugiaino te piste** translate as unmixed, comprehensive in their faith; [6]**agape**, means to lead into rest, the love of God leads us to see in us and others what he sees in us; his rest celebrates our perfection, and [7]**hupomone**, means fortitude, to be steadfast, to remain the same, from **hupo**, under the influence of, subject to + **meno**, to continue to be present.*)

2:3 Instruct the elderly women also to exhibit a consecrated character in all their conduct. Encourage them not to [1]slander, neither are they to get intoxicated with wine; their example makes [2]beauty irresistibly attractive. (*The word, [1]**diabolos**, means devil, accuser, from **dia**, because of, and **ballo**, the fall; the devil and the fall of mankind are no longer our reference in conversation! Gossip (to be double minded about someone) is a form of intoxication to be avoided at all costs! The word, [2]**kalodidaskalos**, means irresistibly beautiful teaching.*)

2:4 They are to radiate a conversation that flows from a mind radically transformed by redemption realities. Their instruction should inspire young women to treat their husbands and children with tender affection. (*The word, **philandros**, and **philoteknos**, connote fond affection for their husbands and children. Paul uses this same combination in chapter 3:4. It is the fondness of God for mankind that persuaded our hearts! [**philanthropos**]*)

2:5 They are to be clearheaded and innocent in heart, creative homemakers, gentle, exclusive in their devotion to their husbands (*not flirting with other men*); nothing in their attitude or actions would distract from the word of God. Domestic life beautifully displays the fascination of the Incarnation.

2:6 In the same manner [1]incite the young men to become acquainted with their redeemed identity. (*[1]Incite, arouse, being alongside, from the Greek [1]**parakaleo**, derived from **para**, a preposition indicating close proximity, a thing proceeding from a sphere of influence, with a suggestion of union of place of residence, to have sprung from its author and giver, originating from, denoting the point from which an action originates, intimate connection, and **kaleo**, to identify by name, to surname.*)

2:7 Being a young man yourself, your day-to-day life mirror-echoes the typical mold into which your message translates [1]without any hint of the fallen mind-set; you excel in distinguished eminence and innocence. (*The word, [1]**adiaphthoria**, means without any hint of the fallen mind-set, from **a**, negative + **diaballo**, through the fall, cast down, devil, accuser, + **phtero**, to waste away, to pine. Neither the devil nor accusation feature in your conversation!*)

2:8 Your wholesome conversation will silence the opposition.

2:9 Employees are to give their undivided devotion to their bosses, making them proud of them in every respect. It is good advice never to give your boss any backchat, even if you think that you are in the right!

2:10 They are to have no hidden agenda, instead in the way they exhibit their faith they are making the message irresistibly attractive in everything they do.

2:11 The grace of God shines as bright as day making the salvation of humankind undeniably visible. *(For God's undeserved kindness has burst in upon us, bringing a new lease on life for all mankind. — Clarence Jordan)*

2:12 [1]The day and age we live in sets the stage for displaying the attraction of an [2]awe-inspired life; our [6]minds are rescued in the revelation of righteousness. We are in the [4]school of grace, instructed how to thoroughly [5]reverse the apathy and [3]indifference that erupts in a [5]wave of lust that would seek to dictate the day! *(The word, [1]aion, as in the day and age we live in; [2]eusebos, meaning godly, the attraction of devotion, awe; [3]asebeia, as in ungodliness, indifference; [4]paideou, training students; [5]arneomai, from a, negative, and rheo, pouring forth of utterance; [5]kosmikos epithumia, worldly lusts; [6]sophronos, saved minds; the revelation of righteousness shows how completely God redeemed mankind in Christ and empowers us to cultivate an innocence consciousness instead of a sin consciousness).*

2:13 Everyone must [1]welcome with open arms the outrageously blessed expectation; Jesus is what the world was waiting for! He radiates the brilliant intent of God, engineered by his greatness to rescue the world in him. *(The word, [1]prosdechomenoi, means to receive to oneself, to welcome with open arms.)*

2:14 He gave himself as sacrifice in [1]exchange for our freedom. We are [1]redeemed from every obligation and accusation under the law and declared absolutely innocent. He defines who we are! [2]Our brand name is "I am." We are exclusively his. We are a [3]passionate people; we excel in doing everything we do beautifully. *(The word, [1]lutroo, means ransom, redemption price, to purchase from slavery; [2]periousios, comes from peri, for sphere, circuit, locality, pertaining to, and eimi, "I am;" [3]zelotes, translates as zealous, passionate; and [4]kalos, as beautiful.)*

2:15 Continue to communicate content in your every conversation; [1]inspire and entreat with conviction and assertiveness; you are not at the mercy of anyone's [2]suspicious scrutiny. *(Encourage everyone to become acquainted with their redeemed identity, [1]parakaleo; and the word, [2]periphroneo, translates as to think beyond what is obvious, suspicious scrutiny.)*

3:1 Remind the Christians in Crete to respect their Roman officials; they must be ready to volunteer for any beneficial service required of them.

3:2 Gossip is out! Never have anything bad to say about anyone! You do not have to win every argument; instead, avoid [1]quarrelling, be appropriate, always show perfect courtesy to one and all. *(The word, [1]mache, means controversial, striving. You don't have to wait for people to change before you are nice to them. There is a big difference between "fake politeness" and perfect courtesy!)*

3:3 Do not be harsh on others. Remember that we, too, were typically foolish; we were stubborn and indifferent to spiritual things, our addiction to the sensual and sexual kept us running around in circles, we were engaged in malice and spiteful jealousies, we were bored and lonely, often utterly disliking ourselves and hating one another!

3:4 But then, oh happy day! It was the generosity of God and his fondness for mankind that dawned on us like a shaft of light. Our days of darkness were over! Light shone everywhere and we became aware: God rescued the human race! *(See 2:11)*

3:5 Salvation is not a reward for good behavior. It has absolutely nothing to do with anything that we have done. God's mercy saved us. The Holy Spirit endorses in us what happened to us when Jesus Christ died and was raised! When we heard the glad announcement of salvation it was like taking a deep warm bath! Our minds were [1]thoroughly cleansed and re-booted into [2]newness of life! *(The word [1]paliggenesia suggests a complete restoration to the original, in modern terms, rebooted. The word [2]anakainosis, from ana, upwards, and kainosis, newness, speaks of a fresh upward focus; a re-engaging with heavenly thoughts. See Col 3:1-3; also 1 Thess 1:5. We realized that we were indeed co-included, co-crucified, and co-raised and are now co-seated together with Christ in heavenly places! [See 2 Cor 5:14-21; Hosea 6:2; Eph 2:5, 6; and 1 Pet 1:3])*

3:6 The Holy Spirit is the extravagant Administrator of the salvation of Jesus Christ; he gushes forth in our midst like an artesian well. *(An artesian well is a well sunk through solid strata of sedimentary rock into strata from an area of a higher altitude than that of the well, so that there is sufficient pressure to force water to flow upwards. From the French word, artesian, referring to the old French province Artois, where such wells were common.*

In John 7:37-39, John records how Jesus witnessed the eighth day, the great and final day of the Feast of Tabernacles, when, according to custom, the High Priest would draw water from the Pool of Siloam with a golden jar, mix the water with wine, and then pour it over the altar while the people would sing with great joy from Psalm 118:25-26, and also Isaiah 12:3; "Therefore with joy shall we draw water from the wells of salvation!" Then, Jesus, knowing that he is the completeness of every prophetic picture and promise, cried out with a loud voice: "If anyone is thirsty, let him come to me and drink! If you believe that I am what the scriptures are all about, you will discover that you are what I am all about, and rivers of living waters will gush from your innermost being!" See Rom 5:5)

3:7 His grace [1]vindicates our innocence. We have also [2]become heirs to the life that we have always longed for, the life of the ages. *(God's gift has restored our relationship with him and given us back our lives. — The Message.*

Both verbs pointing to our righteousness, as well as the fact that by the same grace we have become heirs, are in the aorist tense, [1]dikaiothentes, having been declared righteous, and [2]genethomen, having been begotten. The aorist tense presents an occurrence in summary, viewed as a whole from the outside, almost like a snapshot of the action.

Titus 1:2 This is the life of the ages that was anticipated for generations; the life of our original design announced by the infallible resolve of God before time or space existed.

This life was made certain before eternal time. (BBE). Mankind's union with God is the original thought that inspired creation.)

3:8 You can confidently lean the weight of your being on this word! I want you to be emphatic about this; encourage the believers to be conscious of the fact that they are the [1]custodians of this message. In their day-to-day lifestyle they positively advertise its attraction and beauty. *(The word, [1]proistemi, is protector, guardian)*

3:9 Avoid confusing speculations and debates about genealogies and quarrelsome controversies about the law; it is folly to engage in such [1]useless conversation. It is like chewing chewing-gum that has long lost its flavor! *(The word, [1]mataios, translates as folly, of no purpose, from maten, which is the accusative case of a derivative from the base of masso, to chew, to gnaw, like eating food with zero nutritional value.*

Hebrews 13:9 Do not be swayed by distracting speculations. Any influence foreign to what grace communicates, even if it seems very entertaining and carries the Christian label, is to be shunned. Feast on grace; do not dilute your diet with legalism. There is no nourishment left in the law. What's the use of being busy but not blessed? [Legalism includes any form of self-sacrifice or self-effort with the illusion of gaining further favor from God or improving your spiritual standing before God]).

3:10 If a person continues to be argumentative and factious *(distracting from the essence of the gospel),* **and you have brought it to his attention several times, then it is better to avoid his company.**

3:11 Such a person is obviously out of line and brings himself under condemnation by [1]his own autocratic ruling. *([1]autokatakritos)*

3:12 I will send Artemas to you, or possibly Tychicus, and then I want you to join me as soon as possible in Nicopolis where I have decided to spend the winter.

3:13 Do whatever you can to assist Zenas the Scribe and Apollos with their trip. Make sure they lack nothing. *(Acts 18:24, 19:1, 1 Cor 16:12)*

3:14 Encourage our people to be productive and generous.

3:15 We all send you our fond greetings; salute our friends in the faith. Grace!

The Author

The fact that Paul's message, which is the revelation of our restored innocence, based on the finished work of the cross, as witnessed in all his Epistles, is evident throughout this magnificent study, overshadows the argument that his signature as probable author is absent.

The Sabbath Rest

In Christ the Sabbath Rest is no longer a shadow prefiguring the real, a token holy day in the week, but the celebration of a perfect redemption in which the exact image and likeness of God is revealed and redeemed in human form. Mankind's innocence is redeemed. "Having made purification for sins, he sat down ..." The executive authority of his throne is established on the fact of our innocence! Sabbath is now a place of God's unhindered enjoyment of mankind and mankind's unhindered enjoyment of God. Through the torn veil of his flesh, he has triumphantly opened a new and living way for mankind into the life of their design in the loving embrace of their Maker.

This letter has a Hebrew audience in mind and is written to exhort the Jewish believer neither to underestimate such a great salvation, or to clutter the message with redundant Jewish rituals and sentiments.

Under the dispensation of the law of performance, historic Israel failed to access the redemptive Sabbath of God and remained snared in an inferior slave-mentality, "we are insignificant grasshoppers in our eyes". Numbers 13:33

Let us therefore be prompt to understand and fully appropriate that rest and not fall again into the same snare of unbelief.

The message that God spoke in Christ becomes a living and powerful influence in us, cutting like a surgeon's scalpel, sharper than a soldier's sword, piercing to the deepest core of human conscience to the dividing of soul and spirit ending the dominance of the sense realm and its neutralizing effect upon the human spirit. In this way a person's spirit is freed to be the ruling influence again in the thoughts and intentions of the heart. The scrutiny of this word detects every possible disease, discerning the body's deepest secrets where joint and bone-marrow meet. *(The moment we cease from our own efforts to justify ourselves by yielding to the integrity of the message that announces the success of the cross, God's word is triggered into action.)* What God spoke to us in sonship *(the incarnation)*, radiates his image and likeness in our redeemed innocence. (Heb 1:1-3) This word powerfully penetrates and impacts our whole being, body, soul, and spirit. Hebrews 4:11,12;

Righteousness by faith. Hab 2:4

Hebrews 10:38 Righteousness by God's faith defines life; reverting to the law of works ignores God's work of grace. *(Instead of reading the curse when disaster strikes, Habakkuk realizes that the Promise out dates performance as the basis to mankind's acquittal. Deuteronomy 28 would no longer be the mo-*

tivation or the measure of right or wrong behavior! "Though the fig trees do not blossom, nor fruit be on the vines, the produce of the olive fail and the fields yield no food, the flock be cut off from the fold and there be no herd in the stalls, yet I will rejoice in the Lord, I will joy in the God of my salvation. God, the Lord, is my strength; he makes my feet like hinds' feet, he makes me tread upon my high places. (Hab 3:17-19 RSV)

In the Gospel, the righteousness of God is revealed, from faith to faith. (Rom 1:17) Herein lies the secret of the power of the Gospel; there is no good news in it until the righteousness of God is revealed! *(The good news is the fact that the cross of Christ was a success. God rescued the life of our design; he redeemed our innocence. Mankind would never again be judged righteous or unrighteous by their own ability to obey moral laws! It is not about what a person must or must not do but about what Jesus has done!)* God now persuades everyone to believe what he knows to be true about them. *(It is from faith to faith.)* The prophets wrote in advance about the fact that God believes that righteousness unveils the life that he always had in mind for us. "The just shall live by his (God's) faith." Righteousness by God's faith defines life.

Hebrews 12:1 Look away from the shadow dispensation of the law and the prophets and fix your eyes upon Jesus. He is the fountainhead and conclusion of faith. He saw the joy *(of mankind's salvation)* when he braved the cross and despised the shame of it. As the executive authority of God *(the right hand of the Throne of God),* he now occupies the highest seat of dominion to endorse mankind's innocence.

The Gospel is the revelation of the righteousness of God; it declares how God succeeded to put mankind right with him. It is about what God did right, not what Adam did wrong. The word righteousness comes from the Anglo Saxon word, rightwiseness, wise in that which is right. In Greek, the word for righteousness is dikaiosune, from dike, pronounced, dikay, which means two parties finding likeness in each other. The Hebrew word for righteousness is the word tzedek, which refers to the beam in a scale of balances. *See commentary note on 2 Corinthians 6:14*

Colossians 2:9: It is in Christ that God finds an accurate and complete expression of himself, in a human body! 2:10 He mirrors our completeness and is the ultimate authority of our true identity.

"God desires to show more convincingly to the heirs of the promise the unchangeable character of his purpose." (Heb 6:17 —RSV)

If Christ is both the author and perfecter of faith, self-assessment by any other reference would be foolish. It would be just as impossible to attempt to measure temperature with a ruler. Christ defines our original design and our restored innocence. We find our identity and our destiny there.

We have obtained unrestricted access into the intimate and immediate friendship of God.

Sins were dealt with in such a thorough manner that no further offerings would ever be required. Nothing that we might personally sacrifice could ever add any virtue to our innocence.

A brand new way of life has been introduced.

Because of his torn flesh on the cross, our own flesh can no longer be made an excuse for veiling our experience of his favor and presence.

We have a High Priest in the house!

We are free to approach him with absolute confidence, fully persuaded in our hearts that nothing can any longer separate us from him. We are invited to draw near now! We are thoroughly cleansed, inside and out, with no trace of sin's stains on our conscience or conduct. Our inner thought patterns are purged by the sprinkled blood; our bodies also are bathed in clean water. (Our behavior bears witness to this.)

The Kruger National Park

Lydia and I love the Kruger National Park. It is our favorite holiday destination.

While on a game drive early one morning, I was filled with such gratitude to be there, and to know that we have a valid entry permit; and how the gospel reveals our restored innocence through the successful accomplishment of Christ as the vehicle that gives access to the sanctuary encounter of God.

He secured our right of access to every imaginable blessing. Jesus gives definition to God's eternal love-dream of our unhindered union with him, forever free from the obstructive consciousness of sin.

This is what the theme of the book of Hebrews is all about!

When you visit the Game Reserve you are immediately aware that you are in a very special place. The glossy pictures in the official road map promise glimpses of the enormous variety of game on record. The stage is set; everything is in place. You do not bring anything but your own presence to this Reserve. All its magnificent plant, bird, animal, reptile, and insect species are already there and fully represented. They give unique context to the place. As you drive or sit quietly at your camp or some remote water hole, the sights, sounds and smells are powerful confirmations, complementing and confirming the attraction of the bush.

Here, the roar of the lion belongs to me, the fresh footprint in the sand, the call of the fish eagle, as well as the vastness of the landscape with its magnificent trees. Every sunrise and sunset continues to decorate the canvas of my horizon!

The entry permit gives to every visitor equal access to the Reserve. Yet it takes the keen, observant eye to often encounter the most amazing sightings.

To visit the Reserve simply to tick off the next sighting on your list, certainly does not do justice to the pleasure and bliss to be surrounded by such splendid beauty! The fact that these animals are not caged makes it even more exciting to track them down or be surprised by their sudden appearance in view.

This beats the glossy brochure and the most realistic "zoo" experience.

In traditional church-life we have often sought to confine God's Spirit within the narrow scope of predictable programs and routines.

In Christ, God opened a new and exciting way for us to encounter him without hesitation or restriction! He is not caged in an historic prophetic picture; he is unveiled in pulsating tangible human life!

This Epistle belongs to every believer.

Love kindles faith and faith opens the horizon to explore love's mystery; it is a place where thoughts carve an impression; a place not accessible to the scrutiny of a suspicious academic or religious, guilt- and performance-based approach.

It is a document of profound beauty, leading the student beyond insubstantial religious rituals and sentiments into tangible Divine intimacy.

Someone once commented on the work of Merch: *"It is the work of a guide to lead us to the top of a mountain and then to move aside to let us see the tremendous vistas on every side. What remains is our gratitude to the teacher for bringing us to such a place.*

It is as if he has been saying to each of us, "Look within. Don't be afraid to use your mind to the utmost and to seek your deepest center. Far from this attention to the deepest realm of the human spirit walling you up within yourself, it will open out on to the whole mystery of the universe and the human race. It will show you your union with the forests and birds and distant galaxies, and every other human being who ever was or ever will be. And this kind of metaphysical seeing will give you a tiny glimpse of the fiery mystery of existence from which all things have come and by which they are continually sustained and to which they long to return."

But as splendid as this mystery is, it is meant to draw you into the mystery of Christ. The Word of God has become flesh, and by taking a human form in that very act has transformed it and transforms, as well, the universe and the human race. You have a new being in Christ in which you share through him in the very life of the Trinity." http://www.innerexplorations.com/catchtheomor/m.htm

1:1 Throughout ancient times God spoke in many fragments and glimpses of prophetic thought to our fathers.

1:2 Now, the sum total of this conversation with us, has finally culminated in a son. In his sonship, God declares him heir of all things. He is, after all, the author of the ages.

1:3 We have our beginning and our being in him. He is the force of the universe, sustaining everything that exists by the logic of his eternal utterance! Jesus is the radiant and flawless expression of the person of God. He makes the glorious intent of God visible and mirrors the [1]character and every attribute of God in human form. This powerful final utterance of God is the vehicle that carries the weight of the universe. What he communicates is the central theme of everything that exists. The content of his message celebrates the fact that God took it upon himself to successfully cleanse and acquit humankind. The man Jesus is now his right hand of power, the executive authority seated in the boundless measure of his majesty. He occupies the highest seat of dominion to endorse our innocence! His throne is established upon our redeemed righteousness. *("Having accomplished purification of sins, he sat down ..." More than two thousand years ago the conversation that had begun before time was recorded—sustained in fragments of thought throughout the ages, whispered in prophetic language, chiseled in stone and inscribed in human conscience and memory—became a man. Beyond the tablet of stone, the papyrus scroll or parchment roll, human life has become the articulate voice of God. Jesus is the crescendo of God's conversation with humankind; he gives context and content to the authentic thought. Everything that God had in mind for mankind is voiced in him. Jesus is God's language. His name defines his mission. As Savior of the world he truly redeemed the image and likeness of the invisible God and made him apparent again in human form, as in a mirror.*

The Greek word [1]charakter from charax - to engrave - translated 'mark of the beast' in the book of Revelation. Either the character of the Father or the character of the fallen mind will influence our actions (hand) because it is what engages our thoughts (forehead)

Like in Isa 55:8-11 "Your thoughts are not my thoughts; therefore your ways are not my ways....but my word will incarnate, and saturate earth (flesh) just like the rain and the snow cancel the distance between heaven and earth, so shall my word be that goes forth from my mouth! Instead of the thorn, the fir and instead of the brier, the myrtle!)

1:4 No prophetic or angelic messenger can compete with him in rank or name. This is his rightful portion. *(Whatever the medium was through which God spoke of old, whether angelic or prophetic - recorded scripture is not superior to revealed sonship!)*

1:5 God did not address any of the prophetic messengers when he said, "You are my son, today I have given birth to you! I am to you all that a Father can be to a son, and you are to me all that a son can be to a Father."

(See Acts 13:30-33 But God raised him from the dead; and for many days he appeared to those who came up with him from Galilee to Jerusalem, who are now his witnesses to the people. And we bring you the good news that what God promised to the fathers, this he has fulfilled to us their children by raising Jesus; as also it is written in the second psalm, 'You are my son, today I have begotten you." The resurrection of Jesus represents our new birth and our redeemed sonship. 1Pet 1:3)

1:6 And when he leads his son in triumphant parade, as his firstborn, before the whole inhabited world, he says, "Let all God's messengers worship him in adoration." *(The word often translated worship, [1]proskuneo, from pros, face to face and, I would like to believe to be a derivation of koinonia, joint-participation; rather than the idea of kuneo, or kuon which means dog! I know, some tried to connect the idea of a dog licking its master's hand, which then became a possibility of kissing (!) - yet I would much prefer a face to face koinonia encounter to define true worship! See Ephesians 4:8, Scripture confirms that he led us as trophies in his triumphant procession on high; he [1]repossessed his gift (likeness) in mankind. Quote from the Hebrew text, Ps 68:18, [1]lakachta mattanoth baadam, thou hast taken gifts in human form, in Adam. [The gifts which Jesus Christ distributes to us he has received in us, in and by virtue of his incarnation. Commentary by Adam Clarke. We were born anew in his resurrection. [1 Pet 1:3, Hos 6:2] The fact that he ascended confirms his victorious descent into the deepest pits of human despair [Eph 4:9]. See John 3:13 [RSV], "No one has ascended into heaven but he who [1]descended from heaven, even the son of man." All mankind originate from above; we are [1]anouthen, from above. He now occupies the ultimate rank of authority from the lowest regions, where he stooped down to rescue us to the highest authority in the heavens, having executed his mission to the full. Fallen mankind is fully restored to the authority of the authentic life of their design. [Eph 4:10])*

1:7 Of the angelic messengers he says, I inspire you to be swift like the wind and he fashions those who work his cause like a flash of lightning.

1:8 But when he addresses the son he says, "Your throne, O God, extends beyond the ages. The scepter of righteousness is the scepter of your kingdom" *(Ps 45:6)*

1:9 "You love righteousness and detest evil. Therefore, O God, your God anointed you with the oil of joy to stand head and shoulders above your associates." *(Ps 45:7)*

1:10 "The earth traces its foundation back to you, the heavens also are your invention; they are all hand-crafted by you." *(Ps 102:25)*

1:11 They shall become obsolete, but you will remain; they shall show wear like an old garment,

1:12 and you will eventually roll them up as a mantle; they shall be replaced, but you remain "I am," and your years will never cease. *(Ps 102:26)*

1:13 Neither was it the prophetic messengers he had in mind when he said, "You are my executive authority *(the extension of my right hand)*, **take**

your position and witness how I make your enemies a place upon which you may rest your feet." *(Mt 22:42-45)*

1:14 What role do the angelic messengers play in God's strategy? They are all employed by God in the prophetic-apostolic ministry of the Spirit to help administer the inheritance of salvation that belongs to mankind.

2:1 I have said all this to help you realize the tremendous importance of the message you have heard. Become completely engaged in its meaning and thus you will never drift away from its influence and appeal.

2:2 The words which God spoke through prophetic messengers, were not to be taken lightly; considering the fact that the many and various ways in which God spoke to our fathers, *(1:1-3)* did not compromise the initial intention and [1]resolve of God; neither did the prophetic announcement distract from the [2]ultimate conclusion of the word, [5]realized in the son of God. The prophetic word [2]stands above reproach in every way; the same [3]source is confirmed in our hearing today, and is to be [4]judged in the same integrity. *(Note the words, [1]bebaios, steadfast, from baino, to stand, and [2]parabaino, and [3]parakoo are used here; para, closest possible proximity and baino, footprint, to stand; and then also the word para combined with akoo, to hear, hearing from the original source. The word, [4]endike, from en, in, and dike, judged equal, two parties finding likeness in each other; a scale perfectly balanced. The word, [5]lambano, to receive, to realize, to grasp, to associate with.)*

2:3 No one can afford to underestimate and be blasé about this final message; a salvation of such magnificent proportions! There is no alternative [1]escape. Salvation as it is articulated in Christ, is the message that God spoke from the beginning, and it was confirmed again and again by those who heard him. *(We are [1]rescued from the lies that we believed about ourselves under the law of performance.)*

2:4 The purpose of God in every sign, miracle, and gift of the Holy Spirit was *(not to distract, but rather)* to complement and confirm this great message of salvation.

2:5 God never intended to put the angelic messengers in charge of this [1]new world order that we are speaking of. *(The [1]age and dispensation of mankind's realized salvation.)*

2:6 Somewhere in the scriptures it is written, "What is it about the human species that God cannot get them out of his mind? What does he [1]see in the son of man, that so captivates his gaze?" *(The word [1]episkeptomai, from epi, continual influence upon, and skopos, to view; to observe with interest.)*

2:7 He has made mankind all but equal to himself; he crowned them with his own glory and dignity, and appointed them in a position of authority over all the works of his hands." *(No angel can boast that. [Ps 8:4-6])*

2:8 God's intention was that human life should rule the planet. He subjected everything without exception to his control. Yet, looking at mankind, it does not seem that way at all.

2:9 But what is apparent, is Jesus *(but now God spoke to us in a son ... [Heb 1:1-3])* Let us then consider him in such a way, that we may clearly perceive what God is saying to mankind in him. In the death he suffered, he descended for a brief moment below the lowest ranked angel, in order to taste the death of the entire human race, and in doing so, to fulfill the grace of God and be crowned again *(as a man, representing all mankind)* with glory and highly esteemed honor.

2:10 He [1]towers in conspicuous prominence far above all things. He is both their author and their conclusion. He now summons every son of his, through a perfected salvation, to his own glory. The extent of the suffering he bore is the measure of the perfection of the salvation over which he presides. *(The word, [1]prepo, means to tower; see also Heb 7:26. Who needs a gift, if you can have a reward?! The gift of God, wrapped up in the achievement of Christ, disarms every idea of reward!)*

2:11 Because both he who carried out the rescue mission, as well as those whom he saved and restored to innocence, [1]originate from the same source. He proudly introduces them as members of his immediate family. *(The word, [1]ek, always denotes origin, source, out of; see 1 Corinthians 1:30.)*

2:12 He says, "I will reveal your name to my brothers as being their own; this will fuel my praise in the ekklesia, where I will celebrate God in song." *(This reminds of the emotional moment when Joseph revealed himself to his brothers. [Gen 45:1, Ps 22:22] In Hebrew: "I will inscribe [The word, safar, means enumerate, detail] your name, in the core of my kindred;" tavek, to cut to the core, sever, to bisect, a mathematical term which is the division of a given curve, figure, or interval into two equal parts, the one mirroring the other.)*

2:13 "I will win his friendship again with trust." He says in another place, "I am surrounded by the children which God has given me. I am one of them." *(Rom 5:10, "While we were still hostile, he reconciled us to himself.")*

2:14 Being one with the children of God presupposes the fact that he lived and died in a body exactly like theirs; being as fully human as we are, he is qualified to remove the dominion of death that was introduced [1]as a result of Adam's fall. *(Had he done all this in a superhuman body, the implications of his life, death and resurrection would be irrelevant. The word, [1]diabolos, usually translated devil, literally, dia + ballo, translated as through the fall, or as a result of the fall.)*

2:15 As a fellow human, he re-defined death and delivered them from the lifelong dread of death. *(He brought final closure to the idea of judgment, which is what the system of works is all about. Heb 9:27,28. Evil is not immortal, love is.)*

2:16 This is why it is so relevant to understand that Jesus did not arrive on the planet in an angelic form *(or a Superman-suit);* he embraced the seed of Abraham. *(The seed of faith-righteousness and not flesh-righteousness was preserved. See Galatians 3:16; also 4:21-31)*

2:17 He was obliged to completely assimilate every detail of his brothers' humanity so that, in his position as Chief Priest, his compassion and integrity would prevail effectively over the [1]lies that they believed about themselves, to reconcile them with God. *(The Greek word, [1]hamartia, often translated as sin, is the word, ha, without, and meros, alloted portion; which is the stem of the word morphe, form; thus a distorted form; the lie that we believed about ourselves as a result of the futile ways we inherited from our fathers because of Adam's fall! See 1 Pet 1:18.)*

2:18 He experienced humanity's temptation with the same intensity, and under the same scrutiny, and was therefore qualified to represent them with immediate effect. *(To run to their rescue. See Heb 4:15,16.)*

3:1 Brothers, in the context of our co-inclusion in Christ, we are blameless; we ²participate in his heavenly ¹identity. ⁴Acquaint yourselves immediately and fully with Christ Jesus as the Ambassador and Chief Priest of our ³confession. Our lives co-echo the logic of God's eternal conversation in him. *(The word, ¹kaleo, means to identify by name, to surname; the word, ²metochos, comes from meta, meaning together with, and echo; to hold; to embrace; we echo his conversation. The word, ³homologeo, comes from homo, the same, and lego, to speak. The word, ⁴katanoeio, from kata, in this case a preposition denoting direction towards, and noeo, to perceive, to contemplate; translates as fully acquainted. The aorist imperative is used here, katanoesate, which implies the urgency to get something done once and for all.)*

3:2 Jesus is proof of God's workmanship; he exhibits God's persuasion concerning us. Jesus is what God believes about us. In Moses we have the prophetic model, demonstrated in his complete belief in God's purpose displayed in the meticulous attention to detail regarding the construction of the tabernacle. *(See Heb 8:5 The prophetic model mirrors God's meticulous attention to detail when it comes to every aspect of your life! You are his tabernacle; you are his address on planet earth!)*

3:3 Yet his fame surpasses the glory of Moses, because the one who designs and constructs the house gets the greater glory. *(Heb 1:4; John 1:15)*

3:4 Every house is an expression of someone's design; God is the ultimate architect and creator of all things. *(He owns the blueprint.)*

3:5 Moses took responsible charge of the administration of the tabernacle as a servant of, and witness to the prophetic voice.

3:6 But Christ is in charge of his own household, not as a servant but as a son. Understand this: we are part of this family; this is our real state now; we are not playing a role, or doing the dress rehearsal. We are no longer talking prophetically in figures and analogies. We are bursting with confidence. What good reason we now have for rejoicing! Our expectation, inspired by its foundation in prophecy, has now come to full fruition.

3:7 In Psalm 95:7-11, the Holy Spirit said, "Discern the voice of the shepherd. Grasp the urgency of what God is saying to you today! *(Sonship is the Father's language [Heb 1:1])*

3:8 Therefore, do not be calloused in heart as the people of Israel were: every time they faced any contradiction or temptation in the wilderness, their response immediately revealed their irritation, rather than their persuasion in God's belief.

3:9 Your fathers continued to scrutinize me suspiciously, examining me as though my intentions with them could not be trusted, even though they were eye-witnesses of my miraculous works for forty years.

3:10 They were a generation of people who grieved me deeply; instead of learning my ways, they habitually went astray in their hearts, intoxicated by their unbelief.

3:11 *(Even to this day they are still trapped in the wilderness of unbelief.)* **Hear the echo of God's cry though the ages, "Oh! If only they would enter into my rest."**

3:12 Make sure that none of you tolerates the poison of unbelief in your hearts, allowing callousness to distract and distance you from the living God. *(Unbelief, believing a lie about yourself and your salvation [Num 13:33, Josh 2:11]; unbelief exchanges the living God for a dead god of your own imagination. A calloused heart is a mind dominated by the senses.)*

3:13 Instead, [1]remind one another daily of your true identity; make today count! Do not allow callousness of heart to cheat any of you for even a single day out of your allotted portion. *("To encourage one another daily," from the word, [1]parakaleo, from para, a preposition indicating close proximity, a thing proceeding from a sphere of influence, with a suggestion of union of place of residence, to have sprung from its author and giver, originating from, denoting the point from which an action originates, intimate connection, and kaleo, to identify by name, to surname. Jesus introduces the Holy Spirit in the same capacity, parakletos [Jn 14:16] Greek, hamartia, sin, without form, or allotted portion. Sin would be anything that distracts from the awareness of our likeness.)*

3:14 Who we are in our [1]union with Christ must be taken to its ultimate conclusion. Do not cancel out your confident start, by making a poor finish. *(Starting in faith, then going back to the law of works. Again the word, [1]metochos, is used, from meta, meaning together with, and echo; to hold; to embrace; we co-echo Christ in our union with him.)*

3:15 Every day is an extension of God's today; hear his voice, do not harden your heart. The stubborn rebellion of Israel brought them nowhere.

3:16 The same people who experienced God's mighty act of deliverance out of Egypt under the leadership of Moses were the very ones who rebelled.

3:17 They grieved him for forty years in the wilderness and died there.

3:18 God's invitation does not exclude anyone from possessing the promise of his [1]rest; their unbelief does. Persuasion cannot be compromised by unbelief. *(Our believing a lie about ourselves cannot compromise what God knows to be true about us. Futile striving to become cannot match the bliss of discovering and celebrating who you already are by his design and redemption. [1]His rest declares his perfect likeness revealed and redeemed in human form. [See Gen 1:26, 31, 2:1, 2])*

3:19 The point is this: even though they survived by supernatural means in the wilderness for forty years, they failed to grasp what God had in mind for them. Their own unbelief disqualified them. *(They did not die because of an inferior salvation from Egypt; Pharaoh was taken out of the equation. They died because of unbelief, they believed a lie about themselves! [Num 13:33, Josh 2:11] Don't blame Pharaoh or the devil for your own unbelief! You can experience God's supernatural provision and protection and yet remain outside his rest. The ultimate proof of faith is not experience of the supernatural, but entering into* *his rest. His rest celebrates his perfect work; it finds its definition and reference in Genesis 1:31, 1 Kings 6:7 and Colossians 2:9, 10. He longs for you to discover your own completeness and perfection as seen from his point of view. His rest is sustained in you by what he sees, knows, and says about you in reference to the finished work of Christ. Jesus is what God believes about you.)*

4:1 What a foolish thing it would be if we should now fail in a similar fashion to enter into his rest where we get to celebrate the full consequences of our redemption. *(Why waste another lap in the same wilderness of unbelief!)*

4:2 What God has now spoken to us in Jesus confirms that we were equally included in the prophetic message which was proclaimed to our ancestors; their unbelief disqualified them from possessing the promise; they could not make the vital connection with the promise while they remained enslaved to their dwarfed opinions of themselves! Because the word did not mingle with faith, there was no catalyst to ignite its effect in their hearts, and so the promise did not profit them at all. *(They were absorbed with the typical fruit of the "I-am-not-tree-mentality"; they remained more persuaded about a perception of an inferior identity, than what they were about the largeness of their salvation from slavery, into the freedom of the authentic life of their design. Numbers 13:33)*

4:3 Faith *(not willpower)* realizes our immediate access into God's rest. Hear the echo of God's [1]cry though the ages, "Oh! If only they would enter into my rest." His rest celebrates perfection. His work is complete; the [2]fall of humanity did not flaw its perfection. *(Some translations read, "As I have sworn in my wrath" derived from [1]orge, meaning passionate desire, any strong outburst of emotion. "Oh! If only they would enter into my rest." First Adam failed to enter into God's finished work, and then Israel failed to enter into the consequence of their complete redemption out of slavery; and as a result of their unbelief, they perished in the wilderness. Now let us not fail in the same manner to see the completed work of the Cross. God desires for us to see the same perfection; what he saw when he first created mankind in his image and then again, what he saw in the perfect obedience [lit. hearing] of his Son. God is not "in his rest" because he is exhausted, but because he is satisfied with what he sees and knows concerning us! He now invites us with [1]urgent persuasion to enter into what he sees. His rest was not at risk. "His works were finished from the foundation of the world." The word, apo, translates as away from, before and [2]katabalo, cast down, the fall of humanity, sometimes translated, foundation [see notes on Eph 1:4] "This association goes back to before the fall of the world, his love knew that he would present us again face to face before him in blameless innocence." The implications of the fall are completely cancelled out.)*

4:4 Scripture records the seventh day to be the prophetic celebration of God's perfect work. What God saw satisfied his scrutiny. *(Behold, it is very good, and God rested from all his work. [Gen 1:31, 2:2] God saw more than his perfect image in Adam, he also saw the Lamb and his perfect work of redemption! "The Lamb having been slain from the foundation of the world." [Rev 13:8] "That which has been is now; that which is to be, already has been" [Ecc 3:15] Also 2 Tim 1:9)*

4:5 In Psalm 95 the same seventh day metaphor is reiterated: "O, that they would enter my rest!"

4:6 It is clear then that there is still an opportunity to enter into that rest which Israel failed to access because of their unbelief, even though they were the first to hear the good news of God's intention to restore mankind to the same Sabbath that Adam and Israel had lost. *(Both Adam and Israel believed a lie about themselves. [Num 13:33, Josh 2:11])*

4:7 So, now again many years later, he points specifically to an extended opportunity when he announces in David's prophecy, "Today when hearing my voice, do not do so with a calloused heart. Be faith sensitive."

4:8 If Joshua, who led the new generation of Israel out of the wilderness *(where their parents perished through unbelief)*, had succeeded in leading them into the rest that God intended, David would not so many years later have referred to yet another day. *(This moment still remains as an open invitation to mankind to enter into their rest: the living blueprint of their design. This confirms that the history of Israel was a mere shadow and prophetic type of that Promise that was yet to be fulfilled.)*

4:9 The conclusion is clear: the original rest is still in place for God's people. *(The people of this planet are the property of God [Ps 24:1])*

4:10 God's rest celebrates his finished work; whoever enters into God's rest immediately abandons his own efforts to compliment what God has already perfected. *(The language of the law is "do;" the language of grace is "done.")*

4:11 Let us therefore be ¹prompt to understand and fully appropriate that rest and not fall again into the same trap that snared Israel in unbelief. *(The word, ¹spoudatzo, from spoude, I translated prompt, not labor; this word also reminds of the English word, speed; immediately!)*

4:12 The message God spoke to us in Christ, is the most life giving and dynamic influence in us, cutting like a surgeon's scalpel, sharper than a soldier's sword, piercing to the deepest core of human conscience, to the dividing of soul and spirit; ending the dominance of the sense realm and its neutralizing effect upon the human spirit. In this way a person's spirit is freed to become the ruling influence again in the thoughts and intentions of their heart. The scrutiny of this word detects every possible disease, discerning the body's deepest secrets where joint and bone-marrow meet. *(The moment we cease from our own efforts to justify ourselves, by yielding to the integrity of the message that announces the success of the Cross, God's word is triggered into action. What God spoke to us in sonship (the incarnation), radiates his image and likeness in our redeemed innocence. [Heb 1:1-3] This word powerfully penetrates and impacts our whole being; body, soul and spirit.)*

4:13 The entire person is thoroughly exposed to his scrutinizing gaze. Every creature's original form is on record in the Word. *(Revealing God's resolve to display his image and likeness in human form.)*

4:14 In the message of the incarnation, we have Jesus the Son of God representing humanity in the highest place of spiritual authority. That which God has spoken to us in him is his final word. It is echoed now in the declaration of our confession.

4:15 As High Priest he fully identifies with us in the context of our frail human lives. Having subjected it to close scrutiny, he proved that the human frame was master over sin. His sympathy with us is not to be seen as excusing weaknesses which are the result of a faulty design, but rather as a trophy to humanity. *(He is not an example for us but of us.)*

4:16 For this reason we can approach the authoritative throne of grace with bold utterance. We are welcome there in his embrace, and are [1]reinforced with immediate effect in times of trouble. *(The word, [1]boetheia, means to be reinforced, specifically a rope or chain for frapping a vessel in a storm.*

In his incarnate human body Jesus represents us on the deepest possible level of every detail of our lives, spirit, soul and body. He victoriously faced every onslaught and scrutiny that we would ever possibly encounter!)

5:1 Traditionally a person would be appointed from among their fellows to fulfill the office of High Priest in presenting gifts and sacrifices before God on behalf of the people and for their own sins. *(The High Priesthood of Christ is in sharp contrast to the system of priesthood the Jews were familiar with.)*

5:2 Every Jew felt reassured by the fact that High Priests themselves were hemmed in by the same sins that snared the people they represented. By virtue of their own limitations and inadequacies they were able to sympathize with the ignorance and waywardness of the people under them.

5:3 It was accepted practice that they would offer sacrifices for both their own and the people's sins.

5:4 This honorable office was not by self-appointment but, as in Aaron's case, the priest was summoned to the work by God.

5:5 Neither did Christ assume the high priestly office by his own presumption, but in fulfillment of the prophetic word *(in Psalm 2)* concerning the Messiah, in which God, speaking through David, said, "You are my son, today I have begotten you."

5:6 Just as he has spoken in other scriptures concerning this new priestly order: "Thou art a Priest forever, after the order of Melchizedek." *(By translation, "the King of Righteousness," [Gen 4:18] In these scriptures a new and eternal order of priesthood is introduced. [Ps 110:4] Jesus knew that his priesthood was prophesied in scripture, a priesthood neither passed on by natural birth, nor ending with natural death.)*

5:7 When he faced the horror of his imminent death, he presented his urgent plea to God in an outburst of agonizing emotion and with tears. He prayed with urgent intent to be delivered from death, knowing that God was able to save him. He was heard because of his [1]firm grip on the prophetic word. *(Not because he feared, as some translations have put it, but because he [1]fully grasped that he was the fulfillment of scripture; he knew that he would be raised on the third day; [Hos 6:2] eu + lambano.)*

5:8 Acquainted with sonship he was in the habit of [1]hearing from above; what he heard [2]distanced him from the effect of what he had suffered. *(The word often translated as obedience is the word, [1]upoakuo, under the influence of hearing, or hearing from above. "By" the things he suffered, [2]apo, away from, distanced. "Then I said, I read in your book what you wrote about me; so here I am, I have come to fulfill your will." [Heb 10:7])*

5:9 By his perfect hearing he forever freed mankind to hear what he had heard. *(He now makes it possible for us to hear in such a way that we may participate again in the full release of our original identity; the logos finding voice in the incarnation in us.)*

5:10 The authority of this high priestly order of Melchizedek [1]flows directly from God. *("Called" of God is from the word, [1]prosagereo, from pros, a preposition of direction, towards, face to face + ago, to lead as a shepherd leads his sheep, and + reo (Strong's number: 4482) to flow, or to run like water. His High Priestly office originates in God.)*

5:11 On this subject there remains so much to be said; but oh, how difficult it is to explain something to someone who hears with an indifferent attitude.

5:12 By now you *(Jews)* should have been professors, able to teach the rest of the world, but you are still struggling with the ABC's of God's language in Christ. *(Heb 1:1-3)* The difference between the prophetic shadow and the real is like that between milk and meat in your diet. You cannot live on baby food for the rest of your lives!

5:13 The revelation of righteousness is the meat of God's word. Babes live on milk *(the prophetic shadow of the real, which was to come)*; so does everyone who is not [1]pierced in the ear of his heart by the revelation of Christ. *(The word,[1]**apeiros**, comes from **a**, negative, and **peira**, pierced, not pierced, tested by piercing. God's act of righteousness in Christ restored mankind to blameless innocence [Rom 1:17])*

5:14 This is the nourishment of the mature. They are those who have their faculties of perception trained as by gymnastic precision to distinguish the relevant from the irrelevant. *(The mature are those who know the difference between the shadow and the substance; between the futility of the law of works and willpower to work righteousness, and righteousness revealed by the faith of God in the finished work of Christ.)*

6:1 Consequently, as difficult as it may seem, you ought to divorce your-selves from sentimental attachment to the prefiguring doctrine of the Messiah, which was designed to carry us like a vessel over the ocean of prophetic dispensation into the completeness of the fulfilled promise. A mind shift from attempts to impress God by your behavior, to faith-righteousness in Christ, is fundamental. There is no life left in the old system. It is dead and gone; you have to move on. *(Rom 3:27)*

6:2 All the Jewish teachings about ceremonial washings *(baptisms)*, the laying on of hands *(in order to identify with the slain animal as sacrifice)*, and all teachings pertaining to a sin consciousness, including the final resur-rection of the dead in order to face judgment, are no longer relevant. *(All of these types and shadows were concluded and fulfilled in Christ, their living sub-stance. His resurrection bears testimony to the judgment that he faced on human-ity's behalf and the freedom from an obstructive consciousness of sin that he now proclaims. [Rom 4:25; Acts 17:31; Jn 12:31-33] Jesus said, "and when I am lifted up on the cross, I will draw all judgment unto me!" [Heb 9:28])*

6:3 So it is with God's prompting that we advance. *(From the prophetic types and shadows of scripture into the substance of what God has now spoken to us in his son. [Heb 1:1-3)*

6:4 Now it may be that someone may clearly see the light *(of the prophetic word)* and participate in the Holy Spirit by already having sampled the heavenly gift, *("The prophets who prophesied of the grace that was to be yours searched and inquired about this salvation; they inquired what person or time was indicated by the Spirit of Christ within them when predicting the sufferings of Christ and the subsequent glory. [1Pet 1:10, 11])*

6:5 and they might even begin to feast on the beauty of the Word; already having experienced the power of the age of the promise that all were waiting for.

6:6 If such a person were to insist on relapsing into the old mind-set of legalism, sin consciousness, and condemnation, it becomes impossible for him to be restored again and again to ¹repentance. The principle of repeated ¹repentance, as practiced under the law, does not make sense in the context of the new dispensation, because it would absurdly imply that Christ was being re-crucified and subjected to public shame over and over again. This new order is not to be confused with the old! Grace is not a cheap excuse for sin! C'mon, ¹awaken to faith-conciousness once and for all. You are free from the old rules and bondage of the duty-driven law of willpower. It is impossible for the old system to match the new! *(Under the shadow system of the law, sacrifices were repeatedly slain because no permanent cleansing was possible. [Heb 10:1-4] The word often translated, re-pentance, is the word, ¹**metanoia**, which does not imply pennace at all; let alone, re-pennance! It suggests a radical and total mindshift!)*

6:7 For when cultivated soil is soaked by frequent showers and produc-es the useful, life-giving crop expected by the farmer, the harvest brings much celebration.

6:8 What a complete disappointment though, if the same soil produces nothing but thorns and thistles; it is a worthless yield, and fit for burning; like a dream that has gone up in smoke.

6:9 Having said all this, my dear friends, I am fully convinced of God's love for you; what God accomplished in salvation on your behalf is beyond comparison to anything you were familiar with before. Salvation realities echo what the law could only shadow.

6:10 God is not unfair, neither is he unaware of the affectionate way in which you have honored his Name, and the diligence you have shown in your unrelenting religious service in keeping all the sacred rituals and ceremonies, even to this the present day.

6:11 I urge you to employ that same sincere devotion to now realize the fulfillment of everything that the old system anticipated.

6:12 We do not want you to behave like [1]illegitimate children, unsure of your share in the inheritance. Mimic the faith of those who through their patience came to possess the promise of their allotted portion. (*The word,* [1]*nothros comes from* **nothos**, *one born outside of wedlock, of a concubine or female slave. The child of the law and not of the promise. [Gal 3:29; 4:22-31])*

6:13 God could give Abraham no greater guarantee but the integrity of his own being; this makes the promise as sure as God is. (*Since he had no one greater by whom to swear, he swore by himself.*)

6:14 Saying, "I will continue to speak well of you. I will confirm my intention always only to bless you, and to multiply you beyond measure." (*In blessing I will bless you, and in multiplying I will multiply you.*)

6:15 And so Abraham continued in patience and secured the promise.

6:16 It is common practice in human affairs to evoke a higher authority under oath in order to add weight to any agreement between parties, thereby [1]silencing any possibility of quibbling. (*The word* [1]*peras, means the end of all dispute; the point beyond which one cannot go.*)

6:17 In the same context we are confronted with God's eagerness to go to the last extreme in his dealing with us as heirs of his promise, and to cancel out all possible grounds for doubt or dispute. In order to persuade us of the unalterable character and finality of his resolve, he [1]confined himself to an oath. The promise which already belongs to us by heritage is now also confirmed under oath. (*The word* [1]*mesiteo is used, interposed or mediated. Compare* **mesites**, *mediator, from* **mesos**, *midst. In the incarnation, God has positioned himself in the midst, of his creation.See Galatians 3:20 With Abraham there was no middleman; it was just God! [The Mosaic law required mediators [the Levitical priesthood] because it was an arrangement whereby mankind had a part and God had a part. Mankind's part was to obey the commandments and God's part was to bless. God's covenant with Abraham was a grace covenant pointing to the man Jesus Christ, in whom God himself would fulfil mankind's part and therefore needed no mediator apart from himself.*

In the incarnation he fulfills both the proposal and the "I do!" Melissa Perez]

The Word is the promise; the Incarnate, crucified and risen Christ is the proof.He desires to show more convincingly to the heirs of the promise the unchangeable character of his purpose. RSV

Mankind was not redeemed from the devil; a thief never becomes an owner; neither did Jesus do what he did to change his father's mind about us! It was our minds that needed persuasion! God was not to be reconciled to his creation; God was in Christ when he reconciled the world to himself! 2 Corinthians 5:18-20

6:18 So that we are now dealing with two irreversible facts *(The promise of redemption sustained throughout scripture and the fulfillment of that promise in Jesus)* **which make it impossible for anyone to prove God wrong; thus our persuasion as to our redeemed identity is powerfully reinforced. We have already escaped into that destiny; our expectation has come within our immediate grasp!**

6:19 Our hearts and minds are certain; anchored securely within the innermost courts of God's immediate Presence; beyond the *(prophetic)* **veil.**

6:20 By going there on our behalf, Jesus pioneered a place for us and removed every type of obstruction that could possibly distance us from the promise. In him we are represented for all time; he became our High Priest after the order of Melchizedek. We now enjoy the same privileged access he has. *(He said, "I go to prepare a place for you so that you may be where I am. On that day you will no longer doubt that I and the Father are one; you will know that I am in the Father and you in me and I in you!"[John 10:30, 14:3, 20])*

7:1 This is the same Melchizedek, King of Salem, Priest of the Supreme God, who met Abraham after he had defeated the four kings, and blessed him.

7:2 It was to him Abraham gave a tenth part of all the spoils. To begin to appreciate the significance of Melchizedek, we must first appreciate the meaning of his name: King of ¹Righteousness and King of ²Peace. He is the one who administers God's promise and guarantees his ability to restore us to blameless innocence and wholeness! *(The word, ¹dikaiosune, meaning righteousness, from dike, two parties finding likeness in one another; ²eirene, means peace, from eiro, to join, to be set at one again, in carpentry it is referred to as the swallow-tail joint, the strongest joint in carpentry; to rest. In Hebrew, the word is ²shalom, meaning completeness, wholeness, friendship. The Hebrew word for righteousness is ¹tzedek, referring to the wooden beam in a scale of balances. See commentary note on 2 Corinthians 6:14. The gospel is the revelation of the righteousness of God; it declares how God got it right to put mankind right with him. The English word righteousness comes from the Anglo Saxon word, 1rightwiseness, wise in that which is right.)*

7:3 There exists no record that can link Melchizedek to a natural father or mother; no birth certificate neither any account of his death, nor is there any record of his age. He resembles exactly the Son of God: his priesthood abides without beginning or end. *(This was at a time where detailed records were kept of every genealogy.)*

7:4 Now carefully consider this; the fact that Abraham the great Patriarch gave him a tenth portion of the spoil just goes to show what a distinguished man Melchizedek must have been in Abraham's estimation, and what an impression he had made on him! *(In the Hebrew mind, Abraham was the most important individual standing as a reference to their identity and tradition.)*

7:5 Levi's sons, who were priests by natural descent, were obliged by law to receive tithes from their brethren, even though they were equals and shared a common Father in Abraham.

7:6 However, Melchizedek here receives tithes from everyone associated with Abraham, despite his having no natural link to their lineage. In the blessing that he pronounced over Abraham he recognized Abraham as the holder of God's promises. *(He confirmed the good news of the promise of righteousness represented by Abraham's faith.)*

7:7 In principle, the junior always receives the blessing from the senior person.

7:8 In the case of the Levites, the duration of their priesthood is contemporaneous with their lifespan; but scripture declares that Melchizedek's life has no end.

7:9 My reasoning is that even Levi, who would later receive the tithe, had already paid the tithe to Melchizedek in Abraham.

7:10 When Melchizedek and Abraham met, Levi was already present in the loins of his father. *(By the time Levi was born, Melchizedek was still alive; since he has no beginning of time nor end of life, in him time and eternity meet.)*

7:11 The point that I wish to make is this: if the Levitical priesthood, linked to the law of Moses, was a flawless system *(by succeeding in presenting mankind in blameless innocence before God),* there would surely be no further mention made of another order of priesthood presided over by Melchizedek and not by Aaron. *(Ps 110:4)*

7:12 If there is a new order of priesthood, there must obviously be a new law. *(Melchizedek reveals a new basis for righteousness, related not to a person's effort to keep the law by their own willpower, but based upon the perfect work of Christ. This new law is called the law of faith [Rom 3:27], the law of perfect liberty [Jas 1:25], and the law of the spirit of life in Christ Jesus [Rom 8:2].)*

7:13 The person who is prophetically implicated as being the leader of this new priesthood belongs to a completely different tribe. This implies a complete break with tradition because no one from any tribe other than the Levites ever touched the altar.

7:14 History is clear that the Lord's lineage is from Judah, concerning whom Moses made no mention of a priestly office.

7:15 Of far greater significance and even more apparent is the fact that Jesus is mirrored in Melchizedek in whom the new priestly office arises.

7:16 This new office is not based on the law of precepts constrained by the frailty of the flesh, but by the authority of an indestructible life *(as demonstrated in his resurrection).*

7:17 Thus scripture confirms his perpetual priesthood exactly according to the pattern of Melchizedek.

7:18 This new order brought about an immediate end to the previous inferior and useless system of laws and commandments.

7:19 In its ability to reunite mankind with God, the law did not succeed even once; that is why it was superseded by the introduction of a far superior hope, a new order in which we are perfectly represented before God.

7:20 The previous priesthood was reduced to a mere tradition and passed on through natural descent from father to son. God had no say in the matter.

7:21 To give irrefutable integrity to the new Messianic priesthood, it was written, "The Lord has sworn and will not change his mind, 'You are a priest for ever after the order of Melchizedek.'" *(Psalm 110:4)*

7:22 Melchizedek mirrors Christ in the highest office of priesthood as mediator between God and mankind. Jesus is now the living proof of God's covenanted pledge to benefit mankind in a far better way than under any previous arrangement.

7:23 The fact that there were so many priests shows how frequently they died and had to be replaced.

7:24 But there will be no successor to the Priesthood of Jesus because he remains forever.

7:25 Through him mankind's approach to God is forever secured; he continues to communicate the full accomplishment of their salvation.

7:26 As our High Priest he towers far above every other priestly system in conspicuous prominence and in holy character. His guileless, flawless life on earth was never compromised by sin, and he himself was exalted above the heavens where he occupies the highest rank of authority in the eternal realm.

7:27 Unlike the previous high priests whose system of daily sacrifices was a constant reminder of their own failures, he had no need to sacrifice on his own behalf. The sacrifice he offered was himself for all; a sacrifice never to be repeated.

7:28 Under the law, men were appointed as high priests regardless of their weaknesses. The word of the oath, which succeeded the law, appointed the son in perpetual perfection.

8:1 The conclusion of all that has been said points us to an exceptional Person, who towers far above the rest in the highest office of heavenly greatness. He is the executive authority of the majesty of God. *(The right hand of God).*

8:2 The office he now occupies is the one which the Moses-model resembled prophetically. He ministers in the holiest place in God's true tabernacle of worship. Nothing of the old man-made structure can match its perfection.

8:3 The task of bringing gifts and sacrifices was the duty of every High Priest; with Jesus there would be no exception. *(He would bring the perfect sacrifice.)*

8:4 So here on earth, since he had no further offering to sacrifice *(in terms of the Jewish priesthood),* he would not qualify to be a priest among the Jews, who still have their own priesthood functioning to offer the various gifts presented in accordance with the prescriptions of their law. *(Animal sacrifice was still practiced at the time of this writing, this continued until 70 AD when the Temple was destroyed by the Romans.)*

8:5 They are maintaining a shadow service to God; one which was originally intended as a prophetic picture of the real, just as Moses followed instructions to erect a tabernacle consistent with the accurate pattern that God had shown him on the mountain.

8:6 Jesus is now the fulfillment of all those promises towards which the old practices were merely pointing; as when an arrow strikes the bullseye. The dispensation he now administers is far superior to the old. He is the arbitrator of a more effective covenant; sanctioned by its being an announcement of far greater benefit to mankind.

8:7 If there had been no flaw in the first dispensation, why bother to replace it by a second?

8:8 He had already faulted the first system when he said through Jeremiah, "Behold the days will come when I will make an entirely new covenant with the house of Israel and the house of Judah.

8:9 We will be making a new agreement, completely unlike the previous one based on external ritual. I had literally to take your hand and lead you out of slavery from Egypt; yet you refused to spontaneously follow or trust in me; I could never abide your indifference. *(God prophesies a covenant that will not be subject to the same defect of the previous one; or one that was spoon-fed to Israel and whose obligations they yet failed to meet. God had to take them by the hand to lead them out of Egypt. This time, he promised, I will put my laws into their minds and write them it upon their hearts ...)*

8:10 Now, instead of documenting my laws on stone, I will chisel them into your mind and engrave them in your inner consciousness; it will no longer be a one-sided affair. I will be your God and you will be my people, not by compulsion but by mutual desire.

8:11 Knowing me will no longer be a Sunday-school lesson, or something taught by persuasive words of doctrine, neither will they know me on account of family tradition or door to door evangelism *(each one telling his neighbor)*. Everyone, from the most unlikely to the most prominent people in society, will know me inwardly.

8:12 This knowledge of me will never again be based on a sin-consciousness. My act of mercy, extended in Christ as the new Covenant, has removed every possible definition of sin from memory! *(God's memory of our sins was not what needed to be addressed in the redemption of our innocence. God did not have a problem with sin-consciousness, we had! He wasn't hiding from Adam and Eve in the garden; they were hiding from him! What needed to be addressed were our perceptions of a judgmental God, which were the inevitable fruit of the "I-am-not-tree-system" and mentality.*

Revenge, judgment, guilt, condemnation, inferiority, shame, regret, suspicion etc. could not be treated lightly; they are the enemies of romance! If rules could do it, then the law would be our opportunity to save ourselves, simply by making the correct decisions! If willpower could save us then Moses would be our savior! But, alas! "The good that I want to do I cannot!" See Rom 7

The scapegoat system would be introduced to somehow address and attempt to manage the consequences of sin. The typical "eye for and eye, tooth for a tooth" scenario would be substituted with the idea of a scapegoat. And so, every system of sacrifice carried some significance, but only as far as it pointed to its weaknesses in dealing with the root of the problem, and the need for a better solution! We needed more than forgiveness of our sins; we needed a savior who could rescue us from our sinfulness! This was not merely a means whereby we could get rid of the cobwebs; the spider needed to be killed! The "pay now, sin later-system" had a very real sell-by date!

See Heb 10:2 & 3 Had it been possible to present the perfect offering that had the power to successfully remove any trace of a sin-consciousness, then the sacrificial system would surely have ceased to be relevant. But in the very repetition of these ritual sacrifices the awareness of guilt is reinforced rather than removed.

God does not demand sacrifice; he provides the sacrifice! The ultimate sacrifice for sins would never be something we did, or brought to God, to appeal to him; but the shocking scandal of the cross, is the fact that mankind is confronted with the extravagant, embarrassing proportions of the love of their Maker; he would go to the most ridiculous extreme to finally convince us of his heart towards us! In order to persuade us of our worth to him, he speaks the most severe scapegoat language: "Behold the Lamb of God, who takes away the sins of the world!" This completely disarms religion! Suddenly there is nothing that we can do to persuade God about our sincere intentions; this is God persuading us of his eternal love dream!

God did not clothe Adam with the skin of a slain animal because of a divine need to be appeased, but because of their unconditional love for Adam; they spoke the language of Adam's own judgment: Adam, not God, was embarrassed about his nakedness. The clothing was not to make God look at Adam differently, but to make Adam feel better about himself! And ultimately it was to prepare Adam for the unveiling of the mystery of mankind's redemption in the incarnation. Here Deity would clothe themselves in human skin in a son, and the Lion of Judah, would become the Lamb of God, in order to free our minds to re discover his image and likeness in our skin! Humankind is tailor-made for God!

See also **1 Peter 1:19 but you were redeemed with the priceless blood of Christ; he is the ultimate sacrifice; spotless and without blemish. He completes the prophetic picture!** (In him God speaks the most radical scapegoat language of the law of judgment, and brings final closure to a dead and redundant system! In Psalm 40:6,7, it is clearly stated that God does not require sacrifices or offerings! Jesus is the Lamb of God! He collides victoriously with the futile sacrificial system whereby offerings are constantly made to the pseudo, moody, monster gods of our imagination! This is the scandal of the cross! God does not demand a sacrifice that would change the way he thinks about mankind; he provides the sacrifice of himself in Christ in order to forever eradicate sin-consciousness from our minds and radically change the way we think about our Maker, one another and ourselves! [Sin-consciousness is a works-based consciousness.])

8:13 He announces the new dispensation to confirm that the old shadow system has been rendered redundant.

9:1 The first system followed a specific pattern of worship which was conducted in a specific and sacred place of worship. *(The detail of which spoke in shadows of the new.)*

9:2 The first tented area was called the Holy Place; the only light here came from the lamp stand illuminating the table upon which the [1]showbread was presented. *(The lamp stand was a beautifully crafted golden chandelier portraying budding and blossoming almond branches. Remember that this is also what Jeremiah saw in Jeremiah 1:12, when God said, "I am awake over my word to perform it." The same Hebrew word is used here, **shaqad**; the almond was called the "awake tree," because it blossomed first, while the other trees were still in their winter sleep. The Hebrew word is **lechem paniym,** face bread, or bread of the presence. What happened to us in Christ is according to God's eternal purpose [[1]**prothesis,**] which he has shown in every prophetic pointer and shadow; in the Hebrew tradition the showbread pointed to the true bread from heaven, the authentic word that proceeded from the mouth of God - Jesus, the incarnate word - sustaining the life of our design. The showbread pointed towards the daily sustenance of life in the flesh as the ultimate tabernacle of God, realized in the account of Jesus with the two men from Emmaus; their hearts were burning with resonance and faith while he opened the scriptures to them, and then around the table their eyes were opened to recognize him as the fulfillment of scripture, their true meal incarnated [Lk 24:27-31]. Mankind shall not live by bread alone, but by the authentic thought of God, the Word proceeding from his mouth, the original intent, his image and likeness incarnated, revealed, and redeemed in human life. See note to 1 Cor 11:34.)*

9:3 The second veil led to the inner tent known as the Most Holy Place.

9:4 Therein were the golden altar of incense, and the ark of the covenant. The [1]box was completely covered in gold, both inside and out. In it were kept the golden jar with a sample of the [2]miracle manna from the wilderness, as well as the budding rod of Aaron, as also the two engraved tablets of stone with the ten commandments of the Covenant. *(A "fire-pan" was for the purpose of carrying fire, in order to burn incense on the day of Atonement once a year in the ultimate place of worship. The word, [1]**kibotos,** the wooden box, is the same word used for Noah's ark; the container of mankind's redemption. Gen 6:14 The [2]**manna** prophetically pictured the true bread from heaven, not the bread that mankind's labor produces. John 4:35, 38.)*

9:5 Hovering above and over the ark of the Covenant were the two cherubim, images of glory, intent upon the mercy seat that [1]covered the box on which the blood was sprinkled once a year by the High Priest to cover the sins of the people. Every detail is significant but cannot be discussed at length in this writing. *(The Hebrew word, [1]**kopher,** means to cover (specifically with bitumen), figuratively to cover by legal and equal exchange in order to restore a previously disturbed balance. The rule was an eye for an eye, a tooth for a tooth, a life for a life, etc.*

The ark represented a place of mercy where atonement would be made. Innocence had to be achieved at a cost equal to the replacement value of the peace sought between the different parties. See also Genesis 6:14, where the same word denotes the

[1]*covering of Noah's ark with pitch. The Cross cannot be taken out of the equation of atonement. The first animal sacrifice was when God used an animal's skin to [1]cover Adam and Eve's nakedness.*

St. Cyril of Alexandria [376 – 444] in his work That Christ is One, writes: Christus licet unus sit, multifariam tamen a nobis intelligitur: Ipse est Tabernaculum propter carnis tegumenturn: Ipse est Mensa, quia noster cibus est et vita: Ipse est Arca habens legem Dei reconditam, quia est Verbum Patris: Ipse est Candelabrum, quia est lux spiritualis: Ipse est Altare incensi, quia est odor suavitatis in sanctificationem: Ipse est Altare holocausti, quia est hostia pro totius mundi vita in cruce oblata. "

Although Christ be but one, yet he is understood by us under a variety of forms. He is the Tabernacle, on account of the human body in which he dwelt. He is the Table, because he is our Bread of life. He is the Ark which has the law of God enclosed within, because he is the Word of the Father. He is the Candlestick, because he is our spiritual light. He is the Altar of incense, because he is the sweet-smelling odour of sanctification. He is the Altar of burnt-offering, because he is the victim, by death on the cross, for the sins of the whole world.")

9:6 In the context of this arrangement the priests performed their daily duties, both morning and evening. *(The daily duties included their dress and preparations, baptisms, sacrificial offerings, lighting and trimming, removing the old showbread and replacing it with fresh bread, and sprinkling the blood of the sin offerings before the veil of the sanctuary.)*

9:7 The routine was interrupted only once a year, when the High Priest alone would enter the second tent, the most sacred place of worship, with the blood sacrifice for his own and the people's accumulated errors.

9:8 Already in this arrangement the Holy Spirit indicated that there was a yet more sacred way, beyond the first tent, that was still to be opened. While the first pattern was still being upheld, its fulfillment in truth could not yet commence.

9:9 The tabernacle pattern of that time was an analogy of the hitherto imperfect system in which the gifts and sacrifices presented failed completely to cleanse the conscience of the worshipper.

9:10 All these external rituals pertaining to food and drink and the various ceremonial baptisms and rules for bodily conduct were imposed upon them until the anticipated time of restoration; the foretold moment when [1]all that was crooked would be made straight and restored to its natural and original condition. *(This word, [1]diothosis, is only used in this one place in the New Testament; what was crooked will be made thoroughly straight, restoring to its natural and normal condition something which in some way protrudes or has gotten out of line, as broken or misshapen limbs.)*

9:11 But now Christ has made his public appearance as High Priest of a perfect tabernacle. The good things that were predicted have arrived. This new tabernacle does not derive from its shadow type, the previous

man-made one. It is the reality. *(The restoration of God's original dwelling place in human life is again revealed!)*

9:12 As High Priest, his permission to enter the Holy Place was not secured by the blood of beasts. By his own blood he obtained access on behalf of the human race. Only one act was needed for him to enter the most sacred place of grace and there to institute a ransom of perpetual consequence. *(The perfection of the redemption he secured needs no further sacrifice. There are no outstanding debts; there is nothing we need do to add weight to what he has accomplished once and for all. The only possible priesthood activity we can now engage in is to continually bring a sacrifice of the fruit of our lips, giving thanks to his Name; no blood, just fruit, even our acts of self-sacrifice, giving of time and money, etc. are all just the fruit of our constant gratitude!)*

9:13 The blood of beasts and the ashes of the burnt sacrifice of a heifer could only achieve a very temporal and surface cleansing by being sprinkled on the guilty. *(The word for heifer, is damalis, from damatzo, to tame; this was the most dear and expensive sacrifice. She was a strong, pristine, spotless female calf, she was raised as a family pet; "A Little Princess!" This was the best that the law-system could present; yet, no inner purging of conscience was possible; only the sense of temporal relief; whilst knowing that the entire process would have to be repeated again and again! In this arrangement, God addressed the dilemma of our sin consciousness; the deep-seated stain that it had left, needed to be thoroughly exposed, and then brought to closure. The shadow system with its imperfections, as a possible means of obtaining a lasting and meaningful sense of innocence, had to be exhausted; ultimately proving that no sacrifice that anyone can bring at any expense of their own, could possibly match the sacrifice of God giving himself as scapegoat to the human race in order to persuade us that his love for us would go to the scandalous extreme, where we are finally confronted with the fact that it is not in a sacrifice that we bring where God's mind is favorably influenced towards us; but in the shocking sacrifice of himself, where he forever, in the most radical language, impact our ideas and thoughts about the Father, Son and Spirit's estimate of us. There is nothing dearer in the universe to them, but our redeemed innocence and our individual value realized! See Collossians 2:14,15 in the Mirror Bible.)*

9:14 How much more effective was the blood of Christ, when he presented his own flawless life through the eternal Spirit before God, in order to purge your conscience from its frustration under the [1]cul-de-sac rituals of the law. There is no comparison between a guilt- and duty-driven, dead religious system, and the vibrancy of living your life free from a sin-consciousness! This is what the new testament priesthood is all about! *(Dead works, [1]nekros ergon. A dead, religious-routine system can never compete with the resurrected Christ now realized in you.)*

9:15 As [1]fully representing mankind, Jesus's death brought an end to the old, and introduced the New Testament. He thus redeemed us from the transgressions recorded under the first Covenant and identified us as heirs; qualifying us to participate in the full inheritance of all that he obtained on our behalf. *(The concept of a [1]mediator, **mesites**, in this analogy, is* *not a go-between, as if Jesus had to change the Father's mind about us; it was our minds that needed to be persuaded! Jesus did not save us from God; he is fully God and fully man, and in him mankind is most completely represented. See Galatians 3:20; also Hebrews 6:16-20)*

9:16 For a will to take effect the person who made it must be dead.

9:17 Before the testator dies the will is merely a future promise with no immediate benefit to anyone.

9:18 Even the first Covenant required a death for its actualization; the blood of the animal sacrifice represented that death.

9:19 After Moses uttered the detailed requirements of the law in the hearing of all the people, he would take the blood of calves and of goats, mix it with water and, dipping a bunch of hyssop bound with scarlet wool into the blood-basins, sprinkle the blood on the book and upon the people.

9:20 While performing this cleansing ritual, Moses would solemnly declare, "This is the blood of the covenant which God has made binding upon you."

9:21 The same blood was then also sprinkled on the tabernacle, and on all the furniture and ministry utensils.

9:22 Thus, according to the law, all purging was by means of blood; [1]forgiveness was specifically associated with the shedding of blood. *(The idea of closure to the particular case was communicated in the death of an innocent victim. The blood symbolizes this currency. The word translated forgiveness, or remission is the word [1]aphiemi, from apo, away from, and hieimi an intensive form of eimi, I am; thus forgiveness is in essence a restoring to your true 'I-am-ness.' The injury, insult, shame, hostility or guilt would no longer define the individual.)*

9:23 If the methods of the law were only a shadow prefiguring the heavenly reality, the fulfillment of these examples surely requires a stronger and more efficacious sacrifice.

9:24 In Christ we have so much more than a type reflected in the tabernacle of holy places set up by human hands. He entered into the heavenly sphere itself, where he personally represents mankind face to face with God.

9:25 Neither was it necessary for him to ever repeat his sacrifice. The High Priests under the old shadow system stood proxy with substitute animal sacrifices that had to be offered every year.

9:26 But Jesus did not have to suffer again and again since the [1]fall of the world; the [2]single sacrifice of himself in the fulfillment of history now reveals how he has brought sin to naught. *(The word, [1]katabole, means cast down. [2]God's Lamb took away the sins of the world!)*

9:27 The same goes for everyone: a person dies only once, and then faces judgment.

9:28 Christ died once and faced the judgment of the entire human race! His second appearance has nothing to do with sin, but to reveal salvation for all to ¹fully embrace him. *(To fully embrace, ¹**apekdechomai**, from **apo**, away from [that which defined me before] and **ek**, out of, source; and **dechomai**, to take into ones hands to accept whole heartedly, to fully embrace. In his resurrection he appeared as Savior of the world! Sin is no longer on the agenda, for the Lamb of God has taken away the sins of the world! Jesus Christ fulfilled mankind's destiny with death! [1 Cor 15:3-5, Rom 4:25, Acts 17:30, 31.])*

Note: *(Even in his first coming, he did not come to condemn the world. The Father judges no one for he has handed over all judgment to the son, who judged the world in righteousness when he took their chastisement in his own body. Now in his appearance in us, his body, his mission is to unveil the consequence of redemption through the Holy Spirit.*

*This is not to be confused with the doctrine of his second coming. Many scriptures have been translated and interpreted with only a futuristic value and have consequently neutralized many, like the Jews, to diligently wait for the Messiah still to come. The Messiah has come once and for all as Messiah. Jesus appeared again after his resurrection and now his resurrection life in us as his body is the extension of his second appearance; God making his appeal to an already reconciled world to "be reconciled!" [Acts 3:26, 2 Cor 5:19, 20] The church continued to postpone the reality that God introduced in Christ. We are now already fully represented in his blamelessness! The second coming as doctrine is not in context of these chapters at all! [See 1 Pet 1:10-13] The Aramaic word, **maranatha**, means our Lord has come!*

*See also 1 Thessalonians 2:19 We expect nothing less in the context of the gospel than you enjoying a face to face encounter in the ¹immediate presence of our Lord Jesus Christ! This is our delight and wreath of honor! (The word ¹**parousia** speaks of the immediate presence of the Lord! From **para**, a preposition indicating close proximity, a thing proceeding from a sphere of influence, with a suggestion of union of place of residence, to have sprung from its author and giver, originating from, denoting the point from which an action originates, intimate connection; and **eimi**, I am! There is not even a hint of judgment or punishment in this word! Please do not believe everything you read in Strongs! "G3952 parousia from the present participle of G3918; a being near, that is, advent; often, return; specifically of Christ to punish Jerusalem, or finally the wicked."!!??))*

10:1 For the law presented to us a faint shadow, outlining the promise of the blessings anticipated in the coming of Christ, even detailing its future significance. The mere sketch however, could never be confused with the actual object that it represented. The annual sacrificial rites as shadow of the eventual object would always leave the worshipper feeling inadequate and be a reminder year after year of the sinfulness of mankind. (Barnes Notes on Heb 10:1, "For the law having a shadow: That is, the whole of the Mosaic economy was a shadow; for so the word "Law" is often used. The word "shadow" here refers to a rough outline of anything, a mere sketch, such as a carpenter draws with a piece of chalk, or such as an artist delineates when he is about to make a picture.

He sketches an outline of the object which he desires to draw, which has "some" resemblance to it, but is not the "very image;" for it is not yet complete. The words rendered "the very image" refer to a painting or statue that is finished, where every part is an exact representation of the original. The "good things to come" here refer to the future blessings which would be conferred on mankind by the Gospel. The idea is, that under the ancient sacrifices there was an imperfect representation; a dim outline of the blessings which the Gospel would impart to people. They were a typical representation; they were not such that it could be pretended that they would answer the purpose of the things themselves which they were to represent, and would make those who offered them perfect.

Such a rude outline; such a mere sketch, or imperfect delineation, could no more answer the purpose of saving the soul than the rough sketch which an architect makes would answer the purpose of a house, or than the first outline which a painter draws would answer the purpose of a perfect and finished portrait. All that could be done by either would be to convey some distant and obscure idea of what the house or the picture might be, and this was all that was done by the Law of Moses."

The Gospel is no longer a future prediction; it is a now and relevant revelation. We are talking good news, and not just good predictions! News already happened! Every definition of distance or delay is cancelled in Christ)

10:2 Had it been possible to present the perfect offering that had the power to successfully remove any trace of a sin-consciousness, then the sacrificial system would surely have ceased to be relevant.

10:3 But in the very repetition of these ritual sacrifices the awareness of guilt is reinforced rather than removed.

10:4 The conclusion is clear: animal sacrifices failed to remove anyone's sinfulness or their sin-consciousness.

10:5 So when Jesus, the Messiah, arrives as the fulfillment of all the types and shadows, he quotes Psalm 40:6-8, and says, "In sacrifices and offerings God takes no pleasure; but you have ordained my incarnation!" (Albert Barnes writes the following commentary: A body hast thou prepared me - The quotation of this and the two following verses by the apostle, is taken from the Septuagint, with scarcely any variety of reading: they are widely different in verbal expression in the Hebrew. In the Hebrew text David's words are, **oznayim caritha**

lli, which we translate, My ears hast thou opened; but the writer of this Epistle quotes, **soma** *[body]* **de katertiso moi.** *How is it possible that the Septuagint and the apostle should take a meaning so completely different from the sense of the Hebrew? Dr. Kennicott has a very ingenious conjecture here: he supposes that the Septuagint and apostle express the meaning of the words as they stood in the copy from which the Greek translation [Septuagint] was made; and that the present Hebrew text is corrupted in the word* **aznayim,** *ears, which has been written through carelessness for* **az gevah,** *then, a body... The first syllable,* **az,** *Then, is the same in both; and the latter,* **nyim,** *which, joined to* **az** *makes* **oznayim,** *might have been easily mistaken for* **gevah,** *body; the letter* **nun** *being very like the letter* **gimel;** **yod** *like* **vau;** *and* **he** *like final* **mem;** *especially if the line on which the letters were written in the MS. happened to be blacker than ordinary, which has often been a cause of mistake, it might then have been easily taken for the under-stroke of the* **mem,** *and thus give rise to a corrupt reading; add to this, the root* **carah** *signifies as well to prepare, as to open, bore, etc. On this supposition the ancient copy translated by the Septuagint, and followed by the apostle, must have read the text thus:* **az gevah charitha lli;** Σωμα δε κατηρτισω μοι. *Then a body thou hast prepared me: thus the Hebrew text, the version of the Septuagint, and the apostle, will agree in what is known to be an indisputable fact in Christianity; namely, that Christ was incarnated for the sin of the world.*

The Ethiopic has nearly the same reading: the Arabic has both, "A body hast thou prepared me, and mine ears thou hast opened." But the Syriac, the Chaldee, and the Vulgate, agree with the present Hebrew text; and none of the MSS. collated by Kennicott and De Rossi have any various reading on the disputed words.

It is remarkable, that all the offerings and sacrifices which were considered to be of an atoning or cleansing nature, offered under the law, are here enumerated by the psalmist and the apostle, to show that none of them, nor all of them, could take away sin; and that the grand sacrifice of Christ was that alone which could do it.

Four kinds are here specified, both by the psalmist and the apostle: viz. Sacrifice, zebach, θυσια; *Offering, minchah,* προσφορα; *Burnt-Offering, olah,* ὁλοκαυτωμα; *Sin-Offering, chataah,* περι ἁμαρτιας. *It was impossible that the blood of bulls and goats, etc. should take away sin.)*

10:6 None of the prescribed offerings and sacrifices, including burnt offerings and sin offerings were your request. *(For the use of the word 'request' here, and pleasure in verse 6, see the Hebrew words used in Psalm 40:6, Chapetz - pleasure, delight and Shawal, request, demand.)*

10:7 "Then I said, I read in your book what you wrote about me; so here I am, I have come to fulfill my destiny." *(Ps 40:7, Lk 4:17, Lk 24:27, 44.)*

10:8 Having said what he did in the above quote, that the prescribed offerings and sacrifices were neither his desire nor delight, he condemned the entire sacrificial system upheld by the law.*(These only served to sustain a sin-consciousness and was of no redemptive benefit to anyone.)*

10:9 Also by saying, "I am commissioned to fulfil your will," he announces the final closure of the first in order to introduce the second.

(Grace replaces the law; innocence supersedes sin-consciousness.)

10:10 So, by this fulfilled will, in the mind of God and by his resolution he declares mankind immediately sanctified through one sacrifice; the presentation of the body of Jesus Christ.

10:11 Every priest continually repeats the same daily rituals and sacrifices, knowing that they have always proved incapable of removing sins.

10:12 But now we have an exception. In complete contrast to the previous priesthood, this priest offered a single sacrifice of perpetual efficacy for sins. To celebrate the perfection of what was attained through his single sacrifice, he sat down as the executive authority of God. *(God's right hand [Heb 1:3]. He occupies the highest seat of dominion to endorse mankind's innocence! "Having accomplished purification of sins, he sat down.")*

10:13 His seat of authority is established on the sure expectation that all his enemies will be subdued. He will stand in triumph, his feet on the neck of his enemy.

10:14 By that one perfect sacrifice he has [1]perfectly [2]sanctified sinful mankind forever. *(The word, [2]hagiazomenous, means sanctify, the present participle describes an action thought of as simultaneous with the action of the main verb, "perfectly;" [1]teteleioken, in the Perfect Tense denotes an action which is completed in the past, but the effects of which are regarded as continuing into the present. [See Heb 2:11] For he who sanctifies and those who are sanctified have all one origin.)*

10:15 This is exactly what the Holy Spirit now endorses in us having already foretold it in scripture. *(Jer 31:33, 34)*

10:16 This is my covenant that I will make with you during those days, says the Lord; I will greatly advantage you by [1]giving my laws in your hearts and engrave them in your inmost thoughts. *(The word, [1]didomi, means to give someone something to their advantage.)*

10:17 This is final: I have deleted the record of your sins and misdeeds. It is not possible to recall them. *(Nothing in God's reference of mankind, reminds him of sin. See Hebrews 8:12)*

10:18 Sins were dealt with in such a thorough manner that the idea of having to add any further offerings in future would never again be considered. Nothing that we can personally sacrifice could add further virtue to our innocence.

10:19 Brethren, this means that through what the blood of Jesus communicates and represents, we are now welcome to access this ultimate place of sacred encounter with unashamed confidence.

10:20 A brand new way of life has been introduced. Because of his flesh torn on the cross *(our own flesh can no longer be a valid excuse to interrupt the expression of the life of our design).*

10:21 We have a High Priest in the house!

10:22 We are free to approach him with absolute confidence, fully persuaded in our hearts that nothing can any longer separate us from him. We are invited to draw near now! We are thoroughly cleansed, inside and out, with no trace of sin's stains on our conscience or conduct. The sprinkled blood purges our inner thought-patterns; our bodies also are bathed in clean water. *(Our behavior bears witness to this.)*

10:23 Our conversation echoes his persuasion; his faithfulness backs his promises. *(His integrity inspires our confession.)*

10:24 Let us also think of creative ways by which we can influence one another to find inspired expression in doing things that benefit others. Good actions give voice and volume to the love of God.

10:25 In the light of our free access to the Father, let us extend that embrace to one another. Our gatherings are no longer a repetition of tradition but an essential fellowship where we remind one another of our true identity. Let us do so with greater urgency now the day has dawned in our understanding. *(The prophetic shadow has been replaced by the light of day.)*

10:26 To know the truth, as we now do, and still persist in deliberate sinning is to openly discard God's provision in Christ. But unlike the old sacrificial system, no further sacrifice can be offered in the new.

10:27 To despise and reject his gift inevitably brings the self-inflicted judgment of the law of works; this destructive judgment devours lives like stubble in a fire. *(To know that Jesus bore your judgment and still prefer to carry it yourself by remaining under the law is absurd!)*

10:28 There was no mercy under Moses's law; two or three witnesses could sentence a suspect to death. *([See also Heb 6:6-17; Jas 2:13] Judgment shows no mercy to those who do not walk in mercy, but (the law of liberty) mercy fears no judgment. [Gal 5:22, 23] There is no law against love. [See also 1 Jn 4:18])*

10:29 With how much closer scrutiny do you suppose someone will be viewed who has trampled the Son of God underfoot and scorned the blood of the Covenant by publicly insulting the Spirit of grace. *(Preferring the law above the revelation of grace brings you back under judgment of the law without the possibility of further sacrifice. There is no alternative mercy outside of God's grace gift in Christ.)*

10:30 As Jews we are familiar with scripture, which says that God is the revealer of righteousness, jealous to restore the order of peace. He is the umpire of his people. *(Deut 32: 36)*

10:31 What a foolish thing it would be to deliberately shun the hands that bled for your salvation.

10:32 Remember how strongly you stood against painful contradictions in those early days when you first saw the light.

10:33 As if on a theatre stage, you were publicly ridiculed and afflicted for your faith, both personally and in your association with others that were similarly abused.

10:34 I remind you of the sincere sympathy you felt for me then, during my imprisonment; how you also cheerfully accepted the plundering of your personal property. You were convinced that the treasure you have within you is of far greater and more permanent value, secured as it is in the heavenly dimension.

10:35 I urge you not to relinquish your confident conversation. Persuasion gives substance to every definition of reward and confirms what grace reveals.

10:36 Employ patience as you continue to echo the poetry of God's desire for you to possess the promise. *(The word, [1]poeima, means make poetry of the promise; your doing is to echo the promise and the desire of God! The promise is a gift of faith and not a reward for behavior!)*

10:37 Time becomes insignificant once the promise is realized. Remember how the promise of his imminent appearance was recorded in scripture. *(The arrival of Jesus is the fulfillment of the promise and the realizing of righteousness by faith, as Habakkuk prophesied. [Hab 2:2-4.] He is the fullness of time. [Gal 4:4])*

10:38 Righteousness by God's faith defines life; reverting to the law of works grieves God's work of grace. *(Instead of reading the curse when disaster strikes, Habakkuk realizes that the Promise out dates performance as the basis to mankind's acquittal. Deuteronomy 28 would no longer be the motivation or the measure of right or wrong behavior! "Though the fig tree does not blossom, nor fruit be on the vines, the produce of the olive fails and the fields yield no food, the flock be cut off from the fold and there be no herd in the stalls, yet I will rejoice in the Lord, I will joy in the God of my salvation. God, the Lord, is my strength; he makes my feet like hinds' feet, he makes me tread upon my high places. [Hab 2:4, 3:17-19 RSV])*

10:39 But we are not of the quitting kind; we possess a persuasion of soul that believes against all the odds.

11:1 Persuasion confirms confident expectation and proves the unseen world to be more real than the seen. Faith celebrates as certain what hope visualizes as future. *(The shadow no longer substitutes the substance. Jesus is the substance of things hoped for the evidence of everything the prophets foretold. The unveiling of Christ in human life completes mankind's every expectation. Col 1:27.)*

11:2 People of previous generations received the testimony of their hope in faith. It was faith that made their hope tangible. *(Only the Messiah can give substance to the Messianic hope. No substitute will suffice!)*

11:3 Faith alone explains what is not apparent to the natural eye; how the ages were perfectly framed by the Word of God. Now we understand that everything visible has its origin in the invisible.

11:4 It was faith that made the difference between the sacrifices of Abel and Cain, and confirmed Abel's righteousness. God bore witness to righteousness as a gift rather than a reward! Even though he was murdered, his faith still has a voice today. *(It was not in what they brought, but in Abel's faith that righteousness was revealed.)*

11:5 Enoch enjoyed God's favor by faith, in spite of Adam's fall; he proved that faith defeats death. *(His absent body prophesied the resurrection of Christ; faith does not die!)*

11:6 There is no substitute [1]reward for faith. Faith's return exceeds any other sense of achievement. Faith knows that God is; those who desire to respond to his invitation to draw near, realize by faith that he is life's most perfect gift. *(If he is the desired one then no substitute will suffice. Jesus Christ defines God's faith; he is Emmanuel. He is the substance and evidence of all that God believes. Jesus is what God believes. The word translated "reward" is the word [1]**misthapodotes**. This word is only used once in the Bible and is an interesting combination of two words, **misthoo**, a wage and **apodidomi** to give away; righteousness is revealed by faith as a gift and not as a reward for keeping the law; faith pleases God, not good or bad behavior.)*

11:7 Noah received Divine instruction to save his household from judgment; faith prompted him to construct the Ark immediately, long before the rains were evident. His faith demonstrated the difference between judgment and justification.

11:8 By faith Abraham acknowledged the [1]call of God which gave him his identity and destiny, as evidence of his inheritance as he journeyed into the unknown. *(The word, [1]**kaleo**, means to call, to identify by name, to surname.)*

11:9 Nothing but his faith seemed permanent while Abraham camped in tents like a stranger in the land of promise. His sons Isaac and Jacob joined him as sojourners; equally persuaded that they were heirs of the same promise.

11:10 His faith saw a city with permanent foundations, designed and constructed by God.

11:11 Sarah's testimony of faith is just as amazing: she conceived and bore a child when it was humanly impossible. She believed that God would be faithful to his promise, and ¹gave that belief authority over her life. *(The word, ¹hegeomai, strengthened form of ago, to officially appoint in a position of authority.)*

11:12 Faith brought into reality an offspring beyond calculation; from one as good as dead children would be born more numerous than the stars and as impossible to count as the grains of sand on every distant sea shore. *(The uttermost parts of the earth, bordered by the sea shore, will know the blessing of righteousness by faith which is the blessing of Abraham, meant for the entire world.[1 Pet 1:3])*

11:13 These heroes of faith all died believing. Although they did not witness the promise in their lifetime, they saw its fulfillment in the future and embraced the promise by their persuasion. Convinced of its reality; they declared by their way of living that they were mere sojourners and pilgrims in a shadow land whose geography could neither confine nor define their true inheritance.

11:14 They clearly declared by faith a hinterland beyond their immediate horizon. *(A place of promise where God and mankind would be one again.)*

11:15 They did not regret the country they had left behind. Their faith took them beyond the point of no return. *(Do not allow the contradictions in your past or present to become your reference once again. James says that the person who goes back into an old mind-set immediately forgets what manner of person they are, as revealed in the mirror word, the law of perfect liberty [James 1:24, 25]. The revelation concerning who a person is in Christ declares that the old things have passed away [in his death]. Behold, everything has become new! In his resurrection we were born anew. [2 Cor 5:14-17, 1 Pet 1:3])*

11:16 Their faith saw a greater reality in the spiritual realm than that which they experienced in their present situation; they reached for their true native city designed by God where he himself is proud to be their permanent address. *(The fulfillment of the promise is Christ. He is both our native land and our eternal city!)*

11:17 Faith became a more tangible evidence of the promise than even Isaac could ever be to Abraham. Isaac neither fulfilled nor replaced the promise. Inspired by what faith saw, Abraham was ready to do the ridiculous; to sacrifice his only son, convinced that not even Isaac's death could nullify the promise that God had made to him. *(If Isaac was not the substance of Abraham's faith then who was? Abraham saw beyond Isaac. Jesus said, "Abraham saw my day!" [Jn 8:56-58] "Before Abraham was, I am.")*

11:18 Yet Abraham knew that God had said that his lineage of faith would be traced through Isaac!

11:19 He made a prophetic ¹calculation by faith to which there could only be one logical conclusion based on the word he had received: that God would raise the promise from the dead. *(In the context of Abraham's vision, this was an analogy pointing to the parable of the death and resurrection of Christ. A calculation, logical conclusion, from the word, [1]logitzomai, from logos; God's faith is God's logic.)*

11:20 By the same faith Isaac extended the future of the promise in the blessing he pronounced over his sons, Esau and Jacob.

11:21 In his dying moments, Jacob, in worship to the God of Abraham, as the father of the nations, included in the promise [1]the sons of Joseph who were born in Egypt. *([1]In exalting the two grandsons into the rank and right of Joseph's brothers, he bestowed on them, rather than on Reuben, the double portion of the first-born. Again, faith exceeds the natural. Even though they had an Egyptian mother, they would have an equal interest in all the spiritual and temporal blessings of the covenant of promise.)*

11:22 At the end of his life, Joseph prophetically reminded his sons of the exodus. He had such a firm belief that they would possess the land of promise that he exacted an oath from them: they were not to leave his bones in Egypt.

11:23 By faith the parents of Moses did not fear the king's decree, but hid him from Pharaoh for three months, because they saw a future in the child.

11:24 It was faith that made Moses realize that he was not the son of Pharaoh's daughter.

11:25 By faith he preferred to be associated with the affliction of God's people rather than with the fleeting privileges of Pharaoh's house, which did not constitute the true [1]portion of his inheritance. *(The word, [1]hamartia, from ha, meaning negative, and meros, meaning form or portion, without your portion, to fall short of your portion; often translated as sin.)*

11:26 He was not embarrassed to be associated with the Messianic promise at the expense of the treasures of Egypt. He deliberately looked away from those towards the greater riches of his reward in Christ. *(No reward of the flesh can compare with the wealth of faith.)*

11:27 The rage of the King did not scare him when he abandoned Egypt; faith, giving substance to the invisible, made him brave.

11:28 His faith saw the Paschal Lamb and the sprinkled blood on the door posts as the salvation of the people.

11:29 By faith they crossed the Red Sea on dry ground, but the Egyptians drowned when they followed them.

11:30 By faith the walls of the city of Jericho collapsed when Israel marched around the city for seven days. *(They did not conquer through the strength of their army.)*

11:31 Rahab the prostitute's faith saved her even though her house was built in the wall! While all the other houses collapsed around her, her own remained. She welcomed the spies and acknowledged the God who saved them out of Egypt. *(Josh 2:11)* Her family also was given an equal opportunity to be saved through her faith. *(Imagine their surprise, bearing in mind her life and shameful reputation!)*

11:32 And so the list of faith-heroes continues. There is not enough time to tell the stories of Gideon and Barak and Sampson and Jephtah, of David, Samuel and the prophets.

11:33 These are they who conquered kingdoms by faith. *(Gideon, like Rahab, was in no position to claim any credit for his achievement; faith nullifies boasting [see Rom 3:27, Judg 6:11-16]* They accomplished righteousness by that same faith and thus secured the promise *[by faith and not by performance]. Deborah told Barak the son of Abinoam that, although he would deliver Israel, he would not get the honor, since a woman would do it for him. [See Judg 4:21] In the principle of righteousness by faith, the flesh will take no glory. Barak, means to worship in adoration, and Abinoam means, "my father's delight" or "grace.")* By faith they shut the mouths of lions. *(Samson, whose mighty achievements were immediately accredited to the Spirit of the Lord who moved upon him. Again there was no occasion to glory in the flesh.)*

11:34 Their faith extinguished powerful fires. They escaped from fierce battles. They were empowered in spite of their frailty. They became heroes in battle and caused hostile armies to flee before them. *(Jephtah whose own brothers disinherited him because his mother was a prostitute became the captain of the army of Israel.)*

11:35 By faith women received their children back from the dead. *(1 Kings 17:18-24, 2 Kings 4:32-34)* Others were severely tortured for their faith and refused to accept release when it was offered them on condition that they would renounce their opinions. To have accepted deliverance then could have saved their lives, but their faith saw a more honorable and glorious resurrection.

11:36 Still others were mocked and ridiculed for their faith: they were beaten up, shackled and imprisoned.

11:37 While some were stoned to death, others *(like Isaiah the prophet)* were sawn asunder with a wood saw. There were yet others who were tempted by the promise of possible release from torture, and then were brutally slaughtered with the sword. Many became wandering refugees with nothing but sheep and goatskins for clothing. They lost everything and were harassed and tormented.

11:38 The world did not realize their worth. These faith-heroes were often driven from their homes and forced to live in the deserts and mountains; sleeping like animals in caves and holes in the ground.

11:39 Their lives were trophies to their faith, as the substance of what was visualized by their hope, and the evidence of things their natural eyes never saw.

11:40 God saw the perfect picture in us; we now complete the history of their lives. *(Everything that the shadows prefigured has now found its substance through Christ in us.)*

12:1 So now the stage is set for us: all these faith-heroes cheer us on, as it were, like a great multitude of spectators in the amphitheater. This is our moment. As with an athlete who is determined to win, it would be silly to carry any baggage of the old law-system that would weigh one down. Make sure you do not get your feet clogged up with sin-consciousness. Become absolutely streamlined in faith. Run the race of your spiritual life with total persuasion. *(Persuaded in the success of the cross.)*

12:2 Look away from the shadow dispensation of the law and the prophets and fix your eyes upon Jesus. He is the fountainhead and conclusion of faith. He saw the joy *(of mankind's salvation)* when he braved the cross and despised the shame of it. As the executive authority of God *(the right hand of the Throne of God)* he now occupies the highest seat of dominion to endorse mankind's innocence! *(Having accomplished purification of sins, he sat down. [Heb 1:3, Isa 53:11])*

12:3 [1]Ponder how he overcame all the odds stacked against him; this will boost your soul-energy when you feel exhausted. *([1]analogitsomai, upwards calculation.)*

12:4 Would you be willing to die for your faith? *(Are you as persuaded of your faith in the substance of Christ as your predecessors were in their believing a mere shadow?)*

12:5 The word in scripture that confirms your genesis in God addresses you as sons, "My son do not undervalue the [1]loving instruction of the Lord; neither become despondent when you are corrected." *(The word, [1]parakletos, in the King James Version is translated as exhortation, but here it is translated rather as loving instruction, "comfort" as in John in relation to the Holy Spirit, the Comforter. The word consists of two components, para, a preposition indicating close proximity, a thing proceeding from a sphere of influence, with a suggestion of union of place of residence, to have sprung from its author and giver, originating from, denoting the point from which an action originates, intimate connection, and kaleo, to identify by name, to surname.)*

12:6 For every instruction is inspired by his love, even as a father would discipline his sons with affection, though it might seem harsh at the time.

12:7 Embrace correction. His [1]instruction confirms your true sonship, just as a father would take natural responsibility for the [2]education of his children. *(The word, [1]paideo, comes from pais, for a boy or a girl and deo, to bind, to tie, thus to connect with education, instruction, schooling of a child. In Latin, it is [2]educare, to draw out!)*

12:8 See yourselves as sons, not as illegitimate children *(children of faith, not of the slave woman)*, welcoming your spiritual education together with the rest of the family of faith.

12:9 As we have shown respect to our natural fathers in the process of our education, how much more should we value the instruction of the Father of our spiritual origin who upholds the life of our design.

12:10 In their opinion they gave us the best possible education during the brief time that we were under their roof; God has our ultimate well-being in mind.

12:11 The process of education is not immediately appreciated; at the time it seems to be more pain than pleasure, but it certainly yields the harvest of righteousness for the faith athlete.

12:12 Shake off your weariness, loosen your limbs, catch your breath! *(Get back into faith-mode, quit the flesh-mode)*

12:13 Get rid of all obstacles that could possibly cause you to stumble and sprain an ankle! Don't let a recurrent injury force you out of the race. [1]Recover and carry on running. Don't allow old legalistic mind-sets to trip you up again. *(Isaiah 40:28-31, the [1]kawa principle, [1]intertwining with God's thoughts concerning you immediately causes you to escape the weariness of the old DIY times and mount up with wings like an eagle, to run and not be weary, to walk and not faint! Hebrew kawa, to intertwine.)*

12:14 Pursue peace with all men; true friendship can only be enjoyed in an environment of total forgiveness and innocence. This makes God visible in your life.

12:15 You must understand that this is a grace-race and not a law-race. While we're in compete- and compare-mode we create the opportunity for resentment to flourish and to poison many in the process. *(We are all equally included in the same victory in Christ!)*

12:16 A performance-driven mind-set triggers the law system into action and [1]distorts the picture: suddenly the fleeting moment of pleasure seems more attractive than your true portion This is exactly what happened to Esau, when he traded his birthright for a morsel of meat. *(Sin is a distorted picture; the word, [1]hamartia, often translated as sin is made up of two words, ha, meaning without, and meros, meaning form, or alloted portion.)*

12:17 Esau's regret could not change Isaac's mind. God's mind is made up about our salvation. *(We are saved by faith in his finished work and not by our own works; his system of faith cannot be challenged or replaced by another law system. Sincerity does not influence God; faith does.)*

12:18 We are not talking of a visible and tangible mountain here, one spectacularly ablaze in a setting of dark blackness and tempestuous winds. *(Witness the vivid contrast between the giving of the law and the unfolding of grace; the exclusiveness of the one and the all inclusive embrace of the other. The dramatic encounter of Moses on the mountain is by far exceeded by the mountaintop experience to which we are now welcomed and elevated through Christ! Mankind is now fully represented and co-seated together with Christ in heavenly places! [Eph 2:5, 6, Hos 6:2])*

12:19 Shrill trumpet sounds and a thunderous voice uttering human language. This filled the people with such terror that they begged for silence!

12:20 Beast and human alike felt threatened and excluded from that terrible mountain!

12:21 Even Moses, the representative of the people, was extremely terrified. He was shivering and shaking. Who could approach God and live? How impossible it seemed to find favor with such a 'terrifying' God!

12:22 By contrast, we have been welcomed to an invisible mount Zion; the city of peace *(Jerusalem)*, the residence of the living God, the festive assembly of an innumerable angelic host!

12:23 We are participating in a mass joint-celebration of heavenly and earthly beings; the [1]ekklesia-church of the firstborn mirror-inscribed in the heavenlies. *(Our original identity, [1]ekklesia, from ek, a preposition that always denotes origin, and **kaleo**, meaning to identify by name, to surname], is endorsed by Jesus, patterned in him, the first born from the dead.)*

12:24 Jesus is the spokesman and arbitrator of the New Testament order. His blood signature sanctions mankind's innocence. This is a complete new language compared to the shadow-type message of the blood sacrifice that Abel brought. *(Abel's faith was a prophetic introduction to the sacrificial shadow system of the Old Covenant.)*

12:25 If Jesus is the crescendo of God's final message to mankind, you cannot afford to politely excuse yourself from this conversation. Consider the prominent place that Moses plays in the history of Israel: if you think that Moses or any of the Prophets who spoke with authority on earth deserve honor, how much more should this word that God declared from heaven concerning our sonship, and our redeemed innocence revealed in the Messiah himself, deserve our undivided attention!

12:26 When he introduced the prophetic shadow of what was to come *(the Law system)*, his voice visibly shook the earth. *(Ex 19:18.)* But now the Messiah has come *(he is the desire of the nations; he is what heaven and earth were waiting for [Hag 2:6,7])* The voice of God *(articulated in Christ's birth, life, ministry, death, and resurrection)* has rocked not only the systems on the earth, but also every unseen principality in the heavens, to their very foundations!

12:27 In the words of the prophet, "Yet once more will I shake every unstable system of man's effort to rule himself." God clearly indicates his plan to remove the old and replace it with the new. The second shaking supersedes any significance in the first shaking. Then it was a physical quaking of the earth; now the very foundations of every man-made system was shaken to the core while the heavens were impacted by the announcement of his permanent rule on earth as it is mirrored in heaven.

12:28 We are fully associated in this immovable Kingdom; an authority that cannot be challenged or contradicted. Our participation echoes grace *(and not law-inspired obedience)* as we [1]accommodate ourselves to God's de light, yielding in awe to his firm embrace. *(The word, [1]euaresto, means well pleasing, to accommodate yourself to God's delight.)*

12:29 His jealousy over us burns like fire.

Some hints on practical kingdom living, including family, friends, fellowship, marriage, money and ministry:

13:1 Treasure family bonds and friendship. Family fondness remains the essence of this kingdom. *(Relationship is long-term in every sense of the word.)*

13:2 Treat strangers with equal affection; they could be a messenger of God in disguise!

13:3 Identify with those who are in prison or suffering abuse for their faith as if you were the one afflicted.

13:4 Honor the sanctity of marriage as the exclusive place of intimacy. God does not approve of casual or illicit sex.

13:5 Don't give money a prominent place in your thoughts; realize that what you already have is priceless! He has said that he will never quit on you or abandon you! *(Josh 1:5)* **That is reason enough for total and continual contentment!**

13:6 What he said concerning us gives our confession the edge; we boldly echo scripture, "The Lord is for me, I cannot be afraid of anything that anyone could possibly do to harm me." *(Ps 118:6)*

13:7 Be mindful of those who guide you in the revelation of God's word; follow their faith, consider the conclusion of their lives. *(Do not follow a counterfeit! This would be someone who fakes faith while actually living the law.)*

13:8 Take your lead from Jesus. He is your reference to the most complete life. In him yesterday is confirmed today and today mirrors tomorrow. What God spoke to us in Christ is as relevant now as it was in the prophetic past and will always be in the eternal future! *(Jesus is the same yesterday, today, and forever; there is a history to our salvation that carries more authority and relevance than anything that ever happened in our past, or anything present in time or still to happen in the future. Imagine the enormity of eternity in his sameness before time was; and we were there in him all along! See Rom 8:34 What further ground can there possibly be to condemn mankind? In his death he faced our judgment; in his resurrection he declares our innocence; the implications cannot be undone! He now occupies the highest seat of authority as the executive of our redemption in the throne room of God. See Rom 8: 1, also Rom 4:25. The heavens declare his glory, night to night exhibits the giant solar testimony that is mathematically precise, revealing that God knew before time was the exact moment he would enter our history as a man, and the exact moment the Messiah would expire on the cross and be raised again from the dead!)*

13:9 Do not be swayed by distracting speculations. Any influence foreign to what grace communicates, even if it seems very entertaining and carries the Christian label, is to be shunned. Feast on grace; do not dilute your diet with legalism. There is no nourishment left in the law. What's the use of being busy but not blessed? *(Legalism includes any form of self-sacrifice or self effort with the illusion of gaining further favor from God or improving your spiritual standing before God).*

13:10 For us there is only one altar and one sacrifice; we can never again confuse him with the rituals of the old redundant system. It seems that some would like to eat the meat of their own sacrifices and at the same time indulge in the benefits of grace. This is not possible. *(It is like trying to go in opposite directions at the same time.)*

13:11 When it comes to the sin offering, the carcasses of the slain animals were burnt outside the camp *(no one was permitted to eat from them anyway).*

13:12 According to the prophetic pattern, Jesus, as the final sin sacrifice, was slain outside the city walls.

13:13 There are two opposing systems; you cannot associate with Christ for your convenience while still hanging on to your Jewish sentiment. If you're going to take your stand for Jesus, go all the way. Break your ties with the old shadow-system. Go outside the city-system. Be prepared to share his shame when your fellow Jews mock your commitment to Jesus.

13:14 We are not finding our identity or security in the walled city of popular legalistic religious opinion. Our interest is captured by a different kind of city, much closer to us than the visible one.

13:15 Praise replaces sacrifice; the harvest we bring is the tribute of our lips acknowledging his Name. *(His Name represents the authority of our identity and redeemed innocence.)*

13:16 God delights in good deeds. These deeds are like beautiful poetry giving a voice to your fellowship. *(They are inspired by your innocence; rather than offered as guilt-driven sacrifices.)*

13:17 Trust your guides *(in this grace revelation)* and yield to their instruction. *(Even though it seems different to the law system that you were formerly acquainted with.)* They are genuinely alert to your well-being. *(Just as with shepherds guarding their sheep, you are their total concern.)* They have taken official accountability for you. *(They represent to you all that grace reveals rather than what the law requires.)* It is to your advantage to embrace their care with joy; this makes their work a pleasure and not a burden.

13:18 Worship prayerfully with us; we believe that our joint seeing inspires a beautiful life.

13:19 Pray also that I might be able to re-join you speedily; I can hardly wait!

13:20 This is my prayer for you: that the God who made peace with the human race through the blood of the eternal Testament, who raised Jesus from the dead as the supreme Shepherd of the sheep,

13:21 will thoroughly equip you in the most distinguished way possible, to give expression to his design in you according to his delight realized in Jesus Christ, who is the blueprint of the ages. Jesus is the accurate expression of God's glory. Our lives confirm and echo the Amen!

13:22 My brothers, I have written to you briefly, [1]reminding you of your original identity in order to [2]increase the volume of its resonance in your hearts. *(The word, [2]anechomai, means to hold oneself up against, from ana, often means by repetition in order to increase intensity, and echo, to hold, embrace or echo, resonance. The word, [1]parakaleo, from para, originating from a sphere of influence, and kaleo, to call by name, to surname [see notes on ekklesia, Heb 12:23].)*

13:23 Brother Timothy has already been released from prison; as soon as he arrives we will visit you together.

13:24 Greet all your leaders and the saints; the Italian believers salute you!

13:25 Grace is our embrace! YES!

JAMES - THE BROTHER OF JESUS

Mankind's lost and found identity

From the first and the last verse of James chapter one, it appears that James sets his teaching up against the sense of a lost identity: the twelve scattered tribes, and the widows and the orphans.

To lose your land of heritage or your immediate family would be the greatest and most challenging test or temptation anyone can face: "to forget what manner of person you are." *(James 1:24, Deuteronomy 32:18.)*

As the flesh-and-blood brother of Jesus, there was a time when neither he nor any of his family believed in Jesus. *(John 7:5)* It was only after the resurrection when Jesus appeared to him that the truth dawned on him, that his brother Jesus was indeed the one who all the rumors and prophetic pointers throughout time said he was! Jesus is God unveiled in flesh, the incarnate Word who redeemed the lost identity of mankind in his death and resurrection! James' eyes were opened to the fact that neither Jesus nor he bagan in Mary's womb! 1 Cor 15:7.

Man began in God! We are not merely the desire of a parent, we are the desire of God. Mankind shares a common origin, the *boulomai*, the affectionate desire and deliberate resolve of God, the Father of lights, with whom there is no distortion or hidden agenda. The unveiling of mankind's redemption also reveals our true genesis; we are God's personal invention. We are *anouthen*, from above. We are perfect and complete and lacking in nothing. God's Sabbath is the celebration of our perfection, both by design and redemption. "Every good and perfect gift comes from above, *(anouthen)* from the Father of lights with whom there is no variableness and no shadow due to change, he brought us forth by the Word of truth."

Born from above

John sees the same genesis. He only begins to write when he is already more than 90 years old. Unlike Luke and Matthew, he skips the genealogies of Joseph, he declares, "In the beginning was the Word, what God was, the Word was, and the Word became flesh. He sees that the destiny of the Word was not the book, but human life! God finding accurate expression of himself, his image and likeness revealed in human form. Genesis 1:26 lives again; mankind is standing tall in the stature of the invisible God. "If you have seen me, you have seen the Father!" "Unless a someone is born from above *(anouthen)*, they cannot see the Kingdom of God." The kingdom of God *(the reign of God's image and likeness in human life)* is made visible again on earth as it is in heaven; tangible in human form. *(Jn 3:3)*

In John 3 Nicodemus discovers that his irresistable attraction to Jesus was because of the fact that our natural birth is not our beginning! We come from above! God knew us before he formed us in our mother's womb!

[Jer 1:5] If people did not come from above, the heavenly realm would offer no attraction to them. In our make-up we are the god-kind with an appetite for more than what bread and the senses could satisfy us with. We are designed to hunger for and feast from the Logos that comes from above. From a dimension where the original thought remains preserved and intact without contamination; the Logos that comes from his mouth is the unveiled mirror radiance of our authentic origin, quickening and sustaining the life of our design. "No one ascended into heaven, who did not also descend from heaven, even the son of man." (Jn 3:13)

Paul celebrates the same theme in Galatians 1:15 God's eternal [1]love dream separated me from my mother's womb; his grace became my [2]identity. (*[1]eudokeo: his beautiful intention; the well done opinion. My mother's womb, my natural lineage and identity as son of Benjamin. [2]kaleo, to surname, to summon by name.*) 1:16 This is the heart of the gospel that I proclaim; it began with an unveiling of sonship [1]in me, freeing me to announce the same sonship [2]in the masses of non-Jewish people. I felt no immediate urgency to compare notes with those who were familiar with Christ from a mere historic point of view. (*The Greek text is quite clear, "It pleased the Father to reveal his son in me in order that I may proclaim him in the nations!" [1]en emoi, in me, and [2]en ethnos, in the Gentile nations, or the masses of non Jewish people! Not 'among' the Gentiles as most translations have it. Later when Barnabas is sent to investigate the conversion of the Greeks in Acts 11, instead of reporting his findings to the HQ in Jerusalem, he immediately finds Paul, knowing that Paul's gospel is the revelation of the mystery of Christ in the nations. Col.1:27. No wonder then that those believers were the first to be called Christians, or Christ-like!*)

Paul reminds the Greek philosophers in Acts 17 that we live and move and have our being in God; humankind is indeed the offspring of God. He is quoting from their own writings. [Epimenedes 600 BC and Aratus, 300 BC.] The incorruptible seed of sonship is as much in every person as the seed is already in all soil, even in the desert, waiting for the rain to awaken and ignite its dormant life! Mankind only has one Father! Math 13:44 the treasure was already in the field before it was discovered! 2 Cor 4:4 & 7. God wrote the script of every individual's innermost being when he knitted us together in our mother's womb; the code is "Christ in you!" Col 1:27.

Jesus has come to reveal that the son of man is the son of God. "If you have seen me you have seen the Father! Mat 23:9 "Call no man your father on earth, for you have one Father, who is in heaven." He says to Peter, "Flesh-and-blood cannot reveal to you who the son of man is, but my Father who is in heaven; blessed are you, Simon son of Jonah, I give you a new name that reveals your original identity: you are Rock! (*petros, hewn out of the rock, petra (Isa 51:1, Deut 32:3, 4, 18)*. This revelation is the rock foundation that I will build my identity upon, (*my image and likeness*) and the strong gates of hades, (*ha + ideis, not to see*) that trapped mankind into the walled city of the senses will not prevail against the voice that surnames and summons mankind again. (Mt 16:13, 17) Church, *ekklesia, from ek, denoting source or origin and **klesia** from **kaleo**, to surname or identify by name.)*

Therefore, Paul did not immediately consult with flesh and blood. He deliberately avoided the opportunity to get to know Jesus from a human point of view by visiting the eleven disciples who were still alive and living in Jerusalem. They could have informed him first-hand about the life, ministry, parables, and miracles of Jesus. *(2 Cor 5:16)* But Paul does not make mention in any of his writings even of a single parable Jesus told or miracle he performed, because his mandate and revelation was not to merely relate Christ in history, but to reveal Christ in mankind.

Only three years later he returned briefly to Jerusalem specifically to visit Peter and James, the Lord's brother. *(Gal 1:18, 19.)* One is not surprized to discover that the first believers ever to be called Christians were the Greeks in Antioch who sat under Paul's ministry. *(Acts 11)*

After his encounter with the risen Jesus James writes in Jam 1:17 that the Father of lights brought us forth by the word of truth! When anyone hears this word, he sees the face of his genesis as in a mirror! "for he sees himself".

What James, Peter and Paul had in common was an understanding that their flesh and blood birth did not define them. Jesus came to reveal and redeem humanity's authentic spirit identity.

Mankind share three births:

1/ Man began in God. Mal 2:10. Have we not all one father? Has not one God created us? See Joh 3:13 No one ascends into heaven but he who also descended from heaven, even the son of man. See also Math 22:41-46 and Math 23:9.

2/ The only passport to planet earth is the womb of a mother. "Before I formed you in the womb I knew you." Jer 1:5. It is not our brief hsitory on earth that introduces us to God.

3/ In God's faith every human life is equally represented and included in Jesus Christ. "One has died for all; therefore all have died!" 2 Cor 5:14. "While we were still dead in our sins, God made us alive together with Christ and co-raised us together with Christ." Eph 2:5. We have been born anew through the resurrection of Jesus Christ from the dead. 1Pet 1:3. "Now if all were included in his death they were equally included in his resurrection." 2 Cor 5:15; Hos 6:2.

Paul describes the "metanoia-moment" in Titus 3:4 But then, oh happy day! It was the generosity of God and his fondness for mankind that dawned on us like a shaft of light. Our days of darkness were over! Light shone everywhere and we became aware: God rescued the human race! (See 2:11)

Titus 3:5 Salvation is not a reward for good behavior. It has absolutely nothing to do with anything that we have done. God's mercy saved us. The

Holy Spirit endorses in us what happened to us when Jesus Christ died and was raised! When we heard the glad announcement of salvation it was like taking a deep warm bath! We were thoroughly cleansed and resurrected in a new birth! It was a complete renovation that restored us to sparkling newness of life!

In 2 Cor 5:16 Paul declares: "From now on therefore, we no longer know anyone according to the flesh!"

James says, "We can say beautiful things about God the Father but with the same mouth curse a person made in his mirror likeness." (*True worship is to touch someone's life with the same devotion and care you would touch Jesus himself; even if the other person seems a most unlikely candidate. James 3:9.*)

1:1 My name is James, I am bonded to God and the Lord Jesus Christ. It is in this capacity that I am writing to you, wherever you are. You might even be part of the twelve tribes which are scattered like seed all over the world. I greet you with joyful encouragement!

1:2 Temptations and contradictions come in different shapes, sizes, and intervals; their intention is always to suck you into their energy field. However, my brothers, your joy in who you know you are [1]leads you out triumphantly every time. *(The word, [1]hegeomai, comes from a strengthened form of ago, to lead, thus, to officially appoint in a position of authority; to lead with distinguished authority. Joy is the official voice of faith! "Count it all joy," make a calculation to which joy can be the only logical conclusion.)*

1:3 Here is the secret: joy is not something you have to fake, it is the fruit of what your faith knows to be true about you! You know that the proof of your faith results in persuasion that remains constant in contradiction.

1:4 *(Just like a mother hen patiently broods over her eggs,)* steadfastness provides you with a consistent environment, and so patience prevails and proves your perfection; how entirely whole you are and without any shortfall.

1:5 The only thing you could possibly lack is wisdom. *(One might sometimes feel challenged beyond the point of sanity)* however, make your request in such a way that you draw directly from the [2]source *(not filtered through other opinions).* God is the origin and author of wisdom; he [1]intertwines your thoughts with good judgment. His gifts are available to all, without regret. *(The word, [1]haplous, from ha, particle of union (hama, together with) + pleko, meaning to plait, braid, weave together. See Matthew 6:22, "If your eye is entwined with light your whole body will be full of light." Wisdom that comes from above remains unaffected by the contradictions of the senses. The word, [2]didomi, to give, to be the author or source of a thing — Wesley J. Perschbacher.)*

1:6 Faith must prompt your requests *(not your needs).* Faith is the stabilizing factor; otherwise you become driven by emotions *(inconsistent judgments)* that get out of control like rough seas tossed by tempest winds.

1:7 A haphazard request makes it impossible to interpret God's wisdom accurately; *(faith is the grace that reveals one's capacity to receive from God. The Greek word, para, with the genitive, indicating source or origin, ["coming from" — Wesley J. Perschbacher] and lambano, to receive, to comprehend.)*

1:8 Someone of two opinions remains jittery in all his judgments and seems always lost for direction.

1:9 *(Adverse circumstances can make or break you, depending on how you respond under pressure and allow these conditions to influence your judgment.)* Let the down and out brother boast in his elevation in the Lord. *(God's wisdom makes you see things differently. Begin by seeing yourself co-seated together with Christ in heavenly places! Col 3:1-3)*

1:10 The rich should boast with confidence when things seem to threaten their position of financial strength. Flowers fade; so does fame when wealth is lost. *(Poverty or wealth is not the measure of your life, faith is.)*

1:11 A severe sun combined with scorching eastern winds can completely destroy a harvest before it ripens; something that looked so beautiful and promising the one day, can be gone the next day; even so a wealthy person can suddenly perish in his pursuits. *(A person must have a reference that is more stable than changing conditions.)*

1:12 Blessed is the one who does not lose their footing when temptation strikes; they are [1]crowned the victor; their lives prove the [2]currency and character of their [3]design. The [4]verdict: No contradiction can distract from the love of the Lord. *(Love inspires faith. [Galatians 5:6] The word, [1]stephanos, means a mark of royal rank, or a wreath or garland, which was given as a prize to victors in public games. Yet life as God sees it is a gift, not a reward. [James 1:17-25] Thus even our reward is a gift because our enduring and steadfastness is not something we engage in with our diligence and willpower, but the energy ignited within us by the revelation of the Word of truth. The word, [2]dokimos, means accepted, particularly of coins and money; thus, currency. The Greek word for [3]birth, ginomai. The verdict, [4]epaggello, official announcement.)*

1:13 Do not say, "I am scrutinized by God" when you feel enticed. He is not in the teasing business; evil offers no attraction to God for God to be tempted by it, neither is he experimenting with your design! *(God cannot be both the source of light and darkness. Every temptation is an attempt of darkness to intercept light. [James 1:17])*

1:14 Temptation employs lust to [1]lure someone into a trap *(just like in hunting or fishing)*, one is deceived by the attraction of the [2]bait. Your own private desires can snare you. *(The word, [1]exelko, means to lure as in hunting or fishing, and [2]deleatzo comes from the word, dolos, to deceive by bait.)*

1:15 When passion conceives, it becomes the parent of sin. Sin's mission is to murder you.

1:16 My dear brothers, do not go wandering off into deception. *(By giving credit to temptation, thinking that it could possibly be God's way of speaking to you!)*

1:17 Without exception God's gifts are only good, its perfection cannot be improved upon. They come from [1]above, *(where we originate from,)* proceeding like light rays from its source, the Father of lights, with whom there is no distortion or even a shadow of shifting to obstruct or intercept the light; nor a hint of a hidden agenda. *(The word, [1]anouthen, means, from above. John 3:3, 13)*

1:18 It was his delightful [1]resolve to give birth to us; we were conceived by the [2]unveiled logic of God. We lead the exhibition of his handiwork, like first fruits introducing the rest of the harvest he anticipates. *(The word, [1]boulomai, means the affectionate desire and deliberate resolve of God. Truth, [2]alethea, from a, negative + lanthano, meaning hidden; that which is unveiled; the word of truth.)*

1:19 Consequently, my beloved brethren, *(when you are faced with temptation and contradiction)* ponder the Word that reveals your true origin, do not ponder the problem; that is how frustration is conceived. Rather remain silent than to give anger your voice. *(Quick to hear, slow to speak, slow to anger.)*

1:20 Anger distorts the picture and brings no credit to compliment God's righteousness.

1:21 Get rid of any remaining residue of evil that polluted your life before *(if a quick temper was your problem then, don't make it your problem again.)* Welcome with sensitive embrace the word that powerfully conceives salvation in your soul. *(Saving you from negative thought patterns and depressing emotional traits!)*

1:22 Give the word your [1]undivided attention; do not underestimate yourself. [3]Make the calculation. There can only be one logical conclusion: your authentic origin is mirrored in the word. You are God's poem; [2]let his voice make poetry of your life! *(The word, [1]akroate, means intent listening. James is not promoting the doing of the law of works; he is defining the law of perfect liberty. Doing the word begins with your undivided attention to the face of your birth. [2]A doer of the Word, poetes, means poet. Make the calculation, [3]paralogizomai, from para, a preposition indicating close proximity, union, and logizomai, to reckon the logic in any calculation.)*

1:23 The difference between a mere spectator and a participator is that both of them hear the same voice and perceive in its message the face of their own genesis reflected as in a mirror;

1:24 they realize that they are looking at themselves, but for the one it seems just too good to be true; this person departs *(back to the old way of seeing himself)* and immediately forgets what manner of person he is; never giving another thought to the one he saw there in the mirror.

1:25 The other one is [1]mesmerized by what he sees; [2]captivated by the effect of a law that frees a person from the obligation to the old written code that restricted one to their own efforts and willpower. No distraction or contradiction can dim the impact of what is seen in the mirror concerning the law of perfect [3]liberty *(the law of faith)* that now frees everyone to get on with the act of living the life *(of their original design.)* They find a new [3]spontaneous lifestyle; the poetry of practical living. *(The law of perfect liberty is the image and likeness of God revealed in Christ, now redeemed in mankind as in a mirror. Look deep enough into that law of faith that you may see there in its perfection a portrait that so resembles the original that he becomes distinctly visible in the spirit of your mind and in the face of every person you behold. I translated the word, [1]parakupto, with mesmerized from para, a preposition indicating close proximity, originating from, denoting the point from which an action originates, intimate connection, and kupto, to bend, stoop down to view at close scrutiny; [2]parameno, to remain captivated under the influence of; meno, to continue to be present. The word often translated as freedom, [3]eleutheria, means without obligation; spontaneous.)*

1:26 Meaningless conversation is often disguised in religious eloquence. Just because it sounds sincere, doesn't make it true. If your tongue is not bridled by what your heart knows to be true about you, you cheat yourself.

1:27 The purest and most uncompromising form of religious expression is found at its [1]source. God is the Father of mankind. He inspires one to take a genuine interest in helping the fatherless and the widows in their plight, and to make sure that one's own life does not become blemished in the process. *(The word [1]para, is a preposition indicating close and immediate proximity, intimate connection.)*

2:1 Jesus heads up the kind of faith that does not judge on face value, neither is it influenced by popular opinion or [1]outward appearance. *([1]Face value, prosopolepsia)*

2:2 Here is a typical example: an influential impressive looking man, dressed in glitter and fine jewelry may visit your assembly; then a shabby looking poor man may walk into the same gathering;

2:3 the smart guy gets the best seat while the shabby looking chap gets told to stand in the back or sit on the ground like a slave at your feet.

2:4 To discriminate in your heart against anyone conceives a judgment in you that can cause great ill; can you imagine how it hurts to be rejected like that?

2:5 May I have your full attention on this issue my dear brothers, faith in who you really are according to [1]your original identity is the real measure of your wealth; you might be poor according to the standards of this world but according to God you possess your allotted portion which is the kingdom of his promise to those who love him. *(The word, [1]eklegomai, comes from ek, a preposition denoting origin, and lego, meaning to speak; thus, the original blueprint-word, logos.)*

2:6 But you insult the poor, in your effort to impress the rich; meanwhile you fail to realize that the rich have abused their influence against you. They have conned you into their prejudices and discriminatory judgments. They bought your vote with cheap currency. *(Any value outside of the price God paid in Christ is an inferior value to human life)*

2:7 Their apparent position of influence is just a disguize they employ to blaspheme the name that defines your true identity.

2:8 Scripture confirms that the law of the kingdom is fulfilled in you realizing the same value in your neighbor as you would see in yourself; this is what doing the word is all about, and it makes beautiful poetry. *(Lev 19:18; Lk 10:27, Mt 22:37-40. By not forgetting what manner of person you are, you will not forget what manner of person your neighbor is according to the mirror principle.)*

2:9 To judge anyone on outward appearance is a [1]sin. *(The word, [1]hamartia, from ha, meaning negative and meros, meaning form or allotted portion; sin represents any thing that robs you of your allotted portion which is the true measure of your life.)* This violates the law of liberty and revives condemnation and guilt.

2:10 If you lower the standard of the law in just one aspect of it you have [1]failed entirely. *(To fail, stumble, err, [1]pipto, to descend from a higher place to a lower, from petomai, to fly; thus, to stop flying.)*

2:11 For he who said you shall not commit adultery also said you shall not kill. Here is an example, you might be faithful to your wife, yet you have killed someone; your not committing adultery does not cancel out the murder! *(And vice versa.)*

2:12 Let the law of liberty set the pace *(be the judge)* in your conversation and conduct. *(The law of perfect liberty is the image and likeness of God revealed in Christ, now redeemed in mankind as in a mirror. Look deep enough into that law of faith that you may see there in its perfection a portrait that so resembles the original that he becomes distinctly visible in the spirit of your mind and in the face of everyone you behold. [Heb 1:25])*

2:13 Judgment showed no mercy to those who do not walk in mercy, but mercy triumphs over judgment. *(Those who walk in mercy walk in the law of liberty. [Gal 5:22, 23] There is no law against love. While judgment threatens condemnation, mercy interposes and prevails over judgment. See 1 John 3:20 So, even if our own hearts would ¹accuse us of not really being true to ourselves, God is greater than our hearts and he has the full picture! His knowledge of us is not compromised. (This word, ¹kataginosko is only used three times in the NT, translated, to blame, or condemn. From kata, down and ginosko, to know; thus to know from below; from a fallen mindset perspective) 3:21 Beloved when we know what God knows to be true about us, then instead of condemning us, our hearts will endorse our innocence and ¹free our conversation before God. (The word ¹parresia, from para, a preposition indicating close proximity, and **rheo**, to pour forth; to flow freely, suggesting an unreservedness in speech; bold utterance.)*

Also 1 John 4:18,19 Fear cannot co-exist in this love realm. The perfect love union that we are talking about expels fear. Fear holds on to an expectation of crisis and judgment [which brings separation] and interprets it as due punishment [a form of karma!] It echoes torment and only registers in someone who does not realize the completeness of their love union [with the Father, Son and Spirit and with one another.] We love because he loved us first! [We did not invent this fellowship; we are invited into the fellowship of the Father and the son!])

2:14 My brothers, if your faith *(in your true identity)* is not practical and visible in your conduct it is fake and cannot benefit you in any way.

2:15 Let's bring it closer to home *(I am not even talking about your duty to strangers)*, someone in your own family might be struggling financially to the extent that they do not even have the basics as far as clothes and food are concerned.

2:16 What's the good if you keep your contact with them very brief and distant and wave them goodbye with empty words, something like, "May the Lord richly bless you brother! Be warm, be fed, ok, bye! Have a great day!" A coat and a cup of soup is going to say so much more!

2:17 It is clear then that without corresponding acts of kindness, faith on its own is fake.

2:18 Faith is not in competition with works; the one cannot operate without the other. Faith remains invisible without action; indeed the only way to communicate faith is in doing the things prompted and inspired by faith.

2:19 Congratulations! So you believe in one God; so do demons; however, their belief in God doesn't change them it just gives them the shivers.

2:20 Hey man, if you have nothing to show for your faith your faith is meaningless; it remains a dead doctrine.

2:21 Abraham's righteousness inspired his act of faith when he presented his son Isaac as a sacrifice upon the altar. *(Genesis 15:1, 6 confirms that Abraham was justified long before Isaac was born. God was his reward, not Isaac. No amount of good works can justify a person; good works follow faith, not the other way around! Here James asks the question, "Was not Abraham our father justified by works, in that he offered up Isaac his son upon the altar? The answer is clearly, "No! Abraham was justified when he believed God's Word concerning his offspring, many years before Isaac was born.")*

2:22 His works were in synergy with his faith, and completed it. The one compliments the other.

2:23 Abraham's friendship with God was the fruit of the righteousness he received by faith; this was announced in Genesis 15:6 and prompted a lifestyle that confirmed his faith. *(2 Chr 20:7 calls Abraham the friend of God.)*

2:24 It is obvious then that justification does not stop at faith but continuous into action.

2:25 By protecting the messengers Rahab the prostitute showed her faith in their message and was justified. *(Heb 11:31)*

2:26 Just as the body gives expression to the spirit, so actions give expression to faith.

3:1 My brothers, let's not be quick to assume the title of teacher. Remember when we teach we subject ourselves to greater scrutiny.

3:2 It is common habit to [1]descend from a higher place *(of faith)* to a lower *(of the senses)*, especially in conversation. However, if you want to be in perfect charge of your whole person, the best place to begin is to take charge of your tongue. *(To reflect the word that confirms your true genesis [Jas 1:18, 19]. The word, [1]peripipto, comes from, peri, meaning surrounded + pipto, from petomai, meaning to fly; thus, to descend from a higher place to a lower, to stop flying.)*

3:3 With bit and bridle we are able to direct the strong body of a horse; you see it's the little bit in the mouth that makes the difference!

3:4 Consider the effect of a small rudder on a large ship, when the seasoned captain skillfully steers that vessel on a straight course contrary to fierce winds and weather.

3:5 As small a member the tongue might be it can make great claims. A little fire can go out of control and consume a large forest!

3:6 A tongue can strike like lightning and turn the harmony of your world into chaos; one little member can stain the whole body. It can disrupt the pattern of your design, taking its spark from the smoldering garbage heaps of [1]Gehenna. *([1]The garbage heap outside Jerusalem, commonly related to hell. Gehenna, is the Latin word; Geenas is the Greek word used for the Hebrew "Valley of Hinnom," which is modern day Wadi er-Rababi. A fiery place for the disposal of waste matter from the city of Jerusalem. The "Valley of Hinnom" lies outside of ancient Jerusalem. Thus to slander someone is to reduce that person to rubbish.)*

3:7 From tigers to eagles, cobras to dolphins, mankind has succeeded to curb the wild nature of beasts and birds, reptiles, and sea creatures.

3:8 No-one can tame a tongue though; no human can restrain the evil in its fatal venom. *(The law of works operated by willpower cannot match the effect of the law of perfect liberty! Mirror likeness ignites true freedom to utter that which is precious!)*

3:9 We can say beautiful things about God the Father but with the same mouth curse a fellow human made in his mirror likeness. *(True worship is to touch someone's life with the same devotion and care you would touch Jesus himself; even if the other person seems a most unlikely candidate.)*

3:10 My brothers, a blessing and a curse ought not to originate from the same source. *(Discovering our true source brings true freedom. [Jam 1:17,18])*

3:11 Not even a natural fountain produces both bitter and sweet water.

3:12 As impossible as it is for a fig tree to bear olives, and a vine to produce figs, so a fountain cannot yield salt and fresh water from the same source.

3:13 Humility advertises wisdom; it shows in the quality of your conversation and actions. This distinguishes you with the reputation of someone who is acquainted with wisdom and skilled in understanding.

3:14 If there is any hidden agenda, secretly driven by bitter jealousy and contention, you have nothing to be proud of. Your big talk sounds superficial and offers no disguise. *(The fountain of your heart always shows.)*

3:15 This wisdom does not originate from above, but is clearly reduced to a kind that is earthly, ruled by the senses and dictated to by demons. *(Or **daimōn**; from **daiō** (to distribute fortunes). The Greeks gave the word **daimōn** the same meaning as god. What they meant by the word; however, is still a conjecture. They may have related a demon with **daemmonas**, knowing or being experienced in a thing, or they may have derived the word from **daíomai**, meaning to assign or award one's lot in life (**diaítētai kai dioikemtai tōn ánthrōpōn**), the arbitrators or umpires and governors of men.*

*They conceived of them as those who ruled and directed human affairs, not as a personality, but primarily as a destructive power. Thus they called the happy or lucky person **eudaímōn**, one who is favored by this divine power. The adjective, **daimónios**, was used for one who demonstrated power irrespective of whether it was saving or destructive. The Tragic Poets use **daimōn** to denote fortune or fate, frequently bad fortune, but also good fortune if the context represented it as such. Thus, **daimōn** is associated with the idea of a gloomy and sad destiny independent of a person, coming upon and prevailing over them. Consequently, **daimōn** and **túchē**, luck, are often combined, and the doctrine of demons developed into signifying either a beneficent or evil power in the lives of people. — Zodhiates Complete Word Study Lexicon)*

3:16 An environment of envy and rivalry is conducive to confusion and disorder and all kinds of worthless pursuits.

3:17 The wisdom that originates from above sets the pace in innocence; it loves peace; it is always appropriate *(polite)*; persuaded about that which is good; filled with compassion; these fruits are pure goodness and [1]without discrimination. *(From [1]anhupokritos, without hypocrisy. See James 1:17)*

3:18 Seed always predicts the harvest. Righteousness inspires the kind deeds of those who embrace peace; these are like seeds sown into fertile soil.

4:1 What is it that triggers disputes and fighting? Is it not selfish desires and greedy agendas that ¹both parties host within themselves? Hence wars are born. It is a global identity crisis! *(The word, ¹enteuthen, means, repeated on both sides; also translated, hence, from this point. This is in such contrast to the wisdom from above, see 1:17 & 3:17. Any sense of lack causes you to forget what manner of person you are, and how perfect and complete and without lack you are by design, as mirrored in Christ! This is again the typical arena of the law of works and striving against the law of perfect liberty.)*

4:2 You allow your heart to become so consumed with longing for something until you are ready to kill for it. Then you are still not satisfied. What you want keeps evading you; you quarrel and strive, and you just can't get it. If you are desperately unfulfilled why don't you simply ask God to give you what you need? *(This is in such contrast to the wisdom from above, see 3:17. Also James 1:5, The only thing you could possibly lack is wisdom [One might sometimes feel challenged beyond the point of sanity]; however, make your request in such a way that you draw directly from the source [not filtered through other opinions]. God is the origin and author of wisdom; he intertwines your thoughts with good judgment. His gifts are available to all, without regret.)*

4:3 You have asked, but God seems reluctant to give it to you, you may say. But when your motivation is to get something just so that you can squander it on yourself, you are doing it all wrong! *(This is like expecting God to support your own futile efforts to justify yourself. See James 1:2-4, 17, 18, 23-25)*

4:4 Adultery, whether it is the husband or the wife who does the flirting, is destructive. Can't you see that even though the world system might approve of such behavior, it is contrary to God's design for you? Whose friend do you want to be? Are you prepared to distance yourself from God *(and the life of your design)* just to win the plastic applause of the world?

4:5 Scripture is not quoting empty words when it states that God yearns with jealous expectation over the spirit which he has made to inhabit us.

4:6 His gift of grace *(1:17)* is in direct opposition to the vanity of the proud mindset of self effort, whereby people strive to prove themselves as superior to others! Gift and reward are opposites! Humility attracts grace.

4:7 Your most effective defense against any diabolical mindset, is to yield yourselves in total abandonment to God, and there encounter his dream-life for you. You will witness how effortlessly those thoughts flee from you. *(The word diabollos, from diaballo, dia, because of, and ballo, to cast down; to accuse, to make false and defamatory statements against someone. This points to the develish fallen mindset-system that have engaged generations in the blind-fold mode of pride and accusation, by not seeing the image of God in human life.)*

4:8 Snuggle up to the warm embrace of God; experience his closeness. *(In Christ every definition of distance or delay is cancelled.)* The sinner can come with all stains washed from his hands; the double-minded can come with a purified heart.

4:9 This is not a mere blase yielding. Realizing the misery that you have brought upon yourself and others is often accompanied by intense grief and weeping. This is no place for superficial laughter and make-belief joy; nor any occasion for boasting! (*Your futile efforts to justify yourself through striving and fighting only reinforce your nakedness. The perfect law of liberty, unveiling the mirror message declares your redeemed innocence through the finished work of Christ.*)

4:10 Put down your own efforts to fight for your rights; let him lift you up to the dignity of his [1]presence. (*The word translated, presence, [1]enopion means in the gaze of; face to face. See your own face reflected in his! There is no higher elevation to engage in!*)

4:11 Gossip is out; to bad-mouth and point your finger at your brother is to insult the law of liberty; you put yourself up as a law enforcer and thereby assume that you are above scrutiny.

4:12 God is the one who endorses the law of perfect liberty. That makes him the only judge with power to save. He rendered the law of performance completely irrelevant. He never handed you the power of attorney to judge anyone.

4:13 Hey, you've got your year planner out and can already taste the profits in all your business ventures; you're going big; travel, and trade from city to city!

4:14 Meanwhile, you have no handle on tomorrow! Your life is like a mist that is visible for a short while before it evaporates.

4:15 My best advice for you is to wrap up all your plans and conversations in the delightful resolve of God.

4:16 Don't be so cocksure about your dreams for the future. Plans that presumptuously exclude God's opinion end up to be [1]full of labors, annoyances, and hardships. (*The word, [1]poneros, means full of annoyances, hardships, and labors; often translated as evil.*)

4:17 To turn a blind eye to an obvious opportunity to do good is [1]out of character. (*The word, [1]hamartia, comes from ha, meaning without and meros, meaning portion or form, distorted behavior, often translated as sin.*)

5:1 Your wealth cannot disguise your weakness when calamity strikes. Then it is too late to scream and cry.

5:2 Whatever you have hoarded to show how strong you are financially shows signs of rot; your wardrobes of fine clothing are moth eaten.

5:3 Your tarnished treasures of gold and silver bear witness against you; instead of exhibiting your riches they show off your shame. Your wealth worries have given you ulcers that consume you like a fire from within. You would have thought that you stored up enough insurance to last you to the end of days.

5:4 In the process you have short paid your laborers who reaped your harvests; those wages have now become a loud voice together with the groans of the workers you have cheated and abused; they shout out against you in earshot of the Lord of the masses.

5:5 You have indulged in a delicate lifestyle on all your properties; you have stuffed yourselves; grabbing and looting like soldiers on the battle-field.

5:6 In your quest to get to the top you have stepped on others and ruined innocent lives; while no one opposed you.

5:7 My brothers, if you are the ones abused, remain passionate about the [1]presence of the Lord. Consider how the farmer lays hold of the harvest by patiently letting the early and latter rain do its work in the soil to prepare its precious yield. *(The word, [1]parousia, means presence, from para, closest possible proximity, and eimi, "I am." Sadly this beautiful word has always been traditionally translated to point to yet another future event—the coming of the Lord. Religion thrives on two lies, distance and delay! Emmanuel cancelled both in Christ! Jesus says in John 4, "Do you not say, "there are yet four months then comes the harvest." Yet you are looking at the wrong harvest! Lift up your eyes, look away from your own labor and see the harvest that is already ripe!)*

5:8 Let your hearts also be firm in patience while the [1]closeness of the embrace of his presence sustains you. *(The word, [1]engidzo, means to bring near, reflexively — Strong's Concordance; here translated as "the closeness of his embrace.")*

5:9 When circumstances [1]squeeze you into tight spots, don't make your problem your topic of conversation with one another *(there is no relief in feeling sorry for yourselves)* while the Lord is left standing outside behind closed doors. Let him be the judge of your situation. *(The word, [1]stenadzo, means to groan, complain; from stenos, meaning narrow.)*

5:10 The prophets who spoke in the Name of the Lord are our [1]mentors; consider what they had to put up with and what hardships they went through, and with what fortitude they prevailed. *(The word, [1]upodeigma, means an exhibit, pattern for imitation.)*

5:11 To look back at the faith heroes of yesterday is always an inspiration. Even Job's life was prophetic. Consider how God came through for him in the end; his endurance proved God's extreme compassion and tender mercies. (*The first part represents life under the law of fear, the latter the law of faith.*)

5:12 (*Since you are convinced of God's tender feelings towards you,*) making foolish oaths does not add weight to your intentions! It makes no difference whether you attempt to tap into heaven's magic or swear by some earthly institution, or any other binding authority. Keep it simple, yes cannot mean no at the same time. Swearing silly oaths makes you look phony anyway!

5:13 If anyone is going through a tough time, let him worship; when times are good, sing praises. (*Don't take your lead from your negative or your positive circumstances!*)

5:14 If you feel too ¹weak to ²worship, find encouragement in the care of those who are mature in their faith. Let them anoint you with oil and worship with you in ³prayer. Identify yourself in all that the Lord's name represents. (*The words,* ¹*astheneo, means weak, feeble;* ²*proseuxomai, worship; and* ³*euxomai, prayer.*)

5:15 The prayer (*environment*) of faith shall restore the feeble. The Lord shall revitalize and quicken you; he even forgives you anything stupid you might have done to have caused the situation.

5:16 (*Do not tolerate vibes*) if you have wronged someone talk to him about it; pray for each other to maintain a healthy fellowship. Righteousness is the fuel of effective prayer. (*How right things are, not how wrong things are now motivate your every prayer and conversation! Not the size or the detail of the problem.*)

5:17 Elijah wasn't superman, yet his prayers had supernatural results with global impact. Remember how he prayed. He prayed with such resolve that he stopped the rain for three and a half years!

5:18 He prayed again and everything was back to normal; rain and harvest in season!

5:19 If a brother strays off from the truth, go and fetch him.

5:20 To turn a sinner back from error not only rescues the individual but stops the ripple effect of the rot in a community.

1:1 I am Peter, an ambassador of Jesus Christ to the many ¹foreigners who are scattered throughout Pontus, Galatia, Cappadocia, Asia and Bithynia. *(The word, ¹parepidemos, from para, proceeding from a sphere of influence, originating from; and epidemeo, from epi, continual influence upon, and demos, to bind together; thus, a people who are bound together socially, whilst living in a foreign country. The picture of humanity's scatteredness away from "home-in the Father's bosom", is captured here.)*

1:2 Your ¹original identity is defined by what God, the Father of humanity has ²always cherished about you; how your pre-Adamic innocence would be preserved in the prophetic word, and redeemed through the obedience of Jesus Christ, and the effect of the sprinkling of his blood. Realizing his grace and peace exceeds any definition of contradiction or reward. *(The word ¹eklektos, derives from eklegomai, which has two components, ek, a preposition that indicates source or origin, and lego, to speak; translates, original logic; see John 1:1-3 and 12. The word ²prognosis means to know in advance. Peter emphasizes the priceless value of our redeemed innocence through the obedience of Christ and the shedding of his blood. See 1 Peter 1:18,19; 2 Pet 1:9)*

1:3 So let us ¹boast about it and bless the God and Father of our Lord Jesus Christ with articulate acclaim! He has reconnected us with our original genesis through the resurrection of Jesus from the dead! This new birth endorses and celebrates the hope of the ages; God's eternal love dream concludes in life! *(The word, ¹eulogetos, means to brag, to bless, to speak well of. Jesus reminds Nicodemus that we are born anouthen, from above, [John 3:3,13] and now through our joint resurrection, we are reconnected again to our original identity as sons. The word ²anagennao, from ana, upward, or can also mean by implication, repetition, and gennao, to regenerate, to give birth. As much as his death brought dramatic closure to our futile and failed attempts to justify and define ourselves, our co-resurrection revived the original blueprint of our Maker's image and likeness in us.)*

1:4 We are reintroduced to an ¹imperishable inheritance, which has been ²flawlessly ³preserved for us in the heavenly realm, where neither Adam's fall, nor mankind's failure to justify themselves, could possibly ²contaminate, discredit or diminish the original portion of our true sonship realized in Christ Jesus! *(Here Peter employs three adjectives to reinforce the idea of the absolute imperishable integrity of our inheritance. The word, ¹aphthartos from a + ptheiro, incorruptible, indestructible, that which time cannot decay or decrease; the word, ²amiantos, a + miaino, discredit, dishonor, flaw; also, ³amarantos, from a + maraino, extinguish, neither time nor decay could touch or contaminate it in any way! The verb, teteremenen, is in the perfect passive tense, which translates having been kept. See also Hebrews 6:16,17)*

1:5 Your legitimate inheritance was guarded all along by God's belief in you, to be fully unveiled in the ¹conclusion of time as the perfect solution to mankind's predicament! *(¹Jesus is the incarnate Word, Hebrews 1:1-3; Galatians 4:4)*

1:6 So, regardless of any degree of contradiction, whether prolonged, or swift, your reason for exuberant joy remains uninterrupted; even at times where you might have occasion to feel utterly miserable!

1:7 This will help you in those difficult times: think of your faith as something much more precious than any possible evaluation of gold; remember that fire does not destroy the metal, it reveals it! Now even gold is an inferior comparison to your faith! Gold as a currency has only temporal and unpredictable value; it fluctuates as the market changes. Now, in the same way that fire reveals gold, your faith in the midst of contradiction, makes Jesus Christ visible and gives much reason to testimony [1]stories worth telling. This is what has permanent [2]value, and exhibits the glory of Christ in you! (*The word often translated as praise, [1]epainos, has two components, epi, continual influence upon, and ainos, which often reflects a story worth telling; the word [2]timay, honor, suggests a valuing by which the price is fixed.*)

1:8 So even though you have never seen Jesus in the flesh you love him; even at times where he seems remote and invisible, your awareness of your union in him continues to ignite belief! You are leaping with indescribable and exuberant joy as you hold him in high esteem!

1:9 In this place of joy, you are beyond the reach of any harm. Joy gives your faith a voice announcing the perfection of your soul's salvation. (*Joy celebrates the fulfilment of scripture! Belief gives evidence of everything the prophets pointed to!*)

1:10 This salvation which you now know as your own, is the theme of the prophetic thought; this is what captured the prophets' attention for generations and became the object of their most diligent inquiry and scrutiny. They knew all along that mankind's salvation was a grace revelation, sustained in their prophetic utterance! (*Salvation would never be by personal achievement or a reward to willpower-driven initiative! The law of works would never replace grace!*)

1:11 In all of their conversation there was a constant quest to determine who the Messiah would be, and exactly when this will happen. They knew with certainty that it was the spirit of Christ within them pointing prophetically and giving testimony to the sufferings of the Christ and the subsequent glory. (*Whatever glory was lost in Adam, would be redeemed again in Jesus Christ!*)

1:12 It was revealed to them that this glorious grace message that they were communicating pointed to a specific day and person beyond their own horizon and generation; they saw you in their prophetic view! This [1]heavenly announcement had you in mind all along! They proclaimed glad tidings to you in advance, in the Holy Spirit, commissioned from heaven; the angelic messengers themselves longed to gaze deeply into its complete fulfilment. (*Peter uses the word, [1]anaggello, where the preposition, ana, points upwards to the source of the announcement.*)

1:13 How amazing is that! Jesus is what the scriptures are all about; and you are what Jesus is all about! Now wrap your minds around that! This unveiling is [1]what tied up all the loose ends that would trip you and frustrate your seamless transition from the old to the new! The revelation of Jesus is no longer a future expectation! Do not allow the old mindset of a future tense glory to intoxicate you and distract you from the relevance of this moment! Stop pointing to a future Messiah! You're it! You are who the prophets pointed to! You are the fruit of his sufferings; you are the glorious resurrection generation! Fully engage your [2]minds with the consequence of this grace in the revelation of Jesus Christ! He [3]completes your every [4]expectation! *(The word [1]anazosamenoi, to gird up, is an Aorist participle, which translates, "having girded up the loins of your mind, be sober!" The word [2]dianoia, suggests deep contemplation, thinking something thoroughly through in order to reach a sober conclusion! Then Peter writes, [3]teleios [4]elpisate, this is the completeness of every expectation! See Colossians 1:27.*

In one act of righteousness, God removed every possible definition of distance and delay! Every excuse that we could have to feel separated from God was cancelled! This is what the prophets saw: "Every valley shall be lifted up, and every mountain and hill be made low; the crooked places shall be made straight, even the rough places shall be made smooth. And the glory of the LORD shall be revealed, and all flesh shall see it together, for the mouth of the LORD has spoken." Isaiah 40:4,5)

1:14 Your [1]accurate hearing is what distinguishes you as the resurrection generation; the days of being driven by every [2]desperate, distorted passion of your former ignorance are over! The [3]fashions and patterns of a redundant system are no longer relevant! *(The word, [1]upoakoo is often translated, obedience, from upo, meaning under, as in under the influence of, and akoo, to hear. In the context of this chapter, Peter urges us to hear accurately what was communicated in the prophetic word concerning the life of our design, now rebooted into newness by our joint resurrection with Jesus Christ! The word, [2]epithumia, translates, desire, craving, longing, desire for what is forbidden, lust. The word, [3]suschēmatizō, from sun, union, and schema, pattern; a typical template.)*

1:15 The one whose [1]idea you are to begin with, designed you to radiate his image and likeness; he is the true pattern of your beingness! So, [2]be who you are in realizing the exact detail of your genesis! You are [3]whole and in perfect harmony; seamlessly one with him! *(The word [1]kaleo, to define by name; to surname. The word [2]genethete, referring to genesis, or birth, is in the aorist, passive, imperative case; the distinction between the aorist imperative and the present imperative is one of aspect, not tense. Thus, to get something over and done with! The word, [3]hagios, holy, separate from common condition and use. See Hebrews 10:14-16 Mirror Bible)*

1:16 On the very account that what is [1]written in prophetic scripture, *(and echoed in your innermost being)*, already mirrors the life of your design, you are free to [2]be who you are. As it is written, "I am, therefore you are! I am wholly separated unto you, and invite you to explore the same completeness of your being in me!" *(The word, [1]grapho, to engrave, often refers to the prophetic writings, Old Testament scripture. The appeal of truth is confirmed in* *the resonance within us due to the echo of that which is already written in our innermost being by design! "Did not our hearts ignite within us while he opened to us the scriptures! Luke 24:27,32,44,45. The Textus Receptus uses the word **genesthe**, instead of [2]esesthe, from eimi, as in the Westtcott & Hort text. This makes a massive difference! So, instead of **ginomai**, to become, it is the word, esesthe **eimi**, I am! See note in John 1:1 Three times in this sentence John uses the imperfect of [3]**eimi**, namely [3]**en**, to be, which conveys no idea of origin for God or for the Logos, but simply continuous existence, "I am".Quite a different verb **egeneto**, "became," appears in John 1:14 for the beginning of the Incarnation of the Logos. See the distinction sharply drawn in John 8:58, "before Abraham was born, ([1]**genesthai** from **egeneto**) I am." (The word **eimi**, I am; the essence of being, suggesting timeless existence.)*

1:17 Now since you are defined in your father, who does not judge anyone on face value, but always only according to his work; *(his finished work in Christ)* **wherever you find yourself located geographically or emotionally, [1]return to your 'at homeness' in him; you are not defined by your circumstances.** *(The word [1]**anastrepho**, suggests a radical returning; literally a turning upside down!)*

1:18 It is clear to see that you were ransomed from the futile, fallen mindset that you inherited from your fathers, not by the currency of your own labor, represented by the fluctuating values of gold and silver, and the economy of your religious efforts;

1:19 but you were redeemed with the priceless blood of Christ; he is the ultimate sacrifice; spotless and without blemish. He completes the prophetic picture! *(In him God speaks the most radical scapegoat language of the law of judgment, and brings final closure to a dead and redundant system! In Psalm 40:6,7, it is clearly stated that God does not require sacrifices or offerings! Jesus is the Lamb of God! He collides victoriously with the futile sacrificial system whereby offerings are constantly made to the pseudo, moody, monster gods of our imagination! This is the scandal of the cross! God does not demand a sacrifice that would change the way he thinks about mankind; he provides the sacrifice of himself in Christ in order to forever eradicate sin-consciousness from our minds and radically change the way we think about our Maker, one another and ourselves! [Sin-consciousness is in essence a works-based consciousness.] God did not clothe Adam with the skin of a slain animal because of a divine need to be appeased, but because of their unconditional love for Adam; they spoke the language of Adam's own judgment: Adam, not God, was embarrassed about his nakedness. The clothing was not to make God look at Adam differently, but to make Adam feel better about himself! And ultimately it was to prophetically prepare Adam for the unveiling of the mystery of mankind's redemption in the incarnation. Here Deity would clothe themselves in human skin, in a son; and the Lion of Judah, would become the Lamb of God, in order to free our minds to re-discover his image and likeness in our skin! See 1 Peter 1:2.)*

1:20 He was always destined in God's prophetic thought; God knew before the fall of the world order that his son would be the Lamb, to be

made manifest in these last days, because of you! *(You are the reason Jesus died and was raised!)*

1:21 He is the conclusive cause of your belief in God. Seeing then how perfectly you fit into the scheme of things, it is no wonder that your faith in God's act of raising Jesus from the dead becomes the glorious reference to your own new birth! The glory that God gave Jesus by raising him from the dead, is the conclusion of everything that your faith longed for! *(This is the redeemed glory that the prophets pointed to! Hos 6:2 "After two days he will revive us; on the third day he will raise us up!" Isaiah 40:5 "And the glory of the Lord shall be revealed, and all flesh shall see it together!")*

1:22 As a result of your [1]accurate hearing of the unveiled truth, and through the agency of the Spirit, you have engaged your souls fully with the purifying effect of your inclusion in his glorious work of redemption. *(See [1]commentary note in 1 Peter 1:14. The same Spirit of Christ who spoke from within the prophets of old, now endorses truth within your spirit!)*

1:23 This co-resurrection-new-birth does not compare to the fading qualities of that which is produced by the perishable seed of the carnal works- and performance-based mindsets. The indestructible living seed of the word of God conceives resurrection life within you; this life is [1]equal to its source. *(The word, [1]**meno** means, abiding; or, to remain the same.*

You are giving stature to the rise of a new person; a new resurrection generation of a people who are coming out of obscurity into his marvelous light!)

1:24 "All flesh is grass, and all its glory is like the flower of the field. The grass withers, the flower fades,

1:25 but the word of our God is [1]risen for ever. This word is the [2]exact same message of the glad tidings announced by the prophets and now proclaimed unto you! *(Peter again quotes from Isaiah 40, this time verse 6 and 8. The Hebrew word [1]**Qum**, means to rise up; like in Hosea 6:2, "After two days he will revive us, on the third day, he will raise us up!" Isaiah 40:6,8; also see note on 1:13. The word [2]**meno** is used in the Septuagint and also here in the Greek text, Peter uses the word, **meno**, to remain the same; to continue to be present.)*

2:1 Now, since you are rebooted and redefined in this eternal conversation, any distracting talk is inappropriate. Do away with everything associated with the old performance based mindsets! Anything perverse, all manner of guile and hypocrisies and spiteful jealousies as well as any kind of backbiting is to be shunned. There is zero nourishment in such conversation.

2:2 Imagine how a newborn babe would crave nothing else but pure mother's milk, in just the same way, drink with total abandonment from the unmixed milk of the word. This is your true nourishment! *(Approach the scriptures with an attitude of a new born babe, drawing milk from the mother.)*

2:3 Once you've tasted pure grace, you are spoilt for life! Grace rules! The Lordship of Jesus is established upon the dynamic of his goodness. (χρηστὸς ὁ Κύριος)

2:4 The irresistible attraction seen in him, the living stone, is not at all compromised by the fact that man-made religious structures rejected him; he is esteemed most precious and remains the original and pivotal idea of God!

2:5 Likewise, you yourselves are living stones *(co-quickened in his resurrection; 1:3)* and are co-constructed, and seamlessly joined into a spiritual house; you are a priestly people separated to offer spiritual sacrifices, reflecting God's total approval of Jesus Christ. Everything that was prophetically mirrored in the shadow tabernacle of Israel, has finally found its relevance in Jesus Christ; he fully unveils the real deal; the temple, the priestly-order and the people are all one in him.

2:6 This is [1]central to the prophetic theme of scripture: as voiced in Isaiah 28:16: "Behold, I am laying in Zion a stone, a cornerstone, the [2]exact and precise reference to the authentic thought of God; the one who exhibits the perfect idea of human life indwelt by God. This makes him most precious and desirable; he will not disappoint anyone's belief that he is indeed the Messiah, the Savior of the world! He declares human life to be the true temple of God. *(The word [1]periecho, from peri, which, in compounds, retains substantially the same meaning of circuit (around), excess (beyond), or completeness (through), with echo, to hold, to resonate. The word, [2]eklego, from ek, origin, and lego, idea, thought.*

See Eph 2:20 The first evidence of this building was Jesus Christ himself being the chief cornerstone. He is the first visible testimony to the restored image and likeness of God in human form.

Also Rom 9:33 The conclusion of the prophetic reference pointed towards the rock as the spirit identity of a person. God placed his testimony of their identity in front of their eyes, in Zion, the center of their religious focus, yet, blinded by their own efforts to justify themselves, they tripped over him. But those who recognized him by faith, as the Rock from which they were hewn are freed from the shame of their sense of failure and inferiority. [See Deuteronomy 32:18, "you have forgotten the Rock that birthed you;" and in Isaiah 51:1, "Look to the Rock from which you were hewn."] It is only in him that mankind will discover what they are looking for. Who is the son of man? His physical identity is defined by his spiritual origin, the image and likeness of God, I say you are petros, you are rock [see Mt 16:13-19]. Mankind's origin and true identity is preserved and revealed again in the Rock of ages. The term, rock in those days represented what we call the hard drive in computer technology; the place where data is most securely preserved. Rock fossils carry the oldest data and evidence of life.)

See also Rom 10:11 Scripture declares that whosoever believes in Christ [to be the fulfillment of the promise of God to redeem mankind] will ³not be ashamed (⁴hesitant) to announce it. [See Isa 28:16] These two Hebrew words, ³cush, to make haste, and [Isa 49:23] ⁴bush, to be ashamed, look very similar and were obviously confused in some translations—the Greek from Hebrew translation. The Septuagint was the Scriptures Paul was familiar with and there the word was translated from the word ¹bush.)

2:7 His irreplaceable and priceless value is realized in your conviction; the very stone rejected by the unbelief of the religious leaders of the day, has become the head of the house!

2:8 Unbelief is such a predictable set-up where that which is highly esteemed by faith, seems scandalous and offensive to the self-righteous mind. Since there is no ground left for boasting, grace offends the typical "law of works-mentality." They are the ones who refuse to see the reference to their original identity revealed and redeemed in Christ.

2:9 You are proof of the authentic *[eklego]* generation; you give testimony to the original idea of the royalty of true priesthood *[the order of Melchizedek;]* you are a perfect prototype of the mass of the human race. You are the generation of people who exhibit the conclusion *[eis]* of the prophetic, poetic thought of God that has come full circle. *(See 1:3)* You publish the excellence of his elevation and display that your authentic identity has been rescued out of obscurity and brought into his spectacular light!

2:10 You were once a people without identity, but have now discovered the integrity of your original identity in God; where there was no mercy *[under the cruel judgment of the law of works, sponsored by the "I am not-tree-system,]* **you have now received much mercy!**

2:11 It does not matter how appealing the system of the flesh-glory seems, it can never define or fulfill you; do not allow yourself to be lured into its strategies and sway! You are dearly loved! I urge you from within this place of our joint oneness to remain like pilgrims and strangers to the subtleties of a world-system that is foreign to your design. Avoid any influence that does not ²resonate with your innocence. *(The word, ¹parakaleo has two components; para, suggesting close proximity and kaleo, to surname or to identify by name; suggesting close and intimate companionship; the word ²apechomai, apo, away from and echo, to abstain from that which does not resonate.)*

2:12 The beautiful way in which you conduct yourselves in the company of people who are not familiar with your beliefs, will attract their attention to the resonance of their hearts as they witness for themselves God's intentions as evidenced in your good works. This will be as clear as daylight to them and will completely disarm the evil rumors that they have heard about you.

2:13 Reflect the Lordship of Jesus in your life in the way that you submit to every man-made ordinance, by acknowledging the supremacy of a king.

2:14 Recognize their leadership and structures as their objective to manage the evil doers in a righteous way as well as to commend those who do well.

2:15 God desires that your good conduct will silence those foolish people who see you as a threat to society.

2:16 Yes you are free *(from man-made rules and institutions to govern your behavior)* but do not use your freedom in a way that others may read it as a disguise for an evil agenda! You are God-governed! *(Where love rules!)*

2:17 Esteem all people with equal respect. Love family with much affection. Revere God. Respect the King.

2:18 Servants be subject to your masters in every possible way; not only to those who are nice to you but even to the crooked ones!

2:19 Seeing together with God enables you to suffer wrongfully, gracefully.

2:20 For someone to get beaten up for his sins and then to bear it patiently is one thing; but suffering such abuse while you are doing well is pure grace before God!

2:21 These are defining moments for us, since Christ suffered our judgment in his innocence, thus leaving us a perfect example! In this way, our attitude in bearing insults we do not deserve, reveals the grace of God to the ones mistreating us.

2:22 He never said or did anything wrong!

2:23 Even when they heaped abuse upon him, he never retaliated; he suffered much, but never threatened; instead he fully yielded himself to the righteous judgment of God; which is God declaring the unjust righteous because of what Christ has done!

2:24 In his person he bore our sins in his own body upon the tree and thus [1]brought closure to every distorted pattern of sin's influence upon us; we were made alive unto righteousness; we were healed by the blows he took in his body! *(The word [1]apogenomenos from apo, away from and ginomai, to cause to be, to generate; in giving up his body to death, he removed us from the deadly influence of every distortion that sin could possibly generate in us! See 1 Pet 1:11.)*

2:25 You were completely vulnerable, just like sheep roaming astray without direction or protection, but now you have returned and are restored to the Shepherd and Guardian of your souls!

1:1 I am Simon the Rock, bondman and ambassador of Jesus Christ. We are in this together; God's faith [1]sees everyone [2]equally valued and justified in Jesus Christ our Savior. *(He rescued us from the lies we believed about ourselves. The word, [1]lanchano, means to be measured out beforehand; to be allocated something by allotment. This emphasizes the fact that nothing we did or determined to achieve had any influence upon God to qualify us. Faith is not something we do to persuade God; faith is what happens to us when we realize how persuaded God is about us. Salvation belongs to everyone based on exactly the same merit. God's righteousness persuades us. What God did right in Christ cancels out everything that Adam, or we did wrong! See Rom 1:17 Herein lies the secret of the power of the Gospel; there is no good news in it until the righteousness of God is revealed! The dynamic of the gospel is the revelation of God's faith as the only valid basis for our belief. The prophets wrote in advance about the fact that God believes that righteousness defines the life that he always had in mind for us. "Righteousness by his (God's) faith defines life." The word, [2]isotimos, means to esteem of equal value.)*

1:2 God's [1]desire is that we may now increasingly be overwhelmed with grace as his divine influence within us and become fully acquainted with the awareness of our [2]oneness. The way he has always [3]known us is realized in Jesus our Master. *(The verb [1]plethunthein, meaning to increase, to multiply, is in the Optative mood which expesses a wish. The word [2]eirene, pictures a dovetail joint in carpentry; often translated, peace. The [3]knowledge of God is not our knowledge of him; it is God's knowledge of us! He knew us before he formed us in our mother's womb! Jer 1:5. In this context no one can ever feel ignored or neglected again.)*

1:3 By his divine [1]engineering he gifted us with all that it takes to live life to the full, where our ordinary day to day lives mirror our [2]devotion and romance with our Maker. His [3]intimate knowledge of us [4]introduces us to ourselves again and [5]elevates us to a position where his [6]original intention is clearly perceived! *(I have translated the word, [1]dunamis, power or ability, as engineering, in this context. The word [2]eusebeia means devotion or worship. The word [3]epignoseos suggests an intimate knowledge; here it is in the Genitive case, which means God is the owner of this knowledge. Jer 1:5, 1 Cor 13:12. The word [4]kaleo, means to surname, I translated it, "he introduced us to ourselves again", which reminds of Jesus declaring to Simon, son of Jonah his original identity and thus laying the rock-foundation in our understanding that the son of man is indeed the son of God, now celebrated in the ekklesia, which literally means our original identity. Math 16:17,18. The word [5]arete from aireo means to elevate, to lift one's perspective; often translated, virtue. The word [6]doxa, often translated, glory, from dokeo, original intention, opinion.)*

1:4 This is exactly what God always had in mind for us; every one of his abundant and priceless promises pointed to our restored participation in our [1]godly origin! This is his gift to us! In this fellowship we have escaped the distorted influence of the corrupt cosmic virus of greed. *([1]His image and likeness is redeemed in us. The default settings are restored. We are rebooted to fully participate in the life of our design.)*

1:5 **Now** (*in the light of what we are gifted with in Christ*) **the stage is set to display life's excellence. Explore the adventure of faith! Imagine the extreme dedication and focus of a ¹conductor of music; how he would ²diligently ³acquaint himself with every individual voice in the choir, as well as the contribution of every specific instrument, to follow the precise sound represented in every single note in order to give maximum credit to the original composition. This is exactly what it means to exhibit the divine character. You are the choir conductor of your own life. Familiarize yourselves with every ingredient that faith unfolds! See there how ⁴elevated you are, and from within this position** (*of your co-seatedness in Christ*), **⁵enlightened perspective will dawn within you.** (*The word, ¹epichoregeo, comes from epi, a preposition of position, over, in charge, indicating continual influence upon, + chorus, choir, orchestra, or dance + ago, meaning to lead as a shepherd leads his sheep; thus, the conductor of music. ²"Giving all diligence, extreme devotion." The word, ²spoude, means to interest one's self immediately and most earnestly. The word, ³pareisphero, means to introduce simultaneously. I translated it, to acquaint yourself with every detail of the whole. From para, a preposition indicating close proximity, a thing proceeding from a sphere of influence, with a suggestion of union of place of residence, to have sprung from its author and giver, originating from, denoting the point from which an action originates, intimate connection, + eisphero, to reach inward. Before a performance, the first violinist will give the exact key of the piece to be played; now every instrument can be finely tuned to that note, in the same way the faith of God gives that exact pitch. The word, ⁴arete, often translated, virtue, comes from the word airo, to raise up, to elevate. Faith unfolds the secret of our joint-elevation with Jesus. See yourself seated together with Christ! Colossians 3:1-3. Now from this position of elevation we begin to see new horizons; in fact we begin to see everything differently! There is a level of understanding, ⁵gnosis, a knowing, that can only be accessed by faith. In Hebrews 11:3, "by faith we understand that the ages were framed by the Word of God."*)

1:6 **Here you will realize your inner strength and how fully competent you are to prevail in patient perseverance in the midst of any contradiction. It is from within this place of enlightened perspective that meaningful devotion and worship ignite!** (*Spiritual strength exceeds mind-, muscle- or willpower by far!*)

1:7 **In worship you will find a genuine fondness for others. At the heart of everything that faith unfolds is ¹the agape-love of God.** (*Worship and devotion includes esteeming people and honoring friendship [Jas 3:9]; the same voice that magnifies God cannot insult a person made in God's image. True worship is to touch someone's life with the same devotion and care you would touch Jesus himself; even if the other person seems a most unlikely candidate. The word, ¹agape, is from ago, meaning to lead as a shepherd leads his sheep, and pao, to rest; as in Psalm 23, "he leads me besides still waters, he restores my soul; or, by the waters of reflection, my soul remembers who I am!"*

See The Message translation, " ... each dimension fitting into and developing the other.")

1:8 While you diligently ¹rehearse the exact qualities of every divine attribute within you; the volume will rise with ever increasing gusto, guarding you from being ineffective and barren in your knowledge of the Christ-life, displayed with such authority and eloquence in Jesus. *("These things being in you." The word, ¹uparcho, translates as to begin under, from upo + archomai, to commence or rehearse from the beginning.)*

1:9 If anyone feels that these things are absent in his life, they are not; spiritual blindness and short-sightedness only veil them from you. This happens when one loses sight of one's innocence. *(The moment one forgets the tremendous consequence of the fact that we were cleansed from our past sins, one seems to become pre-occupied again with the immediate sense-ruled horizon, which is what short-sightedness is all about; this makes one blind to his blessings. Spiritual realities suddenly seem vague and distant. Become acquainted with your innocence!)*

1:10 Therefore I would encourage you my fellow family, to make every immediate effort to become cemented in the knowledge of our ¹original identity ²revealed and confirmed in the logic of God. Fully engage these realities in your lifestyle, and so you will never ³fail. *(Your original identity, ¹kaleo, often translated as calling, to surname, to identify by name; ²eklogen, often translated as election; yet the two parts of this word, ek, a preposition denoting origin or source, and lego, from logos, suggests the original word (the logic of God) as our source [Jn 1:1,14]. The word, ³ptaio, means to fail, falter, or get out of tune again in the context of verse 5, literally to fall, lose height, to stop flying.)*

1:11 Thus the great ¹Conductor of music will draw your life into the full volume of the harmony of the ages; the ²royal song of our Savior Jesus Christ. *(In Colossians 2:19, "You are directly connected to Christ who like a choir conductor draws out the music in everyone like a tapestry of art that intertwines in harmony to reveal the full stature of divine inspiration," which is Christ in you. Again the word ²epichoregeo is used, the choir conductor; this time, God is doing the conducting and is leading us into his harmony; ²eis + odos, meaning access into the road. Yet, in this context I prefer the thought that we are led into a song, an ode; a ceremonious lyric poem. The form is usually marked by exalted feeling and style. The term ode derives from a Greek word alluding to a choric song, usually accompanied by a dance; also a poem to be sung composed for royal occasions.)*

1:12 Having said all this I am sure that you can appreciate why I feel so urgent in my commitment to you to repeatedly bring these things to your attention; as indeed you have already taken your stand for the truth as it is now revealed *(in the Gospel).*

1:13 So while I am still in this body-suit, I take my lead from the revelation of righteousness and make it my business to thoroughly stir you until these truths become permanently molded in your memory.

1:14 All the more since I know that my time in this tabernacle is almost done; our Lord Jesus Christ has prepared me for this.

1:15 In the meantime, I will do whatever it takes to make it possible for you to always be able to easily recall these realities even in my absence.

1:16 We are not con-artists, fabricating fictions and fables to add weight to our account of his majestic appearance; with our own eyes we witnessed the powerful display of the illuminate presence of Jesus the Master of the Christ-life. *(His face shone like the sun, even his raiment were radiant white [Mt 17].)*

1:17 He was spectacularly endorsed by God the Father in the highest honor and glory. God's majestic voice announced, "This is the son of my delight; he completely pleases me."

1:18 For John, James, and I the prophetic word is fulfilled beyond doubt; we heard this voice loud and clear from the heavenly realm while we were with Jesus in that sacred moment on the mountain.

1:19 For us the appearing of the Messiah is no longer a future promise but a fulfilled reality. Now it is your turn to have more than a second-hand, hearsay testimony. Take my word as one would take a lamp at night; the day is about to dawn for you in your own understanding. When the morning star appears, you no longer need the lamp; this will happen shortly on the horizon of your own hearts.

1:20 It is most important to understand that the prophetic word recorded in scripture does not need our interpretation or opinion to make it valid.

1:21 The holy men who first spoke these words of old did not invent these thoughts, they simply voiced God's oracles as they were individually inspired by the Holy Spirit.

1:1 The Logos is the source; everything commences in him. The initial reports concerning him that have reached our ears, and which we indeed bore witness to with our own eyes - to the point that we became irresistibly attracted - now captivates our gaze. In him we witnessed [1]tangible life in its most articulate form. (*To touch,* [1]*psallo, to touch the string of a musical instrument, thus resonance.*)

1:2 The same life that [1]was [2]face to face with the Father from the beginning, has now dawned on us! The infinite life of the Father became visible before our eyes in a human person! (*In the beginning "was" the Word;* [1]*eimi, timeless existence, "I am". The preposition* [2]*pros says so much more than 'with,' it suggests towards; face to face. See John 1:1&2. Also John 1:14 "Suddenly the invisible eternal Word takes on visible form! The Incarnation! In him, and now confirmed in us! The most accurate tangible display of God's eternal thought finds expression in human life! The Word became a human being; we are his address; he resides in us! He captivates our gaze! The glory we see there is not a religious replica; he is the authentic begotten son. The glory (that Adam lost) returns in fullness! Only grace can communicate truth in such complete context!" Also John 1:18 "Until this moment God remained invisible; now the authentic begotten Son, the blueprint of mankind's design who represents the innermost being of God, the Son who is in the bosom of the Father, brings him into full view! He is the official authority qualified to announce God! He is our guide who accurately declares and interprets the invisible God within us."*)

1:3 We include you in this conversation; you are the immediate audience of the logic of God! This is the Word that always was; we saw him incarnate and witnessed his language as defining our lives. In the incarnation Jesus includes mankind in the eternal friendship of the Father and the Son! This life now finds expression in an unreserved union. (*We do not invent fellowship; we are invited into the fellowship of the Father and the Son!*)

1:4 What we enjoy equally belongs to you! I am writing this for your reference, so that joy may be yours in its most complete measure. (*In all these years since the ascension of Jesus, John, now ninety years old, continues to enjoy unhindered friendship with God and desires to extend this same fellowship to everyone through this writing.*)

1:5 My conversation with you flows from the same source which illuminates this fellowship of union with the Father and the Son. This, then, is the essence of the message: God is radiant light and in him there exists not even a trace of obscurity or darkness at all. (*See James 1:17, "Without exception God's gifts are only good, their perfection cannot be improved upon. They come* [1]*from above, [where we originate from] proceeding like light rays from the source, the Father of lights, with whom there is no distortion or even a shadow of shifting to obstruct or intercept the light; no hint of a hidden agenda. [The word,* [1]*anouthen, means, from above. John 3:3, 13. Man is not the product of his mother's womb; man began in God."*)

1:6 This is the real deal! To live a life of pretence is a such a waste of time! The truth has no competition. Truth inspires the poetry of friendship in total contrast to a fake, performance-based fellowship! Light is not threatened by darkness! Why say something with darkness as your reference?

1:7 We are invited to explore the dimensions of the same light that engulfs God; when we see the light in his light, fellowship ignites! In his light we understand how the blood of Jesus Christ is the removal of every stain of sin! The success of the cross celebrates our redeemed innocence!

1:8 To claim innocence by our own efforts under the law of personal performance is to deceive ourselves and to deliberately ignore the truth. The truth about you does not mean that you now have to go into denial if you have done something wrong!

1:9 When we [1]communicate what God says about our sins, we discover what he believes concerning our redeemed oneness and innocence! We are cleansed from every distortion we believed about ourselves! Likeness is redeemed! *(The word traditionally translated "confession" is the word* [1]*homologeo from homo, the same, and logeo to speak. In the context of verse 7, this suggests that we say what God says about us!)*

1:10 If we judge ourselves innocent by the law of our own works, then we make Jesus Christ, and what his word and blood communicate within us, irrelevant.*(See John 1:3-5 The Logos is the source; everything commences in him. He remains the exclusive parent reference to their genesis. There is nothing original - except the Word! His life is the light that defines our lives. (In his life, man discovers the light of life.) The darkness was pierced and could not comprehend or diminish this light. (Darkness represents mankind's ignorance of their redeemed identity and innocence [Isaiah 9:2-4, Isaiah 60:1-3, Ephesians 3:18, Colossians 1:13-15])". See also Isaiah 9:2 "The people who walked in darkness have seen a great light; those who dwelt in a land of deep darkness, on them has light shined." Matthew 4:16 The people who sat in darkness have seen a great light, and for those who sat in the region and shadow of death, light has dawned." A new day for humanity has come. The authentic light of life that illuminates everyone was about to dawn in the world!)*

2:1 My darling little children, the reason I write these things to you is so that you will not ¹believe a lie about yourselves! If anyone does believe a ¹distorted image to be their reality, we have Jesus Christ who ²defines our likeness ³face to face with the Father! He is our ⁴parakletos, the one who endorses our true identity, being both the source and the reflection of the Father's image in us! *(The root of sin is to believe a lie about yourself. The word sin, is the word ¹hamartia, from ha, negative or without and meros, portion or form, thus to be without your allotted portion or without form, pointing to a disorientated, distorted, bankrupt identity; the word meros, is the stem of morphe, as in 2 Corinthians 3:18 the word metamorphe, with form, which is the opposite of hamartia - without form. Sin is to live out of context with the blueprint of one's design; to behave out of tune with God's original harmony. Jesus the righteous, iesoun xriston dikaion; the word ²dikaiosune, righteousness is from the root word dike, two parties finding likeness in each other. The preposition ³pros suggests a face to face presentation. [See John 1:1] The word ⁴parakletos comes from para, a preposition indicating close proximity, a thing proceeding from a sphere of influence, with a suggestion of union of place of residence, to have sprung from its author and giver, originating from, denoting the point from which an action originates, intimate connection; and kaleo, meaning to identify by name, to surname. Jesus introduces the Holy Spirit in the same capacity: parakletos, meaning close companion, kinsman [John 14:16]. Sadly this word has been translated as 'advocate' as if Jesus needs to persuade the Father to like us and possibly forgive us!)*

2:2 Jesus is our ¹at-one-ment, he has conciliated us to himself and has taken our sins and distortions out of the equation. What he has accomplished is not to be seen as something that belongs to us exclusively; the same at-one-ment includes the entire kosmos! *(The word ¹hilasmos, means to conciliate, to bring about atonement, from hileos, gracious, merciful. Also reminds of the word hilaros, cheerful, joyous, hilarious!)*

2:3 In this we know that we know him; by ¹treasuring the ²conclusion of his prophetic purpose. *(The word ¹tereo, means to attend to carefully, take care of, to guard, to treasure something with great attention. The word ²entole; often translated commandment or precept; the two components of this word are en, in and telos, from tello, to set out for a definite point or goal; properly the point aimed at as a limit, that is, by implication, the conclusion of an act or state, the result; the ultimate or prophetic purpose. Strong's 5056)*

2:4 To merely claim that you know him, based on your own academic or even sentimental interpretation of him, and not upon the conclusion of his prophetic purpose unveiled in a heart that treasures his truth, is to continue to live a life of pretence! *(As Paul also says in 2 Corinthians 5:16, we once knew Christ from a human point of view but we no longer know him like that! Keep the context of John's writing in mind, 1 John 1:5-8 My conversation with you flows from the same source which illuminates this fellowship of union with the Father and the Son. This, then, is the essence of the message: God is radiant light and in him there exists not even a trace of obscurity or darkness at all. This is the real deal! To live a life of pretence is a such a waste! The truth has no competition. Truth inspires the poetry of fellowship in total contrast to a fake, performance-based friend-*

ship! Light is not threatened by darkness! Why say something with darkness as your reference? We are invited to explore the dimensions of the same light that engulfs God; when we see the light in his light, fellowship ignites! In his light we understand how the blood of Jesus Christ is the removal of every stain of sin! The success of the cross celebrates our redeemed innocence! To claim innocence by our own efforts under the law of personal performance is to deceive ourselves and to deliberately ignore the truth.)

2:5 Whoever treasures [1]the logic of God's authentic thought, has his agape-love fully realized in its most complete context. This is what our association and this union in Christ is all about! *(God's word, or logic, his authentic thought, [1]logos; John 1:1. See John 14:20, "In that day you will know that I am in my Father, and you in me, and I in you!" Also 1 John 5:20 "We know that the Son of God has come, and he has given us understanding to know him who is true, and we are in him who is true!")*

2:6 It is in this place of consciously [1]abiding in the awareness of your oneness that your conversation unveils the same fellowship with the Father that Jesus enjoys, and results in a daily walk that mirrors his; one of living your life in the full [2]benefit of it! *(The word, [1]meno suggests an uninterrupted abiding, a seamless oneness! The word [2]opheilō, often translated, ought to, is from the root word ophelos, which means to advantage, to profit, to gain, to heap up, to accumulate, to benefit!)*

2:7 My beloved family, I know that the words I write to you here may not immediately remind you of the [1]precepts of Moses; this does not mean that it is a new [1]doctrine, it is the ancient [1]conversation that [2]echoes God's voice prophetically! It is indeed the very [1]conclusion of the word, which you have heard from the beginning! *(The word [1]entole is often translated commandment or precept; this word has two components: en, in and telos, from tello, to set out for a definite point or goal; properly the point aimed at as a limit, that is, by implication, the conclusion of an act or state, the result; the ultimate or prophetic purpose. Strong's 5056. The word, [2]echo, to hold, like sound is held in an echo; to resonate.)*

2:8 And yet it is a glorious [1]new [2]message that I am writing to you! You may ask, "How can that which is old, also be new?" Herein is the secret of its newness: whatever is true of Jesus is equally true of you! The days of the [3]dominance of darkness as a reference to human life, are over! The true light surely shines with [4]bold certainty and illuminates your life, as it is unveiled in Christ. *(The word [1]kainos means, fresh, recent, unused, unworn, of a new kind, unprecedented, novel, uncommon. The freshness of this encounter is celebrated in a fellowship of exactly the same oneness enjoyed between the Father and the Son! Again the word [2]entole is used, precept or teaching. The word [3]parago from para, close proximity and agoo, to lead; thus darkness will no longer lead you into its sway. The word [4]ede, even now: - already, by this time; from ē [pronounced ay] an adverb of confirmation; assuredly: - surely; and dē [pronounced day] which is a particle of emphasis or explicitness; now, then, etc.: - also, and, doubtless, now, therefore.)*

2:9 To feel justified in your judgment to [1]dislike a fellow human, is to

continue in darkness, even if you might claim to be in the light! This place of illumination is not cheap talk! It immediately translates into seeing your brother differently! *(See 1 John 1:6, also 2 Corinthians 5:16. [1]It was common among the Hebrews to use the terms "love" and "hatred" in this comparative sense, where the former implied strong positive attachment, and the latter, not positive hatred, but merely a less love, or the withholding of the expressions of affection [compare Genesis 29:30-31; Luke 14:26].)*

2:10 From this conscious union with that which light reveals, there follows a deep love for the very brother who might previously have irritated you!

2:11 If anyone thinks less of his brother than what love reveals, it is proof of a blindfold mode, where reference is blurred by a mind trapped in a maze of dark thoughts, which leads nowhere.

2:12 The reason of my writing is to remind you to live your lives in the innocence of an infant! The name Jesus means that you can rest assured in your salvation from sin's harassment! *(Teknion, diminitive of teknon, an infant.)*

2:13 May my writing also remind you that your fatherhood has its authentic genesis in him who is from the beginning. *(1 John 2:7,8; 5:20)* And to you young men, I write to congratulate you for your victory over the [1]exhausting system of hardships, annoyances and labors. You have discovered your strength in Christ's achievement and not your own efforts! I wrote to all of you as children because you know God as your Father. *(The word often translated evil, is [1]poneros, which according to Thayer's definition means to be full of labors, annoyances, hardships; to be pressed and harassed by labors. This is so typical of the religious system of a works-based self-righteousness, as opposed to faith righteousness. This is the fruit of the I am not-tree-system. The young men who become weary and exhausted under the system of hardships and labor; the law of works, have discovered their eagle wings in Kawa-mode; where God's thoughts entwine with their thoughts, and his strentgh ignites within. Isa 40:31 The Hebrew word, kawa, often translated, to wait, means to entine; to plat together.)*

2:14 What I have written previously will resonate with the fathers whose aquaintance with him is established in the prophetic voice [1]from the beginning. Also the young men will find their strength endorsed in my writing, since they have the word firmly rooted within them as their permanent source and reference. They have defeated the duty-and guilt-driven system that snared them before in the futility of their own efforts. *(The word [1]arche, means to be first in order, time, place or rank.*

2:15 The Father's love does not compete with anything the world-system has to offer! Its cosmetic attraction is surface and external; the Father's love is from within. Do not be lured into an emptiness where love is absent and romance seems lost!

2:16 There is a clear distinction between the [1]biological, physical life that is exploited by the "I am not - mentality" of the world system, and the authentic zoe-life of our design that is sourced in the Father. The one engages the individual with a constant yearning and craving for fleshly gratification, with eyes desperately scanning for recognition; this inevitably results in ²cheap bragging and boastful conversation, which is so utterly boring; while the Father's life satisfies completely! *(The word, ¹bios refers to biological, or physical life; while zoe refers more to spiritual life. The word ²alazoneia, means empty, braggart talk.)*

2:17 The world system with all its glamorous dreams comes and goes; but whoever engages with the poetry of God's desires abides unchanged into the conclusion of the ages.

2:18 Children, this is the completeness of time; the revelation of Christ brings finality and closure to the hour; which makes the anti-Christ system now more apparent than ever, just as it was rumored. There are many who have positioned themselves against the Christ; blatantly opposing grace; this confirms that time has reached its most extreme context! The days of confusion between two oposing systems are over! *(See John 1:17 Against the stark backdrop of the law, with Moses representing the condemned state of mankind, Jesus Christ unveils grace and truth!)*

2:19 Here there remains no room for hiding in compromize mode! Pretence is no disguise; the grace and finished work of Christ has absolutely nothing in common with religious systems that continue to keep people enslaved to their programs and rituals of outdated sentimental ideals! Their departure from amongst us simply reveal that they never really embraced Christ; one cannot be for and against Christ at the same time!

2:20 The Christ anointing within you is evidence that you echo what you carry! The Holy Spirit has made him tangible in your life, and you see clearly.

2:21 My writing to you is not to question your perception of the truth, but to endorse it! No form of deception can possibly co-exist with truth.

2:22 Deception just cannot see that Jesus is the Christ. The anti-Christ system contradicts both the Father and the Son.

2:23 You cannot have the one without the other! To reject the one is to reject the other. What you say about the Son, immediately reflects your opinion of the Father! *(The word, homologeo, from homo, the same, and lego, to speak.)*

2:24 Make that which you have heard from the beginning your permanent reference; and what I have written in the beginning of this letter *(1 John 1:1-4)* will be your testimony too! The same constant that is enjoyed in the fellowship of the Father and the Son is yours!

2:25 This is the essence of the life of the ages which he has announced and purposed from the beginning. *(Amazing thoughts to consider that our Father who knew us individually, completely, long before he formed us, is the same*

Engineer who knew every minute detail of our being as we grew mystically in the secret sanctuary of our mother's womb! And knows us now, and longs to introduce us to ourselves again, so that we may know, even as we have always been known! Jeremiah 1:5, 1Corinthians 13:12)

2:26 My intention with this writing is to nullify the influence of those who wish to unsettle you.

2:27 I am convinced that the effect of his touch within you is permanent; this is the Christ-annointing that teaches you all things, so that you do not need any teacher whose doctrine does not resonate with truth. Deception cannot compete with spirit-resonance.

2:28 So now, just like an [1]infant in a mother's embrace, [2]abide in this place of innocence where his [3]manifest appearance is meant to be fully realized and echoed in unashamed utterance! In his [4]immediate presence there exist no sense of shame or any form of [5]separation! (*[1]Teknion, diminitive of **teknon**, an infant. The word, [2]**meno** suggests an uninterrupted abiding, a seamless oneness! The word, [3]**phanerothe** is an Aorist Passive in the Subjunctive mode, expressing the hypothetical, expected result of the completed action; from **phaneroo**, to appear; to fully realize, to manifest. The word [4]**parousia** speaks of the immediate presence of the Lord! From **para**, a preposition indicating close proximity, a thing proceeding from a sphere of influence, with a suggestion of union of place of residence, to have sprung from its author and giver, originating from, denoting the point from which an action originates, intimate connection; and **eimi**, I am! There is not even a hint of judgment or punishment in this word! Sadly this word has often been translated to yet again point to a future event suggesting the coming of Christ! Please do not believe everything you read in Strongs! For instance: "G3952 parousia, to return; specifically of Christ to punish Jerusalem, or finally the wicked."!!?? The word, [5]**apo**, away from, here translated separation.)*

2:29 To perceive God's righteousness as defining his [1]"I am-ness", concludes that everyone born of him inherently partakes of the same pattern and poetry that his righteousness inspires. Righteousness is our true genesis. (*The word, [1]**estin**, to be, from **eimi**, I am. The word for righteousness is [2]**dikaios**, from **dikay**, suggesting two parties finding likeness in each other, where there is no sense of inferiority, suspicion, blame, regret or pressure to perform. The gospel is the revelation of the righteousness of God as our blueprint identity. See Psalm 23:2 "By the waters of reflection, my soul remembers who I am. He leads me in the footprints of righteousness.")*

3:1 Consider the amazing love the Father lavished upon us; this is our [1]defining moment: we began in the agape of God - the engineer of the universe is our Father! So it's no wonder that the performance-based systems of this world just cannot see this! Because they do not recognize their origin in God, they feel indifferent towards anyone who does! *(The word, [1]kaleo, to identify by name; to surname.)*

3:2 Beloved, we know that we are children of God to begin with, which means that there can be no future surprises; his manifest likeness is already mirrored in us! Our sameness cannot be comprised or contradicted; our gaze will confirm exactly who he is - and who we are. *(See Philippians 2:15 Your flawless innocence radiates life's contrast as beacons of light in the midst of a people who have forgotten their true sonship and whose lives have become distorted and perverse. [In this verse Paul quotes Deuteronomy 32:5 from the Greek Septuagint translation of the Hebrew text, with reference to Deuteronomy 32:4,5 &18. In context, God's perfect workmanship as Father of mankind is forgotten; people have become "crooked and perverse" twisted and distorted out of their true pattern of sonship. Deuteronomy 32:18 says, you have forgotten the Rock that begat you and have become out of step with the God who danced with you! Hebrew, khul or kheel.])*

3:3 And every individual in whom this expectation echoes also endeavors to realize their own flawless innocence mirrored in him whose image they bear. *(The word echo, to hold, to echo, to resonate. John discovered the same "in him" unveiling that Paul walked in! See John 14:20, "In that day you will know that I am in my Father, and you are in me, and I am in you!" Also 1 John 5:20, "And we know that the Son of God is come, and he has given us understanding, that we may know him who is true, and we are in him that is true, even in his Son Jesus Christ. This is the true God, and eternal life. Colossians 2:9,10)*

3:4 [1]Distorted behavior is the result of a warped self-image! A [2]lost sense of identity is the basis of all sin! *(The word sin, is the word [1]hamartia, from ha, negative or without and meros, portion or form, thus to be without your allotted portion or without form, pointing to a disorientated, distorted, bankrupt identity; the word meros, is the stem of morphe, as in 2 Corinthians 3:18 the word metamorphe, with form, which is the opposite of hamartia - without form. Sin is to live out of context with the blueprint of one's design; to behave out of tune with God's original harmony. See Deuteronomy 32:18, "You have forgotten the Rock that begot you and have gotten out of step with the God who danced with you!" Hebrew, khul or kheel, to dance. The root of sin is to believe a lie about yourself. The word often translated, lawlessness, [2]anomia, from a, without, and onoma, name; thus without a name; anonymous.)*

3:5 We have witnessed with our own eyes how, in the unveiling of the prophetic word, when he was lifted up upon the cross as the Lamb of God, he [1]lifted up our sins and broke its dominion and rule over us! *(John 1:29 "Behold, the Lamb of God, who [1]takes away [airo] the sin of the world! The word [1]airo means to lift up.)*

3:6 To [1]abide in him in uniterupted seamless oneness, is to live free from sin. Whoever continues in sin has obviously not perceived how free they are in him; they clearly do not really know him. (*The word,* [1]*meno suggests an uninterrupted abiding; a seamless oneness!*)

3:7 Little children, do not be led astray by any other opinion; his righteousness is the source of our righteousness.

3:8 Sin's source is a [1]fallen mindset, from the beginning! For this purpose the son of God was revealed! His mission was to undo the works of the devil! (*The word,* **diabolos**, *from* **dia**, *because of and* **ballo**, *to cast down.*)

3:9 To discover one's authentic sonship in God, is to discover true freedom from sin. We are born of him and his seed remains in us; this is the only possible reference to sober up the mind from the intoxicating influence of deception. (*The incorruptible seed of our Father carries the exact pattern of the authentic life of our design! Jesus calls the devil, the father of lies.*

John 8:31 Jesus then said to the Jews who had believed in him, "If you continue in my word, you are truly my disciples, John 8:32 and you will know the truth, and the truth will make you free." John 8:36 So if the Son makes you free, you will be free indeed. John 8:44 You are of your father the devil, and your will is to do your father's desires. He was a murderer from the beginning, and has nothing to do with the truth, because there is no truth in him. When he lies, he speaks from his own distorted opinion; for he is a liar and the father of lies.

His intention was to kill mankind's awareness of their god-identity.

John 8:56 Your father Abraham rejoiced to see my day; he saw it and was glad." John 8:57 The Jews then said to him, "You are not yet fifty years old, and have you seen Abraham?" John 8:58 Jesus said to them, "Truly, truly, I say to you, before Abraham was, I am." Two chapters later Jesus adresses the same audience again: John 10:30 I and the Father are one." John 10:31 The Jews took up stones again to stone him. John 10:32 Jesus answered them, "I have shown you many good works from the Father; for which of these do you stone me?" John 10:33 The Jews answered him, "It is not for a good work that we stone you but for blasphemy; because you, being a man, make yourself God." John 10:34 Jesus answered them, "Is it not written in your law, 'I said, you are gods'? John 10:35 If he called them gods to whom the word of God came [and scripture cannot be broken], John 10:36 do you say of him whom the Father consecrated and sent into the world, 'You are blaspheming,' because I said, 'I am the Son of God'?

Here Jesus quotes from Psa 82:6 I say, "You are gods, sons of the Most High, all of you! What does it mean to build your house upon the rock? "Son of man, I say you are Rock; you're a chip of the old block - the son of man is the son of God!" Dig deep = Gaze deeply, intently into the mirror likeness of the face of your birth! Luke 6:48; James 1:18,23-25; Isaiah 51:1; Deuteronomy 32:18 Living your life from who you are in Christ [Grace] beats living your life from who you are in Adam [law of works] by far! Plus it is storm-proof!)

3:10 There is a very visible and vast difference between living one's live from your God identity, or from a fallen mindset; the [1]diabolos-fruit has

nothing in common with ²righteousness; neither does it know anything about brotherly love. *(The children of the devil; here translated the ¹diabolos-fruit; the typical fruit that the fallen mindset bears. Righteousness, ²diakaiosune, from dike, two parties finding likeness in each other.)*

3:11 Our love for one another was the topic of conversation from the start! God had nothing less in mind than a loving family!

3:12 Cain's ¹killing of his brother Abel, is in such contrast to this! His motivation was clearly ²sourced in the ³poneros tree-system; his idea of Divine ⁴favor was to count on his own works as being superior to his brother's faith righteousness. *(Immediately after the fall, Adam named the woman Eloyim gave him, Eve, [in Hebrew Chawah, and in Greek, Zoe.] He thus co-echoes and reinforces the prophetic word that Eloyim gave him: Life in the face of death! "The seed of the woman, shall crush the deceiver's head!" The fallen mindset shall be destroyed! So here, in their two sons, we have the first generation of fallen humanity confronted with their personal pursuit of a lost identity and a lost sense of value and favor. Caleb's motivation was clearly sourced [²ek, out of, origin] in the diabolos [cast down], which is so typical of the ³poneros tree-system. The tree of the knowledge of good and evil [poneros] represents mankind's lost sense of identity and righteousness, where the universal pursuit of humanity would now be their constant effort to achieve righteousness by means of their own works. This inevitably leads to disappointment where shame replaces innocence, and union and fellowship are lost. The word evil, poneros, suggests to be full of hardships, labors and annoyances. Gen 3:19 "In the sweat of your face shalt you eat your bread." The sacrifice of Cain is exactly that! It represents his trust in the fruit of his own toil to gain him a ⁴favorable [charin] standing with God.*

We have the prophetic picture of a scapegoat repeated here in Genesis 4. Not only in the sacrifice that Abel brought; but also in him being murdered by his brother! Just like we would one day murder our brother Jesus! In Genesis 3, Eloyim did not clothe Adam with the skin of an animal because of a divine need to be appeased, but because of their unconditional love for Adam; they spoke the language of Adam's own judgment: Adam, not Eloyim, was embarrassed about his nakedness. The clothing was not to make Eloyim look at Adam differently, but to make Adam feel better about himself! And ultimately it was to prepare Adam for the unveiling of the mystery of mankind's redemption in the incarnation. Here Deity would clothe themselves in human skin in a son, and the Lion of Judah, would become the Lamb of God, in order to free our minds to re discover his image and likeness in our skin! See Revelation 5:5,6.

Only John uses the word, ¹sphatzo, which speaks of a slaying. Four times in the book of Revelation he employs this word in the context of the slain Lamb of God.

See also Hebrews 11:4, "It was faith that made the difference between the sacrifices of Abel and Cain, and confirmed Abel's righteousness. God bore witness to righteousness as a gift rather than a reward! Even though he was murdered, his faith still has a voice today."

Philo a Hellenistic Jewish philosopher says, that in the dispute between Cain and

Abel, Abel attributed all things to God, and Cain ascribed everything to himself; so that the controversy was about grace and works. [Philo lived c. 25 BCE – c. 50 CE]

The tree of the knowledge of good and evil represents a fallen identity; the thought that likeness with God could be earned through good intentions, rather than realizing the gift of life that already defines his image and likeness in us.)

Thoughts on, "Why the other tree and why the temptation in the Garden?"

I think the picture that we are presented with in the garden of Sabbath abundance, and of the 2 trees and the temptation, presents us inevitably with the full scope of our design! We are not robots who are to simply respond to our Maker in remote control fashion.

To give ultimate context to the setting of paradise beauty, we were presented with the opportunity to consciously and spontaneously fellowship with our invisible Maker and to explore the dynamics of our own being there; and from that place of knowing that we are known we would reflect what we discover in fellowship union and intimacy in Eloyim and in one another! We were designed to explore the limitless dimensions of our being as referenced in our Source.

The temptation was to follow the suggestion of an alternative idea that maybe we are not perfect by design; maybe, we thought, even Eloyim knew that we are not really what they had in mind, and would therefore feel threatened by our knowledge of good and evil; maybe that is the reason they didn't want us to eat of the fruit of the "other" tree, we reasoned!

The alternative tree gives us the opportunity to engage an alternative system, whereby we have to now prove to ourselves, and to one another, as well as to our own ideas of deity (religion) that we can manage and possibly master our own being and destiny, independent of our Source!

The quest to prove my I am-ness would now become my constant drive; instead of finding and celebrating me in fellowship with my Maker and my fellow human being, and also in my harmonious co-existence with paradise nature, I have to now strive for it in the fruit of my own efforts to become something I already am by design, perfect and esteemed.

And so we have exchanged Eloyim's perfect approval of us, based on their perfect knowledge of us, for our imperfect knowledge of ourselves and of one another, proved by the inevitable evidence in our disappointment with ourselves and with one another.

The "I am not-tree-system" would continually be re-enforced by feelings of shame, guilt, inferiority and competing, which sadly brings with it every shade of hostility and frustration and the corruption that our history and societies have borne such horrid witness to.

The law expresses and confirms the existence of these systems and their dominance in societies and philosophies for many centuries.

The love of God, the Engineer of our being, demonstrated in the unveiling of our inclusion in the death, decent into hell, the resurrection and ascension of Jesus

Christ, reveals that we are rescued from the lies that we have believed about our-selves, about our Maker and about one another! We are presented with a brand new beginning! The old things have passed away! Behold, everything has become new! 2 Corinthians 5:14-21.

See also 1 Peter 1:18,19 It is clear to see that you were ransomed from the fu-tile, fallen mindset that you inherited from your fathers, not by the currency of your own labor, represented by the fluctuating values of gold and silver, and the economy of your religious efforts; but you were redeemed with the priceless blood of Christ; he is the ultimate sacrifice; spotless and without blemish. He completes the prophetic picture! [In him God speaks the most radical scapegoat language of the law of judgment, and brings final closure to a dead and redundant system! In Psalm 40:6,7, it is clearly stated that God does not require sacrifices or offerings! Jesus is the Lamb of God! He collides victoriously with the futile sacrificial system whereby offerings are constantly made to the pseudo, moody, monster gods of our imagination! This is the scandal of the cross! God does not demand a sacrifice that would change the way he thinks about mankind; he provides the sacrifice of himself in Christ in order to forever eradicate sin-consciousness from our minds and radi-cally change the way we think about our Maker, one another and ourselves! [Sin-consciousness is in essence a works-based consciousness.]

Now immediately engage your thoughts with the reality of your co-seatedness in Christ in the highest dominion of life, and discover there the bliss of your redeemed innocence and your eternal oneness! Colossians 3:1-4)

3:13 It is no wonder then, that the performance-based religious systems of this world loathe you and detest what you stand for! A works-based society finds its leverage in both boasting and condemnation! *(See Romans 3:27)*

3:14 It is clear that we have relocated from a system of dead works into the dynamic of authentic life in the way we love the family. Love is life; not to love is death.

3:15 To hate a brother, is to murder human life; the life of the ages does not echo any resonance in a murderer. It is only in the constant, seam-less resonance of life that agape is realized. *(Agape, from ago, to lead, and pao, to rest.)*

3:16 Love is known in its other-centeredness; just as Jesus laid down his life for us to free his love within us for others.

3:17 The indwelling love of God compels one to live sensitively aware of people around us, and not to exclude those in need.

3:18 My darling children, lets not deceive ourselves by paying lip ser-vice to love while we can truly live the dynamic of love in our practical daily doing!

3:19 In this we know that our beingness is sourced in that which is re-ally true about us; our doing good is not phoney or make-belief; this is who we are in God's sight!

3:20 So, even if our own hearts would [1]accuse us of not really being true to ourselves, God is greater than our hearts and he has the full picture! His knowledge of us is not compromised. (*This word,* [1]*kataginosko is only used three times in the NT, translated, to blame, or condemn. From* **kata**, *down and* **ginosko**, *to know; thus to know from below; from a fallen mindset perspective. See also Colossians 3:9*)

3:21 Beloved when we know what God knows to be true about us, then instead of condemning us, our hearts will endorse our innocence and [1]free our conversation before God. (*The word* [1]*parresia, from* **para**, *a preposition indicating close proximity, and* **rheo**, *to pour forth; to flow freely, suggesting an unreservedness in speech; bold utterance.*)

3:22 Now, instead of begging God, we [1]speak with confident liberty as sons. We also [2]treasure the [3]conclusion of his prophetic purpose [*in redeeming our sonship*] and [4]fully accommodate ourselves to his desires and pleasure! Knowing the warmth in his [5]eyes inspire [6]poetic freedom in our every expression. (*The word* [1]*aiteo, to ask with great liberty and humble confidence; knowing both the desire as well as the ability of the Father to grant us our requests. The word* [2]**tereo**, *means to attend to carefully; take care of; to guard; to treasure something with great affection;* [3]*entole is often translated commandment or precept; this word has two components:* **en**, *in and* **telos**, *from* **tello**, *to set out for a definite point or goal; properly the point aimed at as a limit, that is, by implication, the conclusion of an act or state, the result; the ultimate or prophetic purpose. Strong's 5056. The word* [4]*arestos from* **aresko**, *means to please; to accommodate one's self to the opinions desires and interests of others. The words* [5]**enopion autou**, *means in his sight; face to face. The English word poetry derives from* [6]**poiema**, *to make or do.*)

3:23 And this is the ultimate conclusion of his itention and desire [*entole*] that we [1]would be fully persuaded concerning the name of Jesus Christ who has successfully accomplished his mission as the son of God to rescue mankind's authentic sonship! Our love for one another completes his joy! (*The word* [1]*pisteusomen is an Aorist Passive in the Subjunctive mode, expressing the hypothetical, expected result of the completed action; from* **pisteuo**, *to believe.*)

3:24 Everyone who treasures this final conclusion of God's dream, abides unhindered in seamless oneness in him and he in them. His gift of the Spirit is to endorse our awareness of his abiding within us! (*See John 14:20 In that day you will know that I am in my Father, and you in me, and I in you. Also 1 John 4:13*)

4:1 Beloved do not be swayed by everything that seems spiritual or prophetic; just like with costly metals, there is [1]a reliable test! There are many false prophets who come and go in the religious world-system! They might even sound very inspirational and carry a "Christian" label; this does not mean that God is their source of insight. *(The word [1]dokimatzo, refers to the testing of metals.)*

4:2 This is how you discern the Spirit of God: the incarnation is the central theme of the communication of the Spirit; the fact that Jesus Christ has come in the flesh is what gives legitimacy to every prophetic word. *(See 1 Peter 1:10-14)*

4:3 No so-called "spiritual revelation" that fails to communicate the revelation of the incarnation of Jesus Christ, is of God. This is the anti-Christ spirit that you have heard of and even now witness in the world. Any idea that Jesus Christ is not the incarnate word of God, does not originate in God but is the typical pseudo mindset of the spirit of this fallen cosmic system. *(The Latin rendering from the 2nd century reads, "No spirit that would separate the human Jesus from the divine Christ, is of God.")*

4:4 My darling children, you have nothing to fear; do not doubt for a moment the legitimacy of your sonship! You originate in God and have already conquered the worldly religious system because of the unveiling of Christ in you! His living presence in you is far superior to the futile anti-Christ mindsets present in the world!

4:5 Their conversation mirrors their source and appeals to a common audience; the pseudo-claim of a pseudo-system has blindfolded multitudes to believe a lie about themselves.

4:6 Our beingness originates in God; anyone who knows what God knows about mankind's authentic genesis, hears us; those who do not see their origin in God are deaf to what we communicate. This is the difference between the spirit of truth and the spirit of error. *(The essence of the incarnation is the revelation that Jesus Christ is the word made flesh; [John 1:1-18] he is the one who as the son of God, mirrors and redeems the image and likeness of God in human form. He declares God as the only legitimate Father of the human race.)*

4:7 Beloved, [1]love always includes others, since love springs from God; its source is found in the fellowship of the Father, Spirit and Son. Everyone who encounters love immediately knows that they too are born of the same source! It is not possible to fully participate in love without discovering God. To love is to know God; to know God is to love. *([1]Agape from agoo, to lead, and pao, to rest - love is where the Sabbath of God is perfectly celebrated.)*

4:8 Not to love, is not to know God. There is nothing in love that distracts from who God is. Love is who God is - they are inseparable.

4:9 The love of God is unveiled [1]within us in the Son; he was [2]begotten of the Father in the flesh and sent into the world that we might live because of him. Our lives are mirrored and defined in him. Both his birth in the flesh as well as his commision into the world were [2]entirely God's doing. *(Unfortunately most English translations reads, "The love of God was manifest towards us, or amongst us rather than in us! The Greek word is clear, ἐν ἡμῖν, in us.*

The incarnation is not the genesis of Jesus. The word [2]monogenes, born only of God, or entirely begotten of God, refers to the physical birth of Jesus, which was the incarnation of the Word. See John 1:1 "To go back to the very beginning is to find the Word already present there; face to face with God. The Word is I am; God's eternal eloquence echoes and concludes in him. The Word equals God."[In the beginning, arche, to be first in order, time, place or rank. The Word, logos, was "with" God; here John uses the Greek preposition pros, towards; face-to-face. Three times in this sentence John uses the imperfect of eimi, namely aen [ἦν] which conveys no idea of origin for God or for the Logos, but simply continuous existence, "I am." Quite a different verb egeneto, "became," appears in John 1:14 for the beginning of the Incarnation of the Logos. See the distinction sharply drawn in John 8:58, "before Abraham was [born, genesthai from ginomai] I am." The word eimi, I am; the essence of being, suggesting timeless existence.])

4:10 Love is not defined by our love for God, but by his love for us! It is not our response to God that attracts his attention; we have always had his undivided affection as declared in the prophetic promise and finally demonstrated in his Son's commission and work of atonement for our sins. *(See 1 John 2:2 Jesus is our at-one-ment, he has conciliated us to himself and has taken our sins and distortions out of the equation. What he has accomplished is not to be seen as something that belongs to us exclusively; the same at-one-ment includes the entire kosmos! [The word hilasmos, means to conciliate, to bring about atonement, from hileos, gracious, merciful. Also reminds of the word hilaros, cheerful, joyous, hilarious!])*

4:11 Loved Ones! If this is true about God's love for us, it is equally true of his love in us for others!

4:12 God was never visible to anyone until Jesus brought him into full view; now your love does the same! Our love for one another is evidence of God's seamless union with mankind as witnessed in his love perfected within us! *(See Joh 1:18 Until this moment God remained invisible to everyone; now the authentic begotten son, [monogenes, begotten only of God] the blueprint of our design, who represents the innermost being of God, [the son who is in the bosom of the father,] brings him into full view! He is the official authority qualified to announce God! He is our guide who accurately declares and interprets the invisible God within us.)*

4:13 His own Spirit is the [1]source of this gift, of knowing that we are [2]continuously, seamlessly and very consciously present in him and he in us. *(The preposition [1]ek always denotes source or origin. The word [2]meno means to continue to be present.)*

4:14 We bear witness to that which has [1]arrested our attention concerning the Father's intent in commissioning the Son as Savior of the world! *(John* *uses the word, ¹theaomai, to view attentively, to contemplate, to learn by looking. Realizing authentic, redeemed sonship is what rescues the world!)*

4:15 For anyone ¹to see and to say that Jesus is the Son of God is to awaken to the awareness that we are ²continuously, seamlessly joined in oneness. . *(The word ¹homologeo, from homo, the same and lego, to speak; thus to say the same. The word ²meno means to continue to be present. Young's Literal Translation reads: God in him doth remain, and he in God. [Now God cannot remain somewhere if he was never there to begin with, neither can we!] See John 14:20)*

4:16 And thus we have come to know and believe the love that God has unveiled within us. God is love; love is who God is; to live in this place of conscious, constant love, is to live immersed in God and to feel perfectly at home in his indwelling. *(You're not alone and adrift in the universe; you are at home in the Father's good pleasure - Godfrey Birtill - The Wine is Alive!)*

4:17 So now, with us awakening to ¹our full inclusion in this love union, everything is perfect! Its completeness is not compromized in contradiction. Our ²confident conversation ³echoes this fellowship even in the ⁵face of ⁴crisis; because as he is, so are we in this world - our lives are mirrored in him. *(You are as blameless in this life as Jesus is! In this is love perfected within us, that we may have confidence when we face the scrutiny of contradiction in our ⁵daily lives, because as he is so are we in this world. ἐν τούτῳ τετελείωται ἡ ἀγάπη μεθ᾽ ἡμῶν; notice, the word meth'hemoon, together with us; from meta, together with; to be included in. The word ²parresia, from para, a preposition indicating close proximity, and rheo, to pour forth; to flow freely, suggesting unreservedness in speech; bold utterance, confidence. The word, ³echo, to hold, like sound is held in an echo; to resonate. The word ⁴krisis is often translated, judgment. So, the ⁵day of judgment is translated in the face of crisis, or, facing the scrutiny of contradiction in our daily lives.)*

4:18 Fear cannot co-exist in this love realm. The perfect love union that we are talking about expels fear. Fear holds on to an expectation of crisis and judgment *[which brings separation]* **and interprets it as due punishment** *[a form of karma!]* **It echoes torment and only registers in someone who does not realize the completeness of their love union** *[with the Father, Son and Spirit and with one another.]*

4:19 We love because he loved us first! *(We did not invent this fellowship; we are invited into the fellowship of the Father and the son!)*

4:20 If anyone claims to love God but he cannot stand a fellow human, his love for God is fake; how is it possible to not love someone you can see with your eyes yet claim to love an invisible God? *(Love is not defined by our ability to like or dislike someone; love is a God-thing from start to finish. God cannot make his love for humanity more tangibly certain than what he did in his son Jesus Christ.)*

4:21 God's ¹conclusion on this is clear, loving him includes loving your fellow human - there is no distinction. *(Conclusion, entole)*

5:1 Everyone who believes that Jesus is the Christ, the incarnate begotten son of God, loves the Father and esteems the son with equal affection.

5:2 In this knowing *[of mankind's co-genesis revealed in the Christ-incarnation,]* we love the children of God with the same love that we have discovered in God; we [1]treasure the [2]conclusion of his prophetic purpose with affection. *(The word [1]tereo, means to attend to carefully; take care of; to guard; to treasure something with great affection. Westcott and Hort uses the word poiema instead of tereo. The word [2]entole is often translated commandment or precept; this word has two components: en, in and telos, from tello, to set out for a definite point or goal; properly the point aimed at as a limit, that is, by implication, the conclusion of an act or state, the result; the ultimate or prophetic purpose. Strong's 5056.*

5:3 For the love of God is realized in the way we evaluate his [1]precepts; if love's triumph is [1]the conclusion of every prophetic pointer, how can this be interpreted as an unbearable burden? *(Again the word [1]entole is used.)*

5:4 Whatever is born of God is destined to triumph over the world system. Our faith celebrates a victory that is already accomplished!

5:5 This is the ultimate victory: the certainty that the human Jesus is the divine son of God; *(that he is indeed the incarnate Christ - and the central theme of both the Word that was before time was as well as the key to understanding all of Scripture. He is the Savior of the world. See Luke 24:27 and John 1:1-3, also John 5:39,40)*

5:6 This is he who was to come; he arrived in the flesh via his mother's womb - [1]by water and blood - Jesus Christ. And in his ministry as the Christ, he was not only borne witness to by John the Baptist [2]in the prophetic baptism of water, but he went all the way into his baptism of death, [2]in his shed blood, where he died humanity's death. And it is the Spirit that bears witness according to her own being, which is truth! *(Note the change of the prepositions [1]διά by, used in the sense of accompaniment, also of instrumentality, i.e., by, through, by means of, for [2]ἐν in, clearly pointing to his baptism in water and then in his shed blood! No wonder John writes, "He was not only revealed in water; but also in blood!" If humanity's salvation could be secured only in the incarnation of the Christ and his 3 years of ministry, then his death and resurrection would be irrelevant.*

See John's reference to Jesus' moment of realizing that the hour has come for the son of man to be glorified in the single grain of wheat, falling into the ground, not to abide alone, but to bear much fruit. Then he says, John 12:27 "Now is my soul troubled. And what shall I say? 'Father, save me from this hour'? No, for this purpose I have come to this hour!"

Also John 1:32-34 And John the Baptist bore witness, "I saw the Spirit descend as a dove from heaven, and it remained on him. I myself did not know him; but he who sent me to baptize in water said to me, 'He on whom you see the Spirit descend and remain, this is he who baptizes in the Holy Spirit.' And I have seen and have borne witness that this is the Son of God.")

5:7 There are three witnessess,

5:8 the Spirit and the water and the blood; and these three ¹agree as one! *(καὶ οἱ τρεῖς ¹εἰς τὸ ἕν εἰσιν; the word **eis**, into, indicating the point reached; the one does not distract from the other.*

The only Greek manuscripts in any form which support the words, "in heaven, the Father, the Word, and the Holy Spirit, and these three are one; and there are three that bear witness in earth," are the Montfortianus of Dublin, copied evidently from the modern Latin Vulgate; the Ravianus, copied from the Complutensian Polyglot; a manuscript at Naples, with the words added in the Margin by a recent hand; Ottobonianus, 298, of the fifteenth century, the Greek of which is a mere translation of the accompanying Latin. All the old versions omit the words.)

5:9 Now if it is reasonable for us to be readily persuaded by the evidence that people may lay out before us, how much more certainty is there in the evidence that God has so compellingly borne witness to concerning his son! *(To go back to the very beginning is to find the Word already present there; face to face with God; this Word, translated into the prophetic promise in Scripture and pointing to the Messiah Redeemer for centuries, the Logos, finally became flesh and forever divided human history into a BC and AD. The heavens declare his glory, night to night exhibits the giant solar testimony that is mathematically precise, revealing that God knew before time was the exact moment he would enter our history as a man, and the exact moment the Messiah would expire on the cross and be raised again from the dead! No one has ever known God as Father; Jesus, the humble brother of the human race, [as my dear friend Baxter Kruger would say,] he has revealed him in the most articulate language as our Father. "If you have seen me, you have seen the Father!" John 14:9. "In that day, you will know that as I am in my Father, so you are in me, and I am in you!" John 14:20. The Holy Spirit now endorses in us what happened to us when Jesus died and was raised, and now echoes from within our spirits, "Abba Father!")*

5:10 Whoever shares in the same persuasion concerning the son of God, has God's testimony confirmed within themselves; he who rejects what God believes concerning Jesus sets himself up against the testimony of God and makes God out to be a liar.

5:11 The evidence is clear, God has given us back the life that we have lost, the life of the ages, which is the life of our design; this is the same life on exhibit and mirrored in his son. *(The word ¹didomi can also mean to return something that already belongs to the person.)*

5:12 To ¹mirror-echo the son is to mirror-echo life; those who ignore this ¹inner resonance concerning the son, miss out on the very life of their design! *(The word, ¹echo, means to hold, like sound is held in an echo; to resonate.)*

5:13 My intention in this writing is to endorse your belief in the name of the son of God; *[you are convinced that the name Jesus means that he is indeed the Savior of the world.]* **To know this is to know the life of the ages!**

5:14 Thus we engage in an ¹unreserved conversation, ²face to face with

the father; we know that it is his delight to be our audience in whatever we may ask him. *(The word ¹parresia, from para, a preposition indicating close proximity, and rheo, to pour forth; to flow freely, suggesting unreservedness in speech; bold utterance. The preposition ²pros means towards, face to face. It is not a question of whether we are asking anything according to his will or not; but rather a statement that it is his will to hear us in whatever we may ask of him!)*

5:15 And convinced of his delight with us within this place of intimate conversation, it is clear that our every request is held in the same echo - we already have what we've asked for!

5:16 *(Note on verse 16: The language and sentence construction here is not found elsewhere in the New Testament; ie to sin a sin not unto death, ἁμαρτάνοντα ἁμαρτίαν μὴ πρὸς θάνατον; then again to sin unto death, ἔστιν ἁμαρτία πρὸς θάνατον*

It is my humble thought that this would be another case where a scribe added their opinion and commentary, which became absorbed in the text. The issue of a sin unto death has kept the commentators and theologians busy for many a centuary without any conclusive agreement! Some of the many explanations are as follows: Such sin as God punishes with deadly sickness or sudden death. (!!??) All those sins punished with excommunication. An unrepented sin. Envy. A sinful state or condition. The sin by which the Christian falls back from Christian life into death, etc. etc.

The only time in scripture where a phrase remotely like this is used is, λαβεῖν ἁμαρτίαν θανητοφόρον, to incur a death-bearing sin, which is in Numbers 18:22 [Septuagint] And henceforth the people of Israel shall not come near the tent of meeting, lest they bear sin and die. Henceforth the distinction between sins unto death and sins not unto death became common in Rabbinic writings.

This type of doctrine gave rise to the heresy of indulgences and people getting baptized on behalf of the dead! See my note on 1 Corinthians 15:29.)

5:17 ¹Disharmony in relationship is ²unlike the true rythm of your being. The deception of a distorted image will ³not face death again! *(The word unrighteousness, ¹adikia, from a, negative or without and dikia, indicating two parties finding likeness in each other; thus relationship in conflict. The root of sin is to believe a lie about yourself. The word sin, is the word ¹hamartia, from ha, negative or without and meros, portion or form, thus to be without your allotted portion or without form, pointing to a disorientated, distorted, bankrupt identity; the word meros, is the stem of morphe, as in 2 Corinthians 3:18 the word meta-morphe, with form, which is the opposite of hamartia - without form. Sin is to live out of context with the blueprint of one's design; to behave out of tune with God's original harmony. See Deuteronomy 32:18, "You have forgotten the Rock that begot you and have gotten out of step with the God who danced with you!" Hebrew, khul or kheel, to dance. The root of sin is to believe a lie about yourself. Sin is not unto death or, sin will not ³face [pros] death - this is the whole point of the gospel! Jesus as Savior of the world; the Lamb of God took away the sins of the world; he died humanity's death. See Hebrews 9:27,28 The same goes for everyone:*

476

*a person dies only once, and then faces judgment. Christ died once and faced the judgment of the entire human race! His second appearance has nothing to do with sin, but to reveal salvation for all to [1]fully embrace him. See 2 Corinthians 2:15 We are a sweet savor of Christ unto God evident in everyone we meet. The fragrance of Christ is recognized in all unto salvation. The same gospel that announces the fragrant victory of Christ declares the odor of death; the defeat of destruction in everyone! [This parade of victory is a public announcement of the defeat of the religious systems and structures based on the law of works. Just like it is in any public game where the victory celebration of the winning team is an embarrassment for the losing team. The death of evil is announced in resurrection life! The word, **apollumi**, is derived from **apo**, away from, and **ollumi**, to destroy, to ruin.] The message we communicate is a fragrance with an immediate association; to darkness, it is the smell of doom [the death of death]; to life it is the familiar fragrance of life itself. We are not competing with those who have added their price tag to the gospel. Our conversation has its source in Christ; we communicate from the transparent innocence of a face to face encounter with God. [The law of personal performance or **kapeleuo**, meaning retail; which is a gospel with a price tag.])*

5:18 What was made absolutely [1]clear *[in the incarnate Christ]* **is that whoever is begotten of God cannot be a [2]distorted image of God! Likeness begets likeness. Jesus did not come to reveal the "otherness" of God, but his likeness in human form. There is nothing wrong with mankind's design, neither with their salvation! To [1]see one's true revealed and now redeemed genesis in God, is to treasure the person you really are by his divine engineering and to remain [4]unstained in your thoughts by [3]the "I am not-Tree system." The [3]idea that I am not the expression of his image and likeness can no longer [4]attach itself to my thoughts, neither do I allow it to ignite its destructive cycle of self-righteousness or depression! The system of this world is based on a mentality of separation, which is marked by [3]hardships annoyances and labors! It becomes an all consuming and most exhausting lifestyle of having to prove oneself in every relationship and a futile striving for recognition; with its inevitable results of disappointment, condemnation, rejection and pretence.** *(John begins the 3 sentences in verse 18,19 & 20 with he verb [1]oidamen which is the Perfect Active tense of [1]eido, to see, to observe, to pay attention, perceive, to know as an eye-witness. The Perfect indicative Active tense denotes an action which is perfected or completed in the past, but the effects of which are regarded as continuing into the present. A distorted image is what the word [2]hamartia suggests; from ha, negative and meros, portion or form; thus without form. The word [3]poneros, often translated evil, refers to the tree of the knowledge of good and evil [poneros] which is the fruit of a lost fellowship, identity, value and innocence. Through hardships, labors and annoyances mankind has strived for generations in vain, to redeem themselves from their own judgment and their illusions of separation. The word [4]haptomai means to fasten itself to, or to cling to something; from hapto to kindle a fire; to ignite.*

If there is indeed nothing wrong with mankind's design or redemption, there can only be one problem, we are thinking wrong! See Isaiah 55:8,9; "Your thoughts are not my thoughts, therefore your ways are not my ways!" also Jeremiah 29:11 "For I know the thoughts that I think toward you, says the LORD, thoughts of peace and not of evil, to give you a future and a hope." Isaiah 55:9,10 Just like the rain and the snow bridges the distance between heaven and earth and cancells the drought, so shall my word be, it shall cancel distance and drought and saturate the earth (flesh); every nook and cranny of human life shall be filled in the Incarnation! The word became flesh and indwells us! In the death and resurrection of Jesus Christ, God has brought final closure to the rule of the "I am not Tree-system." The idea of God's absence as well as every definition of distance and separation was canceled. Jesus is God's mind made up about mankind! He is not more Emmanuel to the Jew than what he is to the Gentile. See John 1:14 Suddenly the invisible eternal Word takes on visible form - the Incarnation on display in human life as in a mirror! In him, and now confirmed in us! The most accurate tangible display of God's eternal thought finds expression in human life! The Word became a human being; we are his address; he resides in us! He captivates our gaze! The glory we see there is not a religious replica; he is the authentic begotten son. The glory (that we lost in Adam) returns in fullness! Only grace can communicate truth in such complete context!)

5:19 We know that we have our origin in God; yet the whole world [1]lies trapped in the blindfold-mode of a lost identity; intoxicated by the poneros system of a futile mentality of hardships labors and annoyances! *(The word keimai means to lie prostrate, outstreched; buried.)*

5:20 This is what has become distinctly clear to us: the [1]coming of the son of God is God's mission accomplished! He is the incarnate Christ. The moment all of Scripture pointed to, has arrived! The son is [1]present! In him God has given us the greatest gift, [2]a mind whereby we may know him who is true; and in the same knowing, to find ourselves there in him who is true! Mankind is fully included and located in him, in his son Jesus Christ; this means that whatever Jesus is as son, we are. This is the true God; this is the life of the ages! *(The word [1]heko means to have come, to have arrived, to be present. John uses the word [2]dianoian; deep thought; with dia relating to the means by which we may know; a mind to know; compare metanoia, to know together with; an intwining of thought; the mind of Christ.*

Jesus said, you will know the truth as it is unveiled in me, and that will set you free!

The culmination of the gospel according to John is summed up in these verses: John 14:20 "In that day you will know that I am in my Father, and you are in me and I am in you!" Also 1 John 2:7 & 8, "what is true of him, is equally true of us. 1 John 4:17 "As he is, so are we in this world! Our lives are mirrored in him" as well as here in 1 John 5:20)

5:21 This defeats every image of our imagination that could possibly compete with the authentic likeness of our design! Darling children, distance yourselves from every substitute image, which is what idolatry is all about! *(The word [1]eidolon, often translated idol, refers to image or likeness. Isa 40:18-21 To whom then will you liken God, or what likeness compare with him? The idol! a workman casts it, and a goldsmith overlays it with gold, and casts* *for it silver chains. He who is impoverished chooses for an offering wood that will not rot; he seeks out a skilful craftsman to set up an image that will not move. Have you not known? Have you not heard? Has it not been told you from the beginning? Have you not understood from the foundations of the earth?*

Act 17:28-31 For 'In him we live and move and have our being'; as even some of your poets have said, 'For we are indeed his offspring.' Being then God's offspring, we ought not to think that the Deity is like gold, or silver, or stone, a representation by the art and imagination of human origin. The times of ignorance God overlooked, but now he compells all of mankind everywhere to awaken to their redeemed identity and innocence!)

See John 5:29 - THOUGHTS ON JUDGMENT AND THE RESURRECTION

The word [1]**krisis** *does not mean damnation or condemnation! Judging involves setting affairs right between different parties, deciding an issue, coming to a conclusion. The judgment of Jesus is the acquittal of the human race! "Surely he has borne our iniquities!" Isaiah 53:4,5*

Here is the good news! Jesus boldly announces in John 12:31-33 ... Now is the judgment of this world, now shall the ruler of this world be cast out; and I, when I am lifted up from the earth, will draw all [judgment] to myself." He said this to show by what death he was to die. [Judgment is the subject of the sentence here]

John 16:11 The Holy Spirit will convince the world concerning judgment, because the ruler of this world is judged. [Just like Jesus and the Father - the Holy Spirit will not condemn the world but rather convince the world!]

Isaiah 25:7 And he will destroy on this mountain the covering that is cast over all peoples, the veil that is spread over all nations.

Isaiah 25:8 He will swallow up death for ever, and the Lord GOD will wipe away tears from all faces, and the reproach of his people he will take away from all the earth; for the LORD has spoken.

Isaiah 26;19 but your dead will live; their bodies will rise. You who dwell in the dust, wake up and shout for joy! Your dew is like the dew of the morning; the earth will give birth to her dead!

Hosea 6:2 After two days he will revive us; on the third day he will raise us up!

Ephesians 2:5 This is how grace rescued us: sin left us dead towards God, like spiritual corpses; yet in that state of deadness and indifference, God co-quickened us together with Christ. Sin proved how dead we were (the law confirmed it!) Grace reveals how alive we now are (the gospel announces it!) Before anyone but God believed it, he made us alive together with him and raised us up together with him. (We had no contribution to our salvation! God's master-plan unfolded in the mystery of the gospel declaring our joint inclusion in Christ's death and resurrection; God found us in Christ before he lost us in Adam! [Eph 1:4] In the economy of God, when Jesus died we died. God saw us in Christ, in his death and resurrection before we saw ourselves there! He declared our co-resurrection with Christ 800 BC [Hos 6:2]!) Eph 2:6 (As much as we were co-included in his death,) we are co-included in his resurrection. We are also elevated in his ascension to be equally present in the throne room of the heavenly realm where we are co-seated with him in his executive authority. We are fully represented in Christ Jesus. (Our joint position in Christ defines us; this can never again be a distant goal to reach through religious devotion or striving, but our immediate reference. Col 3:1-3) Eph 2:7 (In a single triumphant act of righteousness God saved us from the "guttermost" to the uttermost. Here we are now, revealed in Christ in the highest possible position of bliss! If mankind's sad history could not distract from the extravagant love of God,) imagine how God is now able for timeless perpetuity (the eternal future) to exhibit the trophy of the wealth of his grace demonstrated in his kindness towards us in Christ Jesus. Grace exhibits excessive evidence of the success of the cross. Your salvation is not a reward for good behavior! It was a grace thing from start to finish; you had no hand in it. Even the gift to believe simply reflects his faith! (By grace you are! Saved by the gift of faith; grace reveals who we are, and the faith of God persuades us of it! You did not invent faith; it was God's faith to begin with! It is from faith to faith, [Rom 1:17] He is both the source and conclusion of faith. [Heb 12:2]) If this could be accomplished through any action of yours then there would be ground for boasting.

Romans 8:34 What further ground can there possibly be to condemn mankind? In his death he faced our judgment; in his resurrection he reveals our righteousness; the implications cannot be undone! He now occupies the highest seat of authority as the executive of our redemption in the throne room of God. (See v 1, also Rom 4:25.)

James 2:13 Judgment showed no mercy to those who do not walk in mercy, but mercy triumphs over judgment. (Those who walk in mercy walk in the law of liberty. [Gal 5:22, 23] There is no law against love. While judgment threatens condemnation, mercy interposes and prevails over judgment.)

*See 1 John 3:20 So, even if our own hearts would [1]accuse us of not really being true to ourselves, God is greater than our hearts and he has the full picture! His knowledge of us is not compromised. (This word, [1]kataginosko is only used three times in the NT, translated, to blame, or condemn. From kata, down and ginosko, to know; thus to know from below; from a fallen mindset perspective) 3:21 Beloved when we know what God knows to be true about us, then instead of condemning us, our hearts will endorse our innocence and [1]free our conversation before God. (The word [1]parresia, from para, a preposition indicating close proximity, and **rheo**, to pour forth; to flow freely, suggesting an unreservedness in speech; bold utterance.)*

Also 1 John 4:18,19 Fear cannot co-exist in this love realm. The perfect love union that we are talking about expels fear. Fear holds on to an expectation of crisis and judgment [which brings separation] and interprets it as due punishment [a form of karma!] It echoes torment and only registers in someone who does not realize the completeness of their love union [with the Father, Son and Spirit and with one another.] We love because he loved us first! [We did not invent this fellowship; we are invited into the fellowship of the Father and the son!])

Colossians 2:13 - 15 You were once spiritually dead, as confirmed in your constant failure; being bound to a lifestyle ruled by the [1]distorted desires of the flesh, but now God has made you alive together with him, having forgiven you all your [2]trespasses. ([1]The uncircumcision of the flesh, i.e., in the Greek, a life controlled by the sexual organs. The word, [2]paraptoma, comes from, para, close proximity, sphere of influence and pipto, to stop flying, from petomai, to fly; thus, to fall from flight or to lose altitude.)

2:14 His body nailed to the cross hung there as the document of mankind's guilt; in dying our death he [1]deleted the detailed [2]hand-written [3]record of Adam's fall. Every [1]stain that sin left on our conscience was fully blotted out. (The word,

[1]*exaleipho*, comes from *ek*, out of, and *aleipho*, with *a*, as a particle of union, and *liparos*, to grease, to leave a stain; guilt was like a grease stain upon the conscience of fallen mankind. The word, [2]*cheirographon*, translates as handwritten. The word, [3]*dogma*, comes from *dokeo*, a thought pattern; thus thought patterns engraved by human experience of constant failure to do what the law required. In his personal handwriting mankind endorsed their own death sentence. The hands of fallen mankind struck the body of Jesus with the blows of their religious hatred and fury when they nailed his bloodied body to the tree; they did not realize that in the mystery of God's economy Jesus was the scapegoat of the entire human race! [Isa 53:4, 5] "The slate wiped clean, that old arrest warrant canceled and nailed to Christ's Cross." —The Message)

2:15 His brilliant victory made a public spectacle of every rule and authority empowered by the fall of Adam. The voice of the cross will never be silenced! (The horror of the Cross is now the eternal trophy of God's triumph over sin! The cross stripped religion of its authority to manipulate mankind with guilt. Every accusation lost its power to continue to blackmail the human race.

Philippians 2:8 - 11 And so we have the drama of the cross in context: the man Jesus Christ who is fully God, becomes fully human to the extent of willingly dying humanity's death at the hands of his own creation. He embraced the curse and shame of the lowest kind in dying a criminal's death. 2:9 From this place of utter humiliation, God exalted him to the highest rank. God graced Jesus with a Name that is far above as well as equally representative of every other name; (The word, uper, means above, also instead, or for the sake of). The name of Jesus endorses his mission as fully accomplished! He is the Savior of the world! Titus 2:11 The grace of God shines as bright as day making the salvation of humankind undeniably visible. See also Eph 3:15, Every family in heaven and on earth originates in him; his is mankind's family name and he remains the authentic identity of every nation.) 2:10 What his name unveils will persuade every creature of their redemption! Every knee in heaven and upon the earth and under the earth shall bow in spontaneous worship! Also every tongue will voice and resonate the same devotion to his unquestionable Lordship as the Redeemer of life! Jesus Christ has glorified God as the Father of creation! This is the ultimate conclusion of the Father's [1]intent!

Romans 5:8 Herein is the extremity of God's love gift: mankind was rotten to the core when Christ died their death.

Romans 5:12 - 21 One person opened the door to sin. Sin introduced (spiritual) death. Both sin and (spiritual) death had a global impact. No one escaped its tyranny.

5:13 The law did not introduce sin; sin was just not pointed out yet.

5:14 In the mean time (spiritual) death dominated from Adam to Moses, (2500 years before the law was given) no one was excluded; even those whose transgression was different from Adam's. The fact is that Adam's offense set sin into motion, and its mark was globally transmitted and stained the entire human race.

5:15 The only similarity in the comparison between the offense and the gift, is that both Adam and Christ represent the masses; their single action therefore bears global consequence. The idea of death and separation that was introduced by one person's transgression is by far superseded by the grace gift lavished upon mankind in the one man Jesus Christ. (But God's free gift immeasurably outweighs the transgression. For if through the transgression of the one individual the mass of mankind have died, infinitely greater is the generosity with which God's grace, and the gift given in his grace which found expression in the one man Jesus Christ, have been bestowed on the mass of mankind. — Weymouth, 1912)

5:16 The difference between the two men is further emphasized in that judgment and condemnation followed a single offense, whereas the free gift of acquittal and righteousness follows innumerable sins.

5:17 If (spiritual) death saw the gap in one sin, and grabbed the opportunity to dominate mankind because of one, how much more may we now seize the advantage to reign in righteousness in this life through that one act of Christ, who declared us innocent by his grace. Grace is out of all proportion in superiority to the transgression.

5:18 The conclusion is clear: it took just one offense to condemn mankind; one act of righteousness declares the same mankind innocent. ("We see then, that as one act of sin exposed the whole race of mankind to condemnation, so one act of perfect righteousness presents all mankind freely acquitted in the sight of God!" JB Phillips)

Romans 5:19 The disobedience of the one [1]exhibits humanity as sinners; the obedience of another man exhibits humanity as righteous. ([1]kathistemi, to cause to be, to set up, to exhibit. We were not made sinners by our own disobedience; neither were we made righteous by our own obedience.)

5:20 The presence of the law made no difference, instead it merely highlighted the offense; but where sin increased, grace superseded it.

5:21 (Spiritual) death provided sin its platform and power to reign from, now grace has taken over sovereignty through righteousness to introduce unthreatened life under the Lordship of Jesus Christ over us.

Hebrews 9:24 - 28 In Christ we have so much more than a type reflected in the tabernacle of holy places set up by human hands. He entered into the heavenly sphere itself, where he personally represents mankind face to face with God.

9:25 Neither was it necessary for him to ever repeat his sacrifice. The High Priests under the old shadow system stood proxy with substitute animal sacrifices that had to be made once a year.

9:26 But Jesus did not have to suffer again and again since the [1]fall of the world; the [2]single sacrifice of himself in the fulfillment of history now reveals how he has brought sin to nought. (The word, [1]katabole, means cast down. [2]God's Lamb took away the sins of the world!)

9:27 The same goes for everyone: a person dies only once, and then faces judgment.

9:28 Christ died once and faced the judgment of the entire human race! His second appearance has nothing to do with sin, but to reveal salvation for all to [1]*fully embrace him. (To fully embrace,* [1]***apekdechomai***, *from* **apo**, *away from [that which defined me before] and* **ek**, *out of, source; and* **dechomai**, *to take into ones hands to accept whole heartedly, to fully embrace. In his resurrection he appeared as Savior of the world! Sin is no longer on the agenda, for the Lamb of God has taken away the sins of the world! Jesus Christ fulfilled mankind's destiny with death! [1 Cor 15:3-5, Rom 4:25, Acts 17:30, 31.])*

Note: *(Even in his first coming, he did not come to condemn the world. The Father judges no one for he has handed over all judgment to the son, who judged the world in righteousness when he took their chastisement in his own body. Now in his appearance in us, his body, his mission is to unveil the consequence of redemption through the Holy Spirit.*

This is not to be confused with the doctrine of his second coming. Many scriptures have been translated and interpreted with only a futuristic value and have consequently neutralized many, like the Jews, to diligently wait for the Messiah still to come. The Messiah has come once and for all as Messiah. Jesus appeared again after his resurrection and now his resurrection life in us as his body is the extension of his second appearance; God making his appeal to an already reconciled world to "be reconciled!" [Acts 3:26, 2 Cor 5:19, 20] The church continued to postpone the reality that God introduced in Christ. We are now already fully represented in his blamelessness! The second coming as doctrine is not in context of these chapters at all! [See 1 Pet 1:10-13] The Aramaic word, **maranatha**, *means our Lord has come!*

See also 1 Thessalonians 2:19 We expect nothing less in the context of the gospel than you enjoying a face to face encounter in the [1]*immediate presence of our Lord Jesus Christ! This is our delight and wreath of honor! (The word* [1]***parousia*** *speaks of the immediate presence of the Lord! From* **para**, *a preposition indicating close proximity, a thing proceeding from a sphere of influence, with a suggestion of union of place of residence, to have sprung from its author and giver, originating from, denoting the point from which an action originates, intimate connection; and* **eimi**, *I am! There is not even a hint of judgment or punishment in this word! Please do not believe everything you read in Strongs! "G3952 parousia from the present participle of G3918; a being near, that is, advent; often, return; specifically of Christ to punish Jerusalem, or finally the wicked."!!??))*

2 Corinthians 5:14 The love of Christ [1]*resonates within us and leaves us with only one conclusion: Jesus died humanity's death; therefore, in God's logic every individual simultaneously died. (The word,* [1]***sunecho***, *from sun, meaning together with and echo, meaning to echo, to embrace, to hold, and thus translated, to resonate. Jesus didn't die 99% or for 99%. He died humanity's death 100%! If Paul had to compromise the last part of verse 14 to read: "one died for all therefore only those who follow the prescriptions to qualify, have also died," then he would have had to* change the first half of the verse as well! Only the love of Christ can make a calculation of such enormous proportion! The religious mind would question the extremity of God's love and perhaps prefer to add a condition or two to a statement like that! Seeing everyone equally valued and included in Christ does not lessen one's passion to communicate Christ effectively, it greatly increases it!)

5:15 Now if all were included in his death they were equally included in his resurrection. This unveiling of his love redefines human life! Whatever reference we could have of ourselves outside of our association with Christ is no longer relevant.

5:16 This is radical, and our most defining moment! No label that could possibly previously identify someone carries any further significance! Even our pet doctrines of Christ are redefined. Whatever we knew about him historically or sentimentally is challenged by this conclusion. (By discovering Christ from God's point of view we discover ourselves and every other human life from God's point of view! Paul sees by revelation that what Jesus redeemed in every person brings absolute closure and death to any other reasoning and judgment we may have had of ourselves or anyone else for that matter! This is our 'metanoia' moment! "From now on therefore, we no longer know anyone according to the flesh, even though we once knew Christ from a human and religious point of view.")

Romans 4:25 Here is the equation: his cross = our sins; his resurrection = our innocence! (Our sins resulted in his death; our righteousness resulted in his resurrection. His resurrection is the receipt to our acquittal. Why was Jesus handed over to die? Because of, **dia**, our sins. Why was he raised from the dead? Because of, **dia**, we were justified! His resurrection reveals our righteousness! If we were still guilty after Jesus died, his resurrection would neither be possible nor relevant! This explains Acts 10:28 and 2 Corinthians 5:14 and 16. And in Acts 17:31, "because God had fixed a day on which he would judge the world righteous [innocent] by a man whom he has appointed, and of this he has given proof to all mankind by raising him from the dead.")

Revelation 5:13 And I heard every creature in heaven and on earth and under the earth and in the sea, and all therein, saying, "To him who sits upon the throne and to the Lamb be blessing and honor and glory and might for ever and ever!"

Francois grew up in a home where Jesus was loved and lived. His parents were in fulltime ministry in an interdenominational mission. His eldest brother Leon, is a missionary in the Ukraine and Russia for many years.

Lydia and Francois met on the 25th of August 1974, while he was working with Youth For Christ. She was sixteen and he nineteen! The following year he studied Greek and Hebrew at the University of Pretoria for three years while Lydia completed her nursing training. In 1978 Francois also spent a year with Youth with a Mission.

They married in January 1979 and are blessed with four amazing children, Renaldo, Tehilla, Christo and Stefan. They worked in fulltime mission for fourteen years, during which time they also pastored a church and led a training facility for more than 700 students over a five-year period.

They then left the ministry and for ten years did business mainly in the tourism industry. They built and managed a Safari Lodge in the Sabi Sand Game Reserve and eventually relocated to Hermanus where they started Southern Right Charters for boat-based whale watching.

In December 2000 Francois began to write the book, "God believes in You" which led to him being invited to speak at various Christian camps and churches.

They are now back in fulltime ministry since February 2004, and travel regularly abroad and into Africa as well as South Africa.

Francois has written several books in both English and Afrikaans, including God Believes in You, Divine Embrace, Done! and The Mystery Revealed. He is currently passionately engaged in continuing with his translation of the Mirror Bible.

His work is being translated into several African languages as well as Chinese, Russian, Hungarian, German, French, Spanish, Polish, Portugese, Dutch and Slovakian.

The Mirror is already completed in Spanish, Shona and Xhosa.

Thousands of people subscribe to their daily posts on facebook and bulk email.

The Mirror Bible is also available on Kindle. Then there is an iPhone or Android mobile app on the following website, www.mirrorbible.com

Should you wish to order printed copies in bulk, [10 or more] pls contact us at info.mirrorword.net

Contact us if you wish to help sponsor Mirror Bibles in Spanish, Shona or Xhosa.

REFERENCES & RESOURCES

Referred to by the author's name or by some abridgment of the title.

Adam Clarke (1762–1832 A British Methodist theologian)

Barnes Notes (Notes on the Bible, by Albert Barnes, [1834], at sacred-texts.com)

BBE (1949, Bible in Basic English)

Breath of life by **Andre Rabe** (www.hearhim.net)

Clarence Jordan (Cotton Patch Gospel - Paul's Epistles by Clarence Jordan - Smyth & Helwys Pub. 2004)

Doddrich (Philip Doddridge 1702-1751 www.ccel.org/d/doddridge)

Dr. Robinson (Greek Lexicon by Edward Robinson1851)

E-Sword by Rick Meyers (www.e-sword.net)

J.H. Thayer (Greek-English Lexicon of the New Teatament By Joseph Henry Thayer, DD - Edinburgh - T&T CLARK - Fourth Edition 1901)

J.B. Phillips Translation (Geoffrey Bles London 1960)

KJV (King James Version - In 1604, King James I of England authorized that a new translation of the Bible into English. It was finished in 1611)

Knox Translation (Translated from the Vulgate Latin by Ronald Knox Published in London by Burns Oates and Washbourne Ltd. 1945)

NEB (New English Bible New Testament - Oxford & Cambridge University Press 1961)

Rob Lacey (The Word on the Street Copyright 2003, 2004 by Rob Lacey)

RSV (The Revised Standard Version is an authorized revision of the American Standard Version, published in 1901, which was a revision of the King James Version, published in 1611.)

Strongs (James Strong - Dictionary of the Bible)

The Message (Eugene H. Peterson Nav Press Publishing Group)

Walter Bauer (Greek English Lexicon - a translation of Walter Bauer's Griechisch-Deutches Worterbuch by Arndt and Gingrich 1958)

Wesley J. Perschbacher (The New Analytical Greek Lexicon Copyright 1990 by Hendrickson Publishers, Inc)

Weymouth New Testament (*M.A., D.Lit. 1822-1902*)

Zodhiates Complete Word Study Lexicon Mantis Bible Study 4 for Apple

CPSIA information can be obtained
at www.ICGtesting.com
Printed in the USA
BVOW11s1808291216
472041BV00003B/17/P